Father Bausch in *Once Upon a Gospel* once again  esty and vulnerability, bringing us ever deeper int r told. Using new stories and familiar ones, he sei , engage, motivate, challenge, and call us to action. I read and re-read his books, always gaining new insights. I have used them in courses taught, in meditation and prayer, I have enthusiastically borrowed and adapted many of his stories and homiletic thoughts, given his books to many as gifts, and continue to remain in awe of this wonderful, faithful preacher and honorable parish priest. Words flow from the pen and heart of Father Bausch.

Reverend Francis S. Tebbe, O.F.M., KHS
President, Catholic Coalition on Preaching

When Nathan had a harsh truth to tell to David, he wrapped it in the folds of a story. Jesus also chose to wrap the truths of the reign of God in stories that he told in major tones and minor, in bold statements and in whispers. In keeping with this tradition, William Bausch, with a finger on the pulse of the human condition and with an ear attuned to God, continues to serve the believing community as its storyteller par excellence. His imaginings elucidate the truth of God's word while edifying and encouraging believers in their daily efforts to live accordingly.

Patricia Datchuck Sanchez
author, *Celebration*

Father Bill Bausch is God's gift to preachers. Don't even hesitate: Just buy *Once Upon a Gospel* and keep it handy if you're a homilist or catechist, or ever in a position to talk frankly with others about faith and life. And if Bausch doesn't make you laugh out loud and weep for the beauty of the gospel message—if you don't feel intensely alive and deeply grateful after reading these stories—then I suggest you need a sabbatical. Come for the stories, learn from the technique, stay for the art of public proclamation. Most of all, incorporate Bausch's honesty and you'll always find your audience.

Alice Camille
author of *God's Word Is Alive* and *Invitation to Catholicism*

Dedication

*To the people of St. Martha's Parish
in Point Pleasant, New Jersey,
who were the first both
to endure and embrace these words*

Excerpt from THE LITTLE PRINCE by Antoine de Saint-Exupery, copyright 1943 by Harcourt, Inc. and renewed 1971 by Consuelo de Saint-Exupery, English translation copyright © 2000 by Richard Howard, reprinted by permission of Houghton Mifflin Harcourt Publishing Company.

Twenty-Third Publications
A Division of Bayard
One Montauk Avenue, Suite 200
New London, CT 06320
(860) 437-3012 or (800) 321-0411
www.23rdpublications.com

The Scripture passages contained herein are from the *New Revised Standard Version of the Bible*, copyright ©1989, by the Division of Christian Education of the National Council of Churches in the U.S.A. All rights reserved.

ISBN 978-1-58595-683-8
Library of Congress Catalog Card Number: 2007939316
Printed in the U.S.A.

Contents

Lent to Pentecost

ORDINARY TIME

Holy Days, Holidays, and Occasions

Funeral Homilies

CRIES OF THE HEART: *Addenda to the Funeral Homilies*

TWICE TOLD TALKS

Preface

One of my homiletic idols, the late Father Walter Burghardt, is famous for his three-point homilies. He self-kids about it, but he continues to enrich us with those three points grounded in Scripture and social justice.

Here I want to justify the use of stories by appealing to the example of Jesus who spoke in parables; indeed he spoke in no other way: "Jesus told the crowds all these things in parables; without a parable he told them nothing" (Matthew 13:34). Also, I have found that parishioners fondly remember and ponder stories. They are the first way that the word of God came to us and, in their own right, have a power of their own.

It has been often noted that the Bible itself is essentially a story book. We find it so hard to realize that it is the product of ancient eastern Semitic thought patterns and not an expression of our either/or Western categories of thinking. The ancients of the East, instead of the analyzing so dear to our digital hearts, simply told stories. Instead of giving a definition of God, they related experiences of God. That's why we get very little description of people in the Bible but we get pages of their conversations. The biblical people were an extremely talkative lot. This is precisely because they were always engaged in some kind of drama with one another and with God where give-and-take is part of the tension. They are, in short, characters in a book and their stories are sources of revelation. And their stories, moreover, wonderful or wicked, were told and retold in oral traditions for centuries. Finally, honed, reshaped, and reedited to fit current political or religious agendas, they were put down in writing. Even then, the written stories themselves, like verbal putty, were altered and configured through the centuries and provoked new insights.

That's because oral stories, sober or fantastical, unlike the printed page, are inherently flexible and malleable. They are multi-leveled and evoke different meanings in different times and places and circumstances. We never exhaust the meaning of a good story. The reason is because stories deal in myth, symbol, and metaphor that resonate in the deeper fissures of our hearts. Think of how a good novel or a good movie rinses through our being, long after we have left them behind. There is, I repeat, never a last word to a story. What I am saying is that story, unlike the proposition, the simple declarative sentence, or the digital printout, continues to live. Truth wrapped in story is irresistible.

That last statement, "*truth* wrapped in story," is more accurate than we think and all the more necessary to repeat, because today's secular educational system teaches that the only truth is scientific truth. The truths of science can be demonstrated and proven, period. Anything else is wishful thinking and private whim. Religious truth especially is considered an oxymoron. We can hold any belief we want as long as we realize it is a private, personally held belief utterly undemonstrable. Only science carries truth. This, of course, is a narrow and debilitating construction of reality. Truth, in fact, comes in many different ways, in many different modes besides science. Are we to say, for example, that the fictional works of Dante, Shakespeare, Dickens, and Wharton carry no truth, no wisdom? Is the fictional story of the Good Samaritan without truth of any sort? Is the wisdom behind Aesop's talking animals useless and silly? Is *To Kill a Mockingbird* simply a good read and not a moral imperative? Is there no truth to Atticus Finch's life?

I say there is and that is why I use stories. Properly related, they wrap the gospel truth in palatable and memorable form. They must do that, of course: relate to the gospel. I work exceedingly hard not to use stories for their own sakes or because they are clever or funny, whether they have anything to do with the gospel text or not. To do that is to curry favor and abandon one's prophetic stance. Which is why I have little patience with preachers who tell clever or funny stories and end each Mass with a joke. That's what people remember and that's what they will remember the preacher for. ("I love Monsignor's Mass. He tells the best jokes.") Taking home the preacher or his joke is a poor substitute for taking home the word of God.

Not all the homilies in this collection use stories, of course. Many preachers hardly use them at all, and their homilies are wonderfully effective. All that I am saying is that I do use stories in my preaching, and I want to justify that. As master storyteller John Shea writes, "We tell stories not to educate or indoctrinate but to illuminate, to coax the reader or listener into another world in the hope that when they emerge from it they do so with an enchanted view of the possibilities in their lives." A good description of a successful homily.

Finally, I would be remiss if I did not wholeheartedly thank my editor, John van Bemmel, for his rigorous and expert scrutiny, gentle patience, and endless hours visiting and revisiting the manuscript.

Introduction

This brief introduction deals with some practical notes. The homilies in this book mostly reflect commentaries on the epistles and gospels (mostly gospels) from Years B and C in the lectionary, although Year A is also tapped. Almost all (ninety-seven percent) of the homilies are new, never before printed (except for the Twice Told Talks section: see below), and all are original. But that statement, that all are original, is not entirely true. I am inspired by a sentence from Walter Burghardt, a thought from Barbara Reid, and insights from William Willimon, James Wallace, John Shea, to name a few. I want to acknowledge their influence. A few homilies, however, have tapped into other past homilies of mine and have been reconfigured for this collection. In addition to the homilies reflecting the liturgical cycle, you will find what I hope is a helpful section of other homilies and related talks titled Holy Days, Holidays, and Occasions, which move outside the cycle and range from golden jubilee celebrations to a class reunion, and holy day and holiday celebrations. There is another section containing funeral homilies, which suggests several ways the preacher can confront the mystery of death.

Finally, there is a section with the strange title of Twice Told Talks. This is basically an emergency anthology of some of my previously printed seasonal homilies, many now out of print. These are not necessarily my best but are simply offered to provide an instant resource for those special occasions when the homilist is looking for material at an especially busy and tense time of the year and doesn't have much opportunity to pull his or her thoughts together. Dipping into this anthology may provide relief. Not a habit to be encouraged, but a help when help is needed.

However one uses this book, I caution that these homilies are not meant to be read front to back like a novel. Doing that makes them sound cramped and cranky. (That was my experience.) Remember also that they were written and delivered over a period of several years and so there will inevitably be some overlap in thought and expression. I suggest that reading them out of the order they appear in the book may be more profitable.

For maximum effect it is wise to pay attention to the scriptural references at the beginning of each homily and read them before reading the homily. Also, referring to the comments and credits at the end of this book will round out the context behind each homily and remind you of the obvious, that the homilies are contextualized by the political and social climate of the time they were delivered and, although the essential insight and message will be valid, adjustments must be made to update the references. Needless to say, we must always remember that these homilies were preached and a great deal is lost by reading them. I especially think of the funeral homilies when my own emotions show through in the preaching—I knew and loved these people—and you simply can't put that on paper. Gestures, voice modulations, and especially pauses in the right places are also lost in the scribal translation, and, therefore, some of the soul. After all, homilies, like stories, poetry, and plays, are best performed. But here they are, all hundred plus of them.

Feel free to take the homilies as they are or modify them. Giving credit would be nice but not necessary. (Worth reading: "Stolen Goods" by Thomas G. Long in *Christian Century*, April 17, 2007, pp. 18ff.)

Finally, there's no escaping the unnerving finger-pointing every time you get up to preach. The words meant for others have a way of coming back to judge the one who spoke them. I just want to note that preaching is a dangerous occupation.

> I went into church and sat on the velvet pew. I watched as the sun came shining through the stained-glass window. The minister, dressed in a velvet robe, opened the golden gilded Bible, marked it with a silk bookmark and said, "If any man will be my disciple, said Jesus, let him deny himself, take up his cross, sell what he has, give it to the poor and follow me." And I looked around and nobody was laughing.

I think this is from Kierkegaard. Ouch.

ADVENT AND CHRISTMAS

Introducing Matthew

"Happy New Year!" is an appropriate opening for this homily. I say this because, as you know, and as you can see from the colors, this is the first Sunday of Advent, which, for Christians, begins a new church, or liturgical, year. We have calendar years, financial years, school years, and so on. So, too, we have our church year. And this less-than-world-shaking fact gives me an opportunity, on this first day of our year, to share with you a rather pedantic classroom lesson as I set you up for what's coming down the calendar pike. It's not exactly thrilling but it's enlightening.

Church years are on a three-year cycle, called, unimaginatively, Years A, B, and C. Each year is devoted to one of the synoptic gospel writers, those three gospel writers whose works are very similar to each other: Year A belongs to Matthew, Year B to Mark, and Year C to Luke. John's gospel, being a different breed altogether, has at times some of its parts scattered among the other three.

Last year, you may recall, we were on Year C and so all year we read from Luke's gospel. Today, our churchy New Year's Day, we begin all over again and start with Year A and that means Matthew's gospel. We'll be hearing from him all this year till next Advent when it will be Mark's turn.

So, our lesson for today: Matthew's gospel. First, who is this Matthew, the one who wrote this second gospel, even though we always list him before Mark, who really wrote the first gospel? The answer is, we don't know. We don't know for sure who any of the gospel writers were, even though tradition has given us the names of Matthew, Mark, Luke, and John. None of the gospels themselves claim authorship or identify its author.

But we're fairly sure our Matthew of the gospel wasn't the apostle Matthew. Why? Well, because he copied so extensively from Mark's gospel, maybe ninety percent of it, supplementing and smoothing it out here and there. The point is, if Matthew had been the apostle Matthew, an eyewitness to Jesus, why would he not tell the story in his own words? Why copy almost entirely from someone who *wasn't* an eyewitness? He copies some 600 of the 660 verses of Mark, which means he simply retells Mark's story for his time and place. No, this Matthew is somebody else.

One thing for sure: it seems that Matthew, whoever he was, was a Jew who had accepted the form of Judaism that Jesus represented. Since he mentions it in his gospel, Matthew evidently wrote after the destruction of Jerusalem in the year 70. Most likely he wrote his gospel around the year 85, some fifty years or more removed from Jesus, outside of Palestine. Antioch in Syria, which had a large Jewish population, is a good guess. And he wrote his revised Mark gospel for his very troubled community. It seems it was made up of Jews for Jesus like himself and Gentile converts to the Judaism of Jesus, consisting of men and women of various civic and ethnic standing. A mixed group.

Matthew's task was a very tough and delicate one: how to reconcile two expressions of Judaism? On the one hand, there were those members of Matthew's community who, like himself, were Jews and proud of it. On the other hand, there were those members of the Pharisees who were Jews and proud of it. But now the situation was different. Formerly many variant strains of Judaism were easily tolerated: the Sadducees, the Zealots, the Essenes, the Pharisees, and so on. They were all part of the mix.

However, after the tragic fall of Jerusalem, when the dust finally settled, the only ones left standing were the Pharisees and the Nazarenes, as the small group of Jesus' followers were called. The Pharisees, regrouping, said that if we're to survive as Jews, we need a united front. Maybe at one time we could tolerate that Jesus group but not now. They've got to go. They're divisive. They are disloyal to the Mosaic tradition. So the Pharisees issued a proclamation saying that the renegades "must be rooted out and the Nazarenes perish and blotted out from the book of life." So, to put it mildly, there was bad blood between the two groups. We see this tension in all those nasty confrontations between the Pharisees and Jesus that Matthew has in his gospel.

But you can sense Matthew's trying hard to counter this excommunication, saying in effect, hey, fellow Jews, we're really as Jewish, as loyal, as you are. Jesus isn't a novelty. No, no, he is an observant Jew fulfilling the law, not abrogating it. Jesus is, in fact, more Jewish than you because he is the authentic interpreter of the Jewish law. Why, more than that, Jesus is another Moses. Look, he too, like Moses, goes down to Egypt. He too escapes a king's wrath, King Herod, who like Pharaoh, kills infants. Jesus also spends forty days in the desert as Moses spent forty years. Like Moses, he even teaches from the mountaintop. You know: those famous beatitudes.

No doubt about it, Matthew is striving to say in his gospel that Jesus stands in an authentic strain of Judaism. Why, he is Son of David, the Jewish Messiah. And accordingly Matthew peoples his gospel with stories of noble and faith-filled Jews. But, for all of this, he still he can't hide the tensions. As the year goes on you'll hear about these hostilities; for example, the famous litany of woes Jesus utters against the Pharisees, which is really Matthew scolding them.

Matthew is also anxious to score another point. He does this by giving us examples of non-Jews who show exemplary faith: the women in Jesus' ancestry, the Magi, the Roman centurion, a Canaanite woman, a Roman soldier. Matthew is saying, Jesus is being faithful to the tradition of Abraham, through whom, God said, all peoples would be blessed. So Jesus, true heir of Abraham, has come for all, Jews and Gentiles alike.

Finally, sensing they're in it for the long haul, Matthew is interested in organization and he is the only evangelist who uses the word church. Peter has a prominent role in this church, this gathering of Nazarenes. He is in fact the rock on which the church is built. Matthew also places heavy emphasis on leadership and discipleship. True disciples are those who hear the words of Jesus and keep them. Matthew's concerns are order, harmony, discipleship, and a Jesus whose parables of invitation and mercy are open to all.

And, interestingly, while in Matthew's gospel and in the other gospels only male disciples are called, entrusted with mission, and play main roles, he preserves a more inclusive tradition where women also play a significant roles in the life of Jesus, starting with the four women in Jesus' genealogy: Tamar, Rahab, Ruth, and Bathsheba. Then there are Mary, Simon Peter's mother in-law, the Canaanite woman, the woman who anoints Jesus' feet, Pilate's wife, the women disciples who witnessed the crucifixion and burial after the men had betrayed, denied, and deserted Jesus, and the two Marys first to see the risen Jesus.

So, what can you expect from Matthew this year? Four things: lots of references to the Old Testament as he tries to validate Jesus as a true Israelite; lots of conflicts with the Pharisees, reflecting the tensions of his time; lots of calls to discipleship to shore up his beleaguered brethren, and, finally, lots of Jesus' parables to bring home his points. Stay tuned.

Speaking of which, to awaken you and give you a change of pace, let me end with a Matthew-type story:

Once upon a time God and a man are walking down the road. The man asks God, "What is the world like?"

God replies, "I'm thirsty and I can't talk when I'm thirsty. If you could go and get me a drink of cool water, we could discuss what the world is like. There's a village not that far away. Go and get me a drink."

So the man goes to the village and knocks at the first house he sees. A lovely young woman opens the door. He is captivated and stammers but finally manages to say, "I need a glass of cool water."

"Why, of course," she says, smiling a dazzling smile, "but it's noon time and happens to be my lunch time. Would you care to stay for some food first?"

"Well, I *am* hungry," he says, looking over her shoulder at a well-set table. "And your offer is most kind."

He goes in and door closes behind him.

Thirty years go by. The man who wanted to know what the world was like and the woman who offered him food have married and raised five children. He is a respected merchant and she is an honored member of the community. One day a terrible storm comes in off the ocean and threatens their lives. The merchant cries out, "Help me, O God!" A voice from the midst of the storm says, "Where is my cup of cool water?"

That's an updated version of Matthew's chapter twenty-five where Jesus says that if you were too distracted or busy to give drink to the thirsty or food to the starving or comfort to the sick, you didn't give these things to him. Bad news. Bad discipleship. Jesus' ringing comment? "Not every one who calls out 'Lord! Lord!' will be saved, but only those who do the will of my heavenly Father."

Welcome to the year of Matthew.

Watch!

Advent. Huge extortion of money for oil sullies the United Nations; sexual scandal shames the Catholic Church; daily suicide bombings scatter death in Iraq; terrorism afflicts Jordan, Spain, and England and worries the rest of the world; AIDS devastates Africa; Avian Flu threatens the globe; an eighteen-year-old kills his girlfriend's parents; greed beyond measure is routine as another businessman, Conrad Black, was recently indicted for stealing more than fifty-one million dollars from his company; Congress wallows in pork; widespread corruption sullies our own state of New Jersey; the rising cost of heating; the pain and scars of divorce; abandoned children; the daily crudity of television; a fifty-seven-billion-dollar porn industry. And if all that were not enough, nature itself also seems to be out of sync: hurricanes, tornados, earthquakes, flooding, global warming.

Are you sufficiently depressed for this first Sunday of Advent? All this is indeed frighteningly bad news. This kind of sick list incites some people to actually embrace today's gospel—"you know not when the hour will come"—and hope with all their hearts it will come and come soon. Why? Because, basically, they *want* the end to come. Because they're disgusted at so much evil—how much worse can it get?—and only God can clear up this moral mess and the sooner Jesus comes, the better.

So they embrace Jerry Falwell's and Pat Robertson's failed predictions of the end of the world and read, to the tune of over seventy million copies, the misguided predictions of the *Left Behind* books whose message is that Jesus is coming soon, very soon. They can't wait. They sport their bumper stickers announcing their readiness, and, of course, their confidence that *their* car will be vacated as they, the favored ones, are raptured into heaven, while others will be left behind on earth to burn. Yes, the sooner Jesus comes back to clean up this mess, the better. So watch!

But maybe we all misunderstand. Maybe, despite all the fearful troubles of the world, Jesus is not referring to his sudden coming next week or next year but to his coming right now, his presence here—today—quietly seeding love and slowly pushing back the darkness. Maybe that is what we should be watching for. Maybe we should look past the daily horrors to those people who give us a hint of his daily presence, who give us hope, encouragement, and challenge.

A man named Ron recalls that when he was growing up, his mother, a nurse, had a real thing about cleanliness. From an early age Ron was taught that when he went through a push door to shove it open with his fist. If the door had a handle, he was to pull it open with his little finger. If he did as his mother instructed, he would not get germs on his hands. Ron never forgot his mother's teaching. "At age forty-eight," he says, "I probably had the strongest little finger in America."

Well, one day Ron was serving a hot meal at a soup kitchen, chili with two pieces of buttered bread. A man came down the line who looked even more scruffy and broken than the others. Ron was overwhelmed by his stench. "Like a pull of a magnet, " Ron recalls, "my gaze went to the dirt and dried blood on his hands." Then before he realized what was happening, the man clasped Ron's hands in both of his.

"Brother," said the scruffy man, "I love you. Thanks for being here."

"I'm glad you came," Ron replied after swallowing hard, trying to smile as the man shuffled over to one of the tables with his meal.

The next man stepped up. As Ron handed him a bowl of chili, a little of the chili spilled on Ron's hand. Without thinking, he licked it off. Then it hit him. That was the hand the other man had just clasped! Ron momentarily froze, repelled to think that he had licked something that smelly old man had just touched. But it was also a moment of revelation for Ron. He said, "The light of awareness changed my vision. No longer was Jesus only the handsome man I had pictured in my mind and seen in paintings. Now he had a scarred, stubbled face and fingers stained yellow; he was dirty, he smelled bad, and he wore cast-off clothes. I had just served Jesus chili and bread."

This is a true Advent man who was watching and so recognized the Lord here and now in the midst of the world's poverty and uncleanliness.

When Bill was born in the 1930s, he was diagnosed with cerebral palsy. The doctor predicted that he would be mentally retarded and urged Bill's parents to have him institutionalized. Fortunately, they ignored the doctor's advice. At first, Bill attended a school for children with disabilities. Later he gained entrance to a mainstream high school. Then, with the help of a counselor, Bill began looking for a career. This effort resulted in little more than a series of humiliations. A job as a pharmacy store clerk lasted less than a day because Bill's trembling hands would not allow him to stock the shelves neatly. A job as a Goodwill Industries cashier lasted three days because Bill's palsied fingers kept hitting the wrong keys.

Bill began combing the want ads himself. Naturally, this met with more rejection. Most times he didn't even get past the initial phone call. Then one day Bill landed an interview with a company, Watkins Products, that sold products door-to-door. "I know I can do this job," Bill confidently told the interviewer.

Bill got his break, but prejudice being what it is, the sales manager assigned Bill to the worst, most hopeless territory in Portland, Oregon, where people lived in dire poverty and the houses were falling down. And the poor man was working on commission. But he had a job. He packed his briefcase with brochures, hit the street at 9 AM and hasn't looked back since. Eventually Bill Porter went on to become one of the top sales representatives ever in the Northwest. ABC's *20/20* told Bill's story on Christmas Eve in 1995 and it was later dramatized on HBO, as some of you may have seen, starring William H. Macy.

Basically, his story too is a story of grace in the midst of prejudice and disability, and therefore it is an Advent sign of the day and the hour of God's presence here and now.

The mother and small child were waiting at the airport. The mother had given the little girl a cup of orange juice and a cookie to keep her occupied. Suddenly someone bumped into the mother who in turn brushed the child and the juice slopped all over her, with the cookie crumbs all over her face and front. A woman who observed all this spotted the father who just got off the plane and was waving to his family. He was sharp and neat in his nice suit, shirt, and tie, carrying his briefcase. The woman thought, "No way is he going near that messy child. He'll stay his distance, peck his wife on the cheek, and take off."

Of course he didn't do any of that. He ran up to the messy child, held her against his white shirt, and whispered loving things in her ear. All the way to the luggage claim area, he never stopped hugging and kissing her, stroking her hair. Surely a reminder of God embracing the morally messy sinner. It is the Prodigal Son story in modern dress and so, once more, a hint of a Presence here and now.

Yes, there are terrible things going on in the world. But faith people like Ron, Bill, and an arms-open father remind us that the hidden Lord is among us: unsung, unannounced, unreported by the media, but here. Be alert for him. Watch!

Finally, this truth is our challenge. Our deeds of charity, our acts of forgiveness, our compassion, our morally lived lives, like pinpoints of light in a morally dark world, must show a weary and anxious people that the Lord really has come and is here, and if there is any watching to be done to detect him, it is to watch us.

The Church's New Year

FIRST SUNDAY OF ADVENT, C, LUKE 21:25–28

There is, as you know, the fiscal year and there is the calendar year and lots of other years—and then there is the church year. That church year begins now, today, with the first Sunday of Advent. Notice that, like people do when the calendar year begins on January 1, we church folk also usher out the old and bring in the new with chaos. We imitate the noise and clatter of New Year's Eve when people bang the drums, blow the whistles, sound the horns, release the sirens, shout the countdown, and wildly throw confetti. It's bedlam time, time to symbolically explode the old, as it were, obliterate the past, so we can make a new, fresh beginning.

The church year is no different. It too always ends and begins with chaos. Recall those terrible apocalyptic images in today's gospel: the sun, moon, and stars will implode. There will be the roaring of the sea and waves. Yes, the very powers of heaven, like a nuclear blast, will be shaken and people will die of fright. Quite a scenario. But the function of these dire images, like the ones of New Year's, is meant to obliterate the sinful past and prepare us to make a new spiritual beginning.

That's what the gospel sound and fury are about. It's about thrashing the old and preparing for the new. Only for us, it is not resolutions to lose weight or be nicer to our mother-in-law. For us Christians, it is the challenge to live the spiritual life better than we did last year.

In a way, I hesitate to use that term "spiritual life," as accurate as it is. The reason is that the term "spiritual life" tends to conjure up floating in la-la land, talking to animals, or pausing to have visions. Or, at least fleeing to the convent or monastery. But the spiritual life is quite realistic, robust, and challenging, and, while it is for everybody, it is not for sissies. Nevertheless, it is a necessity, a goal dearly to be achieved, so we must look at it thoughtfully. And the practical question that will guide our exploration is, how do I know if I am a spiritual person or not? How can I tell? Well, it's really not hard to figure out. In fact, there are five quite sensible and infallible signs that you and I are—or are not—spiritual persons. Listen to this teaching.

First, you are a spiritual person if you have the capacity for transcendence. Simply put, it means that you are aware that there's something more than meets the eye. You are always wonderfully suspicious that something more is going on. This is in contradiction to the out-and-out secularists whose words and actions say quite loudly that there is no God, no afterlife, no meaning, no purpose to life. Life is fundamentally absurd, a cosmic joke. What you see is what you get, period.

But not so the spiritual person. He or she sniffs hidden presences. They sense something in every flower, in beauty, in art, in friendship, in kindness, something that hints at something more to life. In fact, such things hint at Some *One* more. Many a convert became so because, although they were successful in their careers, they felt something was missing and they felt a mystery beckoning them. In Dostoevsky's novel *The Brothers Karamazov*, the priest's brother, who had left the faith and returned during his illness, is dying. Dostoevsky writes:

> The first birds of spring were flitting in the branches, chirping and singing in the windows....Looking at them and admiring, he began suddenly begging their forgiveness. He said, "Birds of heaven, happy birds, forgive me, for I have sinned against you too. Yes, there was such glory of God all about me: birds, trees, meadows, sky; only I lived in shame and dishonored it all and did not notice the beauty and the glory."

The spiritual person notices. The spiritual person has the capacity to perceive beyond and behind.

Second, you are a spiritual person if you have developed a sense of vocation. Which means, for example, that such people tend to see work not as just a job, but as a calling. For them, marriage has a spiritual significance. Spiritual persons feel that they are a part of a higher purpose, that their life, however unfamous, counts, that they were put here for a reason. They have a "purpose driven life," to quote the title of a popular book. As the great Cardinal Newman prayed:

> God has created me to do him some definite service.
> He has committed some work to me.
> Which he has not committed to another.
> I have my mission....
> I am a link in a chain,
> A bond of connection between persons.
> He has not created me for naught;
> I shall do good—I shall do his work;
> I shall be an angel of peace,
> A preacher of truth in my own place.

Spiritual persons have a sense of vocation, of purpose.

Third, you are a spiritual person if at times you experience a heightened state of consciousness. Which means, every now and then—and it's more common than you think—you sense a Presence, a Nearness, a Harmony that all makes sense. At certain times maybe, while engaged in prayer, say, or coming upon a sunset or in a moment of intense friendship or having your child fall asleep in your lap, you sense a Presence, a voice, a summoning, a harmony to life. All, for the moment, is well and for the moment you're pulled into something higher, something quite gracious.

A famous couplet makes its point:

> Two men looked out their prison bars;
> The one saw mud, the other stars.

Every once in a while a spiritual person has a heightened state of consciousness and perceives the stars.

Fourth, you are a spiritual person if you also use spiritual resources to solve problems. You, of course, use all of the wonderful natural helps there are and you turn to those whose skill can help you. But you also turn to prayer, seek solitude, perhaps talk things over with a spiritual director. A spiritual person tries to put life into a larger context.

Fifth, finally and practically, you are a spiritual person if you do decent things. Habitually. It's as simple as that. You engage in virtuous behavior. You actually show forgiveness, express gratitude, display compassion, tithe, bring your religion to the marketplace. You're honest and tell the truth. And, occasionally, you are even heroic.

Darryl Hill, some of you may recall, was the first African-American to play football for the University to Maryland in the early 1960s. No surprise, he received a lot of abuse from people in the South, particularly from the team ironically called the Deacons from Wake Forest, North Carolina. With the pre-game warm up ended and the nastiness in high gear, Hill noticed the Wake Forest captain approaching him. He stopped in front of Hill and said, "Look, I want to apologize for the behavior of my fans." Then he did an astonishing thing. He draped his arm over Hill's shoulder, and began to walk openly with him toward the Wake Forest side of the field where the jeering was at its worst. By the time the two of them reached the middle of the field the rude screaming had dropped to a near silence.

Now, that took a lot of courage for that captain. Who was he? He was Brian Piccolo who years later, as you may recall, would inspire TV's *Brian's Song*, which dramatized his relationship with African-American player Gale Sayers and Piccolo's losing battle with cancer.

A spiritual person is moral and does moral things, even when it hurts.

So, here we are on the threshold of our church's new year, gathered in worship, united in our collective weaknesses and yearnings, yet knowing that we are all called to be spiritual persons, perhaps never as urgently as today when apocalyptic scariness—the hotspots: Iraq, Iran, Israel, and the coldspots: corruption, consumerism, conceit—are threatening to undermine and destroy our lives, indeed our planet.

The spiritual person is the ultimate answer to such threats.

And so, once more, who is that spiritual person? The spiritual person is one:

> who has the capacity for transcendence
> who has a sense of vocation
> who now and then experiences a heightened state of
>   consciousness
> who uses spiritual resources
> and who lives morally.

That is a spiritual person, our goal, our hope for the New Church Year.

The Door Keeper

SECOND SUNDAY OF ADVENT, A, LUKE 3:1–6

In the fifteenth year of Tiberius Caesar
when Pilate was governor of Judea
Herod, tetrarch of Galilee
Philip, tetrarch of Ituraea
Annas and Caiaphas, high priests of the Temple
the word of God came to a desert prophet.

Did you listen to the cadence of this gospel opening, catch its rhythm? Did you sense a kind of drum roll? It's like a metronome. It is gospel writer Luke's way of playing an overture, fanfaring what's to come. It's the blaring graphics and loud music that introduce the six o'clock news or *The O'Reilly Factor* or *Larry King Live*. So, likewise, with this drum roll, Luke is saying, "Here he comes! Get ready for the Messiah!" But note that, in the process, Luke makes two points that will mark the Messiah's story and our story.

First, those names at the beginning: Tiberius Caesar, Pontius Pilate, King Herod, High Priest Annas; yes, psychotic Tiberius, vacillating Pilate, quisling Herod, corrupt Annas—they will be back later at the passion of Jesus. The mention of their names are dark hints of the outcome of Christ's life before he is even born.

Second, when Rome held all the power, when Rome's heel was firmly on Israel's neck, God's word came forth in the wilderness. That is to say, God's word did not stop at war rooms, palaces, and temples. Rather, it searched out a minor priest's son who is dressed in a camel skin and finds him in the desert of an occupied country. Yes, the word of the Lord came to this little speck in the empire who was to prepare the way of One who would straighten broken moral paths, fill valleys of despair, level mountains of trouble, and smooth out the rough ways of wickedness and sin. The word of the Lord had indeed bypassed the high and the mighty and fallen upon a nobody in the unlikeliest of desert places.

Interestingly, unbeknownst to John, the same thing had already happened years earlier to a young illiterate girl in a backwater village called Nazareth. She had a mystical experience and said yes to a vision and the word *to* her became a living Word *inside* her. The Word was beyond spoken. It was made flesh. That was some thirty years before. Now Mary's child was grown up and here was John preparing his way. All that had been set in motion was converging at this moment, and a darkened world saw the glimmer of light and took hope.

What a gospel for our times, for this gospel's Good News is that we should seek hope in our world as well, for the truth is, if you think about it, our world is not much different from John's. The world today is still symbolically the Rome of the Caesars. That is to say, in many parts of the world today the heel of repression and tyranny still grinds firmly upon the necks of its people. There is China with its imprisonments and executions without trials. There are countries in Africa and South America where political and religious freedom do not exist or are brutally repressed. There is Russia which, amidst dire poverty, boasts of 25 newly oil-rich billionaires and 88,000 millionaires who are living luxuriously while the majority are barely eking out a living.

Here in our own country, though blessedly freer and far less overtly brutal, the gap is just as wide. The high and the mighty, often through legal corruption, siphon off our public money and determine our lives. Last year lobbyists spent a record 2.4 billion to get their way, not our way, with the government. The record shows that the richest 300,000 Americans have had their incomes more than triple since 1970 while the real income of the working poor fell. War, crime, broken families abound. Rome lives.

Yet, the gospel news is that, as in the days of Rome, as in the days of John the Baptist, it still happens. What happens? The word of God still comes, and it comes, as it did then, to the small folk and in the unlikeliest of places. In every age it bypasses the boardrooms, complexes, and mega-mansions to lodge in the hearts of the little ones who become pinpoints of light and harbingers of hope. Think of worldly, carefree Francis from Assisi. Think of an ignorant, illiterate girl, Bernadette, from Lourdes. Think of a life-of-the-party playboy, Tom Merton, from Greenwich Village, and an unwed mother, Dorothy Day, from Staten Island, and, yes, even a streetcar conductor named Barney Casey from Milwaukee. All these nobodies received God's word, sometimes reluctantly, and they gave us light and hope. They remain a firm sign of God's presence and power.

Barney Casey? Did you hear me right? Who's he? I know you've heard of the others, so let me tell you about him and God's word and about his being a pinpoint of light. A nondescript kid from Milwaukee at the turn of the last century, a teenager who was the mainstay of his family, Barney Casey worked as a farmhand, lumberjack, brick maker, prison guard, and finally a streetcar conductor. Then one day he witnessed a tragedy that set him on a new course in life.

On a cold rainy afternoon as he guided his streetcar around a curve in a rough part of town, he saw a lot of people gathered on the tracks. He stopped the car, pushed through the crowd to see a young drunken sailor standing over a woman he had assaulted and stabbed repeatedly. He couldn't get the brutal incident out of his mind. He began to pray for the sailor. He prayed for the woman and gradually he felt he must pray for the whole world.

So eventually he quit his job and applied to the seminary. But Barney was not that bright. So the seminary brass dismissed him and told him to go become a brother where the studies were not as rigorous. But Barney, frustrated but not defeated, applied and joined the Capuchin order at St. Bonaventure in Detroit where he got his religious name of Solanus, after St. Francis Solanus: Solanus Casey. Still he really wasn't that sharp and some seminary professors opposed his ordination, but an old priest spoke up for him and he was ordained in 1904. However, the doubts about the intelligence and the abilities of this underachiever still lingered, so the seminary would ordain him only under one condition, that he would remain what is called a "simplex priest," that is, he could celebrate Mass but that's all. He could not hear confessions, preach, or wear the Capuchin hood.

So for forty-three years Father Solanus Casey never heard a confession or gave a retreat or preached a mission, What did he do? He was assigned as a lowly doorkeeper, answering the door and greeting visitors, a no-brainer. He spent his first fifteen years answering the door in Yonkers and in Manhattan and then in 1921 was transferred to Our Lady of the Angels in Harlem.

But in this desert of the ordinary, the word of God bypassed the local bishop and the chancery officials and the abbot and came to Barney, because people were discovering something about this doorkeeper. It was that this simple doorkeeper, having listened so intently to the word of God, turned out to be a wonderful listener to them and an insightful counselor. Word spread and soon many would come, bypass the prior and abbot, and ask to speak with the doorkeeper, Father Solanus. But that wasn't all. Father Solanus—Barney Casey—was also put in charge of the Capuchin Prayer Association, but no sooner did he take charge than miracles began to happen. People were being healed of all sorts of ailments: pneumonia, heart disease, blindness. This doorkeeper turned out to be also a wonder-worker.

His superiors soon transferred him back to St. Bonaventure in Detroit where they could keep an eye and a lid on him. But there he attracted an even larger following and so for the next two decades people trekked literally from all over the world, like the crowds that came to John in the desert, to receive the simple doorkeeper's ministry and hear his words.

Father Solanus—Barney Casey—worked twelve hours a day helping and counseling others. At night he was found praying in the chapel and often sound asleep before the altar. This streetcar driver turned simple priest, not trusted with anything important, died in 1957 and his cause is now up for canonization. Who would have thought, in the car capital of the world, the word of God would come to somebody who answers the door and a light would shine forth?

My point in telling you all this during Advent is precisely the old Christopher point: *Better to light one candle than to curse the darkness.* Times are threatening, times are bloody and dark, but let the word of God lodge in your heart. Pray the prayer, do the good deed, be holy, put yourself in the hands of God. Have a sense of calling.

Be a candle, be a Francis, be a Bernadette, be a John the Baptist, be a simple doorkeeper who lets out the light. And then, lo and behold, you will become today's voice of hope, of one crying out in the desert of our times, "Prepare the way of the Lord, for he is near."

How Starbucks Saved My Life

Matthew, never without Old Testament motifs in his mind, opens up to-day's gospel, as you heard, with John the Baptist in the wilderness. John is dressed like the formidable ancient prophet, Elijah. He is eating inedible locusts, recalling one of the ten plagues that God brought upon Egypt at the time of the Exodus. He has a side dish of wild honey that recalls the bitter scroll that tastes as sweet as honey when swallowed by the proph-et Ezekiel. And John's wilderness is the unforgiving, unrelenting desert, where Moses and the people learned the harsh lessons of dependence on God. Here in the desert John the Baptist, the last great biblical prophet after a hiatus of four hundred years, is inviting people to leave their usual locales and preoccupations and come apart with him, away from the maddening crowd, in order to find themselves and God, for "the Kingdom of God is very much at hand."

So, there we are, Matthew's basic Advent theme in a nutshell: Let go. Let God. It's all so familiar, too familiar, I think, and so I know I must search around to find its contemporary counterpart so you can appreciate John's message anew. And I *have* found it in an engaging book called, of all things, *How Starbucks Saved My Life*. This short biographical book is by Michael Gates Gill. He's the son of the famous literary figure of high society who wrote many years for the *New Yorker*, Brendan Gill.

Now, without intending to plug Starbucks coffee, let me tell Michael's Advent story. He was born into wealth and high society, being pretty much emotionally abandoned by his partying parents. He hobnobbed with the rich and famous all of his life. He eventually went, of course, to Yale and after graduation garnered a top level, high-paying job at a prestigious advertising firm in New York. Clever with words and jingles, he made tons of money traveling to foreign lands selling to high profile customers. He was living the good life.

Michael, I might add here, was not a particularly admirable man. He was unfaithful to his wife and broke her heart and disgraced his four grown children. Later he had an affair with a woman psychiatrist and had a son by her. She eventually tired of him and dropped him. And then his life completely unraveled when a young hotshot took over his company and wanted to project a "youthful" corporate image and so, in the bloodless manner of corporate life where profit, not loyalty, prevails, he fired the sixty-four-year-old Michael Gill.

Here he is: divorced, alienated from his children, father of a small illegitimate son, no benefits, totally broke, living in a one-room flat. The man, in our gospel terminology, has been forced into the desert. But, unknown to him, the Kingdom of God awaits him there. It happens this way.

One day he stops into the Starbucks at Lexington and 78th street for a cup of coffee, totally unaware that it's their hiring week and a young black woman named Crystal, thinking he's applying, offers him a job. To make a long story short, this down-and-out son of wealth and privilege takes the job and very slowly and painfully he learns to live like everyone else. For one thing, everyone at Starbucks is young, mostly African-American and Hispanic, and this white old man sticks out like a sore thumb. What's more, he doesn't know a thing about coffee or the difference between a latte and an espresso.

Now think about it. Michael Gates Gill, always being bowed down to, who never served anything to his subordinates in all his years in corporate life. Now here he is at sixty-four, no longer in a three-piece suit but dressed in black pants, shirt, green apron, and a Starbucks hat making an hour and half commute from his dingy apartment to work for a black woman who was twenty-eight!

He finds himself standing on his feet all day long, learning to master the intricacies of coffee making, serving coffee to the ordinary street folk who rush in daily for their coffees and pastries, and cleaning the bathrooms, at which he learns to excel. He gradually learns the difference between the forty kinds of coffee they serve, but—here comes the grace—as he gets into his job he also learns something more, something novel to him: at Starbucks, as he put it, "it was not about me—it was about serving *others*."

Along the way he learns the Starbucks philosophy, which bowls him over: every customer is called a Guest and is to be treated as such; every employee is called a Partner and you had to cooperate to make it work. Ironclad rule: they must treat Guests and each other with respect and dignity. They must make eye contact and conversation with every Guest. It was a revelation to him, good news, gospel.

He eventually discovers that Starbucks isn't just a job. It is a way of life. It's a key part of people's lives, an important destination for them every single day. By and by he becomes eager to see them. In no time he can call them by name and they begin calling him Mike. He's discovered community. He is totally surprised at how welcome he is made to feel, even though he is the "old man" among a bunch of kids in a low-level job. How different, he recalls, from his boss at the ad agency who once told him, "Fear is a great motivator" and where, he says, the game was win or lose, where, if you got new clients you were the hero, if you didn't you were a bum. As he writes, "There was no in-between. And there certainly wasn't respect or dignity. Those words were literally never mentioned."

Another thing: he was impressed by how the other Partners or employees were truly happy over another's success. He writes, "The advertising world was based on a pyramid where only a few got to enjoy the recognition. At Starbucks everyone was respected and many, if not most, were recognized…not just at special forums, but every day, in every store…."

Well, the book goes on about his struggles and, most of all, about the revelation of a whole new way of life where he was accepted for who he was, not where he came from, where serving people rather than being served blew his mind away, where getting to know and rub shoulders with ordinary people was liberating, and where he found himself, for the first time in his life, being so unbelievably and incredibly happy and fulfilled.

I like what he writes:

> Again, I was struck with the incongruity of my life—ten years
> earlier, as a busy executive, at five in the morning, I might have

been riding the red-eye back from a trip to Los Angeles. Most summer mornings since being fired I would have been sleeping peacefully in our big old New England farmhouse, looking forward to a day of swimming and golf with my contemporaries who were already comfortably retired. Now I was standing in the dangerous dark of a sweaty New York City, waiting for my twenty-eight-year-old boss and scared that I might not be able to do good enough job of opening a Starbucks store. My former entitled and arrogant self would have been appalled.

There is more testimony of his spiritual awakening. He writes,

Crystal and my partners at Starbucks, like Kester and Charlie, had given me a chance to work and live and see things a new way....I *had* been a control freak....I had loved ordering people to work overtime or change a headline or even bring me a cup of coffee....I had been a real bad boss....It was time to be a real good Partner....I had traded in my pin-striped suit for a green apron, a Master of the Universe costume for something that said I was there to serve—not to rule....

Do you notice how unbelievably like Jesus he sounds?

Looking back, he adds, "I could be sincere at Starbucks because I was finally in a work environment that valued those precious moments of truly human interaction. From the moment when I admitted that I was so happy to be there, it had seemed so simple and easy. Why didn't every company work that way?"

I might add that eventually he becomes reconciled with his grown children if not with his wife. They are bemused to see blue blood dad serving coffee to street people—and enjoying it and being affectionately greeted by everyone! They are astounded at his happiness.

There it is, *How Starbucks Saved My Life*. I share this with you because Gill's is an engaging and remarkable story, a secular version, if you will, of the Advent spiritual journey: a man dragged into the desert, forced to let go, stripped of his arrogance, painfully learning what really matters—human relationships and respect—and that life is not all about him.

John the Baptist would have been pleased.

The Ten Commandments of Forgiveness

Second Sunday of Advent, B, Mark 1:1–8

John the Baptist appeared in the desert, proclaiming a baptism for the forgiveness of sins.

It is not without reason, it seems, that the beginning and end of the church's liturgical year talks about the forgiveness of sins. Advent starts, as you just heard, with John's baptism for the forgiveness of sins and Easter ends with the risen Jesus proclaiming, "Receive the Holy Spirit; whose sins you shall forgive are forgiven them." Forgiveness hits a tender spot. We all have done some stupid and immoral things, from sniveling lies to large betrayals—and worse. None of us wants the burdens of shame and guilt as we live. We want forgiveness. None of us wants justice when we die. We want mercy.

Oddly, and perhaps disturbingly enough, at least according to Jesus' teaching, such forgiveness for us depends on our forgiveness of others. Jesus said something to the effect that if our gift is to mean anything at the altar we must first go and be reconciled with one another. He taught us a two-edged prayer asking God to forgive us our trespasses *as* we forgive those who have sinned against us. Since this is so unsparingly true—God's forgiveness depending on our forgiveness—I want to share with you this morning what I call the Ten Commandments of Forgiveness, which a friend, Father Brian Joyce, shared with me. You will not, and need not, remember them all, don't even attempt it. Recall, perhaps, just the ones that strike a chord with you. So, here are the Ten Commandments of Forgiveness.

The First Commandment: Forgiveness is not easy. There is no cheap grace. There is no quick fix. A mother says to her child, "Tell him you're sorry."…"I'm sorry," the kid mumbles reluctantly. Doesn't mean a thing. If it's quick and easy it's not real, especially for deep betrayals and hurts. So we need to ask God for help. We can't forgive on our own. Maybe, like Jesus who said to his Father, "Father, forgive them; they know not what they do," we need to ask God to start the process of forgiveness. First Commandment: Forgiveness is not easy. It takes time.

The Second Commandment: Forgiveness is not forgetting. We say, "Forgive and forget." I don't think so. Forgiveness is about a change of heart, not a bad memory or having a senior moment. The wounds are too fresh or too deep. While forgiveness may not include harboring festering hurts, neither is it about forgetting. In fact, it may be helpful to remember the point from which you have moved on, the occasion that began your journey to full forgiveness.

The Third Commandment: Forgiveness does not overlook evil. It doesn't mean that we accept injustice or naively make believe that all is well when it isn't. It doesn't mean denial. It doesn't mean, "Let's pretend it never existed." So number three is: Forgiveness does not overlook evil.

The Fourth Commandment: Forgiveness is not indifference. What this means is where things are harmful and wrong, we don't just go back to "business as usual," and let the hurt and damage go on. Forgiveness is not indifference, and we should do what we can to make sure the evil won't happen again.

The Fifth Commandment: Forgiveness is not the same thing as approval. We can be forgiving and, at the same time, express our disagreement, express our disapproval of harmful behavior.

O.K. That's the first five. I'm going faster than Moses did.

Forgiveness is not easy.

Forgiveness is not forgetting.

Forgiveness does not overlook evil.

Forgiveness is not indifference.

Forgiveness is not the same thing as approval.

Here are the next five. They are more positive and deeper.

The Sixth Commandment: Forgiveness is based on recognizing and admitting that people are always bigger than their faults. People are always larger than, and they are more than, their mistakes or their wrongdoings. In other words, we don't define somebody and who they are by something they said to us or the way they hurt us. They are bigger than that. Forgiveness is based on recognizing and admitting that people are always bigger and more than their faults and their mistakes.

The Seventh Commandment: Forgiveness is willing to allow a person who has offended us to start over again. You know, the more common thing is saying, "Never again! No way! I will never let that happen again. I will never have anything to do with him again. No way!" Forgiveness means letting go of that. Forgiveness means allowing a person to start all over again.

The Eighth Commandment: Forgiveness recognizes the humanity of the person who has wronged us and also recognizes our own humanity and our shortcomings and our contributions to what went wrong.

The Ninth Commandment: Forgiveness surrenders the right to get even. It's not Eliza Doolittle's, "Just you wait, 'enry 'iggins, just you wait!" "Boy! I'm going to get you back….Payback time!…Revenge!" Or, at least, "Someday you'll be sorry." It means letting go of that and embracing the Christian truth that forgiveness surrenders the right to get even.

And, finally, the Tenth Commandment: Forgiveness means we wish the person who hurt us, or the group that hurt us, we wish them well. In fact, we wish them the best. That's tough, but it's basically letting God be the final judge. We wish them well. We commend them to God's mercy and judgment.

So there are my Ten Commandments of forgiveness:

1. Forgiveness is not easy.
2. Forgiveness is not forgetting.
3. Forgiveness does not overlook evil.
4. Forgiveness is not indifference.
5. Forgiveness is not the same thing as approval.
6. Forgiveness recognizes that people are always bigger than their faults.
7. Forgiveness allows a person to start all over again.
8. Forgiveness recognizes the humanity of the wrongdoer.
9. Forgiveness surrenders the right to get even.
10. Forgiveness wishes the offender well.

The gospel starts off with the desire for God's forgiveness at Advent and ends with bestowing it at Easter. In between, as a necessary connection, lie our Ten Commandments of Forgiveness. You can't have the bookends without the middle.

Wildflowers

Two men looked through their prison bars.
The one saw mud, the other stars.

That's a familiar couplet. It is, I guess, a commentary about attitude: seeing the glass half full or seeing it half empty with the implication that we should be the star gazer, the drinker of life's half-full glass.

Well, true enough. But today, with Matthew's Advent gospel still ringing in our ears, we might consider the other side. We might think of the mud-gazer, the drinker of life's half-empty glass. What I'm leading up to is that we might think this way of John the Baptist as he is presented today: stuck gazing at the mud. In so doing, let's reverse the gospel paragraphs.

"What did you go out to see?" Jesus asked. Jesus answers his own question: not a will-o'-the-whisp reed or a sartorial fop but a prophet, yes, a fearless, assured, strong, confident prophet, taking on kings, soldiers, and Pharisees, giving none of them any quarter.

Yes, but let's go back to the first paragraph of today's gospel. Things are looking a little bit different at the moment. It's all right to be righteous and brave and popular when you're free and in charge and people are flocking to you and hanging on your every word. But it's a different matter to be in a filthy jail cell, looking through your prison bars awaiting execution. No crowds, no press, no affirmations, no Messiah nearby to point to. Just mud.

And time to think, plenty of time to think. And with the thinking comes the doubt. John had announced the Messiah has come. So, now as a rat scurries across the floor and John looks through his prison bars he's asking himself, Where's all the Messiah stuff? Where's the peaceable kingdom?

The blooming desert? Reconciliation, tolerance, brotherhood? Sweet relief? Did I back the wrong horse? Was it all an illusion? Was he the one who was to come? Has Jesus made a difference?

John's questions are so modern, the perfect post-9/11 questions, aren't they? Where's the Messiah and the peace he came to bring? Has anything changed? Look around: We have a long, drawn-out war in Iraq. Terrorism stalks us. Institutionalized corruption is everywhere from Congress to churches, from boardrooms to baseball. Most marriages today, it is reported, don't make their silver anniversaries. We have a bumper crop of fatherless children, many of whom morph into gang members.

We have a technology that gives everyone his or her private hand-held gadget, but we are unable to have any gracious and civil face-to-face communication. We are exposed to a virtual world but cannot achieve and sustain intimacy in the real world. Pornography is so easy to come by, love so hard. Consumption fills our homes and empties our hearts. In a word, we observe along with John that not much has changed in the world. Some messianic times. Some Messiah. Should we look for another? Some have.

For an answer let's go back to Matthew's gospel where Jesus, sensing John's cynicism—maybe ours too—sympathetically responds. He says in effect, "Look, John, I know where you're coming from but you're looking for answers in the wrong place. Really, I'm not what you expected, what people wanted: the tabloid Messiah at CNN, the celebrity survivor, the powerful judge, the warrior to slay dissidents, the master to impose conformity and obedience. I have not come for domination and conquest to enforce virtue and wipe out evil. You won't find me in the halls of power. Remember, I was born in a stable.

"But, I tell you, you *will* find me wherever someone helps the blind to see, the lame to walk, the sick to heal, the deaf to hear, the spiritually dead to rise, and the poor to better their lives. And blessed is the one who takes no offense at my doing it this way."

Father Dan Berrigan knows this. For those old enough, his name still evokes strong emotions. You may remember that he's the peacenik Jesuit priest, activist of the 1960s who spoke out against injustice and protested the Vietnam War. Dan is in his eighties now. Today he works in a hospice for the terminally ill. Each week he spends time sitting quietly at the beside of a young boy who is so totally incapacitated that he cannot speak, hear, or move to respond in any apparent way to those around him.

Father Berrigan says that as he sits there, attentive to the silent powerlessness of this young boy, he experiences the presence of God. Why? Because, he says, that's where God is to be found; because the God who was born in a stable and died on a cross is always present in powerlessness.

That's where the Messiah is. Those who know this and who therefore minister to Jesus in the least of his brethren reveal the messianic presence. On the other hand, if people are still asking where is Jesus in all of this mess, it may be because not enough of us are revealing him through our lives.

But if indeed the blind do see and the lame walk and the sick heal and the poor advance because of us, then these are clear signals of the Messiah's presence among the ruins of our society, and people will know and be lifted up from despair and find hope.

A man remembers. He grew up in a modest household in a very rural area. His parents could not provide much in the way of material goods but they always provided the love, faith, and guidance their son needed to face the world.

One day, tragedy struck the poor family. Their house caught on fire and burned to the ground. The father and son went to town to buy some meager supplies, while the mother sifted through the ashes of their home to find something she could salvage. When the father and son returned from their trip to town, they saw quite a wondrous sight. From the ashes of their cabin the mother had found a few dishes and books and papers. And she had also found a small can that she filled with freshly picked wildflowers from the fields around them. When the boy and his father saw that arrangement of glorious wildflowers in the midst of the ashes, they knew everything was going to be all right.

That's a good metaphor for today's gospel. There are so many—maybe ourselves—asking cynically or despairingly with John the Baptist, Are you the one? Should we look for another? Where is Jesus? But if we make ourselves as wildflowers amidst the ashes of today, people won't have to ask. They will know the Messiah has come.

CEOs: Achievement and Challenge

THIRD SUNDAY OF ADVENT, B, JOHN 1:6–8, 19–28

"Who are you?"
"I am not the messiah."

In a world peppered with grossly dishonest CEOs from Enron, Tyco, Worldcom, and others, it's refreshing to run into Tom Chappell, the CEO of a natural toothpaste company, Tom's of Maine. Eighteen years ago when he was forty-three, he had just guided his company through a period of aggressive growth and now he had more money than a Sultan. But why wasn't he happy? He was feeling drained, emotionally and spiritually. The usual advice for business leaders when they hit that point is to sell the business, buy a sailboat, and travel the world. But Chappell, instead, found direction from a question his pastor put to him. "What makes you think Tom's of Maine isn't your ministry?"

So what this CEO decided to do was to stay with the company, but also to enroll in Harvard Divinity School. The agreement Chappell worked out with his company was that he would spend half of each week in Kennebunk, Maine, doing the CEO stuff, and the other half in Cambridge, Massachusetts, being a theological student. The business ran just fine while he was away, so, explains Chappell, his coworkers suggested that he stay at the seminary and keep praying. So he did.

Four years later, after graduating from the theological school, Chappell asked one of his professors to meet with his company board and help them draft a mission statement and business road map based on moral and ethical principles. As a result Tom's of Maine promised to honor its

30

commitments to all of its shareholders, the community, and the environment. Also, the company promised to start a series of three partnerships each year that promote the common good, such as saving America's rivers, community gardening, and support for a local dental clinic for the poor. In short, Chappell challenged his company to decide what sort of business it would be, one driven only by the bottom line or one with allegiance to other values.

And, in a way, that's the challenge to us all: What sort of person will we be—are we raising our children to be—one driven by the bottom line or one with allegiance to other values?

With that question, let me segue to the more specific topic of children. Recently the *New York Times* ran an article entitled "Kids gone wild" reflecting a poll that found nearly seventy percent of Americans said they believed that people are ruder now than twenty or thirty years ago and that children who haven't been taught the basic rudiments of public behavior are among the worst offenders, especially those of young, status-conscious parents. The article cites the figures: Last year, more than one in three teachers told Public Agenda pollsters that they had seriously considered leaving their profession or knew of a colleague who had left because of "intolerable" student behavior, and nearly eight in ten teachers said their students were quick to remind them that they had rights and could sue their parents if they were too harshly disciplined.

The major culprit of such self-centered rudeness, according to the experts, is the idol, the holy grail, of achievement, and its obsessions for the right schools, the right connections, the right clubs, the right job, the right profession, all of which confer status. The pressure on kids to achieve, they say, to do *well*, is enormous, while the pressure on kids to do *good* is small by comparison. That doesn't show up on college applications, you see. And that's the problem. Parenting today, continue the experts, is largely about training children to compete—in school or on the soccer field—and the kinds of attributes they need to be competitive are precisely those that help break down society's civility. Children are taught to value and prioritize achievement, and achievement is certainly praiseworthy, but the kicker is that it is placed above all else, including respect, love, compassion, and courtesy due to other people.

Dan Kindlon, a Harvard University child psychologist and author of *Too Much of a Good Thing: Raising Children of Character in an Indulgent Age*, puts it this way: "We're insane about achievement. School work is up 50 percent since 1981, and we're so obsessed with our kids getting into the right school, getting the right grades, we let a lot of things slide." Another child psychologist, the popular Wendy Mogel, thinks that the rude, obnoxious behavior of kids who are terribly stressed from academic and sports overload imposed by their parents is a cry to those overinvolved parents to let go and just let them be kids. As she puts it, "The kids need to do fifth-grade level math in third grade and have every gadget, pleasure, and indulgence in childhood, and when they act like kids, we get mad." The article ends by commenting that raising less rude children may mean less pressure-to-achieve time with children, and more time getting them to do the things they don't want to do, like having meals together, sitting up straight, making polite conversation, picking up after themselves, and respecting adults.

Now, so far, all this pulpit commentary, I admit, sounds like a talk for a PTA meeting, not the stuff for a homily in a church, and perhaps you're right to think that. But, on the other hand, the story of CEO Tom Chappell and the observations about an increase of rude children and adults point unmistakably to spiritual foundations and basic gospel truths, and so they do, I maintain, belong in church.

Tom Chappell wanted his company to ask itself what kind of corporation it wanted to be: one driven solely by the bottom line of profit at all costs, or one driven by the values of community, compassion, and reach-out. The gospel asks the same question: What kind of adults do you want to be? What kind of children do you want your children to be? Do you want them driven solely by high achievement or driven by the values of community, compassion, and outreach? Do you want children who have never developed a spiritual life or who have never learned how to pray or handle disappointment? Or do you want children who, in spite of their parent-driven pursuit of scholastic and technical achievement, consider heart, sensitivity, compassion, and caring as even more important, children who have been taught by their parents that they really are *not* the Messiah, but, like John the Baptist, their lives are meant to point to him?

As a summary challenge, let me close with a moving scene from Chaim Potok's celebrated novel, *The Chosen*. A father is wailing to his friend Reuven about the brilliance of his son Daniel. Wailing? Today's parents would be proud to have such an overachiever to show off like a trophy, to have him graduate with honors from Princeton or Harvard. But this father sees it differently. He groans that his son's brilliance is more a curse than a blessing. He recounts to Reuven how his son—when he was only four years old—read a story in Yiddish about a poor man who suffered and struggled to get to Israel before he died. His son not only enjoyed the story but proudly told it back to his father from memory, effortlessly reciting it like a school lesson. And his father remembers how he wept inside himself when he did. He tells Reuven:

> I went away and cried to the Master of the Universe, "What have you done to me? A mind like this I need for a son? A *heart* I need for a son, *compassion* I want from my son, righteousness, mercy, strength to suffer and carry pain: *that* I want from my son, not a mind without a soul!"

What Should We Do?

THIRD SUNDAY OF ADVENT, C, LUKE 3:10–18

There it is, right at the beginning of this gospel, that perennial human question, "What should we do?" Very few of us escape that question sometime or another in our lives. Sometimes it concerns a relatively minor matter: "What dress should I wear?" "What car should I buy?" Other times it concerns more serious religious problems that weigh heavily on people today: "Why are so many young people leaving the church?" "What do I say to my children who no longer believe or go to church?" "How can I trust the church anymore after its cover-up in the sexual scandals?" Sometimes it concerns crucial and life-changing issues of relationships and health. Whatever, we're often in a dilemma. What should we do? Whom can we turn to? Who will understand? Where can I find an answer? Is there an answer?

We observe that Mary in Advent was not beyond such dilemmas. There was this vision with its strange message of motherhood to her, a virgin. There was Joseph's dilemma: Should I marry her or not? Her parents were too close and were worried about her strange behavior. She agonized. What should she do? One thing she does do is to put on her shawl and trek some sixty miles—not a hardship for a peasant girl—to visit cousin Elizabeth. Mary dearly needed a John the Baptist, someone to talk to, someone who would understand, and she knew that kind, older Elizabeth, John's mother, would understand, would help her struggle with what she should do.

Then there are others, like the folk and the soldiers in today's gospel, who came to John the Baptist, who did not have family or economic matters on their minds, but rather the more basic matter of the state of their souls. They were there at a spiritual crossroad. They were there because they knew they needed to change their lives, to get out of the box. They had been stung by John's words. Maybe he was on to something. Maybe it *was* time to get out of their spiritual and emotional rut. So, with some trepidation, they asked John, "What should we do?" And they asked with trepidation because they knew that any answer John gave would cost them something. That just goes with the territory. There would be some pain, some separation involved. A change of heart, repentance, an alteration of lifestyle would be demanded. Were they ready for that? Could they pay the price?

I think of one who did. I think of Dorothy Day, atheist and activist, living with her common-law husband, a man named Forster, on Staten Island. She is pregnant. She had been pregnant before by another man and had an abortion. This time, however, she was in love with Forster and she very much wanted that baby. But during the Advent of her pregnancy, she began to examine her life and the life she wanted for her child. Suddenly she began to pray. She began to read the fifteenth-century spiritual classic, *The Imitation of Christ.* She gradually came to desire that she must baptize her baby and not only baptize her, but baptize her Catholic.

A sister who ran a home for unwed mothers nearby proved to be her John the Baptist. She asked curtly, "How can you have your baby baptized Catholic and not be one yourself?" That is, how can you not change? Dorothy Day thought and prayed. She was at a crossroad. What should she do? She decided to become a Catholic. At the time, of course, she had no notion that she would be up for canonization because of her extraordinary love of and service to the poor, and her holy life. That would come later.

But, meanwhile, it cost her, cost her dearly. Her friends abandoned her. But, most of all, it cost her her live-in husband. Listen to her poignant words from her autobiography, *The Long Loneliness*:

> It was killing me to think of leaving him....getting into bed, cold with the chill of the November air, he held me close to him in silence. I loved him in every way, as a wife, as a mother; I even loved him for all he knew and pitied him for all he didn't know. I loved him for all the odds and ends I had to fish out of his sweater pockets and for the sand and sea shells he brought in with his fishing. I loved his lean cold body as he got into bed smelling of the sea, and I loved his integrity and his stubborn pride.

There's a woman in love! But what should she do? Forster was an anarchist with absolutely no interest in organized religion or organized anything for that matter. And Dorothy? She had found Jesus and she had to make a decision. They parted. The cost was high but she became an authentic, centered, beautiful person.

Now let's put ourselves into this Advent scene. Our questions are: What should I do to be authentic, not just a cookie-stamped consumer living like everyone else, grasping for the latest product that I think will give me some identity, some acceptance? What must I do to live an authentic life, a spiritual life? What should I do?

One who asked this was seventeen-year-old Jim Martin who began his undergraduate studies at the University of Pennsylvania's famous Wharton School of Business, hoping a business degree could get him into any number of lucrative fields. At least he would get a high-paying job. So he took finance and accounting, got his degree, and settled in with a corporate program at General Electric. Pretty good. Of course, being young, he never asked himself the important questions: What do I desire in life? And what does God desire for me?

He was working around the clock making big money, witnessing at times some dishonest and callous behavior in the corporate world but, hey, there was always the paycheck. Still, his life seemed meaningless. One night he came home to his apartment he shared with two other guys and, dead tired, got a drink and turned on TV. He happened to come across a public television documentary on Thomas Merton, the playboy turned Catholic, turned monk, turned mystic who had an enormous influence on millions of people through his writings. Martin bought his autobiography, the *Seven Storey Mountain,* found that Merton had struggled with the same questions as he, and the same addictions to pride, ambition, and selfishness. It made him think and reassess his own life and come back to that haunting question, "What should I do?" Eventually what he did was to quit his big job with the big salary and become a Jesuit who ministers in the poor lands and in the academy and tells people of his fulfilled life now.

We're not that dramatic. We're more in line with those ordinary folk who came to John the Baptist. And John is there to answer us as he did the people who came to him. He was, in his response to them, psychologically right on. He did not offer elaborate programs as an answer. He said in effect, Take it one day at a time and start with the simple things. "Whoever has two cloaks share with someone who had none," he said. We who have more sweaters, coats, and jackets than our closets can handle should give some away. "Stop collecting more than is required," he said to the tax collectors. And we who cut corners for a few extra bucks should take up tithing as a normal part of being a Christian, giving ten percent of our income to charity. "Do not practice extortion, falsely accuse anyone, and don't be greedy," he told the soldiers. And we who watch our leaders double dip, gather multiple pensions, have no-show jobs, and bribe and extort should use our single vote to move them on. And we should look to ourselves if we are doing the same things. Basically, John is saying to us, pick a value, one real value you want to adopt. Practice it. Give it time to catch on.

So, it's Advent and the Advent question hangs there: What should I do? What should I, *must* I, do to be authentic, to live the life God has called me to live?

The old Indian was sharing his wisdom with his grandson. He told the grandson that we have two wolves inside us who struggle with each other. One is the wolf of peace, love, and kindness. The other is the wolf of fear, greed, and hatred.

"Which wolf will win, Grandfather?" asked the grandson.

The wise man gave a John the Baptist answer, "Whichever one we feed."

Overture

FOURTH SUNDAY OF ADVENT, A, MATTHEW 1:18–24

There are some, I suspect, who wonder why we are at church today. After all, we're just twenty-four hours from the vigil of Christmas. Since, as today's gospel appears to show, we're hitting on the same theme both days—it starts, "This is how the birth of Jesus came about"—why not have a holiday special, a "twofer," a two-for-one? Why not one Mass to cover both days?

Good question, but there is an answer—and it's not so we can have two collections! Rather, in our world where the merchants began advertising their Christmas wares at the beginning of September and television was showing all the standard holiday movies such as Dickens' "A Christmas Carol" and Irving Berlin's "White Christmas" two days after Thanksgiving, and where for months stores and the airwaves have been piping in holiday music, a tired, jaded, harried populace has had little time for reflection.

Today might be considered that time for reflection, a welcomed and needed pause in the midst of a hectic and noisy Christmas agenda to sort things out. So look upon today not as an unnecessary duplication of tomorrow, but as a preparation *for* tomorrow, a time-out, free of commercial jingle-belling, to reflect on what it's all about.

And Matthew sets out precisely to tell us what it's about. But, being an ancient writer, he does not do this directly. Rather his birth-announcement gospel of today is more a kind of overture, a symbolic statement of what is to come. He sounds themes that look to tomorrow, themes that explain who and what the child in the manger is and would grow up to be, what we should expect. So, let's unpack Matthew's gospel and his clues. What *is* he trying to tell us about this child when he writes this is "how he came about"?

There are four things to look for hidden in his gospel. The first is a focus on God. Matthew writes, "Mary was found to be with child through the

38

Holy Spirit." The Holy Spirit here is not the third person of the Blessed Trinity. It is simply the divine action that, time after time, *all* throughout Israel's history, has broken into human affairs. Only this time, *this time*, it's unique, it's definitive.

This time God's breaking into the human world is by actually taking on the human condition itself, becoming a human being with all of its fears, joys, and limitations. The world's been waiting for an intimacy like that, although it never dreamed it would take this form, and it will be fulfilled in Jesus. That's Matthew's first point: God is still active, is still longing for us, still taking the initiative. All this drama is God's doing. How God must love us!

Second point. Matthew's angel announces, "Joseph, *son of David*, do not be afraid to take Mary as your wife…" with the emphasis on the phrase, "son of David." These words bring to the fore an important message: Jesus is the fulfillment of the Davidic prophecies. He is not an outsider bearing a new religion. He is not a novelty. He is deeply rooted in his people, in Judaism, in the Old Testament. What was promised of old will at long last be fulfilled in Jesus. Matthew is saying that God has been faithful to his word. Jesus is part of and the climax of God's ongoing love affair with the human race. That's why Matthew throws in that "Son of David."

Third point Matthew is making. He tells us that Mary is found to be pregnant and her fiancé Joseph knows he's not the father. It's a scandalous situation. Either she was raped or she had illicit relations with someone else. But Matthew doesn't linger over the sordid story but wants to say that, yes, God chose to come into the world in scandal. Why would he do that? Because he wants to get us ready for a scandalous God in the flesh.

Jesus, born in scandal, would continue to scandalize. He would challenge the prevailing understanding of the law, break bread with sinners, touch lepers, call tax collectors to follow him, forgive a woman caught in adultery, and make claims that sounded like blasphemy. Matthew's mention of Mary's pregnancy is getting us ready to be scandalized by the Messiah's overwhelming compassion for people like us.

Fourth, Matthew, as you heard, cleverly records a second part of the angelic salutation to Joseph. He has the angel add, "Behold a virgin shall conceive and bear a son and they shall name him Emmanuel, which means

'God is with us.'" Sometimes people ask, "How come Jesus was named Jesus when the Bible says he will be called Emmanuel?" But Emmanuel is not a given name. It's what they call a throne name, a name that sounds a motif, a theme of the person's reign. It's like Angelo Roncalli taking the throne name of Pope John XXIII although his given name remained Angelo and that's what his family and close friends called him. The king we know as Edward VIII of England was actually baptized David, but he choose the throne name of Edward when he succeeded his father George V.

Emmanuel is a throne name, a thematic description that bookends Matthew's gospel. Emmanuel, or "God is with us," is here at Jesus' birth and it will reappear after his death when the risen Jesus tells his followers to go and make disciples of all nations adding, "behold I am *with you* all days till the end." Ever since Jesus, God has been visibly with us in the flesh, in the church. Matthew is saying that, come tomorrow's birth, we human beings will never be bereft of God's presence, God's compassionate presence. In our best and our worst moments, God will be with us. That's what Jesus is all about.

So this thoroughly Advent gospel is full of foreshadowing. It is not the Christmas birth story. It is a pre-Christmas preface. Matthew is telling us what to look for and pray over tomorrow: divine action, divine promises, divine scandal, and divine presence.

Strangely, in a way, Matthew's gospel reminds me of one of those poignant episodes in *M*A*S*H* where the battalion is all set to celebrate Christmas when they receive a new patient, a severely wounded soldier. Despite their efforts, the soldier dies on the operating table in their makeshift hospital. Although it goes against his ethics, the doctor in charge writes an incorrect time of death on the medical records allowing him to tell the soldier's wife and children that he died on December 26. He justifies his action by saying, "No child should have to connect Christmas to death."

Matthew wrote in troubled times—just like ours: war, betrayals, greed, death—and I think he is saying, "In spite of all this, connect the God to life. Believe that God is in the makeshift manger. God is in his promises. God is in these scandals. God is Emmanuel, among and with us. He will save his people from their sins."

Do Not Be Afraid!

In spite of the clear text we just read, centuries of art have done us in. There it is in a thousand paintings: Mary, with a peaceful smile on her face, is looking pious and serene toward a warm light of unknown origin, seemingly on the verge of spiritual ecstasy. So why is the angel saying, "Do not be afraid"? Why doesn't he say, "Enjoy," or add the modern conceit, "You've earned it"?

To understand the angel's words, we have to turn to another artist. Rembrandt pondered the Annunciation and, though he never painted the scene, he did make a sketch of his idea for such a painting. In that sketch, we see the Archangel Gabriel trying to hold Mary up as she falls from a chair. Like Camille swooning in the arms of her lover, she comes near to passing out. The angel has greeted her with "Hail," or rejoice. That was all right. So far, so good. It was the rest that got her. "You have found favor with God." In those days—as in these, if you would but think about it—to "find favor with God" was definitely not always something necessarily to rejoice over.

To be sure, "to find favor with God" meant that God had noticed you and loved you deeply—that was a plus—but it also implied that God had a great task for you, a task that sometimes, maybe often, meant sacrifice and suffering.

That's why you really didn't want God to notice you any more than a rookie wants the top sergeant to notice him for a dangerous mission. Moses tried to duck God's call by protesting that he wasn't a good leader or speaker and would Yahweh consider sending his brother, Aaron, instead, and let him off the hook? No sale. The prophet Isaiah, suddenly finding favor with Yahweh, said, No, don't notice me, please; don't send me, I stutter. And God said, "No problem" and sent angels with burning coals to correct his impediment, leaving Isaiah struggling to come up with another excuse. Jonah did his Robert de Niro thing when he was summoned. "Me? You talking to me, 'cause I'm the only one here," and he ran the other way. Peter put on his best Uriah Heep face: "Depart from me, Lord, for I am a sinner." He said that not because he looked poor next to Jesus, but the Incarnate God had just grabbed him by the hand to pull him out of the waters and Peter knew he was saved for some reason, that he had found special favor, and he was wiggling to get out of it. They were all petrified to have found favor with God. That's the stuff that makes you faint because demands will be made of you.

You get the same idea in *The Lion, the Witch, and the Wardrobe* from C.S. Lewis's *The Chronicles of Narnia*, which most of you will see. One of the children asks Mr. and Mrs. Beaver about Aslan, the Lion, the God-figure.

> "Is Aslan quite safe? I shall feel rather nervous about meeting a lion."
>
> "That you will, dearie, and no mistake," said Mrs. Beaver. "If there's anyone who can appear before Aslan without their knees knocking, they're either braver than most or just plain silly."
>
> "Then he isn't safe?" said Lucy.
>
> "*Safe?*" said Mr. Beaver. "Don't you hear what Mrs. Beaver tells you? Who said anything about safe? Of course he isn't safe. But he's good…."

Mary knew all that. No wonder she swooned and had to be quickly reassured by Gabriel, "Do not be afraid." But she *was* afraid, and it wasn't long after that her fears were confirmed when old Simeon prophesied that a sword would pierce her heart. Mary's "yes," sincere but hesitant, was given at a great price. That's her greatness. We romanticize Mary as having an open, spontaneous, and generous heart singing out her yes. It was indeed generous, but only because it was tinged with fear and laced with trust. She *had* found favor. And she said yes, though surely her next thought was, "What would lie ahead?" Finding favor with God is a mixed blessing.

I make a point of all this to remind you this morning that at one time, perhaps long ago, each of us has had his or her own annunciation. That annunciation is called baptism, when we, having found favor with God, were called, chosen. Perhaps, like the others we mentioned, had we been of age or had our parents fully realized what all this meant, we, too, would have been afraid and asked for an extension, like some of the early Christians who put off baptism because they felt they were not quite ready for all that it entailed.

The fact is, to say yes to the mighty and wonderful God is both liberating and fearful, but we treat it so lightly. Today, because familiarity breeds contempt, the call and response of baptism are taken on easily, almost casually. The transaction has become merely an ethnic or social affair separated from commitment, like the *Godfather* scene of the baptism of Michael Corleone's baby laced with the scenes depicting his father's gang murders. No, to have been found with God's favor is a precious treasure but its ramifications should make us, like Mary, afraid, and yet, at the same time, excited with the challenge of making a difference in this world if we are true to our yes.

A rather simple example from a young man in his late twenties, whom I know:

"I'm looking for another place to work," he told me.

"Really?" I replied, "I thought you were happy here."

"Well, I was happy enough," he went on, "but yesterday, when my boss came in, so excited, he said to me, 'Boy, you won't believe what I got yesterday! You're going to be green with envy,' and stuff like that. Then he pulled out a picture of a car, a Lexus. And he plopped down that picture on my desk and said, 'Eat your heart out. That's what I'll be driving from now on.'

"I stood there stunned at the silliness of this man. His life was actually made better, he really had good reason to go on living for one more day because he got his car! Then he said to me, 'Kid, if you keep your nose to the grindstone, one day you can get to be like me.' He turned and left my office. Those words stuck in my brain. 'Kid, if you keep at it, you will be like me.' I thought to myself, 'Great! One day I'll actually look like you. I'll have no greater point to my life that to get some car and think that it gives me a life worth living.' It was for me an awakening, a moment when everything came into focus. I'm getting out of this job, leaving this office, getting as much distance between me and him as I can. God help me if I ever grow up to look like him!"

He said to me, "Father, I guess I ought to be glad that this old guy said all this to me. For me, it *was* an awakening."

He was right. It was an awakening, basically, to the meaning of his baptismal yes.

Let me give you a parallel example. A man says,

> I grew up in Guatemala and whenever it rained it was also cold. So when I came back from school at the end of a rainy day, my mother would be waiting there for me with a cup of hot chocolate. I appreciated that, though I pretty much took it for granted. That is, until I moved away from home. After being away five years, I went back to visit, and it was cold and rainy when I landed. I got off of the plane and there was Mom waiting for me with a huge smile and a cup of hot chocolate. Now I live in New York and whenever it rains, I think of that special combination of sweetness and warmth.

Looking past the sentimentality of his tale, we affirm, yes, this is what moms do. This kind of natural generosity and love is just who they are. It goes with the territory.

And it should be the same with being a Christian. The moral, ethical life should be a "natural"—things that Christians just *do*—even though it's a bit scary because it requires, out of love for Jesus, being countercultural with all of the ridicule and the rejection, the hoots and hurts, that being countercultural brings.

The bottom line of the Annunciation scene is that in finding favor with God, Mary was at a crossroad. In her song to cousin Elizabeth she sang, "He who is mighty has done great things for me," but she also knew she would have to do great things for God. In virtue of our baptism, our call, so it is with us.

Have an Upside-Down Christmas!

Christmas, A, B, C, Luke 1:39–55

A husband was in big trouble when he forgot his wedding anniversary. His wife told him, "Tomorrow there better be something in the driveway for me that goes from zero to 200 in 2 seconds flat." The next morning the wife found a small package in the driveway. She opened it and found a brand new bathroom scale.

Funeral arrangements for the husband have been set for Saturday.

Now, a bit of "truth in advertising." That joke was a throwaway, designed not only to get your attention, but to give you the only Christmas laugh you're going to have in this homily because I don't want to make you laugh. I want to make you think and to wonder. All right, my cards are on the table. Forewarned, are you ready?

It's a fad. It's different. It will catch on a while and then fade. I'm talking about the upside-down Christmas tree. Have you heard about it? Yes, an upside-down Christmas tree! Some people are actually attaching their Christmas tree upside down with the base on the ceiling and the tip on the bottom looking all the world like an evergreen stalactite. Retailers like Hammacher Schlemmer are actually manufacturing such trees whose cost ranges anywhere from $300 to $600.

Why would anyone have an upside-down Christmas tree? For one thing, it's different and people thrive on novelty. Like being the first kid on the block to have the latest Harry Potter book. Then, of course, you obviously have more floor space to put presents under the tree and, if you're in a small apartment, simply more floor space for its own sake. Then, too, you can put your prize ornaments at eye level where one can see them instead of down below. Of course, it seems to me, there are some serious drawbacks. Who wants to put holes in their ceilings? How do you water it? Where do you put the star that won't poke somebody?

Well, however novel, the notion of an upside-down Christmas tree does provoke a more serious point about Christmas. It reminds us that basically Christmas is precisely about that, about being upside down. The gospel I read is a case in point. In response to Elizabeth's words of blessing, Mary, as you heard, sings her famous song of subversion:

> My soul magnifies the Lord and my Spirit rejoices in God my Savior. Why? Because he who is mighty has done great things not for the emperor or the king or Donald Trump, but for me, a slave, a handmaid, a nobody. What's more, God has scattered the proud and cast down the mighty, but he has lifted up Rosa Parks. He has filled the hungry poor while sending Goldman Sachs away empty. Why, he has even bypassed mighty Rome and he has come to the help of Rome's conquered outpost, little Israel, as he promised our ancestors he would.

Mary, the revolutionary, sang of God's upside-down values.

Yes, the upside-down Christmas tree and the upside-down ways of God that Mary sang about are profoundly serious correctives to what Christmas has become: awash in sentimentality, a gauzy card, a glut of gluttony, a spree of spending, and silly sitcoms. Last year, I recall, the holiday TV season began with a squishy story of a dead woman training to get her angel wings by helping a family cope with a mother's death. The woman in training who was awarded her wings was none other than Dolly Parton who wound up fluttering them softly and singing the "Hallelujah Chorus." And they all lived happily ever after.

Well, it's not exactly what Mary sang about or what Christmas, with its hard edge, is really about. Mary's child, this Jesus to come, this child we celebrate today, was no TV character, no sweet spirit from sitcom land. No, make no mistake about it: He came to turn things upside down and, on Christmas day, even though I know you were hoping for a warm fuzzy homily, we ought to bite the bullet, review his program, as it were, and measure ourselves against it to see if we understand Christmas.

Mary's child preached love over vengeance, and we can't get enough of *The Sopranos*. He said hard things like loving one's enemies and praying for one's persecutors, and we have Iraqis killing Iraqis. He urged forgiveness to the seven times seventh degree, and Hutus hate and kill Tutsis in Rwanda. He said don't go to Communion unless you first are reconciled to your brother or sister. Then you could come back and offer the gift of yourself at the altar, and we harbor grudges. He said that one more electronic gadget will not make us free—to the contrary—but that the truth will make us free, that truth being paraphrased by St. Augustine who said, "We were made for Thee, O God, and we are restless till we rest in Thee." He said to us (who in the report that came out last week are dubbed the fattest inhabitants on the planet and spend more than half our lives—half!—watching television, using computers, listening to the radio, and going to the movies) that if we didn't get up and feed the hungry and give drink to the thirsty and visit the sick and imprisoned we would feel the flames. He said that, flat out.

Some Sweet Christmas-card Jesus, huh?

He said that the first would be last, and we adore celebrities, can't get enough of them. He himself washed grimy feet and then had the nerve to tell us to do the same. If we say, "to the strong go the spoils," Jesus counters and says that the meek will inherit the earth. If we embrace the compulsory Brass Rule that self-actualization, self-assertiveness, and self-measurement—the self posted on the Internet—are the marks of a go-getter, successful person, Jesus shakes his head and says that the one who hugs himself to himself like that will lose his life, while the one who loses his life for his sake will find it.

If we think Christmas is about being happy, Jesus says it's about being obedient. If we live for brand names—and we do—and wrap our identities around them from the earliest age, Jesus cautions that we do not live by bread alone but by every word that comes from the mouth of God. If we measure success by what we consume, Jesus measures success by what we give. If we greet only those who greet us, and lend only to those who lend to us, Jesus asks wryly, what's so great about that? Even the members of Al Qaida do that. Our hearts should be wider.

It seems everything we hold dear, Mary's child turns upside down.

Not much "ho, ho, ho" here, is there? Jesus comes off sounding like the Grinch. But that's because we have been brainwashed to think that happiness lies in what we have and not in what we are, even though that belief lets us down every time. But Jesus is not joyless. On the contrary. Far from it. He offers the world true joy, a joy, he says, that no one can take from us. It's the old story of the nun in poorest Africa washing the disgusting wounds of a wasted person and a visiting onlooker commenting, "I wouldn't do that for a million dollars" and the nun happily responding, "Neither would I." Or, more season-appropriate, it's mournful Jacob Marley who, when alive, hadn't a clue he was forging each link of his chains with selfish greed and indifference to his fellow human beings, while his partner, Ebenezer Scrooge, at the last minute, managed to embrace the selflessness that gave him a giddy joy he never knew before, the joy Jesus spoke about.

So there you are. Mary was right when she sang about a whole new order of things. Her child was not to be a comfort. He was to be an intrusion and Christmas would be about that. In short, Christmas in the Bible is not like Christmas in the mall. Christmas is not a once-a-year winter wonderland, family gatherings, and nostalgia. It is not holiday camaraderie, church, cards, carols, candles, and crèche.

Please understand me. These things are important and beautiful and should be embraced, but you must know in your Christian hearts that they are only a sign, a sign of what things should be like all the time; a sign that, for the moment at least, we have caught the real meaning of Christmas and have lived the upside-down life.

A Merry Upside-Down Christmas to you all.

The Bells of Christmas

Matthew 1:1–16

Caution: I am about to read St. Matthew's genealogy gospel with its lists of unpronounceable Semitic names, names that will bore you because they go on and on. But I ask you to listen anyway because this gospel is more revealing than you think.

I ask you, wasn't that genealogy thrilling? Well, actually, in its way, it was, and moreover, according to the ancient style of writing, it was artfully designed to lead you somewhere. To discover where, let me first offer you a more agreeable story, a retelling of an old familiar Grimm Brothers' tale that you've heard before many times.

Once there was a fisherman who lived with his shrewish wife in a little broken-down hut by the sea. Every day he went fishing. Well, one day he sat fishing for a long time, catching nothing until his line jerked violently. He drew it up and there was a very large fish who said to him, "Fisherman, I beg you, let me live for I am an enchanted prince turned into a fish. Let me go and I will grant your every wish." The fisherman said, "Why not? Any fish who can talk deserves to be tossed back. And as for my wish, my tiny hut is very much in need of repair. I would wish for a cottage, a small cottage."

"All right," said the fish. "You live in a cottage."

When the man got home there was no longer the falling-down hut but a lovely cottage with flowers outside, and there was his wife dressed in fine linen. He explained to his astonished wife what had happened.

But as time passed the wife grew discontented and said, "Hey, stupid, come to think of it, why did you settle for a cottage? You go back and tell the fish we want to be a duke and duchess and live in a mansion." Horrified, he resisted, but her persistent nagging finally drove him back to the water where he found the fish and, embarrassed, asked for a mansion.

"You've got it," said the fish as he swam away.

He went back home to find a huge McMansion with a fireplace, an oriental rug, plasma TV, and he and his wife were media celebrities. All went well for a while until she badgered him to go back and ask for a castle where she would be a queen. Back he went and the fish said all right and when he went home there it was. Trumpeters announced his arrival and he was ushered into the great all where there was his wife, a queen!

All was well when one day the queen ordered her husband to go back and tell the fish she wanted to be *pope*! "Oh, I couldn't do that," he protested, but she wore him down. He went back to the fish and when he went home there was a cathedral with prelates of all kinds filling the place. He bowed to his wife, the pope.

Well, one day his wife demanded that he go back and tell the fish that she wanted to be God! Nothing less would do, she insisted. After much protestation, the fisherman reluctantly returned to make this final request. "So she wants to be God, does she?" said the fish.

"I'm afraid so."

"Very well," said the fish as he swam away for the last time.

The fisherman dragged his heels going home, afraid of what he might find. But as he drew near, he found nothing. He no longer saw the cottage, the McMansion, the castle, the cathedral. Amazingly, in their place, there was nothing but a small cave and inside that cave was a feeding trough for animals and inside that feeding trough lay a tiny baby. The fish had granted his final wish.

And *that* sums up Matthew's genealogy story. That is to say, at Christmas a helpless, infant God is seen as joined to humanity with all of its limitations, violence, and betrayals. Descending from the tainted, and birthing in a smelly and disgusting cow stall rather than a castle or mega-mansion, God powerfully revealed that he would be no stranger to the lowliest of all: to the hurting, the down-and-outers, the marginal, the poor, the addicted, the fearful, the skeptical, the sinful—in short, to all of us here today.

Yes, we found Jesus' genealogy tedious and pointless because we insisted on hearing it as a boring prelude to his birth. But it's not about a birth. It's not about DNA and biology. It's about a list of the in-laws at a wedding—God's wedding—to humanity in all its terrible follies and noble deeds. At the birth of Jesus, it's wedding bells, not jingle bells, we're hearing.

How did Matthew convey this? Look again at Jesus' ancestry. Contrary to the patriarchal mentality of the time, Matthew has inserted four women into a long list of men—and what women they are! There is, for example, Tamar who tricked Judah into marriage after she pretended to be a prostitute. There's Rahab who actually was one. There's Ruth who was married to Boaz after they had an illicit affair and the son that was born was Jesse, the father of King David. There's Bathsheba who committed adultery with David and gave birth to Solomon, while David, Jesus' ancestor, shamelessly had Bathsheba's husband murdered.

Not only were these women unsavory, to say the least. They weren't even bluebloods. They weren't even Hebrew. They were Gentiles, foreigners, outsiders! And then finally we get Mary, found to be pregnant, and her conceiving through the power of the Holy Spirit was probably no more believable then than it would be today.

So Jesus' family had plenty of skeletons in the closet. He came from some mixed, suspect stock—cattle rustlers and horse thieves dotted among the noble as we would put it—and was born in a stinking stable. And that meant, and still means, to put it bluntly, that there is no moral stench in our lives that is alien to him. None. Do you understand this?

The gospel good news is that the God of the shady ancestry, the God of dank stables and bottom-feeder shepherds, is one of us. This God has entered into our humanity, our lives, and has taken us for better or for worse, richer or for poorer, in good times and in bad, in moral sickness and in holy health. And why? Because all that this God-in-the-flesh wants, has *ever* wanted, is a return of his love and there's no place he won't go to get it, no level to which he will not descend. That's the meaning of Christmas in a nutshell. It's about love.

Let me close with a kind of Christmas story about one very reluctant bride as we might call her. Her name is Anne Lamott, an outrageous writer who has influenced many. In her book *Traveling Mercies* she tells us that she grew up in a hippie household in California—where else?—that provided no boundaries for her.

Her parents occasionally went to church for show, but both were atheists. In fact, most of her friends were atheists. She learned a bit about the Bible from the mother of a girlfriend who read stories when Anne was there for sleepovers. But that's as far as her contact with religion went.

When she attended school on the East Coast she came to believe in the existence of a supreme power, but it was not something that made a big difference in how she lived. Following graduation, she returned to California where she became a writer and where she adopted the hippie life she knew. Which means she used cocaine, became addicted to alcohol, slept around, got pregnant, and had an abortion. A sordid, stable-like life.

Now and then she kind-of attended a small Presbyterian church. I say "kind-of" because she mostly stood in the doorway in the back and listened to the choir she liked. But sometimes, in spite of herself, she heard something more than sweet music, something as low and persistent as a heartbeat, but she shook it off and always left before the sermon.

Well, one night, after some heavy drinking, she became aware of a presence in her room. She knew instinctively, beyond any doubt, that it was God-in-the-flesh, Jesus, in her shabby room! And she was appalled. Horrified. No way was she ready for him. What would her hippie, liberal friends think if she had Jesus for a friend? If, even worse, she ever became a Christian? She turned to the wall in rejection of Jesus and cried out loud, "No way. I would rather die!"

But all was not over. Not by a long shot. Try as she might she could not shake the feeing that in her tortured life Jesus was following her, stalking her, as it were, "like a little cat," as she put it. She wrote, "It was as if God wanted me to reach down and pick it up, wanting me to open the door and let it in. But I knew what would happen: You let a cat in one time, give it a little milk, and it stays forever." She didn't want that to happen. But she underestimated Jesus who had already descended into her promiscuous, alcoholic life.

About a week later she went back to the little church, so hung over that she had to sit. This time, too drowsy to move, she stayed to the end. The last song of the service moved her deeply. She ran home but had a sense that that little cat ran with her. She writes, "I walked past dozens of potted flowers, under a sky as blue as one of God's own dreams, and I opened the door to my house and stood there a minute. Then I hung my head and said, 'I quit.' Then I swore and said, 'All right! All right! You can come in.' This was the beautiful moment of my conversion."

This wasn't the end. Things weren't smooth or easy. After the honeymoon, as it were, she fell. She had to go into recovery, but for all of that, she was hooked. She, down in the moral dumps, had finally said yes to the God of the suspect genealogy and the foul birthplace, and she was never the same again.

Matthew's account all over again, isn't it? What can I say except to urge you once more to remember that the bells you are hearing these festive days are not jingle bells. They are wedding bells. *The Word was made flesh and dwelt among us.* Yes—*us.*

Same Time Next Year

Did you know that in a recent newspaper poll the three most irritating Christmas songs we heard this season are "Do You Hear What I Hear?", "The Little Drummer Boy," and "The Twelve Days of Christmas"? They were played and sung so much that people grew sick of them.

Well, here we are, five days after Christmas—probably exhausted—and we know what they mean. Since early September we've been dunned to death with Christmas catalogs, jingles, songs, and advertising, knowing that, even now as we sit here, the poinsettias are being replaced by Valentine candies, which will quickly give way to Easter lilies, which in turn will give way in July to back-to-school sales. We have no time to savor the holidays because of the dizzying hectoring of noise and pressure to consume around the clock.

Anyway, it's post-Christmas, and with the manufactured nostalgia and commercial overlay dimming for the time being, it might be worth our while in hindsight to take a second look at Christmas past. What we learn may help our perspective—and our spiritual strategy for next year.

The fact is that much of what we love about Christmas predates Christmas and has nothing to do with Christianity. Yes, what we Christians call the Christmas season traces its origin to the Roman midwinter pagan festival called Saturnalia which ran from December 17th to the 24th and was filled with eating and drinking, gift giving, evergreen wreaths, and concern for the less fortunate.

Among the Christians, outside of some pious personal remembrances of Jesus' birth, the church at large was not particularly interested in the Saturnalia and lived quite comfortably enjoying the secular festivities. In fact, it took it some four hundred years to discover that interest and come up with what we call a Christian Christmas. Why the delay? Because for the first four hundred years the church had other, more urgent, interests and was busy absorbing the mind-blowing impact of the resurrection of Jesus and figuring out who and what he was. Christians were also busy trying to stay alive during the many persecutions. It was only in the fourth century, when Christianity became a legal religion and Christians could catch their breath, that there was the time and leisure to turn to the question of Jesus' birth. Gradually they began searching for a proper day to celebrate it. By that time, nobody knew the exact date, of course, so they came up with all kinds of symbolic speculations, among them January 6, April 20, May 20, March 29, and September 29.

Finally, in 354 the Roman bishop, Pope Liberius, ordered all his people in Rome to celebrate December 25th as the correct day of Christ's birth and over a period of time, because of Rome's standing, this date gradually spread over the rest of the Christian world. But why December 25th when nobody knew for sure when Jesus was born? Because the pope was shrewdly trying to keep the momentum of the Saturnalia going and at the same time co-opt that date, because, you see, the Romans had a longstanding festival on December 25th called "the Birthday of the Unconquered Sun." They noted that the days had grown shorter and so therefore the sun was being "defeated." But now the days were getting longer and so the sun was regaining its strength and would conquer the darkness. Well, that was a pretty good scenario for the Christians to adopt so they simply changed the letter "u" in the word "sun" to the letter "o" and you had the unconquered Son, S-O-N, of God to celebrate on December 25th.

Still this identification of the birth of Jesus as the December 25th Son did not inspire any special religious festivities—the secular ones were still in place—and some ignored it. In short, Christmas as we know it was yet a minor issue for most of Christianity.

In the early Middle Ages it was Epiphany that became the really big feast. It took a while for Christmas to come into its own. Charlemagne was crowned emperor on Christmas Day in the year 800. That was a boost. King William I of England was crowned on Christmas Day in 1066. That too was a boost. But then Francis of Assisi came along and introduced the crèche, or manger scene, in the thirteenth century, and Christmas caroling was added in the fourteenth century. The feast as a religious celebration was starting to catch on.

The word itself, "Christmas," also appeared at this time. It came from the medieval celebration of a special Mass said at midnight on the eve of Christ's birth. Since this was the only time in the Catholic church year when a midnight Mass was allowed, it soon became known in Old English as Christ's Mass, from which we get the word Christmas.

But then came the Protestant Reformation of the sixteenth century and the Reformers immediately condemned Christmas as being excessive and much too popish. Besides, they noticed, folks were putting something into their eggnog and smiling a lot. So the seventeenth-century English Protestants wound up passing laws banning Christmas. Shops *had* to stay open on Christmas Day and Parliament deliberately met on that day. The Puritans of England banned Christmas in 1647 and the Puritans of *New* England followed suit. It was outlawed in Boston from 1659 to 1681 and in the Plymouth colony William Bradford made keeping Christmas a criminal offense. The Catholic Church reacted by emphasizing even more the religious aspects of Christmas, but it still didn't catch on that much.

Anyway, by the 1820s some began to worry that Christmas was dying out altogether and they tried to revive it. Well, to their surprise, a big boost came from the stories of Washington Irving who wrote of Sinterklaas who rode through the sky with a horse and wagon and dropped gifts down chimneys. Then came Clement Clarke Moore's popular 1823 poem "A Visit from St. Nicholas," more popularly known as "'Twas the Night Before Christmas."

But the biggest boost of all came from Charles Dickens' "A Christmas Carol" in 1843. Then in the 1860s the artist Thomas Nast gave us the popular visual image of Santa Claus that evolved into the obese red-union-suit character we have today. The Scandinavians added the yule log, the Germans the Christmas tree, the Mexicans the poinsettias, and hordes of Catholic immigrants to this country began putting pressure on others to celebrate the religious feast day, and Christmas has been on a Victorian roll ever since.

Not to lose customers, the Protestant churches soon went along with the trend. Religious Christmas had settled in alongside of secular Christmas.

Finally Christmas was declared a United States federal holiday in 1870 by President Ulysses S. Grant and, although often challenged by secularists, it was reaffirmed by the Supreme Court in 1999 and again in the year 2000.

Today, Christmas as we know it lives in an entirely different imbalance. It is now a frantic merchandising venture fueled by around-the-clock advertising. Carols singing of the Little Town of Bethlehem or Hark the Herald Angels Sing have given way to Red-nosed Rudolph and Mommy, the Desperate Housewife, Kissing Santa Claus—whether it's Daddy or not is another question. Christ as "the Reason for the Season" is simply out-classed and out-glitzed.

"Too bad," we say. Yet, instead of just lamenting the fact, let's strategize for next year. Yes, the hype will reappear—we know that—but before we're overwhelmed, let's ask now, while we're in let-down time, how can we comfortably celebrate the pagan Saturnalia and *still* make a statement for faith for next year? There are several practical suggestions. Three of them.

First, make up your mind now to use religious stamps and to send religious Christmas cards next year. Enough of dogs, Santas, and snow scenes. You're a celebrating *Christian*. Don't worry about what your friends will think. Don't be afraid to announce your Christianity. They will admire you for it.

Second, plan to shop, party, and visit but, along with your lights and decorations, also display the crèche in your house and in your window or on your lawn. Yes, we shake our head and annually grouse about the secular fanaticism of the ACLU, how it is stealing Christmas and how religion is being systematically subtracted from the public square.

But think for the moment. The nation is eighty percent Christian. Think of the impact we'd have if eighty percent of the nation's Christians displayed crèches instead of those huge inflated Snoopys, Santas, or Snowmen that cover our lawns. What a powerful visual impression, a wonderland of faith, that would make. But as it is—and we know this is true—people can go around our neighborhoods and get absolutely no indication that we, or most of our neighbors, are Christian. No clue at all that makes us stand out from the Disneyfied crowd.

We have to face it. The honest truth is that the secularists haven't stolen Christmas. Christians have given it away and the next time we decry another lawsuit removing a tree or crèche from the public square, let's first look at our own homes and our own private square. If Christ is absent in our private "here," we should make no fuss if he's absent in the public "there."

Third, target a charity now and lead up to it all year, like having the family toss loose change into a coffee can for the next eleven months.

So, there we are, post-Christmas, looking forward to the next one and considering three things: Christian signals in our choice of stamps and cards, Christian displays on our lawns, Christian charity in our hearts. Next year these three should add the needed touch of holy day to a wonderful holiday.

Josephs

"Son, why have you done this to us?…Your father and I have been looking for you," said Mary. Said Mary. Mary said a lot of things: things to the angel Gabriel, to cousin Elizabeth, now to Jesus. But what about Joseph? Have you noticed? Joseph said nothing, says nothing. He has no speaking parts in this drama of Jesus' birth and boyhood. Not one word. He even gets the news secondhand, suffers humiliation and embarrassment in silence. He is famously always in the background, just being there, listening to his quiet dreams, embracing rather than dismissing Mary, leading her to Bethlehem, assisting at the birth, sniffing out Herod's threats against her child, guiding her to a foreign country to hide out, coming back to Nazareth, providing a living, teaching Jesus a trade. Joseph, the Quiet Man. Hidden. Ordinary. Obedient. Someone caught up in the grand purposes of God without really understanding what was going on.

Even in later artwork anonymous Joseph is often pictured in the background or in the shadows while the spotlight falls on Mary and Jesus. With him there are no angels, no candle, no book. Just, maybe, some tools. He's just there to protect and support the wife and child with his labor and show Jesus how to make a living. He comes and he goes quietly. We know nothing of his death, except it was likely before the deaths of Jesus and Mary.

That's St. Joseph, and most of us, I believe, probably identify with him. Most of us are ordinary. We live and work in ordinary places. Most of us rarely are the first to get the news. We mind our own business. We too live the hidden life. We're background people. But, oh, it is into such hidden lives that grace comes. That is my dear and daring message for today. Yes, I tell you, it is in the hidden lives that the true stuff of living, learning, and loving are to be found. It is in the ordinary lives where daily, quiet heroism flourishes, where most of us find an anchor for our lives, where—dare I say it?—saints are made. We have to be humble about this, humble enough to recognize this great truth.

This wonderful truth is annually bought home to me every Christmas. Like you, I get the seasonal Christmas cards, a good number of which contain personal messages, progress reports, if you will. It's been a long time since I've seen some of these people—friends and mostly former parishioners—and we exchange where we are right now in life and how time has challenged or altered us. None of my correspondents are celebrities. All are ordinary people. Most, in truth, are Josephs and, I tell you, these hidden saints with their taken-for-granted heroisms, dedications, and faithfulness make me feel quite humble. I am very, very, grateful for knowing them.

So, I want to try something. I want you to use your imagination and picture my friends variously standing or kneeling around a large manger scene. Listen as I open each one's card and read his or her message. I will let you peek over my shoulder.

"Dear Father," writes Steve—he's the middle-aged man kneeling by the shepherd figures—"it's been eight months now. Advent was tough to get through with all the Christmas parties, but I made it. It's hard, but, as they say, one day at a time."

Steve. Steve is an alcoholic. He's fallen off the wagon several times. But he's made it eight months this time and every day he stops in church and prays for strength. Every day he sees himself as a rag-tag lowly shepherd in need of redemption, in need of Jesus, and that puts him high on my list, way above those who think they are self-made and need no one. I love Steve.

"Dear Father, we haven't seen each other for a long time and we never really talked, although you were my favorite priest. And now, after so many years, I am writing to you. I am dying of pancreatic cancer and would like to talk to you. Marion and I have never been married in the church and we would like to get that straightened out. I would like to see you. David." I never knew about his marriage. They went to church. Good people. Quiet people. I see David standing with the Magi at end of their journey, the end of his journey. David is a wise man.

"Dear Father," writes Joan with joy. She's standing near Mary. "Dear Father, I am so happy. After all these years I'm pregnant. Bob and I feel like Elizabeth and Zachary. Our prayers have been answered. You married us and we would love it if you could baptize the baby." The biblical story repeated. Worth rejoicing over.

"Dear Father, sorry we did not make your 50th. Valerie has Alzheimer's. Was diagnosed in 2002. Most days are good. Please keep her in your prayers. Ray." I was stunned to get this card. Before they moved to Indiana, Valerie and I, many years ago, worked in the diocesan Family Life Bureau. Val was one of those very bright, talented, vivacious outgoing persons. She wrote and traveled here and abroad giving talks. She was a delight to be with. It's hard to picture her in twilight living, not even recognizing her husband and children. But, I tell you, it's also easy to picture her husband, Ray, as Joseph. I can see him quietly ministering to his wife, there in the background, faithful in his devotion as he was in his marriage. The quiet man who will be there to the end. A saint.

"Dear Father, I wanted to tell you that Robert is making his confirmation this year and guess what? The name he is taking in William, after you! He says he always remembers you being there from the beginning." I married Robert's parents. The mother nearly died in giving birth and wavered between life and death for a long time afterward. I baptized Robert and gave him his First Communion and have photographs of me holding him as an infant and a toddler. His father, Dave, is a Joseph, fearing for his wife, staying with her all through the tough times, kneeling with her every Sunday at Mass. A quiet man, too. A background man you could count on. I'm glad I know him.

This one, after a brief message, signs himself facetiously, "Saint Jeff." Jeff is in his early thirties now, married. I remember him as a college student. He would be the one standing around the manger scene with skepticism. Why skepticism? Well, you see, Jeff went to college. There, as in every college, where diversity and political correctness rule, he was taught that there are no absolute truths. Everything is relative. One opinion is as good as another. It was considered the height of intolerance, for example, to express the thought that Shakespeare was the greatest writer of English who ever lived, lest you offend someone who thought Stephen King was. As a valedictorian from Harvard once said in his address, "At Harvard they teach you that you can believe anything you want, as long as you don't believe it's true." Anyway, Jeff was there with his parents at Christmas Mass and stood with them afterward at the manger scene and was not impressed. But after college, living a real life, he found common sense, found truth in the people around him, in the stories of heroism and devotion, in falling in love, and we talked about that and he quietly came home.

"Dear Bill, Sunday December 10 I had two heart attacks. This led to one week in Methodist hospital, dozens of exhausting tests, surgery, a pacemaker. I'm 103 pounds now. Kudos to Pat. He hardly ever goes out but he got out to see me via car service with mail, daily needs, and newspapers. He was—and is—a gem. Still, may God be blessed and praised. My trust in him is everlasting." Signed, Kevin. Kevin was a classmate in the seminary who joined after a stint in the military. He is eighty-four now. He left the seminary early on and went back to his native Brooklyn where he lives now in an assisted living arrangement with his partner, Pat. Kevin is gay and has been with Pat, also in poor health, for nearly forty years. He prays the divine office daily, attends the Episcopal church faithfully. (A conservative traditionalist, he left the Catholic Church when it made all those changes.) He does charitable deeds quietly, loyally, and faithfully for others. Like all of us, he trusts that God will write straight with the crooked lines of his life. He can't stand or kneel now. He is sitting around the manger scene near Joseph, praising God and quietly waiting to go home.

"Dear Father, I went to see Michael yesterday as I do every day. I clean him up and comb his hair. Then I stand back and say to myself, 'My, he looks so handsome!' Father, I'm so proud of him! You should see him. Marge." What you don't know and I know is that Marge goes to see her son in the nursing home. Her son is forty-five and has been schizophrenic since his early adolescence. Marge sees him every day, whether he knows her or not and she is so proud when he "looks so handsome." She is near the manger looking at Jesus and thinking of the baby who didn't turn out quite as she had hoped, but she keeps faith.

"Dear Father, I am doing well. The kids have been great. Joe was so much a part of everyone's life that he is missed. Holidays are hard, as you know, but somehow the Good Lord gets us through them. Love, Rose." A widow's lament and trust. She lost Joe, her husband of fifty years, four months ago.

Finally, there is "Dear Father, here's a picture of the clan and the new grandchildren. Aren't they precious! Merry Christmas, Rita and John."

These are your Christmas cards too, aren't they? This is the stuff of living. This is the stuff of being human. Victory lies with the Josephs of this world, the hidden presences who made our beds, put food on the table, who were there when we needed them most, cried and laughed with us. They are the background, behind-the-scenes saints, out of the spotlight, but in the soft shadows of our hearts. Today we remember them, members of our holy family; and, because of them, as my friend said, "May God be blessed and praised."

The Teddy Bear

EPIPHANY, A, B, C

When I lived a brief time in Boston, I had the occasion to visit Massachusetts General Hospital. On the tenth floor there is a glass display case with various plaques and artifacts. One display was particularly interesting, in fact, astonishing, maybe humorous. But, I'm ahead of myself. Let me go back.

Six-year-old Tony was born with an eye problem; he was almost totally blind. His doctor had read in the *New England Journal of Medicine* of a new surgical procedure at Mass General that might help. He sent the boy's medical record and in due time a decision was made to try the surgery.

Tony had a favorite teddy bear he kept with him at all times. This teddy bear had begun to show signs of wear. One eye was missing, one ear was chewed off, and the stuffing was oozing out through several holes. Tony's dad offered to buy him a new one but he didn't want a new one, so the old one went with him to Boston and remained close all through the x-rays, tests, and consultations. In fact, the boy and his teddy bear were not separated until the anesthesia was applied for the surgery itself.

With the surgery completed, Tony was heavily bandaged and had to remain still for a couple of days. But each day the surgeon was in and out of the room to encourage him. Finally came the day for removing the bandages. For the first time in six years Tony could see. Though his vision was blurred at first, it gradually clarified and for the first time Tony could look into the faces of his parents.

Before long it was time for Tony to be discharged and to go home. On that final morning the surgeon signed the necessary discharge papers and gave Tony a big hug and said, "Listen, I own stock in you, I expect to get letters from you regularly. Do you understand?" Then Tony did something totally unexpected. He said to his surgeon friend, "I want you to have this," and he handed him his teddy bear. The surgeon's first impulse was to say, "Oh, no, I can't take that." But something stopped him. With a flash of sensitivity the surgeon understood what Tony was trying to do. He wanted to give his dear surgeon friend the most precious gift at his disposal, so full was his heart with love. The wise surgeon accepted the teddy bear with a hug and a thank you, assuring Tony that he would take mighty good care of his friend.

For over ten years that teddy bear sat in that glass case on the tenth floor, one eye missing, one ear half chewed off, and stuffing oozing out of several holes. In front of the teddy bear was the surgeon's card and just beneath his name he had written this caption, "This is the highest fee I have ever received for professional services rendered."

Now slowly and reluctantly let me break the spell of this story by adding that that incident of mutual kindness in one place in one city in one country took place during the Vietnam war where life was being violently extinguished; in Africa, where tyrants were massacring millions of people and fearful repressions and crimes were occurring all over. Yet, in the midst of all this global darkness, this teddy bear light shone. It was a pinpoint of brightness joined with millions of others and it still remains a sign of God in this world. That's why I tell the teddy bear story on Epiphany, a feast of revelation, light in the darkness, and travelers who followed the star to seek out that light that would make a difference. As someone said, the candle says to the darkness, "I beg to differ." The Wise Men wanted to differ with the world's dark deeds and not just bemoan its terrible state. They would be a candle, a sign of God's presence and, as such, an example and pattern for us.

For as we look at our dark world today, the war in Iraq—Iraq, ironically the Magi's home as well as, you know, the home of the Garden of Eden, Noah, Abraham, Jacob, Rebekah, and Rachel; visited by Jonah, Daniel, Ezekiel, and St. Peter, and where the Hebrews were captive for seventy years—and as we look at the genocides in Darfur and Ethiopia and the threat from Iran, we too desperately seek the light, must *be* that light and add to the witness of Tony and his teddy bear and his gentle surgeon.

Or, to change the imagery, we know of a dark cave in Afghanistan, in the White Mountains of Tora Bora where some suspect, stuffed with arms and weapons, a Muslim named Osama bin Laden is hiding, hiding because there is a twenty-five-million-dollar bounty on his head. Hiding because the Administration wants him dead from a bullet, a bomb or an American court of justice. We know of another cave in the Middle East, in a little town called Bethlehem, that has no weapons. Only an animal or two and now a husband and his pregnant wife. Here a child is to be born, a Prince of Peace, the Light of the World. Question: How do we journey from the one cave to the other?

Along with little Tony, Marion Hill tells us how. Let me tell you her story. She was born into wealth and prestige and literally in a Hungarian castle. Her first spoon was not silver but solid gold. She went to school in Vienna and became an actress. There she fell in love with a young law student named Otto. Otto and Marion married and went to live in Hollywood. There they set up house and gradually he began to dabble in movies. In fact, he became so interested in the movies that he gave up his medical practice and went on to become the famed and formidable director, Otto Preminger.

Marion's beauty, wit, and charm got her everything and she became an international hostess. But the truth was she couldn't handle the fast life. She slipped into alcohol, drugs, and sexual affairs. She divorced Otto, attempted suicide three times before moving back to Vienna. There, like Tony and his parents, she met another doctor and she went to him for counseling. But this was not any doctor. He was the famed Dr. Albert Schweitzer, and when he went back to his heroic mission to the poorest of darkest Africa, she went with him. Marion, the rich, celebrated. In fact, Marion, spent the rest of her life as a hospital servant. She wrote a book called *All I Want Is Everything*, a title inspired by Dr. Schweitzer who once told her, "There are two kinds of people. There are the helpers and the non-helpers." Marion says, "I thank God that God has allowed me to become a helper and in helping, I found everything."

Let's go back. I asked before, concerning the two caves, one of darkness and one of light, how do we, like the Wise Men, travel from the one to the other? Now you know the answer: a teddy bear at a time.

LENT TO PENTECOST

No to Yes

First Sunday of Lent, B, Mark 1:12-15

We have begun the season of Lent and it's best viewed as a journey, a journey from no to yes, from dead ashes to living water. Noah's world of the first reading was ashes: deceit, infidelity, betrayals, broken relationships, injustice, murder. He had to rise from those suffocating ashes and set out for a new life. It took him forty days. Our world, alas, is the same.

This past Wednesday we took the ashes of destroyed cities, the dead babies of Darfur, the broken trust of CEOs, clergy, and politicians, the moral destroyers of our society, the sins of our own souls and smeared them where all could see. We are now, like Noah, out to seek the Easter waters, forty days hence, that will wash them away. On Easter Sunday we will be challenged to start all over again as we are asked:

> Do you renounce Satan?
> And all his ways?
> And all his works?
> Do you believe in God the Father...
> in Jesus Christ...
> in the Holy Spirit?

We get forty days to work up to our answer, to say yes.

To be sure, we all have our own lenten strategies to make the journey from no to yes. Permit me to offer my own suggestions, six of them, three to do and three to start.

First one to do: Say no to indiscriminate television watching. TV is commercial television, designed to create needs and make you buy what you don't really need. Much of it is filled with soft and hardcore pornography and values that are contrary to the gospel. You really can't absorb those powerful images and secular values day in and day out without being affected and spiritually desensitized. I don't say cut out television altogether—for most, I think, that would be serious withdrawal—but I suggest that for Lent you limit yourself and your children to an hour or two a day. Be selective.

Second one: If you say no to television, say yes to spiritual reading. Buy a little pocket New Testament and read a passage a day from the gospels. If you subscribe to any Catholic magazines you'll find recommended spiritual reading. Also, listen to audiotapes or CDs on the way to work, school, or shopping.

Third: Coffee-can the table. That is, put a coffee can or other container on the family table and every day have each one empty his or her change into it. That goes to the poor. You might even cut out from the newspapers those awful and pathetic pictures of starving children and paste them on the outside of the coffee can to keep you focused.

So, three to do right away: No to TV, yes to spiritual reading and donations to the poor. Now we come to three that are a little more personal, a little more difficult, a little more long-range, but at least let's consider them seriously.

Fourth suggestion for Lent: Be a stitcher, an encourager. That is, at home, at work, at school give the encouraging word, the encouraging deed, at least once a week. For example, make the Wednesdays of Lent your encouragement day.

This man gives a lovely example. He remembers when he was sitting on the antique window seat that his wife, Helen, had treasured through the years. A heavy storm was in progress and he sat staring at the rain pelting down on dead autumn leaves. He writes:

> The gloomy look of the garden seemed to match the mood of hopelessness that had come over me. Problems at work had made me fearful of the future. Basic questions that surface with the coming of middle age had made me fearful of life itself.
>
> I started to light my pipe and accidentally spilled some hot ash which burned a hole right in the middle of the window seat cover. Seeing what had happened, Helen calmly threaded a needle and

stitched a beautiful flower over the charred spot. When I looked at the finished work, I realized what a striking symbol it was. I had married a repairer of broken spirits, a healer of wounds, a harbinger of hope in times of darkness and despair.

So, on Wednesdays at least, be a repairer of broken spirits, a healer of wounds, a harbinger of hope. Pick up what others drop on the floor. Speak an encouraging word for every put-down remark. Give a pat for every shove. Be a stitcher.

Fifth suggestion—and this is tough: Prepare to heal, work up to it. That is, make an attempt at reconnecting a broken connection that often, in my experience, starts out with a misunderstanding.

Sixth and final suggestion: Reconnect basics. Put aside a day every week or two when friends, spouses, or families reconnect. Or, I guess I'm saying, review the reason you're doing all that work and all that running around like crazy to begin with. To get at what I mean, let me tell you about a woman named Marjorie Tallcott. She was married and had one child during the Great Depression of the 1920s. The family managed to scrape their way through the year, but as Christmas approached one year Marjorie and her husband knew they would not be able to buy any presents. So, a week before Christmas they explained to their six-year-old son, Pete, that there would be no store-bought presents this Christmas. "But I'll tell you what we can do," said Pete's father, "we can draw pictures of the presents we'd like to give to each other."

That became a busy week. Marjorie and her husband set to work. Christmas Day arrived and the family rose to find their skimpy little tree made magnificent by the picture-presents they had adorned it with. There was luxury beyond imagination in those pictures: a black limousine and red speedboat for Dad, a diamond bracelet and fur coat for Mom, a camping tent and a swimming pool for Pete.

Then Pete pulled out his present, a crayon drawing of a man, a woman, and a child with their arms around each other laughing. Under the picture was just one word: "US." Years later Marjorie writes that it was the richest, most satisfying Christmas they ever had. Pete's card summed it up: "Us."

No things, notice. Just people. Too often today it's no people, just things, lots of them. Time to go back to basics.

So, my six lenten suggestions. The first three: no to TV, yes to spiritual reading, and the coffee can on the family table. The second three: be a stitcher, work at healing a broken relationship, and reconnect as a family. All six are ways of getting from Ash Wednesday no to Easter yes.

Take Congress

First Sunday of Lent, C, Luke 4:1–13

The other day a mischievous friend asked, "Why are there no Wal-Marts in Afghanistan? Because they're all Targets."

Well, now that I have passed on his joke, I am going to turn serious and, perhaps quite uncomfortably, talk about Lent in this year of 2007, offering some suggested areas of resolution and penance centered around four contemporary realities. Hang on.

Item 1: Take Congress—and it's hard not to add Henny Youngman's, "Please!" With great fanfare, the new 110th Congress opened with the passage of new rules to curb lobbyists' influence by prohibiting them from treating those who make our laws to meals, trips, stadium box seats, or the discounted use of private jets with their enormous use of fuel.

That was show. The reality: By the simple subterfuge of paying political fund-raising committees instead of the legislators themselves directly in the past two months, according to the *New York Times* (February 11, 2007), "Lawmakers invited lobbyists to help pay for a catalogue of outings: lavish birthday parties in a lawmaker's honor, martinis and margaritas at Washington restaurants, a California wine-tasting tour, hunting and fishing trips, weekend golf tournaments, a President's Day weekend at Disney World, parties in South Beach, concerts by The Who and Bob Seger and even Broadway shows…."

Apparently it's hard to let go, not to sell oneself and one's influence for money and high living, not to mention that all that bribery money should have found its way to the causes of the poor and needy. The sad thing is that the people in Congress feel a sense of entitlement, not shame. They're not serious about reform.

Item 2: A man at the airport security areas, about to put his shoes into the tub, spots printed across its bottom an advertisement for Rolexes. It suddenly jolts him to the realization that there is no half inch on earth that does not have an ad enticing us to buy. Arenas, stadiums, theaters, school book covers, movies, TV, radio, and on and on. Three decades ago we saw 2000 ads a day. That's a lot. Today we see, absorb, ingest, and breathe in 5000 advertisements each day without even realizing it. And they do affect us.

Those silly intellectuals who say they don't ought to warn those corporations who spent 2.6 million dollars for a thirty-second commercial during the February 4 Super Bowl and are shelling out 1.7 million dollars per thirty-second commercial for the upcoming Oscars that they're wasting their money. But, of course, they're not. They know they'll manipulate our fears and poor self-esteem and we will buy their brands if we want a happy life, enhanced figures, good sex, and financial rewards—the hallmarks of success. All this reminds us that every day we are being brainwashed into the secular gospel that we *do* live by and are judged by bread alone. Christians should be alert and take some countermeasures.

Item 3: Author and columnist Tom Friedman writes that when he was recently in Paris his African-born taxi driver talked ceaselessly on a phone while watching a dashboard mounted TV. Meanwhile, in the back seat, Friedman typed on a laptop while listening to an iPod. "Technology is dividing us as much as it is uniting us," he reflects. The taxi cab driver could have been talking to relatives in another continent and Friedman was sending a story to New York, yet the two of them communicated hardly at all. And both were sitting two feet from each other.

We see it all the time. Watch friends walking down the street, each one separately talking into a cell phone, in effect being everywhere but where they are. Watch a couple at an intimate dinner with one of them on the cell phone, and the other reduced to a place setting. Friedman suggests that "continuous partial attention disorder" is the disease of the Internet Age (*Times*, November 1, 2001). Less time, less space, for family, for people, for God.

Item 4: This one is physically and emotionally close to home. Ready? When New Jersey allowed casino gambling for Atlantic City in 1977 the idea was that a portion of its gigantic revenues would help relieve the terrible poverty and decay of that city and other blighted areas. Today, apart from the Boardwalk, the blight, the poverty, the drugs, the homeless, and prostitution are still very much there. What happened?

What happened is that the money never reached its destination. Casino officials got the law changed that allowed the Gambling Authority to take the money earmarked for the poor and funnel it back to the casinos themselves. Translated, that means that as of last month, some $400 million dollars have gone for casino projects: new hotel rooms, an IMAX theater, parking lot beautification, and so on. The Authority, with a straight face, says that the money diverted from the poor to the casinos is needed to help Atlantic City to move forward and maintain its image, as if the casinos could not take some portion of the their 5.2 billion dollars in revenues they made last year to do their own improvements, instead of robbing the poor.

Well, there you are, perhaps disturbingly, real life, the context of Lent this year. Now keeping in mind these four categories as a conscience backdrop, allow me to offer a regimen for Lent. I will offer various suggestions from the difficult to the moderate, and you can pick and choose, mix and match.

First, Congress. Unlike Congress, be serious, really serious about change, about reform, about recovering your spiritual balance, about making this a good Lent. That might be shown in the following ways in descending order. Make a day of recollection or a few days retreat where you can step back and do some introspection, take a tally of your spiritual life and monitor your seriousness about reform. Do daily spiritual reading, such as the gospel of Luke or the popular book, Jim Martin's *My Life with the Saints*. Visit a nursing home or hospital weekly. Make a daily or weekly visit to church for some quiet time.

Next, those 5000 daily, unrelenting, value-shaping, consumer-inducing commercials. In protest, react to them by practicing biblical tithing. Give ten percent of your income away to charity. Not just for Lent but as a way of your Christian life, sending the message that you do not live by bread alone. How about this? Give up TV for Lent or, if it's too hard to break that addiction—and you should realize that it is that—then take one day a week, say, a Wednesday, when you don't watch TV at all. Fill in the time with spiritual reading or comforting the sick. Make that Wednesday, in other words, a special reminder of Lent.

Third, that multi-tasking, that "continuous partial attention disorder" we're afflicted with. You know: those "partial attentions" that are letting human relationships wither. In reaction, for Lent form a small group, perhaps in church or at your homes and spend an hour a week discussing the Sunday readings or a good spiritual book. And are you ready for what separates the wimps from the athletes? Never, never bring your cell phones—or allow others to bring them—to the dinner table. That is sacred space, at home or out with friends. You're not that important. People are. Attend to them.

Finally, Atlantic City: Ah, a touchy subject. You're thinking, "Thanks a lot for making me feel guilty." Sorry about that, but, you know, depriving the poor is not morally neutral. So, for the truly serious, the heroic, boycott it—cold turkey—for as long as there is injustice. For addicted aficionados, at least go less often or, if you do go, be sure that you not only visit the casinos but ride or walk around the few blocks down and witness the poverty and depression of the poor and disenfranchised. You've got to see where your money is not going. Who knows what Christian decisions you might make?

There you are. The lenten point remains that we are really indistinguishable from the rest of the world in our attitudes, values, and consumption. And we ought not to be. What kind of witness is that? What kind of Christianity? Lent is the time to recover ground, to be different, to be visible Christians, not just on ash-marked Ash Wednesday.

Let me end with these words from the Rule of St. Benedict:

> In these days of Lent
> Let us add something beyond the normal measure
>   of our service,
> Such as private prayers
> And abstinence in food and drink.
> Let each one, over and above the measure prescribed for him
> Offer God something of his own free will
> In the joy of the Holy Spirit.

Stars and Mud

There is a fun article by a couple of guys named Tim Sims and Dan Pegoda titled *101 Things to Do During a Dull Homily*. I suppose I shouldn't really tell you this, but here are some of their suggestions:

- Pass a note to the organist asking whether he plays requests.
- See if a yawn really is contagious.
- Slap your neighbor. See if they turn the other cheek. If not, raise your hand and tell the preacher.
- Using church bulletins for raw materials, design, test, and modify a collection of paper airplanes.
- Start from the back of the church and try to crawl all the way to the front, under the pews, without being noticed.

Well, I hope *this* homily isn't dull, but I admit it isn't that spiffy either. Let's just say it's thoughtful.

Note, we have two mountain stories in today's reading. They both present a problem. Take the first one: God ordering Abraham to execute the human sacrifice of his son and then changing his mind. Everybody has trouble with this. What kind of sadistic God is this to put a father through such emotional agony? Especially since this boy, Isaac, has been a longed-for son promised to a post-menopause Sarah and a seventy-five-year-old Abraham?

His birth is miraculous and he is now about ten or twelve, the apple of his parents' eye, the guarantee of their grandchildren to untold generations. And after all this, God wants the father to kill his only son? No wonder the rabbis and the great reformers like Calvin and Luther didn't know what to make of this. It's a puzzling and alarming episode.

Nowadays, when we know that the Bible is a book of stories, we sense this incident as a parable, a story with a strong point, the way the original people would have understood it. And that point is one that we moderns have a hard time with, that God is God and we are we. The story says this is not your usual mountain god that Abraham knew as the Sumerian nomad he was. This is a God beyond mountains and sky, who cannot be manipulated, a unique God of times and seasons, principalities and powers, of life and death. Abraham, on the other hand, is a totally dependent being who is challenged to cling to this utterly sovereign God in good times and in bad, for better or for worse, for richer or for poorer, no matter what. Trust Yahweh.

In other words, the hard lesson of this mountain experience story for us is to open ourselves to the God who cannot be understood, who is beyond all our scheming, who rains on our picnics, who allows humans to be inhuman. Only this God is worth my life and allegiance. This mountain God is the alpha and omega, the first and the last, the beginning and the end, Master of all. Trust him.

It is this truth that is revealed in this story. Our insufferable pride makes it difficult to bow to this reality, but somewhere along the line, says the story, we must cry out with Abraham, "Here I am!" and kneel down.

The second mountain story is, of course, the gospel, the gospel of the Transfiguration as we call it. This too is a story, given to us by Mark, and it contains two themes.

The first is grasped easily by those of you who have ever seen Stone Mountain in Georgia. For those who haven't, Stone Mountain is something of a geological oddity. It is a bald and rounded mass of granite, a mile and a half long and nearly a thousand feet high. Eons ago, molten rock pushed up from the earth's core to the surface and then bubbled out and hardened into a monolith. Given the very flat landscape around it, what one notices first about Stone Mountain is how *unexpected* it is. This isolated mass of stone stands all alone, sticking out like a blister on a thumb.

So it is in Mark's gospel. Jesus has been doing his ministry in the lowlands of rural Galilee with no mountain in sight. Suddenly and without warning, the grade in Mark's narrative turns sharply upward and we find ourselves with Peter, James, and John on a high mountain apart, seeing things we never expected to see or missed on the lowlands.

And this event becomes a symbol of the need to come apart and look at things from a different angle of vision. It's an invitation to scale the heights so that we can see what we cannot see in the valley. In other words, this story is the lenten motif: Come apart, spend some quiet time in prayer, make a day or evening of recollection. Ascend the mountain to refresh your spiritual vision and recapture the splendors, the brightness, the wonders and insights you have lost down in the busy valley.

The other theme rests on cleverly noticing that only three of the twelve apostles were taken as witnesses to this new vision. Did you ever wonder why? Why these three, Peter, James, and John? Why not Nathaniel or Matthew or Jude? Jesus chose Peter because he was the head of the apostles, John, because he was the beloved disciple; and James, because he would be the first apostle to die for the new faith.

But Jesus, knowing human nature, had other reasons, more ironic. These three had witnessed a powerful experience and insight on Mount Tabor into who Jesus really was. They were rightly overcome by such splendor, such privilege, but eventually they became cocky, oversure of themselves.

You see, later on, when Jesus predicted that his apostles would flee in his dire hour of need, Peter was very vocal in saying, "Though all should deny you, I will never deny you." And the other two, brothers James and John, perhaps still remembering that mountain vision they, unlike the others, were privileged to witness, would shamelessly ask for places at Jesus' right and left hand in his kingdom and, when challenged if they could accept his chalice, announced to all that they indeed could and would drink of the chalice Jesus was about to drink from, the chalice of suffering and death.

Jesus made a wry face at that and decided to test them. So, when it came time once more he deliberately took these very same privileged three apostles with him, this time not to the stars, but to the mud; not to the mountain, but to the ground in the garden of Gethsemane—and let's see now how these fair-haired apostles fared. Answer? They failed him; they fell asleep.

And there was more, for afterward, you recall, Peter would deny Jesus, and James and John would flee, and in their promised spots at Jesus' right and left, two thieves took their places. So much for pride and shallow promises.

And once more, the gospel becomes a story, a parable of pride coming before a fall; a warning to us and a reminder that, for all of our baptismal promises, we too have broken them, have fled Jesus, have gone back on our word and that is why we have Lent: to repent, as eventually did a more humbled Peter, James, and John.

As Peter said in the gospel, "Lord, it is good for us to be here." So it is good for *us* to be here on this Second Sunday of Lent to be reminded of our need to repent, to return to the splendors of the mountain.

Fourteen Generations

My sister sent me this email called "The Five Best Things to Say If You Get Caught Sleeping at Your Desk." They're listed in ascending order.

Number Five in the countdown: "They told me at the blood bank that this might happen."

Number Four: "This is just a fifteen-minute power nap they raved about in the time management course you sent me to."

Number Three: "Whew! I guess I left off the top of the Wite-out. You probably got here just in time."

Number Two: "Did you ever notice sound coming out of these keyboards when you put your ear down real close?"

And the all-time Number One: You raise your head slowly and say, "…in Jesus' name. Amen."

We are masters of excuses, especially when it comes to Lent. We mean to do well, give up this or that, and never quite keep our word. One of the reasons for our failures is that we focus on the negative. "I won't watch TV. I won't take any alcohol for Lent. I'll give up munchies." Well, that's OK but, in a sense, it's like digging holes but never planting anything in them.

The point is not what we get rid of, although that is essential; it's what we want to replace it with, namely, with God and God's love, with virtue. That's why if people tell me that they're giving up chocolate for Lent, I tell them that's fine provided it helps them think about God more often. If all it does is make them think about chocolate, forget it and try something else.

The fact is, the more profitable penances focus on the positive, the goals we want to achieve. "I want to cut down on the computer and cell phone so that I can have more time with God, with family, with friends, with the poor and needy. I want to be free of my inordinate desires so that I can desire the one thing necessary. I want to shut down television so that I may discover Jesus Christ." That sort of thing.

So, with the positive in mind, let me suggest three creative and off-beat penances for Lent, something you wouldn't normally think of.

First, release the secret and let it go in peace. Many years ago in a small pond near where I was stationed an eight-year-old boy drowned; Chris, let us call him. He was with his three friends and they were looking for golf balls. The three friends said that when Chris had slipped into the pond they thought he was horsing around and playing a trick on them. A sad and terrible tragedy.

But I have to tell you that it was a double tragedy because it wasn't altogether true. A dozen years later the three boys came to me—and I give them credit for that—and confessed that one of them had pushed Chris into the pond. In those twelve years each of them had suffered long-term emotional damage from the secret they had been carrying. Their confession was the first step to their healing.

So, if there is a short- or long-term secret that rankles, expose it. Tell a friend. Tell it in confession. Find out where they're having a parish mission and go see the priest you don't know and who doesn't know you and you'll never see again. That's what I would do. And, remember, it's not only a matter of unloading a dreaded secret. It is a matter of making room for God's presence and peace. That's the goal.

Second, try your hand at restorative justice. Restorative justice is a legal term that means setting up meetings between perpetrators and victims so that perpetrators can learn and see firsthand how their sins and crimes have damaged people's lives, in the hope they would feel some remorse.

A good thought for us. Often we have distanced ourselves from the ones we hurt by our lies, greed, or emotional or physical abandonment and, as a result, have zero empathy. But to look into the eyes of our victims, to stand face to face, to perceive the hurt, to see the wounds, to feel what they felt from our unkindness, helps us to stand in their shoes, empathize, and repent. This makes room for compassion. If we can't do this physically— and often we can't—we can do this in our imaginative prayer. Imagine the other sitting across from you and read their face and heart. Get into their skin and weep. Spiritual restorative justice is a good lenten exercise.

Third and last for Lent, try hard to take the unique and long view of your existence. To show you what I mean, let me turn to the Franciscan nun and part-Seneca Indian, Sister Jose Hobday. She tells of how her mother passed on to her the concept of the Fourteen Generations. The idea is simple: You pay reverence and respect to the seven generations that have gone before you and the seven generations that will come after you. That is, you keep seven generations, forward and back, in your mind and heart in everything you do and live accordingly.

Sister Hobday says that when she learned this from her mother she focused on the seven generations of her ancestors, feeling that she had been loved and cared for even before she was born. Her mother had told her that, if she lived with her ancestors in memory, it would give her power she would not otherwise have. And she did. She lived with awareness of the ancestors that went before her, knowing that they wanted to pass on to her all they had, that she was a part of a process, a procession, a communion of saints, the recipient of all they had loved and labored for. She was never alone. Many had brought her to this moment. It was a concept she cherished.

But, no surprise, as she grew older, she began to shift her focus. She started to become more aware of the Seven Generations to come after her, and so slowly she moved from contemplating the receiving side to the giving side. Instead of just feeling empowered by her past, she now saw herself with the mission of trying to empower those to come. She wanted them to know her traditions, stories, wisdom, rituals, her love of nature and her faith, desiring that the Seven Generations to come would have the same natural gifts and beauty she had.

In other words, early on she learned to see herself not as an isolated individual, a concept so prevalent today, but as a torchbearer, someone blessed by those who had gone before and someone with a mission to those to come. She knew she was a link in a chain, a bridge, a connector of generations. She was important. What a spiritually thrilling and energizing concept!

Wouldn't it be nice, then, as a goal for Lent, to strive to shift our sights, to realign our self-centered, navel-gazing attitudes to those of being part of the Fourteen Generations? To savor the love and sacrifice that brought us here, to have a deep responsibility for those to come? To know ourselves as part of a larger whole, a people with a calling, grateful to the Seven Generations before, committed to the Seven Generations after? It's a good and holy stance to take in life, one worth striving for in Lent.

So, there we are, with three offbeat suggestions: Release the secret, seek restorative justice, and become a part of the Fourteen Generations. "In Jesus' name. Amen."

Lenten Anger

John, the storyteller of this gospel, sets Jesus' action and words "in the Temple." Yet, notice, that when Jesus speaks of the same place, he calls it "my Father's house." And here is the central conflict and central theme of the gospel story. What's going on in the Temple area is not appropriate for my Father's house. It has no place there. It must be overturned.

So we see Jesus, who in another gospel described himself as "meek and humble of heart," making a whip from thick cords and cracking hard across the tables, overturning them, spilling everything, shouting, "Stop making my Father's house a marketplace." The money-changers were there because people had to pay the Temple tax for the sacrifices carried out each day. Because these Jews were from all over and all had to use the Roman coin with Caesar's image on it—Caesar being considered a divinity—their coins had to be converted to the imageless Temple money of the Jewish exchange. That was understandable. It was the gouging, the exorbitant rates, the fleecing of the pilgrims that got to Jesus. In the holiest of places yet! The Temple precincts had become a veritable mall of ATMs, a circus of noise and transactions. Holiness had been replaced by hokum. Jesus was merely acting in the ways of the prophets of old.

Seven centuries before, the prophet Isaiah declared God's scorn for such Temple shenanigans: "What to me is the multitude of your sacrifices?" says the Lord! "I have had enough of burnt offering of rams and the fat of fed beasts. I do not delight in the blood of bulls or of lambs or of goats. Bring no more vain offerings....it is mercy, not sacrifice that I desire." Prophetic anger is what Jesus was showing, outrage at what should not be, but was. God's honor and God's people should not be treated like that.

This incident tells us something about Jesus, and something about ourselves. You see, people are measured by what angers them. True, anger can be dangerous. So can food, sun, and water. But anger that leads to reform and betterment is a respectable and desirable emotion.

So it comes down to this: We are basically judged by what angers us and what does not. Anger becomes the primary lenten emotion and forms the basis of a litany of reflective questions for this season. Such as: We get angry if we get stalled in traffic and miss the first episode of *The Sopranos*. But are we angry over injustice, over the millions of children starving in our own country, the land of plenty? The massacre in Darfur, the massive greed of so many politicians: Jack Abramoff seeding corruption; former U.S. Representative Randy Cunningham pleading guilty to accepting two million dollars plus in bribes; Michael Milken, Ivan Boesky, Ken Lay, and Bernie Ebbers fleecing their companies and our pocketbooks?

Are we angry that there are homeless in our own land of mega-mansions? Over the graphic violence and mindless sex in the media, the corruption of sports, the vast and growing chasm between the very rich and very poor? Are we not just merely disgusted, a feeling that stays within us, but angry, which moves us to action? Are we angry over our own buying into the culture's norms of success: high consumption, low reflection, fierce competition, tepid cooperation, materialism? Are we angry over our selfishness and petty jealousies, our picayune lying and cheating, our lack of a generous spirit, our failure to develop a truly spiritual life?

I don't know if you ever looked at it this way before, but Lent is the church's official time to get angry enough to overturn old tables and set up new ones. What new ones might we set up? I suggest five.

First, I will love things that are worth loving. Some things are *not* worth loving, like SUVs or celebrities. The things worth loving are family, faith, God, Jesus, friends, to name a few.

Second, I will put first things first. Remember, Jesus said, "Seek first the kingdom of God and everything else will be added to you." For a Catholic, celebrating the Eucharist on Sunday comes before anything else. Putting a golf outing or a soccer game before that is not a Christian priority. Being present to our children comes before any self-regarding pursuits by a parent.

Third, I will cultivate spiritual insight. This means seeing beyond the flesh and blood realities we can see, the wood and plaster of the buildings we live in, to the Ultimate Spiritual Reality behind them all, God. It means seeing our fellow human beings as they really are, as children of God, made in the image and likeness of God, and treating them accordingly.

Fourth, I will strive for integrity of character, meaning that I will not do anything that will compromise my integrity. If I'm Pete Rose I will not gamble on baseball. If I'm Barry Bonds I won't use steroids. I won't cheat in exams. I won't do anything to get ahead or gain the whole world at the expense of my own soul.

Fifth, I will enlist in causes that benefit the community and to which one can give one's loyalty. I'll join Bread for the World to help stamp out hunger in the world, or I'll support Catholic Relief Services, one of the most efficient and effective organizations that help all over the world. Or maybe I'll have time to join the PTA or the parish council or Meals on Wheels. Whatever one needs to lift oneself out of oneself for the sake of turning the Temple back into "my Father's house."

These are some new tables to replace the old. Let me repeat what lenten anger might strive for:

First, I will love things worth loving.

Second, I will put first things first.

Third, I will cultivate spiritual insight.

Fourth, I will strive for integrity of character.

Fifth, I will enlist in causes that benefit the community.

It's time to turn the temple of my life into "my Father's house."

Transformation

A thumbnail lesson for today: Did you ever wonder how Lent began? It began in the early centuries when, as more and more people wanted to become Christians, a formal process of preparation was developed for them, a process designed to culminate in the candidates' baptism on early Easter morn. This arduous process, often lasting for years, ended with a final forty-day marathon of studying, fasting, scrutiny, prayer, and charity before baptism was finally administered on Easter. It was this final forty-day push for the candidates that became our standard Lent for all Christians. And the designated word "Lent" was a good one: It comes from an old word meaning "lengthen." It refers to the lengthening of daylight, the start of spring and therefore new beginnings, the whole idea of Lent.

In the course of history, Ash Wednesday was attached to Lent as an official introduction, a name given by Pope Urban in 1099. It could start as early as February 4 or as late as March 10, depending on the Easter date, which in turn depends on the moon's cycle.

End of thumbnail. But now we have to add that, unfortunately, during the course of the centuries, Lent's purpose and meaning hopped the track as its main focus moved to penance, to giving up something, to fasting. By defining penance and fasting as Lent's exclusive purpose we lost what it was really all about. The real purpose, the real goal of Lent goes back to Jesus' words often translated as, "Repent and believe the good news." But the word translated as "repent" in the original Greek is *metanoia*, which really means "a change of mind and heart."

In other words, Lent's intent doesn't have anything to do with penitence and fasting as such, but with changing our way of life. Fasting, penance, and good deeds are only the means, not the end. The end, the goal of Lent is transformation: to be a different person, to lose our self-centeredness and the habit of measuring everything by our needs and feelings in order to become a caring, compassionate person.

Lent, then, is about a radical change of mind and heart, of learning to see the world as God sees it, of becoming—let me use an old word here—noble; of learning to withdraw from the relentless narcotics of consumption and greed, of me-first, and simply becoming a good human being—again, to use an old word—a saint. Once more, Lent is about transformation, when someday kindness and charity will become second nature to us.

Lent's charter story is Ebenezer Scrooge, an Easter rather than a Christmas figure. His terrible penitential visions were but the means for his transformation from a miserly skinflint to a compassionate human being. Scrooge is not the perfect Christmas character, he is the perfect lenten pilgrim.

So, at the end of Lent we are not to tally up on our spiritual scorecard how many things we gave up or how many devotions we took part in, how many good deeds we did. At the end of Lent what matters is if all these things brought a change of heart and mind, a transformation.

And that brings us to our final point. Transformation indeed is the goal of Lent, but the truth is that transformation is a slow, quiet affair that usually takes place as a result of repeated small moments, not the one-time big ones, and we've got to get over our fantasies that it will be otherwise. By that I mean that, like Christian Walter Mittys, we tend to fantasize that someday we will be part of a mighty drama and all the world will applaud and we will be different as a result. We will discover a cure for cancer. Out of nowhere we will step in front of the president or pope and take the bullet. We will pray over a person and they will be cured. We will find a way to reverse global warming. We will be nominated the American Idol of the year who on TV announces to a stunned world that we are giving up fame and fortune to become a priest or a nun to work among the poor in Africa. You name your own fantasy, but there we are, on the cover of *Time* magazine, transformed from nobody to somebody.

It's a fun but a futile fantasy. Transformation is seldom instant: very few St. Pauls are knocked down by a vision. Rather, transformation is a result of many little acts of kindness, unnoticed charities, secret prayers, quiet compassions.

Okay, it's story time, time to let a story say what I just said, only more memorably. Listen.

It's a story of a night-shift cabbie who, on a late August night, picked up a woman. He was responding to a call from a small brick complex in a quiet part of town and he assumed that, as usual, he was being sent to pick up some hung-over partiers or someone who just had a fight with a lover, or a worker heading to an early shift in the industrial part of town.

When he arrived at 2:30 AM the building was dark except for a single light in a ground floor window. Now, under the circumstances, most drivers would just honk once or twice, wait a minute, and then drive away. But this cabbie was different. He had seen too many impoverished people who depended on taxis as their only means of transportation or people who needed assistance. So he got out, walked to the door, and knocked.

"Just a minute," answered a frail, elderly voice.

He could hear something being dragged across the floor and, after a long pause, the door opened. There was small woman in her eighties wearing a blue print dress and a pillbox hat with a veil pinned on it, looking for all the world like somebody out of a 1940s movie. By her side was a small nylon suitcase.

He got a glimpse of the apartment that looked as if no one had lived in it for years; the furniture was covered with sheets. There were no clocks, knickknacks, or utensils on the counters. In the corner was a cardboard box filled with photos and glassware.

"Would you carry my bag to the car?" the woman asked. So he took the suitcase to the cab, then returned to assist the woman who took his arm as they walked slowly toward the curb. When they got into the cab, she gave him an address, then asked, "Could you drive through downtown?"

"It's not the shortest way," he answered.

"Oh, I don't mind," she said, "I'm in no hurry. I'm on my way to a hospice." When he looked in the rearview mirror he noticed her eyes were glistening. "I don't have any family left," she continued. "The doctor says I don't have very long."

The cabbie then quietly reached over and shut off the meter. "What route would you like to take?" he asked.

For the next two hours, they drove through the city. She showed him the building where she had once worked as an elevator operator. They drove through the neighborhood where she and her husband had lived when they were newlyweds. They pulled up in front of a furniture warehouse that had once been a ballroom where she had gone dancing as a girl. Sometimes she'd ask the cabbie to slow down in front of a particular building or corner and would sit staring into the darkness, saying nothing.

As the first hint of sun was lighting up the horizon, she suddenly said, "I'm tired. Let's go now."

They drove in silence to a small convalescent home. Two orderlies came out to the cab. They were solicitous and intent, watching her every move. They were obviously expecting her.

The cabbie opened the trunk and took the small suitcase to the door. The woman was already seated in a wheelchair. "How much do I owe you?" she asked, reaching into her purse.

"Nothing," he said.

"You have to make a living," she protested.

"There are other passengers," he responded.

Almost without thinking, he bent over and gave her a hug. She held him tightly. "You gave an old woman a little moment of joy," she said. "Thank you." He squeezed her hand then walked into the dim morning light. Behind him, a door shut. It was the sound of the closing of a life.

Now let the cabbie finish this story in his own wise words:

> I didn't pick up any more passengers that shift. I drove aimlessly, lost in thought. For the rest of that day, I could hardly talk. What if that woman had gotten an angry driver or one who was impatient to end his shift. What if I had refused to take the run, or had honked once, then driven away? On a quick

review, I don't think that I have done anything more important in my life.

Then he added a capsule of this homily. He said, "We're conditioned to think that our lives revolve around the great moments. But truly great moments often catch us unaware, beautifully wrapped in what others may consider a small one."

Transformation, friends, is the goal of Lent and it's Lent's small acts of kindness that get you there.

God So Loved the World

John went to visit his ninety-year-old grandfather in a very secluded, rural area of Georgia.

After spending a great evening chatting the night away, John's grandfather prepared breakfast of bacon, eggs, and toast. However, John noticed a film-like substance on his plate, and questioned his grandfather, "Are these plates clean?"

His grandfather replied, "They're as clean as cold water can get them. Just you go ahead and finish your meal, Sonny!"

For lunch the old man made hamburgers. Again, John was concerned about the plates since his appeared to have tiny specks around the edge that looked like dried egg and asked, "Are you sure these plates are clean?"

Without looking up the old man said, "I told you before, Sonny, those dishes are as clean as cold water can get them. Now don't you fret, I don't want to hear another word about it!"

Later that afternoon, John was on his way to a nearby town and as he was leaving, his grandfather's dog started to growl and wouldn't let him pass. John yelled and said, "Grandfather, your dog won't let me get to my car."

Without diverting his attention from the football game he was watching on TV, the old man shouted, "Dang it, Coldwater, leave that boy alone and go lay down! "

The humor, of course, lies in the misunderstanding, in the delightful confusion of the words. Humor turns to tragedy, however, when we confuse the words of Scripture's best known sentence found in today's gospel: "God so loved the world that he gave his only Son so that those who believe in him may not perish but have eternal life." Yes, this is the famous John

3:16 that you see unfurled at stadiums, ball parks, and rallies. It's been used, abused, flaunted, and bannered.

It's been flung out there by some to say "accept Jesus or wind up in hell," its latest incarnation being that of the president of the Southern Baptist Convention saying on television that Muslims cannot be saved. That is not funny. Surely that is a perversion of what Jesus meant, for is not the rest of the quotation: "For God did not send his Son into the world to condemn the world but that the world might be saved through him"?

To unlock the real meaning of this short and memorable passage we must note that there are two key words. The first key word in John 3:16 is among the smallest, the two-letter word "so." God *so* loved that…that *what*? That he would go this far, go the distance, go to the cross—and what a comfort that is for us.

Anglican theologian John Stott speaks for all of us when he says that if it were not for the cross, he could never believe in God. He writes:

> In the real world of real pain, how could one worship a God who was immune to it? Rather than gaze on a serene Buddha, legs crossed, arms folded, detached from the agonies of this world, I have always turned instead to look at that lonely, twisted, tortured figured on the cross. That is the God who laid aside immunity to pain to enter into our world of flesh and blood, tears and death. When I look upon him, I know and believe I am loved, healed, forgiven and delivered.

Chuck Colson, former Nixon aide and the founder of Prison Fellowship, visited a prison in Brazil that is operated by Christians and founded on Christian principles. This is what he found:

> When I visited this prison, I found the inmates smiling, particularly the murderer who opened the gates and let me in. Wherever I walked, I saw men at peace. I saw clean living areas, people working hard. The walls were decorated with biblical sayings from the Psalms and Proverbs. My guide then escorted me to the notorious prison cell once used for torture. Today, he told me, that area houses only a single inmate.

As we reached that cell, he paused and asked, "Are you sure you want to go in?" "Of course," I replied impatiently. "I've been in isolation cells all over the world." Slowly the guide swung open the massive door and I saw the prisoner in that punishment cell: a crucifix beautifully carved by the inmates, the prisoner Jesus, hanging on a cross. The guide said softly, "He's doing time for the rest of us."

Yes. God so loved the world that he gave his Son.

God so loved the world. That last word is our second key word: God so loved the *world*. All of it. His love is inclusive. He did not come to condemn but to save.

Back in the late 1980s, some may recall, there was the world's most unwanted ship, the *Pelicano*. Some twenty years ago, from 1986 to 1988 she was the hobo of the high seas. No one wanted her. Sri Lanka didn't. Bermuda didn't. The Dominican Republic turned her away. So did the Netherlands, the Antilles, and Honduras.

The problem was not the boat. Though rusty and barnacled, the 466-foot freighter was seaworthy. The problem was not the ownership. The owners kept the license current and taxes paid. The problem was not the crew. They may have felt unwanted, but they weren't inefficient. Then what was the problem? What was the reason for these three years of rejection? Waved away in Sri Lanka. Turned away in Indonesia. Rejected in Haiti. Why was the *Pelicano* the most unwanted ship in the world?

Simple. She was full of trash. Fifteen thousand tons of trash. Orange peelings. Beer bottles. Newspapers. Half-eaten hot dogs. Trash. The trash of Philadelphia's long summer of 1986. That's when the municipal workers went on strike. That's when the trash piled higher and higher. That's when Georgia refused it and New Jersey declined it. No one wanted Philadelphia's trash.

That's when the *Pelicano* entered the picture. The owners thought they would turn a quick buck by transporting the rubbish. The trash was burned, and the ashes were dumped into the belly of the boat. But no one would take it. Eventually it was too old. Who wants potentially toxic trash? Finally, it is said, the owners resorted to dumping their unwanted cargo into the depths of the sea.

Within the context of our gospel, the boat becomes a parable. God would have taken it, for God so loved the world that he sent his Son not to condemn, but to save. In the same way, God would take us even with whatever toxic sin we carry.

The late Lewis Grizzard was a newspaper columnist and essayist known for his offbeat, often outrageous, Southern humor. Beneath the laughter, however, there was sadness, a life of personal suffering and loss. Some of Grizzard's pain came from his troubled relationship with his father, an alcoholic who left the family when Grizzard was a boy. "Before he died," he wrote, "I asked Daddy a thousand times, 'What is wrong? Why can't you stay sober? Why can't you stay in one place? What can be so bad you can't talk about it?'" His father would never give a direct answer.

One day, Grizzard pleaded desperately with his father to tell him what was wrong in his life. He told him that it didn't matter what it was, no matter how terrible, that he loved him whatever the awful truth was. But his father could not respond. He could only weep, sobbing out the words that he had made a mistake, "a bad mistake."

"That's all I ever got," said Grizzard. "The man died, as far as I know, with his secret. What terrible secret did he have? Did he kill somebody? Did he rob or cheat somebody? Was he a child molester? I can think of no more unthinkables. No matter. Whatever his sin, his secret, I loved him—and I love him—anyway."

Whatever his sin, I loved him—and I love him—anyway.

This is a moving tribute from a son to a wayward father. In a vastly more powerful way, it is a genuine description of John 3:16, of the unwavering love of Jesus Christ for all of us, all of us who, like Lewis's father, have secrets too shameful to tell.

The "God so loved the world…" is the translation of: "Whatever his sin, I love him anyway."

So, there we are. The famous gospel sentence, "God so loved the world that he gave his only Son so that those who believe in him may not perish but have eternal life." These are profound words of invitation: invitation to gratitude, invitation to trust, and, finally, invitation to repentance for having been indifferent to such love.

Losers

Fourth Sunday of Lent, C, Luke 15:1–3, 11–32

It will help you to get over the dull familiarity of this beloved tale if you realize that it is the last episode in what we might call "the loser cycle" that Luke uses in his gospel. One after another, in a kind of rhythmic pattern, he has presented us with losses: the lost status, the lost coin, the lost sheep, and, today, the lost son.

The lost status came quickly when Jesus was found letting a woman of the streets touch him, washing his feet with her tears and drying them with her hair. His host had invited him because he thought he was a prophet. Now he knew better. He'll never invite *him* again. Jesus lost his status as a prophet.

Later, as we heard at the beginning of the gospel, Jesus went and ate with the enemy, the tax collectors, and sinners. Tax collectors were notoriously corrupt besides being despicable lackeys for the occupying Romans. And here was Jesus eating with one of them. He lost his status as a Jew.

In rapid story succession, Jesus lost his name, a housewife lost her coin, a farmer his sheep, and now, in today's story, a father lost his son and his son lost his soul and his brother lost his humility.

Loss all over the place. What in the world is Luke trying to tell us? Believe it or not, I think he's trying to tell us the same thing that that bigot Ted Turner said, although he, of course, didn't mean it in the same way. Ted Turner famously or infamously said, if you recall, "Christianity is for losers." And like wisdom out of fools' mouths, he was dead right and Luke would agree with him. Turner thought what he said was an insult. Christians think it's good news. The fact is, Christianity *is* for losers, for those who have lost virtue, hope, pride, position, wealth, health, and life. It is for those who have lost everything and found themselves, as a result, open to God's tender mercies.

Let me tell you about two losers, one from fact, the other from fiction.

I'll begin with Steven Cook. Steven lost one of the worst things you can lose, his integrity. He lied and his lie cost another person terrible, terrible pain. Steven, you may recall as I unfold the story, was a former seminarian and he said that his seminary professor had sexually abused him. That was bad enough, but now this professor was no longer a professor, but the Cardinal Archbishop of Chicago himself, Cardinal Joseph Bernardin.

The accusation, of course, made the headlines and crushed the cardinal, who in turn lost his good name. Finally, in February 1994, Steven Cook who had lost his innocence, retracted his accusation and admitted he had lied.

But this cardinal did not gloat. Like the father in the parable he took the initiative and in December of that year arranged a meeting with his false accuser. He ran to meet his wayward son. At that meeting Cook, like the Prodigal Son, apologized to Bernardin in a way that was simple, direct, and deeply moving.

Then, having the reconciliation he so ardently sought, Bernardin offered to celebrate Mass of thanksgiving with Cook right then and there, but Cook was unwilling because, he said, of his long alienation from the church. The cardinal did not push him but simply brought out from his briefcase a Bible and a chalice which someone, whom he did not know, had sent him, asking him to use it for a Mass for Steven Cook. Holding them in his hands, the cardinal said, "What do you say, Steven?" At that point Steven broke down and asked to participate in the Eucharist. But first, he received the anointing of the sick from his victim because he was ill with AIDS and then Mass was celebrated and the prodigal loser became a winner because of the love of his spiritual father. Christianity was in his corner.

The fiction story I want to tell you comes from an old, old movie entitled *Stars in My Crown*. In one of the episodes in the little southern town where the movie's story takes place there was a black man who had been a kind of "Uncle Remus" figure—a father like the father of the gospel—to several generations of the children who had grown up there. He was good to them, generous with them. He told them stories, taught them to hunt and fish, and in general was greatly beloved.

Now he owned a little cabin and some land, and after his wife died, he continued to live there alone. One year a very valuable deposit of copper was discovered that ran through his property. Some of the business leaders of the town came to the old man and offered to buy his land so they could start a mining operation. The old man had not been raised in a money culture. He simply wanted to live out his days in the only house he had ever known, and so, with total naiveté, he refused to sell. Ah, but since a great deal of money was at stake—greed is a terrible thing—the atmosphere eventually turned ugly. When the businessmen could not buy him out, they resorted to nasty threats.

Sadly, many of the very people whom he had befriended all his life, the very ones who were his spiritual sons, turned prodigal, wanted his inheritance, fled their father, and became his foes. It finally came down to the point where they said, "If you are not off the property by sundown tomorrow night, we are going to come and lynch you!"

Well, the old preacher in town got wind of what was happening and went out to the black man's house. Then, the next day, at the appointed sundown hour, the executioners rode up, hiding behind their white hoods and masks. The old preacher stepped out on the porch with the man at his side and said, "John knows that he is going to die. He asked me to come out today and write his last will and testimony. He wants me to read it to you." They all stood there in silence. The preacher continued as he read the will: "He wants to give his fishing rod to Pete, because he remembers the first bass he caught with it. He wants to give his rifle to James, because he remembers using it to teach him to shoot. He wants to give his shovel to Seth because he taught him how to till his land."

And so it went: Item by item the old black gentleman proceeded to give in total love to the very people who had come to take his life. Well, I needn't tell you that the impact of this open generosity was more than even the hardened spirits of his prodigal sons could handle. One by one, shamed to the core by such unconditional love, the would-be executioners turned away in silence, burdened with the realization that they had sinned against their father, and yet he had still loved them. No one was left.

The man's little grandson had been watching this whole drama from a distance. After the crowd had dispersed, he ran up on the porch and said to his grandfather, "What kind of a will was that?" The old grandfather answered gently, "It was the will of God, son, the will of God."

Yes, it is the will of God, revealed in this beloved gospel, that no prodigal child should go unembraced by God's unconditional, overflowing love. Thus, friends, this gospel is more than a wondrous story. It is an invitation.

The Stations Pilgrims

On this fifth Sunday of Lent let us pause to consider a Christian tradition, the Stations of the Cross. Journeying the Stations of the Cross is a time-honored devotion among Christians, especially during this holy season.

The Stations were popularized by the Franciscans. In early and medieval times the pilgrimage was a very popular pious devotion. Remember, they didn't have 747s then to jet them across the waters and air-conditioned buses to meet them and take them around. No, they walked or rode mules or took slow boats. Such pilgrimages, done with the greatest devotion, therefore were a matter of months and years and were frequently fraught with dangers.

One of the favorite pilgrimage goals was the Holy Land. There people wanted to visit the very spots Jesus walked and especially his torturous way to Calvary. But it was far away across the waters and many people were unable to make such a long, arduous journey. So artists among the pilgrims who did go began to sketch those Holy Land sites associated with Jesus' passion and death, usually under the care of the Franciscans who would bring the sketches back to Europe. They would hang these pictures along roadsides and eventually inside churches. The number of such pictures varied from seven to twenty-four, but eventually settled at fourteen to become our standard fourteen Stations of the Cross today.

But here is something you may not know about. It was important then as it is important now to understand the "rules" of these fourteen Stations. They are just that, stations or *stationary standing places*. The pilgrim of yesterday and today is to stand before the depiction of Jesus' way to the cross for two reasons. One is to meditate on the scene before him or her, but the other, far more important, is to enter into it. That is, to be a participant, to take on the role of some character or other. Let me illustrate that by asking you in your mind's eye to journey with me along seven of these stations. Here you are, standing at:

The First Station: Jesus is unjustly accused by Pilate. Have you have stood any time in your life, falsely accused, when rumors spread about you, when you were the victim of false gossip? And no matter how hard you tried to explain, no one seemed to believe you? How about all those in prison falsely accused, like the two Catholic bishops in Chinese prisons right now, accused of being spies for America? All those sent to their deaths like St. Thomas More on trumped-up charges? If you've been there, unjustly accused by gossip or innuendo, how do you act? Do you identify with Jesus before Pilate, keeping silent and offering up your humiliation for the sins of the world, or at least knowing that he's been there before you, knowing that God will have the last word?

There's the poignant Fourth Station: Jesus meets his mother. Mary's heart was broken not only because she saw her son publicly disgraced and humiliated, going to his death as a common criminal, but, most of all, that she could not help him. How gladly would she have changed places with him, but she was restrained by the rough soldiers.

Mary is every parent unable to save their children. Every parent who watches by the hospital bed, every parent who has buried a child, every parent who stands by helplessly to watch a child disintegrate with drugs or alcoholism, whose unending prayers plead with God for a son or daughter living a sinful lifestyle, or who have departed from the faith, or whose marriage is falling apart. Mary is every parent with arms achingly outstretched because they want so badly to save their child and can't, at least not right now. They instead silently offer their prayers and their tears and we know that many a last-minute Good Thief is snatched to paradise because some mother or father, perhaps now long since dead, earned mercy for them.

The Fifth Station: Simon is forced to carry Jesus' cross. These who stand a long time at this station are all the people who carry crosses they did not want or ask for or bargain for. No one wanted the sick parent, the retarded child, the cancer, the addiction, the divorce, the job loss, the depression—unwanted crosses of all descriptions. Too many of us have the name of Simon of Cyrene, and we're angry at God and frustrated. But the longer

I stand here, the more I absorb the tradition that says that if Simon started out with anger—he wanted no part of Jesus' cross; he was forced into it—after a time of carrying the cross with Jesus, he moved to understanding, and from understanding he moved to love, and from love he moved onto his own salvation and became, as it were, a co-redeemer with Jesus. Could this too be my calling?

The Sixth Station: Veronica wipes the face of Jesus. Veronica is a composite of the women of Jerusalem in Scripture who wept over Jesus. The simple truth of the legend of her veil is as brief as it is powerful. It is meant to say this: All who show compassion are imaged in the likeness of Christ. An essential part of discipleship is to have a well-used veil. How's mine?

The Ninth Station: Jesus falls the third time. People who spend time here readily say: I recognize this station from experience, for here I stand with my habits of sin: the nasty word out of my mouth before I can stop it, the quick judgment, the ongoing gossip, the addiction—and it is that—to internet pornography, to anger. No matter how hard I try, no matter how many times I confess it, no matter how bad I feel afterward, I can't seem to shake my favorite sin. I keep falling, like Jesus. But as I stand here long enough I begin to perceive that this station really has a different focus. It really should read, "Jesus *gets up again,* the third time."

"How about it, Lord? One more time? Don't let me get discouraged. I will make my favorite prayer once more: O God of the Second Chance, here I am again!"

The Twelfth Station: Jesus dies on the cross forgiving his enemies. I stand here accused, I who still hold grudges and harbor a hard heart. How far I am from the unknown woman in the Ravensbruck concentration camp who wrote this little prayer and pinned it to the dead body of a little girl there.

> Oh, Lord, remember not only the men and women of good will, but also those of ill will. But do not remember all the sufferings they have inflicted on us. Remember, rather, the fruits we have bought, thanks to this suffering: our comradeship, our loyalty, our humility, our courage, our generosity; the greatness of heart that has grown out of all of this. And when they, our torturers, come to judgment, let all the fruits we have borne be their forgiveness.

Jesus, hanging on the cross and forgiving his enemies, is that "deeper still" love. How can I be unforgiving?

Finally, there's the Fourteenth Station: Jesus is laid in the tomb. Many people at this one. They're there crying, "This is my time of despair and dryness. I don't know what to do. I'm at my wit's end. There seems no way out of my tomb. It's dark and dry. I'm caught in a loveless marriage, a dead-end job, a soured relationship, an unethical business deal; I can't seem to break them off, like an addiction." Or, "It's dark and dry in my life and in my soul. I can't pray. I get no answers when I do. God seems to have abandoned me. My faith is routine and empty. Like the people who placed both Jesus and their hopes in the darkness of the tomb and rolled a heavy stone over both, I feel a stone rolled over my heart."

But these same people are in for a surprise. "O God of Surprises, find me soon! Find me soon!"

You see, the fourteen Stations are more than a simple pious devotion. They are life. They are where we are. They reflect our pain, but they give us hope, for there is a fifteenth Station called the Resurrection.

In any case, as we approach the great theme of Jesus' passion and death you might reconsider the Stations, taking one each day to contemplate. It's a good devotion to prepare yourself for Easter.

Lazarus: Death and Life

FIFTH SUNDAY OF LENT, A,
JOHN 11:3–7, 17, 20–27, 33–45

A little boy was afraid of the dark. One night his mother told him to go out to the back porch and bring her the broom. The little boy turned to the mother and said, "Mama, I don't want to go out there. It's dark. The mother smiled reassuringly at her son. "You don't have to be afraid of the dark, dear," she explained. "Jesus is out there. He'll look after you and protect you." The little boy looked at the mother real hard and asked, "Are you sure he's out there? "Yes, I'm sure. He is everywhere, and he is always ready to help you when you need him," she said. The little boy thought about that for a minute and then went to the back door and cracked it a little. "Jesus? If you're out there, would you please hand me the broom?"

In two weeks we will recall the death of Jesus, but today we are confronted with the death of Lazarus. It seems we're being asked to think about what we would prefer not to think about: death. And to ponder the little boy's question, "Jesus are you out there in the dark?" Really?

In answer, let me offer some suggestive images for you that indicate that Jesus is out there in the dark. Years ago, I had the opportunity to make a trip to Washington, D.C., with some friends. Part of our itinerary was to visit the Vietnam Memorial Wall. As you may know, the monument is a long black granite wall with thousands of names of those who lost their lives in the war. As I walked the grounds of the memorial, a couple of things stood out.

The first thing I noticed was the silence. As crowded as it was, there was a hush of reverence over the whole setting. The next thing that caught my eye was how different people approached the wall. Some were obviously just there as spectators. They could touch lots of names on the wall, pass

104

them over quickly, and have no reaction whatsoever. To them, the names were just letters carved in a granite wall.

But to others, those names, or rather, *this* name, was a reason to pause, to cry. They moved very slowly as if approaching something sacred and then touched the name. Some wept, others were just still, lost in grief or reverie. Some stood quietly as they ran their fingers gently over the letters. Some even knelt. As I watched this ritual unfold, I couldn't help but wonder what the relationship was between the living person and the name: husband, son, father, brother, friend. It had to be something special or it would not have solicited such a reaction.

Of course, the answer is that to those who knew the person behind the name, it represents all the memories, the history, the personality and intimacy created between these two people. It is the depth of the relationship that makes the connection, the investment of life one person made in another person. It represents someone who made a difference to the one who knew that person.

And so too, Jesus. He said, "I know mine and mine know me." "I no longer call you servants but friends." So we are not anonymous to him. He runs his fingers over our names and claims us as his own before and after our deaths. That is our hope.

Another image. In a cemetery in Hanover, Germany, is a grave on which were placed huge slabs of granite and marble cemented together and fastened with heavy steel clasps. Why? Because it belonged to a woman who vehemently did not believe in the resurrection of the dead. So she directed in her will that her grave be made so secure that if there *were* a resurrection, it could not reach her. On the marker were inscribed these words: "This burial place must never be opened."

Ah, but in time, you see, what happened was that a tiny, infinitesimal seed, covered over by the stones, began to grow. Slowly it pushed its way through the soil. As it grew and its trunk enlarged, the great slabs of the grave were gradually shifted so that eventually the steel clasps were wrenched from their sockets and then, one day, there it was: the grave was exposed. A tiny seed had pushed aside those enormous stones.

Faith says that if nature can move huge stones, God can move the huge stone at Jesus' grave. And ours as well. Such is the force of God's love.

A third image. The luminous paintings of the great artist Renoir, are, as you know, aglow with life and light and color. He seemed to put light inside the people he painted. Remarkably, as you may also know, for the last twenty years or so of his life—his most productive years—Renoir was terribly crippled with arthritis. His hands were twisted and gnarled. His wrists, his arms, even his spine were ravaged by the disease. He couldn't even stand as he worked.

He had to sit as he painted and be shifted about in his chair by assistants. At times the pain was so great as he worked that beads of perspiration would stand out on his face. On one occasion, one of his students said to him, "Why do go on and torture yourself like this?" Renoir looked at the canvass he was working on and replied, "The pain passes, but the beauty remains."

That is the promise we have. "Untie him and set him free." That is to say, after the ravages of sickness and death, the beauty of love and eternity remain.

A fourth image. A celebrity of his time, playboy, wit, editor of the famous British publication *Punch*, Malcolm Muggeridge, much to the chagrin of his worldly friends, became a Christian. In fact, he became the worst kind: he became Catholic. He did so because he was inspired by the presence and work of Mother Teresa. Anyway, elderly when he converted, he wrote many lovely things, including these words of imagery:

> As I approach my end, I find Jesus' outrageous claim ever more captivating and meaningful. Quite often, waking up in the night as the old do, I feel myself to be half out of my body, hovering between life and death, with eternity rising in the distance. I see my ancient carcass, prone between the sheets, stained and worn like a scrap of paper dropped in the gutter and, hovering over it, myself, like a butterfly released from its chrysalis stage and ready to fly away. Are caterpillars told of their impending resurrection? How in dying they will be transformed from poor earth crawlers into creatures of the air with exquisitely painted wings? If told, do they believe it?

I imagine the wise old caterpillars shaking their heads—no, it can't be;

it's a fantasy. Yet in the limbo between living and dying, as the night clocks tick remorselessly on, and the black sky implacably shows not one single scratch of gray, I hear those words: "I am the resurrection" and then I feel myself to be carried along on a great tide of joy and peace.

Faith asks, "If caterpillars, why not we?"

A final image. A long time ago there lived a little boy whose parents had died. He was taken in by an aunt who raised him as her own child. Years later, after he had grown up and left his aunt, he received a letter from her. She was in terminal illness and, from the tone of her letter, he knew she was afraid of death. This man whom she had raised and touched, wrote her a letter in which he said:

It is now thirty-five years since I, a little boy of six, was left quite alone in the world. You sent me word that you would give me a home and be a mother to me. I've never forgotten the day when I made the long journey of ten miles to your house. I can still recall my disappointment when, instead of coming for me yourself, you sent your servant, Caesar, a dark man, to fetch me. I well remember my tears and my anxiety as, perched high on your horse and clinging tight to Caesar, I rode off to my new home.

Night fell before we finished the journey and as it grew dark, I became even more afraid. "Do you think she'll go to bed before I get there?" I asked Caesar anxiously. "Oh, no," said Caesar, "she'll sure to stay up for you. When we get out of these woods, you'll see her light shining in the window."

Presently, we did ride out into the clearing and there was your light. I remember that you were waiting at the door; that you put your arms tight around me; that you lifted me—a tired, frightened little boy—down from the horse. You had a fire burning on the hearth; a hot supper waiting on the stove. After supper you took me to my new room. You heard me say my prayers. Then you sat with me until I fell asleep.

You probably realize why I am trying to recall this to your memory now. Very soon, God is going to send for you, and take you to a new home. I'm trying to tell you that you needn't be afraid of the summons or of the strange journey or of the dark messenger of death. God can be trusted. God can be trusted to do as much for you as you did for me so many years ago. At the end of the road you'll find love and a welcome waiting. And you'll be safe in God's care. I'm going to watch and pray for you until you're out of sight. And I shall wait for the day when I make the same journey myself and find you waiting at the end of the road to greet me.

Notice the symbols; Caesar, the dark figure, is death; the light at the end of he journey is Jesus, the light of the world; the house is the "many rooms" in the Father's house that Jesus promised; the supper is the heavenly banquet; God is the loving aunt. It's a homecoming story. It is gospel. It is hope. It is promise.

The little boy's question, "Jesus, are you out there?" must have been Lazarus' question. The Good News is that he was: for Lazarus, for you, and for me.

Easter

A, B, C

"My son Bobby got sick last week," says this father. "I took his temperature, and it was 102.5. Out came the children's Advil. He slugged down a dose, and fifteen minutes later his fever was back down to 100. Just before bed, I checked his temperature again. It was back up. More Advil. I checked again forty-five minutes later; now it was 103. By midnight, his skin was hot, he was lethargic, and his temperature was 104. I called the hospital. 'Bring him in as soon as possible,' they said.

"I told Bobby we were going to the doctor. He looked at me with weary, wondering eyes and said, 'Am I going to die, Daddy?' Immediately, I had three reactions. Common sense: 'No, you are not going to die. We just need to get this fever down.' Emotional: 'I'm scared.' Visions of children with bizarre diseases flooded my heart. Spiritual: 'Dear Jesus, cover him. Heal him. Love him.'

"'No, Son, you're not going to die,' I told him. I didn't want to scare him. I was fairly certain his fever was not life-threatening. But my mind flashed to the many parents in this world who have had to look at their children, knowing that the ultimate answer to that question is yes. And I wonder if in the heavenly places there was once a conversation between the Father and the Son, when the Son asked the question, 'Am I going to die, Daddy?' and in his heart the Father knew the answer was 'Yes.'"

My friends, we have just finished a week—Holy Week we called it—in which that "yes" was worked out in a sad and sickening way: the betrayal on Wednesday, the agony on Thursday, the horrific, brutal death on Friday, the stillness and grieving on Saturday. But then, the burdened body, carrying our weight, rose anew on Sunday, the one we call Easter, the one that has brought us here today in all of our finery because we are spiritually

109

rejoicing over the opportunity for the newness of life, grateful that, because of Jesus who "bore our infirmities," death no longer is the final word. *This* is gospel, Good News indeed, and alleluia is the only response.

This we acknowledge. But in the long run, for the mind, these are often mere words, familiar words that have perhaps lost their power from that very fact, words we know and casually recite in our creed. But it takes more than the head to sense the love, the very deep love that is evident in the Son's yes. It takes the heart. It takes the heart to be moved to embrace the love that took on our burdens and redeemed them. No, we need a symbol, a powerful image to make us both weep and rejoice in gratitude. And make us remember.

Since I have found no greater image to do this necessary task, I find that I must, once again, reprise the ancient story I have shared before. Listen anew with your imagination, with your Easter heart.

Even before the dawn one Friday morning, I noticed a young man, handsome and strong, walking down the alleys of our City. He was pulling an old cart filled with clothes both bright and new and he was calling in a clear, tenor voice, "Rags! Rags! New Rags for old! I'll take your tired rags!" Now this is a wonder, I thought to myself, for the man stood six-feet-four, and his arms were like tree limbs, hard and muscular, and his eyes flashed intelligence. Could he find no better job than this, to be a Ragman in the inner city? I followed him. My curiosity drove me. And I wasn't disappointed. Soon the Ragman saw a woman sitting on her back porch. She was sobbing into a handkerchief, sighing and shedding a thousand tears. Her knees and elbows made a sad X. Her shoulders shook. Her heart was breaking.

The Ragman stopped his cart. Quietly, he walked to the woman, stepping around the tin cans, dead toys, and Pampers. "Give me your rag, " he said so gently, "and I'll give you another." He slipped the handkerchief from her eyes. She looked up and he laid across her palm a linen cloth so clean and new that it shone. She blinked from the gift to the Giver. Then, as he began to pull his cart again, the Ragman did a strange thing. He put her stained handkerchief to his own face and then *He* began to weep, to sob as grievously as she had done, his shoulders shaking. Yet she was left without a tear.

This *is* a wonder, I breathed to myself, and I followed the sobbing Ragman like a child who cannot turn away from mystery.

"Rags! Rags! New Rags for old!"

In a little while, when the sky showed gray behind the roof tops, the Ragman came upon a girl whose head was wrapped in a bandage, whose eyes were empty. Blood soaked her bandage. A single line of blood ran down her cheek. Now the Ragman looked upon this child with pity, and he drew a lovely yellow bonnet from his cart.

"Give me your rags, " he said, tracing his own line on her cheek, "and I'll give you mine." The child could only gaze at him while he loosened the bandage, removed it, and tied it to his own head. The bonnet he set on hers. And I gasped at what I saw, for with the bandage went the wound! Against his brow it ran a darker, more substantial blood—his own!

"Rags! Rags! I take old rags!" cried the sobbing, bleeding, strong, intelligent Ragman. The Ragman seemed more and more now to hurry.

"Are you going to work?" he asked a man who leaned against a telephone pole. The man shook his head. The Ragman pressed him. "Do you have a job?"

"Are you crazy?" sneered the other. He pulled away from the pole, revealing the right sleeve of his jacket—flat, the cuff stuffed into the pocket. He had no arm.

"So," said the Ragman, "give me your jacket and I'll give you mine." Such quiet authority in his voice! The one-armed man took off his jacket. So did the Ragman—and I trembled at what I saw, for the Ragman's arm stayed in the sleeve, and when the other put it on, he had two good arms, thick as tree limbs, but the Ragman had only one. "Go to work," he said.

After that he found a drunk, lying unconscious beneath an army blanket, an old man, hunched, wizened, and sick. He took the blanket and wrapped it round himself, but for the drunk he left new clothes.

And now I had to run to keep up with the Ragman, Though he was weeping uncontrollably and bleeding freely at the forehead, pulling his cart with one arm and stumbling for drunkenness, falling again and again, exhausted, old, and sick—yet he went with terrible speed. On spider's legs he skittered through the alleys of the city, this mile and the next until he came to its limits and then he rushed beyond. I wept to see the change in this man. I hurt to see his sorrow. And yet I needed to see where he was going in such haste, perhaps even to discover what drove him so.

The little old Ragman—he finally came to a landfill. He came to the garbage pits. And then I wanted to help him in what he did, but I hung back, hiding. He climbed a hill. With tormented labor he cleared a little space on that hill. Then he sighed. He lay down. He pillowed his head on a handkerchief and a jacket. He covered his bones with an army blanket. And then he died.

Oh, how I cried to witness that death! I slumped in a junked car and wailed and mourned as one who has no hope because I had come to love the Ragman. I sobbed myself to sleep.

I did not know—how could I know?—that I slept through Friday night and Saturday and its night too. But then, on Sunday, I was awakened by a violent light. Light—pure, hard, demanding light—slammed against my sleeping face and I blinked and I looked and I saw the last and first wonder of all. There was the Ragman folding the blanket most carefully, a scar on his forehead but alive! And, besides that, so healthy! There was no sign of sorrow or of age, and all the rags he had gathered shone with cleanliness.

Well, I lowered my head and, trembling for all that I had seen, I got out of the junk car and walked to the Ragman. I told him my name with shame, for I was a sorry figure next to him. Then I stripped myself of everything and I said to him with yearning in my voice, "Dress me. Make me new again!"

He dressed me, my Lord. He put new rags on me and I am a wonder beside him.

Thus, in parable, the story this week: We have traveled from the burdened Ragman to the risen Christ. From "Crucify him" to "alleluia." From fear of death to hope of resurrection.

It's been a great triumph for divine love. No small wonder that we can wish each other "Happy Easter."

Easter: God's Choice

A, B, C

Up front, let me tell you how hard it is to resist preaching to you sentimental stories of butterflies and bunnies on a family Easter Sunday and send you home smiling and me home feeling good about myself. But I decided that I will not do that. Instead I want to offer you what you may not be prepared for and did not come here for today: a teaching.

And if that sounds too much like a boring classroom lecture—and my homily may turn out that way—then let me put it to you another way: I want to offer you a different take on Easter, another point of view, in order to help us all to come to terms with the meaning of this greatest of Christian feasts, the heart of our religion.

So follow along with me. We must go back to Holy Week, starting with Palm Sunday, the day Jesus went up to Jerusalem to die. Now, what was in Jesus' mind when he mounted a donkey and deliberately went to the very seat of the Roman power? Answer: He went to confront. He went to confront Roman imperial power and all misused power and the religious collaborators with it. And he did so as the basic, fundamental Jew he was, a Jewish prophet, steeped in the heart of Judaism, which always pitted the kingdom of God against any kingdom of force, fear, greed, and exploitation.

Here's how the opening salvos developed that fateful week. It was quite dramatic. On Palm Sunday *two* processions entered Jerusalem at Passover, a tinderbox time, when the people celebrated their deliverance from the past Egyptian Empire and not so secretly hoped to be delivered from the present Roman Empire. Protests were inevitable and so at each Passover the Roman governor—Pilate in the time of Jesus—rode up to Jerusalem from the imperial capital on the coast at the head of a 600-plus cohort of imperial cavalry and troops to reinforce the local riot squad.

113

Pilate's procession—try to picture it—arrived from the west where Rome and imperial power was. Jesus' procession, significantly, entered the city from the east, a counter-procession. And whereas Pilate rode into the city on a warhorse, Jesus rode in on a donkey. Jesus quite consciously planned the contrast that way, very much mindful of the prophet Zechariah who speaks of a king of peace on a donkey who will banish the warhorse and battle from the land. Are you starting to get the picture of what's going on?

What is going on is that, in this public drama—and it was that and was understood as such—the gauntlet has been thrown down and the contrast is clear. Jesus versus Pilate, the nonviolence of the kingdom of God versus the violence of the empire. That was the contrast: two arrivals, two entrances, two processions, two ways of life, two choices represented by these two processions on Palm Sunday.

Well, the next day, Monday, Jesus deliberately takes on the Temple authorities' collaboration in the domination system, chiding them for making the Temple a den of thieves, meaning it was not a place where robbers rob but where they fled after having robbed elsewhere.

On Tuesday Jesus entered into a series of debates with the Temple authorities who desperately wanted to seize him but were afraid of the crowd. Here I want to make a correction. I want you to note that, from the day he entered the city, Jesus was consistently protected by the crowd. They stood by him all the way. They were *not* the fair-weather friends so loved by preachers: "Hosanna one day, crucify him the next day." No, the people were with him from beginning to end.

That's exactly why on Wednesday, when Judas went secretly to make a deal to betray Jesus, the plan was for the soldiers to come to the Garden of Gethsemane on Thursday at night time when the crowd who loved and protected Jesus had dispersed for the day.

On Friday, therefore, Jesus stands before Pontius Pilate and a second, smaller crowd, one gathered in Pilate's courtyard, which was closed to the public but open to these hangers-on and supporters of the Temple authorities. In other words, it was an in-the-pocket, bought crowd and it was this second crowd who shouted crucify him, not the people, not all the Jewish people. And so Jesus, the innocent, is gruesomely and wrongly executed by imperial power between two thieves.

But on Sunday, the day we're celebrating, the Sunday we call Easter, spectacularly, Jesus—*not the bad thief, notice*—is raised from the dead by divine power. And here we're at the heart of the matter: What does this raising of Jesus by God mean? It means that God said a resounding "yes!" to Jesus and all he stood for, and a firm "no!" to the powers that killed him. Easter means that God is on a collision course with injustice, with violence, with exploitation. That's the other point of view.

God is against the betrayal of Judas, the denial of Peter, the complicity and corruption of power in Pilate and Herod. He is against Jesus being beaten in jail, mocked by Herod's court, and flogged by Herod's soldiers. He is against the politically correct judgment of Pilate, who had initially judged Jesus innocent of capital offense. He is against an innocent man being exchanged for another prisoner guilty of murder, Barabbas.

And now, are you ready for this? To translate what I just said into our dreary contemporary terms, God is against betrayals like San Francisco's mayor who had an affair with his trusted campaign manager's wife. He is against the denials, lies, and corruption among some of our officials, the billion-dollar sport-betting ring, the double dipping, multiple pensions, the top official of the Smithsonian enjoying his $747 a night luxury hotel while much of the world is homeless. He is against the top three Viacom executives who received 52 million dollars in compensation while shares fell, financially hurting many people. He is against those people who shelled out $45,000 for a limited Louis Vuitton tote bag—a *tote* bag, for cryin' out loud!—when that money would have kept two families in Jamaica well off for two years.

God is against the leaders of the noble Shriners who diverted much of the money meant for children's hospitals and lavished it on liquor parties and luxurious travel expenses. God is against the murders and violence of our streets, the vulgarity of our discourse, the moral and physical abuse of spouses and children, the misuse of power.

The Easter story, in other words, is basically a potent story of where God stands, and that stand is clear in the resurrection. He approvingly raises up a Jesus who told us to turn the other cheek; go two miles with one who forces you to go one; give someone your coat who asked for your shirt; that one should go first and be reconciled with one's brother or sister and then come and offer one's gifts at the altar. Who said, be a Samaritan, do not seek revenge. And do not return evil for evil, but cry out with him on the cross, "Father, forgive them; they know not what they do." Put away the sword of violence, he told us. Feed the hungry and give drink to the thirsty and always remember that in the end it profits you nothing to become Paris Hilton but wind up losing your own soul. This "Jesus-way-of-life" the Father raises up. In other words, Easter, beyond its tremendous mystery, is as we say these days, a statement, a divine statement of divine values.

See, by now—I can feel it—you really *are* missing the Easter bunnies and butterflies! They're much nicer, much safer, much more comfortable, much more Disney, aren't they? But look, the truth is that Easter—Christianity—is about joyously sterner, deeper stuff. It's about life and death, right and wrong and, mostly—and here comes the zinger—which side we're on, which entrance we have taken into the holy city.

The fact is, the day Jesus entered Jerusalem from the east on a donkey and Pilate from the west on a warhorse was the day you and I were confronted with the choice: Which entrance shall we take, which procession shall we follow? Easter is the day God announced *his* choice. What is left is *our* choice.

Have a happy, right-choice Easter.

The Thomas Syndrome

Item One: Old backwoods Clem decided it was time to purchase a new saw to help clear his heavily timbered property. A salesman showed him the latest chainsaw model and assured him that he could easily cut three or four cords of wood a day with it. But the first day Clem barely cut one cord of wood. The second morning he arose an hour earlier and managed to cut a little over one cord. The third day he got up even earlier but only managed to achieve a total of one and a half cords of wood.

Clem returned the saw to the store the next day and explained the situation. "Well," said the salesman, "let's see what's the matter." He then pulled the cable and the chainsaw sprang into action.

Leaping back, Clem exclaimed, "What the heck is that noise?"

Item Two: Once there was a man who dreamed of nothing but gold. He was obsessed with it. Morning, noon, and night he dreamed of gold. One day he got up from his desk and ran to the marketplace. He ran through the crowd to the table where the man was selling gold coins. He swept them all into his little bag and ran away. A policeman was standing right next to the table and nabbed him.

He took him to the police station and as he was locking him up he said to the man, "I can't understand it. There you are, me right next to the merchant's table and at least 100 witnesses and you steal something right in front of them!"

The man replied, "I never saw any of them. I only saw the gold."

Item Three: On Friday evening, April 7, NBC's anchor Brian Williams commented that it was a rough week for Christians: On the front page of the *New York Times* there appeared successively the story that Jesus really did not walk on water. A scientist claims that there was a freak storm that turned the lake to ice and so Jesus walked on ice. No miracle here. Then there was the discovery of a missing-link fish with opposite fins indicating that they were to be used for walking and so we have proof of evolution. Finally, he said, there was the publication of *The Judas Gospel*, a work claiming to rescue Judas from the role of a craven traitor to an obedient disciple following Jesus' orders.

Item Four: Every Christmas and every Easter, like clockwork, the major weekly magazines feature Christian themes on the cover and as the lead article. *Time, Newsweek, U.S News & World Report* all follow the same well-worn pattern: three-fourths of the article raises new theories that debunk traditional Christianity along with gorgeous artwork, boxed quotes to catch the eye, attractive layout, and lots of coverage of the new ideas, followed at the very end by the usual, "Of course, some noted theologians and Scripture scholars disagree." But by that time, the impression has been made and the doubts sown.

Item Five: All this is occurring in the context of great publicity about Pope Pius XII and the Jews, the gospels of Thomas, Mary Magdalene, and other Gnostic gospels, not to mention the enormous popularity of *The DaVinci Code*, a book filled with gross misinformation passed off as fact, which has been on the *New York Times* bestseller list for some 156 weeks and has earned its author over forty million dollars and has just come out in paperback as more huge sales continue. There is also the blockbuster movie which even one of its co-producers, John Calley, admits is "conservatively anti-Catholic." And, of course, reflecting a profitable market, a spate of anti-Christian, anti-Catholic books are riding the trend as bestsellers.

Five items and five challenges. No doubt about it, people in general and especially Catholics are puzzled and confused, since most of the books, TV fare, and movies are specifically about the Catholic Church. Worse, most Catholics not only have read these books and read the newspaper and magazine articles about them, but many half-believe them, just as they read and half-believe the outrageous, half-baked bestselling *Left Behind* books. They all sound so plausible. Who can contest them?

And there's the issue, the big, big issue: Who can contest them? Sadly, very few; for the fact is that most Catholics suffer from the Thomas Syndrome. What is the Thomas Syndrome? It's what we find in today's gospel. "Thomas, called Didymus, one of the Twelve, was not with them when Jesus came." That's it: The Thomas Syndrome means the Thomas Absence. He was absent when the risen Jesus came and so did not get to see him or hear him and his message. And so, not knowing, he had no defense against false information or false rumors about Jesus, and so his faith wavered.

And there *we* are. That's us. Absent Thomases. Not seeing or hearing Jesus or learning about him, we see and hear everyone else and have no way of knowing whether what they're saying is true or not. Not having seen and touched Jesus and the church tradition about him, not knowing his mission and message, we have no comeback, nothing to draw on to critique what is being said. We have, in short, no tools to measure the absurd or ridiculous, the false from the true. No wonder what we are bombarded with today sounds so plausible.

What I am saying is that we are absent from sufficient knowledge about our faith, that we have to admit we are religiously illiterate. Clueless to our own tradition, how could we possibly evaluate *The DaVinci Code*, the annual magazine temptations, or any other new claim down the pike? It's been a long time, hasn't it, since we checked our religious facts or studied our faith? Can we speak intelligently about it? Are we still trying to live an adult Christian life based on spotty grade-school religious knowledge? The answer for many is yes, but that just won't work anymore.

Imagine being similarly illiterate in our work. Imagine we're a mechanic still using the tools and knowledge when we worked on model Ts in the early 1900s, trying to figure out the electronic hybrid car before us. Imagine being a doctor, engineer, lawyer, teacher, or tax assessor without having upgraded ourselves in current skills and knowledge. The point is, we keep up with everything but our faith.

Sure, the whole world knows, eagerly and deliciously, that unmarried and divorced Tom Cruise and his unmarried partner had a baby, that unmarried and divorced Brad Pitt and Angelina Jolie also had a baby out of wedlock. How could anyone not know? It's the daily, unrelenting input of our lives. We relish every detail. And we can give chapter and verse on who's on or off *American Idol* and the latest CD rage and can tick off the Oscar winners.

In the way of the world, in the realm of entertainment trivia we are masters. When it comes to our faith, however, afflicted with the Thomas Syndrome, we are dunces. Maybe that's too harsh, but it seems to be largely true in many cases. We have to ask ourselves, when was the last time any of us read a book about our faith, took a course, or took part in a Bible study group, upgraded our religious knowledge? Do we even have good general Catholic magazines in our homes, such as *The Liguorian*, *Catholic Digest*, or *St. Anthony Messenger*, that might offer a countercultural view of life and answer our questions?

You get the point: All the stuff avalanching out of the secular media is overwhelming. It sows doubt and confusion because, like Thomas, we were not with the disciples when Jesus came. We really don't know who he is or what he said or what he wants. We can't evangelize because we don't know what to say. We're like Clem in the joke: Nothing in his experience prepared him for the electric motor. We're like the man so indoctrinated, so programmed to see only one thing, gold, that he missed the truth.

Today's gospel about Thomas is, in its way, a wake-up call. It's time for us who are absent from knowledge about our faith to learn why we are Catholics, why we believe what we believe, and do what we do. Time to gain sufficient knowledge to discern the true from the false, to be able to refute the nonsense and affirm and explain our faith. It's time to subscribe to good magazines and books, perhaps join a Catholic study group, to listen to religious tapes as we drive to work or shopping.

Today's gospel reminds us that the Thomas Syndrome is a timely affliction, one we can't afford to ignore. It's time to deal with it so that, cured, we can exclaim once again with conviction, "My Lord and my God!"

Behind Closed Doors

SECOND SUNDAY OF EASTER, C, JOHN 20:19–31

There they were, behind closed doors, out of fear. What were the apostles afraid of? Probably several things. They were afraid that those responsible for the death of Jesus might hunt them down, get rid of the whole movement, root and branch, once and for all. They were afraid of public ridicule. You know: "You hitched your wagon to a lame horse. You're a bunch of losers." They were afraid go home—after all, they had left all things to follow Jesus—and admit they were wrong. Better to hide till it was all over.

Fear is a terrible thing. We all have our fears. In spite of being incessantly distracted by a frivolous, profit-driven media that squeezes every last drop out of the latest celebrity scandal du jour, we fear the real growing threat of terrorism, Iran's potential for nuclear warfare, the seduction of our children, the vulgarity of civil discourse. We fear increasing taxes, identity theft, unsafe streets, loss of health and income, aging, dying. And we fear matters of the heart.

Virginia, nineteen and pregnant, victim of neglect, abuse, bureaucratic failure, was with her fifteenth set of foster parents. The new foster mother asked Virginia, "Are you frightened, Virginia?"

"Kinda," she replied without looking up. "I've been in lots of homes."

"Well," the sympathetic woman tried to reassure the mother-to-be, "Let's hope this time turns out for the best."

Virginia simply said, flat and without change of tone or even lifting her head, ""Hurts too much to hope."

"Hurts too much to hope." What a terrible burden to carry. There's a young woman locked in fear.

I read once about a man, Janez Rus, who feared punishment for his wartime activity in support of the Nazis. He was a young shoemaker when

121

he went into hiding at his sister's farmhouse in June 1945. He was found thirty-two years later. He said he used to cry when he heard happy voices outside. He didn't even dare to go to his own mother's funeral. Throughout those years he never left the house, a victim of his own fears.

Then we fear God's love and all its demands. A famous therapist named Rollo May, recovering from a nervous breakdown, went, even though he was a non-believer, to visit Mount Athos, a peninsula of Greece inhabited exclusively by monks. He happened to arrive when the monks were celebrating the Greek Orthodox Easter. The ceremony was thick with symbolism, thick with beauty. Icons were everywhere. Incense hung in the air. And as the height of that service, the priest gave everyone present three Easter eggs, wonderfully decorated and wrapped in a veil. *"Christos Anesti!"* he said, "Christ is Risen!" And the people, including non-believer Rollo May, responded, "He is indeed." May writes, "I was seized then by a moment of spiritual reality: What would it mean for our world if he *had* truly risen?" We too fear it might be true and what would that demand of us?

We fear intimacy—and lots of uncommitted sex is a favorite way to cover up that fear—and we fear betrayal and being made a fool of, of not fitting in or, society's worst sin: we fear not feeling good about oneself, looking good. And so in many ways we withdraw, take no risks, and hide behind the closed doors of our own making, pretending to be cool, sophisticated, life of the party, or aloof, reserved, a deep thinker. But it's all a façade. We're afraid. As Bette Midler sang in the movie, *The Rose*, "It's the heart afraid of breaking that never learns to dance / It's the dream afraid of waking that never takes a chance."

Fear. We are looking for someone to walk through the doors we've closed and call us out of our fears. Someone who understands because they've been there.

Let me tell you the story of an extraordinary woman. Her husband had been injured in a fire while attempting to save his parents from a burning house. They unfortunately perished, and his face was terribly burned and disfigured. The man in fact was so self-conscious that he wouldn't let anyone see him, even his wife. Finally, after weeks of his self-imposed exile, the wife went to Dr. Maxwell Maltz, a plastic surgeon and well-known author. He told the woman not to worry, that he could restore her husband's face.

But she replied. "You don't understand, Doctor. He won't let anyone see him. He won't accept any help."

"Then why are you here?" asked the doctor.

She replied, "Because I want you to disfigure my face so I can be like him. If I can share in his pain then maybe he will let me back into his life."

Dr. Maltz says he was shocked and told her that he could never do anything like that. But he was so moved by this woman's love that he went to speak to the husband. Knocking on the man's door, he spoke loudly, "My name is Doctor Maltz. I am a plastic surgeon and I want you to know that I can restore your face." No response.

"Please come out." No response.

Still speaking through the door, Dr. Maltz told the man of his wife's proposal. "She wants me to disfigure her face like yours in the hope that you will let her back into your life. That's how much she loves you."

There was a brief moment of silence and then, ever so slowly, the doorknob began to turn.

Let me move quickly to the gospel point of all this and tell you about Jesus. His disciples were like the husband: hiding in fear behind locked doors, disfigured with their own betrayals and cowardice. Jesus appears in their midst—and here you *must* notice, cannot fail to notice—he appears with his wounds! Maybe, Jesus feels, if he, like the wife of our story, can appear before them disfigured, they will let him back into their disfigured lives.

Are we getting the message? When it hurts too much to hope, when life has wounded us, when faith is exhausted, know that the risen Jesus with disfiguring wounds is waiting to get into our disfigured and fearful lives and call us out of our fears.

Jesus got his wounds on Good Friday so that, now being like us, we might let him in on Easter Sunday. He is willing to come through the doors we've used to shut him out and is standing outside with those terrible wounds searching out *our* terrible wounds, letting us know he understands where we're coming from and that he can give us peace and wholeness.

So, even if you can't or don't feel like praying, go apart and simply repeat the last three words of the Bible, "Come, Lord Jesus!" Give your wounds to the wounded Lord.

Threes and Tragedies

Sometime after Sidney died, Tillie was finally able to speak about what a thoughtful man her late husband had been. "Sidney thought of everything," she told her friends. "Just before he died he called me to his bedside. He handed me three envelopes. "Tillie," he said, "I have put all my last wishes in these three envelopes. After I'm dead, please open them and do exactly as I have instructed. Then I can rest in peace."

"What was in the envelopes?" her friends asked.

"The first envelope contained $5000 with a note: Please use this money to buy a nice casket." So I bought a beautiful mahogany casket with such a comfortable lining that I know Sidney is resting comfortably.

"The second envelope contained $10,000 with a note: Please use this for a nice funeral. I arranged a very nice funeral for Sidney, very dignified, and bought all his favorite foods for everyone attending."

"And the third envelope?" her friends asked.

"The third envelope contained $50,000 with a note: Please use this to buy a nice stone."

Holding her hand in the air, flashing a ten-carat diamond, Tillie said, "So how do you like my stone?"

You caught the humor, but I confess, I was really pitching something else. I was trying to call your attention to a common human metaphor that made the story work: the use of the number three. Did you notice Sidney left three envelopes, not two, not four?

You see, in storytelling, three is one of those symbolic numbers meaning "just right," just right to make something complete. As in those Jesuit-Dominican-Franciscan jokes, or an Irishman-an Italian-a Jew jokes, there are always three because three is just right for the tension. Two is not enough; there's not sufficient play. Four is too much; it throws the story off balance. But three is just right. It has nothing to do with a unit of measurement; it's a cryptic, symbolic sign that has everything to do with making just the right point.

The passion-death-resurrection story of Jesus has a right point to make and therefore it uses three all the time. Jesus returns to his prayer in the Garden of Gethsemane three times. He takes three apostles with him. Peter denies him three times. Piety has Jesus fall three times on his way to his death. Three are crucified together on Calvary. Jesus hangs three hours on the cross. The threes of these stories are just sufficient to get our attention and emphasize the depth of what's going on.

After his death and resurrection Jesus appears three times in the guise of a gardener, a housebreaker, and a chef. And all three appearances coincide with the threefold times of grief, discouragement, and hunger. He appears to Mary Magdalene who is so full of grief that, through her tears, she thinks Jesus is the gardener. He housebreaks through locked doors into the upper room to the discouraged apostles listlessly hanging out there, wondering where they go from there.

Finally, in today's gospel he appears on the shoreline as a chef with food for the apostles who were trying to go back to their former lives, but their hearts aren't in it. They were hungry for something more. As John wrote in today's gospel, "This was now the third time Jesus was revealed to his disciples after being raised from the dead."

The three appearances are just enough to make the point: Jesus has been raised up and is there, will ever be there, to counter those three things: grief, discouragement, spiritual hunger.

Grief. Think of the parents and loved ones of those thirty-two slain and injured students and staff at Virginia Tech in Blacksburg, Virginia, not long ago, the deadliest shooting rampage in American history. Think of how, when such tragedy beyond words happens, those who relentlessly work at removing any mention of God or religion from the public square fall silent and threaten no lawsuit as every publicly elected, publicly funded official, from the President of the United States to the President of the University, to mayors and politicians, anchors and commentators on radio and television, openly and ceaselessly promise prayers to the affected, implicitly acknowledging a God to be prayed to.

They do so because some things are too large for the human mind to understand or prejudice to challenge. Stunned before such massive evil beyond our comprehension, beyond any rational explanation, we instinctively and humbly fall to our knees. We are like Mary Magdalene at the tomb, full of questions and tears.

We have to trust that somehow, the shadowy one who told Mary not to weep over her loss is not unmindful of our loss, our tears, our shock. It is in grief time that Jesus makes his appearance in many mysterious ways.

Discouragement. The disciples were in the Upper Room, completely empty, numb, discouraged. They had left everything to follow Jesus and now he has left them in death. Could he not have prevented his own death? Did he lie to them? Where was he when they needed him most? What were they going to do now? As we saw, some, as if in a fog, routinely went back to the trade they knew, but they were just going through the motions.

The questions remain. Could not God have prevented the Virginia Tech massacre? We always ask those questions in time of tragedy. Where was God when we needed him most? What do a grieving people do now? Like the disciples, we're behind the impenetrable doors of doubt and fear, asking what is happening to us as a nation: Imus in the morning, massacre in the afternoon, and salacious sitcoms in the evening.

But Jesus who penetrated the doors of fear and uttered his one word of hope, *shalom*—peace—breathes into us his Spirit and lets us know that pain and death, ever since his resurrection, are not the last words and that we have now abiding with us the Steadfast Spirit who will not go away, who is incapable of leaving us. Through the doors of a dark, hollow room the wounded risen Jesus has spoken peace and he does so to us now.

Hunger. On the road to Emmaus the two hungry, discouraged disciples finally recognized Jesus in the breaking of the bread. On the shoreline, one of the dispirited disciples recognized Jesus and said, not "It is Jesus!" but "It is the *Lord!*" Yes, Lord, a transformed Jesus beyond what they knew. And another jumps into the water to get to him while all the while Jesus is calmly setting up a cookout for them, for he knew they were hungry.

They were hungry for answers. More. Like us, they were hungry for meaning. Life is not, cannot be, about endless consumption, conceit, and competition. We do not live on bread alone, even with seventy-five varieties to choose from. We are hungry for relationships that do not exploit, friendships that do not betray, and a God who will make all things new again, even out of senseless tragedies like Virginia Tech.

Jesus' cookout is not an answer but a reassurance. It is another form of his, "I am the bread of life...he who eats this bread will never die." Which is to say, his life, teaching, death, and resurrection are nourishment even, maybe especially, in times of tragedy.

This is a gospel made for today, highlighting three fundamental human emotions: grief, discouragement, hunger. It is also a gospel of three appearances: do not weep, *shalom*, come and eat. Three words, just right for these troubled times.

The Good Shepherd

When I was a full-time pastor, a word that means shepherd, I thought I was a pretty good Good Shepherd. That is, until the day some friends and I went to a small restaurant. We were seated in a booth where, behind us in another booth, as it so happened, was a man who obviously had too much to drink. He was very loud, vulgar, abrasive, and at times obscene. The waitress who knew me went over to the man in the booth and said, "Sir, do you know a priest, Father Bausch, is sitting in the next booth?" The man got up, turned around, draped himself on the corner of our booth and shouted, "Father Bausch! I'm so glad to meet you. I attended one of your talks and it changed my life!" The Good Shepherd lays down his life for his sheep. For him, I would have made an exception.

But I want to tell you perhaps a familiar story about one who did, a story told and remembered by a man named Ted Wotjkowski. Ted Wotjkowski considered himself an ordinary man. He came to Chicago from Poland after World War II. He worked as an engineer and raised a family. But what I want to tell you is that as a young man Ted was a special witness to one of the great Good Shepherd heroes of the twentieth century. Go back to 1939. In September of that year German tanks rumbled into Poland. The first village attacked by the Nazis was Wotjowski's home. He was then twenty years old. He went underground, manned a shortwave radio to gather war news from London, and secretly printed leaflets to let the villages know what was happening. Things gradually became too risky for him so he hopped on his father's bicycle and headed toward Hungary and then to France where he hoped to join the Polish army. But he was caught at the border, jailed, and then in May 1940 was sent to the dreaded Auschwitz concentration camp.

Auschwitz was not yet a killing ground for Jews, but a place for criminals and enemies and critics of the Nazi regime. Many priests were there. Wotjkowski lived in a two-story barracks with eight hundred other prisoners. He was sent out daily to build more barracks. The Nazis treated the prisoners cruelly, saving their special hatred and punishment for priests.

Whenever a prisoner escaped, all the others had to stand in the sun for days with their hands on their heads. After a second escape, ten prisoners were machine-gunned. The third escape occurred around July 1941. The punishment for this third infringement was that one hundred soldiers from Wotjokowski's barracks were forced to stand in rows of ten. Ten of them would die. Wotjkowski stood in the eighth row. The camp commander ordered each row, one after another, to step forward. He then began a random selection: one, two, three were pulled from each group. Wotjkowski hoped that the ten would be already singled out before the commander reached his row.

A fourth, fifth, and sixth man were picked. The sixth man broke down sobbing, "My wife, my children! Who will take care of them?" Suddenly a prisoner from the sixth row spoke up. He turned to the commander and said. "I will take the place of this man with the wife and children." Everyone looked. Wotjkowski in particular noticed that there was something serene and remarkable about the volunteer's demeanor. The commander, however, was not impressed. "You must be one of those vermin priests," he snarled. But he accepted him as one of the ten. All ten, this volunteer and the nine others, were locked in a bunker to starve to death. They would not waste bullets on them.

That man, that volunteer, was indeed a priest. But he wasn't just any priest. He was the well-known Franciscan Father Maximilian Kolbe. He was a leader and a gifted man. He published religious magazines and newspapers read by more than one million Poles. He was widely admired, running the largest Catholic religious house in the world. Intensely devoted to the Blessed Mother, Kolbe supervised 650 friars at an evangelization center near Warsaw. Naturally the Nazis regarded Kolbe with suspicion and mistrust after they invaded Poland. When he resisted pressure to apply for German citizenship, for which he was eligible, he was arrested on February 17, 1941.

Back to the incident. When the guards were out of earshot, the prisoners swapped information with one another about the fate of those ten men in the bunker starving to death. It turned out that Kolbe was leading the doomed men in prayer and hymns. A piece of bread had been smuggled in to be used in a Mass. After three weeks, all the men had died except Kolbe who was near death. The Nazis, impatient to use the bunker to punish others, had a doctor inject poison into Kolbe to finish him off.

The man Kolbe had saved, whose place he took, was but a poor anonymous peasant farmer. Kolbe, on the other hand, was a renowned man, only forty-seven, one of the most well-known and accomplished men in Poland. Yet he exchanged his life for the other. Truly a Good Shepherd. He saved not only that peasant but also Wojtkowski himself who, inspired by Kolbe's act, endured years of backbreaking labor and abuse in the camp. Finally, in 1945, while being force-marched to Dachau, he escaped and took refuge with a German priest who hid him and fed him until the Allies rolled into Germany. Wojtkowski finally got to the United States and moved to a Chicago suburb with a large Jewish population. He kept a scrapbook on Father Kolbe and a piece of his clothing and an original signature. A large painting of Kolbe hung in his study.

A heroic story. The Good Shepherd lays down his life for his sheep. I think—I hope you won't think me too self-serving—that with all the terrible scandal in the church where some priests have shamed us all, that you remember there are good shepherds, lots of them: Father Maximilian Kolbe, canonized in 1982 by his fellow Pole, who literally laid down his life for another; that German priest who hid and fed Wotjkowski at the peril of his own life; the many priests you knew as you were growing up, the faithful ones who baptized, married, and anointed family members, who guided and encouraged your journey. They are legion.

Good Shepherd Sunday is a good time to pray for the good shepherds as well as the bad ones; and a good time to realize in this messy family of ours we call the church that *the* Good Shepherd walks with us still.

Vine, Branches, and Compartments

Fifth Sunday of Easter, B, John 15:1–7

They deal in extortion, prostitution, drugs, and murder, yet in the cinematic *Godfather* series the Corleones are Catholics, baptizing their babies, having First Communions, and receiving honors from the Vatican. In the movie *The Sting*, Doyle Lonnegan, played by Robert Shaw, deals in bribery, extortion, and murder, and he is a Fourth Degree Knight of Columbus. In real life it is said that Eichmann, after a day of murdering Jews at Auschwitz, would go home and tenderly play with and be affectionate with his small son. I understand that Jack Abramoff, who cheated and bribed in the billions, goes to Temple.

What is happening here? Perhaps it's best explained by the tale of Aldrich Ames, who, you might recall, pleaded guilty to giving up the CIA's most precious secrets for money from the KGB. Ames was asked how he could do such a terrible deed, despite his sacred oath of loyalty to his country, knowing that his spying would jeopardize the futures of his wife and son, and knowing that his deeds cost the lives of at least eleven people. The spy calmly responded: "I tend to put some of these things in separate boxes, and compartmentalize feelings and thoughts."

And there it is. What these people have in common is that all of them seem to have two boxes in their lives and rationalize evil conduct because the two compartments don't seem to be connected. They separate their lives into "church" and "world" and one has nothing to do with the other. They cut their lives into separate compartments: my church life, my work life, my professional life, my entertainment life—all little boxes that don't touch one another. The Corleones and Lonnegans, Eichmanns and Ameses

131

are living examples of this and, consequently, are under the judgment of today's gospel. They are, in Jesus' metaphor, branches cut off from the Vine and so, even when they look prosperous, they wither and die. The fictional Corleones and Lonnegans, the real-life Eichmanns and Ameses are dead men walking, acting as if they are not connected to the world and the community and to the people they hurt.

And when you disconnect like that, you are a branch cut off. Jesus warns against this: "Be whole. Remain in me," he urges, "as I remain in you. Just as the branch cannot bear fruit on its own unless it remains on the vine, so neither can you." In short, stay connected and be mindful of the connection.

The great Christian truth is:

We are connected to something larger than ourselves.

We are connected to the millions of South Africans who lined up for hours to vote freely for the first time in their lives.

We are connected to the thousands who are dying in Bosnia, Iraq, and Sudan.

We are connected to children we dare not hurt by our hands or words.

We are connected to the earth, we dare not pollute by our selfishness.

We are connected to animals that we dare not make suffer needlessly.

We are connected to nature, to all of creation. St. Francis of Assisi reminded us of this when he spoke of Brother Sun and Sister Moon and preached not just to people but to animals. In spite of current philosophy, we are not atoms, separate little egos grasping and hugging everything to ourselves, touting Number One, the self-centered, navel-gazing Dives totally unmindful of Lazarus at the gate. We are an interconnected human community, our brother's keeper, part of a global family. Our actions have consequences.

Christians especially, who are reminded that they are a People of God, the Mystical Body of Christ, the Vine and Branches, should not have separate little boxes in their lives, separating beliefs from actions, their church going from their church living, their lives from the lives of others. We are a communal people responsible for one another, whose actions affect others. Therefore what you and I do and say here should be the same as what we do and say when we leave here. The unity of Vine and Branches does not allow us to make compartments of our lives.

I remember once giving a retreat to a group of men. One of the organizers of the retreat was a lawyer who was very active in church affairs. He belonged to a prayer group, hosted seminars, was a lector. One day I complimented him on his loyalty to the church and then casually asked, "How does all this affect your job as a lawyer?" He rolled his eyes and replied, "I don't even want to go into that!" And I was stunned. Here is an active Catholic who's basically telling me, hey, business is business and religion has nothing to do with that.

On the other hand, a few years ago, the CEO of Baxter International, a medical supply company, made a decision that cost his company $189 million. I know what you're thinking. You're thinking, like many crooked CEOs who have been in the news lately, that Baxter's CEO Harry Kraemer must have done something unethical. He must have cooked the books, or drained the company accounts in order to finance his own luxurious lifestyle.

No, that's not it at all. It was Kraemer's honesty, his high sense of ethics and his refusal to separate his life from his work that caused him to make such a momentous decision. Executives at Baxter International learned in 2001 that one of the products they manufactured, a filter for a kidney dialysis machine, may have been defective. Some dialysis patients using the Baxter International filter had died of unexplained causes. Rather than covering up the situation, Kraemer recalled all of the filters and instituted a rigorous investigation into the problem. This recall and investigation cost the company $189 million.

Kraemer also recommended that his performance bonus for that year be cut, because this situation occurred under his leadership. And to top it all off, he informed all his competitors in the medical manufacturing business of the possible flaws in Baxter's filters, so that they could benefit from the research his investigation turned up.

"I am the Vine, you are the branches." You can even take those words to mean branch as in a branch office. There's main headquarters and then there are its branches that are supposed to reflect the product and philosophy of the main corporation. We are branches of Jesus. The Vine. We are supposed to reflect his values and his mission. To be true to Jesus, we cannot chop up our lives into little compartments as if one had nothing to do with the other. You and I are Christians seven days a week, all the time. People should be able to tell from how we act. That's what the gospel's all about.

Let me end by recalling a strong parable in a classic film of the past. See how good your memories are. It's Federico Fellini's ground-breaking film, *La Dolce Vita—The Sweet Life*—hailed by critics as one of the most important films ever made. As the film opens, viewers see a helicopter towing a statue of Jesus across the Italian sky. Soon, a second helicopter appears carrying a writer named Marcello. Marcello, raised as a country boy, longed for more excitement than his rural beginnings could offer. So he was moving to the big city in search of the "sweet life" he dreamed of. However, there Marcello eventually lost his roots, his faith. He's disconnected. His hopes of fulfillment eventually dissipated into emptiness.

As the film strikingly ends, there is this powerful scene where Marcello is alone on the beach, looking down at and pondering the fate of a large dead fish washed up on the shore. Cut off from the sea and its source of life, the fish had died. Fellini ends the movie there leaving his viewers to make the connection between the dead, decaying fish and the empty, faithless, cut-off Marcello.

Like the fish on the shore and like Marcello without his faith are those who, like a branch separated from the vine, separate themselves from Christ, and try to build compartments where there should be none.

The Ninety-Seven Percent Solution

Fifth Sunday of Easter, C, Acts 14:21–27

Warning: What I'm about to share is a "think" piece, not everybody's cup of tea. That is to say, my words today are not an exhortation to virtue or an inspiration to live the Christian life, or a story to catch your heart, but, if you will, simply a classroom subject, something for us to think about. Every once in a while I like to toss these things out to give you a headache.

My words are inspired by Luke's Acts of the Apostles that we're hearing these post-Easter days. Here in Acts we are treated to the ongoing saga of the trials and tribulations of the early church. But also, as an ongoing subtext in Luke's account, there lies the very critical issue of leadership, our subject for today.

Now be it noted that in the early Christian church, leadership developed slowly in three phases. The first was what we call the charismatic phase. Here different gifted persons, many of whom were original companions of Jesus and some not, like Paul and Barnabas, became the natural, looked-to leaders in that small, loose, and exuberant confederation of believers. And that was sufficient for a while.

But as time went on and numbers and complexity grew, it was evident that some kind of order and stability was needed. So to establish that order and stability, the charismatic leaders, who by nature moved around and moved on, sensibly appointed and left behind a council of elders. You heard precisely that in today's first reading: "Paul and Barnabas appointed elders in each local church, then they traveled on…." These elders were called in Greek, the presbyters, from which we would get our term priests. It was governance by council.

135

Gradually the third form of early church government to evolve was the single bishop. The name means "overseer" or in Greek, *episkopos*, hence our word bishop. It seems that he might have been originally a kind of the chairman of the board of elders, but soon, by the end of the first century, he emerges as a single in-charge bishop presiding over the local church. This final form of church government, the single local bishop, soon became the norm at the beginning of the second century and you can find mention of this office of bishop in the pastoral epistles of Sts. Paul, Peter, and Jude, and in other early Christian writings outside the Bible.

In short, what developed quickly is what scholars call the emergence of "early Catholicism." Our current form of church authority, therefore, has solid biblical foundations and is in historical continuity with the church of the apostles.

That's what happened historically. Now, the interesting part: *How* did the system work through the ages? Here I offer just three comments you might ponder.

First, the election of these bishops. Let us remember that originally, and for more than a millennium and a half thereafter, bishops were nominated not by the pope, but either by public acclamation—as in the case of St. Ambrose who wasn't even a baptized Christian when he was acclaimed bishop by the people and had to be given a hasty RCIA run-through—or by the local clergy or by the emperor or civil magistrates. In fact, it was only in the nineteenth century that the novelty of the pope nominating and appointing *all* the bishops of the world emerged. Or, let me put it to you this way: 175 years ago, out of the 646 bishops in the world, only 24 of them were directly appointed by the pope.

Since this is historically so, some think that it's time to return to the ancient tradition and let others have some say in the process of making bishops. Not necessarily to do the actual appointing any more as they used to, but, more modestly, simply to be apprised of who the candidates are and have some input.

Just as they used to publicly issue the banns of marriage for engaged couples, so they should issue banns of intent for episcopal candidates so that, sensibly, people, especially those who have firsthand experienced and witnessed his abilities, compassion, and pastoral skills—or lack thereof—

could have an opportunity to share their assessment of his worthiness and fitness for the job. That makes good sense and might prevent some disastrous leadership.

A few quotes from the past to remind us of the way it was: In the fifth century, the bishop of Rome, Pope Celestine I said, "No bishop is to be imposed on unwilling subjects, but the consent and wishes of clergy and people are to be considered." And Pope Leo of the same era adds, "On no account is anyone to be bishop who had not been chosen by the clergy, desired by the people, and consecrated by the bishops of the province." And while we're at it, let's add the words of a sixth-century church council that decreed, "No one is to be consecrated as a bishop unless the clergy and the people of the diocese have been called together and have given their consent." When did *you* ever hear such words? We've come a long way and maybe we should travel back.

Second, having authority not only does not preclude but actually includes dialogue and, moreover, in an official, certified, institutional way. So far there's really no efficient institutional forum for the leaders and people to dialogue. Not that people want to vote on doctrine and discipline; doctrine is not up for popular vote. Not at all, but they would like a respectful input about the practical ramifications of such doctrines and disciplines and how they might impact their lives. They would like to exchange and measure the realities of their life's experiences with the theories of any official teaching and decree. As ninety-seven percent of the church, it would seem eminently wise for the laity to have a voice, wouldn't you think?

Third, having authority does not preclude oversight. In fact, it invites it. The people are the church and, for example, they are entitled to some accountability from the people whose salaries they pay and to whom they entrust their money for drives, appeals, and causes. Furthermore, they would like to know and discuss practical diocesan and parish policy. They would like to have avenues in which to affirm the good clergy and to challenge the bad clergy. So far, such avenues of accountability are not in place in ways that are encouraged and accessible, and they should be. They might have prevented a lot of scandal.

So, there it is: Luke's early church history provoking some latter-day thoughts such as: assessing episcopal candidates, having a forum for dialogue, and demanding accountability. These sensible ancient principles would seem to be the very least that both clergy and laity should embrace to make a faith community open and responsible.

Anyway, all this should make for interesting conversation at your dinners this evening and, if it does, Luke and I will have done our jobs.

Photo Ops

Sixth Sunday of Easter, C, John 14:23-29
Mother's Day

"...we will come and make our dwelling with you...do not let your hearts be troubled or afraid...my peace I give you."

Just as in your homes I have photographs peppered around my house. Mostly, I don't even notice them. They're just part of the background, the furniture. But every once in a while, for some reason, even if I'm doing something else, I find my eyes straying and fixing on one or another photograph that happens to be in view. I stare, for example, at my parents' sepia wedding picture in their 1925 tux and gown and wonder, did they ever think they would have had six children or know the precious influence they had on our lives. So many words of wisdom, so much common sense, such faith, such examples of hard-working, honest people.

I spot a picture of my rotund Aunt Celesta, my mother's sister, who had the heartiest laugh in the world, and at once recall how, every Sunday, we rode from New Brunswick to South Amboy for Sunday dinner where her little house was crowded with cousins, other aunts and uncles, and Lord knows who else.

My childhood memories there are of a large table with a humongous platter of ziti in the center and how, at the beginning of the meal, a large loaf of Italian bread was passed around and each one tore off a piece and passed it to the next person. Then we each drank wine. The kids on this occasion were allowed a sip; we were not permitted wine or coffee until we were in college. We all ate of the same loaf and drank of the same cup and, you know, it wasn't until I was an adult that I realized we, as a family, were really celebrating Eucharist—sharing the bread and drinking the cup that made us one.

And I remember there was talk, lots of talk, shouting at times, and laughter, constant, uproarious laughter, and when they didn't want us kids to know what they were saying—perhaps something risqué—they spoke in Italian and let out a whoop. I remember, most of all, that I knew with the certainty of a child's instinct that every aunt and uncle was a parent and they scolded you sometimes when needed, but at all times they loved you to death.

I spot a photo of Nonna, sitting tall and straight in her chair in her long dress, not looking too happy to be photographed. I remember her vaguely, and from what I learned about her she put me very much in mind of that old song, "No Mirrors in My Nana's House." I don't know if you know the song or ever heard about it. The origin of that song is interesting. A little girl grew up in her grandmother's house in a very poor neighborhood. She said her grandmother's house had no mirrors. One of her friends asked, "Then how did you know what you looked like?"

"Well," said the little girl, "my Nana told me. You see, every morning I would get up and get dressed and comb my hair, and then I would go to Nana and I would say, 'How do I look?' And she would tell me I was beautiful. She said my skin was smooth and golden brown, kissed by the sun, and she said my eyes shone like the silver moonbeams. In my Nana's house, there were no mirrors, so I saw myself through my Nana's eyes who loved me." I gathered Nonna was like that.

There's one of my dad. It's funny the things you remember. I recall as a kid telling my dad that it was great that we were giving the stuff we didn't sell at our bakery to the poor every week. Being a good Catholic boy I said to dad, "We're passing out food so that we can tell them about Jesus." My dad simply looked at me and said matter of factly, "Son, we don't give food to the poor to tell them about Jesus. We give food to the poor because they're hungry." All right.

Another time, I recall overhearing him give advice to my married brother who was asking him what to get his wife for Mother's Day, a fitting time to recall this. Dad said this to my brother: "Whatever you do, don't buy anything that plugs in. Anything that requires electricity is seen as utilitarian. And avoid anything you think is useful. The new silver polish advertised to save hundreds of hours is not going to get you brownie points. And, for heaven's sake, don't buy anything that involves weight loss or self-improvement. That won't go over big. And, whatever you do, son, don't buy her jewelry. The jewelry your wife wants you can't afford. And the jewelry you can afford she doesn't want."

Then there's mom in her round frame. She probably would resonate with the list someone just emailed me:

You know, you're a mom when…

Your feet stick to the kitchen floor and you don't care.

You can't find your cell phone so you ask a friend to call you and then you run around the house to locate the phone in the downstairs laundry basket.

You have the local pizza dealer's phone number memorized.

You're willing to kiss your child's boo-boo regardless of where it is.

Spit is your number one cleansing agent.

Photo ops. I usually take all these photos for granted but, as I said, every once in a while, one photo catches my eye and I find myself pondering it—smiling or misty-eyed or even outright laughing. Sometimes one photo provokes another and I take a fresh look at all of them and, when I'm through, I am awed by the cumulative effect they have had on me. I find myself filled with the love that I have received and, most of all, I have a deep sense that I am not alone.

Does this trip down memory lane have anything to do with today's gospel? Yes it does, for it is times like these—photo gazing, Mother's Day—that this gospel comes alive. The gospel we heard at the beginning is a kind of verbal photo: Jesus is speaking to his soon-to-be-bereaved friends, telling them not to be afraid, for the Father will make his dwelling in them and that his Spirit will, like old photographs, remind us of God's love, God's presence, and God's gift of peace; and, mostly, that we should remember to see ourselves through God's eyes because, in God's house, there are no mirrors.

Promised Presence

ASCENSION, C, LUKE 24:46-53

A hodgepodge of thoughts runs through my mind when I think of the Ascension, and this hodgepodge, I confess, makes for a dull homily: a little teaching, a little statistical information that you should know, a little challenge. That's it. But you've heard dull homilies before, so hunker down and put up with it. It will be short.

I start off by observing, considering how Jesus was treated the last week of his life, that he was probably happy to move on. Now he could take it easy, so to speak, and sit quietly at the right hand of the Father until Judgment Day. I think also of the nervous disciples asking if he's going to restore the kingdom soon, because this mismatched, less-than-perfect bunch are not sure they can hack it alone and, without Jesus, they might as well go home.

But then I reflect that the Ascension does not close the chapter on Jesus or his followers. Far from it.

Jesus' promise is that he not only actively continues to intercede for us, but also, through the gift of his Pentecostal Spirit, he lives in and among us, his disciples, in every age. After all, why else would he reply to Paul, stricken on the road to Damascus and asking the vision who are you, "I am Jesus whom you are persecuting"?

Jesus? He was dead and gone as far as Paul was concerned. But Paul soon learned that, in fact, in persecuting Jesus' followers, he was persecuting Jesus himself. There was a connection, a bond, an intimacy, an enduring presence. That's why Paul would later write to his converts and remind them that they are of the Body of Christ, such was the close unbreakable identity between Jesus and his followers.

This powerful presence of Jesus and his abiding Spirit reveal the fundamental reason why the church has endured throughout the centuries. It has survived, sometimes barely, the external onslaughts of emperors, kings, heretics, wars, famines, and diseases. It has survived its own internal corruptions, prejudices, sins, scandals, and misjudgments.

And today, as we well know, the church continues on its bumpy road. As you are well aware, it has shrunk to a pinpoint in secular Europe and is dwindling in South America where Pope Benedict XVI is trying to shore it up from the vast inroads of Pentecostalism. The church has lost considerable ground here in secular America where books on atheism flourish and where only twenty-six percent of us Catholics go to church regularly, Catholic marriages have fallen to half their usual numbers, baptisms are declining, and the youth, who are notoriously religiously illiterate, are drifting away.

But then, when I say that, some perspective is in order, namely, that you should know that we sixty-five million plus Catholics in the United States represent only six percent of the global Catholic population—did you know that?—we who always think that the whole world revolves around us and our needs. Which somewhat explains, by the way, why during the clergy sex abuse scandals, Rome was slow to act; it had the other ninety-four percent of the Catholic world to think about. Another statistic: Although we are only six percent of the Catholic world, we have twelve percent of the bishops in the Catholic Church. We do have a priest shortage here, but not a bishop shortage.

But the real truth you should absorb lies in this reality check: while Catholicism is losing ground in the northern hemisphere, it is flowering in the southern hemisphere of our globe. *There* is the future of the church in this millennium. There the church is thriving and growing in a wonderful way.

For example, listen to this: Africa went from a Catholic population of 1.9 million in 1900 to 130 million in 2000, a growth rate of over six thousand percent. Think about that. This is the most rapid expansion of Catholicism in a single continent in two thousand years of church history. How about this: Did you know that thirty-seven percent of all baptisms in Africa today are of adults? Contrast this to the average worldwide adult baptisms which are 13.2 percent. Yes, there, in the southern hemisphere, lies the future of the church which, in fact, until the Muslim onslaught in the sixth century, at one time had a glorious Catholic past and flourished as the home of St. Cyprian, St. Augustine, the desert fathers, and the monastic movement.

But what about us, where affluence and secularism have muted the presence of God in our part of the world? All is not yet entirely lost. History has shown us that, even in our worst moments, Jesus' ever-present Spirit can break through and raise up saints who turn things around and call us back to the gospel. That gives us hope.

A Francis of Assisi pops up out of the moral mess of the twelfth century. Maximilian Kolbe steps forward from the Nazi madness to die as a martyr. Thomas Merton emerges from the nihilism of Greenwich Village. Weary Rosa Parks says no to racial prejudice and refuses to move to the back of the bus. Nelson Mandela rejects apartheid and goes to prison for twenty-seven years.

Ascension and Pentecost tell us that God is still present, still speaks, still sends out disciples to make a difference, still calls, not just the Mertons and Kolbes and Parkses, but you and me. Jesus is here and still seeks witnesses. What he said in the gospel to his disciples on Ascension Day still remains valid and indispensable: "You are witnesses of these things." We should remember that.

If we do, it wouldn't be the first time in our long history that we arose from the ashes.

The Holy Spirit and Papa God

PENTECOST, A, B, C, JOHN 14:15–16, 23–26

Priests have always been targets. Not just in persecution times because they were leaders—think of the countless Polish priests who died at Auschwitz under the Nazi terror—but in benign times. Because the Roman collar and black suit mark out the priest, kids stare at him and slightly tipsy women at wedding receptions, glass in hand, weave their way over to him to ask him to hear their confessions. The men remark with knowing looks that, now that Father's here, they'll have to watch their language and off-color jokes, and the hosts see that he is seated with "safe" people.

Priests don't mind. It's a minor misery. They expect that. It goes with the territory. But they brace themselves for the inevitable angry bore—not infrequently an ex-Catholic—who spots the collar from across the room and makes a beeline for his target. "Why in the hell are you wasting your time in that stupid church? I finally wised up and got out."

Then, obviously having read Dan Brown, Richard Dawkins, and Christopher Hitchens, he goes on to spout the familiar litany of all that is wrong with religion in general and the Catholic Church in particular: the Inquisition, the Crusades, the bad popes, sinister bishops, Vatican conspiracies, the clerical sex scandal, the degradation of women, dull Masses, lousy sermons, money-grubbing clerics, and so on. I think the church was even blamed for Donald Trump's hairdo.

Of course, I am familiar with that litany of accusations. The church has had and does have many problems and too often is like a dysfunctional family. So why stay, why put up with such misery? Why? Because of Jesus'

145

words in today's gospel, "I will give you another Advocate to be with you always." *Always*, notice.

This always-abiding Presence, this Holy Spirit of Pentecost, makes the difference. *That's* why we put up with it. Jesus promised to be with us no matter what we may be like on any given day, when we're good and when we're bad; when we're heroic and when we're cowardly; when we're faithful and when we're not.

Now you can choose to believe or not believe in this presence of the Holy Spirit. If you choose not to believe you can checklist the church's problems and walk away in disgust: The church is nothing but a pack of barking dogs baying at a silly monkey atop a tree. But if you choose to believe, then you must look not only for signs of church failures, but for signs of the life-giving Spirit.

Then you will begin to notice, with great regularity, in the worst of times and in the depths of misery, how God has a tendency, out of nowhere, to raise up holy ones who advertise the presence of the Holy Spirit: a Catherine of Genoa in the kitchen, a Charles de Foucauld in the desert, a Damien in the leper colony, a Mother Teresa in the slums, a Thomas Merton in the Village, a reformed alcoholic priest in the debris of 9/11.

Pentecost, friends, celebrates that. It celebrates the abiding presence of Jesus, the persistence and surprises of the Spirit that give us reasons to remain Catholic.

This truth calls for reinforcement so I have a parable for you. It's a folktale from Haiti. As you listen, I ask you to think Pentecost.

Once upon a time, in the middle of a great forest, there lived an old woman who kept hives of bees. By the end of the summer she had more honey than she could use. Every jar, bowl, and barrel were filled to overflowing with the sweet golden honey. The old woman kept some for herself. The rest she poured into a great pot, lifted the pot on top of her head, and set off to market. Off she went through the great forest for days with the pot balanced on her head.

But just as she neared the marketplace she accidentally caught her foot on a tree root and went flying. There was a great crash. The pot had fallen and smashed to the ground, oozing the sweet sticky honey all over the forest floor. The woman just sat there and began to cry.

"Oh, misery!" she moaned. "Papa God, you sent me too much misery!" After a long while, she finally got up, trudged home with a heavy heart crying all the while, "Misery! Oh, misery! Papa God, you sent me too much misery!"

Now it so happened that a little monkey, sitting high among the branches, saw the whole thing. As soon as the woman was out of sight, he swung down to the ground. He looked and looked at the strange sticky stuff. He had never seen anything like it before. Cautiously he dipped one of his fingers into it and touched his lips. "Oh, my," he exclaimed to himself, "this misery is good! I've never tried misery before." He scooped up a whole handful and swallowed it. He ate and ate until he got down to licking the pot until there simply wasn't any more. Oh, but there had to be more. "I want more!" he cried.

And then he remembered overhearing the old woman saying. "Papa God, why'd you send me so much misery?" He scratched his head. So that's where misery came from!

"Maybe," he thought to himself, "maybe if I paid Papa God a visit he'd give me some more misery." And the more he thought about it the better the idea seemed.

So off he went. Back to the trees and then to the mountains and he climbed and climbed until at last he came to Papa God's house. And there was Papa God himself, sitting in the garden just watching the world.

"Beg your pardon, Papa God," he shouted.

Papa God turned and saw him and smiled. "Ah, little monkey, what do you want?"

"Begging your pardon, Papa God," said the little monkey, "more than anything else, I want misery."

Papa God looked puzzled. "You want misery, little one?"

"Oh yes, sweet sticky misery. I want as much as you can give me, Papa God."

Papa God got up, thought a minute, and said, "Well, it just so happens that I have got some special misery made just for monkeys. Are you sure you want it?" The monkey nodded his head. So Papa God went inside his house and, after a spell, returned carrying a leather bag. He said to the monkey, "Little monkey, this bag is full of misery. Now you must pay attention and do exactly what I tell you. First of all, you must carry this bag to the middle of a great sandy desert where there are no trees and where, in fact, they can't grow. Then, once you're there, you will slowly open the bag and inside you'll find more misery than you ever dreamed of."

The monkey was delighted and wasted no time. He took the leather bag and climbed back down to the world and he ran and ran until he came to the edge of a great desert and then he ran and ran some more until he came to its very center. Exhausted, he sat down. His hands were trembling in anticipation of all that misery. So he opened the drawstrings of the bag just as Papa God had told him and out came real monkey misery...*dogs*! One, two, three, up to seven huge, hungry black dogs!

The monkey screamed, dropped the bag and ran literally for his life. The seven black dogs were snapping at his tail. They were getting closer and closer. And just when he thought he could go no farther and the dogs were sure to get him...a tree appeared!

Out of nowhere a huge, great tree appeared, right there in the middle of the desert where trees, of course, do not grow at all. The monkey scampered up the tree as fast as he could, leaving the seven snarling dogs leaping up and down the trunk.

And for the rest of the day he sat in the tree branches, quaking with fear until the sun went down, and the dogs, frustrated, eventually slunk away. As soon as they were gone and the monkey thought it was safe, he climbed down and ran for the forest as fast as he could and never looked back.

Now, the question—the Pentecostal question—is this: Where did that tree come from? Who put that great tree where trees don't grow, right there in the middle of a hot, dry desert?

I'll tell you. Papa God put it there. Why? Because Papa God knows that too much misery is not a good thing, even for a monkey.

Message: We rejoice in the mercies and put up with the miseries of our church because we believe with all our hearts that, true to Jesus' promise, the always-present Spirit continues to grow trees where they don't grow.

The Doors of Pentecost

A, B, C, JOHN 20:19–23

Archbishop Thomas Kelly of Louisville, Kentucky, tells a story about the day he was appointed bishop. He made it a point, on the morning the news was made public, to have breakfast with his mother so that he could be with her when she heard the story on the radio.

So there they were having breakfast when her son's appointment was announced during the morning news. Mrs. Kelly was thrilled. She leaned across the table and asked,

"What is it like for you to be made bishop?"

Kelly explained to his mother how he felt, and as he spoke, his mother sat with her chin on her hand, seemingly in reverie.

When he had finished, there was a pregnant pause. Mrs. Kelly sighed and said, "You know, Tommy, if I had known that one day you would become a bishop and have your picture in the newspapers and on television, I would have had your teeth straightened."

Well, it wasn't quite what he expected. A bit of a surprise I would say.

For a real surprise, let's return to the gospel we just heard. It's a story of shut and open doors. The disciples of Jesus were hiding in fear behind closed and locked doors, shutting out the rest of the hostile world, a world for them full of suspicion and accusation. They felt better, safer, huddled together in isolation.

And then, a surprise! Into their isolation Jesus bursts. Through closed doors he walks. Past locks he breaks in. Oblivious of barriers he comes. Surprised and fearful, the disciples are stunned. *They* thought it was all over between Jesus and themselves. After all, their conduct these past few days had been anything but sterling: denials, betrayals, flight, leaving Jesus to go it alone, die alone. The only thing they had left was their embarrassment and guilty consciences. Truly, this bunch of failures deserved to be behind locked doors. Who wanted them? Who would speak to them? Let it cool off and they would slink away and go into hiding somewhere and be forgotten.

And yet. And yet there he was. He sought them out in their weakness, ignored the doors they thought would keep him out. Yes, he was there, and there to speak of forgiveness and, above all, to give them the gift of the Spirit: the Spirit of the Second Chance, the Spirit of a love greater than their shame, a Spirit that would break down doors and send them out, now as a community of wounded, forgiven healers, to preach the Good News of God's love. Oh, what a beginning, what a Pentecost that was!

Yet, I confess, I never realized fully what that all meant, how profound a story it was, until a priest friend told me the story of Tom. And on Pentecost, I want to share it with you. Here's my friend's story:

Tom was a forty-one-year-old man, dying of AIDS. His family was in total denial. His parents literally had him locked in an upstairs bedroom, although they did care for his basic necessities, like food and water. The first time I visited Tom at his parents' home, I was brought up to his bedroom. This huge, rather handsome man was now terribly thin and looked lost in his king-sized bed. I bent over to kiss him on the forehead and then sat beside his bed. I took his hand and said, "Now tell me what you want me to know." He said with tears in his eyes, "No one touches me any more." I continued holding his hand and let him unravel his story.

Eventually, Tom became so ill that it was necessary to hospitalize him. Each day I would drive over to visit him in the hospital. I would try to engage his mother and father in conversation. Nothing seemed to work. Knowing it was therapeutic for all of them to be able to talk about Tom's condition, I tried many different techniques. I was successful with his brother and sister-in-law, but the parents had built high walls around the subject.

Meanwhile, Tom's condition worsened daily. After about five weeks, the family seemed to look forward to my arrival at the hospital each day. There were times I spent alone with Tom. He wanted and needed to tell me other pieces of his story. He was a wonderful man who had made one decision that left its mark on him. Apparently he felt safe with me. I did not judge him. We even found things to laugh at, at times.

But what came across was that Tom feared that that he had been a failure. Though everyone who knew him described Tom as generous, kind, thoughtful, and attentive to others, Tom focused on the "mistake" he had made. He shared how embarrassed he was. What would others think of him? Tom never gave many details. I never really found out how Tom developed AIDS. Tom also worried about his friends from whom he had pulled away. So many unanswered telephone calls and notes! He admitted that he had gone behind closed doors, as it were, to protect himself. He went through waves of despair. He shared the loneliness that all of this created for him.

One day, Tom asked me to contact his friend Anna and ask if she would like to visit him. Tom and Anna had been very good friends but had not seen each other in over two years. Too ashamed, he never told her about his condition. When I contacted Anna, she felt betrayed. "Why didn't he tell me what was going on?" she cried. I wasn't sure if Anna would even go to visit Tom.

The next morning, however, Anna called me and asked what time visiting hours were at the hospital. I agreed to take her over when I went for my visit. When we walked into the room, at first both old friends seemed very frightened of each other. But when they embraced, the conversation immediately came more easily.

"What did I ever do that you cut me off?" Anna asked.

"You didn't do a thing," Tom replied. "I was so ashamed to tell you about myself."

Anna said, "It doesn't matter to me. I've missed you and have worried about you so."

All Tom could say was, "Anna, I'm glad you came. I'm so sorry. Please forgive me." Tears flowed. Two friends were reunited.

One of Tom's last conversations was with his brother. Tom told him, "I *do* have AIDS. But I know I am a good person, and I hope you love me."

Tom's brother went over to his brother's bedside and embraced him. "Yes," he said, "I love you. I love you so much. I don't care what you have. I love you."

Tom's father was a holdout. He still remained distant, but it seemed to me that even he and Tom had somewhat repaired their rift by the time of

Tom's death. I recall the night of Tom's wake when his father embraced me and said, "You know, I wanted a perfect son. For a while I thought he was a failure. But these weeks in the hospital I started to learn who my son was again. I loved him so much. He was a good boy. I am proud of my son." Tom had died knowing that his father accepted and loved him and that even when we make mistakes we can be perfect.

When I heard this story, friends, I could not get it out of my head how much it was like the Upper Room that first Pentecost. Failure and shame and all kinds of doors. But, one by one, those doors opened as the Spirit exhaled its love, like the wolf in the fairy tale that huffed and puffed his way in. Once more, in the person of my friend and eventually Anna and his brother and his father, doors were gone through and with them Jesus walked in and breathed on Tom and said, "Tom, receive the Holy Spirit. Your sins are forgiven."

It's a Pentecost story. One by one my priest-friend, the brother, the sister, Anna, the father went through the closed doors. They had been sent by the Spirit. Pentecost is precisely that. It is about the birth of a sent community—you and me—whom the breath of God has touched, a community called church, a gathering of people inducted through baptism, sent to open shut doors and let out sin and despair and let in the Good News.

It's a formidable job we have been given, but we are not alone. As church, we have the Spirit, for as the Mexican poet Amado Nervo puts it: "Alone we are only an anthill / but in the Spirit we are a mountain." And he goes on to move us from drop to fountain, from feather to wing, from beggar to king. All because we have the Spirit.

Yes, and more. In the words of St. Peter, we are a royal priesthood, a holy nation, a people set apart. We are church.

Moorings

There is an extraordinary movie you will likely never see. There are several reasons for this. First, it has, at least so far, a very limited distribution. You won't find it in many theaters. Second, there is very little talking in the movie. Third, it has no background music. Fourth, it has no plot as we understand it. And, finally, to cap it all off, it is three hours long!

No wonder you'll never see it or want to see it. What possessed the director to make it?

Yet, the movie called *Into Great Silence* has packed people into New York's Film Forum and was held over for weeks. The film has been a huge hit not only in New York, but also, surprisingly, in secular Europe. It is, believe it or not, a film about life in a monastery of Carthusian monks, contemplative monks. The opening scenes of fire and snow and eventually the passage of time in slow seasonal changes set the mood. Then there are the measured rhythms of the monks' communal liturgical hours, the solitude of the monks in their hermitages, their prayer and study. It's a quiet, riveting, compelling film, a slow-motion call to awareness of what really counts.

It's clearly a movie that's in sharp contrast to so many of the graphically cruel, torturous, and nihilistic movies we are offered, like *Kill Bill 1* and *2*, or *Hostel*, or the movies full of unending violence, action, exploitation, greed, and betrayals.

Into Great Silence reminds us, as columnist John Garvey writes, that "we are called into being from nothingness, and the monks face this as a vocation. They have tried in the life they have chosen to eliminate the distractions that keep us from being what we are called to be. Not all of us are called to this way," he continues, "but they are engaged in a central truth

153

about life…a moment-to-moment acknowledgment of our absolute contingency, our dependence on the will of God."

Maybe that's the surprising appeal of the movie to overactive worldlings and sophisticates who have a deep, holy longing inside of them but are unable to name it. The yearning they seek to assuage in sex and drugs and "extreme realities" is the yearning for God and they don't know it.

And for all of us too, in a world where people kill each other, where students are slaughtered at the hands of a madman, where people in high office betray us, where greed covers everything like a sticky paste, where infidelity is celebrated and celebrity is an idol, it is a source of some hope to know that, in such a world where these horrors exist, there's a place where people still make the sign of the cross and sit in silence before the triune God.

The great truth that the monks teach us is that we need a center; we need to get in touch with that God who anchors our lives and gives them meaning. Lacking this holy anchor—and we see it frequently enough—so many anchorless children, full of anger at being abandoned, are unknowingly clutching their cell phones, iPods, and blaring CDs to drown out their spiritual loneliness and emptiness.

Maybe, too, that is why half of full-time college students, according to the recent report of the National Center of Addiction and Substance Abuse, binge drink and abuse prescription and illegal drugs. Shockingly, the report says, each year more than 1700 students die from alcohol poisoning and alcohol-related injuries. Each year 700,000 of them are assaulted by classmates who were drinking and each year almost 100,000 students become victims of alcohol-related sexual assaults and rapes.

The students gave the reasons they take alcohol and drugs. They say they take them to relieve stress, relax, have fun, forget their problems, be one of the gang. Interestingly, college women's focus groups said they drink because they wanted to keep up with the guys (even though one drink for females has the impact of two drinks for males). They also said that they were under enormous pressure to have sex, so they used alcohol as a disinhibitor.

Besides the complicit toleration of college presidents and deans who look the other way, it seems that the students have not had much contact with the Great Silence to discover there, rather than in alcohol and drugs, an identity, a vision, a sign that might anchor them.

A storyteller named Dan Yashinsky, backs up my point. He relates that he was telling stories at a downtown arts center when a restless group of kids stomped in. They were ten-year-olds from a Catholic school in a new housing development. In they came, munching potato chips and blowing bubble gum, clearly not in a listening mood. Since it was close to Halloween, Yashinsky wisely lit a candle, turned off the lights, and started telling ghost stories and it wasn't long before they were hooked.

He wound up telling them one of those summer camp scary stories where, you know, the narrator's voice gets quieter and quieter until the moment when the ghost grabs the poor victim, and then he raises his voice loudly and says something like "I gotcha!" and the kids scream and jump into one another's laps. Which is exactly what happened.

Well, when the lights came on the children lined up to leave, talking excitedly about their shocking experience, Yashinshy noticed one girl standing quietly, holding something around her neck. He asked her if she liked the stories and she said, "Oh, yes, but when you told the last one I didn't jump."

"I noticed," he said, "How come?"

"Because when I knew it was going to be scary, I held the Blessed Virgin Mary." She showed him the medal she was still holding. "You should get one, too."

"I'm not sure I should," he answered. "I'm Jewish."

"That's okay, " she said sagely, "get a Jewish one."

Then he makes this appropriate comment: "Writing this book about storytelling as an art and way of life, I have often remembered the girl's good counsel. When you know something scary is coming, you must find and hold onto your own source of reassurance and wisdom. You must have a steady beacon to guide you through perilous waters."

The monks remind us of who that Beacon is, without which our souls shrivel and life becomes unmoored.

This truth was again brought home when one day a renowned theologian went to visit the monks. He did not want to see the abbot—a mere manager, he said—but the master of novices. He asks him, "What is the novices' biggest complaint?"

The master says, "They complain they have to be up at 2:30 AM to attend the divine office and sing matins and lauds. They aren't too happy about it. They tell me that it's so much better when they're out in the fields and they feel ecstasy and love for God and alleluia and so on. So I said to them, 'All right, I forbid you to come to any services, then, except for Mass.' Well, after a short while they came back and said, 'We didn't come here to be farmhands.'"

"What happened to your ecstasies?" the master asks.

"They dried up," said the novices.

So the master wisely told them, "Of course, now you realize that what you are doing at 2:30 AM is what gives you the ecstasy in the fields."

Going into the Great Silence, connecting to the Beacon, the Anchor, the Center gives you the ecstasy in the fields of your life. You won't need alcohol and drugs.

ORDINARY TIME

The Call

The first reading is the winsome story of a call that took place some 1100 years before Christ called his first disciples. Young Samuel was sleeping at a local shrine, long before the Temple in Jerusalem was built, when he heard a voice. He was living at the local shrine because his mother, Hannah, childless at the time, had been praying for a son and promised that if God gave her one, she would have her first-born reared near God. She went on to have five children.

So little Samuel was sleeping in the Holy Place where the ark was kept when he heard the voice that called him. Eventually he recognized whose voice it was and quickly gave the response old Eli told him to give, "Speak, Lord, for your servant is listening," a bit different from some modern prayers which say, "Listen, Lord, for your servant is speaking." Samuel accepted his call and went on to anoint Israel's first king, Saul, and its next and greatest king, David, from whose line Jesus would be born.

And when Jesus was born and grew up, he in turn called others and that's today's gospel reading. He called his first disciples: John and Andrew who were at the time hanging around with John the Baptist. They left John and followed Jesus who at one point turned around and asked them what they were looking for. What did they want, really want? They said they wanted to know where he stayed. This was no passing fad. They wanted to spend some time with him and learn what he was all about. And learn they did, and were so captivated that John remembered all the details even to the time of day when he first met Jesus.

And Andrew? He proves to be one of the most attractive characters in the New Testament. For one thing, he was always content to play second fiddle to his brother, Peter. For another, he simply couldn't keep the good news to himself and seemed delighted to introduce people to Jesus. The New Testament mentions him three times and each time that is what he does. He brings the boy with the five loaves and two fish to Jesus. He brings inquiring Greeks to see Jesus and, in today's gospel, he runs and gets his brother, Simon, to meet Jesus. When Simon arrives, Jesus changes his name to Peter, a sign that when God looks at people, he sees not only what they are but also what they can become.

I'd like to share some true stories about people who were called in various ways, people who were called and became. Oh, not dramatically like Samuel or directly like Peter, Andrew, and John, but more subtly and persuasively by example and circumstance, like most of us are called.

About ninety years ago a man picked up the morning paper and, to his horror, read his own obituary! The newspaper had reported the death of the wrong man. Like most of us, he relished the idea of finding out what people would say about him after he died. He read past the bold caption, which read "Dynamite king dies," to the text itself. He read along until he was taken aback by the description of him as a "merchant of death."

He was the inventor of dynamite and had amassed a great fortune from the manufacture of weapons of destruction. But he was moved by this description. Did he really want to be known as a "merchant of death"? It was at that moment that a healing power greater than the destructive force of dynamite came over him. It was his hour of conversion, his call. From that point on, he devoted his energy and money to works of peace and human betterment. Today, of course, he is best remembered not as a "merchant of death," but as the founder of the Nobel Peace Prize, Alfred Nobel.

Let me tell you about a lady who way back knew Josephine. Josephine was only a little girl when her family moved to California. She was in the third grade and every day the bus would pick her up, like it did all the other kids, and drop her off. In her case, when the bus came back from school in the afternoon, her brother was waiting for her by the fence that surrounded the house. He was a year or so older than Josephine but he didn't go to school.

Some of the other students on the bus used to look for him and when they saw him they would laugh. They laughed at him because somehow they recognized that he was different. He looked and acted differently from the other kids. The kids on the bus didn't know why, they didn't understand, so they laughed. They would wave to him and sometimes they would call out to him and he in turn would wave back to them, only making them laugh more. But when Josephine got off the bus her brother would jump up and run to meet her. And to the other students' surprise, Josephine didn't seem at all embarrassed, though she knew that behind her the kids on the bus were having a great time. She would greet her brother and hug him, and often she would just drop her books on the ground and throw both arms around her brother. And then, hand in hand, the two of them would march into the house.

Josephine was only a little girl, of course, but she had learned a very human lesson of love. And it took time—the rest of the school year, as a matter of fact—for the others to learn, but toward the end the other students gradually seemed to understand a bit more and their mocking behavior began to subside. Obviously some of the students' parents had heard about this and had spoken to their children. And then some of the other more perceptive children felt that somehow it was not right to be mocking this kid, and their example affected some of the others. Therefore they began to show a little kindness and compassion.

When anyone would ask Josephine about her brother, she would simply say that her brother was retarded and would never be like the other kids, but he was her brother and she loved him. Later on, even a couple of the girls would come over and play at the house and they got to know Jimmy and would play with him as well. The children on the bus would still wave at Jimmy, but this time it wasn't in mockery; it was with a little more gentle kindness and he would wave back.

And Josephine rode that bus for many years until finally her family moved away. But the image of Josephine embracing her brother and the evolving reaction of the kids on the bus remained in the memories of those students for a long time. Else you would not have heard this story which a now sixty-five-year-old woman told me. She was one of those students on the bus and found herself subsequently called to a very compassionate life.

Finally, let me tell you about a bishop of the last century and how he got his call, his vocation. He was a noted evangelizer, making it his special outreach to cynics, unbelievers, and scoffers. He liked to tell the story of a young man who used to stand outside the cathedral shouting derogatory remarks at the people entering to worship. He would call them fools and all kind of names. The people tried to ignore him but it was difficult. So finally the parish priest went outside to confront the young man, who simply ranted and raved against everything the priest told him. Finally the priest addressed the young scoffer. "Look, let's get this over with once and for all. I'm going to make a deal with you. I'm going to put you on a dare and I bet you can't do it."

The young man shot back, "I can do anything you propose, you black-robed wimp!"

"Fine," said the priest. "All I ask you to do is to come into the sanctuary with me and I want you to stare at the figure of Christ and I want you to scream at the very top of your lungs, as loud as you can, 'Christ died on the cross for me and I don't care one bit.'"

So the young man screamed as loud as he could, looking at the figure, "Christ died on the cross for me and I don't care one bit."

The priest said, "Very good. Now do it again."

And again the young man screamed, with a little more hesitancy, "Christ died on the cross for me and I don't care one bit."

"You're almost done now," said the priest. "One more time."

The young man raised his fist, kept looking at the statue, but the words wouldn't come. He just could not look at the face of Christ and say that anymore.

The real punch line came when, after he told the story, the bishop said, "*I* was that young man. That young man, that defiant young man was me. I thought I didn't need God, but found out that I did."

People are called in various ways. The burden on us, dear friends, is two-fold. First, we must consistently and personally answer the call to a moral, decent, and holy life. Second, our Christlike lives, by their very nature, ought to be a call to others.

Beyond the Pew

THIRD SUNDAY IN ORDINARY TIME, C,
1 CORINTHIANS 12:12–30

In today's epistle, written in the middle of the first century, St. Paul famously tells the people at Corinth that they are the Body of Christ.

Now hold that declaration in mind while I skip to the twenty-first century, to today. I'm quoting from a section in *Newsweek* magazine that is self-consciously listing the most influential people of the new year. Among them is a woman named Ingrid Mattson. She is a white Canadian Catholic woman who grew up attending daily Mass. Or, at least she used to be. She is still white and Canadian but she is not Catholic any longer. She is a convert to Islam and a professor at Hartford Seminary in Connecticut.

Her story is that at a certain point she no longer believed in the God they talked about in the Catholic Church. So she abandoned religion altogether until she met some kindly Muslims who led her to the mosque where she felt close to God. Then she says something as if grasping it for the first time. She says that she discovered that God was no longer in the church, but he was everywhere: in nature, in art, and in the welcoming faces other Muslims. She converted at twenty-three.

Where has she been? It was a remarkable thing for a former Catholic to say and one wonders what she learned from them, because, for all of its faults, the one thing the Catholic Church is famous for is its sacramentality. That is to say, its Catholic imagination. The Catholic Church has always been an extremely sensuous church, unlike other forms of Christianity which rejected art, wine, oil, candles, statues, stained-glass windows, incense, and the world. The Catholic Church has always held that the world is bursting with hidden signs of a gracious God.

Francis of Assisi was its spokesman when he sang of Brother Sun and Sister Moon. Joseph Mary Plunkett was its poet when he wrote:

> I see his blood upon the rose
> And in the stars the glory of his eyes.
> His body gleams amid eternal snows
> His tears fall from the sky.
> I see his face in every flower…

Or Jesuit poet, Gerard Manley Hopkins, who wrote:

> The world is charged with the grandeur of God.
> It will flame out, like shining from shook foil.

In other words, the church has always held that God is *not* confined to church buildings or churchy institutions. It is not the church's view that we live in a world devoid of divinity and come to church to find refuge from the world. On the contrary, in the church's eyes, our life, our holiness, our sanctity, our witness are to be found outside these walls, in the arena of our lives. Our sense of God's presence is to be found in our prayer, relationships, work well done, virtue in hostile places, and in the beauties of nature and art.

If this is so, why, then, do we go to church? The answer is that here in church, as an assembly, we get refocused, empowered, renewed, nourished, and fed in order to be the Body of Christ when we leave here. Here we are vitally reminded that we are more than the sum of our individual selves. Here we are reminded who we are, what we are: a People of God. With this knowledge reaffirmed, we are thus strengthened to return to our place of God-discovery and God-witness. With our sense of God's special presence here, we are ready to see his face in every flower there.

But there's one more thing, as Columbo would say, why we go to church. We go to church to be released from our self-delusions that we are the center of the universe, always a temptation. We are here to be challenged by the simple presence of others who are different from us and whom we are forced to rub shoulders with, whether we like them or not. Going to church, you see, is going to a place not of our choosing, to be with people not necessarily of our choosing, and breaking bread with people not of our choosing. In short, going to church keeps us humble, makes us realize we belong to more than those in our gated communities and that we are a part of a worldwide family past, present, and future. Being here reminds us that we are united with those in every corner of the world, from basilicas to barrios, from palaces to prisons, who, at this very moment, are celebrating Eucharist, and we are they and they are us. We are here as the Body of Christ. We are here to reaffirm this truth: No one travels to God alone.

This belief, you must realize, effectively undermines the popular slogan so commonly embraced today, "I am spiritual but not religious. I have no need of organized religion. I'm a player and move on a different plane." What a deception! It is a common conceit tailor-made for the "Me Generation" where the self is the sole measurement of existence. It sounds so "free." In this spiritual world there is no one to challenge you. "If it feels good, do it." In this spiritual world you don't have to sit with those "others." You can hang around with your own like-minded group.

In this spiritual world you are not beholden to anyone but yourself. In this spiritual world no one is going to point an accusing finger, because who can judge the self? In this spiritual world everyone's opinion or truth is as good as another's, so all is flattened out. Judgments and social actions are both unnecessary and arrogant. In this spiritual world no one is ever wrong—they're just in a different place—and, of course, consequently, no one is ever right either. In this spiritual world truth is what I believe it to be, morals are what I determine. In this spiritual world it's Me and God and I don't have to deal with that smelly person off the street who came in and knelt behind me and struck his breast and cried, "O God, be merciful to me, a sinner."

Religion for these "spiritual" players is too much work. After all, religion is pot-luck suppers and disciplines and dogmas and pews full of those other people. Spirituality travels lighter. It dabbles in the esoteric, in secrets hidden from those "others."

In this "I-am-spiritual-but-not-religious" world it's not St. Paul's insight that we are the Body of Christ. It's the self-serving slogan, "I am an army of one." But the church says no. There is no army of one. That's delusional and dangerous. Rather the church offers memories, traditions, links to ancient wisdom, and pits our lives against those of our contemporaries and predecessors in the faith. It demands communal living, understanding, and worship and gives challenge to our lives. As T.S. Eliot wrote:

> Why should men love the church?
> Why should they love her laws?
> She tells them of life and death
> and all they would forget.
> She is tender where they would be hard
> and hard where they would like to be soft.
> She tells them of evil and sin
> and other unpleasant facts.

Solo "spiritual" persons conveniently don't have to listen to that stuff.

We are the Body of Christ. We are here communally to celebrate Eucharist and gospel, to take courage from each other's presence and, thus braced, to be sent out—"Go, the Mass is ended"—with new eyes: to see the grandeur of God, to bring God to home, neighborhood, school, and workplace so that others too might see what we see; so that people looking at us might see what that former Catholic saw in those Muslims: that God is not confined to church. God is here in nature, in art, and in the welcoming faces of other Catholics.

Dreadful Love

Fourth Sunday in Ordinary Time, C,
1 Corinthians 12:31—13:13

There it is as you heard, that second reading, St. Paul's famous passage on love. I can't tell you how many times it's used at weddings or how many times Paul's word "love" has been distorted from his original intent.

The word "love," as you know, has been co-opted by Madison Avenue to sell us products that, they promise, will deliver love. Love, according to them, is to be found in cologne, chocolates, and roses. In media land, love is equated with sex and the one with the most cosmetic surgeries, makeovers, clothes, cars, implants, and a year's supply of Viagra wins. And so there they are, young people on TV, selling themselves around the approved criteria of being lots of fun, a swinger, fond of fondue and funky rock, judging one another on looks and sex appeal and declaring they're in love.

Needless to say, such "love," defined as surface glitz and "personality," is shallow and no love at all. It is as far from real love as you can get. So let's get at St. Paul's truth about love.

The fact is, love is not in the feelings or the glands, although they are important and a marriage without sentiment and sex is a poor one. But the point is, they are not primary. They do not ultimately define love. Love, to sound pedestrian, is in the will, in the decisions we make, and the harder the decision in spite of the feelings, the greater the love. Love can operate, often does operate, when feelings are fearful, timid, or sad. That's why the Russian writer Dostoevsky still has the best line on love. "Love in action is a harsh and dreadful thing..." he wrote.

The alcoholic lawyer, Sydney Carton, in Dickens's *Tale of Two Cities*, who heroically takes the place of another at the guillotine, is right when he says, "It is a far, far better thing that I do than I have ever done." His decision to do so is love. St. Maximilian Kolbe, trembling in his shoes, steps forward to die in place of a prisoner in a Nazi concentration camp. That's love. In fact, according to the highest authority, "*Greater* love than this no one has than to lay down his life for his friend."

Before, during, and after his hanging, I prayed for Saddam Hussein. He was a wicked, depraved man that evoked nothing but feelings of revulsion. So why did I pray for him? Because Jesus said to. "Love your enemies. Pray for those who persecute you." Jesus didn't ask how I felt. He simply told me to love, a dreadful task.

When William Stafford, the American poet and pacifist of the last century, was a boy he came home from school and told his mother that two new students had been surrounded on the playground and taunted by the others because they were black.

"And what did you do, Billy?" asked his mother.

"I went and stood by them," Billy said.

Sick in the stomach at the thought that he too would be beat up, Billy decided to stand by them. He loved.

Karl Downs, a pastor in Oakland, California, died at an early age of a heart attack. Several years before that, he was asked by Juvenile Court to take responsibility for a young man who was always getting into trouble. With misgiving, he accepted that responsibility and, in a tough love way, became a substitute father for that boy. No one remembers Karl Downs, but we all remember the name of that boy. He was Jackie Robinson, the first black man to play major league baseball, an outstanding athlete and a good man.

Martin Luther King was a seriously flawed man, yet his love for his people and his thirst for justice let him to express that love in a harsh and dreadful way: He knew he would be killed. "We have some difficult days ahead," he said, "but it doesn't matter with me now. Because I've been to the mountaintop. I just want to do God's will. I'm not fearing any man." His feelings were ones of apprehension. His decision was to love. And it cost him.

In *To Kill a Mockingbird*, you recall, the bigoted man spits in the face of Atticus Finch. It didn't make Atticus feel very good, but his love for justice and the brotherhood of man was worth the price.

At the funeral of a boy who died of an overdose, his friend turns and says to me, "I loved him, Father; he was my best friend." Well, it was not the time or place for me to say what was burning in my heart, namely, that that kind of so-called love killed his friend. He knew he was taking drugs. Why didn't he tell someone, get him help? I'm sure he felt he didn't want to rat on his friend, but that kind of weak love is no love at all. If he really loved his friend, he would have ignored his feelings and made the decision to do precisely that. "Love is a harsh and dreadful thing." Ask Jesus on the cross.

Love, as Thomas Aquinas reminds us, is in the mind, in the will, in the decisions we make. Feelings are wonderful and necessary and they embellish love and we would be enormously poorer without them, but they should not be identified with love. They should not be identified with the decision to do what is best for the beloved, which is why parents drag their kids to the dentist.

Well, all this has been a little heavy, so let me ease your pain and end with a fairy tale. Once there lived a beautiful princess. Among the many young men who fell in love with her were three handsome brothers. Often she invited them to visit her and they regaled her with songs and stories of magic. When it came time for her to marry, she knew she would choose none other but one of the handsome brothers. But which one? She loved them all. So she decided on a test. Whichever one brought her the most marvelous gift would have her hand in marriage.

The three brothers were best friends, wished each other luck, and agreed that before they presented their gifts to the princess they would meet back home to show each other the gifts they brought back from all parts of the world. One brother traveled to Asia where, after many searches, found a magic carpet. He bought it and set out for home. Another brother went to Egypt where a magician showed him a shiny mirror. You had only to think of a place you'd like to see and then look and there it was in the mirror. The lad bought it and set out for home.

The youngest brother traveled to the lands of Arabia. There he met a farmer who took him to a corner of his farm where from a small and lovely tree hung a single apple. "This," the farmer told him, "is an apple that once grew in the Garden of Eden. It will cure any illness and pain. But be careful when you use it, for its magic will work only a single time." The youngest son gave his fortune for the apple.

The three brothers met back home and revealed their prizes. One of them suggested they use the magic mirror to find the princess. And when they looked they did see the princess, but she was ill, she was dying. So quickly they mounted the magic carpet and arrived where the princess lay. The youngest brother then took the magic apple from his bag and said, "Here, this will make you better." She bit the apple and magically she was healed. The next day in the garden each brother told her how each had purchased his gift. Then they reminded her that without the mirror they would never have known the princess was dying. Without the carpet they would never have gotten to her bedside. Without the apple she would have died. She agreed. Now whom would she choose as husband?

The princess loved them all but could only marry one. She then embraced the oldest brother and thanked him for saving her life with the magic mirror. Then she hugged the second brother and thanked him for the magic carpet that had also saved her life. Then she looked into the youngest brother's eyes and said, "I have chosen you. For the magic mirror performs its magic as often as you need it, for me or for anyone, and the carpet also will help anyone fly. But the apple…the apple can be used only once. You could have saved it for yourself, for the time when you would need it. But you didn't. You gave it to me."

If you heard my message at all, you know that the youngest son gave the apple with feeling. But the love was not primarily there. It was in his decision to give it at all.

A Day in the Life of Jesus

FIFTH SUNDAY IN ORDINARY TIME, B, MARK 1:29–39

Typical of Mark's style, this gospel might well be called, "A Day in the Life of Jesus," as a TV documentary might show us "A Day in the Life of Steven Spielberg" or "A Day in the Life of Tiger Woods."

The ever-staccato Mark gives us lots of breathless movements: Jesus leaves the synagogue, Jesus enters Simon Peter's house, Jesus cures his mother-in-law, Jesus then cures many in the crowds, Jesus silences the demons, Jesus runs off to a lonely place, and then Jesus takes off on a round of preaching and teaching. We thought *we* lived busy lives!

But all, as usual in the gospels, is not as it seems, and you might miss some of Mark's hidden messages that are worth pondering, and so I invite you, like Jesus in prayer, to slow down your mind and attend to what's really here.

Let's start with Jesus' cure of Peter's mother-in-law. As the gospel says, "He approached her, grasped her hand and helped her up. Then the fever left her…and she waited on them." Some women are apt to comment, "Sure, what's new: a bunch of men come home. There's no lunch waiting for them so, instead of fixing some food for themselves, they have Jesus cure the lady of the house and, sure enough, 'the fever left her and she waited on them.' They should have gotten their own sandwiches."

The women may have a point, except that's not the conceit or language of Scripture which, as I said, always has deeper meanings. Here the episode means that once one is touched by Jesus Christ—"he grasped her hand and helped her up"—once one answers that call, then one immediately becomes a disciple and consequently has no choice but to serve others. In short, the fever leaves and service begins. God's service to her becomes her service to others. In short, Mark's message is not about chauvinism, but about discipleship.

Then there's that mysterious phrase, "He drove out many demons, not permitting them to speak because they knew him." They knew he was the promised Messiah, God's own Son, but the point is that Jesus didn't want that to get around just yet.

He didn't want to be a revealed celebrity because, although he may call followers, he does not court fans. Fans scream until the next idol comes along, but followers take up the cross. Mark is asking, what are we: genuine followers or mere fans?

Next, there is the sentence, "Rising very early before dawn, he left and went off to a deserted place where he prayed." Jesus needed time out to clarify who he was, to discover his mission, what it demanded, where it was taking him. He needed to resist the fans and the growing fame to follow something deeper.

Older parishioners here will remember the name of Carl Perkins. He was a popular rockabilly singer from the 1950s and the author of "Blue Suede Shoes," which was one of Elvis Presley's first big hits. As a guitarist, Perkins influenced many of the next generations of Rock 'n' Rollers, especially George Harrison of the Beatles. Perkins never quite attained the fame of his more notorious colleagues. He once explained it like this: "I never envied Elvis, his mansion and all that. All those boys—Elvis, Jerry Lee Lewis, Roy Orbison—they all lost their wives, their families. People say to me, 'What happened to you, Carl? All of them went to superstardom. Where'd you go?' I say, 'I went home. And that's a good place to be.'"

Mark is saying that it takes some quiet time, some prayer time, to find our true home, to grasp one's identity and mission in life. Mark is asking: Do we know where home is?

Finally, laced all through this brief road schedule of Mark's is the motif of healing, and that brings us to the careful and significant difference between curing and healing.

Ram Dass, an American spiritual teacher in the Hindu tradition who suffered a debilitating stroke in 1997, makes the distinction well: "While cures aim at returning our bodies to what they were in the past, healing uses what is present to move us more deeply to Soul Awareness....[A]lthough

I have not been cured of the effects of my stroke, I have certainly undergone profound healings of mind and heart." In other words, healing, which refers to the soul, can happen without cure, which refers to the body. In fact, it is often in the uncured sickness that the healing begins.

A man named Michael Lerner, who works with people diagnosed with cancer, offered this description of what he would do if faced with a cancer diagnosis. "I would pay a great deal of attention to the inner healing process that I hoped a cancer diagnosis would trigger in me. I would give careful thought to the meaning of my life, what I had to let go of and what l wanted to keep."

In his poem "Fever," John Updike, in an almost playful way, tells about one facet of the inner healing that may accompany sickness:

> I have brought back a good
> message from the land of 102 degrees:
> God exists.

Lying meditatively on his sick bed a long time, he cites the witness of the bedposts, blankets, and the trees outside the window, finally observing:

> ...[Yes] it is truth long known,
> that some secrets are hidden from health.

He's right. Some patients report a greater sense of being alive and in communion with others when they were sick. When they were cured, they returned to normal life, a life often characterized by numbness and rote obligation. Cure of the body actually threatened healing of the soul.

This was the case with a man by the name of Fred. He was diagnosed with terminal cancer. After an initial period of distress he says, "Something amazing happened. I simply stopped doing everything that wasn't essential, that didn't matter." His terminally ill life became vital and peaceful. But the doctors changed their mind. He was *not* terminally ill. He had a rare but curable disease. "When I heard this over the telephone," he said, "I cried like a baby—because I was afraid my life would go back to the way it used to be."

Jesus cured some, not all. He was more interested in healing, healing the soul, in driving out many demons, such as thinking that you are the center of the universe, collecting things and discarding people, selecting pornography and passing up truth, excusing vice and ignoring virtue, a constricted heart over a generous one. Sometimes, gospel wisdom tells us that an uncured body brings about a healed soul.

So I guess that, according to Mark, that old prayer is right after all:

> I asked God for strength that I might achieve;
> I was made weak that I might learn humbly to obey.
> I asked for health that I might do great things;
> I was given infirmity that I might do better things.
> I asked for riches that I might be happy;
> I was given poverty that I might be wise.
> I asked for power that I might have the praise of men;
> I was given weakness that I might feel the need for God.
> I asked for all things that I might enjoy life;
> I was given life that I might enjoy all things.
> I got nothing that I asked for,
> But everything I had hoped for.
> Almost, despite myself, my unspoken prayers were answered.
> I am, among all people, truly blessed.

Jesus Includes

SIXTH SUNDAY IN ORDINARY TIME, B, MARK 1:40–45

Before reading the gospel: "This is an enormously visual gospel. As we unpack it, try to see it all in your mind. Put yourself into the scene. Get into it. Use your imagination. Now listen."

The ancient Hebrews did not have our medical knowledge or know about bacteria, but they observed people getting sick from eating pigs so they invented kosher laws forbidding the eating of pork. There were a good many other diseases that were the object of such laws: tuberculosis, smallpox, and so on. And there were also people with skin diseases that they called by the general term of leprosy: acne, ringworm, scabies, psoriasis. And, of course, there was real leprosy, Hansen's disease, ironically not as contagious as the others but an especially horrific disease with its running sores, decaying, disfiguring flesh, and fearful odor: people with partial limbs and half faces. Leprosy, then, was uniquely despised because it was so ugly and lepers were repulsive, unlovable, even perceived as evil.

Unfortunately such sicknesses also came to be seen as divine punishment and so were a matter not for the physician, but the priest; hence, he figures in the gospel.

Lepers had no hope of receiving love, no hope of being accepted as persons, no hope of enjoying ordinary human companionship. The bottom line is that the Hebrews lived in double terror of such lepers and made all kinds of laws to segregate them. The book of Leviticus forthrightly states the fate of the leper (13:45–46): "The person who has the leprous disease shall wear torn clothes and let the hair of his head be disheveled; and he shall cover his upper lip and cry out, 'Unclean, unclean.' He shall remain unclean as long as he has the disease; he is unclean. He shall live alone; his

174

dwelling shall be beyond the camp." These instructions make the leper the ultimate outsider.

And yet. And yet this leper in our gospel story came to Jesus and knelt as he offered his prayer, "If you wish, you can make me clean." Why did he make such a tabooed, forbidden move? Because he heard of Jesus' power to heal. More important, he heard that Jesus cares about those no one else cares about. He heard that Jesus includes the excluded, and who was more excluded than himself? This emboldened the leper to come forward.

So, to the chagrin of the onlookers, the leper moved closer. To their double horror, Jesus stretched out his hand and touched the man. He actually touched an unclean leper who was looked upon with fright if not hatred by the medical and religious authorities. The leper was suspected of having committed some kind of terrible sin to warrant this disease and had gone beyond his legal rights in even speaking to Jesus.

But Jesus was there for him as he was for so many outcasts. He reached out and touched the leper. In place of isolation he gave companionship. In place of rejection he gave acceptance. In place of disgust he gave compassion. That must have been far better for the man than any physical cure could possibly mean.

Yes, the real power of this gospel is not that a sick man was made healthy, but that a person universally held to be repulsive, unlovable, even evil, is in fact loved, is the object of God's mercy and compassion.

The leper brought the dark and frightening side of his nature and laid it out before Christ and was touched. Is there anyone here who would do the same?

The medical profession has done a lot for body leprosy, ringworm, acne, and so on. It has humbly done less for soul leprosy, the leprosy of rejection and exclusion. If, for example, you have ever felt anonymous, abandoned, a non-person, you have had a feeble hint of what it was like to be a leper in days of yore.

I suspect that most of us have experienced at one time or other the castaway sensation. As a child, to be second banana to a preferred sibling. Later, to be passed over for promotion after twenty loyal years, while a young hotshot, only six months with the firm, gets your coveted prize. Or to be downsized out after thirty grinding years, and now you are over fifty-five! Or betrayal by a spouse or friend or the disappointing sin you thought you'd never commit. The feelings of guilt, unworthiness, isolation, loneliness, spiritual flatness, perhaps even self-loathing, shame, and disgust, a deep sense of unloveableness lie hidden underneath our bright exterior.

Yet this gospel tells us that we can bring the dark and frightening side of ourselves and present it to Jesus.

And this is where the visualness comes in: In prayer, in quiet, in the confessional, see yourself presenting your dark side to Jesus who embraces what others reject and touches what others shun, who ignores the labels, slurs, and categories others construct. "Come to me all of you who labor and are burdened by hurt and isolation and carry the wound of being cut off and I will refresh you."

Oh, what a gospel this is! The untouchable "I" touched by love! Why do I hesitate to come to Jesus?

But there's more. I must point this out lest you miss the supreme irony in the story. Remember, as the gospel story opened, Jesus was in community and could move about freely and the leper was cut off, excluded. By the time the story ends, the situation is reversed; the leper went off into the company of people, while it was impossible for Jesus to enter a town openly. Jesus had taken the leper's place. Having touched the leper, *he* was now under the sentence of exclusion. The cleansed leper can now enter the town while the one who cured him cannot. Truly he has taken upon himself our infirmities. He feels what we feel.

I have a story to end with. A man by the name of Bob Considine tells of the time he accompanied an infant Vietnamese orphan to the U.S. so she could be adopted after the Vietnam War. In the long flight to the U.S. the baby's eyes overflowed with tears but she made absolutely no sound. Considine found the stewardess and asked her what the problem was. The stewardess had seen war orphans before and was quick to tell Considine that this was normal. As she said, "The reason they don't make a noise when they cry is because they learned a long time ago that nobody will come."

The message of the gospel, friends and fellow lepers, is to cry our tears. If no one else, Jesus will come. Jesus *will* come.

Valentines

"Cursed is the one who trusts in men....He is like a barren bush in the desert that enjoys no change of season but stands in a lava waste, a salty and empty earth."

And a Happy Valentine's Day to you, too, Jeremiah!

"Woe to you who are rich, woe to you who are filled now, woe to you who laugh now and a double woe when everyone speaks well of you."

And a Happy Valentine's Day to you, too, Jesus!

Don't look for these Sunday readings on your Valentine cards this week.

On the other hand...on the other hand, if you dig deep enough, there *is* a valentine card buried here in these words. To discover it, you have to remember, of course, that the Bible is basically a love story, a story about God's love for us, even if we haven't always reciprocated. But God seems never to give up and keeps on sending valentines through his prophets who, on his behalf, keep saying in many ways at many times, "Hey, look at me! Forget political alliances, the latest distractions, false promises and self-preening. Woe to that sort of thing. Be *my* valentine."

Valentine. The word itself conjures up memories. Way back when Abe Lincoln and I were classmates we used to have a box in the classroom, like a ballot box. One of the kids' fathers made it. For a week or so before Valentine's Day we all brought homemade Valentine cards—no one would think of buying one—and put them into the box's slot.

On Valentine's Day the box was ceremoniously opened as we all nervously waited for the competition to begin. Would I get any cards? Would I get many to prove I was the Casanova of the fourth grade? More important, would I get a cherished one from that certain girl who was my current love, even though she probably didn't know it? Or, horrors, would I get a syrupy one from another certain girl I couldn't stand? And then, who would get the most cards and be on top in the popularity contest? We would all mentally count as our names were called and furtively glance at one another. Everyone, even the geekiest, got at least one card. Sister Margaret Mary saw to that. It was altogether a bittersweet delight, an episode in the journey to finding oneself.

When I grew up I would sometimes wonder if God felt like that. He stuffed our boxes with his valentines: his word, his prophets, his sacraments, his saints, his coming among us in Jesus and giving his life for us. Sometimes we stuffed his box too. Gradually, however, as time went on, it became a cursory, slipshod valentine or none at all.

We did, though, give a lot of valentines to money and fame. Not bad things at all, but they tended to be greedy and demanding and kept asking for more and more of our time, more and more of our dedication, more and more of our attention, more and more of our love. The result was that there really wasn't much love left or time left to drop a valentine into God's box. And things got woeful.

I got a strong sense of this sort of spiritual free fall when I read an article that appeared in the newspaper called, "Life After Football." It was about football players when they retire from the game. It's kind of frightening. Listen:

Sixty-five percent of National Football League players leave the game with permanent injuries.

One in four players reports financial difficulties in the first year after he retires.

The suicide rate for active and retired football players is six times greater than the national average.

And this one: Seventy-eight percent of NFL players are unemployed, bankrupt, or divorced within two years after their last game.

They became Jeremiah's barren bushes in a salty desert. In their heyday they were rich, filled, laughed, and spoken well of. Woe to them. They stuffed the wrong box, and God was left to lament his empty box and they their empty lives. So no wonder Jesus called blessed the poor, the hungry, the weeping, the disdained. It's not that poverty, hunger, and grief are good—decidedly not—it's just that the folks who live this way have no illusions. They know they need God. They know they are dependent. They know that only love will save them. Freed from clutter, false promises and self-importance, they are more apt to be open to God's call, God's valentines.

Let me revisit valentine memories. I mentioned before that every kid in our classroom would get at least one card. Sister, I said, saw to that. She stuffed the ballot box with cards for the least likely to get one. But I tell you from personal experience, she needn't have bothered. My mother, like some other mothers, made sure I put in several valentines for the losers, as we unkindly called them. Mothers stayed home in those days and so had a keen knowledge of who was in and who was out.

My protests, of course, counted for nothing. Mom was not going to let some child get hurt and I had better shape up. That, in hindsight, is where I learned the Beatitudes.

Like when we had class parties I always had to bring an extra box of cupcakes just in case some mother was too busy to bake some for their kid to bring. Which meant, as I learned when I grew up, mom knew whose mother was too drunk to bake anything and whose kid would have to arrive emptyhanded. Like when I had to invite Gerard, the dirty kid with the ill-fitting clothes, to my birthday party and with the threatening, not-to-be-disobeyed, "You be nice to him and include him." And at the school picnic: "You go up and talk to Jack if he's standing alone by himself and none of the kids will play with him. You don't have to stay, just say hello." And she would be there, of course, to monitor the situation, because Jack was "different," slow, with that silly look. Or when my dad said we would swing around and pick up Kenny in case his dad was busy, knowing all the while that Kenny's dad was out of work and could not afford to run his old jalopy.

Blessed are the poor, the hungry, the weeping, the unemployed, the kids with alcoholic parents, the hated....I learned these Beatitudes firsthand, even though I didn't know it at the time.

Some, sadly, never learn the Beatitudes or send valentines. Let me close with an instance. There was an interesting article in *People* magazine. It was about a young man, eighteen-year-old Kevin Hines who decided to give up his fight with depression by jumping off San Francisco's Golden Gate Bridge. As he paced and cried along the bridge sidewalk, Kevin looked for someone who would talk him out of his crazy decision. If even one person expressed concern for him, then Kevin was prepared to back down. But not one passerby gave Kevin a second glance, with one exception—a tourist asked him to take her picture. Not one person, including the tourist, cared enough to try to intervene to keep him from killing himself. Finally, Kevin Hines climbed up on the guardrail and threw himself 220 feet into the waters below.

I can hear Jesus: "Woe to you who are rich with life, too rich to rescue another's. Woe to you who are filled with satisfaction, too filled to share with an empty heart. Woe to you who laugh, too giddy to sense despair and sadness."

Anyway, miraculously, Kevin survived his jump, although he suffered very serious injuries. While recovering from his injuries, he received some encouraging advice from a visiting priest: "You are a miracle. Now go out and save lives." He took the advice to heart. Today, according to *People* magazine, Kevin Hines has gone back to school and is working to put the priest's words into action in his life and in the lives of others. He is determined to live the Beatitudes and stuff boxes.

So! From Jeremiah, Jesus, Sister Margaret Mary, my mom, my dad, and Kevin: A Happy Valentine's Day!

Conscience

There you are: in front of millions of people on television. The show is *Who Wants to Be a Millionaire?* You are given a sentence, "No one puts new wine into old wineskins." Who said that? You have four answers and only one is correct:

- a. Moses
- b. John the Baptist
- c. Elijah
- d. Jesus

On that show, as you know, when a contestant is not sure of the correct answer he or she has three lifelines. The "50/50" lifeline removes two wrong answers thus improving one's chances. The "poll the audience" option allows a contestant to ask the audience for help with the answer. The remaining lifeline is the "call a friend" option, which allows the player to phone someone for an opinion.

And that clever introduction, friends, is my segue to talking about something much misunderstood and much in need of clarification, at least as much as I can manage within twelve minutes or so. So prepare yourselves today not for an elegant homily, but for a rather dull classroom instruction, although I'll try to sweeten it with some stories. Sorry about this, but it's the only chance I have to hit a wider audience. Take a nap if you wish.

My topic is conscience. And we need some instruction because conscience today has been twisted out of all recognition. Conscience has come to mean, "If it feels good, do it" or "If I think it's right, then it's all right." Thus the I, the me, the self, frighteningly, is the measurement of all things.

181

With that measurement, people justify doing the most terrible and hurtful things; those who kill, rape, steal, cheat, lie, betray, and abuse go out afterward without a pause or blink and enjoy a hearty meal. Some, like the Sopranos who deal in death and destruction, are even romanticized into celebrities.

Conscience is tougher than that. It is far too important to be left up to the self alone, where there are too many built-in tendencies to self-interest and self-deception. We need to look beyond ourselves.

So, to the classroom. Let's take a look. God, like Regis Philbin, has given us precise lifelines when we're not sure of the answer, what to do or how to act, what's right and what's wrong. Four of them, in fact. Yes, there are four consultations every person must take advantage of before a serious decision, and then, whatever you decide, even if it's mistaken, will be morally sound.

The first step is to consult the church. Not that the church is always right—it can make a bad call—but it has 2000 years of accumulated wisdom and teaching and you ought at least to look at that. After all, it has mystics and saints who struggled with the same problems and you ought to see how they handled them. How did St. Elizabeth Seton handle the death of her husband, Rose Hawthorne her divorce, Monica her wayward son, Augustine his guilt, Theresa her terminal illness, Ignatius the loss of a job, or John of the Cross his depression? So seek out the church's teaching and collected wisdom as one element in the formation of conscience.

Second, consult the community. "Poll the audience." Not that the community is always right either, especially in our saturated media climate where moral issues are clouded and manipulated by sound bites and celebrity endorsements and can turn wrong to right within a decade or two. I think of the latest poll, for example, that shows that three-fourths of teenagers—taught by celebrities like Madonna, Jodie Foster, Michael Douglas, Tom Cruise, and others—think it's morally all right to have a baby out of wedlock, in spite of the terrible proven social consequences related to poverty, crime, and gang warfare.

Still, in spite of this media brainwashing, there's always a substratum of common sense within the community, a certain communal "feel" that can cut through the sound bites and we ought to seek that out.

Third, within the community there are always the wise to be consulted. "Call a friend." You know, those who "have it together," who have deeper spiritual insight, who live beyond the pressures of advertising and the tyrannies of possessing the latest "must-have" fashions. Wise people who have experienced life and its pains but have found a center. People, for example, like author Anne Lamott, an unusual character who had a terrible conflict with her mother, Dorothy, a major character in her books. In her latest book called *Plan B*, her mother has been dead for two years. "I prayed for my heart to soften," Lamott writes, "to forgive her and to love her for what she did give me: life, great values, a lot of tennis lessons, and the best she could do. Unfortunately, the best she could do was terrible…and my heart remained hardened toward her."

For the first two years after her death, Dorothy Lamott's ashes sat in her daughter's closet. Lamott recounts moving them at last to a corner of the living room A small thing? No. A huge thing. "Jesus," Lamott says, "understands that things like forgiving your mother take a long time."

"I don't think Jesus was rolling his eyes impatiently at me while she was in the closet," she writes. "I don't think much surprises him: This is how we make important changes—barely, poorly, slowly. And still, he raises his fist in triumph." We need such lived wisdom from the wise wounded.

And from those who have known pain. Listen to this sad story:

There was once ancient temple bell famous for its beautiful tone. It had been commissioned by a king as a way of showing the people's devotion to Buddha; for the king's advisors had told him that making a huge temple bell in honor of the Buddha would secure the nation from foreign invasion. So the king approached the greatest bell maker in the realm. This man worked hard and produced many bells, but none that was extraordinary, none that had a special tone.

Finally, he went to the king and told him that the only way to get the kind of bell he wanted was to sacrifice a young maiden. So soldiers were sent to find and fetch a young girl. Coming upon a poor mother in a farm village with her small daughter, they took the child away, while the mother cried out piteously, *"Emille! Emille!"*

"Mother! Oh, Mother!" the girl replied.

When the molten lead and iron were prepared, the little girl was thrown in. At last the bell maker succeeded. The bell, called the Emille Bell, made a sound more beautiful than any other.

When it rang, most people praised the art that had produced such a beautiful sound. But whenever the mother whose child had been sacrificed heard it, her heart broke anew. She could not hear the beautiful tone without pain.

You see, only those who understand the sacrifice can feel the pain. Others just enjoy the sound.

The moral: Seek out not those who merely enjoy, but those who can feel the pain, the truly wise. In other words, you don't ask Hugh Hefner. You ask Atticus Finch.

Finally, the fourth to consult is the Holy Spirit. We must not rush into judgment, but the first step is to pray for guidance. Seek the Holy Spirit's help not only in prayer but also in the Spirit's sacred word, the Scripture, and its secular word, the story of depth. For example, this one:

Writer Gordon MacDonald paints a heartbreaking picture of children in Ethiopia when that country was experiencing devastating hardship. He tells of one occasion when several thousand starving and homeless people came to a mission during the night, hoping to find food and shelter. (Think New Orleans and Hurricane Katrina.) These desperate people had only the clothes on their backs, and most had slept on rock-hard ground. As one worker made his way through the crowd, dozens of children crowded around him. Those who were closest managed to grab at his hands, while others put their arms about his legs and waist. The worker, quite flattered, commented to a doctor that these were some of the most affectionate children he had ever seen.

The doctor made a wry expression as he shook his head and answered matter-of-factly, "Look, it isn't affection they're seeking," he said. "They need your body warmth. They're absolutely freezing to death, and it's worse because they're so hungry." And Spirit stories like that put your problems into perspective and give you a broader vision of where your decision might fit.

So, there you are: Morality 101 on conscience. Conscience is not whim and it certainly is not that insidious pride of only consulting with one's self or how one feels. No, conscience is a process, a necessary process of consultation in four areas: the church, the community, the wise, and the Holy Spirit. Then, no matter how grievous a mistake you might make in your final decision, you did your moral best. God is pleased and raises his fist in triumph.

What Simon Saw

You all remember it fondly, the Oscar-winning musical *My Fair Lady*. It gets replayed a lot on television. You recall the plot. Professor Henry Higgins takes from the gutter a lowly, uncouth flower girl, Eliza Doolittle, and turns her into a lady. Even after the triumph of the ball where Eliza was declared a princess by that "dreadful Hungarian," Karpathy, and they all return home ecstatic, Higgins still sees Eliza as a successful experiment, an artifact he has cleverly created, and he treats her as such. His friend, Colonel Pickering, on the other hand, takes another view. He chides Professor Higgins and insists that Eliza has feelings and should be treated as a human being. Henry Higgins airily dismisses such a thought.

A glorious play that, in a way, puts to music today's gospel. For, in the long run, both the musical and the gospel are about the same two people: Higgins vs Pickering, Simon vs Jesus. For both pairs the issue is seeing.

In the gospel, as you heard, Jesus asks Simon pointedly, "Do you see this woman?" Yes, as a matter of fact, Simon did: Professor Higgins-like, he quite clearly saw an inferior person, a sinner and, what's more, he just as clearly saw Jesus as a fraud, a phony prophet, because if Jesus saw what Simon saw he'd have nothing to do with this woman.

But Jesus *did* see. He had no illusions. He saw that the woman *was* a sinner. But he saw something else too. He saw tears. He heard a kiss. He smelled oil on his feet. He felt hair used as a towel. He sensed genuine repentance in the air. He recognized love.

It is Simon's blindness that makes him see what the woman before him is and not what she can be. It is Simon's blindness that prevents him from seeing who Jesus really is. That's why he played it cool and he, the correct and perfect host, did not give Jesus the customary amenities of water and towel for his feet, the greeting kiss, or oil for his head, the very things the sinful, inferior woman did give.

Simon, in short, is one of those who puts people in categories and identifies them by race, sex, age, economic status, or their mistakes. Simon doesn't seem able to see beyond the woman as she is, or the great love she can show.

Simon, to turn to another movie comparison, puts me in mind of Rod Steiger who plays Marlon Brando's greedy and manipulative brother in the classic *On the Waterfront*. He sees Brando as a meal ticket as he makes him lie and cheat and throw fights, and Brando, like a sinful woman, utters those immortal words in the back seat of the car, "I could have been a contender. I could have been somebody." Simon could simply not see that far, that this woman could be a contender for holiness, a somebody other than what she was, a sinner.

And what about the woman? How did she see herself? As only a sinner, or possibly a forgiven sinner? When she boldly approached Jesus, did she have in mind the story of David of our first reading who sinned grievously but through the prophet saw his evil ways and repented? Could she hope for a replay here? How did she see Jesus? Simon saw Jesus as a deluded fraud. But the woman saw him as mercy incarnate because she had heard rumors, good things, about him.

And how about this: Years later, I wonder if that other forgiven sinner of our second reading, Paul, heard both stories, the story of David and the story of this woman, and with great relief saw that his ways and his sins need not define him forever. Whatever. All this is indeed good news, that Jesus sees differently, that he's no Professor Higgins or Simon the Pharisee. No, he sees us not only as we are or have been, but as we can be and so he sets the stage for forgiveness.

To continue a colorful trajectory, let's move to the next century. To Rome. Many of you who have visited the Eternal City have visited one of its most popular sites, the fascinating catacombs of Pope St. Callixtus. He wasn't always a pope. He was once a slave. He wasn't always a saint. On the contrary, he started out as a first-class embezzler, cheat, and fraud. He was David, the woman, Paul, before his discovery of forgiveness.

His story goes like this. Around the year 190 a man named Carpophorus set up a bank for his fellow Christians, particularly widows who needed a safe place to keep their limited funds. He had a slave named Callixtus who had some experience in managing money, so he put him in charge. Callixtus made some bad investments and also managed some of the money right into his own pocket. For this bit of sleight of hand Carpophorus sent him to jail to do hard labor. But eventually the ruined depositors prevailed on Carpophorus to release Callixtus in the hope that the wily man might recover some of the pilfered money.

The first thing the newly freed Callixtus did was barge in on a Jewish service one Saturday, trying to get back some of the funds from Jewish investors. A brawl ensued and Callixtus was nabbed once more and sent to do hard labor in the salt mines on the island of Sardinia. That should have been the end of him. But somehow he conned his guards to let him sneak out with some visitors. But it seemed prison life tempered the man and he seemed to be repentant of his former life.

Carpophorus, the Professor Higgins and Simon of his time, was not convinced and still saw his former slave as a sinner and was duly scandalized when a priest named Zephryrinus, following Jesus, saw love and offered forgiveness. Eventually, as pope, Zephryrinus not only ordained Callixtus a deacon, but he put him in charge of a Christian cemetery on the Appian Way, the famed catacomb of St. Callixtus. There's more: When Zephryrinus died the Roman clergy elected Callixtus pope! Talk about Eliza Doolittle going from rags to riches! That's nothing compared to going from con man to pope.

So, there we are: David, the nameless woman, Paul, Callixtus, and so many others down through history. The story is always the same. Seen by so many others as irredeemable sinners, they were seen by Jesus as potential saints. My message is that it is comforting to know that one of the gospel's chief messages is that Jesus sees differently.

The Touch of God

There are two interwoven stories in this gospel: the man of prominence who is the leader of a synagogue and has a name, and the woman of no account with no name. They do not know each other, do not travel in the same circles, yet they share two things in common: They both have a desperate need and both believe Jesus can help them.

The prominent man with a name, Jairus, the synagogue leader, is unlike the other synagogue leaders. They do not beseech Jesus. They stand around and watch disapprovingly. They discredit Jesus, what he does, the unsavory group he hangs around with. But this leader, Jairus, breaks rank. He doesn't care. He is desperate. His daughter is dying and he had heard that God is working through Jesus and he wants his daughter to live and so, position or not, he finds himself at the feet of Jesus. He makes his case and Jesus agrees to go with him. When he arrives at the house, he touches the daughter, not so much to cure her as to make her and her family know that God is present.

But on the way a nameless woman interrupts their journey.

Yes, she, the one with no name, comes up behind Jesus and says to herself, "If I but touch his clothes, I will be made well." Touch. That word keeps reappearing. The physicians touched her, but to no avail. The crowd, pressing in on Jesus, touched him but that led to nothing. But she—it was different, and when Jesus asked, "Who touched me?" he did not mean physical touch, skin against skin, clothes against clothes. His disciples take it this way. No, the woman touches Jesus in a different way. She is not just touching his clothes. She is touching divine presence and that's all the difference. She is touching the heart of Jesus, acknowledg-

188

ing his compassionate love and her willingness to receive it. And when she touched that way in faith, at that precise moment Jesus unveiled this nameless woman's true identity, namely, that she was never simply an unclean woman with uncontrolled bleeding. No, she has an identity. As burdened as she is, she is a daughter. She is a daughter of God whose faith has made her whole.

What can we learn from these powerful incidents? Three things. There is the courage of Jairus. He, a man of standing, risks human respect and public opinion to break rank, to make a public act of faith, to acknowledge Jesus and, in front of everybody, bow before him. It would be like Prince Charles falling down and kneeling before the pope. And so the first thing we learn is that sometimes, perhaps often, we too must break ranks and take the public risk of "bowing before Jesus." Before others, often before your friends, to back off from the dishonest or hurtful deed, to take a stand against the smut and mockery of the conversation: that kind of public witness. I know a gifted young man at Monmouth University, an aspiring actor, who finally got a break to play the lead in a play. But when he learned that the play was one of those scurrilous, mocking ones, he refused the part. He took the loss and the public ridicule. His name is Matt but when I see him, I call him my Jairus.

Second, we learn from his gospel that Jesus does not discriminate. All, even the lowliest, have a claim on him. The important official must step aside while Jesus gives his attention to an unimportant woman. Jesus will do the same for me.

The third thing we learn is about the importance and power of touch. Here let me take time to explore something we all experience. Most of us feel painfully awkward and tongue-tied in the presence of a family member or a friend who is in serious or terminal illness. We reluctantly pay a visit—not too often—and don't know what to say, what to talk about at the bedside.

There they are, our loved ones, once so self-sufficient and strong, now shorn of almost every human dignity, dependent as a baby who can't even do bodily functions without assistance. What do you say to them? And they in turn, embarrassed, often prefer isolation rather than expose their need, their condition, the poor shadow of their former selves.

But this gospel would remind us that we are there not primarily to talk, but to touch and, through touch, to communicate that they are not just a sick or dying or hemorrhaging patient. They are daughter or son of God, and we by our touch indicate the presence of God in Jesus. We let them know that they are recognized for who they most deeply are, and are never alone.

Physician Rachel Naomi Remen tells a story she calls "Kissing the Boo-Boo." She writes:

> Mary had suffered a temporary bowel obstruction from adhesions that has been caused by the radiation used to treat her cancer. When the pain began she packed a small overnight bag and drove herself twenty miles to the hospital. She had to pull over several times to vomit. Then she spent one full day in the emergency room. When I asked her why she did not call any of her friends, she said they were all working and besides:
>
> "None of my friends knows a thing about intestinal obstruction."
>
> "Then why didn't you call me?"
>
> "Well, it's not really your field either," she replied.
>
> "Mary," I said, "even children instinctively run to others when they fall down."
>
> With a great deal of heat Mary said, "Yes, I've never understood that. It's so silly. Kissing the boo-boo doesn't help the pain at all."
>
> I was stunned. "Mary," I said, "it doesn't help the pain; it helps the loneliness."

We are there simply to touch and in touching to remove the loneliness and communicate the presence of Jesus, even when they are by themselves. Our touch is to give them the assurance of Jesus in their distress and their true identity in their weakness.

This man tells a true story:

> My father-in-law was a pediatric anesthesiologist, working with a boy who had continually recurring cancer. The treatments were very painful, but in this boy's case, my father-in-law could usual-

ly alleviate the pain. One day the boy caught a cold, but he had to have the treatment. His name was Brian, eleven-year-old Brian. And my father-in-law can't give him the anesthesia because, with a cold, it can be extremely dangerous.

So my father-in-law sits the boy down and he says, "You know, Brian, I love you very much and I have to give you this treatment. But I can't give you the anesthetic this time. I can't take the pain away. But every time I apply the treatment, I'm going to hold you. I'm going to hold you through the whole thing. And each time the pain comes, I'm going to be there and hold you and you'll feel better."

By the sickbed we are often uncomfortable, knowing that we can't take the pain or the approaching death away. But take the lessons of this gospel with you. That hurting or wasting body is a son or daughter of God. As such, they necessarily catch the attention of Jesus. When we touch them we touch them in faith, we hold them in their pain. And when we do, Jesus is present calling them "daughter," "son." And that's enough, if not for them, but for you to know, and that's why you are there: to make this gospel live again.

Legends

Today, an instruction. We all remember the story of the Arabian Nights. The sultan wed many wives and killed many wives. Till he met Scheherazade. Every night she told him a story, but left it unfinished until the next night. The sultan would not dare kill her, for he wanted to know the ending and so she strung him along for a thousand nights. By that time, of course, he fell in love with her.

We human beings all carry the sultan's instinct. We have an insatiable curiosity. We're never content to let a story lie still. We're always asking, "And then what?" And where a story is too brief or too sparse for our liking, we flesh it out and add to it. This is the way legends are born. Legends circle around, heighten, elaborate a truth. They, as we might say, add technicolor to basic black and white facts.

So legends may indeed be fanciful but—and this is important to remember—they must always be anchored to a core truth. So, for example, whether George Washington chopped down the cherry tree and confessed that he did it may be legend, that is, it may not have factually happened, but it does encase the basic truth that 1) there *was* a George Washington and 2) he indeed was a man of great integrity, the whole point of the story.

Legends, then, must stay within character and stay within the fundamental message. So there was a St. Nicholas, a slim third-century bishop, who did in fact give to poor children. The saint eventually became Santa who lavished gifts on children as, through the centuries, he morphed into a roly-poly, red-suited FedEx driver. The Santa legends are not factual, of course, but they are true to the extent that they elaborate the initial kindness and givingness of a holy man who was living out the gospel. You get the point? Dig behind a legend, however wild, and you will find the solid fact that launched it.

I spin this elaborate introduction because it helps us understand both the apocryphal gospels and the legends of the saints. The four canonical gospels—Matthew, Mark, Luke, and John—are sparse. They do not, for example, give a description of Jesus, tell us what happened to Mary and Martha, Lazarus, the twelve apostles, the people in today's gospel who asked to follow Jesus. Somehow we feel unsatisfied. We want to know. "But then what happened?" The later apocryphal gospels were invented to answer this question.

Now some of these gospels kept the rules: They spun fanciful stories around the core truth. For example, they gave names to Mary's parents. No problem. She *did* have parents, so why not give them names? Others, alas, such as the Gospel of Judas or the Gospel of Peter, wandered from the core truth into wild unorthodoxy and, even though they had some interesting things in them, they went overboard and so were rejected by the church. It would be like making Santa not only a gift-giver, but a child molester. Whoops! With that you just stepped over the truth line. You may be telling a story, but it's not tradition's story.

So, with that being said, let's do an exercise in legend. For example: Jesus was crucified between two thieves, a nameless good thief and a nameless bad one. The bad one mocks Jesus and tells him to save himself and them. The good thief rebukes him and then, turning to Jesus, says, "Lord, remember me when you come into your kingdom."

Thus the wonderful core truth of last-minute redemption and mercy. Still, it is rather an intriguing story. People pondered: It's too bad we don't know more about those two thieves. Were they Clint Eastwood or Tony Soprano types? Butch Cassidy and Sundance? How did they become that way? Where were they from? It drove the early Christians crazy until around the year 600 an apocryphal book appeared called The Arabic Gospel of the Infancy of Our Savior.

The book covers Mary and Joseph's escape journey into Egypt with the Christ Child. As Mary and Joseph are wandering through Egypt, looking for some place to call home, at least temporarily, the locals warn them about a certain stretch of desert that is teeming with robbers. Hoping to pass this stretch unnoticed, Mary and Joseph decide to travel by night. But they come upon two highwaymen blocking the road ahead of them. The highwaymen, the robbers, in this apocryphal gospel, are named Dismas and Gestas.

Gestas is ready to get down to business to rob the Holy Family, but Dismas intervenes. "Let these persons go free," he says, "so that our comrades (who were sleeping nearby) may not see them." A strange request from a hardened criminal, and Gestas dismisses it out of hand. So Dismas ups the ante. He says to Gestas, "Look, take these forty drachmas from me instead," and he tosses in his valuable belt as well. The drachmas and the belt are an offer Gestas can't refuse, so he stands aside and lets the Holy Family go, free and unmolested.

So now comes the tie-in. Before they continue on their way, Mary prophesies to Dismas, "I promise you, because of your kindness, the Lord God will sustain you and will grant you remission of your sins." And a precocious Christ Child adds an aside, "Thirty years hence, O my mother, these two robbers will be raised upon the cross along with me, Dismas on my right hand and Gestas on my left, and after that day, Dismas shall go before me into paradise."

Now we can imagine how it all began and we feel more satisfied. Legend that this is, it has become an acceptable story because it has kept the core truth in focus, the focus on mercy, forgiveness, and love.

If you want a quick P.S., at some point—when is hard to pinpoint—Dismas segued into *Saint* Dismas and he eventually became the patron saint of thieves in particular and criminals in general.

An example. There is a priest named Emil Kapaun from Kansas. He is being promoted for sainthood. He was a military chaplain during the Korean War. In November 1950 the North Koreans captured him and 1200 American fighting men. The American POWs got so little food they were on the verge of starvation, so every night Father Kapaun crept out of the barracks to steal corn, millet, and soybeans from the guards' storehouse to feed the soldiers. Before Father Kapaun went out to steal, he prayed to St. Dismas, the Good Thief.

Thus, in this instance, the initial true event of Calvary fleshes out into legends, which in turn spill over into stories, which in turn inspire new ways of forgiveness and compassion. The point of today's instruction: Unravel the legends of the saints and you'll find a gospel truth.

Out of the Box

Is he not the carpenter?...And they took offense at him.

They knew him growing up. They knew his family. They had him figured out. So where did he get off teaching them in the synagogue? Who did he think he was? Jesus was someone in a box. That's where he was in their eyes. He was in a familiar place. I say "familiar" because being in a box and putting others in a box is a human inclination, a human impulse, a human habit.

Think of yourself. We all conform to what others have decided who we are. Have you ever noticed how we talk differently with different groups who have different boxes for us? We may use some salty or off-color language with friends we would never use at home or talking to me. We may do some things totally out of character with one group but totally in character with another.

The fact is that we are always more than people think. People are always more than we think. You may never know that I struggle with doubts about my faith. I may never know that you struggle with depression or addictions. You may never know what I give quietly to charity and I may never know that every day you take care of an elderly parent and clean their house and get their groceries. You may never know my secret fantasies and desires, weaknesses and strengths, nor I yours.

The point is that we are indeed more than people think and sometimes, you know, it breaks out. Sometimes some strikingly wicked or heroic deed pops out to challenge others' assessments and they exclaim about us, "We never knew you had it in you." And likewise, in a similar situation, we say of them, "We never knew they had it in them."

195

This was what was happening to Jesus. Anyway, the truth is that people are always more than we think and therefore we must always grant them transcendence, that extra dimension of being. We must never lock them in the box, nor should they lock us in.

Popular fiction is full of box-breaking precisely because it caters to our secret desire to be more than what people think of us; it caters to our fantasies of moving away and getting a new start, a new identity where we can be our true selves. So, Clark Kent, boxed by everyone as the mild-mannered reporter, breaks free and literally soars. No one in the world thinks Wart, the pint-sized squire, has it in him to become King Arthur; nor dirty Cinderella a shining princess, nor the ugly duckling an elegant swan. No one ever dreamed that a kid down on the Kansas farm named Dorothy Gale would get to visit Oz; or an overweight old maid, Charlotte Vale, played by Bette Davis, would turn into a striking woman in love in *Now, Voyager*. We love these stories because the people in them have done what we find ourselves powerless to do: break out of the box and show people that there really is more to us than they think.

Yet, this is precisely the belief of the gospel: We are more than we show. This is precisely the call of the gospel, to be more than people think, to be, in fact, exactly as God thinks, as God sees us. And real life offers us examples. Womanizing Thomas à Becket was the carousing and drinking companion of King Henry, but when he became Archbishop of Canterbury he wound up defending the church against Henry and gave his life for it. Stunned, Henry never thought he had it in him.

Who would have thought that a rich, popular, spoiled, dissolute kid, baptized Giovanni di Bernardone, running with his rat pack, would break rank, as it were; that he would heed a dream in which a voice told him to "serve the Master, not the man," a dream that slowly got to him and made his old life of partying less and less attractive until one day, breaking out of his playboy image, he got off his horse and embraced a leper? He then went home, rejected his inheritance and walked away forever from his riches to become Francis of Assisi. And his shocked friends thought they knew him!

Unlettered, ignorant Bernadette held fast to the vision of the Lady at Lourdes and withstood ridicule and persecution from the high and the mighty. Everybody thought she would fold. Nobody ever thought she had it in her to be so steadfast.

That gaunt woman in the photograph wearing a cheap, dark wool cap over her white hair, her hands thrust into the pockets of an old tweed overcoat covering a dark, drab dress: a rebel who had an affair and an abortion was boxed in forever as a loser until she met Christ. She became a Catholic, and succumbed to a lifelong affair with the poor and downtrodden and, as a result, was shot at, investigated by the FBI, and imprisoned for her participation in a United Farm Workers rally, supporting the rights of migrant workers. She co-founded the *Catholic Worker* newspaper and many houses of hospitality for the poor and is up for canonization. Who would have thought this of a woman from Brooklyn, Dorothy Day?

Of Jesus they said, "Where did he get all this?" We thought we knew him. We had him in his proper box. But, like all of us, he was more than they thought. And so must we liberate this deep truth in ourselves and in others.

What I am saying is that there is in each of us an authentic call to holiness, to quiet heroism. We have it in us. Every one of us. *One of these days* we have to walk away from the routine sins, the worship of consumerism and celebrity, the indifferent life, and our gray, lackluster spiritual existence. We have to answer that call to embrace in a very public way the truism that we really do not live by bread alone; that we are called to live beyond the box, do the unexpected, the heroic deed, take the unpopular stance, express the transcendence within us, and allow others to do the same.

The gospel message reminds us that we are always more than people think. We are, in fact, exactly as God thinks. We must take the step to let God's assessment show. And if it causes our friends to wonder, so much the better.

Nevertheless

In the ancient biblical world, it was believed that there were just seventy-two nations. That is, if you count all the descendants of Noah's three sons—Shem, Ham, and Japeth—you come up with seventy-two, the only survivors of the flood and therefore the ancestors of the human race. So the number seventy-two came to represent all the nations. Thus in his gospel Luke is saying that in choosing the seventy-two Jesus is sending his disciples not only to Israel, but to the whole world.

So, as we heard, he sends them out two by two, just like the Mormons and Jehovah Witnesses, who knock at our doors. Speaking of which, one humorist says one day he was late leaving home for work when there was a knock at his front door. It was wet and cold outside. He opened the door and there were two Jehovah Witnesses damp and shivering in the cold. They asked if they could come inside. Well, he just couldn't just leave them standing there, so he said okay. He brought them into his living room and offered them a chair. They were quiet for a long time, so he asked, "What happens now?" The older one said, "We don't know. We never got this far before."

Anyway, as you heard, the disciples came back jubilant at their success but they were caught up short when Jesus told them not to be so happy that spirits were subject to them, but rather because their names were written in heaven. That is to say, they should rejoice because they made a difference to someone beyond themselves, they were part of something larger.

And that, in the most profound sense, is the *Christian* formula for success. Make a moral difference, be a part of something larger. It's a simple teaching and yet it is as far as you can get from the world's criteria of success, which is having for oneself lots of money, position, consuming a lot, being a celebrity, an army of one. Forget the Band of Brothers.

Yet, when it is tried....I know a man who is a member of what we call today the "Greatest Generation." He served in World War II, was in the Normandy invasion and D Day. He tells me of the sufferings, the deprivation, the horror of the war. But then he always says, "Still, I look back on those four years as the very best years of my life. For once in my life I really had the feeling that I was part of something bigger than myself. I was on the move. We had a mission. Maybe it's sad to say, but I look back upon those years as the best of my life."

Notice what he said. The best part of his life was when he was "part of something bigger...we had a mission." Today when so many measure everything by something smaller—that is, themselves, their needs, their wants; when any sense of what is best for the common good is simply not on their mental radar; when education and advertising are geared toward "the good life," which means one of endless self-fulfillment—few lives are successful in the gospel sense, in the human sense.

To be currently specific: the people who made millions in the Oil-for-Food scandal at the United Nations; money stolen from the poor people of Iraq; corruption at the World Bank; the 210-million-dollar separation package given to the head of Home Depot, who was fired for doing a poor job; and the other thirty-six chief executives ousted last year who walked away with over a billion dollars among them; public officials routinely convicted of corruption; Congress wallowing in shameless earmarks and lobbyists' money. Did you know that there were sixty-two lobbyists in 1968 but that today there more than 15,000 of them, including some 2400 former public officials and some 240 ex-members of Congress? The pharmaceutical lobby, for example, has two lobbyists for each of the 535 member of Congress.

University officials steering unsuspecting students into taking loans from banks in which they have a financial interest, doctors pushing drugs from companies from which they have received extravagant perks and gifts, the obsessive idolatry of high self-centered consumers like Paris Hilton—all these high salaried, high-positioned people are not only mired in irresistible greed but, gospel-wise, they reveal themselves as morally incapable of purpose or any sense of the common good. Yet, by the world's standards, they are considered "successful."

That's why it's troubling that, according to the *Los Angeles Times*, a new study indicates that young adults today are more narcissistic and ego-driven than the previous generation. Some suggest causes such as permissive parenting, increased materialism, the fascination with celebrities. Certainly there's the almost total immersion in the self-centered world of cell phones, iPods, BlackBerrys, iPhones, and other solitary electronic games making a new generation decidedly less interested in giving their time to others or being a part of something larger and, who, therefore, quotes the report, "tend to have less interest in emotionally intimate bonds."

I remember a college girl telling me that, unlike her sister who went a few years ago, *she* definitely was not going this year with us on our parish-sponsored Jesuit Volunteer Program to work in a poor country. "Why?" I asked. She said, "Because Jane went with you to Honduras and it totally destroyed her life. When she came back she wasn't the same person. She changed the course of her life and upset everybody."

Well, that was the best reason I ever heard for actually going. Jane did drop out of the me-alone generation and wanted to do something with her life and become a part of something larger. Yet Jane's attitude should be a normal part of being a Christian, not a cause for concern.

Anyway, to test your spirituality, ask yourself: How passionate am I to make a moral difference with my life? Does the common good figure in my decisions or only "What's in it for me and mine?" If someone remarks that you are "successful," what do they mean? Money, big house, exotic vacations, prestigious job, promotions, upscale neighborhood, three cars?

Would you be defined as successful in terms of your consumption *or* in terms of your life, that it matters, really matters in the good that you do, the time you give, the care, concern, and compassion you show for others? Has your life at this stage transcended itself and become a part of something bigger, grander, than your needs? Have you a sense of mission, of being chosen and sent?

This gospel raises these very questions and so, as usual, it turns out to be more subversive than we think. "Rejoice that your names are written in heaven."

Dust

We sometimes secretly flatter ourselves that we are the Scarlet Sinners of the county. But I daresay that there are not too many hit men, drug dealers, or Madams here today. Truth to tell, our sins are not scarlet. They are pink. The poet James Thomson wrote these lines:

> Once in a saintly passion
> I cried with desperate grief,
> "Ah, Lord, my heart is black with guile,
> Of sinners I am chief."
> Then stooped my guardian angel
> And whispered from behind,
> "Vanity! my little man.
> You're nothing of the kind!"

And the angel's right. We're nothing of the kind. We are far more like a house that is neat but a long time abandoned and we may not notice that a layer of fine dust has settled in every nook and cranny of our lives. Dust: soft, fine dust, but it's on everything. It has taken the luster off our spiritual lives. If we are spiritually out of kilter, it's usually not because of the burdens of *horrible* deeds. It is because of the fine, accumulated human dust of *weak* deeds. Our house *is* in order, but, as I said, moral dust has settled everywhere. Listen:

We had been childhood friends. She was in a nursing home. I went occasionally to visit her. When I entered, she stood there, defiant as ever, half expecting my embrace. But I averted my eyes and we sat down. She always had a sharp tongue and she went on about life's ingratitude, her unfaithful lovers, the deplorable people here. After a half hour, I rose to leave. Again, the half expected embrace side-stepped. Suppose she broke down and cried? I couldn't handle that. And, then, her sharp tongue. What would she say? So I pleaded I had to get home to attend to things, it would be hard to get a taxi, I would be late, I really had to go, and so on. We shook hands politely and I left. Two months later I called. The nurse informed me that my friend had committed suicide. I killed her. I mean, I didn't drop poison in her water or slit her throat, but I killed her. I starved her to death. She was hungry for company, friendship, a touch, an embrace, a kiss, my time, my time, my time. And I couldn't give any of those things. I just couldn't. I killed her.

The difficult people, who are just that: surly, clinging, manipulating, maddening, often relatives, we really don't want to be with them. It's so unpleasant. They are so unpleasant. They always push our buttons. But as a disciple of Jesus, do we reach out nevertheless, *not* because we see them as obnoxious, but because we see them in need of redemption? No big scarlet sin. Just an understandable human situation. Just the dust of measuring love only by *my* feelings.

"I am going home to Denmark, son, and I just wanted to tell you I love you." In my dad's last telephone call to me he repeated that line seven times in a half hour. I wasn't listening at the right level. I heard the words but not the message, and certainly not their profound intent. I believed my dad would live to be over 100 years old, as my great-uncle lived to be 107 years old. I had not felt his remorse over Mom's death, understood his intense loneliness as an "empty nester," or realized that most of his pals had long since died.

"Dad's dead," sighed my brother Brian.

My little brother is a witty lawyer and has a humorous, quick mind. I thought he was setting me up for a joke and I awaited the punch line. There wasn't one. "Dad died in the bed he was born in, in Denmark," continued Brian. "The funeral directors are putting him in a coffin and shipping Dad and his belongings to us by tomorrow. We need to prepare for the funeral." I was speechless. This wasn't the way it was supposed to happen. If I knew these were to be Dad's final days, I would have asked to go with him to Denmark. I would have offered consolation during his final hour. Dad announced his departure as best he could and I had missed it. I felt grief, pain, and remorse.

Why had I not been there for him? He'd always been there for me. In the mornings when I was nine years old, he would come home from working eighteen hours at his bakery and wake me up at 5 AM by scratching my back with his strong hands and whispering, "It's time to get up, son." By the time I was dressed and ready to roll, he had my newspapers folded, banded, and stuffed in my bicycle basket. When I was racing bicycles, he drove me fifty miles each way so he could watch me. He was there to hold me if I lost and shared the euphoria when I won. Later, he accompanied me to all my local talks. He always smiled, listened, and proudly told whomever he was sitting with, "That's my boy!" My heart was in pain because Dad was there for me and I wasn't there for him.

Again, no big scarlet sin. We're all busy. But it bothers us because we sense that we're less somehow for our neglect and the excuses for our neglect, which like so many small particles settle like dust on our soul.

It's the early 1900s in New York City with street merchants hawking their wares all over the place because it's Christmas. Moss Hart, the famous playwright, remembers when he was a boy of ten straining against the cold wind with his father as they start down the rows of pushcarts. He would pause before this or that pushcart to pointedly admire a chemistry set or stamp album or printing press. His father, getting the hint, would also pause, ask the pushcart man the price, stand there a moment, then shake his head and move on. Once in while, Hart recalls, his father would pick up a little toy of some kind and glance at him as if he might want it, but Hart says he was too old for that kid stuff. His heart was set on bigger things, but those bigger things always cost too much money.

Finally they came to the end of the carts and he heard his father jingle some coins in his pocket. He suddenly realized that his dad had managed to get together about seventy-five cents for a present for him, only to find that nothing could be bought for that small a price, at least not for a ten year old. He saw his father's hurt and disappointment, and gratitude and love welled up inside him and he wanted to throw his arms around his father and tell him that all the toys in the world didn't matter. His father loved him and that was all that mattered. He wanted to shout out loud, "It's all right, Dad. I love you." But he didn't.

Moss Hart goes on:

> But instead we stood shivering beside each other for a moment. Then we turned away from the last two pushcarts and started silently back home.…I didn't even take his hand on the way home nor did he take mine. We were not on that basis. Nor did I ever tell him how close to him I felt that night, that for a little while the concrete wall between father and son had crumbled away and I knew that we were two lonely people struggling to find each other.

No scarlet sin here. Just the sad, pink, festering hurt of wanting to love and to be loved, but being unable to elicit either. Just the dust of emptiness that we could fill, but find ourselves unable to do so, unable to say, "I'm sorry" or "I love you" or "You mean more to me than anything else in the world."

We are those people and we share their dust, dust that takes the luster off our spiritual lives.

Jesus urges in today's gospel. "Shake off the dust." Now we know what he means. The dust of:

apologies withheld,

the dust of comfort suppressed,

the dust of affirmation denied,

the dust of embraces ungiven,

the dust of love unspoken.

Shake them off!

The View from the Ditch

We've heard the parable of the Good Samaritan all our Catholic lives and there is no one who does not know its story line. So well known is it that the very phrase "good Samaritan" has fallen into our common vocabulary and people who do good deeds are called Good Samaritans and even hospitals are named Good Samaritan. And over the years we've heard endless homilies about the priest or Levite who passed the beaten man by, the oddity of a Samaritan being kind to his nemesis, a Jew, and so on. And all these perennial homilies have one thing in common: They have been preached from *our* point of view and, as a result, we have pointedly been accused of identifying with the priest or Levite, when we should identify with the Samaritan. Shame on us.

But I want to challenge that. I want you to consider that this gospel takes on an entirely different focus if we can appreciate how this parable must have played out before the ones who first heard it, Jesus' original audience, Jewish Galilean peasants. How did *they* understand and respond to it? That focus gives us a whole new insight into this familiar parable.

So let's enter into the mentality of the original audience and when we do, the first startling truth that emerges is that, unlike ourselves, these Jewish peasants from Galilee would never have identified with the priest, the Levite, *or* the hated Samaritan. On the contrary, the character with whom they would have identified would be the victim, the man mugged by the robbers and left for dead. Yes, these first Jewish hearers would have instinctively identified with the Jewish victim; they would have adopted the view from the ditch, as it were.

They would easily imagine themselves lying there on their backs in the depths of need, having been stripped of all their resources and, then, opening their eyes, looking up and forced to see, horror of horrors, one's hated enemy as the merciful face of God! It was their worst ethnic nightmare. As the victim, unable to resist, they are forced to accept godly mercy from one regarded as beyond the pale. They would have shuddered at the thought. But once they got over the shock, then sooner or later they would come to the slow realization that sometimes it is possible to accept God's healing and forgiving mercy only after one has reached the depths of need, having been stripped of everything, including one's hates and prejudices.

That's the way the first audience would have heard this shocking parable. They immediately would have identified with the Jew in the ditch being utterly humiliated and taken aback to discover God's compassionate love in the face of the Samaritan enemy. And they would know then and there that accepting mercy from one regarded as an enemy would challenge them to see every person as a neighbor and to become themselves a doer of mercy across any boundary of separation, hate, and prejudice.

So you see, this parable would have knocked them off their feet. And Jesus' "Go and do likewise" did not mean for them to imitate the Samaritan but to imitate the victim: If compassion and love can come from one's enemy, then no one is enemy. Everyone is neighbor. Quite a lesson!

This theme has been played out often. For example, no one here, I presume, is unfamiliar with Dickens's novel *Great Expectations* or David Lean's masterful movie version of it. Pip, you recall, a young orphan, living with his nasty sister and her gentle husband in the marshes of Kent, is at the cemetery one day at his parents' grave when a fearsome escaped convict grabs him and orders him to bring some food, and a file for his chains. Pip obeys and brings the food but the convict is eventually captured.

One day soon after this episode, Pip's uncle brings him to the house of the eccentric and one-time jilted Miss Havisham. There he meets her ward, cold and contemptuous Estella, who scorns him, although Pip falls in love with her and dreams of some day becoming a gentleman to come back and marry her. But in due time Miss Havisham sends him away to apprentice as a blacksmith to his brother-in-law.

One day Mr. Jaggers, a lawyer, appears to the now grown-up Pip, saying that a secret benefactor has left him a fortune and he must go to London to learn how to become a gentleman. Pip is overjoyed and knows in his heart that Miss Havisham is that secret benefactor and indeed wants him to come back as a gentleman and marry Estella.

So he goes to London, lives it up, and when twenty-one gets a regular generous allowance. Several years (and adventures) go by when one day a bear of a man bursts into Pip's apartment. Pip is horrified at this rough, uncouth character and backs away until the man reveals that he is the convict from long ago that Pip fed.

He has never forgotten the boy's kindness, even when he fled to Australia and made a fortune, so that he indeed, not Miss Havisham, is the source of Pip's mysterious wealth. But Pip by this time has developed into a haughty, self-important snob, and is appalled at this seedy character; and when the generous convict-benefactor moves gently to embrace him, Pip steps aside. He wants nothing to do with this creature so beneath his station. He is Samaritan to Pip's Jew.

Anyway, to make a very long story short, Pip gradually comes to see good in the convict and begins to care for him and helps him escape the clutches of the police who learn that he is in London. The plan fails and the convict dies in jail in peace in Pip's arms. Pip has lost his benefactor and his fortune, but love for this Good Samaritan, this generous convict, has forever changed him.

Just like the parable from first-century eyes. Pip, the victim, having been beaten up by life's twists and turns, looks up out of the ditch of despair and loss and sees the face of his enemy, the fearsome convict who offered him love, friendship, and fortune and now he knows that all barriers must dissolve.

Let me share, if you don't mind, another, more earthy, example. It never happened before and he can't understand it, but an utterly mortified nine-year-old boy in the third grade has wet his pants. His heart has stopped because he can't imagine how this has happened. He knows when the boys find out he'll never hear the end of it and when the enemy camp, the girls, find out, they'll disdain him. He puts his head down on the desk and prays, "Dear God, this is an emergency. Please, I need help now!"

He looks up from his prayer and here comes the teacher with a look in her eyes that says he has been discovered. As the teacher walks toward him, a classmate named Susie is carrying a goldfish bowl that is filled with water. She tries to sidestep the teacher who twists around to let her by but accidentally knocks her with her hip, causing Susie to dump the bowl on the boy's lap. The boy pretends to be angry but all the while he's saying to himself, 'Thank you, Lord! Thank you! Thank you!"

Now instead of being the object of ridicule, he's the object of sympathy and while the teacher sends him downstairs to change into his gym shorts, back in the classroom Susie, the stupid girl, is being reviled for being such a klutz.

Finally, at the end of the day, as they are waiting for the bus, the boy walks over to Susie and whispers, "You did that on purpose, didn't you?" Susie whispers back, "I wet my pants once, too." He looks into the face of his enemy and says, "Thank you."

Thus the famous parable Jesus told is not so much about the kindness of the Good Samaritan as about the conversion of the Challenged Victim, shocked to find mercy where he felt it could never be found and forced to see a neighbor in one he considered an enemy.

Sabbath Rest

It was then that the fox appeared.

"Good morning," said the fox.

"Good morning," the Little Prince responded politely, although when he turned around he saw nothing.

"I am right here," the voice said, "under the apple tree."

"Who are you?" asked the Little Prince, and added, "You are very pretty to look at."

"I am a fox," the fox said.

"Come and play with me," proposed the Little Prince. "I am so unhappy."

"I cannot play with you," the fox said. "I am not tamed."

"Ah! Please excuse me," said the Little Prince. But, after some thought, he added: "What does that mean—'tame'?"

"It is an act too often neglected," said the fox. "It means to establish ties."

"'To establish ties'?"

"Just that," said the fox. "To me, you are still nothing more than a little boy who is just like a hundred thousand other little boys. And I have no need of you. And you, on your part, have no need of me. To you, I am nothing more than a fox like a hundred thousand other foxes. But if you tame me, then we shall need each other. To me, you will be unique in all the world. To you, I shall be unique in all the world.... Yes, it will be as if the sun came to shine on my life and I shall know the sound of a step that will be different from all the others. Other steps send me hurrying back underneath the ground. Yours will call me, like music, out of my burrow."

The fox gazed at the Little Prince a long time. "Please, tame me!" he said.

"I want to very much," the Little Prince replied, "but I have not much time….I have a great many things to understand."

"One only understands the things one tames," said the fox.

"What must I do to tame you?" asked the Little Prince.

"You must be very patient," replied the fox. "First you will sit down at a little distance from me—like that—in the grass. I shall look at you out of the corner of my eye, and you will say nothing….But you will sit a little closer to me every day."

And that classic story, *The Little Prince*, my friends, is a variation of today's gospel and a good summer reflection.

"Come away by yourselves to a deserted place and rest a while," invites Jesus. A deserted place is not where food is normally found nor rest easy to come by. Therefore the deserted place becomes a symbol for learning how to be fed by God. And the rest is not more time to sleep and play. It is Sabbath Rest, learning how to be sustained by the goodness of creation, learning to center down to God's presence, and learning to be free of the idolatry of work. As one spiritual writer says, "The Sabbath is there to stop you from being absorbed in the success story, to prevent you being enslaved to productivity and profit." In the context of our story, the deserted place, or the Sabbath Rest, is any time we turn to people, any time we take to tame our foxes, any time we take to get to know ourselves, God, our family, and our neighbors.

But, alas, we are famously programmed Little Princes. We protest, "I have a lot of things to do. I'm busy, busy, busy. Catch up with you later. I simply don't have the time to sit down with you and move a little closer every day." The result has long been noted by sociologists that Americans are among the loneliest people on earth; that we are workaholics, multi-taskers; that we are racing too fast to establish ties—one-night stands, maybe, or several marriages and lots of acquaintances, but very few real friends. It is interesting that current TV advertisements are trying to get families to eat together even as they pass in the night, nuke TV dinners, and ship the kids off to multiple activities.

But as Jesus advised, we need to go apart. Ann Morrow Lindbergh, married to an aviation hero, mother of a kidnapped and murdered child, and mobbed by crowds, wrote her famous book *A Gift from the Sea* on the need to get away from it all and the need to take time to respond to the needs of love. In a reflection on a moon shell she found, she writes, "Solitude, says the moon shell. Every person, especially every woman, should be alone sometime during the year, some part of each week, and each day." She took the moon shell back to Connecticut to remind her of her need for the Sabbath Rest. She says to the moon shell, "You will remind me that unless I keep the island-quality intact somewhere within me, I will have little to give my husband, my children, my friends, or the world at large."

How true that bit of gospel wisdom is. We have lost the island-quality, the Sabbath Rest, the ability to sit down on the grass and move closer to God every day, to family, to friends. As a result we have little left to give others. And then we wonder why we are spiritually tired or depleted. We wonder why our relationships are so shallow, why we really don't know each other, or why "image" is so perversely and obscenely important to us. It's because it covers up that we are hollow inside.

And the pity is we teach our children that always being active, always being on the go, always being involved in as many projects as possible is the epitome of success. This is how, we tell them, they acquire all the achievements they can proudly list on their resumes to be sure they get into a good college, the door to the good life and good income. And ultimately, at the end of the day, all too often these so-called successes can't handle their personal lives or lack the spiritual resources to endure pain, suffering, and disappointment or the spiritual vision to put compassion, honesty, family, and friends first. But such spiritual resources are acquired only by "coming apart for a while."

Summertime *is* a time to travel, to hit the beach or the mountains or relax with a good novel. Why not? But sometime during the year, winter or summer, we must heed Jesus' invitation to come apart, to learn once more how to establish ties—with God, with others.

The gospel reminds us that it's time not just to vacation, but to embrace the Sabbath Rest.

Yin and Yang

In many ways, this Martha-Mary story has got to be one of the most annoying episodes in the gospels. Annoying because it always seems to leave you between a rock and a hard place. If you're too much like active Martha, then you're ignoring your host. If you're too much like passive Mary, then you're sitting on a chair with dog hair all over it. Martha may be Martha Stewart, but you hate her for it. Mary may have chosen the better part, but the Board of Health is banging on the front door. They tried ringing the bell but it's broken.

I tell you, I've been to Martha's house. She's someone I haven't seen in a while and I want to do some catch-up time. She has welcomed me with great enthusiasm and has put out the best china and linens and great desserts and every time I look, my coffee cup is miraculously refilled. And she pops up and down to check the stove, the refrigerator, the microwave, talks while moving about until I've had it and finally exclaim, "For cryin' out loud, will you just sit down and talk with me!" After all, I did come to be with *her*, not her dishes.

I have also been to Mary's house. The moment I arrived she grabbed me by the arm and ushered me to the couch. We sit and talk and talk and sit, sit and talk and the hours go by and by and I'm getting hungry and I have to cough before a glass of water is offered. The room grows cold and the window is open and she doesn't get up to close it or put up the heat. Well, I guess we had a good visit but I leave cold, hungry, and uncomfortable.

In popular misconceptions Martha and Mary come off like that: the Oscar Madison and Felix Unger of the first century. They're both wrong, of course, if they go to extremes, but, even so, it's Martha who usually gets the bum rap here: too busy with practical things. Why can't she be more like Mary? Why can't we?

Well, that's the usual "moral" of the story, but before we deal with *that*, I want to tell you that there is really much more to this gospel and these two sisters than you think. Behind its short sentences, there are some surprisingly deeper revelations going on that first-century Christians would have, with some initial amazement, immediately picked up and discussed. So let us twenty-first-century Christians discover what it was that caught their attention.

First, Mary. Take another look at what she is doing, where she is. "She had a sister Mary who sat beside the Lord at his feet listening to him speak." Given the customs of the time where male and female roles were strictly demarcated, with women confined to the kitchen and the men to the living room, Mary is remarkable for crossing the boundaries. She boldly came in where Jesus was and did what only men were allowed do: She sat at the feet of Jesus. This was the customary symbolic sign that someone wished to be a master's student, his disciple, something open only to men. There is, after all, that verse in the Talmud that states, "It is better to burn the Torah than to teach it to a woman."

But Mary ignored all this and presented herself as a disciple, and thereby assumed equality with men. Jesus not only allowed it, but praised it and so, once more, he turned the world upside down. And that openness, that mutual respect, that acceptance, that equality is a powerful between-the-lines subtext of this gospel, something you should not let pass by unnoticed.

Then there's Martha [our parish patron]. She comes across, perhaps, as a Type A personality who can't sit still. But this is to underestimate her position, her passion, and her faith. To gain an appreciation of Martha, recall her in another well-known gospel story. She appears in John's gospel where she and her sister Mary are grieving over the death of their brother Lazarus.

Do you recall that it is forceful Martha who speaks up and dares to scold Jesus, "Lord, if you had been here my brother would not have died"? But, more than that, it is Martha who on this occasion winds up making a stunning profession of faith every bit equal to that of St. Peter, who at the village of Caesarea Philippi, in answer to Jesus' question, "Who do people say I am?" responded, "You are the Messiah, the Son of the Living God."

Well here, near her brother's burial place in the village of Bethany, Martha says the same thing to Jesus. After Martha's complaint, Jesus had said to her, "Everyone who believes in believe in me will never die." And then he asked her, "Do you believe this?" And Martha responded, "We have come to believe you are the Messiah. Yes, Lord, I believe that you are the Messiah, the Son of God, the one coming into the world." And there she is proclaiming the same words, the same faith, as Peter, thereby becoming his female counterpart and a co-founder of the faith.

You see, between the lines, as we said, there is something revolutionary being said here in this brief, familiar gospel story of the two sisters. You should be alerted to it, and now you are.

But let's go back and take the both of them at the more familiar face value and learn a lesson here as well. From them we learn that we have to stop making a false opposition between the activism of Martha and the quietude of Mary—action and contemplation—as if one were better than the other.

Jesus' remark that Mary had chosen the better part is not to dismiss the business of Martha, but is meant to underscore *balance*, as if Jesus were saying to the Marthas of the world, "Stop what you're doing and reclaim your center. What are you doing all this for? Have you lost a sense of life's purpose? What motivates you? How does your life, your work, fit into the larger picture?"

These questions are especially relevant to those who are in church ministries of any sort. Fidelity and competence are not enough. You must get at the center of it all. When I was a pastor we had a cardinal rule that members of every ministry had to go away twice a year on a day of recollection in order to reclaim *why* they're doing *what* they're doing. They, the parish Marthas, were to play "Mary" for a day so that mere busy competence would not subvert spirituality; so that, in short, in their work for the Lord they wouldn't forget to pay attention to the Lord in their work. All Marthas, and the center evaporates and burnout sets in. All Marys, and charity and service go undone.

And so with all of us. This gospel calls for balance in our lives. After all, try to recall that today's gospel follows last week's gospel of the Good Samaritan where, at the end of his parable, Jesus commanded, "Go and do likewise." Yes, do the works of mercy and compassion, but don't let your good deeds get separated from the word of God, from the reason for it all. That is why, for all of us Marthas, it is imperative to frequently play Mary's role in our lives. That is why all of us must take time for prayer, spiritual reading, and recollection.

These two pioneering women, Martha and Mary, aren't opposites and we should not separate them. They are the yin and yang of a balanced spiritual life.

Treasures

Buried treasure, a pearl of great price, a storeroom full of choices—these are the themes of today's gospel I would like to explore with you in several stories. And, straightforwardly, I use these figures of speech to represent the beginnings of morality, of character, and the critical part you play in the making of moral people, of which we seem to be in short supply these days.

Michael Jordan's father, James Jordan, you might remember, was murdered in the summer of 1993. Before that happened, Michael said this to columnist Bob Greene:

> My heroes are and were my parents....It wasn't that the rest of the world would necessarily think that they were heroic. But they were the adults I saw constantly and I admired what I saw. If you're lucky, you grow up in a house where you can learn what kind of person you should be from your parents. And on that count, I was very lucky. It may have been the luckiest thing that ever happened to me.

To Michael Jordan, good parents meant as much to him as his incomparable basketball skill. Early on, he was given a pearl of great price, a moral treasure—character and honesty—to draw on when he grew up.

My point is that the moral person of character is the result of drawing from the storeroom of treasured, witnessed experiences and memories buried early and daily in his heart by his parents and mentors and other significant adults. My point is that the greatest gift we give the next generation are moral treasures in the storeroom of their psyches that they can discover and draw on in later life. The real tragedy in some of today's kids is there *is* no treasure in the field, only an empty field. That is, their moral storeroom is empty. There is no deep, subconscious resource to plumb, because they have been raised in a moral vacuum by poor models, or they have been physically, emotionally, and morally abandoned by their parents, and so are left only with the constructed celebrities of Paris Hilton and Donald Trump as guides.

We count. Our example, our witness count and have effects we don't always realize. I remember years ago some reporters were interviewing Russian Premier Boris Yeltsin, asking him what gave him the courage to stand firm during the fall of communism in the former USSR. Interestingly, he credited the electrician from Poland, Lech Walesa, who started the downfall of communism there. When Walesa was interviewed and asked what inspired him, he said it was the civil rights movement in the United States led by Martin Luther King. When King was interviewed and asked what inspired him, he said it was the courage of one woman, Rosa Parks, who refused to move to the back seat of the bus.

Is it too much of a strain to say that the moral courage of a brave little woman in the South brought about the downfall of communism? Hidden treasures are like that. And that is the lesson for us. How valuable the little things we do, the people we influence!

Famous evangelical minister Bill Hybels writes:

> Recently my brother and I spent a lunch hour discussing the mark our dad left on our lives....Dan and I reminisced about the times we had sailed with him on Lake Michigan. We remembered violent storms with fifty-mile-an-hour winds. All other sailors would dash for the harbor, but Dad would smile from ear to ear and say, "Let's head out farther!" We talked about the tough business decisions we had seen him make.
>
> We winced when we remembered his firm hand of discipline that blocked our rebellious streaks. We never doubted it. Dad was strong, tough, and thoroughly masculine.
>
> Yet for twenty-five years he spent nearly every Sunday afternoon standing in front of a hundred mentally retarded women at the state mental hospital. Gently and patiently he led them in a

song service. Few of them could even sing, but he didn't care. He knew it made them feel loved. Afterward he stood by the door while each of those disheveled, broken women planted kisses on his cheek. As little guys, Dan and I had the unspeakable privilege of watching our six-foot-three, two-hundred-twenty-pound, thoroughly masculine dad treat these forgotten women with a gentleness that marked us.

A personal story. When I was about eight or nine, my friends and I found a high mound from a house excavation. So we simply had to climb it see who was going to be "king of the mountain." Once on top we surveyed our domain. That's when some girls walked by. The nerve of them to enter our territory! So we hurled dirt bombs down on them.

Needless to say, within hours the entire story had found its way through the neighborhood telegraph to my mother. Her reaction was instantaneous. "Did you boys throw dirt at the girls?" After some hesitation I admitted we had. "Well, that's not right. I will not have you doing that. Right now you are marching down the street to apologize to the girls. And you are going to tell them that you won't do it any more." Was this intervention really influential in my life? Well, I still remember it! And I think I'm a little less inclined to throw dirt in any sense of that term as a result of this childhood experience.

What I'm saying is that wise parents, wise adults provide this sort of training all the time, getting their children to act with virtue and thereby developing their abilities to do so on a regular basis. Thus:

"I know you don't feel like doing your home work right now. You'd rather watch television or go out and play. But I want you to stick to the work for another half hour. Then you can join your friends down the street."

"I know you don't like the sweater your grandmother sent you for Christmas. But she gave it to you out of love. So you *will* write her a thank-you note nonetheless."

"I know you've received a last-minute invitation to go on this exciting weekend trip. But when you agreed to join the soccer team you made a commitment to your teammates. You don't have to play soccer next year if you don't want to. But for this year you made a commitment and you must fulfill it. So, no, you cannot skip the game to go on the trip."

Would you say that? If you wouldn't, what's the message? It's okay to break your commitments, your word? Later on, when their marriage breaks up, you'll ask, where did they learn that?

Early moral-treasure burying is critical. Listen to this man, now married and a father:

> Of course kids don't want to be like their parents! For a decade I had hair down to my waist in defiance of my parents and everything they represented. For today's adolescents, it's body piercing. God knows what my little [two-year-old] Catherine and her peers will come up with to torture me and my wife in our dotage.
>
> But I also know that, despite my best efforts to the contrary, my parents have had a big effect on me. I'm able to teach Catherine about tools today because my dad put a hammer in my hand when I could hardly lift one. I'm able to pass along some sense of ethics in part because when my mother caught me using fake credit card numbers to make long-distance phone calls in high school, she gave me a lecture about honesty that I'll never forget.
>
> ...And because my parents hugged openly and often in our home I learned firsthand that one of the best ways to raise a happy and secure child is to raise that child in a loving home.

What are you putting daily into the moral storeroom of your children or grandchildren or pupils, the next generation? When they look for treasures, will they find any? Or let me put it this way: Do you think the little girl called Scout could ever forget what she witnessed in her father, Atticus Finch?

The kingdom of God is like the pearls of example and wise counsel buried deep in the hearts of the little ones.

Snakes and Fish

A husband and wife are discussing their living wills. The husband is adamant about his desires. "Just so you know," he says, "I would never want to live in a vegetative state. I would never want to be dependent on some machine and fluids from a bottle. If I ever get to that state, I just want you to pull the plug." His wife thought about this for a moment, got up, unplugged the TV, and threw out all his beer.

When I start with a joke, it's usually because I have a dense homily to follow, one you won't necessarily take to. You see, I've been doing some research for a talk and am about to inflict some of its data on you, data that, in its own way, reflects that part of today's gospel that says, "What parent among you would hand his son a snake when he asks for a fish? Or hand him a scorpion when he asks for an egg?"

So, here's some things I found out, truths, I suspect, we already know in our hearts. In our system we can't get richer, at least for long, without impoverishing the physical and emotional world around us, without depleting the earth's limited resources, without working long hours and continually widening the gap between ourselves and our family, our friends and the community. That seems to be a daily observable truth.

Even though our world tells us that we are what we spend, the fact is that our spending doesn't make us more satisfied or holier. We Americans own cars, drive more than anyone else in the world, use our multiple plastic cards with abandon, and live in very big houses. In 1900 the average American lived in a house the size of today's typical garage.

Today our homes are enormously bigger, have doubled, in fact, since 1970, even as the average number of people living in each one has shrunk;

and even though we have all that extra space, it's *still* not enough to hold our excess, with the result that we have spawned a whole new industry, that of the storage locker, which has spread like mushrooms all over the land. But all this stuff, by all accounts, hasn't made us happier.

No wonder, I learned, the pollsters find that at least two-thirds of Americans dread the onset of the Christmas season simply because it *does* add more stuff to their lives. The poll found that people were desperately looking for permission to celebrate Christmas in a new way that fits better with what they actually need: time with family, time with real friends, silence for reflection, connection with nature. Interesting.

Along the same line, the U.S. Census Bureau tells us that the average density of cities, suburbs, and towns in 1920 was about ten persons per acre; by 1990 it had dropped to four persons per acre, even though the population doubled, and today there are on the average two people in very large houses per acre. That is to say, fewer and fewer people are occupying eight times more developed land than they did eighty years ago. But we're no more neighborly.

In fact, the statistical chances of sighting, bumping into, or knowing your neighbor are meager. Studies have shown that, as urban neighborhoods became more heavily used by cars instead of pedestrians, the average person saw the number of friends and acquaintances they had in the neighborhood drop from nine to four.

Yes, say the reports, growth has built mega-mansions in the field behind your house, but you can't see the horizon anymore. Condos have risen on the shoreline, but you can't see the ocean any more. Strip malls offer convenience but the trees are gone and the animals' habitats as well. Big box stores like Wal-Mart and Target have swallowed up acres and acres of fields and compact downtowns. Upscale housing developments with no interior centers force us out daily into four- or six-lane congested highways to go shopping, those very same highways that effectively chop up and segregate communities. We own two or three cars but traffic is dense, the roads are gridlocked, and carbon dioxide emissions pollute the air and add to global warming.

One calculation I came across says that an American family will consume more fossil fuel between the stroke of midnight on New Year's Eve to dinnertime on January 2 than a Tanzanian family will use in an entire year. We eat more than the rest of the world and struggle with overweight and a costly obesity epidemic. But we're no more content.

More data: We are beyond a doubt the most comprehensively entertained people in history and there is no musical sound emitted by anyone anywhere on the planet that is not available to us, yet it's harder to communicate with a child or hear much about our neighbors or our immediate vicinity. We do have more of everything, from entertainment around the clock to cars and flat screen TVs, but again, all this affluence really doesn't seem to make us fulfilled.

Not to mention that, hectored by the more than 5000 commercials we ingest each day, to acquire more and more goods, we have to work longer hours. We have added 199 hours to our annual schedule, the equivalent of five forty-hour weeks, and ironically much of the money we make is meant for services that make it possible for us to work those long hours: more child care, more prepared meals, more professionally run birthday parties, more pet sitters. The amount of time parents spend with their kids has steadily decreased and studies show that children in affluent suburbs are more likely to be depressed and on prescription drugs than children living in inner-city poverty.

In a word, we are the first mass affluent class in world history, yet none of this has made us happier. In 1946, for example, the social scientists tell us that the United States was listed as the happiest country among four advanced countries; thirty years later it was eighth among eleven counties; a decade later it ranked tenth among twenty-three nations, many of them from the third world. What happened?

Yet stubbornly in every survey asking about satisfaction and happiness and "quality of life," people still continue to name family, home life, health, being married, and friends as fundamental factors. Income hardly registered as a factor in the survey, yet, in its pursuit, all the "real" happiness factors are made to take last place. Something is very wrong.

In other words, having more *does* make things better and more efficient, but only up to a point. As the economists point out, money consistently buys happiness right up to about $10,000 per capita income and after that point the correlation disappears. As income steadily increases, family and community life decrease, people travel farther away from home, more people have fewer close friends, and families no longer eat together.

In still other words, the social scientists tell us, we have kept on doing something way past the point where it once worked. To switch at last to gospel language, we have given one too many snakes in place of nourishing fish, too many scorpions in place of life-giving eggs.

All this data I've uncovered is hardly happy talk, but I guess for us believers it has its point, for this unsettling social snapshot is a gospel invitation to reflect on our lives, how busy, fast, and artificial they have become and how devoid of real sustaining and fulfilling relationships they are. The point is to reconsider what really matters and recognize how much we long for real values: a united family, time out, true and fast friends, the delights of nature, the closeness of God, and the interaction of a good supportive community whose faces and names we actually know. We want to bequeath good spiritual gifts to our children, to our friends, to our community.

The data seems to suggest that if only we could slow down, surrender the brand names, and stop the addiction of more and more! Simply put, we need to live more simply, spend time with loved ones, linger long over a meal, savor a sunset, experience the intimacy of family and friends, and, mostly, have a sense that we belong to something larger than ourselves.

So, to paraphrase the gospel, ask for less and not more and you will receive; seek what matters and you will find; knock on the neighbor's door and it will be opened to you. If, as Jesus says, you learn to give good gifts to others, the Father in heaven will give the Spirit.

Believing Is Seeing

Eighteenth Sunday in Ordinary Time, A, John 6:24–35

We just heard a familiar story from the New Testament. On the surface it's a story about a crowd that had been fed by Jesus the day before, tracking him down and looking for a rerun the next day. The story quickly moves beyond the surface with Jesus wryly commenting to the crowd that they are looking for him for the wrong reason, because they got a free meal. But that's not what he's all about. He cautions, "Seek rather the food"—a different kind of food—"that endures."

Jesus is engaged in what we moderns call "consciousness raising," moving people from one level to another, helping them see differently, to see beyond and behind things. Every disciple of Jesus aims at this goal: to see as Jesus sees. The saints are simply those people who achieved this. For example, some people saw a disfigured leper. Mother Teresa saw Jesus. The mob saw a fallen woman and was about to stone her. Jesus saw a repentant sinner. Learning to see beneath the surface, behind things, as it were, is the condition for wisdom and spiritual growth.

Let me give a simple illustration in the story of The Rabbi and His Daughter, followed up by an example:

> One day Rabbi Meir of Rothenberg sat at his desk studying the Holy Books. The morning light streamed through the window, casting a golden glow on the high wooden shelves and leather-bound volumes that covered the walls of his room. As he pondered over the meaning of the words that lay before him, he heard a knock on the door.
>
> "Who is there?" he asked, and smiled when he heard the reply.

It was his youngest daughter, Rachel, coming to see him for a morning visit.

Rabbi Meir held out his arms as the young girl ran to greet him. Rachel was a curious child. She was bright and quick, and showed wisdom beyond her years. On her own (for it was not usual for girls to study the Torah in those days), she had learned to read in Hebrew and Aramaic. She knew all the prayers for weekdays, Shabbat, and the holidays and could recite whole passages in the Torah from memory. But Rachel knew, as did all the children in her family, that the most difficult challenges of all were to be found in the study of the Talmud. Most of all, Rachel wanted to join with her father in that study, but girls almost never had that chance.

Standing next to Rabbi Meir's chair, she asked him, "Father, teach me, how do you study the Talmud?"

In the quiet of the study room, he answered, "Talmud is very difficult. It requires that you not only read and memorize, but also that you think."

"Please, Father," Rachel begged, "let me try!"

"Very well, my daughter. I will give you a lesson. Now, listen carefully. Two men working on a rooftop fell down through the chimney. When they landed on the floor, one had a clean face, and one had a dirty face. Which one went to wash his face?"

(The answer to this question seems obvious, but is it? What do you think?)

Rachel puzzled for a moment to herself. The dirty one, of course. Everyone washes his face when it's dirty! Right? But then she had a second thought and said eagerly, "I know, Father. The one with the clean face went to wash!"

Rabbi Meir said, "And how do you know that is the answer?"

Confident now, Rachel replied, "Because he looked at the dirty face of his friend and thought that his must be dirty too, whereas the dirty one looked at the face of his friend and thought that his face must be clean!"

Rabbi Meir smiled at his daughter. "That is good thinking, my child," he said, "but to study Talmud you must think a little harder than that."

"Why, Father?"

"Because," said Meir, as he stroked her hair, "if *two* men fall down a chimney, how is it possible that only one of them would have a dirty face?" Rachel's face fell when she heard the reply, but her father consoled her: "You did very well. But always look for the question behind the question."

Spiritual insight does precisely that, it looks behind things; it tries to see the hand of God, the breath of the Spirit, deeper meanings. So let me conclude with my story.

A woman spoke quietly of the death of her father. He had been a proud man, she said, a man who spent all his work days tilling the soil of a Carolina farm and all his Sabbaths praising God for life and seed and family. A final bout with cancer sent him to the hospital, never to come home again, and in the last week of his life the disease provided the added indignity of a stroke that robbed him of his speech. As his family visited his bedside, his eyes would moisten with frustration and grief as he tried in vain to speak to those he loved so dearly.

On his last day alive, the attending physician had issued the signal and the family had gathered in his room, the daughter and her two brothers. With strength fading, the father motioned to his son that he wanted a glass of water. The son hastened to the sink and returned with a full water glass, which he held toward his father's lips. But the old man pushed the glass away and moved his finger from the glass toward his son, as if to say, "You drink it."

Hesitant and uncertain, the son lifted the glass to his lips and drank from it. Then the father motioned toward his daughter, indicating that she should drink some, too. Sensing what his father wanted, the son passed the glass to his sister, and she drank. Now the father pointed toward the other son, and the daughter suddenly saw what was happening. "My God," she gasped, "he is serving communion!" The act remained the same but a whole new level had been reached.

There in the face of death, this father summoned a sacramental water glass to administer the feast of life. And so the episode, the story, becomes not simply a moving account of a father's death, but a higher revelation of how this man saw his last journey and ultimately how his children saw it.

Now anyone looking through the window of their house would see only some family members having a drink of water. Perhaps they were thirsty. But those with spiritual insight would realize that this was no longer an episode about a dying man asking for a glass of water. It was a story about Eucharist, the foretaste of the eternal banquet and sign of that man's faith, hope, and love.

We must try to cultivate through prayer and meditation a Christian way of looking at the world, looking beyond surface and image. For us, the old adage must be true: It's not the world's "seeing is believing." For us, it's faith's "believing is seeing."

Higher Calling

Eighteenth Sunday in Ordinary Time, C, Luke 12:13-21

Take care to guard against all greed, for though one may be rich, one's life does not consist of possessions....You fool! This night your life will be demanded of you and the things you have prepared....

With a gospel like that, you know what you're in for, so let me begin. A few summers ago, the sophisticated *New Yorker* magazine, in its August issue, had a cover of a beach scene. There were four adult figures towering over a little girl standing on the sand. Three of the adults, since it's vacation time, naturally have cell phones glued to their ears with the now familiar cocked elbow. They all are looking anxious, nervously pacing back and forth. The fourth adult is intently seated at his laptop. The child, however, has a smile on her face. She has a conch shell listening to the sound of the ocean. The artist has named the drawing "Higher Calling."

And that's the meaning of today's parable. Notice that Jesus does not criticize the farmer's wealth, nor does he imply that he has gotten it dishonestly. The man probably worked very hard, very diligently, and was rightly named "Farmer of the Year." He's obviously a good manager. Nor is there any complaint about a well-deserved, relaxing retirement. Then why he is called a fool?

He is called a fool because of his deafness to a higher calling—his cell phone to his ear instead of a conch, as it were—his narcissism. Notice how many times the pronoun "I" is repeated: What shall I do?...I shall tear down my barns...I shall store my grain...I shall say to myself, live it up. It was the "me" and "mine" that stand out; the self-absorption, the self-centeredness, living only for oneself. There was no sense of a higher calling.

228

The farmer's barns, even the mega-mansioned ones, are symbolically too small. The whole world should be his granary.

Whenever I hear this gospel of the man and his barns I always think of the flamboyant Liberace who became the highest paid performer in the world and who at his height spent five million dollars a year; and when he died in 1987 he left behind eight overloaded warehouses full of stuff that could not fit into any of his five fully furnished residences. An engaging, colorful fool.

What we're basically talking about here is greed and greed's chief product, desensitization. Greed blinds one to the higher calling, which means other people. Countries and marriages and families have been devastated by greed: working too many hours, buying too much, running up credit card debt, grasping too much busyness, stimulation, and novelty—extreme this or that—which very soon becomes an addiction, always needing more to get the same kick.

Most if not all our political and financial scandals are about self-directed greed: the double dipping, the multiple pensions, the embezzlement, fraud, duplicity, skimming.

And in all of this, always, one grows more distant from family and friends, home and community.

Yes, greed earns "the good life." But that good life, which has made us, as someone put it, "leisurely, large, loaded and lonely," has substituted for the shared blessed life. Greed pushes us to spend an inordinate amount of time trying to be better off instead of simply trying to be better, of making a living instead of a life. Other people are not even on the radar. And a sixty-billion-dollar-a-year "I'm Number One" TV advertising makes sure we don't see them.

And I hate it when they target the kids. A case in point. These next six weeks, for example, will stimulate high anxiety among the kids. Advertising even now is subtly warning them to have the approved brand name clothes and brand-name knapsacks and brand-name cell phones to go to school with or else be relegated to the eternal shame of nerddom. It's not that they won't have a basic pen and pencil; it's that they won't have the politically correct pen and pencil.

Reminds me of the story of the teenage girl who left for school wearing one yellow and one orange sock. Her mother, noticing this, headed her off at the front door and asked why she was wearing two different colored socks. The teenager responded, "I have a right to be different if I want to." Then she added, "Besides, all the kids at school are doing it."

The pressure is enormous and my heart goes out to them, and even competition among adults is fierce, especially in the suburbs. Who wants to be the last in the development to have the super-model, chrome-plated, gourmet outdoor grill that spouts out stock quotes even though last year's model is perfectly good? The summons to the Higher Calling gets lost in the hype.

You know, the irony is that we Christians started out so dedicated to the Higher Calling that by definition we were notoriously counterculture. The pagans were astonished how we lived simply, shared goods, practiced open charity, and even died for the faith. In their Playboy culture they were puzzled by—even as they admired—celibate monks engaged in communal work and prayer.

In fact, knowing how much pressure they would be under, the early church made it very difficult for people to join, requiring years of preparation. The whole point was to get candidates conditioned to live by a different code, a different set of values, and to learn how to endure being out of place. Let me put it this way: All the early Christians were the Amish of their day with their quaint morals, communal living, and simple lifestyle. All the early Christians, if you will, had conch shells to their ears while others had cell phones.

Alas, today, if Christian churches are faltering, it is because they have joined the secular parade, have themselves become greedy for money, power, and prestige and no longer show us how to live. One thing is for sure: It is apparent that we no longer have the Amish reputation.

How do we regain it, how do we prevent being called fools, especially from the one Person we never want to hear it from? I have some half-dozen practical suggestions for you and myself. Are you ready?

First, share your bounty. Regularly give to St. Gregory's pantry or a similar program.

Second, tithe. Give ten percent of your income to charity. And teach your children to do so from the start. For example, if you give a child a dollar for his or her First Communion, you say, "Remember, ten cents of that is for the poor." If you give the Confirmation youngster five dollars you remind him or her, "Remember fifty cents of that is for the poor." If you give a birthday present you say, "Now you have a new present. Which one of your old ones do you want to give to a child who has none?" Imagine hearing that for the first ten years of your life! Get them in the habit early of thinking that way.

Third, learn to form the habit of asking, "Do I really need this? Can I do without it? Could I not give this money to a worthy cause?"

Fourth, go through your closet and drawers once a year. If you didn't wear a piece of clothing that year, give it away. General rule: If you haven't worn it in a year, it belongs to the poor. You're hoarding their property.

Fifth, make the comparison test. Be honest. That is to say, check how your charitable giving compares with other items. How does your charitable giving equate with eating out, entertainment, grooming, hobbies, clothing, and so on? How, to give a practical example, does what you give in the collection compare with what you'll casually spend on tonight's drinks and dinner?

Sixth and finally, Christmas is coming. Yes, brace yourself for the annual mind-numbing hectoring starting in September, if not earlier. But my point is that, right now, before you're zombied out, while you're still somewhat immune to *Rudolph* and *Jingle Bell Rock*, decide to set a strict limit on family and friends' presents—how many more things do they need?—and give the rest to charity.

Perhaps, in their name, you might make a donation to a charity and write that on your Christmas card. Or how about making the decision now to match whatever you spend on gifts with local or national charities?

So there you are, six things to duck being called a fool: First, share your bounty. Second, tithe (and get your kids hooked). Third, ask the questions. Fourth, annually check closets and drawers for unused clothes. Fifth, compare your charitable giving with your spending on luxuries. And sixth, transform excessive Christmas spending into Christmas giving.

Do these things, listen to the Higher Calling, and, in the gospel expression, you will be rich in what matters to God.

Elijah

Nineteenth Sunday in Ordinary Time, A, 1 Kings 19:4-8

The first reading will occupy our time. The prophet Elijah is at his lowest ebb, contemplating suicide. As the story tells us, he's discouraged. The wicked Queen Jezebel is after him. All his work seems down the drain. Nothing is going right. He's at a very bad part in his life. So he treks across this desert, physically and mentally exhausted, sits beneath the broom tree, and as you heard, asks God to take his life. He's had it: "Enough already; I'm ready to die!" He's given up. He's in despair. He is one tired and desperate prophet.

His mood is not unknown to us. It is found everywhere today, communally and individually. The press reported this week that the ugly and horrible war in the Mideast has already killed more than one hundred Israelis, most of them military, and over fifteen hundred Lebanese, most of them civilians. Or as the Jesuit magazine *America* says, "Lebanese casualties have outnumbered Israeli deaths more than ten to one. A third of them have been children." Factions in Iraq are routinely killing thirty-five to fifty people a day. Iran is making nuclear weapons. Terrorists are emboldened and airports are fortresses. Gas prices keep climbing. Daily revelations of corruption in the corporate, sports, political, and professional worlds are numbingly commonplace. The vulgarity and sleaziness of the media disgust us. Thus subconsciously burdened, we all feel an unspoken unease as we go about our lives.

Then there are our personal lives which force us brooding beneath the broom tree. There are those who have suffered loss, the loss of a child or spouse through death. The loss from divorce. The loss of physical or mental health. The loss of a job or an opportunity. The loss of virtue. Loneliness.

Betrayals and disappointments, addictions, and simply spiritual flatness plague many. Some people are sick and tired of being sick and tired. We all have Elijah moments. So let's go back to the Elijah story and see what we can learn. Two things, in fact.

The first thing we learn is the value of Elijah's solitude, the time when one is forced by circumstances "to be still." Elijah sat exhausted beneath the broom tree, but in that stillness he had a chance to regroup and recover, to listen to the Lord. One of Grace Noel Crowell's poems speaks of his condition—indeed of life itself—as a reservoir that needs filling up just like a slow rain fills an empty cup. She proposes:

> Hold up your cup, dear child, for God to fill.
> He only asks today that you be still.

That's a lovely metaphor. It's starting to rain after a long dry period, one or two drops and then more, and you turn your cup upside down; and gradually, drop by drop, the cup begins to fill again. Those of you who are hurting, grieving, in sorrow, or just struggling with something, the poem says that maybe you need just to sit awhile and rest, and turn your cup upside down to God; and little by little, let your dry reservoir fill up again. *Be still.* Stop trying to control. Be still.

The second thing we notice is that as the exhausted prophet wakes up from his stupor of despair he unexpectedly spots a little hearth cake and water. Where did that come from? Maybe it was there all along but he never noticed. Being so "down," that was the last thing he expected, but there it was and it picked him up a little. In discouragement, the Elijah story says, be alert to the little signs.

Here's another example: a pagan philosopher of some note, a man with a reputation of some fame, yet he's unhappy. His life is a shambles, his religious doubts are plaguing him, his personal life is a disaster. His relationships—with the woman he is living with and his illegitimate child—are strained to the breaking point. He's depressed. To throw him into further despair, he's just received news that two common Roman soldiers had converted to the Christian faith. Here these ignorant soldiers have found something and they're happy, and he, Augustine, the great intellect, is in a terribly depressed state. Dejected, he goes into his garden and just sits under *his* broom tree, and great man that he is, he puts his head in his hands and he simply weeps. As he's weeping, he tells us, he hears a small voice saying, "Take and read, take and read," on the other side of the garden fence.

So in a half daze he goes into the house and picks up the Christian Bible, and in his own words in his autobiography he says,

> I seized, opened, and in silence read that section on which my eyes first fell: "Not in rioting and drunkenness, not in chambering and wantonness, not in strife and envying, but put on the Lord Jesus Christ." No further would I read, nor needed I, for instantly at the end of the sentence, by a light, as it were, of serenity infused into my heart, all the darkness of doubt vanished away.

Under his broom tree of despair, prompted by a child's voice, he found a new direction in life.

So for this woman. It was one of the worst days of her life. Newly separated, she was tired, sick, lonely, hot, and discouraged. It was all she could do to lift her little boy into his highchair for dinner. She put his food on the tray and began to read the mail. Another bill she could not pay; it was the last straw. She leaned her head against the tray and began to cry. The little boy looked at this sobbing mother, then took the pacifier out of his mouth and offered it to his distraught mother. She began to laugh through her tears and hugged the source of such total unconditional love. Again, the lesson to learn in times of being at the end of one's rope is to be alert to the small signs.

So in bad times, be still. Maybe bad times are a sign that you're running on empty and simply need the time to hold your empty heart up to God to be refilled. Second, notice the little signs: summer, spring, flower, a kindness.

There are all kinds of people sitting under the broom tree. I suggest when shortly I lift up the paten and the chalice, you might think of someone under the broom tree and say in your heart: "I am placing Mary or John on this paten and in this chalice. May they too be lifted up to God." Or when you approach for Communion, bring someone in your heart with you. Let them share the "hearth bread" of life, this sign that they are not alone.

Thus strengthened by that food, may they begin to walk forty days and forty nights to the mountain of God.

Reference Point

"Much will be required of the person entrusted with much, and more will be required of the person entrusted with more."

You know, that's kind of a scary saying. Sounds like a basic requirement at the Pearly Gates. We wonder how some will make out as we all shake our heads, hearing, to the point of numbness, of one more politician, one more CEO, one more manager, one more steward filling their pockets at others' expense.

To paraphrase the gospel, "If that servant says to himself, 'The auditors are delayed in coming' and begins to fleece the servants and eat high, get drunk, and travel to exotic places on public credit cards and lobbyists' perks, then the master will come and assign him a place with the unfaithful." That's a good gospel word: unfaithful. They, the stewards of public and private trust, have broken faith with the people, with God. Do they even think in those terms? Have they no moral sensitivity? Not likely.

For example, I read with dismay the other day how credit card companies fleece their customers. There's the man who told a congressional hearing how he exceeded his charge card's $3000 limit by $200 and wound up paying $7500 in penalties and interest.

I learn how the credit card companies ratchet up interest rates as high as thirty percent, how they apply penalties to purchases that were made before the penalty was incurred, in effect increasing the price of the product *after* it was sold, and how they deal in what is known as "double cycle billing," whereby a cardholder who pays $450 of a $500 balance is charged interest on the entire amount as opposed to the unpaid balance.

What stuns me is that somebody, some living human being, some steward in a big office, who lives in a mega-mansion suburb and has villas in Florida and Tuscany, concocts these schemes. They have to know that their legal corruption is wrong, is hurting people, usually those who can least afford it. Or, then again, do they? Are they so far insulated from everyday life, living in rarified luxury on the backs of the people they exploit, that they simply don't see? Do they no longer believe in a Master to whom they are responsible and who will come on an unexpected day? Probably.

But let's leave the stratosphere of the rich and powerful and descend to our everyday lives where stewardship is wanting. Here's a disturbing home-grown example found in two similar stories, both in last week's newspapers: one in the July 30 issue of the *New York Times* and the other in the July 27 issue of our local paper, *The Ocean Star*, and later in the mainline New Jersey newspapers.

The headline in *The Ocean Star* was "Jenks [local amusement enterprise], cops unite to curb teen drinking." The article concerns the growing trend of teenagers abusing alcohol before attending the popular non-alcoholic teen night at the beach, with many thirteen- to seventeen-year-olds drinking before the event. Some were so drunk that they had to be transported to the hospital. Some, the story says, come down by train from local towns and they drink on the train and arrive intoxicated. Jenks is thinking of canceling the teen night, and the police complain that, with everything else, they don't have the manpower to monitor the teens.

Hold this in mind as we turn to the story in the *Times*. It concerns the death of a girl in Italy, sixteen-year-old Claudia Muro, who was killed by a drunken driver on her way home from a nightclub. The driver had a blood alcohol three times over the legal limit and had already had his license suspended several times for driving intoxicated. This death has finally shaken the Italians, whose level of drunken driving and teenage alcohol abuse has risen dramatically with some 6000 people killed each year on their roads. An extensive survey there of some 50,000 young people leaving bars and discos and nightclubs found that half were drunk. Mind boggling!

However, the trend of underage drinking by teens and its attendant tragedies are not my concern here. What is of interest are the remarks on both sides of the Atlantic. The local chief of police remarked that the teens coming to the Point Pleasant teen night were drinking beforehand while unsupervised. But he added, "We have found that kids who are dropped off or picked up by their parents have no issues and are not drinking." In short, those who had stewards were all right.

In Italy, the president of the Province of Rome said the kids drink because of "a lack of a reference point, one that they don't find in the family or in school or in other institutions, and therefore their idea of community is to stay together in the piazzas getting high." The man from Rome and the chief of police from Point Pleasant Beach are on to something. Some kids have no reference point. That says it all. They are without stewards.

One of the more chilling memories I have of this is when I was a young priest, ordained maybe only three or four years, and I had to go to the police station to talk to a teenage boy who was in very serious trouble. He did have a mother and father but they were out all the time, going here and there, doing this or that. They were fairly absent from his life and they raised him with no particular set of teachings or guidelines. They just let him do what he wanted. Anyway, he was very distraught and after a bitter outburst, crying, he put his head in his hands and said to me, "I wish I had been raised a Nazi. At least I'd have something to believe in!"

I thought of him recently when I was watching one of those nature programs that was dealing with a severe problem. It seems that a group of adolescent bull elephants were rampaging, wreaking havoc among the other animals. They were wounding and killing the rhinoceroses and hippos and other animals and were quite out of control. The gamekeepers tried everything, but nothing worked. Until an old native told them what to do. So they brought in a half-dozen mature bull elephants and within two weeks things had calmed down. The old elephants were simply not going to put up with such adolescent nonsense. They restored order and the young bulls themselves were better off for it.

Human children without stewards, adults without stewards, without a reference point, fare the same way.

For ourselves, the gospel just wants to remind us all that we *do* have a reference point. We have Jesus who is the way, the truth, and the life; who said, "Come to me all you who labor and are burdened and I will refresh you." We have a reference point that tells us that we are beloved by God, that God has chosen us for a work, that we have a purpose in life, that our lives are meaningful, that we are answerable to the Master, that when we fall, there is a Divine Mercy to lift us up and that, finally, we are never alone. There is a huge community of saints who surround us, a church that invites us, and a demanding set of corporal and spiritual works of mercy that calls us beyond ourselves. That's the creed we live by, or should. That's *our* reference point.

And by our word and example we should get out the good news that, on all levels, faithful stewardship is the way to go.

I Beg to Differ

It's August but think Christmas. Think of the angelic choir singing to the shepherds, "Glory to God in the highest and peace on earth…" Think of Handel's *Messiah* and think of its majestic words, "King of Kings!" and later, "Lord of Lords!" Then quickly fast forward to today's gospel with Jesus' words, "Do you think I have come to establish peace on the earth? No, I tell you, but rather division, so that even families will be divided among themselves." Strange words from the Prince of Peace! Until you remember that in John's gospel, on the night before he died, Jesus said, "I will ask the Father and he will give you another Advocate to be with you forever. Yes, this Spirit of truth whom, alas, the world cannot receive…."

That's the key, the word "truth." Prince of Peace that he is, Jesus would nevertheless speak truth, for peace cannot be built on a lie, and his Spirit would remind us of truth—but *that*, as Jesus noted, would be precisely the problem. The world cannot receive it and so would be divided. As the old Turkish proverb puts it, "Whoever says the truth will be chased out of nine villages." The world, it seems, cannot stand too much truth and the one who speaks it will often be tossed into the cistern, as was Jeremiah in today's first reading or, like Jesus, sent off to Calvary.

The fact is, the title "Prince of Peace" never implied that Jesus was harmless. The fact is truth-telling peace would always come at a price, because it would mean we would have to give up our habitual participation in the conspiracy of silences we maintain, silences we justify by saying, "Well, we want to keep the peace. We don't want to cause division. We don't want to rock the boat." But, for example, somewhere along the line the family has to stop pretending that Mom's drinking is not really a problem, the community has to stop pretending that it doesn't harbor racism, and the nation has to stop pretending that its economy is not based on the oppression of certain groups.

Sometimes the searing spotlight of truth is forced upon us like the recent, unspeakable horror of the abuse and killing of a mother and her two daughters in Connecticut. We see now that the criminal justice system failed, and failed miserably, to treat the two monstrous perpetrators as serious offenders, despite long, long histories of continuous, multiple crimes, repeatedly setting them free each time on parole. Like the devastating collapse of the Minneapolis bridge that has thrown the spotlight on lawmakers' shameless multi-billion dollar earmarks for pet political, vote-getting projects at the expense of the more unglamorous but basic maintenance of roads and transit projects badly in need of repair and upgrading.

The divisions truth causes go on. As I speak to you, Christians in the Sudan, China, and Saudi Arabia are literally dying for their faith. That's perhaps hard for us to understand, we who, in the name of tolerance, are afraid of alienating anyone, but the fact is, there will always be a sense of exclusion for anyone who holds a truth. Orthodox Jews don't want to be forced to give up their dietary laws. Quakers don't want to be forced to serve in the military. Fundamentalist Christians don't want evolution taught to their children. We don't have to agree with them, only to acknowledge the fact that openly adhering to a belief system is what religion is all about and it *does* cause division. Yet we know that if we dare to speak truth we may earn the dreaded label of intolerant.

But we must remember that "intolerance" means disagreement with punishment, as pogroms, inquisitions, and forced sensitivity training sessions testify. True tolerance, on the other hand, is disagreement but *without* punishment. But it's still disagreement and we are right, without rancor and with charity, to make challenges and to bear witness. We can't do this, we can't set the world on fire, if we have politically corrected tolerance to mean "live and let live."

A false tolerance means no judgment, no witness, no truth, no divisions. False tolerance says, "You must approve of what I do." The Christian response is, "I must do something harder: I will love you even when your bad behavior—and it *is* that—offends me." False tolerance says, "You must agree with me." The Christian response is, "I must do something harder: I will tell you the truth because I'm convinced the truth will set you free." False tolerance says, "You must allow me to have my way." The Christian response is, "I must do something harder. I will plead with you to follow the right way because I believe you are worth the risk." False tolerance, in a word, seeks to be inoffensive; Christian tolerance takes risks. False tolerance costs nothing; Christian tolerance costs everything.

In our misguided and intimidated commitment to false tolerance we duck even the minor divisions. Unlike that famous *Saturday Evening Post* magazine cover by Norman Rockwell, we are afraid to bless ourselves and say grace at Wendy's or McDonald's, much less at an upscale restaurant lest we offend somebody. When we're greeted with the politically correct "happy holidays," we hesitate to respond with a pleasant "Merry Christmas." We send our secular friends secular Christmas cards so we won't upset them, rather than bless them from our tradition.

Some of our bedrooms are devoid of crucifixes and our homes frequently religiously sanitized so that no one who doesn't know us suspects we're Catholic. Our magazine racks contain everything from *O* to *Vogue*, *Newsweek* to *Newsday*, but nothing to hint that we are committed to a different way of life. We sometimes, even passively, participate in the worst kind of smutty conversation because walking away or protesting would make us appear intolerant or earn us unsavory labels. We're not always much good in establishing division, the line between vice and virtue, good and evil, right and wrong. We're no Rosa Parks in December 1955 who divided a nation when she offensively clung to her seat when ordered by the bus driver, J.P. Blake, to the back of the bus.

"He offended no one" is, when you think about it, a rather accusatory motto on a gravestone. And far, far from the true peace that brings division.

The fact is, we are known as much as for our silences as for our actions, for our efforts at peace as well as for the truth that divides and challenges. As another old proverb goes, "The candle says to the darkness, 'I beg to differ.'" Our Christian lives should be a candle—"Let your light shine in the darkness," Jesus said—and if the darkness is offended, so be it. Setting the earth on fire is a skill Christians have to acquire.

Saved or Spent?

Twenty-First Sunday in Ordinary Time, C, Luke 13:22–30

Way back before the anti-discrimination laws, Mrs. Rosenberg was stranded one night at a fashionable resort on Cape Cod, one that did not admit Jews. The desk clerk looked down at his book and said, 'Sorry, no room. The hotel is full."

The lady said, "But your sign says that you have vacancies."

The desk clerk stammered a bit and finally said, "Look, you know that we do not admit Jews. Please try the other side of town."

Mrs. Rosenberg stiffened. "I'll have you know I have converted to your religion."

The desk clerk replied, "Oh, yeah? Let me give you a little quiz. How was Jesus born?"

"He was born to a virgin named Mary in a little town called Bethlehem," she replied.

"Very good," the clerk said. "Tell me more."

"He was born in a manger."

"That's right," said the clerk. "And why was he born in a manger?"

Mrs. Rosenberg said loudly, "Because some idiot behind a hotel desk wouldn't give a Jewish lady a room for the night! Any more questions?"

"No."

"Didn't think so."

Then there's the story of the evangelical conference. A man was late and arrived to find the huge auditorium packed to the brim until he spotted a chair way up front. He slowly edged his way up so as not to disturb the speaker, leaned over to the woman next to it and whispered, "Is this chair saved?" She whispered back, "No, but we're praying for it."

That disposes of the issue of exclusivity, the issue about who's saved and who's not, who's in and who's out. It's a fruitless and irrelevant question, asking how many or how few, and Jesus, whose audience was very clannish, rightly ignored it. His response was to say bluntly, Forget the arithmetic and check your own behavior. God calls every human being to salvation and so the real issue is not numbers or trying to find out if we'll be in the final count, but fidelity. How have we embraced God's invitation and have we calculated the cost?

As the man replied when asked if he were saved, "I'm still trying to figure out how to be spent!" Spending is the gospel issue, not saving. Claiming kinship or proper credentials earns a withering, "I do not know you or where you're coming from if you're all saving and not spending."

Or, as Matthew's gospel has it, "As long as you did it to the least of my brethren, you did it to me"—or not, as the case may be. In other words, the crucial question is, How did you spend yourself in service to others? Or was everything saved for one's own self? Mouthing "Lord, Lord" or claiming that you shared a few drinks is not going to cut it.

And that phrase, "sharing a few drinks," allows me to move to a concrete example of one who went beyond empty words and foolish numbers. So let me introduce you to an alcoholic by the name of Matt Talbot, an Irishman who was born north of Dublin in 1856 to very poor working-class people during very hard times. Matt went to school off and on and at age twelve took his first job and his first drink. It wasn't long before the twelve-year-old was coming home drunk. Shocking, but hardly unlike today's drunken fourteen-year-olds getting off the train to go to teen night. Matt's father, himself a heavy drinker, beat him to no avail.

Matt later went to work at a brickyard and proved to be a good worker. Now in his late teens with his steady pay he, like so many others, headed for one of Dublin's two thousand pubs. Alcoholism was a major problem in Ireland and one record from 1865 showed that police arrested some 16,000 Dubliners for drunkenness, a third of them women.

No wonder alcohol was called a demon. Even though the clergy preached against intemperance, it was uphill because the laborers were paid in the pubs and so the paycheck seldom left there. Matt Talbot was in the forefront wasting his pay on drink, money desperately needed at home. His addiction was such that sometimes he sold his boots or his shirt for a drink. To feed his habit, he once even shamelessly stole a fiddle from a blind man who earned his living playing in the streets.

No one knew then that alcoholism was an illness, a terrible craving arising from a complex disease involving heredity, emotional factors, and the makeup of the brain. Way back in 1784 Dr. Benjamin Rush of Philadelphia wrote a pamphlet suggesting that alcoholism was an illness rather than a moral failing, but it took nearly two centuries, 1958, for the American Medical Association to finally get around to that opinion.

Anyway, one Saturday night Matt and his hard-drinking brothers went to the local pub. They were broke but expected their drinking buddies to treat them. They didn't. Matt was so angry that he left in a huff and trudged home and told his mother that he was so mad that he was going to take the pledge and stop drinking. His mother said, "Go in God's name, but don't take it unless you intend to keep it." Matt responded, "I'll go in God's name." His mother said as he left, "God give you the strength."

And keep it he did. From that point on he never took another drink. Withdrawal, nausea, and all the horrible aftermath followed but Matt held fast. They didn't have AA or Al-anon or the Twelve Steps in those days. No friends of a New York stockbroker and a Ohio surgeon who founded AA in 1935 were around. Matt had to go it alone. But not quite. He had God and a devotion to Mary.

Up to this point Matt had been a nominal Catholic (after all, alcohol was his god and the bar was his altar), but after his conversion, he drew close to God. He started going to daily Mass. He would kneel on the steps a half hour before church opened. He made the Stations of the Cross, prayed the rosary daily, joined Catholic sodalities, and gave much of his money to the poor. He followed ancient penitential practices, like sleeping on a plank instead of a mattress, and although barely literate, he did spiritual reading and found a wise spiritual director in a Monsignor Michael Hickey. He did this for years. A reformed alcoholic and a quiet saint on the streets of Dublin, he had no time and less patience about who is saved or not. Just prayer and service were his concerns.

Matt had a heart and kidney condition and, at age sixty-five, on Trinity Sunday, 1925, on his way to church Matt fell in the street and died. He was given the last rites, taken to hospital, but having only a rosary and a prayer book on him no one knew who he was until his sister identified him. When his body was undressed at the hospital it was found that he was wearing chains, an old form of Irish monastic asceticism. People at the hospital were astounded and soon word got out. Shortly after his death, people hearing of the chains got interested in him and stories of his holiness spread eventually right to the Vatican. He is now Venerable Matt Talbot.

"Lord, will only a few people be saved?" And Jesus said, "It's a non-question, for people will come from the east and the west, from the north and the south, from Cape Cod and Dublin, and will recline at table in the kingdom. You've been invited. How you respond, how your life is spent, not saved, is the only issue. End of discussion."

End of homily.

Hypocrisy

"Well did Isaiah prophesy about you hypocrites...."

Harsh words, but we all disdain hypocrites, people who say one thing and do another. Hypocrisy. So for our reflection today we might note that there are usually three degrees of hypocrisy. First, there is the deliberate, calculating, conscious hypocrisy. Dickens's Uriah Heep is a classic example. Second, there is the indifferent and somewhat semi-conscious hypocrisy, and third, there is the unaware hypocrisy, the hypocrisy that exists but is not yet recognized or challenged.

As for the first: In 1990, some of you more hip folks might recall, the group known as Milli Vanilli caused quite a music controversy. The duo of Rob and Fab had exploded on the pop music scene. They had five big hits, including three number-one songs. Then it was discovered that they weren't really singing on their records or at their concerts. They were simply lip-synching. The *actual* vocals were by two former American soldiers who just didn't have the "look" the record producer wanted. People in the recording industry were outraged, and Milli Vanilli had to give back the Grammy Award given to them for Best New Artist.

In today's gospel, Jesus says that the Pharisees, like Milli Vanilli, were doing an Old Testament lip-synch. They were mouthing the appropriate words, but they were not singing God's song.

This first type of hypocrisy is distasteful, to say the least, a moral fault that promotes cynicism and distrust.

The second type of hypocrisy concerns a dullness of spirit, a failure to understand the gospel fully.

246

G.K. Chesterton's ditty catches what I mean:

> The Christian Social Union
> was very much annoyed
> because there were some evils
> we really should avoid
> and so they sang another hymn
> to help the unemployed.

There's a soft hypocrisy here that's he's lampooning. Prayer that has become a mere moving of the lips with no effort to make change of heart, all talk and hymn-singing, but no action to help.

Once there was a little church situated near a bad curve in the road. Routinely accidents, some fatal, would occur and the good people of the parish would go out and generously help the victims and return to church and piously pray for them. This went on a long time; it made them feel good to do such compassionate work.

One day a visitor at the church who witnessed another accident and heard stories about all the previous ones, asked why the good people didn't go to the town hall and petition to have the road straightened out. With that simple bit of justice they wouldn't need their charity. Well, it so happened that the mayor, a parishioner, owned a very lucrative farm market right where the road needed to be adjusted, an adjustment that would reroute traffic away from his business. So, after long deliberations it was decided to leave the road as it was and the good people of the parish would go on nobly performing their charitable deeds of rescue and piously saying their prayers for the victims. It made them feel good.

This type of hypocrisy is perhaps not thought through, but it is a failure of discipleship.

Finally, there is the third type, the quite unconscious hypocrisy, one needing only a prophetic voice to call us to awareness of what's going on in our lives. Listen to this story.

Every night, when my father came home from work, he would do the same thing. I was six and every night I watched him. We lived on the second floor. I could hear him coming up the stairs before I could see him. When he came through the door, I was there. He would pat me on my crew cut and take off his hat and plop it on my head. All this was done while he was making his way toward the bedroom, while I was following, pushing the hat back to see. My father was a policeman. He carried a gun in a holster at his hip. Once as we were walking toward the bedroom, I asked him if he could draw fast enough with the gun that high. "It's not like that," he said.

On the top shelf of the closet in my mother and father's bedroom was a wooden safe. My father had it made to size and it was a snug fit, perfect height and perfect depth. On the shelf next to the safe was a key. With his back to me, my father would open the closet door, take the key off the shelf, and open the safe. Then he would take off his belt and holster and take the gun out of the holster. The holster and belt would be rolled up and stuffed way back in the safe. Then he would open the cylinder of the gun. The bullets would slide out into his free hand. He would put the bullets in a dish that was inside the safe. Then he would put the gun into the safe, lock it, and put the key on the shelf. This is what he would do every night when he came home—as I watched.

Well, one night, after he had put the bullets in the dish, he turned and walked over to me. He was holding the gun by the barrel. Without saying anything, he offered me the handle. I took it. Its heaviness surprised me. My arm fell to my side. I quickly heaved my arm up. It was all I could do to hold it upright. My father took it out of my hand, opened the cylinder, and rolled it.

"This is where the bullets go," he said. "When you pull the trigger the chambers move."

He paused. "Do you want to play with it?" he finally said.

I nodded.

He gave me the gun. "Don't pull the trigger."

I went to window and pointed the gun at the two flats next door. I looked at my father. He was watching me, but he said nothing. I went over to the bed, hid behind it, then popped up and aimed. My father said nothing.

I put the gun in my pocket and jerked it out. Fast draw. My father said, "Are you done?" I nodded and handed him the gun.

He turned and went to the safe. As he was locking the gun away, with his back to me, he said, "There. Now you don't have to be figuring out how to get it all the time."

His words stunned me. It was not because they were critical or unkind. They were not. In fact, they were said in a completely matter-of-fact voice. There was no judgment in what he said. There was something far more shocking than judgment. There was truth.

He was right. I was a junior hypocrite, pretending only to watch on the outside while plotting on the inside. The truth was, I *was* figuring out how to get it. But until he said it, I didn't know that was what I was doing. I did not know my watching was really a spying. I was "casing" the closet for a future raid, but I didn't know it. He knew me before I knew myself, and he gently showed me to myself, gently challenged my hypocrisy.

We have to be aware of this kind of subtle hypocrisy in ourselves.

So, there we are: hypocrisy—calculated, thoughtless, or hidden—but it's still hypocrisy. We need to be aware of it in our lives and align our actions with our faith, our deeds with our talk, our hearts with our image.

Moving Up Lower

Twenty-Second Sunday in Ordinary Time, C, Luke 14:1, 7–14

"On a Sabbath Jesus went to dine at the home of one of the leading Pharisees, and the people there were observing him carefully."

In Luke's original Greek, "observing him carefully" has the same meaning as Obama observing Hillary Clinton carefully or Giuliani observing Romney carefully. They were not observing to pick up pointers. They were watching carefully for their opponents to trip themselves up: some politically incorrect slip of the tongue, some gaffe, some slight contradiction. And then they would pounce. That's the "watching carefully" of the gospel. The irony, of course, was that, at the same time, Jesus was watching *them* carefully.

What he saw was the usual social climbing and jockeying for position. That's normal human pride at work and it's something to be dealt with, and so, on this level, Jesus offers some practical wisdom which adds up to, "Don't embarrass yourself. Don't sit at the head table only to be publicly escorted to the main dining room when the guest of honor arrives. Don't be like the latecomer at a wedding who sits in the empty seat in the front pew, the one reserved for the bride's mother. Don't rush into the taxi waiting to pick up a celebrity. And don't park in Father's spot!"

That's everyday etiquette advice to soften up his audience. Then Jesus hits them with the real point: Don't always invite your in-group against whom you are always measuring yourself, but measure yourself against the less fortunate; that is, let your heart, your charity, and your compassion move beyond the people who can pay you back. Jesus says in effect, "Be like your heavenly Father who sends rain on the just and unjust alike and invite the least of your brethren, those who have no voice, those who never receive an invitation and from whom nothing can be expected.

A strong gospel point, so let me give you an example of how it's done. I'll tell you about a man who heroically extended a lifelong invitation to those with absolutely nothing to offer. His name is Peter Claver, a seventeenth-century Spaniard, whose feast is on September 9. *His* invitees were slaves.

For over a thousand years, slavery, long an institution, had died out over time, slavery in Europe at least. By the twelfth century it was virtually unknown. But then, dramatically, in the fifteenth century, European exploration and exploitation of Africa, Asia, and the Americas revived the slave trade with a vengeance. The Portuguese explorers who followed the coast of Africa in search of new trade routes to Asia saw money-making opportunities everywhere they went. With their superior weapons, it was easy to conquer the local people, and it was a short step from subduing a population to enslaving them.

As one of the first new lands colonized by the Portuguese, the Canary Islands became the first place where slavery was reintroduced. But when word of the situation reached Pope Eugenius IV in 1435, he fired off a letter to the local bishop denouncing the enslavement of the Canary Islanders and demanding that they be set free. His plea fell on deaf ears as the Portuguese and then the Spanish pushed farther and farther into fabulously wealthy unknown lands and the temptation to exploit the riches of these territories through the slave labor of the local population became irresistible. Besides, the explorers argued, those American Indians, Africans, and Asians were clearly less than human, quite inferior, brutish, primitive beings. Pope Paul III fired back with a 1537 document that asserted that "the Indians themselves indeed are true men" and that "no one in any way may presume to reduce said Indians to slavery."

Forget the pope. In spite of papal condemnations, greed won out and the international slave trade flourished among Catholics and Protestants for another four hundred years and often, by the way, with the cooperation of the native blacks who grew rich by rounding up and selling their fellow citizens.

In the midst of all this, a son, Peter, was born to the Clavers, a farming family who worked the land in the province of Catalonia in Spain. He was a bright, religious lad, but like Hamlet, he found it very hard ever to make a decision and stick with it. His parents eventually sent Peter to a school run by the Jesuits in Barcelona. At that time the Jesuits were still a relatively new religious order in the Catholic Church. They soon became not only renowned teachers and shock troops against the Protestant Reformation, but famous as missionaries and convert makers as well.

Such an active, exciting, varied life appealed to Peter. He talked a lot about joining but could never quite commit himself. Finally, after vacillating for several years, Peter Claver asked to be received as a Jesuit novice. But, typical Peter, he had barely entered the novitiate when he began once more to second-guess himself. What if he was not cut out for an active life as a missionary or parish priest? Maybe this, maybe that. He drove everyone crazy.

Fortunately, help was nearby in the person of the college doorkeeper, a seventy-two-year-old lay brother named Alphonsus Rodriguez. Brother Alphonsus had had a family and a career, but after his wife and children all died, he gave up his business and entered the religious life. Although he was a Jesuit brother now, he hadn't lost his ability, cultivated over many years as a businessman, to judge character. Nor had he lost his knack for handling a customer who couldn't decide what he wanted. So it was Brother Alphonsus who assured Peter that he did indeed belong with the Jesuits and, moreover, that Peter should ask his superiors to send him to the Americas as a missionary. Peter was stunned. But Brother Alphonsus insisted that the way to overcome fear and indecision is make a bold move.

So Peter summoned up his courage and asked his superiors to assign him to the American mission. They gave their consent and sent him to Cartagena, Colombia, as an unordained novice.

Now Cartagena's location on the Caribbean Sea made it one of the principal ports for the slave trade in the New World: twelve thousand enslaved Africans were unloaded in Cartagena every year. You can imagine that, after weeks crammed together in the dark holds of the slave ships, these tragic people were filthy, weak from hunger and dehydration, and half mad with fear. Many were sick. Some were dying. Yet, whatever their condition, all were driven like cattle into holding pens near the dock to be sorted out and sold later. The only white man who treated the Africans kindly was a

Jesuit priest, Father Alphonsus de Sandoval. When he heard the roar of the harbor cannon that signaled the arrival of another slave ship, Father de Sandoval gathered up food, water, and medicine and hurried down to the harbor. The comforts Father de Sandoval could offer the Africans were meager, yet he cared for his "parishioners," as he called them, day after day until they had all been sold off and the pen was empty.

When Peter Claver, the apprehensive new Jesuit recruit from Spain, arrived in Cartagena, Father de Sandoval made him his assistant. At first glance it would appear that the priest had made a terrible mistake. Yet this turned out to be the turning point for Peter. The work in the slave pen transformed him, this well-off, middle-class young man. Once he recognized that he could do something for God and his fellow man, all doubts, all qualms, all uncertainties vanished. He asked his superiors in Cartagena to ordain him and to permit him to serve the slaves. A saint-in-the-making had been born. He would spend the rest his life inviting to the Lord's banquet the poor, the crippled, the blind—those who could never repay.

Every time a slaver sailed into Cartagena's harbor, Peter took the pilot's boat out to the ship and began his work at once down in the hold. On shore, as sailors and soldiers herded the slaves into the pens, Peter went with them. Over the years he built up a team of interpreters who could speak the languages of Guinea, the Congo, and Angola, the lands from which most of the captives came. Through his interpreters Peter tried to comfort the Africans and learn what they needed. Every day Peter and his interpreters returned with more food, more water, more medicines, and as he treated the Africans, he explained to them the basics of the Catholic faith. It is said that during the forty-four years Father Claver served in the slave pens, he baptized over one hundred thousand Africans. Whatever the number of converts may have been, Peter regarded them as his parishioners. He kept up a steady round of visitations, saying Mass for his converts, bringing them the sacraments, and continuing their religious instruction.

No surprise, Peter Claver's devotion to his African converts enraged the white population of Cartagena. The charges: He was keeping slaves from their work. He was contaminating churches and chapels with his congregations of unwashed Africans. He was profaning the Blessed Sacrament by giving Communion to these "animals." Some well-born ladies even refused to enter a church if Father Claver had said Mass there for slaves. Even some of Peter's brother Jesuits thought he was excessively devoted to the Africans. No matter. After years of wavering, Peter Claver had found his vocation, and he would not be deterred from it.

Peter kept up his exhausting routine until one day, when he was seventy-four years old, he collapsed in the slave pen. Back at the Jesuit residence he lay on his deathbed, abandoned by the white Christians of Cartagena. The only one who tried to nurse the dying man was an African servant. The end came quickly. Late in the evening on September 7, 1654, Peter Claver received the last sacraments, then fell unconscious and died shortly after midnight. A crowd of slaves broke down the gates of the Jesuit residence so they could see their saint one last time.

On January 15, 1888, the people of Rome witnessed a double canonization as Pope Leo XIII declared that Peter Claver and Alphonsus Rodriguez, banquet throwers for the poor, were saints.

And that, my parishioners, is this gospel of the Lord.

"Oh"

*"You gave me no water, you gave me no kiss, you did not anoint
my head."*

To get across my double message today, let me share some obtuse moments
from my past.

When I was a little boy there was a man who lived on our street, a Mr.
Hill. He used to walk his dog by the house The dog was as old as he was and
they shuffled along together at a slow pace. The little dog had a harness and a
leash. The leash was not to control the dog but to find it. Every afternoon he
came along, but one day my mother said, "Mr. Hill hasn't been by today."

"You probably missed him," I said.

The next afternoon my mother said, "I didn't see him today either. I'm
afraid he's sick." So the next afternoon when I came in, my mother said, "I
want you to take this down and see Mr. Hill." She had wrapped an apple
pie from our bakery shop. He was not ill but I discovered what the problem
was. When I went inside the door I saw a little harness that had been on the
dog hanging on a nail.

We visited a bit. He was alone. When I got back home I, with a kid's
black-and-white mentality, asked my mom a kid's naïve question, "What's
he being punished for? I never see anybody there. I never see any cars. I
never see anybody come from the church. What's he being punished for?"

And my mom said, "You see, what he did was, he got old."

I said, "Oh."

Then there was Mrs. Patterson, a pillar of our church, Sacred Heart, in
New Brunswick. I remember as a boy I caught the flu or something. In any

case, I had to stay at home for five days. Each day I looked out the window and would watch Mrs. Patterson go out for her mail. The rural mailbox was a bit high for her. She would open up the lid and reach inside. Then she would go inside her house and get a stool and bring it out and step up on it and forage inside, in case there was some piece of mail stuck near the back. There was never anything there except a few advertisements. Sometimes I would see the mailman coming and he would stop and flip through his bundle, shake his head, and then move on. Nothing for Mrs. Patterson.

For five days I saw her shuffle to the mailbox. For five days I saw her mount the stool searching and come up empty. For five days I saw the mailman shake his head and move on.

When I went to church the next time I asked our pastor the same naïve question. "Mrs. Patterson, what'd she do wrong?"

He said, "Arthritis. She's not able to get up the church steps."

I said, "Oh."

When I grew up I was still short on wisdom. Years ago, after I had preached at a certain parish, a woman invited me to lunch. She was a widow and was alone. We went into the house and she told me, "Go into the den and read the paper or watch TV. I'll have it ready in a minute." She put on her apron and she busied herself in the dining room.

I saw where she had gone, so I went in there and said, "Now, Marie, don't fix up all this. We can eat in the kitchen. That's where I always eat." But she ignored me and pulled out a drawer in the dining room, a buffet or sideboard or whatever you call it. She took out napkins and linens. She put the cloth on, the napkins on, and then opened a beautiful case with curved glass and took out stemmed glasses.

She wiped the dust out and I said again, "Look, really, don't fuss. I eat in the kitchen at home all the time." Ignoring me, she went right on. Again I tried, "Look, I mean, after all, it's just the two of us. I really *am* used to eating in the kitchen." She turned around and with a level gaze said to me, "Father, will you shut up and sit down!" Startled, I said, "Well, if that's what you want." She said evenly, "Do you have any idea what it's like fixing a meal for one?"

I said, "Oh."

And so we ate in the dining room with stemmed glasses and candles and linens.

Three people: Mr. Hill, Mrs. Patterson, Marie. Once active people, active parishioners. They all made the mistake of getting old or sick or widowed, and so a world that thrives on "what have you done for me lately" forgot them. The church forgot them. And *that*, I think, is what separates us from the saints. Saints remember. Saints take to heart the words from the epistle attributed to St. James (2:14): "What good is it, my brothers and sisters, if you say you have faith but do not have works? Can faith save you? If a brother or sister is ill-clothed and lacks daily food and one of you says to them, 'Go in peace, keep warm and have your fill' and yet you do not supply their bodily needs, what is the good of that?"

Indeed, what good are mere words? Saints wed word and action. They wash, they kiss, they anoint. And a nice side effect—to move to my second point—is that those saints who act on their faith beget other saints. People become saints because they meet saints, not because they read books.

Author Robert Ellsberg is typical when he tells of his own spiritual journey that took him, a college dropout, to the Catholic Worker "house of hospitality" on Manhattan's Lower East Side. He was searching for meaning beyond books and lectures. He was wary of his self-centeredness and wanted to give himself to something larger than himself. That's what brought him to the Catholic Worker's outreach. Well, he wound up staying there for five years and eventually he found what he had been seeking. He also became a Catholic, but not because he comprehended Catholicism intellectually. Rather, as he wrote: "The attraction of Catholicism had little to do with doctrine or the church's teaching authority, of which I comprehended very little. It had much more to do with the wisdom and example of its saints."

Jack Casey was employed as an emergency worker on an ambulance rescue squad. When Jack was a child, he had oral surgery. Five teeth were to be pulled under general anesthetic, and Jack was fearful. What he remembers most, though, was the operating room nurse who, sensing the boy's terror, said, "Don't worry, I'll be right here beside you no matter what happens." When Jack woke up after the surgery, she was true to her word, standing right there with him.

Nearly twenty years later, Jack's ambulance team is called to the scene of a highway accident. A truck has overturned, the driver is pinned in the cab and power tools are necessary to get him out. However, gasoline is dripping onto the driver's clothes, and one spark from the tools could have spelled disaster. The driver is terrified, crying out that he is scared of dying. So Jack crawls into the cab next to him and says, "Look, don't worry, I'm right here with you; I'm not going anywhere." And Jack was true to his word; he stayed with the man until he was safely removed from the wreckage. Later the truck driver told Jack, "You were an idiot; you know that the whole thing could have exploded, and we'd have both been burned up!" Jack told him that he felt that he just couldn't leave him.

Many years before Jack had been treated compassionately by the nurse, and because of that experience, he could now show that same compassion to another. Grace is contagious.

So, back to my double-message personal stories: There are people who are lonely and needy. They were once shakers and movers and now they simply shake and move slowly. They are feeble or alone. We must raise our gospel sensitivity and minister to the has-beens, the invisible, the forgotten. Secondly, we must do so because there is a desperate need for models of caring and compassion in our world of "Me First."

Being reminded of that should lead us to say, "Oh."

Shoot the Lawyer

Twenty-Third Sunday in Ordinary Time, C, Luke 14:25–33

Question: You are stuck in an elevator with a tiger, a lion, and a lawyer. You have a gun with just two bullets in it. What do you do? *Answer:* Shoot the lawyer twice to make sure he's dead. With apologies to the lawyers here; it could have been any public professional. With this joke I wanted to make a point as a way of understanding today's outrageous gospel. So listen up.

First, notice that as soon as I started my introduction, you immediately and unconsciously suspended judgment. You knew right off that I wasn't speaking factually or literally. After all, a tiger and a lion in an elevator? You're carrying a gun? A lawyer present? Violence? No, you sensed right away that a story or joke was coming and so you automatically shifted perception gears as you waited for the punch line. You knew we were in storyland, not newspaper land. And we all enjoyed the joke and laughed because deep down it touched our hidden universal disdain for sleazy and unprincipled lawyers or politicians or whoever, and it was our way of getting back at them.

You've got something like this going on in the gospel, a gospel that, startlingly, has a loving Jesus preaching hate as he announces to the crowd following him that unless they hate their parents and family they can't be counted as his disciples. What kind of talk is that? It's elevator talk, if you will. It's ancient non-literal Semitic talk, the kind of exaggeration or hyperbole a first-century Jew would use to press a deeper point, like "If your eye is a source of scandal, pluck out; your hand, cut it off."

So what precisely is that deeper point here? It is one, as a matter of fact, repeatedly made by Jesus here and there in the gospels. In one place, Jesus said to leave father and mother and possessions behind and come, follow him. In another, when his mother and relatives want to see him he turns and waving his arms around to the crowd asks, "Who are my real mother and brothers and sisters?" And he answers his own question by saying, "Those who hear the word of God and act on it." And another time when someone shouts, "Blessed is the womb that bore you and the breasts at which you nursed," Jesus counters, "Rather, blessed are those who hear the word of God and observe it."

All these sayings, in one way or another, affirm that it is not blood ties that bind one to Jesus, but rather obedient response to the word he proclaims. And that's the message you get once more in today's gospel with its exaggerated talk of hating one's family and renouncing possessions. Underneath it's about commitment, observing priorities, allegiance. The bottom-line challenge to us is this: What is the cost to us of being a Christian? Has our fidelity to the gospel ever cost us money, reputation, the possibility of advancement, property, and even family harmony?

I have a friend who is a junior executive at a big company. She happened to mention a point from a homily she had heard the previous Sunday. Well, you'd think she had belched in public. Everyone around her reacted as if she had dropped from some weird planet and said disdainfully, "*You* go to church?"

Some years ago a radio station invited people to call in and tell them the first thing they said when they woke in the morning. The responses, as desired, were usually funny: "Do I smell the coffee burning?" "Honey, did I remember to put out the dog last night?" One morning the station phone rang and the perky DJ said his usual, "Good morning. This is station FM 106. You're on the air. What's the first thing you said when you rolled out of bed this morning?" A voice with a very pronounced Bronx accent said, "Hear, O Israel, the Lord our God is one; you shall love your God with all your heart, with all your soul, with all your mind, and with all your strength." He was, of course, a devout Jew reciting the Jewish *Shema*, or holiness prayer. The DJ didn't know how to handle this and, after a moment of embarrassed silence, said, "Sorry, wrong number," hung up on him, and cut to a commercial.

Then there's Elizabeth Ann Seton from high society, linked to the first families of New York, married at nineteen, and who eventually found herself at age thirty widowed and penniless, with five small children to support. While in Italy with her dying husband, she met several Catholic families whose kindness, charity, and devotion impressed her. In March 1805 she became a Catholic. By and by she lost a husband and two daughters and bore the cross of a wayward son.

She went on to found the first American Catholic community of sisters in America and she also opened the first Catholic school and Catholic orphanage. She is, as you know, the first American-born citizen to be canonized. But it wasn't easy, and she knew this gospel well. Perhaps her hardest cross was when she first became a Catholic and many of her family and friends turned their backs on her. But she clung to her newfound faith. She was forced to accept the "hate" of her family in order to be a disciple.

The gospel message is cost. Being ridiculed, being called a wrong number. Does being a Christian cost us anything? Look back over the past week or month and examine your life. Ask yourself: Was there any time you felt you had to pay a price, even a small one, for being a Christian? Think about it.

Remember South African writer Alan Paton's story about Robert Mansfield? Mansfield was a white man in South Africa and headmaster of a white school who took his athletic teams to play cricket and hockey against the black schools. That is, until the department of education forbade him to do it any more. So he resigned in protest. Shortly after, Emmanuel Nene, a leader in the black community, came to meet him. He said, "I've come to see a man who resigns his job because he doesn't wish to obey an order that will prevent children from playing with one another."

"I resigned because I think it is time to go out and fight everything that separates people from one another. Do I look like a knight in shining armor?"

"Yes, you look like a knight in shining armor, but you are going to get wounded. Do you know that?"

"I expect that may happen," Mansfield replied.

"Well," Nene said, "you expect correctly. People don't like what you are doing, but I am thinking of joining with you in the battle."

"You're going to wear the shining armor, too?" Mansfield asked.

"Yes, and I'm going to get wounded, too. Not only by the government, but also by my own people as well."

"Aren't you worried about the wounds?"

"I don't worry about the wounds. When I get up there, which is my intention, the Big Judge will say to me, 'Where are your wounds?' and if I say, 'I haven't any,' he will say, 'Was there nothing to fight for?' I couldn't face that question."

Is there nothing to fight for? Or as the gospel would put it, is there nothing worth being hated for?

Who Do You Say I Am?

Twenty-Fourth Sunday in Ordinary Time, B, Mark 8:27–35

That's an interesting question in today's gospel: "Who do you say that I am?" Have you ever tried to answer that question? Who do *you* think Jesus is? Think!

Down through the centuries there have been a thousand answers. Jesus in fact has been like a living Rorschach test: Everyone tends to see him as they are, as they want him, need him, to be. Every era, in short, makes Jesus over to its own image and likeness. So, in one era, Jesus is a fearsome deity like Zeus waiting to hurl lightning bolts; or he is a suffering servant in agony on a wooden crossbeam; in another era, he is a manicured man hanging from a $22,000 gold cross from Tiffany's.

For some he is the Jewish version of Che Guevara, a revolutionary promoting violence. He is a capitalist. He is a philosopher. He is a social worker. He is the Long Ranger riding in to save us from danger. For moderns, he is the Godspell hippie. He is Superstar, Aquarian, the blond Nordic, the neat guy playing the outfield with the kids. He is Dear Abby, Dr. Phil, dispensing warm fuzzies. He is androgynous, he is gay, he is a Hollywood idol, the soft-curled hermaphrodite found on cards, calendars, and crafts—you name it.

Our current age is no exception to the self-projection rule. For us today, as George Carlin would have it, he is Jesus Lite. Yes, Jesus is our buddy, the friend who gives a thumbs-up and winks. He is sweet, non-judgmental, a "live-and-let-live" kind of a guy. A pussycat. A heck of a nice fella, but not one who, in the long run, really inspires you and certainly not someone you would die for—or live for, for that matter.

Very recently the *National Study of Youth and Religion* was published; it is the largest study of religious practices among American youth to date.

The study, which surveyed 3200 American teenagers by phone and interviewed more than 250 in face-to-face conversation, reports good news: Adolescents are not hostile toward religion. The reason teenagers are not hostile to religion? Because they have no reason to be. According to the vast majority of teenagers interviewed for this study, religion is simply not a big deal and, except for the evangelical kids, Jesus is not a big deal, and, although an important person, he is not very strong, not very challenging, and certainly not demanding. Professor Kenda Creasy Dean, Associate Professor of Youth, Church, and Culture at Princeton Theological Seminary, reports that in her classes she hears young people casually say, "Well, it doesn't really matter. Everyone goes to heaven when they die. Jesus forgives everything we do in the end."

Isn't that comforting? What an easygoing Jesus! And when asked to describe this gentle Jesus, students, just like their parents would, write on the blackboard words like, "loving, forgiving, kind, friendly, merciful, generous." Bottom line? You couldn't ask for a nicer guy. You wonder: Just who *is* this Jesus, this wan, sweetheart of a man, this overgrown sponge the youth describe and we embrace? He's nothing like the gospels tell us.

Youth, by definition, is passionate and we serve them up a passionless Jesus, one full of platitudes but no prickles, crèches but no crosses? Youth want to make a difference and we offer them lifeless liturgies. They don't want to be told simply to go to church or increase their donations. They want a hands-on experience of feeding the poor. They are generous. They want authenticity, which is why for years a million of them on World Youth Day flock to a septuagenarian pope. He stands for something. They want a hero, and we give them a toothy Paul Lynde with a halo.

This soft version is not a Jesus to get excited about, get passionate about. I tell you, the bland, cool Jesus we embrace ourselves and offer our young people is not the awesome one of the gospels. He's not the one we find there who came to bring a sword, not peace, or who shouted at us to tear out our eye if it was accessing porn on the internet. He is not the one who told us to shun the revenge and violence so dear to the TV, movies, and video games, to turn our one cheek when the other is slapped, to offer no resistance, to feed the hungry, give drink to thirsty, clothe the naked of the world, visit the imprisoned, and forgive Saddam Hussein from the bottom of our hearts. Or else, no doubt about it, we're going to burn in hell. This very unbland Jesus said all this. It's right there in the gospels: Matthew 25.

In constructing our colorless Jesus you would think we had never heard his sharp words on Sundays about the doomed, materialistic rich man and Lazarus, about the Son of Man who casts evildoers into eternal fire (Mt 13:42), the Lord who hands the unjust servant over to the torturers (Mt 18:34), and tosses the man without the wedding garment into the outer darkness (Mt 22:13). How about his unnerving parables of the Master who cuts into pieces the faithless servant (Mt 24:51) and throws into outer darkness the parsimonious servant (Mt 25:30)? Or, in Luke's version: "But as for those enemies of mine who did not want me to be king over them, bring them here and slaughter them in my presence" (Lk 19:27)? How about his pointed words, "What does it profit us if we gain the whole world and lose our very souls?"

You think we never heard Jesus telling stories about destroying nasty tenants (Mk 12:9), declaring that unbelievers will have to endure God's wrath (Jn 3:36), that he has come to set a son against his father and a daughter against her mother (Mt 10:34–35). This so-called sweet Jesus calls his opponents liars (Jn 8:55) and has a sustained role as terrible judge in the book of Revelation (1:13–14; 1:16; 19:15, 19:17–18).

Would this kind of Jesus go to Atlantic City? I don't think so. Unless it were to sit in the middle of the road with a half-fed child between his knees, midway between the casinos and the squalor a few blocks away in silent witness until they carried him away for disturbing the peace. The Jesus of the gospels is countercultural and brave and courageous and strong and determined—or he would never have endured his excruciating passion and death. And after his resurrection he proudly wore his scars as a sign that the kingdom of God is won with a lot of sweat, not given.

He's about a way of life. He's about the decisions we make at business and school. He's about honesty and caring and concern for others. He's about whistle-blowing and ethics. He's about chastity and fidelity. He's about truth. He's about making relationships work. He's about keeping one's word. He's about life, life here and hereafter, for those who listen to him, and not much life for those who don't.

And he's principled as well as merciful; demanding as well as forgiving, provided we repent; full of love indeed, but a tough love that is *not* content to look the other way but which desperately wants us to grow, to be decent, to be holy, to be saints. He will settle for nothing less. *That's* the Jesus of tradition, of the gospels, quite different from our rose-colored image of him. Look, if we don't have this kind of a Jesus worth dying for, then he is not worth living for either and our youth, alas, have not met that Jesus and I wonder if we have.

"Who do you say that I am?" What would you say to him? How do you depict Jesus? I want you to wrestle with this question all week. When you meet with friends, discuss it. At the lunch break, discuss it. Around the table, discuss it. See if the Jesus you know excites you, challenges you, makes you very nervous with his demands, yet at the same time makes you want to know more about him and follow him and love him. A lot rides on your answer to his question: Who do you say that I am?

Divine Obsession

We have today's familiar gospel about a sheep, a coin, and a son. Now right at the beginning let me tell you up front that the focus of all three parables is not on the sheep, the coin, or the son but on the shepherd, the housekeeper, and the Father—all three being the same seemingly obsessed figure we call God. That having been said, let's detour to take a look at some intriguing biblical background beginning with that dinner party where these stories were first told.

The Pharisees were fuming. But these Pharisees were not scandalized that Jesus was not observing food purity regulations. They didn't care about that. Rather, in ancient times, it was understood that likes eats with likes; that is to say, meals were a way of celebrating group cohesion. The Pharisees were upset then because Jesus was identifying with obvious sinners and extending membership in his kingdom to them. And, what was worse, they observed, he wasn't even asking them to make restitution—especially those notoriously corrupt tax collectors who by all accounts should restore their extorted money.

Not that Jesus was indifferent to that, but that was not the point at the moment. The point was that by choosing to eat with them at all Jesus was, as we say, making a statement. He was saying that sinners who heeded and needed him, regardless for the moment if they repented or made restitution, would be included in the call to the kingdom of God. "I have not come to call the righteous but sinners." *That* upset the Pharisees: Jesus' guest list, his eating buddies, his roll call, not food etiquette.

Second, I can't let this pass by: you shouldn't miss Jesus' implied insult to the Pharisees. Looking them straight in the eye he begins, "What man among you having a hundred sheep…" This zinger is lost on us but think of it: Jesus is inviting the proud Pharisees to imagine themselves as lowly shepherds. "How nice," we think. That's because we have been raised on romanticized Christmas cards and think shepherds are adorable. But in reality shepherds in Jesus' time were as popular as child molesters. They were thought to be dishonest and thieving, poaching on other people's lands, stealing their sheep. They were scum. To ask the Pharisees, then, to imagine *themselves* as shepherds is like asking the governing board of the ACLU to imagine themselves as traditional Catholics.

But let's move on to the parables themselves. The first parable of the lost sheep assumes the common custom of several shepherds caring for a large flock, so leaving the ninety-nine in the care of others to search for the lost one was sensible and expected. The main focus of the story, however, is the effort of the shepherd. He would have to traverse over craggy hillsides and deep ravines, rocks and stones, and search dangerous caves, all the while keeping an eye open for predators. And finally to carry back a sixty- or seventy-five-pound sheep on one's shoulders over such ground is no small thing. The point of the story is the exhausting effort, the drive, the sacrifice, the dedication, the passion of the shepherd for one lost sheep. Keep that in mind.

The second parable of the woman of the lost coin is a variation on the shepherd story. Once again, notice, the emphasis is on the great effort the woman expands to find it. I want to remind you that houses in the first century were dark. They had small high windows and very little light. The woman has to use up expensive precious oil to search. Moreover, floors were packed dirt and had cracks and corners making seeing very difficult. Yet, she looked and looked. Again, the point is the enormous amount of energy she spends in searching. Are you starting to get the picture?

The third, last and most famous parable is that of the Prodigal Son story. Again, he is not the point. The Father and his efforts are. We are asked to imagine his going outside every night to watch for a hoped-for son who never comes. His sleepless nights. His anxiety. Until one day, just when he's given up, he spots a figure. It's his son turning into the farm and the father himself, an old man, forgets his dignity and runs down the stony path through prickly bushes, out of breath to embrace his son and, like Jesus at the dinner table, does not even allow for any apology or a repentance speech but silences his son's stammerings with kisses. Right now, all that counts is that the son is home and the family household is complete. Again, the emphasis is on the worriment, the concern and the effort of the Father.

I tell you, whenever I hear these parables I think of Francis Thompson's famous and memorable poem. It centers around this very theme of divine pursuit. He called it, fittingly, "The Hound of Heaven." In the poem he compares Jesus to a bloodhound who won't let go of the trail no matter what it cost him even as he, the poet, slipping into drugs and alcoholism and all kinds of evil, flees him and leads him on a merry chase. He writes:

> I fled Him—Jesus, the Hound—I fled Him down
> > the nights and down the days;
> I fled Him down the arches of the years;
> I fled Him down the labyrinthine ways
> Of my own mind; and in the mist of tears
> I hid from him…
> …From his strong feet that followed, followed after.
> But with unhurrying chase
> And unperturbed pace
> Deliberate speed, majestic instancy
> They beat….

At the end of the poem the poet, lying sick and exhausted on the ground in a dirty alley, sees Christ, the Hound of Heaven, standing, panting over him. The tireless Hound of Heaven has finally cornered his prey. The Hound of Heaven is none other than the shepherd, the woman, and the Prodigal Father.

I think, when I hear these parables, of how many people waste their time trying to earn forgiveness and reconciliation. They plot and plan. How can I get back with God, what steps must I take? Do I begin with prayer? Do I go see a priest? These parables tell us: stop trying to earn reconciliation. Just abandon yourself to God's searching mercy. God is seeking you more than you are seeking God so "here I am as I am" is all one can say or need say. This gospel is indeed a deep, profound revelation about an obsessed God.

Let me end with a little biblical insight on this very point. In ancient times the numbers ten and a hundred were symbolic numbers denoting completeness. That is why the shepherd simply had to leave the ninety-nine to find the single lost one because otherwise his flock would not be complete and that was intolerable. So too with the woman. It wasn't the amount of the coin that mattered. It was that things just weren't right with only nine coins. They weren't complete. Something was off center. And the father: the household was incomplete with one of its members missing and that was driving him to distraction.

Thus these parables seem to be depicting God as anxious as the shepherd, the housekeeper, and the father that all should be just right, complete, and imply that God's a nervous wreck until they are. That's what makes these parables, in the last analysis, mind-blowing stories about God's passion—or shall we say "obsession"?—for you and for me. It is, when you think of it, an overwhelming and humbling thought, and, I would add, a motive for surrender.

A Trickster Tale

Ever since it was told, this parable has driven everyone crazy, including the people who wrote it down. All kinds of face-saving interpretations have been offered throughout the centuries to try to explain away Jesus commending a crook. None of these explanations are completely satisfactory and I think we just have to live with its perplexing challenge.

But among the various guesses there is one educated guess I find more appealing than the others and would like to share with you. It is this: long before Luke wrote this gospel, in his world there was an ancient and venerable tradition of what we call "trickster" tales. That is, stories that for the moment neatly reversed the accepted power structure. Kings fell, slaves rose. The powerful with their armies failed, the servant with the quick wit succeeded. That sort of thing. So Aesop's fables, for example, which go way back before Luke, were telling tales of servants who fell into a master's disfavor and by cleverness and cunning, which the master grudgingly admired, not only restored themselves but gained higher positions and responsibilities.

The Old Testament has its share of "trickster" stories. Joseph the slave in Egypt who rises to royal position and power by interpreting the Pharaoh's dreams while the wise men couldn't, and the shepherd boy who was first passed over and becomes King David are such stories.

In folklore there is Wart, the lowly page, who pulls out the sword and becomes King Arthur, while the mighty warriors fail to do so. Scullery maid Cinderella marries the prince. Coyote and Brer Rabbit outfox the fox. Brash con man Groucho Marx as Dr. Hugo Z. Hackenbush bedazzles aristocratic Margaret Dumont. Eliza Doolittle sings "Just you wait 'enry 'iggins, just you wait" and recounts how one day their positions will be reversed.

The trickster tales, often humorous, provide us with the fantasy that, just for once, everything is turned upside down, the powerful get their come-up-pance while the powerless rise to the top, masters are conned and servants are masters. That's why we delight at those vaudeville-like exchanges:

Officer: "Sailor, do you have change for a dollar?"
Sailor: "Sure, buddy."
Officer: "That's no way to address an officer! Now let's try that again! Sailor, do you have change for a dollar?"
Sailor: "No, SIR!"

Or: "What's wrong, doctor? You look puzzled."
"I can't figure out exactly what's wrong with you. I think it's the result of heavy drinking."
"Well, then, I'll just come back when you're sober."

A little drum roll as we enjoy the tables turned. As peasant girl Mary wistfully sang to her cousin Elizabeth in Luke's gospel, "He has lifted up the lowly and put down the mighty."

So, back to this parable. Read in the light of a trickster tale, the storyline is that the servant has manipulated his master's money and is summarily dismissed, as he should have been. He did an immoral deed. So out of a job, ashamed to beg, and unable to dig, what does the wily servant do? He adds insult to injury. Knowing that his master's debtors have not yet heard about his dismissal, he quickly calls upon them. They in turn, thinking he still is legitimately acting on behalf of the master, are delighted when they are called in one by one to rewrite the terms of the notes more favorable to themselves.

The deed is done, and now—and here is the heart of the matter—the master, when he finds out he has been tricked, is caught in a bind. Being very much a macho Mediterranean man, he can't very well lose face and let his debtors know that his dishonest servant pulled a fast one on him, had outfoxed him, had shamed him. He has a reputation to maintain and doesn't want to be known as a fool who can't even control his own servant. In a word, he's been had and he has to live with it.

The servant scored one on the master, the lowly over the great. More than that, the master later reconsiders it all, looks at his servant with a wry smile, and commends the servant, "Well, I've got to hand it to you. I guess if I were in your shoes I would act the same way." And the devious servant bows and turns away with a smile on *his* face. We presume the master kept him on.

Now the thing to note is that in Jesus' parable, the servant plays the role of a trickster. That is to say, the servant is portrayed not necessarily as a decent person to be imitated in his moral conduct, but rather as one more example of someone who subverts normal expectations and in *this* role he is commended because he sounds a familiar gospel theme, one we've heard often before. You know: the first—the master—will be last and the last—the servant—will be first; sinners will enter the kingdom before the so-called righteous. Those invited to the banquet will be excluded, the bums in the alleys will take their place. The boastful Pharisee up front will not enter the kingdom, the lowly publican in back striking his breast will. Rich Dives will wind up in hell; poor Lazarus, in Abraham's bosom.

And so here also. The message is this: In Jesus Christ's tricky kingdom be prepared to expect and do the unexpected and put one over on the so-phisticates, the scoffers, the movers and the shakers. Be spiritually clever and live by the surprises of the gospel where people forgive seventy times seven, go two miles when forced to go one, return good for evil, pray for enemies, choose the last place, wash feet like a slave, and throw banquets for those who can never possibly repay. *That* will turn things upside down and unnerve your worldly masters.

Why? Because, to their amazement, you chose the road less traveled. You choose to live the paradoxes of the gospel and to that degree, in gospel terms, you have acted prudently.

Jesus and Warren Buffett

This is a very visual, very powerful gospel with an old, old pedigree. A similar storyline of a rich man and a poor man having their positions reversed in another world can be commonly found in ancient Egypt, Greece, and Rome. Jesus probably knew these stories and gave his own twist to them.

The contrasting details are strong: the rich man, to whom St. Jerome in the fourth century gave the name of Dives, is dressed in royal purple. The only purple Lazarus has is his ulcerated sores. The rich man has plenty to eat. Lazarus has to compete for food with the dogs. The rich man lets the scraps from his dinner fall to the ground. For Lazarus, the scraps *are* his dinner. And, you should know, those scraps were not leftover food. No, they were edible "napkins." That is, the diners would wipe their hands and mouths with loose bread and then throw these scraps down on the floor where they were swept outside. Lazarus was glad to eat these discarded bits of bread still smelling of Dives's breath and stained with food.

Lazarus was poor. We're not told how he became poor. We can only surmise that the original hearers of this parable probably saw him as the usual victim of over-taxation or famine or, more likely, the victim of a powerful landowner who cheated him out of his land, reduced him to a tenant and finally to the precarious status of a day laborer hanging out, like some of the migrant workers of today, waiting for someone to come along and hire him. In any case, it seems he was at the bottom of a downward spiral.

Dives was rich. We are not told how he became rich and we must not assume it was by dishonest means. And the judgment given him was not that he was rich or that being rich was a moral fault, for in the Bible possessions themselves were not good or evil. What counted was what one did with them. That's where Dives fails. His fault was his self-indulgence brought on by his blindness.

And here the parable by its very nature quickly escalates—somewhat uncomfortably—into our lives. We are reluctant to acknowledge it, but like Dives we too are caught in a self-indulgent world. It's not just that Leona Helmsley left her dog twelve million dollars or the duPont "registry for the ultra affluent" has offerings like a $30,000 platinum cell phone, a $1 million Patek Phillippe watch, a $2 million luxury sports car, and $300 million yachts or that, inevitably, human beings have also become commodities so that we can buy human ova and sperm, rent wombs, trade in human organs, and sell persons, the latter exchange more specifically known as trafficking.

It's not just these gross realities. It's that Lazarus still lives and we don't like to admit that. He lives in the children who are dying each day from hunger, abuse, disease, and neglect; in the refugees and people displaced by war and repressive governments; in the homeless on the streets; in hospitals and convalescent homes where no one visits; in those uninsured and in the one billion really poor of this globe at the bottom of the pile.

And then there's that door symbolism. *"And lying at his door was a poor man named Lazarus."* The door, the gate, the barrier so that one doesn't see the other. Out of sight, out of mind. That is, as we indicated, Dives's besetting sin: moral blindness. He lives in a social cocoon. He lives in a gated community, socializes with his circle of like-established friends, converses with his equals, dines with his companions, and lives, like his children, if he has any, with a very strong sense of entitlement. Just as we do. *Of course* he'll buy his son a new car upon graduation from high school. *Of course* his daughter will have the latest laptop. *Of course* they will have high definition TV. *Of course* they will vacation in the Bahamas. The "of courses," the taken-for-granted entitlements, keep Dives and his family and friends self-focused, self-enclosed, self-enchanted. They never met a poor person. How could they?

Like ourselves, they are good people. That's not the issue. The issue is that, behind the high walls of privilege and high consumerism they are blind to the needs of others. The gospel parable is telling us that it should not be this way for him or for us. Every now and then—like now when we are apart from our homes and toys and under the scrutiny of the Lord—we should look up from our affluence and see, notice Lazarus.

We don't normally see him because we also live in a highly segregated society. We are balkanized into low-scale or upscale housing developments, socially defined neighborhoods, day care and nursing homes, school systems, income brackets, and brand names. It is sobering to think that we live in a country where, combined, the top 400 wealthiest people have as much money as the lowest 210 million. These poor are invisible to us. Television, for example, dislikes poor people, not personally, but because their appearance is a downer and, according to rating meters, causes viewers to hit the remote. Politicians overlook them because poor folk vote in small numbers and have no lobby. The poor remain beyond our experience.

For example, it was hard for us, when hurricane Katrina hit New Orleans, not to think in our terms. When a hurricane is approaching we of course will call our relatives on our cell phones to tell them we're leaving, load the family in our SUVs, fill it up with $100 worth of gasoline, stick some bottled water in the trunk, use a credit card to check into a hotel on safe ground and call our insurance agent. Of course. We can't begin to imagine not having a phone, cell or otherwise, an SUV, money, credit cards, insurance Are there really people in our own country who live without them? Yes, every day. Too many of them.

Let me end with, of all things, a reference to Warren Buffett who again made this year's list among *Forbes'* 400, He said candidly at a $4600-a-seat fundraiser for Hillary Clinton: "The 400 of us pay a lower part of our income in taxes than our receptionists do, or our cleaning lady for that matter." Then, Jesus-like, he added this gospel's message. He said, "If you're in the luckiest one percent of humanity, you owe it to the rest of humanity to think about that other ninety-nine percent."

That's really all the gospel is saying for now: Think about the ninety-nine percent. Open the gate. Lower the bridge. Notice Lazarus. And then, to the best of your ability, do something about him.

The Next Time Charles Gets Married

Twenty-Seventh Sunday in Ordinary Time, B, Mark 10:2–16

In the year 1981…
   Prince Charles got married
   Liverpool was crowned soccer champions of Europe
   Australia lost the Ashes Tournament
   The pope was shot

In the year 2005…
   Prince Charles got married
   Liverpool was crowned soccer champions of Europe
   Australia lost the Ashes Tournament
   The pope died

Lessons learned? The next time Charles gets married, someone warn the pope!

"The next time Charles gets married."

In the context of Charles's marriages and his siblings' divorces—Andrew and Anne—and, more to the point, in the context of some of your divorces and certainly your children's and grandchildren's divorces, we uncomfortably must come to terms with Jesus' pronouncement of no divorce. Preachers usually avoid this hot-button issue, but let's plunge ahead.

First, some context to a gospel that ties in the two episodes of Jesus' hard teaching and his soft blessing of the little children. In ancient times, in Jesus' society where women rarely, if ever, owned property and had no independent means of living, marriage was a savior. It meant a guarantee of support for the most vulnerable members of society, women and children. For their sakes, therefore, marriages *had* to be stable. Laws against divorce, in other words, said that women and children should not be so easily thrown aside and left unattached and unprotected. So, you see, in criticizing those who advocated easy divorce—and there were many in his day who did—Jesus was putting himself, as always, on the side of the weak and vulnerable. He is not once-and-for-all condemning divorced persons, but is coming down squarely on the side of the defenseless. "Don't do that to women!" is his stern message. Seen in this context, then, Jesus' words are consistent with his gentle mercy. Which is why at the next moment, to emphasize his point, he embraced the most defenseless of all, little children. He knew divorce hurt them then as it surely does so today. Bottom line: In his time, Jesus' words against divorce are words of compassion: Be good to defenseless women and children. Don't cast them off into poverty and need.

Now fast forward to the present where Jesus' social context no longer prevails. Today we have lots of divorce and it's a touchy subject. We live in a world where people make and break promises, where people find it difficult to keep their commitments, and where people have promises broken by other people, where people who, for a variety of reasons, have felt it necessary to break their marriage vows and divorce.

Yet, even they know that Jesus is fundamentally right in proclaiming marriage's sanctity and that a faithful and enduring marriage is ideal. In fact, in Catholic theology, marriage is a sacrament, a powerful image, or sign, of God's fidelity to his people, whom God has pledged to take in good times and in bad, for richer and poorer, in sickness and in health, until he gathers them to himself. A good and faithful marriage, in other words, is a living sign of a good and faithful God. So, a lifelong committed marriage is good for the world. No dispute about that.

Still, the ideal falters. There *is* divorce, some forty to fifty percent, and children always get wounded. Anyway, the causes of divorce in our day are easy to spot. First, there is a highly mobile society that seldom allows people, even married couples, to really know and communicate with one another.

I read an article recently where, after sixteen years of marriage, Suzanne and Jim Shemwell of Idaho were ready to call it quits. But then on March 5, 2003, while on a snowmobile trip in Boise National Forest, they became stranded in a blizzard. Trapped in a forest and fighting frostbite, hunger, and injuries, they stopped arguing and began cooperating. Back home their conversations were filled with insults and discouraging comments, but in the woods, they focused on encouraging and comforting each other. By the time they were rescued on March 10 the Shemwells were wondering why they had ever wanted to separate in the first place. They made plans to renew their wedding vows on March 10 the next year.

Next, there is a highly pornographic and secular society which mocks that fidelity and in fact encourages infidelity.

There is also consumerism which begins with a $30,000 wedding ceremony and puts a couple on a lifelong treadmill to possess more and more and forces them work apart more and more, longer and longer, to acquire all the things they think they need and that deaden their souls and their relationship.

And, next, in a society where image is the end-all and be-all, there is the tendency to marry an attractive, surgically altered shadow over deeper substance. Most don't tap into Dr. Neil Clark Warren's "eHarmony" compatibility matching system with its "Relationship Questionnaire" that screens applicants on as many as twenty-nine dimensions of compatibility, including values, character, education, spiritual beliefs, and family background. It should, I think, be required for all engaged couples.

Finally, in a culture of individualism, there is seldom a third party at any wedding. That is to say, the focus is entirely on the individual selves. Each is expected to provide the other with every physical, sexual, emotional, material fulfillment—an impossible task of course. The understanding is that they are two people over and against the world, rather than in service to it. There is seldom a sense that in marriage they are committing themselves to something greater than themselves; that they are connected to and responsible for others; that they are not in this for themselves alone, but rather have bonded to combine their growing love into the service of others: children, the poor, the future, God, the betterment of society. A dedicated commitment to something or Someone greater than themselves is often the glue that keeps them together, and makes them holy in the process.

That's why, were I the church's witness at a wedding, I would say something like this to the couple: "Stephen and Nancy, God has gifted you in wondrous ways: a good family, a good education, the support of friends, jobs that excite you. Still, such gifts are not to be clutched possessively but to be shared generously. Not only with dear ones, but with the crucified strangers of our world. I commend to you especially America's children. Did you know that every forty-four seconds, an American baby is born in poverty? Every minute a baby is born without health insurance? Every two minutes a baby is born at low birthweight? Every eleven minutes a child is reported abused or neglected? Every two hours and twenty minutes a child or youth under twenty is killed by a firearm?" I would, of course, soften these unsettling statistics as I went along—after all, it is a happy occasion—but I would want to make the point that they are not embarking on a marriage for two but on a joint commitment to many. Failure to recognize and embrace this is to court failure in the marriage. You need a third party in every marriage to make it work.

All right, these are the ideal. They don't always hold up. And when they don't, you now want to know how you stand with a broken marriage in the light of Jesus' prohibition against divorce? The answer is twofold.

At the official level, according to the Catholic Church, anyone who divorces is still a good Catholic in good standing. If, however, they remarry—presuming there is no annulment—they are considered living in sin and may not go to Communion. Still, to give the official church its due: It does hold fast to the ideal of a lifelong faithful marriage as both good for children and society and, in these casual days, it performs a valuable service in doing so. It would be, I think, a tragic mistake to weaken that ideal simply because many don't follow it. It has promoted serious marriage preparation courses, a kind of a Catholic "eHarmony" system; it has promoted many compassionate support groups for the divorced and remarried.

Unofficially, in the day-to-day care for divorced people, many priests leave the question of remarriage and church participation up to the careful and thoughtful consciences of those people who 1) know that their first marriages are irretrievably lost; 2) who have tried, but have no official recourse to change their status; 3) who are sincerely desirous of participating in the life of the church; and 4) show solid signs that their second marriage, even though it cannot be celebrated by the church, will in all other respects be a Christian marriage.

We cannot soften Jesus' words. Divorce is a failure and remarriage is something less than the ideal. On the other hand, in one way or another, we all fail to live up to the ideal of the Christian life as found in the Beatitudes. How many of us live by them day in and day out? How many of us live by the ideal of nonviolence and always turn the other cheek? How many of us will give away a coat when someone asks for our shirt? How many of us have never looked at another with lust or called another a name in anger? The fact is we all fail one way or another, yet we all believe in God's mercy and forgiveness and continue to live as members in good standing in the Christian community. Why should the question of divorce and remarriage be treated differently?

It would seem, in short, that the Christian community must not only hold firmly to the ideal but must also care tenderly for the wounds and nurture the hopes of the persons who are caught up in less than the ideal. Just as Jesus would.

The Rich Young Man

You may have missed a significant moment in this well-known gospel. Recall: The man has just told Jesus that he has lived a decent moral life from his youth. Right away, Jesus is smitten with such candor and grace and the gospel pointedly records, "Jesus, looking at him, loved him." And then—here's the punch line—having felt such love, Jesus dumps on him! "Go sell what you have and give to the poor." No pat on the head, no "right on" exclamation, no thumbs up. Instead, "*Because* I love you, I'm telling you this."

It's an old posture that many of you have used many times. "If I didn't love you I wouldn't care so. No, you can't go out tonight. You have home-work to do."

"I know this will hurt, honey, but we have to get that tooth taken care of."

"I can't let you do that to yourself!"

Why all these imperatives? You know why: because if you love some-one you want what is best for them. You can't just stand by and let them settle for less. If you didn't care, then let them go jump in the lake. But you do care. You love them enough to care, and therefore to make demands. Now do you see why the gospel follows Jesus' feelings of tender love with a strong command to give away what that man cherishes? Jesus loves him too much to let him settle for just being "a good man," period. "Hey," says Jesus, "you can do better than that."

Jesus is speaking to us, you know, and that's the lesson of the gospel. We too, like the man in the gospel, are good people, but we can do better than what we are doing, especially in the way that we—Christians that we are—imitate the possessiveness and consumerism of our culture. So this gospel, as you first are inclined to suspect, is not about riches per se, but about this truth: what can we (no matter where we stand on the economic ladder), what must we, let go of for the sake of greater love, growth, witness? The gospel is about love's challenge, about identifying with the man in the gospel who was willing to do more but was unable to do with less. This gospel, in short, is about three things.

First, it's about escalation. It's about consumption, competition, about keeping up with the Joneses at the cost of making us camouflaged Christians, less visible disciples.

There is a story about an old monk who had been mentoring a young disciple. Finally he told the disciple he was ready to strike out on his own. So the young disciple goes into the wilderness and lives in a simple lean-to near the river bank. Each night, happy as a lark, he puts out his simple tunic, his only possession, to dry. One morning he is dismayed to find that it has been shredded by rats. So he begs a second tunic from the villagers, but when the rats destroy that too he decides he must get a cat. But now he has to beg food not only for himself but also milk for the cat. To get around that, he buys a cow. But he now has to seek food for the cow. So he works the land around his hut and that takes all his time to grow the crops to feed the cow. The operation expands. He hires workers. He marries a wife who keeps the household running smoothly. Pretty soon he is one of he wealthiest people in the village. Several years later his old mentor comes back to find a mansion where the lean-to had been. "What is the meaning of this?" he asks. The disciple replied, "Holy Father, there was no other way for me to keep my tunic."

A perfect parable for us: I have to keep up appearances, have to maintain my status, have to have what everyone else has, accumulate what everyone else accumulates, increase my social profile, fill our houses, making it necessary to rent out mini-warehouses to contain our excesses. So we, good people, rationalize and no one ever suspects that Jesus is looking at us with love, saying we can do better than that, that we are not everybody else. We ought not to identify with the old Mort Sahl one-liner, "Ask a Californian who he is and he points to his car." Love says we must point elsewhere.

Second, the gospel is about how far are we willing to be different, to march to a different drumbeat from what the advertisers tell us we need in order to be accepted, "successful." Or, to put it another way, what is standing between us and a more fundamentally gospel-lived life?

A friend comes to mind. When I was in Middletown, I met a twenty-five-year-old financier who helped in our youth ministry and visited jails and nursing homes. This gospel struck him like a lightning bolt and he made a radical decision to go to Covenant House in New York City to work with the runaway kids. He liquidated his debts by working two jobs, gave away his sports car, and when I drove him to New York all his possessions were in an overnight bag. He has never regretted his decision to march to a different drumbeat. And people have no trouble identifying him as a disciple.

Third, the gospel asks: are we really willing to share what we have with the poor? This in practice means one thing: do we tithe? Tithing is an ancient spiritual remedy for selfishness and loss of Christian identity. Tithing should be as natural for us and our children as breathing. It should be built into our lifestyle.

Two college students are riding a subway in New York. A homeless man approaches them, asking for money. One of the college students adamantly rejects the man in disgust. The other whips out his wallet, pulls out a couple of dollars and gladly hands the money over to the homeless man with a smile. The homeless man thanks him kindly and then continues on to the other passengers. The first student is outraged by his friend's act of generosity. "What on earth did you do that for?" he shouts. "You know he's only going to use it for booze." And the second student replies, "And we weren't?"

That's us. Let me tell you something. Whenever I'm away and attend church as a "civilian"—I like to sit in the pew and see what the people have to put up with—I always give a twenty-dollar bill in the collection. Why not? Like the college student, I know that after Mass I'm going to drop forty or fifty dollars or more for drinks and food at Shipwreck Grill or the Grenville Inn. I should spend less on God than myself? Tithing, ten percent of your income given to charity, no matter how meager, helps us to put our lives in perspective and reminds us of who we are. It should be as natural for us as being a Christian. It's something we should teach our children.

Yes, friends, Jesus looks upon us with love us but it's not the simpering, gushy love of the greetings cards or insipid hymns. It's a tough love that reminds us that, good people that we are, we can do better, must do better.

Don't walk away sad. Accept the gospel challenge.

Outcasts

This familiar gospel of the nine Jewish lepers and the lone Samaritan one who returns at the end of the story to give thanks has rightly inspired countless homilies and reflections about gratitude. But I'm not interested in the end of the story where gratitude is praised. It's the beginning, the more challenging part, that intrigues me, where isolation is taken for granted.

At that beginning we have a familiar scene: lepers ostracized from the community, living in tombs or in segregated sections of the city, prohibited from getting too close to others so that they had to bellow out, "Unclean! Unclean!" and wear bells around their necks shouting for alms at a distance. Lepers, according to biblical law, were excluded, marginalized outcasts.

Jesus happens to meet a group of them on his way into a village. The lepers were, of course, not living there but were begging or foraging at the town dump on the outskirts. Looking up, they saw Jesus and his band and they began their chorus from a distance, "Have pity on us!" Jesus motions his band to stop. He sees what they see: outcasts: nine Jews and one obviously a Samaritan, all pariahs, all dreaded lepers. Jesus should move on but does not. Instead he astonishes his followers by speaking to the lepers. More than that, he sends them to the priest who had the power to notarize any cure. This would permit them back into normal society.

With faith in Jesus' word they go off and on the way they are cured. They, of course, were happy not so much because they were cured bodily, but because, at long last, their status as outcasts was ended. They were now accepted, full members of the community. Their isolation was over. Pitiable and disgusting as they were, someone had reached out to them.

And once again in this gospel you realize that there is Jesus deliberately making a point he has made over and over. Recall, he choose a shunned and despised tax collector for an apostle, got a nasty reputation for welcoming and eating with sinners, allowed another outsider, "that sinful woman," to break into a Pharisee's house to anoint his feet, cured the servant of the hated occupying-Roman centurion, and later, near the end of his life, on the way to Calvary, he accepted the help of a foreigner from Cyrene and died with two outcasts on either side. No question about it: Jesus constantly calls outsiders inside and ministers to them.

To state the obvious, ours is also a world of outcasts: Israelis and Palestinians, Sunni and Shiite Muslims, homeless and housed, imprisoned and free, black and white, criminal and law-abiding, poor and rich, gays and straights, sinners and saints, wicked and worthy.

Still, with such divisions we Christians are not free to duck the gospel's implied challenge: How do *we* treat those we consider outcasts? People, even Christians, generally respond in one of two ways. They are either judgmental or permissive. The judgmental response says, "Look, they're child molesters. Jail them and throw away the key." "They got AIDS? Let them pay for their sin." The permissive response says, "Well, deep down they're nice people. They had an unhappy childhood or were poor or deprived. Just keep an eye on them. Put them on probation and let them go."

But like Jesus who told the woman caught in adultery to sin no more, we don't soft-pedal or deny crime and evil, but once the crime or evil is fully acknowledged, we have to respond to the unspoken cry, "Jesus, Master, have pity on us!" and minister to the outcasts. And accept them not as model citizens—hardly—but as those for whom Christ died. We believers have to bring these outsiders inside, at least inside of a faith community that will offer them help, prayer, and ministry.

This is an uncongenial teaching, so let me unpack it gradually. Parents will resonate with this familiar example. You've told your six-year-old it's cold outside and looks like rain; be sure to put on your jacket and raincoat. But when you're not looking, off he runs outside where it is cold and he has no sweater or jacket and it begins to rain and he splashes around in the puddles. Of course he comes down with a bad cold. Serves him right. That's what he gets for being naughty, disobedient. But what do you do with little sinner? Throw him out? Disown him? Lock him away? No, you care for him, sit endless hours by his bed, call the doctor, take his temperature, baby him. More than anything else, you want him to get well again so you can kill him.

But notice the dynamics for this diminutive outcast: He was wrong, he did something bad—no fudging that—but your love leads you to bring him inside and minister to him.

Let's escalate to a case that made headlines a while back. Brian Nichols killed four people in Atlanta, a terrible deed. A fugitive, this murderer accosted a young mother, Ashley Smith, and held her captive in her home for seven hours. Captive, she asked Nichols if she could read. He nodded, so she went over and got her copy of Rick Warren's bestseller, *The Purpose Driven Life*, and began to read aloud these words:

> We serve God by serving others. The world defines greatness in terms of power, possessions, prestige, and position....Jesus, however, measured greatness in terms of service, not status. God determines your greatness by how many people you serve, not how many people serve you.

Nichols listened intently, hearing such words for the first time and asked, "Will you read it again?" Smith read it to him again. There was silence. Then they talked throughout the night. When morning came, Nichols let her go.

Here was a woman, rightly repulsed by his crime, who nevertheless saw more than a terrible murderer. Here was a man who, tutored by her ministry, came to the realization of a different way of life. In one way, of course, nothing's changed. He is still a horrid murderer and must go to jail, but this outcast had received the attention of one of Jesus' followers and was invited into conversion.

Those of you who are engaged in prison ministry have no illusions about the guilt of the prisoners. All that you know is that they are moral lepers, outcasts, cut off from community, and like Jesus you offer them acceptance and another community, a community of faith where people will visit them, write to them, pray for them, take away the pain of their isolation.

The movie *Philadelphia* with Tom Hanks playing a lawyer with AIDS is a powerful exposé of the wounds of exclusion and discrimination. To counter this, the late Cardinal John O'Connor emptied the bedpans of AIDS patients—today's lepers—at St. Vincent's Hospital. He was not interested at the moment *how* these men contracted the disease. All he knew was that right now they were isolated and needed care and companionship. They were outcasts and he was inviting them to a community of compassion and into a church that opened its heart for those wretched who need it most.

Otherwise, to harbor only hatred and turn our backs on the "enemy," we unwittingly defeat the gospel and validate Oscar Wilde's painful words: "As one looks through the pages of history, one is positively sickened, not by the crimes of the wicked but by the punishments of the just."

Harsh, judgmental, excluding, unforgiving attitudes, having no faith in the spirit of the Crucified One who offered a last-minute rescue to a despicable man, feeling no compassion for a fellow sinner, refusing to minister to moral lepers is clearly not the way of Jesus.

We may like this gospel where it reminds us to give thanks. Yeah, we can do that once in a while. We may not like its "forgive your enemies, pray for those who persecute you" teachings. But when we dismiss such teachings, then we ourselves become spiritual lepers cut off from the gospel and then *we* need to cry out, "Jesus, Master, have pity on us."

Servant Leadership

I suppose that James and John were not nicknamed elsewhere in the gospel "Sons of Thunder" for nothing. Apparently these two brothers had a reputation for being somewhat overbearing hotheads. Why they were chosen by Jesus in the first place is a minor mystery, but perhaps no more than his choosing a blundering Peter, an unsure Thomas, and a turncoat tax collector named Matthew. Anyway, diplomacy not being their strong suit, and knowing they were part of the inner circle—after all, James and John, along with Peter, witnessed the Transfiguration—these two ask, right in front of the other ten, to sit at Jesus' right and left hand when he finally makes it big. Now that's *chutzpah*!

Pointedly Jesus replies that in his kingdom it is not about sitting. It's about standing. Can you, will you, stand by me, stand *for* me, stand for what I am all about? And what is Jesus about? He is about servant leadership, a concept worlds apart from what we experience. We too often experience authority as rank without responsibility, comfort without conscience, crown without compassion, and greed without grace.

Let me share something, something you probably don't want to hear, to demonstrate this. I used to clip out newspaper stories about the misuse of authority until, I confess, the sheer volume of them threatened to take over my office. Besides, it's depressing.

Here's but a small sample. There's Congressman Randy Cunningham in jail for accepting two million dollars in bribes for directing seventy million dollars to two favored military contractors; Congressman Ney is on his way to jail, admitting conspiring with lobbyist Jack Abramoff to corrupt public officials; the ex-governor of Illinois, George Ryan, in jail on corruption charges; legislators are in bed with developers; and this week a Queens union leader was indicted for siphoning off two million dollars from labor unions and contractors. There's the Kentucky executive charged with bribing Louisiana Representative William J. Jefferson; the mayor of Bridgeport convicted of sixteen charges of corruption; an Ohio fundraiser pleading guilty in a campaign financial fraud; a former New Jersey governor giving a high-paying job to his unqualified boyfriend; and that recent report about "breathtaking" fraud in the Katrina hurricane aid program.

On the local scene, to name a very, very few, Jack Westlake of the Monmouth Board of Taxation pleads guilty to tax evasion; Thomas Broderick, former Monmouth County assistant highway supervisor, sentenced for a money laundering scheme; the president of Atlantic City's City Council and a former Camden council member pleading guilty to federal corruption and bribery charges; a priest, Father Joe Hughes of Rumson, jailed for embezzlement; and a couple of Fannie Mae executives charged with cooking the books to reap outrageous bonuses.

Well, I won't go on with this familiar litany. You get the unnerving point. These people, these leaders, are highly educated at the very best universities, highly degreed, wealthy, affluent, well housed, well positioned. To say that, for all of that privileged living, they lack ethics is obvious; to say they are awash in greed is an understatement. To say that they are arrogant and proud doesn't cut it. Trapped in their egos, they have abused power. They are far, far from Jesus' teaching, "Whoever wishes to be great among you will be your servant, the slave of all."

Leaders, of course, are essential. Power is necessary. Power moves and gets things done. But, to quote Lord Acton, all power eventually corrupts and absolute power corrupts absolutely—unless it is grounded in the teachings of Jesus Christ. And leaders, remember, include us, not just the high and mighty CEOs, but us: parents, principals, managers, teachers, board members, policemen, scout masters, pastors, doctors, anyone who has charge of or determines the lives of others. In the Christian scheme of things, all such leaders, including you and me, are basically servants who are there "not to be served but to serve and to give their lives as a ransom for many." That radical teaching—and it is outrageously radical if you think about it—is a deep spirituality to live by, a necessary and humble interior balance a Christian must embrace. The more power I have the more respect I must show, the more service I must render, the more aware of others I must be.

So certain practical guidelines for Christian living surface:

First, servant leaders pay attention to the rank and file folks. These rank and file people are not the potentates who get chauffeured away for Executive Development, but the ones who stay behind and clean up. How do leaders see and treat their daily laborers? How do we?

A quiz was given to a new class of nursing students in their first year of training. Most of the students did well on the quiz, until they came to the last question that they all left blank. That question was, "What is the name of the woman you see every morning who cleans the school?" The students thought that the question was a joke until they found out that the professor was counting the question against them. When they protested, the professor said, "In your careers, you will meet many people. All of them are significant. They deserve your attention and care, even if all you can do is smile and say hello." Servant leaders notice the marginal.

That bit of spiritual advice is played out in those old folktales where the high and the mighty decide, in a moment of grace, to go in disguise among the "ordinary" people to get their perspective on life. In the movies you have *Sullivan's Travels* where a movie producer puts on the clothes and lifestyle of a bum; *The Prince and the Pauper* where twins, one a prince and one a pauper, change places; soon we'll be hearing the story of Ebenezer Scrooge who is forced out of his isolation to witness the household of Bob Cratcthit. All learn to see through others' eyes, and they become wiser and better leaders for it. That's why I've always thought that every five years, every CEO and every bishop should be required to live six months in a row house in poor neighborhood.

Second, servant leaders learn to think communally, not selfishly. What, in other words, goes into the their moral judgment call? Is it only about profit, sales, career advancement, getting ahead, one-up-man-ship? Are there any considerations as to the long-range impact on the family, on the community, on the environment, on public health? What we see so often today is short-term gain. Get your money and run. And generations suffer as a result of such self-centered decisions.

Third, servant leaders strive for that humility which leads them to ask occasionally if they are part of the problem, and do they have mechanisms that provide a forum to deal with this question? Without feedback, you become a tyrant. I remember a friend of mine who was made a bishop lamenting that, now that he's bishop, this is the last time he will hear the truth. His minions, like so many others in public life, will tell him what he wants to hear, not what he needs to hear.

Finally, servant leaders submit to accountability. Without accountability you are left with your own pride, self-interest, and self-serving viewpoint. Church leaders come up short here.

Back to James and John who wanted privilege, power, and position without the cross; who wanted leadership without the service, the "slavery" of love. Well, they must have been totally embarrassed and shamed when, at the end of the day, there were two down-and-out thieves, one at the right and one at the left in Jesus' kingdom. Not quite what they first imagined, but it made Jesus' point.

A quick postscript: Did James and John and the others eventually get the message, get to drink the chalice Jesus drank? I think so. About twelve years after Jesus' death, James was the first apostle to suffer martyrdom. Tradition adds that Andrew was tied to a cross, Bartholomew was skinned alive, Peter was crucified upside down in Rome, the other James was thrown from the Temple pinnacle, Thomas was run through with a lance in the East Indies, Matthias was stoned and beheaded, Jude was pierced with arrows, Philip was hanged in Phrygia. Only John escaped his torture.

Well, we don't have to go that far but we do have to recognize that the gospel message clearly is that power and position are the other side of servant leadership: Followers of Jesus do not sit. They stand in solidarity with the world's most famous foot-washer.

The Justice Woman

It was the annual celebration at the Cathedral for those married twenty-five or fifty years. The bishop had singled out a Golden Jubilarian, Luigi, asking him to take a few minutes to come up to the microphone and share some insight into how he managed to stay married to the same woman all these years. Luigi said to the congregation, "Well, I've a tried to treat her well, spend-a the money on her, but da best-a is-a dat I took her to Italy for the twentieth anniversary." The bishop immediately commented, "Luigi, you are an amazing inspiration to all the husbands here. Please tell the people what you are planning for your wife for your fiftieth anniversary." Luigi proudly replied, "I'm-a gonna go and a-get her."

Well, neither the bishop nor we expected that! We can picture the bishop coughing and two hefty monsignors quickly hustling Luigi from the sanctuary.

But there's a point to the story, namely, its unexpected twist, the precise mechanism needed to unlock today's puzzling gospel with its challenging parable. So put the story aside and open your hearts.

You heard the gospel: A proud judge who feared no one, neither God nor man, is unwilling to hear the pleas of a poor and defenseless widow, one without a man, without protection, without status. But she persists until she gets justice and the judge gives in, not out of principle, but because he fears the woman will get violent. It is interesting to note, by the way, that in the original language, when the judge says to himself, "I shall deliver a just decision for her, lest she finally come and strike me" the words colloquially mean, "lest she come and give me a black eye!" or, as we would say, "lest she come and punch me out!" Jesus' audience must have chuckled at that line.

In any case, I suspect that all over Catholic Land today, having read this gospel, preachers will be comparing the judge to God and urging the faithful, who are compared to the widow, to be similarly persistent in prayer and not give up. I don't know. I have reservations. This equating the judge with God is very shaky. After all, the Bible is full of lines saying that God hears the cry of the poor, that God is eager and willing to give good things to those who ask. So it's hard, when you really look at it, to equate the insensitive judge with God.

In fact, the storyline says twice that the judge is not exactly a sterling character, for he neither "fears God nor respects man." And besides, is the message that if you badger God long enough you can eventually wear God down and get what you want? Is it right to make God a punchy old man who needs his sleep and if you play your radio loud enough he'll give in? Is the parable saying that you can bribe or bargain with God? And it really doesn't do any good to go through the back door and say, well, the point is that if an insensitive clod of a judge will finally answer the widow's plea, how much more will God? But that too, I think, is straining the comparison.

I suggest that there is a more fruitful and less obvious—and unexpected—way to understand this gospel. Why not see the *widow* as the image of God, not the judge? Once you reverse characters, then a whole new perspective emerges. That is to say, that when the widow is seen as a God-like figure, then the message of the parable becomes crystal clear: Anyone who determinedly resists injustice, faces it, names it, and denounces it until right is achieved, is acting as God does, is God-like.

Powerless as Jesus on the cross who defeats the power of death, the widow achieves victory for right. Through her persistence the widow becomes a kind of Gandhi or Martin Luther King figure. Against all odds she will endure until justice is done and God will be present.

So the parable is not about strategies to wear down a reluctant God with non-stop prayer or threatening black eyes, but it's about justice, about us little people who act like God whenever we persistently seek, often against terrible odds, to have justice done; whenever—to update the story—we hold self-serving politician's feet to the fire, work to have children insured and free of violence, uncover the greed and corruption that siphons off money from the poor, improve education, and break down barriers that separate people.

A black man and his family were traveling through the South in the 1950s. They stopped to rest a few moments at a park along the highway. His daughters spotted a swing set on a playground in the park and pulled their father toward the swing. They were too young to read the signs that warned that this playground was for "whites only." Sadly but patiently the man told his daughters that they could not play there and explained why. This was their first encounter with racism and they burst into tears. So, much as his mother had done for him when he was a child, the man gathered his children into a warm embrace and said to them "Listen, you little girls are somebody. In fact, you are so important and so valuable to God and so powerful that it takes the governor, the lieutenant governor, and the whole state police force to keep you girls off those swings."

One day because another widow named Rosa Parks would persist, those girls would grow up to see justice done and the signs taken down and God would be present.

So, once more, the judge is anyone who thwarts justice and the woman of our gospel is anyone who acts like God in her pursuit of justice.

This woman is formidable. I wonder though: Was she the only one to take on the judge, the only one to hunger and thirst for justice? She shouldn't be. She should have us for company. And *that's* what this gospel is really all about.

Sight and Insight

Think of the classic Abbott and Costello routine of Who's on First, What's on Second, and I Don't Know's on Third and you get a pretty good idea of one of the favorite themes in St. Mark's gospel. That theme is that the apostles consistently misunderstand Jesus. They never quite seem to catch his meaning, his message, or his mission. They, like Lou Costello, constantly get him wrong. In Mark's gospel—the other gospel writers are kinder—the apostles are portrayed as dense, and Jesus, like Bud Abbott, is portrayed as saying for the umpteenth time, "Don't you get it?"

Besides saying it outright, which he does many times—that the apostles keep misunderstanding—Mark further makes his point by telling two blindness/seeing stories. Just a few paragraphs before today's story of Bartimaeus, Jesus cures another blind man but in stages. At first the blind man sees fuzzily, and, squinting, he says that people look like trees walking around. Then Jesus places his hands on him and then the man sees clearly.

In recounting this first incident, Mark is clearly insinuating a parallel with the apostles. They are also blind and their faith in Jesus, like this man's, is coming very slowly, in stages. In today's second story, however, where Bartimaeus sees instantly, Mark seems to be admitting that the apostles seem to be finally getting it.

And what are they getting? Listen to this: Discipleship with Jesus means an upside-down world where the first are last and the last first, where one forgives one's enemies seventy times seven times, where the one who loses his life will save it, where the miserable, chest-striking publican in back of the Temple is more worthy than the triumphant Pharisee in front, where proud fathers run to their wayward sons instead of the other way around, where one gives his coat when only asked for a shirt, where enemies are to be prayed for, good deeds are to be done in secret, and the one who wishes to rule over all must be the servant of all.

Talk about subversive teaching! Think about what you just heard. That's a tough Christian mission statement and, I tell you, it surely won't get you very far in a world of greed and me-first. No wonder the apostles had trouble seeing Jesus and his message and, maybe, if they *did* see, they didn't want to and pretended to be blind. Yes, seeing like Jesus, brings a lot of difficulties.

Example: I know a woman who spoke up in a business meeting, opposing a policy that the company was considering. When asked why she was so adamantly against this policy, she said simply, "Well, for one thing, I'm a Christian and, the way we look at it, we just don't believe in taking advantage of the weaknesses of people." The next day the boss called her into his office and told her, "You ought not to wear your religion on your sleeve. If it happens again, you might look for another company."

It has been noted that Jesus has many admirers but not many followers. This woman's a follower. So is Bartimaeus, because the gospel says, "Immediately he received his sight and followed Jesus on the way. "On the way" is early Christian code for going all the way, sincere discipleship. It's not easy to see right, to stay on the road, to go all the way. Not in a culture that celebrates the Self and does everything to keep us from seeing beyond our own selfish wants and desires.

Let me share a shameful story of how some people see. In May 1945 a young soldier named Stephen Shields was part of the American troops that entered the town of Nordhausen where they liberated the infamous concentration camp where thousands of Hungarian Jews had been murdered. Battle-hardened soldiers were stunned at what they saw. A few hundred prisoners were all that remained and they were walking skeletons. Shields says they didn't even have the strength to speak. They just moved silently, zombie-like, through the open prison doors and started waking toward the town of Nordhausen. They were silent. The only sound they made was the rustling of their long, ragged coats against the grass of the fields. They looked like an army of scarecrows, a column of living cadavers.

Shields says that on the road between the concentration camp and the little village, the ghostly prisoners were encountered by two teenagers about fifteen years old. They were blond, strong, and healthy looking. The teens gaped at the column of starving Jews walking along the highway. They stopped in their tracks and then, says Shields, incredibly, they began to laugh. They nudged each other, pointed at the pitiable prisoners, made comments, and continued to laugh uproariously. To them that sickening, suffering parade was just too funny for words. Shields says that of all the horrible experiences of the war, the banality, the lack of empathy, and the ridicule in the face of evil was the worst he experienced. Where Shields saw tragedy, the boys saw comedy. Where a Mother Teresa would have seen the suffering Christ, the boys saw the stuff of mockery. They sorely needed to pray, "Master, I want to see."

This week there was a sad article in the paper about a father at a youth football game in Philadelphia for six- and seven-year-olds. The father pulled a gun on the coach because his son wasn't getting enough playing time. What did his seven-year-old son see? This is how you express your frustration, pull a gun on someone? This is a life lesson his father wants to teach him? Will he bring a gun to school someday? Doesn't the father see what he is doing? Is he like Mark's apostles? Doesn't he understand?

The fact is that slick advertising, routine violence, and examples of greed and exploitation blindside all of us. Eventually we become like Mark's version of the apostles: slow to understand the message of Jesus Christ, slow to see what he sees, what the saints have seen. That's why periodically we need to hear a gospel like today's. We need to enter into it. We need to identify with Bartimaeus, begging on the side of the road. We need to sense that Jesus is passing by in this Mass, in this assembly of yearners and believers. The truth is, if we will admit it, that in some areas of the heart, in some areas of the spirit, like the apostles in Mark, we have misunderstood Jesus and his message, that we have spiritual blind spots.

But Jesus in this liturgy is calling us. "What do you want me to do for you?" he asks. Right away we can think of a million things, but surely a more true, a more reflective response should be that of Bartimaeus: "Lord, I want to see."

Britney and the Publican

It may surprise you to learn that this particular Pharisee of the gospel was not praying an unfamiliar prayer. He was, as a matter of fact, praying in a way that expressed the sentiments and values found in the later Jewish Talmud where, for example, we find this similar prayer:

> I thank thee, O Lord my God, that thou hast given me my lot with those who sit in the seat of learning, and not those who sit at the street-corners; for I am early to work and they are early to work, [but] I am early to work on the words of the Torah, and they are early to work on things of no moment. I weary myself and they weary themselves, [but] to no profit. I run and they run, [but] I run towards the life of the Age to Come, and they run towards the pit of destruction.

Another prayer runs like this: "Praised be the Lord that He did not make me a gentile, for all gentiles are as nothing before Him; praised be He that He did not make me a woman for woman is not under obligation to fulfill the law; praised be He that he did not make me an uneducated man for the uneducated man is not cautious to avoid sins." To thank God for not being a heathen, a woman, or ignorant was commonplace. It wouldn't fly today.

So the Pharisee is only praying in a traditional way when he says, "I thank you for not making me like the rest of humanity, like this Publican who is clearly outside the pale and uneducated in the law." Why, then, do we traditionally dump on the Pharisee? Why is he, as Mark Twain put it, "A good man in the worst sense of the term"?

299

I would suggest that the Pharisee in this parable is best understood as a variation of the rich man from another familiar parable: you know, the self-centered rich man who never even saw Lazarus begging at his gate. The Pharisee in today's parable, I maintain, is a twin to that man in that he also is guilty of spiritual imbalance. That is to say, he too is so distracted with himself that he is blinded to the presence and needs of the larger world, and that cramped his spirituality.

So, let's turn sober and serious as I update the Pharisee of today's gospel, master, as he is, of the unbalanced blindside. For this I turn to an author by the name of Jake Halpern. Halpern has written an interesting book called *Fame Junkies*. As the title suggests, it's a book on why Americans are obsessed with celebrities and the troubling political and spiritual ramifications of this obsession. In his book Halpern demonstrates what we all know from everyday experience, namely, that the TV networks spend far too much time covering the lives of Hollywood celebrities instead of reporting the hard, significant, and challenging news. There are, for example, the genocide in Dafur, uninsured children, poverty, the buying and selling of human beings, the breakup of the family, most marriages not making even the silver jubilee, the threat of gangs, the plight of the middle class, and the like. Not that we want to hear this stuff all the time—that would be depressing—but we need to hear enough, more than we're hearing now, to make us reflect and act.

Anyway, the producer of CNN heard about the book *Fame Junkies*, thought it was worthwhile and newsworthy, and asked Halpern to appear on TV to discuss it. But guess what? When Halpern arrived at the studio, he learned that his segment had been canceled. Why? Here's the reply from CNN: "Why didn't you hear? Britney Spears just lost custody of her kids and we're running that instead!" So ironically his important story of significance got bumped—as do many stories that really matter—to make room for the frivolous. Halpern shook his head. It only proved his point.

He goes on to wryly observe that the fate of Ms. Spears's children and her antics are not "just a breaking news story," but a news extravaganza. He points out that it was the top news story on CNN, *Larry King Live*, *Anderson Cooper*, *Nancy Grace*, *Showbiz Tonight*, and was announced as breaking news by *The Situation Room*. The news networks devoted thirty-seven times more coverage to Spears than they did to the ongoing conflict in Iraq. And it's far from over as you are well aware. Halpern further asks us to look at the record. Listen to this: in 2004 the nightly news shows on the three major networks spent a total of just twenty-six minutes covering the bloody conflict in Darfur but some one-hundred-thirty minutes on the Martha Stewart scandal.

Another report that monitors TV news shows revealed that recently the story that commanded the most time on the nightly news shows was not the unveiling of the Hillary Clinton health plan, or the racial feuds in Jena, Louisiana, or the Fed's eagerly awaited interest-rate cut, or the breaking of the Blackwater scandal in Iraq, but O. J. Simpson's arrest for robbery. And we all remember the endless news blitzkrieg of Anna Nicole Smith.

Well, let's back up and take the large view. The truth is that from time immemorial stories about the rich and famous have irresistibly drawn us. It's just human nature. We have a built-in interest in celebrities and will always want to know if Brad Pitt and Angelina Jolie have really split. This celebrity gazing, this adoration, is part of us, but the hidden message of our gospel warns that it shouldn't take over our lives.

The spiritual damage arising from this addictive fascination is that when entire networks, on which we rely to get the news, allow real and impacting stories to be pushed aside in deference to Britney Spears, Paris Hilton, and high ratings, then we are diminished: diminished as human beings, diminished as thoughtful people, diminished as citizens, diminished as Christians. The shallow and the frivolous fill our minds and hearts, dim our moral vision, dull our consciences, and, as one commentator put it, we wind up "entertaining ourselves to death"—spiritual death.

Look at it this way. If it's all Britney Spears, we can never learn of Dorothy Day and her work among the poor. If it's all Paris Hilton, we have no room left for compassion for the plight of the homeless. If it's all O.J. Simpson, we have no time for the lives of the saints or the gospel of Jesus. If it's all "infotainment," as it's accurately called these days, we have no time for serious reflection. And that leaves us all poorer as a nation and as a church.

Or, to put it another way, if our mental and moral diet is *Desperate Housewives* and *Grey's Anatomy*, then our empathy quotient shrinks and we will not be able to notice Lazarus at the gate or an unwashed tax collector beating his breast in humble confession, challenging us to do the same. How can we see the needs of others or hear the cry of the poor when Britney Spears is crowding the screen? That's the danger to anyone who wants to be a good citizen and live the gospel.

The thing is that all of us here are good and decent people but we have to be alert how every day we are seduced into wallowing in trivia at the expense of truth, glitz at the expense of good, celebrity at the expense of concern, and passivity at the expense of justice. Celebrity fixation, propagated by newsrooms, does us no service.

I know all this sounds sober and serious, as I said in the beginning, and there's nothing wrong about being interested in celebrities—but only up to a point. If we exceed this point, as we often do, we'll eventually become brand name minds along with brand name clothes. The gospel's subtle warning is that we will morph into the Pharisee whose mental and spiritual horizons don't exceed himself or his TV screen.

And *that*, the gospel says, is too narrow a world for a disciple of Jesus, and we won't go home justified if we live in that world.

The Two Great Commandments

"You shall love the Lord your God with all your heart, with all your soul, with all your mind and with all your strength." The second is this: "You shall love your neighbor as yourself."

The scribe, a sincere man who asked Jesus if he could boil down the 613 commands of the Torah into one pithy summary got his answer. Then, true to his listening skills he got in therapy class 101, he repeats Jesus' words to show that he got his message and was really listening to him. Jesus is pleased that he has been heard and understood and the incident ends. Class dismissed. And there it is, this teaching, forever enshrined in our texts and in our liturgies. But it's a truth that needs to be enshrined in our lives. It needs the dress, the clothing, the flesh and blood of everydayness to get into our hearts, into our conduct. I therefore ask you to listen with your heart.

Go back forty or more years. It is the court martial after the My Lai massacre. Do you remember the incident? Lt. John Calley, accused of the massacre of innocent Vietnamese civilian villagers, is testifying. "An enemy I couldn't see, I couldn't feel and I couldn't touch: nobody in the military system ever described the enemy as anything but communism. They didn't give it a race, they didn't give it a sex, they didn't give it an age." Yes, anonymous, faceless life is cheap, except for the double edge commandment, "love of God, love of neighbor," which demands a face, race, gender, age;

303

in short, the acknowledgment of the other as neighbor, a brother or sister in the Lord.

"You shall love your neighbor as yourself."

My own failure in this matter was brought home to me when I was a college student in Baltimore and in my neighborhood there was a fair amount of ill and handicapped people who would beg. One man had no legs below the knees and he would sit outside the Walgreens I visited daily to pick up the paper. He would arrive in his wheelchair and, with powerful upper body strength, lift himself out of the chair and onto the ground. He did this in winter as well as in summer. A large plastic cup was placed between the stubs of his knees. I tell you I felt pretty good about myself because I always tossed him some money on my way out the store

Then one day as I was approaching the store, I saw a woman squatting down next to him and talking with great animation. As I turned to go into the store I heard her say, "So you haven't always lived in Baltimore…?" She was inquiring about his life, caring for him in a personal way. The money I later tossed into the cup somehow seemed impersonal, even demeaning. All those times, I realized, I never saw the man as a neighbor. I didn't even know his name or where he was from.

"You shall love your neighbor as yourself."

One woman tells this story: "I am a forty-six-year-old woman, divorced, with three grown children. After several months of chemotherapy following a mastectomy for breast cancer, I was starting to put my life back together when my doctor called with the results of my last checkup. They had found more cancer, and I was devastated. My relatives had not been supportive. I was the first person in the family to have cancer and they didn't know how to behave toward me. They tried to be kind, but I had the feeling they were afraid it was contagious. They called on the phone to see how I was doing, but they kept their distance. That really hurt.

"Last Saturday I headed for the laundromat. You see the same people there almost every week. We exchange greetings and make small talk. So I pulled into the parking lot, determined not to look depressed but my spirits were really low. While taking my laundry out of the car, I looked up and saw a man, one of the regulars, leaving with his bundle. He smiled and said, 'Good morning. How are you today?' Suddenly I lost control of myself and blurted out, 'This is the worst day of my life! I have more cancer!' Then I began to cry.

"He put his arms around me and just let me sob. Then he said, 'I understand. My wife has been through it, too.' After a few minutes I felt better, stammered out my thanks, and proceeded on with my laundry. About fifteen minutes later, here he came back with his wife. Without saying a word, she walked over and hugged me. Then she said, 'I've been there too. Feel free to talk to me. I know what you're going through.' I can't tell you how much that meant to me. Here was this total stranger, taking her time to give me emotional support and courage to face the future at a time when I was ready to give up."

"You shall love your neighbor as yourself."

When I was in another parish I saw the large van pull up in the church parking lot. A bunch of teenagers got out. They were part of our youth group. They got out with bedrolls and paraphernalia and, I must tell you, they looked awful. They looked like refugees. They were dirty and smelly, clothes messed up. They all looked like they just came from a brawl. It was the most awful bunch of kids you've ever seen, and they were ours. I said, "What's this?" "What's this," I knew, is that they just returned from Appalachia. There for one week, along with other groups, they had helped the people clean up and repair homes, and clear out tons of debris. Now they were back home sitting on their bags, waiting for their parents to pick them up. I said to one of the boys, "Are you tired?" He said, "Man, I'm dead. I'm more than tired!" But then he added gospel words without realizing it: "But this is the best tired I've ever felt."

Why the best? Because he had loved his neighbor as himself and in the loving he had found God. I guess the old Persian proverb has it right after all:

> I sought my God,
> my God I could not see.
> I sought my soul,
> my soul eluded me.
> I sought my neighbor
> and I found all three.

It Might Have Been

This very colorful and visual gospel, so congenial to the imagination, raises interesting questions, at least a half dozen of them. For starters: why did Zacchaeus climb the sycamore tree? The first answer that comes to mind is that he was, as the gospel notes, short and couldn't see over the crowd. But that's only part of the answer.

Remember Zacchaeus is not only a tax collector on behalf of the occupying Romans and considered a betrayer of his nation and a despicable thief, but he is listed as the *chief* tax collector, which puts him beyond the pale. So he is in danger from the crowd, should they recognize him. So, to avoid being seen and beaten up, he gets out of their way and climbs a tree to hide among the branches in safety.

Second question: why did he want to see Jesus in the first place? The first answer that comes to mind is that he was curious. Jesus was a minor celebrity, a wonder-worker, so he heard. Jesus happened to be passing through his hometown of Jericho and so natural curiosity drove Zacchaeus.

But that's only part of the answer. Zacchaeus wanted to see Jesus not merely in the sense of sighting, but in the sense of trying to psych Jesus out, where he's coming from, get the mettle of the man, see what he was like inside. Yet, as we said, because of the hostile crowd, he hesitated and almost decided to stay home. What if the crowd saw him? Ridiculed him? What if Jesus detoured another way? What if he turned out to be nothing? Better to be safe than sorry and stay put.

Well, thank heaven, what might have been wasn't, and Zacchaeus finally made his decision and climbed that tree, for what he saw from his vantage point was someone among the rabble, not above them. He heard him preach, saw his compassion, his kindness to those in need, and he was captivated by what he saw. It changed his life.

Third question: what happened next? Well, anyone who goes through all that trouble deserves more than a passing glance. And so the tables are turned. Zacchaeus sees Jesus. Now Jesus sees Zacchaeus. He looks up and calls him by name. This calling by name is a rare occurrence and happens only once or twice in the gospels. And then Jesus tells him to come down among the hostile crowd and so, with hesitation, he does. Then Jesus boldly tells Zacchaeus that he's just invited himself to his house to break bread.

Fourth question: what about that unfriendly crowd? They remain unfriendly. They start to murmur. Murmur, murmur, murmur all over the place. The gist of the murmuring is that their hero has gone to eat at the house of a sinner. But Jesus corrects them and reminds them that, even so, Zacchaeus too is a descendant of Abraham; that is, he too, in spite of whatever wrong he has done, is a child of the promise. That would be equivalent to a Christian reminding a murderer that, even so, Jesus died for his sins.

Fifth question: what happens next? Zacchaeus proclaims his innocence: "I don't think I have, but *if* I have extorted anything from anyone I will repay several times over." Whatever the case, Jesus reminds the murmuring crowd that he has come to seek and save those who are lost. Lost here does not mean damned, but means "in the wrong place" and Zacchaeus was certainly there, and now he was in the right place, with Jesus.

Now the final and most significant question: What does this Zacchaeus episode mean for us? Let me suggest an answer by way of a story. In the 1800s the poet John Greenleaf Whittier wrote one of the most quoted poems in the English language. The poem was titled "Maud Miller." You've never heard of it? Actually not many people remember this rather sorrowful poem, but I tell you generations of people have quoted two famous lines from its final stanza.

"Maud Miller" is about a young maiden who, while working the fields one day, sees a handsome young judge riding on horseback. She offers him a cool drink of water. Their encounter lasts only a few moments, but it makes a deep impression on both of them. Maud is greatly attracted to the judge and she dreams of marrying someone of his gentleness and integrity.

She could leave the fields behind and live as the wife of a wealthy and powerful man.

At the same time the judge is attracted to Maud. He is tired of his career and he dreams of marrying a warm, compassionate woman like Maud and setting into a simpler life in the country. But neither Maud nor the judge acknowledges their attraction to each other. They are from different social classes. They cannot risk breaking the bonds of social conformity. For us, think of Audrey Hepburn and Gregory Peck in *Roman Holiday* and you get the picture.

Anyway, Maud later marries a man who brings her much pain and hardship. The judge also enters into a loveless marriage. In the final stanza of the poem Whittier offers us this famous warning: "For of all sad words of tongue or pen, the saddest are these: 'It might have been!'" "It might have been." One of the things about the Zacchaeus story, as we saw, is that he finally set his jaw and took the plunge. He decided to take the risk. Not knowing what he might encounter, he dared to go out in public to see, embrace, follow Jesus and discover a new way of life.

And in this story there *we* are, always on the verge of commitment, always close to the decisive act, the heroic deed, the real holiness to which we feel attracted but, like Zacchaeus, hesitant to embrace. Why? The truth is that what haunts us is what haunted him: what of the crowd?

Murmur, murmur, murmur. "Hey, I see you got religion. What happened to you? Don't be a party pooper." And all because you decided to go out on a limb. All because you decided to go to church. All because you joined a prayer group. All because you pray. All because you won't take drugs or do things that hurt people. All because you won't talk dirty talk. All because you have become an advocate of the poor. All because you love God and it shows. And all because you don't want to have to say at the end of your life, "It might have been. If only I had answered the call, the impulse, to see Jesus Christ and follow him!"

So the Zacchaeus story winds up challenging us to go out on a limb. It is, in the last analysis, an invitational story. Its message is: beware of the "might have been" and embrace St. Paul's words, "Now is the acceptable time."

A Couple of Sit-Ins

Thirty-Second Sunday in Ordinary Time, B, Mark 12:38–44

"Mr. Johnson," said the judge, "I have reviewed this case carefully and I've decided to give your wife $800 a week alimony." Mr. Johnson answers. "That's very generous, your honor. And, believe me, I'll try to help out a little myself now and then." That's not quite what the judge had in mind.

I tell that story as a warning because I'm going to pull something like this joke with this gospel's well-known and well-beloved incident of what we call "the widow's mite." We've heard it year after year and, year after year, have taken away the moral of the heroic generosity of a woman who had next to nothing and gave what she had to the Temple treasury. Why can't we be like that? It's a good, familiar, conventional lesson, but I'm going to pull a "Mr. Johnson" and stand this gospel unfamiliarly on its head. To understand this mild shock to your expectations, you must remember the opening of the gospel. Jesus is spitting out some acid comment. "Beware of the social-climbing scribes who hanker after the trappings of position and respectability, while all the while they exploit poor people, especially vulnerable widows."

Ah, there's the context. These scribes and Sadducees were all part of the political-religious Temple complex that, like the old Tammany Hall or Enron or Congress, had grown corrupt. They had their lobbyists, briberies, and scandals. It was an open secret, yet people could do little about it. One group called the Essenes found the Temple so corrupt that they moved out. They went and settled in the environs of the Dead Sea and, as you know, we found their scrolls in 1947. Others stayed and gave passive resistance. Jesus is one of them. Jesus, recall, "sat down opposite the treasury." That is, he is there is silent protest. He is opposed to the whole Temple atmosphere around money, with the rich parading their large sums. He is, in effect, doing a sit-in just as he is obviously watching who is putting what in.

Along comes a widow, one of those exploited. Poor as she is, she drops in two coins out of the religiosity of her heart. Jesus sees this, shakes his head, and speaks out his words: "This poor widow put in more than all the others...from her poverty, she has contributed all she had...." I ask you to hear these words not as words of praise, but as words of lament. Yes, lament, spoken with a heavy heart. Jesus is sorrowful, even angry, that this devout woman has unwittingly put money into a system in which the scribes devour the houses of people like her. Moreover, she has given her all to a Temple that will soon be destroyed. In this different interpretation, Jesus is feeling bad that this woman had just innocently contributed to a corrupt system that will turn right around and use her money to buy longer and more expensive robes and pay for their high life, that she unknowingly has cooperated in her own exploitation. It's not uncommon. The exploited are often so co-opted, so helpless, that they do not see what is happening. Needless to say, Jesus' public sadness, his sit-in, and his open criticism of the political powers caught their attention. Sooner or later they would have to deal with him.

So, now seen in this light, this incident of the "widow's mite" is really not a story about a poor woman's generosity. It's a story about the exploitation of a poor woman and the meanness and greed of the system that exploits her. Jesus' words are not words of praise, but, as I suggested, words of sadness. And it's not a stretch to think that today Jesus sits opposite some corporations, government buildings, state houses, and even some churches and laments over the taxpayers and impoverished who must support them.

In fact, I tell you, he does so in his followers, his true followers. Let me mention one example. It's about a Hispanic man named Oscar, Oscar Romero. In 1977 he was appointed archbishop of El Salvador at a time of severe upheaval and a cruel oppressive government. But Romero was chosen because he was a safe, party man, a good choice by the powers that be who wanted to make no waves. Then to this safe, conventional party man three things happened and happened traumatically that turned him around. First a Jesuit priest he admired, a staunch defender of the exploited workers and peasants, was killed by the military. This priest was killed for nothing more than siding with the poor, as Jesus had taught him to do. Bereft now of a courageous leader, the poor came to their archbishop and asked him if *he* would now be their defender. Me? A defender of the poor? This was a moment of decision for a privileged man who had every expectation of living the privileged life of a Temple scribe. He thought, he prayed, and he said yes.

The next year the second thing happened. Three bishops condemned a people's popular movement, saying it was too communist sounding. Archbishop Romero broke ranks and said no. He said, and said loudly, that it was a movement for simple justice for the exploited. The government took note.

The third and final event came in 1979 when the military police opened fire on a large political gathering of unarmed people. Romero was absolutely saddened and appalled at this slaughter of the innocent and from that moment on became ever more publicly outspoken in defense of the poor.

Well, obviously he was becoming too bold and too public a figure to be sitting there every day opposite the treasury, as it were. Like the scribes of Jesus' time, sooner or later the political powers would have to deal with Romero. And they did. In March 1980, while he was celebrating Mass uttering those words, "This is my body given for you," soldiers burst into the church and shot the archbishop to death. He slumped over the altar of sacrifice, his blood staining the white altar cloths. His cause is up for canonization.

So it turns out that this familiar gospel is not so familiar after all. Maybe it's not just about the simple message of a simple woman of great heart who shames the ostentatious high and mighty with her two small coins. Maybe it's about legal corruption and a Jesus who is saddened that good people are exploited by the system and must pay into it. I suspect we kind of like the old interpretation. In a way it's safer. But this one is more spiritually challenging. It challenges us to challenge evil where we find it, to sit across from the treasury, to lament, to do what we can to cleanse the Temple and bring justice for the poor and marginal. In short, it challenges us to be like Jesus.

Where's Bob?

THIRTY-SECOND SUNDAY IN ORDINARY TIME, C, LUKE 20:27–38

The skeptic confronted the priest. He said, "If you really believe what you preach, then I make you a challenge. Drink this poison here and if you don't die, I'll believe." The priest retorted, "I have a better plan. You drink the poison and I'll raise you up!"

We're going to talk about the resurrection, something we hope is considerably down the road. Concerning the resurrection, there are two major points to make. First, when we recite our creed and proclaim, "I believe in the resurrection of the dead," most of us, I suspect, mean what Plato meant: "I believe in the immortality of the soul."

But that decidedly is *not* the Christian belief. Christian belief is not that the soul, apart from the body, lives on. No, the Christian belief is that the whole embodied person lives on. Who and what we are now, as an embodied person, will live on. Just as Jesus' resurrection offered the entire Jesus as risen with a glorified body that ate and to which he invited his apostles to feel and touch, so, like Jesus, the "total we" will be raised up, not just the soul.

This profound sense of embodiment, you should recall, is fundamental to our religion and is its underlying motif. It structures our liturgical year where we have the three major embodiments of the Christian faith: the Incarnation, God taking our flesh; the Eucharist, "my body given for you"; and the resurrection, the raising of Jesus, the victory over death and limitation—all dealing with the body, Christ's and ours. So, once more, we as a totality, body and soul, will be raised up, not just our souls.

The second point is that, in talking about the resurrection of the dead, the focus must be entirely on God and God's promises. This is critical to grasp.

God is Emmanuel, "God with us." That description was given at Jesus' birth—
"You shall call his name Emmanuel, which means 'God with us'"—and closes
his death and resurrection, after which he reminded us, "I am with you all
days, even till the end of time." He added, "So do not be afraid. I go to prepare
a place for you." And those promises in fact resonate with us.

Why? Because we all have a deep down hankering not only to survive
but also to find completion and permanence in an ever-changing world.
We have an almost genetic capacity, a yearning, for growth. Becoming is
never finished. All these yearnings suggest a place prepared for us, a resurrection, an eternity. As C.S. Lewis once wrote, if the duck has a yearning to
swim, well, there is water; a flower to grow, well, there is sunlight; a child
to love, well, there is mother. Likewise, if we have a yearning to live forever,
to be, to become more beyond this world, why should there also not be
something to satisfy *these* longings? Some may scoff over people declared
clinically dead who describe having seen a bright light and feeling a deep
sense of peace, but they cannot explain or deny the universal expressions
of life after death.

So we Christians resonate with God's promises to love and cherish us, to
be with us beyond the grave, knowing such promises are not conditioned
by boundaries, space, or time. God is faithful and that's all we need to know
and that is cause enough for joy. Having created us, God is simply unwilling to let us go—ever. Remember that.

Otherwise, if we lose this insight, this truth, and shift our focus from
God to ourselves, *then* we get bogged down in all those "me" questions.
Will I still need glasses? Will I look like I am now or when I was twenty-
six and tall and straight with jet-black hair? What about those cremated,
those eaten by sharks, those pulverized by explosives? Will Rick, my dog,
be there? Will I know my friends?

As curious as we are about these things and fruitlessly wonder how God
can "reassemble" bodies, we must accept the fact that these are really not
primary questions because, as I said, the resurrection is not about us. The
resurrection is about God and God's fidelity, God's promise never to abandon us. God will work out the logistics.

True enough, Hollywood offers us its solution of ghosts, ghouls, zom-
bies, and dead baseball players on fields of dreams, and literature offers

us Hamlet's father and Washington Irving's Headless Horseman, but these concoctions really don't say much about people of the resurrection.

And Jesus himself, you notice, doesn't reveal much either, except to say that eternal life will be different, a dimension beyond our comprehension. So he tells the Sadducees who bring him the absurd case of the seven men with one wife, a parody on the first reading of the seven brothers. Jesus simply tells them that they are wrongheaded. The continuation of life through marriage and children is not needed in the afterlife where extinction is not the issue. People will be more like angels. It will be a whole new order of existence.

Occasionally, though, we get hints of that new order. We get intimations of closeness and contact. For example, I know a woman who had lost her husband, Bob, and was deep into grief and anger. One day she lost her car keys. She searched everywhere. She began to cry over her loss of Bob and the keys. Suddenly she became angry with Bob for leaving her alone and she found herself shouting at him, "Find my damn keys! If there's anyone out there, if there's any love left in this universe, find my keys!" She calmed down and a year later she found her keys in a most unexpected place: peeking through a hole in a poster that hung on the inside of her closet door. How silly. How in the world could they have gotten there? Who would be so mindless as to put them there?

Of all the speculations, she did not dismiss the thought that it might be her husband. Bob had a tendency to procrastinate, and he had a unique sense of humor and it would be just like him to have taken a year to get around to giving the keys back in a clever fashion. She's not saying it was Bob, or wasn't, only that life is unpredictable and uncertain and that if there is uncertainty there is also, as she put it, "ravishing mystery." In other words, she was not ready to put a period to death.

Nor should we. Jesus said, "I am the resurrection and the life. He who believes in me shall live forever." That's a promise that will be kept.

Christic the King

Go back to the year 1925. It's several years after the Great War, World War I. Pope Pius XI is sitting in the Vatican looking around the world, particularly at Europe, and he is worried at what he sees. Mussolini is parading around Italy with arrogance. A man named Hitler in Germany has just been released from jail and his scary Nazi party is gaining strength. People everywhere seem to be losing faith and perspective. The pope feels he must come up with some sign, some symbol, to remind people what life is about and to whom they truly belong.

What did he choose? He finally hits on a popular symbolic term: king. That should do it. After all, there were kings of the past and present and there were mythical kings to come: Good King Wenceslas would brighten holiday times, Old King Cole was a merry old soul. Clark Gable was Hollywood's king to be followed by Elvis, the king of rock and roll, and the soft melodies of Nat King Cole, not to mention the most formidable king of them all, King Kong. So the concept "king" had a lot going for it, and so in 1925, as a reminder to whom we subjects should pay our respect, whose commands we should follow, the pope instituted the feast of Christ the King: king of our hearts, our souls, our lives. It was meant to jar us to get our priorities straight, to remind us of the ultimate object of our allegiance.

This is that feast of Christ the King that we are celebrating today. It has nothing to do with crowns, palaces, or robes, concepts foreign to us Americans. Rather, it has to do with the basic question: to whom or to what do we give our allegiance? This is a pretty basic question. It deals with how, we, on the everyday level, act or should act. It deals with the daily decisions we make when we leave here, decisions that reveal the allegiance we have.

Let me give you two practical examples of allegiance. When Pius XI's apprehension proved right and Hitler rose to power, he overran Europe. There were many heroes who resisted. One of them was a king, King Christian of Denmark, aptly named, a person of character and principle. One famous story tells of the time when the order came from the Nazis that all Jews were to identify themselves by wearing armbands with the yellow Star of David. King Christian, whose tiny country had been occupied in 1940, said, No, it's not right. One Danish person was the same as the next one, he declared. So what did he do? He put on the first Star of David and let it be known that every loyal Dane should do the same. The next day in Copenhagen almost the entire population was walking around wearing the yellow Star of David armbands. As a result, the Danes saved ninety percent of their Jewish population. Later, the Nazis decided that all 8000 Jews would be rounded up and sent to concentration camps. King Christian again reacted. He organized a resistance effort that smuggled 7500 Jews to Sweden within a two-week period.

It goes without saying that he suffered for his allegiance to principle rather than to Hitler. He was imprisoned for two years and, after his release when the Third Reich fell in 1945, he died a few years later from his ill treatment. As I said, the feast of Christ the King asks to whom or to what do we pay our allegiance, what guides our life? Well, for King Christian of Denmark it was justice and charity, the very things Jesus preached.

Let's move to today's headlines. A father attacks the coach of his seven-year-old because he's not giving him enough playing time. Another father knocks out a referee for what he thinks is a bad call in a football game. It's a game for seven- to nine-year-olds, for cryin' out loud! A psychologist on a talk show laments the harm such actions do to those kids. Football, he says, is a game full of precise rules and regulations. Therefore the kids watch in utter confusion as their fathers violate the rules of the game and the rules of fair play and character building. These fathers, the psychologist adds, not only cause moral confusion by their acts of violence but are teaching their sons that this is the way you settle scores. In our terms, for them, violence is king, not Christ.

Now, keeping these incidents in mind, skip over to West Nickel Mines School in Lancaster, Pennsylvania. Ten young Amish girls were shot by an insane non-Amish assassin. But revenge and counterviolence did not rule here. What did the Amish do? They forgave the man! Not only did they forgive him, but they brought food to his wife and children who lived not too far from the school.

Now I just said that easily and you listened to that easily, but did it sink in? Think. Put yourself in their place. You have just rung the doorbell of the family whose husband and father brutally murdered your nine-year-old innocent daughter and here you are bringing food and forgiveness for them. Could we reach that level of faith the Amish did, these very same people who have also asked that some of the money that has been raised for their grieving families be given to the family of the man who killed and wounded their daughters? Would you and I, *could* you and I, do that? How different the Amish are from the brutish fathers who beat up on their kids' coaches and referees!

Well, the Amish are different, aren't they? They live apart from us, living a life they feel God wants them to live. They take King Jesus at his word when he says we should forgive our enemies and did so as he reigned from the cross. They do not actively try to convert anyone, believing their lives are testimony enough. I think they just proved that. They accept a core set of rules. They are people of peace. They, as you may know, do not serve in the armed forces. They do not accept Social Security or purchase life insurance. They vote, pay taxes, but do not hold public office. They forgive their enemies because they believe they cannot enter heaven if they hate anyone. For them, the matter is simple: Christ the King has spoken.

There's no question but that here's a people who have every right to rant and rage, to blame and yell and lash out. But not for them the football fathers' way. They will not serve the demons of anger and revenge. They serve Another. We Catholics should envy their reputation.

So, there you are: King Christian of Copenhagen, Denmark, and the Amish of Lancaster, Pennsylvania. Today on this feast let us collectively pray for the courage to add our names to these faithful followers of Christ the King.

Heart Transplant

CHRIST THE KING, C, LUKE 23:35–43

We Americans have always been suspicious of kings ever since we jettisoned them in 1776. We find it amusing rather than impressive, for example, when in that stunning movie *The Queen*, Prime Minister Tony Blair and his wife are instructed by the protocol office on how to leave the queen. They are to back out of the room never showing their backs to the Queen. It was hilarious to watch both a distinguished head of government, Tony Blair, and his wife, no friend of royalty, walking awkwardly backward out of the room while the Queen gazed imperiously at their stumbling departure.

Kings and queens are not for us and we save those titles for our adored celebrities, for example, King of Rock and Roll, Queen Latifah. We talk of being a royal pain you-know-where. Kingship doesn't cut it with us.

But it did back then when Pius XI invented the feast of Christ the King. At his time there were kings and dictators and some were repressive and cruel beyond belief. The pope wanted to set up a counter royalty to let them know that they were under judgment. He wanted to give them a different view of what it meant to be king. So he chose Jesus. The choice was wise because there couldn't be more of a contrast.

Jesus did not have a scepter but he did have a towel.

He did not have people bowing backward from his presence but he himself bowed instead and washed their feet.

He had no army but he did have disciples.

He sat on no throne but rather on a donkey's back.

He wore no crown of gold but one of thorns.

He did not take life. He gave it.

He did not set boundaries but included prostitutes, tax collectors, foreigners, and good thieves in his kingdom.

318

He did not exploit people but spoke sympathetically of widows' mites, prodigal sons, good Samaritans, and poor farmers.

He did not wield the sword but mercy. "Today you will be with me in paradise."

He did not force. He invited. He seduced his subjects.

I think of one such subject, Anne Lamott, a writer who has influenced many. In her book *Traveling Mercies* she describes her very unwilling encounter with Christ.

She grew up, she tells us, in a hippie household in California—where else?—that provided no boundaries for her. Her parents occasionally went to church for show but both were atheists. In fact, most of her friends were atheists. She learned a bit about the Bible from the mother of a girlfriend who read stories when Anne was there for a sleepover. But that's as far as her contact with religion went.

When she attended school on the East Coast she came to believe in the existence of a supreme power, but it was not something that made a big difference in how she lived. Following graduation, she returned to California where she became a writer and where she adopted the hippie life she knew. Which means she used cocaine, became addicted to alcohol, slept around, got pregnant, and had an abortion.

Now and then she kind-of attended a small Presbyterian church. I say "kind-of" because she mostly stood in the doorway in the back and listened primarily to the choir she liked, a motley group of five black women and one Amish-looking man, who sang sweet gospel music. But sometimes, in spite of herself, she heard something more than sweet music, something as low and persistent as a heartbeat, but she shook it off and always left before the sermon.

Well, one night, she relates, after some heavy drinking, she became aware of a presence in her room. She knew instinctively, beyond any doubt, that it was Jesus. And she was appalled. Horrified. No way was she ready for him. What would her hippie, liberal friends think if she had Jesus for a friend? If, even worse, she ever became a Christian? She turned to the wall in rejection of Jesus and cried out loud, "No way. I would rather die!"

But all was not over. Not by a long shot. Try as she might, she could not shake the feeling that Jesus was following her, stalking her, as it were "like a little cat," as she put it. She wrote, "It was as if God wanted me to reach down and pick it up, wanting me to open the door and let it in. But *I* knew what would happen: You let a cat in one time, give it a little milk, and it stays forever." She didn't want that to happen. No way.

Well, about a week later she went back to the little church, so hung over that she had to sit. This time, too drowsy to move, she stayed to the end. The last song of the service moved her deeply. She ran home, but had a sense that that little cat ran with her. She writes, "I walked past dozens of potted flowers, under a sky as blue as one of God's own dreams, and I opened the door to my house and stood there a minute. Then I hung my head and said, 'I quit.' Then I swore and said, 'All right! All right! You can come in.' This was the beautiful moment of my conversion."

This wasn't the end. Things weren't smooth or easy. She fell. She got pregnant again, and she had to go into recovery, but for all of that, she was hooked. She had said yes to the King who was gently but relentlessly calling to her.

The feast of Christ the King, though sounding stilted and obsolete to us, is meant to say how we too should surrender to a different and often unpopular way of life where we make deliberate decisions to follow Jesus' Golden Rule, rise above "what's in it for me?", choose honesty and fidelity rather than deceit, forgiveness rather than revenge, serve rather than being served, engage in peacemaking, and yes, even dabble in heroism.

These attitudes do not make for a popular kingdom and won't get you far in a world of greed and conquest, but it's part and parcel of Jesus' kingdom and the world needs it, really needs it.

Let me illustrate it this way. In December 1997, you may recall, a young man in West Paducah, Kentucky, took a gun to school and killed seven of his classmates. Parents came from all over the community, frantically praying a parent's most heartfelt prayer: "Not my child. Please don't let anything happen to my child."

One mother's prayer was not answered that day. Her son died in the shooting. In spite of her shock and grief, the mother didn't hesitate when doctors asked if she would donate her son's organs to someone else in critical need.

Many months pass, and the mother discovers that some of her son's organs went to a Methodist pastor. She contacts him and asks to meet him.

The day of their meeting, the grieving mother and the grateful pastor talk and pray and celebrate the life of the precious son who died. And then the mother startles the pastor by making a strange request. She asks: "Can I put my ear to your heart? Can I hear my son's heart beating, one more time?"

We are called to be that person who has the transplanted heart, the heart of Jesus. There are so many people today who are so discouraged with the present war and the threat of more war, corrupt leaders, overwhelming greed, the grossness of society, and the absence of morals that they desperately need to hear the reassurance of that heart. They need to put their ears to our hearts and know that Jesus Christ still reigns.

Holy Days, Holidays, and Occasions

Operation Encouragement: New Year's Day

Two quotations to start off the New Year: Ralph Waldo Emerson wrote, "Our chief want is someone who will inspire us to be what we know we could be." Basketball coach Jim Valvano said, "My father gave me the greatest gift anyone could give another person: he believed in me."

Since this is the day for resolutions, I suggest, in the light of these quotations, one overriding one: Be a bearer of joy and encouragement this year. I think of some events and persons who have brought me joy since we met last New Year's.

When I visited my cousin in Bordentown, I was told that, as a sign of the town's growing sophistication, a second "adult" store was opened in a small strip mall. Scarcely had it opened, however, when an imaginative follower of Jesus opened a storefront church right next to the porn store. This storefront church announces itself to be "Christ the Redeemer Ministry." It'll be interesting to see who wins this battle, God or Mammon? Either way, my heart was filled with joy and encouraged by the creative audacity of the minister.

Then there was the Christmas card I received from a friend a few weeks ago. My friend, a recovering alcoholic, wrote in the card: "Father Bausch, I'm happy to tell you that both my sons, in their thirties, have checked into the program and have now been faithful members of AA for two years. This Christmas will be the first one in thirty-five years that all the members of the family have been sane and sober. Joyful news!"

I visited a poor, elderly woman called Bea. She is crippled with arthritis and needs a walker to get around. She said to me: "Father Bausch, did I ever tell you that God is my walker?" "No," I said. Then she launched into this poem she wrote herself:

> I trust my walker to lead me—
> it never fails me, always keeps me strong.
> My walker, like my God, is my pilot.
> My walker is my support—
> like God, it leads and I follow.
> I depend on it for every step I take.
> It keeps me steady—I'll never fall.
> It gives me confidence and strength.
> We walk together, hand in hand,
> and I'll tell all the Good News, that God is my walker.

This past year, I met Father Jack Corcoran. He was home on leave from his mission in Nepal. When he first went there twelve years ago, he said, he found, among other things, fifty-two severely mentally ill women chained up in prison....Their families had been unable to control them. In prison they were kept on earth-floored cells covered with straw. Father Jack sought out a doctor who prescribed medication for the women, and before long they were all joyfully able to go back to their families.

Stan Gaede, an old gent I visited in a nursing home, remembers when he was thirteen years old and sitting in the driver's seat of his father's pickup truck. He wasn't old enough to be driving. He was barely able to look over the steering wheel. Nonetheless, he was driving right through the middle of town. His father sitting in the back of the truck, was delivering 100-pound bags of potatoes to friends, relatives, and needy people in their town. He recalls his dad running back and forth from pickup to house and back again, toting those one-hundred-pound bags on his shoulders.

At first, he says, he was embarrassed by his father's actions. After all, his father was a fairly successful farmer, with land and employees and social standing. Yet there he was, "running around town with sacks of potatoes on his shoulder, making a spectacle of himself." It was an act of love, though. Stan would never forget the joy his father experienced giving away 100 pounds of potatoes, a joy he continued in his own life.

Finally, it was a joy to read about Pierre Toussaint, who likely will be the first black American saint. There will be dancing in the streets from Harlem to Bedford Stuyvesant. "He was a very holy man who reached out to help everyone who needed any kind of help, and it never made any difference to him about the color of the other person's skin," explained Monsignor Robert O'Connell, the vice postulator for Toussaint's cause and the pastor of New York's oldest church, St. Peter's in downtown Manhattan where Toussaint attended daily Mass for almost seven decades. He was no Reverend Al Sharpton or Reverend Jesse Jackson but, like most saints, he quietly let his actions leave their own eloquent message as his legacy.

Born into slavery in the French colony of Haiti in 1766, Toussaint was among the 800,000 slaves who made it easy for the French plantation owners to amass huge amounts of wealth from their coffee and sugar crops. But when the French revolution exploded and the slaves lashed out with their own uprising, many of the slave owners packed up and fled. And John Berard du Pithon, Toussaint's master, fled to New York City with his wife, his sister, four slaves, and Toussaint.

And when du Pithon fell on hard times in the city and eventually died, Toussaint stayed on with his master's family and, for the next twenty years, supported them with the money that he earned as a hairdresser. And even beyond that, Toussaint and his wife, Juliette, who was also a slave, made their modest home a haven for orphaned black children, raised them, and eventually even found jobs for them. He also raised enough money (through his wealthy customers) for a special home for orphans that had been built by a priest and that helped those who needed food, medicine, or clothing.

When, on her deathbed, his late master's wife arranged for his freedom, Toussaint dedicated the rest of his life, and much of his money, toward ransoming the freedom of other slaves. He also spent the lion's share of his time visiting and nursing those who had been struck down by yellow fever or cholera.

Pierre Toussaint died in New York City in 1853 at the age of eighty-seven. In reviewing Toussaint's life, both blacks and whites readily agree that nothing seemed more personally important and critical to Toussaint than sharing joy by helping others, even his own slave masters.

Well, it's good to remember that Jesus brought joy to all he met—except his enemies. Imagine the joy of the blind whose sight Jesus restored, of the deaf who could suddenly hear, of the lame who could throw their crutches away! Jesus was the personification of joy to the world.

For 2006, make it your mission to bring joy and encouragement to others. They are so sorely needed.

Mother's Day

FIFTH SUNDAY OF EASTER, B, JOHN 15:1–8

I had a good and serious homily prepared for today's striking gospel of the Vine and the Branches. But then it dawned on me: it's Mother's Day and I'm seasoned enough to know that, if I am to get paid this week, I dare not omit saying something about Mother's Day in relation to this gospel. Still, any preacher who dares to get up and speak on Mother's Day faces at least three problems, or dangers. The three dangers I am speaking of are the danger of "being an expert," the danger of using *Mary* as the model of motherhood, and the danger of facing a very mixed congregation.

The danger of being an expert: you all know the story of the priest who got up and spoke at great length on the glories of motherhood. And when he walked outside a woman came up to him and said, "Father, I wish I knew as little about being a mother as you do." Or the other priest who preached about Mary as the perfect model to be a wife and mother. And a woman came up to him, carrying one baby and with four other children following her, and said, "It's easy enough for her with her one child."

And then, our congregation is mixed. We celebrate Mother's Day. We talk about and honor mothers. And yet many of our congregation are *not* mothers, and some, like myself, are not married and are not women. Nevertheless, what we all have in common is we've all had a mother. We've all had the experience of a mother and that justifies speaking about her.

Two verbs come to my mind when I think about the experience of being raised and growing up and becoming an adult and, in my case, letting go of a mother. The first verb is to treasure. We treasure the memories, the importance, the impact, and the love of our mothers.

The second verb is to remember because, despite what it says on the Hallmark greeting cards, mothers are not perfect, and they should not be expected to be perfect, and they are never going to be perfect, and we remember that. And what that truth does, later on as we go through life, is make us look back and smile at the things our mothers taught us.

For example, someone compiled a list of the Ten Things Mothers Always Say. See if any of these sound familiar to you:

1. Because I said so!
2. Cupcakes are *not* breakfast food.
3. I'm doing this for your own good.
4. You could catch your death of cold out there.
5. Close the door. We don't live in a barn!
6. If you're too sick to go to school, you're too sick to play outside.
7. If you're too full to finish your dinner, you're too full to have dessert.
8. Don't talk with your mouth full.
9. Someday you'll thank me.
10. All I do is follow you around all day, picking up after you like some maid.

What would we do without these pearls of wisdom? Think of the potential mess the world would be in if we defied our mothers' instructions and the things they taught us:

They taught us *logic:* "Come down immediately. All right, if you fall out of that tree and break both your legs, don't coming running to me!"

They taught us *medicine*: "If you don't stop crossing your eyes, they're going to freeze that way."

They taught us *ESP*: "Put your sweater on; don't you think that I know when you're cold?"

They taught us *to meet a challenge*: What were you thinking? Answer me when I talk to you and don't talk back to me!"

They taught us about *genetics*: "You are just like your father!"

They taught us about the *wisdom of age*: "When you get to be my age, you will understand."

They taught us about *anticipation*: "Just wait until your father gets home."

They taught us about *receiving*: "You are going to get it when we get home."

And my all-time favorite, they taught us *justice*: "One day you will have kids and I hope they turn out just like you. Then you'll see what it's like!"

And sometimes they make it happen. A woman writes, "When my three-year-old son opened the birthday gift from his grandmother, he discovered a water pistol. He squealed with delight and headed for the nearest sink. I was not so pleased. I turned to mom and said, "I'm surprised at you. Don't you remember how we used to drive you crazy with water guns?" Mom smiled and then replied, "I remember."

Some mothers are clever. Some are devious.

There's a story about a young man who was walking through a supermarket to pick up a few things when he noticed an old woman following him around. Thinking nothing of it, he ignored her and continued on. Finally he went to the checkout line, but this older woman got in front of him.

"Pardon me," she said, "I'm sorry if my staring at you has made you feel uncomfortable. It's just that you look like my son, who just died recently." And she wiped away a tear.

"I'm very sorry," replied the young man. "Is there anything I can do for you?"

"Yes," she said with a sigh, "As I'm leaving, would you say 'Goodbye, Mother!'? It would make me feel so much better."

"Sure," answered the young man. As the old woman was leaving, he called out, "Goodbye, Mother." She waved back at him and disappeared through the supermarket door.

As he stepped up to the checkout counter, he saw that his total was $127.50. "How can that be?" he asked, "I only purchased a few things!"

The clerk looked over the top of his reading glasses and said, "Your mother said that you would pay for her."

For most of us, our mother is the Vine of today's gospel. We carry her vitality with us wherever we go, even after our mothers have passed on. No matter how far we may stray from our mother's home or our mother's teachings, we still are the Branch that is attached spiritually to that Vine. It still gives us life.

And so I end with one daughter's remembrance of her life-giving mother, Sister Jose Hobday, a Franciscan nun whose mother was a Seneca Indian. And what she writes is for all of us, mothers or not. She writes:

> I was about six years old at the time. I was sitting outside on a
> block of concrete, and I was crying. I don't even know why. I was

just crying and crying. My mother came along and said, "What's the matter?" I said, "Nothing. Leave me alone!" She did—and then I really started crying. About fifteen minutes later she came back and sat beside me. "You know," she said, "I have to tell you something. There are going to be a lot of times in your life when you are going to cry, and you won't know why. You won't understand and neither will anybody else. You can marry the nicest man in the world, but at times like this, he won't know what to do to help you stop crying."

Then she said she was going to teach me a prayer for the times when I was crying and didn't know why. She made me get off the cement block and stand up. She said, "Now put your arms around yourself. " I did, but it wasn't good enough for her. "You're just folding your arms," she said. "Put them all the way around yourself. Cuddle your body. Hold yourself the way you would hold a baby in your arms. Now after you have a real good hold of yourself, close your eyes and begin to rock yourself. Rock yourself real good, the way you would a baby, and just keep doing it. When you grow up, no matter how old you are, and you find yourself crying and you don't know why, I want you to rock yourself just like this. And as you do it, remember that you are God's little girl, and that God understands why you are crying, even if no one else does. And remember, too, that God holds you close, just the way you are holding yourself, because God loves you very much. Then just keep rocking yourself and be comforted."

Sister Hobday adds:

Isn't that a good prayer? I still say it today when I feel bad. I recommend it for you, too. Just stand wherever you are—in the kitchen, in the shop, or in the bathroom—and wrap your arms around yourself as tightly as you can. Rock yourself. Before long you will be able to feel God holding you in the same way you are holding yourself. You will be comforted the way you were comforted as a child when your mother held you in her arms and rocked you.

Father's Day: The Men

It's Father's Day and to speak of fathers in particular and men in general I want to go back six months and pick up the story of three famous men. We call them Astrologers, Kings of the Orient, Wise Men, Magi. Whatever we call them, there are three obviously identifying things about them that will form our rather offbeat reflection for today, namely, they are male, they are active, and they are on a journey. And these are the three things I want to talk about in the hope that my remarks will provoke your follow-up, whether agreeing or disagreeing, dismissive or thoughtful.

The Magi are male, which means that they are traversing the desert, not standing in the temple, not sitting in church. And they are in the majority. The Gallup Poll shows that only thirty-seven percent of adult American Catholic men go to church—and it's far less in other countries. In Latin American churches the pews are largely the domain of women. Even in once Catholic Ireland, the tradition is for men to stand outside the church on Sunday and smoke and chat while their women pray at Mass.

The question arises, Why are men, along with young adults—the other big group—absent from church? There are several reasons. First, there is the liturgy. It is largely a feminine construct. Father Richard Rohr, who has done pioneer work on male spirituality, writes, "Church became a women's thing in most countries because most official church rituals appeal much more to the feminine psyche than to the masculine."

Yes, the leadership may be male but the worship service—with its incense, candles, art, ritual, movement, themes, and hymns—appeals to a feminine consciousness. From the beginning, Christianity has always been acknowledged as more of a woman's religion, but today, with the priest shortage, women have substantially added an official presence by being dominant in ministerial positions once held by men.

For example, eighty-five percent of lay ecclesial ministers, as we call them, are women. Women are also now in the majority as theologians, Scripture scholars. and, as always, teachers in school and religious education. It is common today for commentators on both sides of the liberal-conservative spectrum to speak of "the feminization of the church." And this has an impact on men.

As I wrote in my book *Brave New Church*:

> Taught for most of their lives by women in school and CCD, soon to be tutored by Catholic theologians who will be predominately female, what do the men and boys who *do* go to church see? If they see the dominance of a female congregation, female acolytes, female Eucharistic ministers, female lectors; if the iconography and hymns are feminine; if the liturgies are feminine, executed by priests who bring feminine sensitivities to the service; if the gospel message of sweet consolation is not matched by St. Paul's masculine call to strive like an athlete and lay aside sin; if little boys who are invited to kneel quietly at the shrine of Mother Faustina but not allowed to wield, so to speak, the ax of St. Boniface; if the call is to be like "Sweet Jesus" and not to honor and valor; if the number of priests who serve as role models continues to decline; finally, if we take into account the current sociological context—namely, that the young males may be among the one out of every four babies born without a father, or part of the large cadre of households led by females only—then common sense tells us that the church really has nothing to offer men but more of the same.

A little colorful, but it makes the point: One reason men do not go to church, scholars of both genders contend, is Christianity's feminine face and feminine liturgy. This, by the way, is in contrast to Islam that from day one is decidedly a masculine religion. We're not making judgments here, just observing the obvious imbalance and lack of appeal to men.

Second, men by nature are outdoors, active, competitive. Once they had an outlet in the church as they filled the religious orders such as the Jesuits, for example, who called themselves "*Soldiers* for Christ" and were under a superior *general*. And they battled the elements, traversed the world, and fought off the pagans, and we had priests like Issac Jogues and his lay companions in our own country, who embraced the rigors and martyrdoms of the new world. That's action. As one author bluntly sums it up, "Women go to church, men go to football games."

Today such men would be busy climbing the corporate ladder, and Christianity's concepts of vulnerability, turning the other cheek and opening oneself to God speak a language that women are more likely to embrace, not young men competing in a winner-take-all world.

Third, men are on a journey and initially they're quite preoccupied with it: sex, career, marriage, mobility, upscaling. But, you should note, as men get into middle age and beyond, they are more apt to turn reflective. Their children, along with their hair and waistline, are gone. They are dealing directly with mortality, with the deaths of their parents. "What's it all about?" and "Who Am I?" loom now and then, and since men find their identity in their work, *that's* where they're going to find the answers and live out their faith, not in church.

Yes, not many of them are likely to go to church to discover that identity. The church doesn't seem to say much to them and, besides, the clergy sexual scandal, still smoldering, has turned many of them off. No, to do any kind of God talk, men need to go beyond parish walls. They need other formats, not only to talk openly about getting off the career merry-go-round, but also to talk about the spiritual dimensions of their work, its ethical side, and how leadership and honesty interact. The Baby Boomers in their fifties and sixties are getting anxious about how they'll be remembered and how to pass on life lessons to younger members. They are concerned about "leaving a legacy."

Since all this is so—think of your grown sons, grandsons, sons-in-law, nephews—how can the parish help these modern-day Magi? For one thing, the church's liturgies and rituals need to begin to address the world of work beyond Sunday. It needs to give men courage and inspiration to transform the world through their work.

Second, the parish needs better iconography; that is to say, statues, paintings, hymns, and homiletic themes that are more vigorous, more concerned with people in the marketplace, rather than in the convent or monastery. Remember, men, like our absent young adults, are not looking for refuge from the world. They love it. It's the church they're not sure of. They want to know how to live honorably in the busy world they know.

As Father Richard Rohr observes, "Masculine spirituality emphasizes that doing or acting is the primary way of developing a spirituality—not hearing, not talking, not reflecting." He notes that for many men reflection comes after the action. You know, just like the National Football League is geared to intense activity followed by analysis.

Third, as men get older, the parish needs to offer concrete outlets and challenges for them to share their skills and experiences. I know accountants who help people with their finances; a mechanic who looks out for the elderly in his neighborhood, men who help with youth sports. The parish bulletin ought to constantly list helpful books, such as Richard Rohr's *Adam's Return*, and Gregory Pierce's wonderful book, *The Mass Is Never Ended*, which address work beyond Sunday, or useful Web sites, such as livingfaithatwork.org.

Well, there we are: today's Magi, a traveling band of male seekers. Men are still looking, even when they don't realize it.

True, as we saw, they are not here among us in any significant numbers, but we who *are* here can provide a needed invitational balance through a kind of Martha-Mary parish that respects the contemplative and celebrates the active, that embraces both monastery and marketplace, feminine and masculine spiritualities, and that has a strong sense that the ideal parish is not a goal but a means, a means to find common support in prayer and worship in order to transform the world. The motto is and remains: The Mass is ended. Now go. For *God's* sake, go!

Hurricane Katrina

"Where two or three are gathered in my name, there I am in the midst of them."

On September 11, 2001, the United States suffered the worst terrorist attack in its national history. Hijackers commandeered huge jet passenger planes and flew them into the World Trade Center Towers, the Pentagon, and a field in Pennsylvania. It was a tragic, tragic day in our nation's history. Nearly 3000 lives were lost.

Twelve days later, the *New York Post* published a picture of a large perfectly formed cross planted upright in a pit in the rubble of Building 6 of the World Trade Center. It was one of several that had been discovered by a construction worker in the ruins of that building. The large, cross-shaped metal beams just happened to fall that way when one of the towers collapsed. As word of the cross spread at Ground Zero, exhausted and emotionally overwhelmed rescue workers flocked to the site to pray and meditate.

The man who discovered the pit where the crosses were found is a Brooklyn-born hard hat, a gentle giant named Frank Silecchia. He found the crosses on the Thursday morning immediately following the collapse of the towers. He marked the site by spray-painting on a nearby wall the words "God's House," and a directional arrow. "The crosses are just shards of steel that came from Tower One, and went right through the roof of Building 6 and destroyed the entire center of it," he explained. "When I first saw it, it made me cry for about twenty minutes. It helped me heal the burden of my despair, and gave me closure on the whole catastrophe."

336

In subsequent days, Silecchia led his fellow rescue workers and others, many of whom were grieving the loss of loved ones, to the crosses. The grieving included a veteran firefighter who had been digging through the twisted metal for his lost firefighter son. It also included an angry cop who lost someone in the collapse, a Vatican representative who photographed the crosses for the pope, and ABC's Barbara Walters. He says they all left in peace.

"Barbara Walters's niece lost her son in the building," he said. "Barbara told me she wanted people to see the House of God, so people who needed healing could find it." Also, it is interesting that that evening, forgetting all the church-state haggling, more than three hundred members of Congress gathered spontaneously on the steps of the Capitol and sang "God Bless America."

About the horrors of 9/11, everyone, of course, was stunned. This was the first time in our history that our country had been subject to a massive terrorist attack on its own soil. Suddenly we were exposed as vulnerable, and that day, as a result, has been referred to as "the day the world changed." And indeed it has.

And now, added to this man-made devastation and loss of life comes nature's turn in the form of Hurricane Katrina. At this point we still have no full accounting of the devastation of property and the degradation of living and loss of human life which, so far, is approaching the four hundred mark. As we sit open-mouthed looking at the television, we can scarcely take in the apocalyptic landscape. Where there once were homes, there is a water-wrecked earth. Where there once were buildings, there is rubble. Where there once was law and order, there is anarchy in the streets with armed thugs and greedy looters causing havoc everywhere. Where there once was life, there is death. Over four states, it looks like a vast war zone. It's among the greatest destructions in history and certainly in our history.

And what of the people? Hundreds are dead, buried in the debris. Those who are alive are homeless, possessionless, hungry and despairing, in serious danger of disease and starvation. Within the span of a few days they have joined the pitiable refugees of the world seeking food, shelter, and lost family members. It's an unsettling double blow to us and our complacency: internal terrorism at our shores spawning security check points, surveillance, armed guards at airports and train stations—and now this huge gaping external wound in the underbelly of our country, which will take years, perhaps decades, to heal.

In such terrible, uncertain times, we all seek some assurance, some answers, some sign that God has not abandoned us; that, at the very least, somehow God cares.

The small indications that God is not absent in our tragedies lies in the small hints, hidden signs, unexpected breakthroughs, which speak to us here and there. There are, for example, those strange, coincidental crosses boldly standing amid the devastation of the Twin Towers, like the crucified Jesus hanging on a lonely hillside. There were those heroic firefighters and police.

In the middle of and in the aftermath of Katrina, shameless looters were vastly outnumbered by shameless lovers who put their lives on the line to rescue, save, and comfort others. And our country as a whole, even with inexplicable delays, has pressed in on those four states by foot, land, air, and sea, with a huge armada of supplies and personnel such as the world has never seen. And there is that daily, enormous outpouring of donations and volunteers.

And when you begin to perceive these things, you begin to perceive that what Jesus promised is beginning to seep through: "Where two or three are gathered among the ruins in my name, there I am in the midst of them." Such massive evils as terrorism and hurricane destructions are an awesome mystery and we'll never understand it. Only our faith tells us that God is not indifferent, not absent from it. Not as long as there are Good Samaritans in the midst of it all.

But another thing as you watch it all on TV. You begin to perceive that life *is* a matter of choices and you ask yourself, What led the looters and the lovers, the swindlers and the saviors, the rapists and the rescuers, to act as they did? Why did they choose such different paths? And then this one: Are we aware that every day, we are guiding our children, by our example and lifestyles, toward one of those paths? And then we ask, What would we have done? What is our habitual way of acting? With love or selfishness?

Were we there in New Orleans or Biloxi, what would we have taken with us as we fled? Ask yourself that.

And, lastly, what memories, joys and regrets—especially if, for the moment, we can't find them and are wondering where they are and *if* they are—what memories, joys, regrets concerning my spouse, my children, my friends, my neighbors would I have: the time I spent or did not spend with them, where they have fitted into my priorities, and the last time I said to them, "I love you"?

The tragedies of 9/11 and hurricane Katrina become a forceful meditation on the three fundamental "Fs" of human existence: Faith, Family, and Friends. These three values are the difference between those who believe and live as though Jesus were in their midst and those who do not.

9/11 Anniversary and Father Mychal Judge

In September, 2006, on the fifth anniversary of 9/11, a film was distributed. Its title is *Saint of 9/11,* a touching elegy for the late Father Mychal Judge, the much-loved New York City Fire Department chaplain who was one of the first to die at the World Trade Center when debris fell on him as he was following firefighters into the lobby of the North Tower. A famous photograph—you may remember it—shows a dead Father Judge, head slung to the side, being carried out by four firemen, looking for all the world like a modern pietà.

Let Jesuit priest, Father John Dear, tell the story as he experienced it.

> On the morning of September 11, 2001, I was having breakfast with my parents at their hotel in Manhattan when we heard that a plane had crashed into the World Trade Center Towers. My parents left town before both buildings collapsed, and I went downtown to St. Vincent's Hospital to try to help. In two days, Red Cross officials asked me to help coordinate chaplains at the main Family Assistance Center. I worked there fulltime for three months with over five hundred chaplains of all religions and counseled some fifteen hundred relatives and fifty firefighters and rescue workers at Ground Zero.
>
> After leaving Ground Zero on Friday afternoon, September 14, I stopped by the Church of St. Francis of Assisi on West Thirty-First Street, near Madison Square Garden, to attend the wake of Franciscan Father Mychal Judge, the chaplain of the New York

Fire Department, one of the first New Yorkers killed that terrible morning. The next day, September 15, over three thousand people attended Father Judge's funeral, which was broadcast live around the world. He was hailed as a real hero.

Who was this man Father Dear speaks of? Mychal Judge was born in Brooklyn on May 11, 1933, the son of Irish immigrants. He lost his father when he was only six and missed him terribly, missed, as he often said, having his father to look up to. When he grew up he entered the Franciscans in 1954 and was ordained in 1961. He then served as pastor of two New Jersey parishes. In 1986, he was assigned to St. Francis of Assisi Church in Manhattan, and in 1992 he was named chaplain to the New York City Fire Department. "I always wanted to be a priest or a fireman," he said at the time. "Now I'm both!" Within a short time, he gained the respect of every firefighter in New York City. It was easy to see why. Mychal Judge was exceptionally outgoing, friendly, open, and extroverted. He was a great raconteur whose gift of gab was complemented by a rollicking sense of humor. He regularly talked to thousands of parishioners, the ill, firefighters, other Franciscans. One Franciscan recalled later that he "treated everyone like family."

In 1996, when TWA flight 800 crashed off Long Island killing 230 people, Mychal spent long days consoling distraught relatives. He told them, "God is present, loving, smiling, having received our loved ones. They are in his presence, illumined by his smile and warmed by his love. His kingdom is enriched this day, so enriched by so many beautiful souls, so much beauty."

Interestingly, about a month before he died, Mychal Judge had a strong sense from his prayer that his life would soon end, so he decided to give away his few possessions. A friend of his even received a box full of his books. Then, when word came that a plane had crashed into one of the World Trade Center Towers on the morning of September 11, Mychal immediately went downtown with other firefighters. Mayor Giuliani saw him rush by with several of them and grabbed him by the arm. "Mychal, please pray for us," he said. "I always do!" Mychal responded with a nervous smile.

A few months after the catastrophe, a documentary on national television showed footage of the lobby area inside the first tower only minutes before it collapsed. Father Mychal Judge is seen walking by slowly, looking distressed and worried, his hand and lips moving slowly. Many presumed he was saying the rosary. Moments later, he went outside to bless the bodies of a firefighter and a woman. Just as he removed his helmet, steel debris fell on him, striking him in the back of the head, killing him instantly. That photograph of firefighters carrying his dead body minutes later to nearby St. Peter's Church traveled around the world. Father Mychal Judge was sixty-eight years old.

Father Dear reminisces:

> During the weeks after September 11 I met hundreds of firefighters at Ground Zero and the Family Assistance Center. On several occasions, I came upon a circle of ten or twenty firefighters, standing together in silence, in a state of shock. I did not know what to say to them, so I would ask them about Father Mychal Judge. Immediately, their faces would light up. They always knew him. More than once, I was told about how he would enter a hall during some firefighters' banquet and announce in a loud voice, "You are all doing God's work. Therefore, all your sins are forgiven!" Father Judge had run-ins with church authorities. He routinely gave this general absolution. When the cardinal of New York heard about it, Mychal was called in, reprimanded, and told never to do it again. But he disobeyed and continued to offer firefighters the mercy of God's forgiveness. Many of them spoke of how grateful they were.

But it must be said that this man of many good deeds did not achieve his life of grace without struggles. He had to battle his twin demons of alcohol and homosexuality. He kept his vows; he did not carouse or seek sexual adventures. He kept his celibacy but it was a struggle. Because of his own struggles he worked sympathetically and closely with the gay Catholic organization, Dignity. That, of course, brought him into conflict with the conservative Catholic establishment. He even marched in a St. Patrick's Day parade organized by a gay activist.

In the early days of AIDS when even the medical personnel were fearful of physical contact, Father Judge ministered to the dying men at St. Vincent's hospital and physically embraced them. Even when he encountered hostility from patients who wanted nothing to do with religion, he discovered that rubbing their feet with holy oil before he talked with them would usually break down their resistance. That was heroic. As to his alcoholism, at the time of his death he had been sober for twenty-three years and had saved countless people by taking them to AA. One man remembers living in a box until Father Judge found and rescued him.

Quite a man. The bottom line came from a fire captain who said, "Father Mychal was the kindest guy in the world. He always had time for everyone." Mychal once told one of his friends that when he got up in the morning, he allowed himself two minutes for "a pity party, to feel sorry for myself." After that, he went to work, helping and serving those in need, whomever he met.

Mychal Judge, a flawed man, gave his life in loving kindness, selfless service, and steadfast compassion. He is a witness to gospel love, to the greatest love of all: laying down our lives in love for others.

Mychal Judge said in a prayer he once wrote. "Lord, take me where you want me to go. Let me meet who you want me to meet. Tell me what you want me to say, and keep me out of your way."

St. Mychal Judge, pray for us.

Memorial Day

Those of you old enough to remember will recall that Bob Hope's signature song was "Thanks for the Memories." Memories are precious, challenging, and defining. A people, a nation is what they are by what they choose to remember and celebrate. For us, I suggest, there are three sets of memories that define us: the memories that made us, the memories that make others, and the memories of a nation.

First, the memories that made us, the horrid ones and the good ones. The horrid ones can leave us scarred, like the memories of broken homes, emotional or physical abuse, or failure. But we can grow out of them into someone deeper and better, as did denying Peter, worldly Ignatius, promiscuous John Newton, Communist Dorothy Day, and divorced Rose Hawthorne, the daughter of novelist Nathaniel Hawthorne. Bad memories show us where we have been and, by the grace of God, where we are now. The good memories are to be cherished because they have made a positive difference to us as they did for Robert Maynard, a writer for the *New York Daily News.* He relates how he came to choose to become a newspaperman. A mason made the difference.

As a boy, he remembers, he was walking along one day when he came upon an irresistible temptation. In front of him was a fresh piece of gray cement laid down to replace a broken piece of sidewalk. Maynard stopped and began to scratch his name in the wet cement. Suddenly, he became aware that the biggest mason he had ever seen was standing over him, holding a garbage can lid as his choice of weapon for little boys that day! He tried to run, but the big man grabbed him and shouted, "Why are you trying to spoil my work?" Maynard remembers babbling something about just wanting to put his name on the ground. Then a remarkable thing happened.

The mason released his arms, his voice softened, and his eyes lost their fire. There was now a touch of warmth about the man." What's your name, son?" the man asked. "Robert Maynard."

"Well, Robert Maynard, the sidewalk is no place for your name. If you want your name on something, you go in that school over there. You work hard and you become a lawyer and you hang your shingle out for all the world to see." Tears came to Maynard's eyes, but the mason was not finished yet. "What do you want to be when you grow up?"

"A writer, I think," Maynard replied.

This time the mason's voice burst forth tones that could be heard all over the schoolyard. "A writer...well then, be a writer! Be a real writer! Have your name on books, not on this sidewalk."

As Robert Maynard walked away across the street, he paused and looked back. The mason was on his knees repairing the damage Maynard's scratching had done. He looked up, saw the young boy watching, and repeated, "Be a writer." And so he did and never forgot the inspiration of a man who challenged him to a better way.

It's a good day to bless the masons in your life, to remember the people who have challenged, encouraged, guided, loved, and made a difference to you.

Next, there are the memories we create and are creating, must create.

Bonnee Hoy was a gifted composer who died in the prime of her life. At her memorial service, a friend told of a mockingbird that used to sing regularly outside Bonnee's bedroom window on summer nights. Bonnee would stand at the window peering into the darkness, listening intently, and marveling at the beautiful songs the mockingbird sang. Being a musician, Bonnee decided to respond musically. So she whistled the first four notes of Beethoven's fifth symphony. With amazing quickness, the mockingbird learned those four notes and sang them back to Bonnee. Then for a time, the bird disappeared. But one night, toward the end of her life, when Bonnee was very sick, the bird returned and, in the midst of its serenade, several times sang the first four notes of Beethoven's fifth. The friend then said, "Think of that! Somewhere out there in this big wide world there is a mockingbird who sings Beethoven because of Bonnee."

There we are—or should be: creators of good memories, making it our goal every day that somewhere out there in this big wide world there will be people singing because of us; people who are caring, honest, loving because of the song we sang to them.

Finally, there are memories that define us as a nation. We are celebrating such a memory this weekend, on what is aptly called Memorial Day. We are remembering those who made it possible for us to be here today and worship freely. We are recalling that, since the Civil War, more than 1,100,000 men and women have lost their lives in service to this country. We tend to take this for granted, but we should not.

Listen to this high-school girl who previously did not really know or, truth to tell, really care too much about wars and those old veterans. After all, *she* has never known what it means to live unfree.

Well, it so happened that this girl had the opportunity to witness a memorial service in San Francisco, aboard a submarine that was used in World War II and in Korea. At first she was bored and was ready to check her cell phone messages when the National Anthem was played over the speaker system. She says she looked up and around and noticed that some of the veterans were actually crying as they remembered what they gave for their country and they thought of their fallen comrades. "I never cried when it was sung," she thought to herself, but suddenly "I began to think about how many men and women had made the ultimate sacrifice of their lives so that I might be here and have the things I have."

Then as the group began the Pledge of Allegiance, she looked around and saw on the veterans' faces a thoughtful, respectful look, a look of such sadness.

> Suddenly, I started to cry myself with the realization of what it all meant to them. All those old sailors, my dad included, standing on the deck of an old submarine holding the flag with such pride and stillness. I was overcome. Then the speakers got up to give their speeches about their experiences and the meaning of Memorial Day. They talked about the hardships and struggles and the fact that they were lucky to be alive when so many of their brothers had fallen victim to the war, how it was up to them, the

veterans, to teach our children about the sacrifices made by so many.

I left the service a little different. So many of the speakers spoke about America with so much pride that it was hard not to think about all the people, including myself, who have no idea what this holiday is really about. While people go to their barbecues and beaches and store sales, I hope some remember all those who have fallen and remember those who still live and live with the cost.

So, there are three memories to remember this weekend. First, we need to remember the bad memories that are thankfully past, the present grace that brought us here today and we need to remember the good memories that still nourish us. Second, we must remember our task, our challenge, our mandate, to create good memories for others, to sing a song that will endure. Third, we must remember those who have died in the service of this country, so that we might live.

To forget to remember any or all of these is to die spiritually. To remember these things is to live: as disciples, as a people, as a nation.

Thanks for the memories.

All Saints

This is a brief homily because this was not a holy day but a weekday and people had to leave for work or school.

At first there was Jesus. Then came those who died like Jesus, that is, doing the Father's will, the martyrs. They were honored as heroes in the early struggles of the nascent church. In fact, thanks to the imperial persecutions, there got to be so many of them that around the year 397 the church appointed a particular day, the first Sunday after Pentecost, as a common day for all martyrs. Then, some 300 years later, Pope Gregory III consecrated a new chapel at St. Peter's in Rome to all the saints, not just the martyrs, but also to those who would have been martyred for boldly confessing their faith in the face of persecution and opposition—the confessors we call them—and they were added to the list. And then eventually came the holy monks and hermits and men and women of heroic lives. One hundred years later Pope Gregory IV set the celebration for all saints of every stripe on November 1 and for the last twelve hundred years we've been doing just that.

Since the Christian calendar, in imitation of its Jewish roots, always begins a liturgical celebration the evening before, Christians from the start began celebrating the feast of All Saints then. They called it "all blessed eve," "all hallows eve" or, as we say it, Halloween. Well, that hallowed eve, as we know, has completely lost its religious roots, substituting witches or superheroes for saints and becoming, as so much else in our time, a lucrative commercial enterprise, so much so that Halloween, which generates fifty-one billion dollars in sales each year, is financially second only to Christmas.

Well, Halloween is over. Our tricks and treats are ended. Our money is spent. But here we are, much to our credit, not only American consumers, but Catholic Christians giving testimony by our presence to the original meaning of it all. We just know there is something more to life than the latest car or Victoria's Secret. We know that there have been, and are, flesh and blood people like ourselves who decided, perhaps after living lives less than Christian, to live a counterculture life. It wasn't easy but they had a deep joy and laughed often and we envy them for their integrity.

And they are ours: Augustine, Francis of Assisi, Theresa, Elizabeth Ann Seton, Thomas Aquinas, and those in the making: Thomas Merton, Pope John XXIII, Oscar Romero, Dorothy Day, Mother Teresa. They fit into these definitions: "The saint loves people and uses things. The sinner loves things and uses people." How true that is. And this more profoundly: "A saint is someone through whom we catch a glimpse of what God is like—and what we are called to be." Yes, the fact is that most saints have been inspired by the example of other saints. Most have been touched by what they heard and saw in others. Let me share two brief examples.

Paul Rusesabagina is an African. He is the heroic hotel manager in Rwanda, and an engrossing movie named *Hotel Rwanda* was made about him. In 1994 Hutu militants began a brutal assault against their Tutsi neighbors. More than a million people were murdered, if you can image that horror. In the midst of this terrible slaughter over twelve hundred desperate people took refuge in Paul's hotel. Daily, Paul had to face down armed troops who wanted to invade the hotel and kill the occupants. Courageously, in peril of his own life, Paul defended and protected the refuges.

How did this modern saint get this way? Paul credits the example of two heroes, his father and Nelson Mandela. His father had been well respected in the community. He was a wise man and he always told the truth. When there were disputes in the community, the elders called on Paul's father to mediate. He was so honest that if one partner in a dispute was lying, they often confessed their lie as soon as they saw Paul's father. (Fathers, note: Your actions can make or break future saints.) Then there's Nelson Mandela, former president of South Africa. He inspired Paul because of his long imprisonment and his use of nonviolence to bring peace between enemies. These two men were Paul's inspiration. Indeed, saints beget saints.

The second example is the Christian author Philip Yancey. In his book, *Disappointment with God,* he relates a touching story from his own life.

One time on a visit to his mother—who had been widowed years earlier, in the month of Philip's first birthday—they spent the afternoon together looking through a box of old photos. A certain picture of him as an eight-month-old baby caught his eye. Tattered and bent, it looked too banged up to be worth keeping, so he asked her why, with so many other better pictures of him at the same age, she had kept this one. Yancey writes, "My mother explained to me that she had kept the photo as a memento, because during my father's illness it had been fastened to his iron lung."

During the last four months of his life, Yancey's father lay on his back, completely paralyzed by polio at the age of twenty-four, encased from the neck down in a huge, cylindrical breathing unit. With his two young sons banned from the hospital due to the severity of his illness, he had asked his wife for pictures of her and their two boys. Because he was unable to move even his head, the photos had to be jammed between metal knobs so that they hung within view above him, the only thing he could see. The last four months of his life were spent looking at the faces he loved.

Philip Yancey writes:

> I have often thought of that crumpled photo, for it is one of the few links connecting me to the stranger who was my father. Someone I have no memory of, no sensory knowledge of, spent all day, every day thinking of me, devoting himself to me, loving me. The emotions I felt when my mother showed me the crumpled photo were the very same emotions I felt one February night in a college dorm room when I first believed in a God of love. Someone like my father is there, I realized. Someone is there every day thinking of me, loving me. It was a startling feeling of wild hope, a feeling so new and overwhelming that it seemed fully worth risking my life on.

And, that, friends, says it all. Saints are those who have taken the risk.

All Souls

John 11:28–44

Because All Souls falls on a weekday, many people are under time constraints to get to work, so the homily is brief. Preachers may find its fourfold outline useful, if not its words. It may give them something to hang their own words on.

For two thousand years this gospel has resonated with the Christian people. The reason is obvious: The same four characters in it are present at every funeral. Let's look. First, there is Lazarus, a beloved family member. We can imagine him slowly wasting away each day. Like those burial bands, he is wrapped tighter and tighter with limitations until, finally, the last band is in place and he is dead.

So it is, was, with our Lazaruses. Outside of a sudden death by accident or heart attack, many of us have witnessed our parents, our spouse, son or daughter or sibling slowly dying. We recall too well the medications, the procedures, the operations, the doctors, the visits, the hospital, hospice; like so many bands, these things are wound round and round until our Lazarus died. It was hard to watch. We felt so helpless. We tried to make the transition easy, but our Lazarus is dead and we are here today with that memory in our hearts.

Then there are Martha and Mary, the grieving relatives. We are they. Now every morning we wake up in an empty bed. Every evening we wrap our arms around the pillow wishing it were him or her, but it's only a pillow and we cry. There is the favorite chair unsat in, the empty place at the dinner table, the loneliness, the ache in the heart. We don't like cooking for one. There is his favorite jacket or her favorite dress. We don't have the heart to throw them out. There is the son or daughter who won't be home any more for Thanksgiving and Christmas, the child who died much too young. Maybe, to add to the burden, there was a suicide and we still, after all these years, have mixed feelings about that. There are, in a word, our tears, grief, memories, and, yes, anger. "If you had been here my brother would not have died. What kind of friend are you?" We feel Martha's anger at God. We'd like to shake a fist, but we're afraid to. We are Martha and Mary.

Next there is the crowd who came to comfort Martha and Mary. Remember, they are the folks who brought food to the house and sandwiches for all after the funeral. They are the ones who sent us Mass cards, called and asked if there was anything they could do. They sympathized with our loss and felt helpless in the face of our grief. Bless them for being there. But when they left, it was lonely.

And finally there is Jesus in the gospel story. He's crying. He isn't crying like our Western males, a trembling lip kept in check, a muffled sob. No, this is a Mideastern Jew of two thousand years ago who, like all his contemporaries, throws his head back and lets out a primal scream. This was his friend, remember, and he loved his friend. But, we note, this Jesus not only has tears, he has compassion. He has pity. He has power that wells up from his love. So Jesus has them bring out the corpse and he prays and he speaks and he dips into his life-giving love and calls out, "Friend Lazarus, come forth." And when Lazarus does, Jesus simply says, "Untie him and set him free."

We are here to remember that Jesus has said the same thing to our Lazarus. "Come forth. Untie him. Untie her. Set them free." And off came the bands: the medication, the intravenous lines, the tubes, the bed, the bandages, the hospital, the restrictions, the depression. And there stands our Lazarus, *our* Lazarus, free and shinning. Our husband, our wife, our child, our sister, our brother, our mother, our father have known the love-tears of Jesus and the power behind them. They have been untied, freed. The gospel lives once more and we are assembled on this feast of All Souls to affirm it, embrace it, and find comfort in it and remember it.

Yes, we are all here today with memories and prayers, and, if our loss is fresh, with tears. But at this liturgy this gospel, as I said, has been re-played once more. Lazarus, Martha and Mary, friends, and Jesus have again marched across the stage. Lazarus, our loved one, so cherished in memory, Martha and Mary who are us, supporting friends in this congregation, and Jesus, Jesus whose words still echo, "Untie them and set them free."

Thanksgiving: Together in Kindness

Luke 1:39-55

Thanksgiving is a time when we traditionally reflect on our blessings. Blessings. It's a word we trip off our tongues easily enough: "Bless us, O Lord, and these thy gifts…." We bless ourselves with the sign of the cross, and we say, "God bless you" when someone sneezes. But this Thanksgiving I want to turn your minds and hearts to seeing blessing differently. I want you to see blessing not as words that we say or something that one person gives to another. Rather, I ask you to think of blessing as "being together in kindness." Yes, I want you to see that blessing is not something you do, but as something you are to another. I want you to see that blessing, like the encounter of Mary and Elizabeth, is a moment of meeting, a relationship that acknowledges one's worth. It *is* being together in kindness.

A simple example of what I mean comes from writer Patricia Livingston. She tells about a time in Florida just before a hurricane. They were preparing for the third major storm within a month. One sensible, necessary task, as you know, was to have your car filled with gas because you might suddenly have to evacuate and gas simply might not be available for a long time. Pat Livingston says she had been waiting for over an hour in a line that stretched for blocks leading to a gas station. Finally, at last, she had inched up to being second in line. The woman in front of her was swiping her credit card and reaching for the fuel nozzle. Unbelievably, her tank opening was on the other side. There was no way the hose would reach to the far side of her sleek black car. In desperation she tried the other two hoses but they were also too short. Frustrated after waiting all that time, the woman collapsed against the gas pump pounding it with her fists crying, "No! No!"

Pat says the young lady looked in her twenties, had long black hair, and was dressed in a short professional suit and high heels. She first wondered how a smart yuppie like that could not know where her gas tank was. Then she thought, maybe it wasn't her car. Maybe it was her boss's car that she had been told to take out and fill with gas.

Anyway, when the distraught young woman finally started to get back into the car to drive off, Pat jumped out of her car and called out, "Why don't you just pull up and turn around, and come back on the other side?"

"You mean you're willing to wait while I do that?" she asked, stunned.

"Of course," Pat assured her. Then she paused and added, "Don't forget, we're all in this together." Instant tears streamed down the young woman's face. She sobbed, "That's the nicest thing anyone has said to me in a long time." After she filled her tank, she walked over to Pat and said, "Thank you. I really mean it. Thanks." It was a little thing, Pat commented, but the point is that a blessing had been exchanged. Two people had come together in kindness and that was cause for thanksgiving.

It seems to be that way in all creation. Listen to this. I recently read a story about a female humpback whale that had become entangled in a web of crab traps and lines off the coast of San Francisco. The lines were all wrapped around her and one line was through her mouth. A fisherman had sighted her and alerted an environmental group for help. When the team arrived they had to dive in with knives to untangle her by hand, a very dangerous task. After hours of work, the whale had finally been cut loose.

But then something unusual happened. When the whale realized she had finally been freed, she swam joyfully around in circles. Then, amazingly, she came back to each and every diver, one at a time, and nudged them, pushed them gently around. In other words, she thanked them. Some said it was the most incredibly beautiful experience of their lives. The diver who cut the rope out of her mouth says her eye was following him the whole time and that he would never be the same.

We bless one another when we meet in kindness. I remember a short scene from one of my favorite movies, *Now, Voyager*. Bette Davis, as Charlotte Vale, a mousy maiden lady shakily turned into a self-assured woman, has returned home to her domineering mother. The mother's new nurse, played by Mary Wickes, in her best, no-nonsense, matter-of-fact manner, tells an apprehensive Charlotte not to pay too much heed to her mother's latest attention-getting sickness. Charlotte says appreciatively to the nurse, "Dora, I suspect you're a treasure."

Yes, people are treasures to us, are blessings to us. So this Thanksgiving is a good time to remember and cherish the people in our lives who, in need and in deed, in sickness and in health, were with us in kindness and let us know we count.

An illustration. A relationships expert named Gary Smalley conducts seminars. For one session he borrowed a friend's Stradivarius violin to use as an illustration. His friend had the violin flown in, complete with its own security guard! During the seminar, Smalley held up the violin for the audience to observe without revealing its true nature. It was old and scratched up, with no strings, so it didn't look particularly impressive. As he held it up, he noticed that the audience response was minimal. All they saw was an old violin. Then he began to explain that this was not just an old violin that he was holding. He told how there were only a few of them left in the world, and it was valued at millions of dollars. He then showed the audience the tiny inscription that said Stradivarius. There was spontaneous applause and a noticeable catch of breath throughout the crowd.

Just a few moments before it was just an old violin, not worthy of special honor. But by attaching that word Stradivarius to it, it suddenly was given a high place of honor.

Thanksgiving is a time to remember those who have attached words to us, words like "May I help?" and "I'm right here," and "Blessed are you among women"; and labels like friend, beloved, special, lover, the best, treasure, one in a million, heart of my heart. We may have been, and maybe are "an old violin" to others, but from those who have been together with us in kindness we learned that we each are a Stradavarius.

Today, then, while we will thank God for many *things*, let us remember *people*, especially those who have been with us in kindness and who, in that encounter, have blessed us.

Golden Jubilee: Priesthood

Some four hundred friends from my last parish where I had been pastor for twenty-one years threw a celebration for my fiftieth jubilee. My thank-you response was to recall my very first homily at the parish in which I read an excerpt from the classic child's tale The Little Prince *as a kind of mission statement and hope of what my ministry might be. I offer the excerpt for any new pastors who might want an inaugural theme for their ministry and for any new silver or golden jubilarians who are searching for a theme to reminisce by.*

Last month I received a little note from Joan Henderson. It was, of all things, a twenty-year-old bulletin clipping stuck in the pages of her copy of *The Little Prince*. That book is significant and, as you can see, I still have—and cherish—the specially bound copy the people gave me. It was significant because it was the book I used at my very first homily at St. Mary's in February 1972, when I faced a people whom I did not know and who did not know me and were wondering just what they were getting.

Nervously, I recall, I had turned to the place in the story where the planet-hopping Little Prince meets the fox for the first time. I read the following excerpt:

> It was then that the fox appeared.
> "Good morning," said the fox.
> "Good morning," the little prince responded politely, although when he turned around he saw nothing.

"I am right here," the voice said, "under the apple tree."

"Who are you?" asked the little prince, and added, "You are very pretty to look at."

"I am a fox," the fox said.

"Come and play with me," proposed the little prince. "I am so unhappy."

"I cannot play with you," the fox said. "I am not tamed."

"Ah! Please excuse me," said the little prince. But, after some thought, he added: "What does that mean—'tame'?"

"You do not live here," said the fox. "What is it that you are looking for?"

"I am looking for men," said the little prince. "What does that mean—'tame'?"

"Men," said the fox. "They have guns, and they hunt. It is very disturbing. They also raise chickens. These are their only interests. Are you looking for chickens?"

"No," said the little prince, "I am looking for friends. What does that mean—'tame'?"

"It is an act too often neglected," said the fox. "It means to establish ties."

"'To establish ties'?"

"Just that," said the fox. "To me, you are still nothing more than a little boy who is just like a hundred thousand other little boys. And I have no need of you. And you, on your part, have no need of me. To you, I am nothing more than a fox like a hundred thousand other foxes. But if you tame me, then we shall need each other. To me, you will be unique in all the world. To you, I shall be unique in all the world. But if you tame me, it will be as if the sun came to shine on my life and I shall know the sound of a step that will be different from all the others. Other steps send me hurrying back underneath the ground. Yours will call me, like music, out of my burrow...."

The fox gazed at the little prince a long time. "Please—tame me!" he said.

"I want to very much," the little prince replied, "but I have not much time. I have friends to discover, and a great many things to understand."

"One only understands the things one tames," said the fox....

"What must I do to tame you?" asked the little prince.

"You must be very patient," replied the fox. "First you will sit down at a little distance from me—like that—in the grass. I shall look at you out of the corner of my eye, and you will say nothing. Words are the source of misunderstandings. But you will sit a little closer to me every day...."

And for some twenty-one years we slowly moved closer and closer until we quite tamed one another and the sun came out and shone on our lives. I remember on my twenty-fifth anniversary, arriving for morning Mass to find pasted in the sanctuary the words, "One only understands the things one tames." Twenty-five years later, here we are—not all, for many have gone to their rest—and we know the full meaning of those words.

Well, if the saying is true, and I can vouch that it is, that "inside of every old man is a young man asking what happened," I tell you this: Through my store-bought glasses, looking past my liver-marked hands, ignoring for the moment the calendar that puts me closer to eighty than to seventy, and pondering fifty years of priesthood, the answer is clear: Grace happened.

How else to explain the taming that has gone on and God's writing straight with the crooked lines of my life? I look at these liver-marked hands—symbol of all of my imperfections, shortcomings, and sins—and marvel as I think of all the children over whom they poured the baptismal waters; some of your children, in fact. I think of a half century of signing the cross over repentant sinners, pressing the healing oils on the foreheads of the sick, offering the Sacred Host to nourish the yearnings of pilgrims, joining other hands in matrimony, holding the hands of those in excruciating pain or grief or despair and, not the least of which, gesticulating to urge on the homiletic word, the point in the classroom, the lecture, the conferences—thousands and thousands of them—or to tap the keys that eventually morphed into books. Imperfect, wrinkled hands with crooked, arthritic fingers—they become a symbol of an undeservedly graced priesthood.

Then, too, I look back at my tilting at the ecclesiastical windmills, sometimes foolishly—maybe more than I realize—sometimes prophetically; and I wish I could say they were the passions of my youth, except I still find myself, perhaps with less vigor, doing so. Ironically, at precisely the same time I was being ordained, 1955, that irenic and fantastic Catholic writer, Flannery O' Connor, was penning these words: "It seems to be a fact that you have to suffer as much *from* the Church as for it." Had I known of these words at the time I would have adopted them as my coat of arms!

What kept me going all through these years was the taming that went on, the grace caught from you, the people, like a holy contagion. It's only these past years of retirement, so-called, that going around celebrating Mass, or giving talks and retreats here and there that I run into grace's children. I run into people who ask if I remember them from St. Mary's; they mean fifty years ago at St. Mary's, New Monmouth in Middletown, my first assignment! I usually clear my throat and say, "Well, I've changed." I really mean, of course, you're out of your mind! *You've* changed, you look different from fifty years ago. How do you expect me to remember? Sometimes, oftentimes, I do remember the names, if not the now weathered and lined faces.

But I am more put off when they then proceed to ask me if I ever realized how much I meant to them, how much I helped them. And the answer, of course, is that I do not. I never had the foggiest notion that I made an impact. Bumped-into parishioners from other parishes remind me of how I visited their sick mothers or buried their fathers or baptized them. *That* hurts when, to me, they look older than I do! And there are those with those photographs—a pox on Thomas Edison—showing me with my arms wrapped around them dressed in their First Communion regalia. It's not that they are such children. It's that I don't recognize that young priest there. Mid-life adults I taught long ago at St. Joe's, Keyport, Our Lady of Perpetual Help in Maple Shade, St. Benedict's in Holmdel, Red Bank Catholic, or gave retreats to at the Christian Brothers Academy, golden-year adults to whom, traipsing up and down New Jersey, I gave Cana Conferences to—all startle me with the same news and, once more, I sense that hidden grace was at work.

I am especially touched when full grown men, like Jeff Senn, for example, now in his thirties whose marriage I just witnessed last week, had searched me out to do the honors because he claims to have been so influenced by me and signs off his letters to me with, "I love you, Father." That quite dissolves me. My friend, Msgr. Tom Dentici, whom some of you might recall—he was pastor of St. Robert's in Freehold and now has worked in the Diocese of Denver, Colorado—my very talented friend and co-worker when we both worked for the Family Life Bureau and whom I always counted among the best priests in the country, wrote me explaining why his health problems prevent him from being here, also wrote these words: "In my view, you are one of the best parish priests I have ever served with." And I didn't know that at the time either. But, unknowingly, he hit on the one thing I have always cherished as my fondest identity: a parish priest.

So grace, I have learned, is a hindsight thing. Like wallpaper over wall cracks, it smoothes over the stupidities, mistakes, lapses, and sheer nonsense that's a part of your life, helps you suppress them and allows you to focus on what God can do, has done, in spite of it all.

I keep coming back, fondly, to the people, to you, to the foxes of my sunlight and now of my evening shade, who remind me of this truth, who concoct such holy festivities like today, who are repositories of graced memories and who are ultimately a comfort to me. A simple remembered childhood poem by Longfellow will have to say what I can't:

> I shot an arrow into the air,
> It fell to earth, I know not where;
> For so swiftly it flew, the sight
> Could not follow it in its flight.
>
> I breathed a song into the air.
> It fell to earth I know not where;
> For who has sight, so keen and strong
> That it can follow the flight of song?
>
> Long, long afterward, in an oak,
> I found the arrow still unbroke;
> and the song, from beginning to end,
> I found again in the heart of a friend.

For which, dear foxes, I thank you.

Class Reunion

This homily was preached at my sixtieth (!) high school reunion at St. Peter's Church, whose high school we attended. I built it on a former homily used for All Saints Day and gave it a new twist.

When I was ordained in 1955 I was sent to New Monmouth, at that time a sleepy village with no sidewalks and three stores down at the junction: Wasserman's, the general store; a barber shop; and a liquor store. Shortly after arriving I needed some things, so I drove down to the junction. All the parking spaces were filled except the one in front of the liquor store and so I parked there and went about my business.

Before long, much to my amazement and chagrin, word had gone around the town that the new priest had a drinking problem! I who enjoy a Manhattan now and then and that's all! Well, I soon traced the rumor to two maiden sisters who lived together who were the self-appointed moral guardians of the parish. So one evening—my pastor pleaded with me not to do this, but I could tell he was not sincere—I drove my car to the junction and parked in front of the sisters' house and walked home, leaving it there all night. I never heard from them again.

A few years later I was invited to share the platform at a Columbus Day parade that went down Livingston Avenue here in New Brunswick. I don't know if any of you remember those parades, but they were the event of the year. Some background: previously I had been counseling Maria and her husband, Pasquale, who were desperately trying to have a baby but without success. I gave them blessings and told them to go home and I would pray for them. They left the rectory, grateful but sad. So, here I am, months later, standing with all these dignitaries on a public platform, when who comes along marching in the parade but Maria, obviously very, very pregnant. Spotting me, the exuberant Maria pointing to her extended womb shouts at the top of her voice for all the world to hear, "Father Bausch, thanks to you!"

It's good to hear you laugh for laughter is most appropriate at class reunions. There's so many memories, escapades, teachers, pranks, crazy classmates. Of course, sorrow also surfaces, as it must, as we remember our deceased classmates in this Mass, not to mention our own personal losses: spouses, children perhaps, health, opportunities, unfulfilled dreams, fractured journeys.

But I want to invite you to put all this—the laughter and the tears, the memories and the senior moments—into a larger context. I'm thinking of one of the more endearing teachings of the Catholic Church, the one we call the Communion of Saints, and I want to explore that with you. Yes, I can hear you groaning now: Just what we need, a catechism lesson from Sister Agnes Gabriel!

But hang in there and check out the compassionate truth of the Communion of Saints and where reunions fit into it. To catch its import, the Communion of Saints concept is best imagined as an endless line of pilgrims stretching from the fathomless past to the unknown future, like cars as far as you can see stuck on the Parkway, singing a song of faith. But note: because each of us in the pilgrim march is gifted with only a partial sight, partial understanding of the mystery of God, within that endless chorus— and depending where one is: at the beginning, middle, or end—one sings with great gusto and assurance, but another sings with little attention and conviction.

But the Communion of Saints says that others sing what we cannot and others supply what we are lacking. Which is to say, others chant the song of faith with us when we can join them and they hum the song of faith for us when we cannot. Or, let me put it this way. Five years ago a friend of mine lost her son in the Twin Towers on 9/11. She says that she can no longer believe in God, in a God who would let her son lose his life, especially since she and her family are faithful Catholics and good churchgoers. How could God do this to her? There are three responses to this woman.

The first is to say, "Well, if you can no longer believe, you are no longer a Catholic. You no longer belong." That's a harsh view. That's to deny the seriousness of her loss. A second response is to say to her, "You haven't really lost your faith. You're just temporarily depressed. Everything will be fine." Everything will *not* be fine. This is to deny her pain. But the third response is to honor her losses, the loss of her son and the loss, or at least, the shock to her faith. The fact of the matter is that tragedy has indeed broken her trust in a loving, provident God. How could it be otherwise? Meanwhile? Meanwhile, the community believes for her. The saintly chorus picks up her faltering verses.

The collective faith of the pilgrims sustains her though her period of unbelief; and as she slowly encounters these saints of yesterday and today, she will begin to see their scars and sense their resilience and they will help her believe once more, in the face of tragic absurdity, in a new and different way. They will help her sing with a different modulation. They will sing louder the phrases that she can only sing softly, if at all. In short, the chorus, or the community of saints, sings when you and I are unwilling or unable to do so.

Peter sang for Doubting Thomas until he could believe again. Thomas sang for Denying Peter until he could embrace again. Monica sang for sinful Augustine until he could repent again. Clare sang for sad Francis until he could laugh again. We are a whole community who pick up for each other. We are a chorus of pilgrims. We support each other and we become more than the sum total of our individual selves as the Communion of Saints.

You exhibit the gifts I don't have and I exhibit those you don't have. You cry the tears I cannot cry and I laugh the laughter you cannot laugh. You believe when I struggle with doubts. I believe when you struggle with doubts. You smile when I am in tragedy. I grieve when you are in joy. Our individual pieces are partial. Our faith, our hope, and our love are quite incomplete. But the Communion of Saints, the vast pilgrim chorus—past, present and future, those in heaven, earth, and purgatory—tells us something. It reminds us of our faith family, that we belong to a vast community of eternal time and space—those gone before us, those here, those to come—and it picks up for us, fulfills what is lacking in our lives. The Communion of Saints becomes a revelation and a comfort. It tells us a mighty truth: together we sing more than we sing individually. The Communion of Saints says that we are never alone.

And so class reunions, to get to the pitch after a long windup, are simply a celebration of our place in the vast pilgrimage. Reunions take time to locate us within the larger picture. Beyond the absences—who's here, who's not, who died, who is ill—beyond the "you look wonderful" to people whose identities we're not sure of, beyond the losses of spouses, children, health, and dreams, lies a greater reality. Our lives are not a collection of isolated incidents. They are not over. We are *not* fading into mere oblivion. We are just at a different place in line and our reunion celebrates that place with its own peculiar challenges and graces. We remain forever a part of a huge God-given pilgrimage. We are here today specifically to be re-united with our sixty-years-ago past at St. Peter's and with our present as we enjoy our repast shortly. We are also here with our future, knowing that our deficiencies are canceled by others' fullness, our sins are wiped out by others' virtues, our declining years are made fruitful in the legacies we have left others, and our future is redeemed by those who have gone before us.

Reunions, in short, spotlight our time and place in the pilgrimage line where our unique sadness, gladness, and nostalgia are some of the verses we add to the over-all chorus. In sum, we make beautiful music. And that, classmates, is what we're here to celebrate: *our* time, *our* place, *our* uniqueness, the people who made us who we are, and the people we made who they are.

If we're at the stage where a clear conscience is the sign of a bad memory, we're also at the stage where a good memory is why we have class reunions. We are here like a link in a chain, but it's *our* link, *our* life, *our* contribution, *our* place in the Communion of Saints. Blessed be God forever. Amen.

A Wedding Homily

There's the woman who accompanied her husband to the doctor for his physical. The doctor asked her for a private conversation before they left the office. "Your husband, " the doctor said, "is under great stress and you must devote your life to sheltering him. Don't argue or disagree with him. Get up early each morning and fix his favorite breakfast. Spend the morning cleaning the house, but have a nice lunch ready at noon if he happens to come home. The afternoon you can spend on outside work, but make sure there is a special dinner waiting for him when he returns. The evening hours may be spent watching a game with him on TV, followed by romance, should he be interested. This must be your schedule to help him through this."

The wife left the office, picked up her husband, and drove him home. "Well," said the husband anxiously, "what did the doctor say?" "He said," replied the wife, "that you're going to die."

Nancy and Dan, I'm not going to stand here and tell marriage jokes, although humor will be an essential ingredient in any happy marriage. The jokes, like gallows humor, are a cover-up because we really don't know how to handle the deep experiences, the profound joys, the sacredness and the spiritual challenges of marriage. So we kid about it to hide our discomfort. But now that I have you captive I want to put the kidding aside and I want to share with you not some foolishness, but some wisdom about marriage.

Your first impression when I make that august pronouncement is accurate. I know what you're all thinking. I am likely the only professional bachelor in this church and where do I get off trying to instruct you about married life? Am I about to share my ignorance?

No, I know I don't have direct experience, but I have drawn upon the wisdom of those who are married. I want simply to share what these successfully married folk have taught me. And what they have taught me are three wisdoms which in turn I pass on. Surprisingly, they're all old sayings I've heard before, and most likely you have too, but these folks took them over and gave them a twist for their own marriages.

The first wisdom is this. "Life is what happens to you when you're making other plans." Yes, the plans, the dream: house, pool, rose garden, adorable kids.

Well, the dream house turns out to be a cold water flat in Camden; the closest thing you come to a pool is your septic tank; the rose garden is poison ivy, and the two adorable children are two homely, rope-haired kids who aren't too bright at that. Whom do you blame? The immature go around with a backhand against the forehead, declaring that life in general and marriage in particular are unfair and maybe we should look elsewhere.

But the mature, the spiritually mature, realize that "life is what happens to you while you're making other plans," and they tough it out to eventually discover deeper love, deeper dimensions, and a deeper self.

The man who shared this wisdom with me is writer Mitch Finley. He himself wrote these words on the tenth anniversary of his marriage. He's married twenty-five years now.

Two of the most famous quotations in English literature are found in the same book, one at its beginning and the other at its end. "It was the best of times, it was the worst of times…it was a season of light, it was a season of darkness…." "It is a far, far better thing that I do than I have ever done…." The source, of course, is Dickens's *A Tale of Two Cities*, a novel about the French Revolution. Yet these familiar words come to mind as I pause to reflect on a marriage now ten years old. These years have been for me, the best of times and the worst of times, mostly the best of times. The vow I spoke ten years ago was, in retrospect, a far, far better thing than I had ever done. The ten calendar years that my life companion and I have lived through together have marked seasons of light and seasons of darkness, mostly light. These ten years stand as witness to the truth [that]…marriage is our last best chance to grow up.

Nancy and Dan, life will happen—for better or worse, for richer or poorer, in sickness and in health, as the old wisdom put it—but together, if you turn to the grace of the sacrament you are about to receive, you will seize the chance to grow in ways you never dreamed.

The second bit of ancient wisdom a woman told me with a smile on her face. She said the secret of a good marriage is to remember that "Even a stopped clock is right *twice* a day." I think I know what she meant. Frequently I meet a couple whom I had married. We go through the usual light talk: how's things, how are you, and so on. I listen, for, sooner or later, I will catch the word I'm waiting for: "Everything's wonderful, fine, great…*but…*"

"But" means that they discovered that, in spite of what the other told them, they did not marry God. They married someone less than perfect and the clay feet are beginning to show up.

But then, always optimistic as lovers are, they add the phrase, "Give me enough time and I will change my partner." Translation: "Give me enough time and I will make my partner perfect, that is, like me!" Which, when you come to think of it, is a very frightening thought. I mean, consider: How would you like to be married to you?

Anyway, even those of you married for a short time can laugh up your sleeve at that one. This is a far cry from the long-married couple.

This is the husband, say, married twenty-five or more years who props himself on his elbow and looks down at his sleeping wife and says to himself, "Well, there she is. She's still can't cook like my mother. She's still not the world's greatest housekeeper. In spite of Miss Clairol the gray is showing through and crow's feet are around the eyes—but I love her."

And she looks down at her husband and says, "Well, there *he* is. He stays out more than he should. Sometimes he drinks more than he should. He's getting thinner on top and thicker around the middle—but I love him." You see, they have moved away from the immature "I will change my partner" to the exceedingly mature " I have accepted my partner"; they have come to realize and accept that "Even a stopped clock is right twice a day."

The woman who told me that is famed author Madeleine L'Engle and she puts it more elegantly. She wrote these wonderful words about her forty-eight-year-old marriage with her now deceased husband.

> Our love has been anything but perfect and anything but static. Inevitably there have been times when one of us has outrun the other, and has had to wait patiently for the other to catch up. There have been times when we have misunderstood each other, demanded too much of each other, been insensitive to the other's needs. I do not believe there is any marriage in which this does not happen. The growth of love is not a straight line, but a series of hills and valleys. I suspect that in every good marriage there are times when love seems to be over. Sometimes those desert lines are simply the only way to the next oasis, which is far more lush and beautiful after the desert crossing that it could possibly have been without.

Nancy and Dan, divorces occur between the oases. Hang in there. The next oasis is always better and deeper. And that's for sure. Some of the most passionate and deepest lovers I know are golden jubilarians.

The third and final bit of wisdom I would share comes, I admit, from a bachelor, but he had seen a lot and knew what he was taking about and he did practice what he preached. He said in the gospel we read to introduce this talk, "This is my commandment. Love one another *as* I have loved you." If you want to see the force of that "as," look at Calvary. And that is the measurement Jesus offers: to go that far for one another, or, as his disciple St. Paul expressed it, love is bearing one another's burdens.

I have a final love story that takes Jesus' words seriously.

Two centuries ago there lived a very famous German-Jewish philosopher named Moses Mendelssohn. Moses Mendelssohn was brilliant and compassionate, but he had one flaw. He was a small, hunchbacked man. Hunchback that he was, he fell in love with a beautiful and charming young woman named Gretchen, the daughter of a prosperous banker. Several months after he had met Gretchen, Mendelssohn visited her father. He asked him, very cautiously, how his daughter might feel about the possibility of marrying him, for he had come to love her very much. "Please, tell me the truth," Mendelssohn insisted.

The father hesitated and then replied, "The truth is that the girl is frightened of you because...because..."

Mendelssohn finished his sentence for him, "...because I am a hunchback?"

"Yes," said the father, "because you are a hunchback."

Mendelssohn paused. Then after some silence he asked permission to see the daughter on the pretext that he wanted to say farewell to her. The father agreed. Mendelssohn went upstairs and found Gretchen in a room where she was busy with needlework. She avoided looking at him during the conversation, which Mendelssohn eventually directed to the subject of marriage.

In the course of the conversation, the young woman asked him if he really believed in the old saying that "marriages are made in heaven."

"Of course," he replied. "And while we're on that subject, I might as well tell you that something unusual happened to me. As you know, when boys are born the angels in heaven call out for all to hear, 'This little boy is destined to have this special girl for a wife. It is decreed from all eternity and no one may change it.' So when I was born, the angels made the usual announcements about me and the name of my future wife was announced. But then the angels paused and added, 'But alas, Mendelssohn's wife will have a terrible hump on her back!'

"Then I shouted out loud before the court of heaven. I cried, 'Oh, Lord, no. No. A girl who is hunchbacked will very easily become bitter and hard, and the object of awful jokes and hurts. No, Lord, a girl should be beautiful. Oh, Lord, please, please give the hump to me and let her be well formed.' And you know what, Gretchen? God heard my prayer and I was glad. I am that boy and you are that girl."

Gretchen was deeply moved. She saw Mendelssohn in a whole new way, and so she became his faithful and loving wife and they had a long and loving marriage.

Moses gave his wholeness to ransom Gretchen, Gretchen gave trust to ransom Moses, and both, in the exchange and in the sharing, found love.

So, Nancy and Dan, if you are willing to embrace life as it happens, willing to seek out the right when so many things go wrong, willing to carry each other's burdens, then you will become the sacrament of marriage, an outward sign of the way God loves us. For that is precisely why marriage *is* a sacrament: to show in a concrete way that, if mere human couples are capable of forgiveness, forbearance, patience, and love in spite of all, well then, how much more can we catch a glimpse of how much God must forgive forbear and love us? As St. Paul said, It's a great mystery, your ability to mirror and reveal God.

So, let the revelation begin....

Golden Jubilee 1: Marriage

The justifications for this homily for a couple married fifty years are the initial trip down memory lane of the cultural artifacts of half a century ago—the current homilist can update the material by searching on the internet—and the use of Madeleine L'Engle's wonderful quote. A possible drawback is the use of the section from The Velveteen Rabbit (also used in the other anniversary homily that follows), but it was so germane that it was difficult to avoid. I started out with the italicized opening, stumbling over the words as if having a hard time reading them.

> *"Kay and Carl Simone are a brilliant, outstanding, handsome couple who today, after fifty years of noble and unselfish devotion— though you would hardly believe that such a young-looking couple could be married that long—are humbly here before you...."*

I'm sorry. This is the way I was supposed to begin, but even with my glasses it's hard to read Kay's handwriting. So let me jettison that introduction and start my own way: In 1809 in Hardin county, Kentucky, a man asked his neighbor, "Anything new?"

"Naw," said the man, "nothing ever happens around here. Only thing I heard was that the Lincolns had a boy the other day."

It was the same fifty years ago. Nobody noticed what was going on at Holy Ghost Church in Brooklyn on September 2, 1950, when a young couple stood before beloved Father Fogerty to pronounce their wedding vows. People had other preoccupations, other things on their minds.

372

People, for example, were busy flocking to the movies to see Walt Disney's *Cinderella*, *Cheaper by the Dozen*, *Father of the Bride*, *Born Yesterday*, *The Asphalt Jungle*, *Sunset Boulevard*, and *All About Eve*, which was awarded the Oscar for best picture of the year. *Guys and Dolls* opened on Broadway, William Faulkner was awarded the Nobel Prize for Literature, Dunkin Donuts appeared on the scene, and Charles Schultz's *Peanuts* made its debut in that fateful year of 1950. And people were humming the new songs: "Rudolph the Red Nosed Reindeer," "Mona Lisa," "Harbor Lights," and "Tennessee Waltz." Most of all, television—black and white and no remote control—grew very popular that year, and soon after so had new electronic neighbors: the Ricardos, the Kramdens, the Goldbergs, Howdy Doody, Rod Serling, and Sargeant Joe Friday.

Then, too, when folk went out for a Sunday drive in those less congested times, they encountered for the first time the distracting novelty of those new-fangled, engaging road signs that both made them think of a product and put a smile on their faces at the same time:

The whale put Jonah down the hatch

But coughed him up

Because he scratched.

Burma Shave.

or: Altho insured, remember, kiddo

They don't pay you.

They pay the widow.

Burma Shave.

That kind of thing. And, most meaningful for Kay and Carl, the Brooklyn-Battery Tunnel opened up.

But there were the serious things happening too fifty years ago. Mother Teresa founded the first mission of Charity in Calcutta. President Harry Truman ordered the army to seize control of the nation's railroads, Alger Hiss was convicted, and then, of course, in 1950 the Korean War broke out.

With all these distractions, it's understandable that, outside of a few family members and friends, not that many took note of Kay Wilson and Carl Simon exchanging their wedding vows on a hot Saturday morning. Just another bride and groom. There was no inkling whatsoever at the time of future greatness, that in later years, for example, *he* would gain fame as

King of the Computers and *she* as Queen of the Casseroles. But for now, the couple did not realize that, and like Abraham and Sarah in our first reading, they had just taken the first step in their physical and spiritual migration to a far-off country. And, like that ancient couple, they would soon have company.

Their migration began modestly enough. The church was directly across the street from Kay's house and, as her father sensibly suggested, she could just walk over. It would be practical and cheaper. But that, of course, was a man's point of view. No way, doing her Rufus walk, was she going to traipse across the road in her wedding gown. So she walked out her front door, got in to the limousine and was driven around the block and deposited in front of the church on the other side as a proper bride. She was early.

Actually, so was Carl. They had planned to be married in October, but that Korean War intruded and Carl was soon to be drafted and so they moved up their wedding a month. Then, following the insistent call of Uncle Sam and later the more alluring call of Ma Bell, the migration began in earnest: Brooklyn, Manhattan, Florham Park, Morristown, Long Branch, and finally Colts Neck. And along the way, like Abraham and Sarah, they would have company. Peter, Paul, and, all too briefly, Matthew, Jeanne, and Andrew.

And then, in the course of time, we at St. Mary's, the final destination of their journey, would discover the treasure these immigrants from Brooklyn were. I mentioned, for example, that they were married at Holy Ghost Church in Brooklyn. That name, under the impetus of Vatican II, has been renamed Holy *Spirit* Church. That's an apt symbol of Kay and Carl. Coming as they did out of the conservative forties and fifties, they would live through the Vatican II of the sixties and become what they never dreamed of: the avant garde quintessential parish ministers of the seventies, eighties, and nineties. They would be new church at its best.

And they were. And I tell you here and now that I, privileged to be their pastor for most of that time, have always been deeply inspired by them and always felt that, as have so many of you, they were there with me each step of the way as we broke new ground here at St. Mary's. I have learned to rely on them, respect them, and finally, to love them. Most of all, outside of their contributions to community and church, I think, their ultimate gift is that they would eventually display a steady witness of fifty years that would be a beacon in the world that has trouble making a five-year commitment. Their marriage has steadily become more and more of a sacrament, an outward sign of grace, a hint that, in the fidelity, forbearance, love, and forgiveness of each other, this is what God must be like toward us.

Well, it's been a long journey, peppered by many, many hardships and heartbreaks, which some of us know but, out of respect, do not speak of. But at this stage of their lives they display the truth of something I often quote at weddings in the vague hope that the starry-eyed youngsters before me might remember it. It's from someone seasoned like Carl and Kay: Madeleine L'Engle talking about her marriage of forty-eight years. They didn't make fifty because her husband died. But reflecting on those years, she spoke for many:

> Our love has been anything but perfect and anything but static. Inevitably there have been times when one of us has outrun the other, and has had to wait patiently for the other to catch up. There have been times when we have misunderstood each other, demanded too much of each other, been insensitive to the other's needs. I do not believe there is any marriage in which this does not happen. The growth of love is not a straight line, but a series of hills and valleys. I suspect that in every good marriage there are times when love seems to be over. Sometimes those desert lines are simply the only way to the next oasis, which is far more lush and beautiful after the desert crossing that it could possibly have been without.

I think that's about right. And here are Carl and Kay, at last on the other side of those desert lines, with a depth and commitment not possible without the hills and valleys of life. And like Abraham and Sarah, all through they have unknowingly entertained God. Which is to say, the one constant in their journey has been a bedrock faith and the faith community that has supported it.

I must end now and let me tell you that I really struggled to avoid the temptation to end with a cliché, and perhaps for many of you, a now tiresome story; but because it's so apt, so evidently true here today, it kept coming back to my mind and I finally gave in. So I ask your indulgence. If you will think of Carl and Kay and try to listen with fresh ears, you'll feel, once more, I hope, the strength of its truth, *their* truth.

It's that particular scene, you recollect, when the Velveteen Rabbit and the Old Skin Horse are lying in the pantry, and the young Velveteen Rabbit is starting to make conversation to while away the time, and asks:

"What is real? Does it mean having things that buzz inside of you, and a stick-out handle?"

"Real isn't how you are made," said the Old Skin Horse. "It's a thing that happens to you. When a child loves you for a long, long time, not just to play with, but really loves you, then you become real."

"Does it hurt?" asked the rabbit.

"Sometimes," said the Old Skin Horse, for he was always truthful. "But when you are real, you don't mind being hurt."

"Does it happen all at once, like being wound up," he asked, "or bit by bit?"

"It doesn't happen all at once," said the Old Skin Horse; "you become. It takes a long time. That's why it doesn't often happen to people who break easily, or have sharp edges, or have to be carefully kept. Generally by the time you are real, most of your hair has been loved off, your eyes drop out, you get loose in the joints, and very shabby. But these things don't matter at all, because once you are real, you can't be ugly, except to people who don't understand."

"I suppose you are real," said the rabbit, and then he wished he had not said it, for he thought the Old Skin Horse might be sensitive.

But the Old Skin Horse only smiled. "The boy's uncle made me real," he said. "That was a great many years ago, but once you are real, you can't become unreal again. It lasts for always."

It is at this point, therefore, that I ask two of the most real people I know to come forward, almost fifty years later to the day, to renew *their* vows and to restore our faith.

Golden Jubilee 2: Marriage

GENESIS 18:1–10

The Sarah and Abraham theme plus, once more, the oft-used Velveteen Rabbit *excerpt are a good combination for this occasion.*

I would like to reflect with you on that first reading. You heard that Abraham and Sarah had left their ancestral home and were now typical nomads wandering the deserts of the Middle East. On one occasion they were suddenly aware that three strangers had come their way, not knowing that the strangers were God's angels. Nevertheless, very typically, they welcomed the strangers and they pressed their hospitality upon them.

It is important that you recognize that in the Middle East, even to this day, hospitality is *the* hallmark of a very true and noble human being, the highest form of charity. To give hospitality is a profound and esteemed virtue. It's difficult for us to understand how profound it is until you remember that the people of Abraham and Sarah's era lived in very harsh and barren times. Food was extremely scarce and hard to come by. No one ever had enough. So, in effect, you see, what hospitality says is: "When I take my food—little that it is and as much as I need it in order to live, this food that keeps me alive—I share it with you. I am thereby sharing something of my life, my very self." And such hospitality, a concern for others at a real cost to self, was, as I said, the highest form of love and charity.

As I was reflecting on this Scripture passage of Abraham and Sarah and their entertaining the strangers at their own expense, I could not help but think that this is what marriage fundamentally is all about, isn't it? Marriage is, when you come right down to it, hospitality: ongoing, profound,

377

consistent hospitality. Nothing comes close to marriage and family life as the practice of hospitality. And when I put it that way, you not only admire Sarah and Abraham for *their* hospitality but also their counterparts of another century, Irene and Frank Shallis, two very hospitable people. In fact, the similarities between the two couples are striking.

First of all, like Abraham and Sarah, they too were nomads who also left their ancestral home, Frank with his family of seven and Irene and her family of nine. They said goodbye to the wonderful folks who had raised them. Their eventual journey away from home began innocently enough. It started when they met on a blind date and canny Irene knew instantly—before the highly intelligent Frank knew it—that this was the man she was to marry. He found out later.

Then after marriage, like Abraham and Sarah, came the migrations: Buffalo, Jersey City, Madison Township, and, finally, last but not least, Colts Neck, where I was very fortunate to meet them. And at each stop they practiced hospitality. They typically gave of themselves from raising a growing family to coaching Little League to the feeding and caring for six eventual children.

Of course, like Abraham and Sarah, they too had obstacles along the journey of life: damaged legs, heart transplant, heart attack, but also like Abraham and Sarah, they too had a beautiful and unfaltering faith and a deep commitment to one another and to marriage that got them through each crisis.

I guess what I'm saying in all this is that for fifty years Irene and Frank Shallis have shown hospitality, have *been* hospitality: to one another, to their six children, to their grandchildren, to their friends, to the stranger, to this community, to this parish, and to those in need. They have given of themselves, they have shared from their needs, they have sacrificed necessities and luxuries, they have put others first. That's hospitality. That's marriage. Quite a record. Quite a record, not too often matched these days.

I want to recall to you an interesting development, as you heard at the end of the Abraham and Sarah story. You remember that after their generous and gracious hospitality, the stranger, who is God, says to elderly Abraham and Sarah, "You've been so good to me that this time next year I will come back (a long pause) and Sarah, in her old age, will bear a child."

Now, don't get panicky! What seems to be going on here, what God is really saying is that because of the hospitality of your marriage I will give you new life.

New life means not just the reward of heaven, but here and now, the life of the Spirit, the life of promise, the life that has, at last, become so real that we stand in admiration of it and feel the need to celebrate it. We feel that we must simply acknowledge that this couple here before us today, no longer the fifteen- and sixteen-year-olds on their first date, no longer the youthful bride and groom, no longer the vigorous mother and father, but, like many of us, showing the beautiful signs of wear and tear of time, have grown into worthy, precious, and genuine human beings. They have journeyed into something wonderful and real and we love them for it.

And *that's* why, even though I know that by now it's something of a cliché, I have to say that when I was thinking of Abraham and Sarah, when I was thinking of Irene and Frank, I simply could not avoid also thinking of the old beloved Velveteen Rabbit story, especially one episode, and I will end with its message. And although it's been told many times—this story of the workings of grace—I ask you to listen to it with fresh ears because it's so applicable. It's that particular scene, you recollect, when the Velveteen Rabbit and the Old Skin Horse are lying together in the closet, and the young Velveteen Rabbit is starting to make conversation to while away the time, and asks:

"What is real? Does it mean having things that buzz inside of you, and a stick-out handle?"

"Real isn't how you are made," said the Old Skin Horse. "It's a thing that happens to you. When a child loves you for a long, long time, not just to play with, but really loves you, then you become real."

"Does it hurt?" asked the rabbit.

"Sometimes," said the Old Skin Horse, for he was always truthful. "But when you are real, you don't mind being hurt."

"Does it happen all at once, like being wound up," he asked, "or bit by bit?"

"It doesn't happen all at once," said the Old Skin Horse; "you become. It takes a long time. That's why it doesn't often happen to people who break easily, or have sharp edges, or have to be carefully kept. Generally by the time you are real, most of your hair has been loved off, your eyes drop out, you get loose in the joints, and very shabby. But these things don't matter at all, because once you are real, you can't be ugly, except to people who don't understand."

"I suppose you are real," said the rabbit, and then he wished he had not said it, for he thought the Old Skin Horse might be sensitive.

But the Old Skin Horse only smiled. "The boy's uncle made me real," he said. "That was a great many years ago, but once you are real, you can't be come unreal again. It lasts for always."

Let me tell you this: Irene and Frank Shallis are among the realest people I know, and it is a privilege to ask them to step forward and renew their vows.

Second Time Around: Marriage

JEREMIAH 31:32–34; ROMANS 12:1–2, 4–8;
LUKE 24:13–35

In the presence of such august company—the bride and groom, clergy, yourselves—and considering the gravity of the celebration, one hesitates to start off the nuptials of Elizabeth Moody Schmalz and Thomas George Ferguson, Betsy and Tom, with a tale, much less than an elegant one, but counting on your good breeding not to throw the programs at me, I will do so. Besides, the kids may enjoy it and the adults might ponder it. The story goes like this:

Once upon a time, a poor but hardworking woodcutter was walking home from the forest, with an ax strapped to his back. Suddenly he came upon a large old pot made of brass. It was the biggest pot he had ever seen. "What a fine pot!" he exclaimed. "But how will I get it home? It's too heavy to carry. Wait, I know."

He untied his shoulder strap and dropped the heavy ax into the pot. He proceeded to tie one end of the strap through one of the pot's handles and the other end around his waist. Then he began the hard work of dragging the clumsy pot down the path to his small house.

The woodcutter's wife was most pleased to see the pot and said, "What a fortunate day, husband. You found a wonderful old pot and another ax."

"No, wife, I just found the pot. I had the ax before."

"But there are *two* axes in the pot," she said.

The woodcutter looked inside and was speechless. Sure enough, two identical axes sat side by side. As he leaned down to pull them out, his

381

straw hat fell from his head and into the pot. Now *two* hats rested near the axes.

"Wife! The pot is haunted!"

"Or it's magical!" she said happily. "Let's put tonight's dinner inside and see what happens." One dinner became two. "Quickly," said the wife, "get our savings from the jar on the shelf!" The handful of coins doubled.

"It is magical!" cried the woodcutter. "What shall we put in next?"

"The money, of course," said his practical wife. "Let's get rich while we can." They placed the coins inside repeatedly, and the amount doubled each time. An hour later every jar, pan, basket, pocket, chest, shelf, and shoe they owned was filled with money. They were, indeed, rich!

"Dear wife," said the woodcutter, "we can build a fine house and have a big vegetable garden, and I won't have to work so hard from now on. Oh, I'm so happy I could dance!" Then he grabbed her around the waist and began to dance around and around the small room.

Suddenly he slipped on some loose coins and accidentally dropped his wife into the pot! He tried to pull her back out, but it was too late. He now had *two* wives. They stepped out of the pot and looked closely at each other. It was impossible to tell them apart. "What have I done?" cried the woodcutter. "Can a man live with two wives at the same time?"

"Not in my house," said the first wife.

"Not in my house," said the second wife. Both women looked at each other, smiled, and grabbed the woodcutter and made him get into the pot. Two woodcutters climbed back out. "Can two families live in the same house?" asked both of the men.

"No," said the first wife.

"No," echoed the second wife.

Half the money was given to the second couple and they built an elegant house. It was right next to the first couple's fine, new house. Ever since that time, the people of the village have remarked on the strong resemblance of the woodcutter and his wife's new relatives, the ones who must have brought them all that money!

A charming Chinese folktale, is it not? I thought I would amuse you with it, at least the children, but I also thought that in a way it fits what we're celebrating today.

That is, everything's doubled: a second chance, a second love, a second marriage. We have two people who separately knew loss but who, through the labyrinth of place and circumstance, together found gain in each other. We had double sorrow, now we have double joy. We have two families now where once there was one, each enriching the other. The magic pot has struck again.

We, of course, call it grace, a grace reminiscent of the first reading from Jeremiah where the prophet speaks of a new covenant between two houses rising from the loss of the old one. Here Israel and Judah will have a covenant written in their hearts where they will be God's people and he will be their God. So with the houses of Schmalz and Ferguson.

But it was, I'm sure, a while coming. I'm sure that not so very long ago, when Betsy and Tom began their solitary journey, they couldn't envisage being joined in a new covenant standing here before God in the presence of their families and wonderfully loyal friends.

At one time, I imagine, at that point when they both lost their beloved spouses of many years, joy seemed something forever lost to them. They have each been through their own Good Friday experiences. But now, today, it is like Easter for them. God has turned their mourning into dancing as the psalm says (30:11).

Gradually, unsuspectingly, unintentionally, they stumbled over the magic pot of divine providence, and sorrow halved and love doubled. They began to heal, at least to the point where they were able to laugh, to love, and finally to make plans, to hope. Now God, who is able to do far more than all we can ask or think, has given you each a precious companion to share your life. And two families, the Schmalz and Ferguson families, have emerged side by side.

Betsy and Tom, you know far better than I that the future will be different from the past in ways that both please and displease you. All newlyweds, even mature ones, face the challenge of adjusting to many changes all at once, some expected and others that will surprise you. After all, you each are conjoining families with cherished traditions, and each of you will continue to embrace forever powerful memories of your former spouses.

That is sacred, inviolable territory and always will be. And the children who have experienced the loving breath and depth of *their* father and *their* mother will surrender no loyalty, no affection, no precious memory—nor should they—as they strive to embrace the biblical wisdom that it is not good for man or woman to be alone, and that includes their mother and father. Treasured memories are not to be displaced but shared, like showing off family jewels.

No journey is free from peril or conflict *or*, as our woodcutter found out, surprises. But, Betsy and Tom, as someone said, the concept of two people living together without ever having a cross word suggests a lack of spirit. And I offer you these wise words for your marriage: "Love is not blind. In fact, it sees more, not less. But because it sees more, it is willing to see less."

It's all a restatement of St. Paul who said in our second reading, "Rejoice in hope, be patient in suffering, persevere in prayer." Finally, as the post-Easter gospel of loss and gain reminded us, you will not journey alone.

Like Cleopas and his wife starting on their Emmaus journey after the death of their Beloved Companion and at one point are joined by the Stranger, so you are here today in church to begin your journey with that same Stranger at your side. You are asking him, as you confer this holy sacrament of matrimony on each other—your meeting point—to walk with you, to be your third Partner, to set *your* hearts on fire.

You are asking that invisible Stranger to come and stay with you, for the evening draws near. At times, I warn you, he will seem absent, but I also remind you that you can always recall him and be aware of him whenever you break bread and share it with each other and with your neighbors in need.

Well, now, with all that having been said—story and truth, truth and story—it's time for doubling in reverse: to make each as no longer two, but one. So I shall ask Betsy and Tom to step forward....

FUNERAL HOMILIES

I have included the following funeral homilies with some hesitation. The hesitation is due to the fact that funerals are so exquisitely personal. They necessarily abound with personal references, local color, inside knowledge and jokes. Reading these funeral homilies, then, might seem a bit like reading another's mail. So why did I include them in this collection? I did so because I am convinced that behind and beneath the very specific person and circumstances the reader does not know lie a universal pattern and framework for another homilist's reworking. In other words, I feel that the creative homilist can extract the personal names and histories and discover a fundamental structure, an outline, a homiletic lead, a meaningful story on which to build his or her own thoughts and apply them to the here and now.

Introducing each homily will be a brief background of the type of person who is deceased. Such an introduction may guide another's thoughts. It is imperative, by the way, that one looks up and reads the Scripture reference.

"It's All Right"

Mark 16:1–8

"Will anyone remember?" I thought to myself. "But what if they do?"

Not too long ago a Soviet satellite with an atomic reactor aboard got into trouble and disintegrated over Canada, then fell to earth. I remember the fears of both the Soviets and the North Americans because of panic and because of the danger to health. Reading about that sort of thing reminds us that, not too far underneath the surface, all of us live with a great deal of fear. The fear of atomic hardware falling out of the sky.

And the everyday fears: the fear of losing our jobs; the fear of losing our health; the fear of losing our life's savings; the fear of another war; the fear of accidents; the fear of misfortune coming to our husbands, our wives, our parents, our children; the fear of being rejected, being unwanted; the fear of growing old and dependent, of being left alone without friends or family or loved ones. And finally, of course, there is the fear of loss: the loss of our faculties, the loss of our hearing, the loss of our mobility, the loss of memory, the loss of our loved ones, and the loss that we call death.

Even after we suffer these losses, particularly the loss of death, then there are other fears that creep in, fears we don't always express: the fear of losing control. Why couldn't I have done more? The fear of admitting our feelings of anger against God, especially in the suffering and death of innocent ones. If there is a God, why can't that God prevent babies from dying, or people from having cancer, or war or pestilence or hunger or famine, and all the other ills we suffer?

We want to shake our fist at God. We want to yell and scream and get terribly annoyed with God. And then sometimes after that there's a fear of a weak faith. "What kind of faith do I have? It's all right when I talk to others, but when it hits home, can I come to terms with all of these realities?"

386

It is all these kinds of fears that like so many mountains fall upon us, and like the people in our gospel, faced with the huge, great stone covering the tomb, they say, "Who's going to lift the stone?"

God says, "I will." Because from the fear of being unwanted or unloved, from the fear of death and all its anxieties, from the fear that there's no more to life than a bunch of molecules and ashes left over, God says through the prophets, "Tell the people: 'Behold, I have loved them with an everlasting love.'" And through Isaiah the prophet, God says, "Tell the people: 'Is it possible for a mother to forget the child of her womb? And even if it were possible that a mother could forget her own child, I shall not forget thee.'"

So it is God who is the one who will lift our fears, and we must believe that. One of the greatest teachers of this century was the great philosopher and theologian Karl Barth. In his old age, as people are wont to do, someone asked him what was the most important truth he had learned in all of his vast study and thinking. And Karl Barth answered by quoting that old Protestant hymn that he learned in childhood. He said, "It's all in these words: 'Jesus loves me, this I know.'" That was the conviction of decades of learning and studying, and he believed that.

You see, the whole point of faith is that when we are met with this fear of darkness and death, we are not ashamed to call out, because the whole point of believing is the conviction that there is someone there to answer. It's what you parents have experienced when your children were very small and the lights went out at night and they got scared. Those little back-up night lights were all right, but they were a short-term solution. The only way the children's fears could possibly be allayed was for Mommy and Daddy to go in and soothe the children, and pat them on the head, and soothe away the bad dreams, and tuck them in bed all over again, and give them those famous centuries-old words of reassurance, "Now, now, it's all right, it's all right."

And the secret of allaying those fears is, of course, love. It is the love of the mother and the love of the father that eventually still the children's worst anxieties, and put them back into that sleep of innocent peace.

It's the same way with us: When we are faced with this great anxiety called death, we tend to run the whole gamut of acceptance to anger, to disbelief, to hurt, to bewilderment, because, after all, in death we always lose a person. But we have to remember that we never lose our relationship to

God. We still have someone who says, "It's all right." That someone is God: God present in his word, in the Spirit, and in the church.

And it is in all these ways that God pats us on the head, and tucks us back into bed, and says, "Even though you have fears and anxieties, it's all right." Jesus made it all right, because it's this kind of love that burst the bonds of death. It is the kind of love that Jesus had that simply took away death's final word and made God's comfort the final word—instead of the grave. And this is what we must believe. Jesus said in the gospel, "Do not fear, little flock. It has pleased the Father to give you the Kingdom."

That's what we celebrate at a liturgy like this. Many of you are old hands at liturgies like this. You know well enough why we sing "Alleluia" as we enter the church. We sing that "Alleluia" because through our tears we believe that God has made it "all right" for the person who has died.

We wear the white vestments and put out flowers, not because we're insensitive to human grief, but it's our limited way of saying, "Now, now, it will be all right." We cover the dark coffin with the white cloth of the dead person's baptismal innocence because that's our way of saying, "It's all right." We bring the body and put it in front of the baptismal font beneath the crucified Savior because John says that out of Jesus' side flowed that blood and water with which we have been renewed. And that's our way of saying, "It's all right."

And finally, we're at this Mass where bread and wine shall be brought up and changed into the body and blood of Christ, and broken and crushed and given, because today Jesus is still saying, "This is my body given for you. This is my blood shed for you and for the one who has died." And this, above all, is our greatest assurance that God pats us on the head and says, "It's all right."

So we go back to the altar with that double stream of feeling: human grief and loss, especially having known someone who suffered a long time, and a sense of relief that it's all over because it's been a long, hard road for everybody. A sense of bewilderment, facing death so squarely and closely. But above all, I hope, a sense of faith. Faith that God gives us in our collective selves and this ancient liturgy. And faith in the promises that God made, the pat on the head, the allaying of our fears, the uplifting of our hopes, the forgiveness of our anger, the strengthening of our faith, and the promise that through Jesus, as our liturgy says, life is never ended but merely exchanged. And so for N _____, as for us, "It's all right."

Sue Van Benthuysen: A Name on the Wall

JOHN 15:12–17

The deceased is a middle-aged woman who worked for Meridian Health Services, heroically battling cancer before succumbing. She was a wonderful amateur artist whom I met in art class and then recognized as a parishioner. The chief imagery here is the Vietnam Wall.

A few years ago, I had the opportunity to make a trip to Washington, D.C., with some friends. Part of our itinerary was a visit to the Vietnam Memorial Wall. As you may know, the monument is a long black granite wall with thousands of names of those who lost their lives in the war. As I walked the grounds of the memorial, a couple of things stood out. The first thing I noticed was the silence. As crowded as it was, there was a hush of reverence over the whole setting. The next thing that caught my eye was how different people approached the wall, once they found the name of a loved one. They moved very slowly as if approaching something sacred and would then touch the name. Some stood quietly, running their fingers gently over the letters. Others wept, and some even knelt.

As I watched this ritual unfold before my eyes, I couldn't help but wonder what the relationship was between the living person and the name. It had to be something special or it would not have solicited such a reaction. After all, there were literally hundreds of people milling about the wall and some were obviously just there as spectators. They could touch lots of names on the wall and have no reaction whatsoever. To them, the names were just letters carved in a wall. But to others, those names, or rather, *this* name, was a cause for tears.

When I go to cemeteries at someone's funeral I have noticed a similar response when people come to pay their respects to a loved one. Out of the corner of my eye I see them walk past rows and rows of names on monuments and crypts looking for just one. Then they stop. They approach a special stone with reverence and run their fingers over the carved letters that spell out the name of their loved ones. Some weep, others are just still, lost in grief or reverie.

So where is the connection? As I said, it is in the relationship. To those who knew the person behind the name, it represents all the memories, the history, the personality and intimacy created between these two people. It is the depth of the relationship that makes the connection. It isn't just in the name. It represents the investment of life one person made in another person. It represents someone who made a difference to somebody.

That's the way it is here this morning. To many, to most perhaps in Point Pleasant, Sue Van Benthuysen is but a name on the wall, a name in the obituary column of the *Press*, some person who died much too young at age fifty-four. But for us, it's different. There are enough of us here in this church today who do have cause to remember Sue, who run our fingers over her name and pause, and weep and pray and smile and remember.

As we touch those letters, we conjure up memories of this little girl who at the tender age of five moved with her family from Newark to Point Pleasant. Some remember her graduation from Georgian Court, the birth of her son, the loss of her father seven years ago, the devotion of her mother and siblings, the delight of her nieces and nephews. We know also that, beyond her immediate family, there are many acquaintances, for Sue was, like a child gathering snowflakes, a natural gatherer of friends. She worked for the Meridian Health Systems for many years and had many friends there, some of whom are here today. She had special friends, among whom Rosemary Doherty stands out. My own memories of friendship as I run my fingers over her name are that of a gracious, generous, and talented lady whom I met, of all places, at art class. I had almost no talent. Sue had a great deal of it. I used to silently watch with envy her painting come to life as mine languished in dullsville. Soon we became acquainted and I felt more comfortable watching her, openly hoping to get some hints. She was a wonderful painter.

Then almost accidentally we began to meet here at St. Martha's and she suddenly realized that the bumbling pupil was a priest and I suddenly realized that she was a gentle person of gentle faith, a wonderful woman. As time went on, she told me of her cancer, her battle, her remission, and then, lately, its return; as it turned out, its final return. We met. We talked about it. We prayed. She knew time was short and tried to prepare herself. I hadn't seen her at church for a while, figuring that we missed each other, until her mother called last Friday to say that Sue was dying and I went over to the house and gave her the sacrament of the sick and dying. She, my good friend, died the next day.

And as I say this, I remember: there's that word again, the one that appeared in our gospel: "I have called you friends....you did not choose me but I chose you and I appointed you to go and bear fruit, fruit that will last." This woman, Sue, had the greatest Friend of all. She *was* chosen, chosen at her baptism and she has remained true to her call and God has remained true to her. That white cloth over her coffin is but her original baptismal dress stretched large to remind us that she ends up where he began: in God's house, as God's child, as God's friend. The white vestments of joy that I am wearing are a symbol of the happiness of that enduring friendship, a reminder that the fruit of her life lives on in so many here. The flowers you see here are a sign that her life has bloomed. The light of the Easter Candle here is a sign of new life and, at the same time, a guarantee what she is now with the One who chose her, bright with love.

As the poet says:

> Is there a leaf upon the tree
> The Father does not see?
> Leaves fall, so do we all
> Return to earth, to sod.
> Sparrows and kings,
> And all manner of things
> Fall, fall into the hands
> Of the living God
> She has fallen. She has been caught.

May she rest in peace in those Loving Arms. Amen.

Mike Capenegro: In Need of a Story

JOHN 14:1–3

The focus for the homilist here is the wonderful story by Arthur Gordon and its connection to the gospel. It's a great and comforting story and can be used in many configurations for a funeral.

I noticed in his official obituary that Michael Capenegro, *Colonel* Michael Capenegro, had a distinguished career. He was an infantry officer for twenty-five years and he was a professor of Military Science and, after military retirement, he taught at St. John's School of Business, not to mention that he was also mayor of this township for more than ten years. Impressive. I strain to picture this talented man in these challenging roles, imagining him both in and out of uniform as straightforward, competent, undertaking his various duties with confidence, and doing his tasks with level-headed integrity. I am indeed taken with his bio and am in awe of his achievements and appreciate them dearly. His was an admirable and useful life.

But I have to confess that this marvelous resume I try so hard to keep in mind keeps dissolving into the wellsprings of my emotions, perhaps because I did not know him as a colonel or professor or politician. The fact is, whatever his achievements, I knew him simply as a man and I loved not the colonel or the professor or the politician, but Mike. Just as, I know, his family knew and loved him as husband, father, brother, cousin, grandfather. These levels, these heart connections, these poignant memories—each one cherished to the point of tears, each one turned over, examined, held tightly and traded these past few days—no obituary can capture.

As for me, we met casually and respectfully in his post-military days when I first came to St. Mary's. But over the years we drew closer as I sensed something special and honorable about him. When his lovely wife, Ramona, died, I presided at her Mass as I am, sadly, doing at his; and I got to know him better, bound by a common event.

Then, in the course of time a widow from Middletown, Peg Boyle, caught his eye. This was another link because I knew Peg and her husband and family previously when, as a young priest—alas, a long time ago—I was stationed in St. Mary's in Middletown. A good woman from my past and a good man from my present built a new life, a good life, as they should have, and I was a part of it. But I think the bond was cemented because of two things. First, Mike was a faith-filled man. I admired that. He was true to his religion, loyal to his parish, and regular in his worship, and that's no small thing, no small witness. Second, most of all, as far as I was selfishly concerned, he liked me. He was very supportive. He backed up my efforts, praised my homilies, volunteered, like so many, for parish projects. He, like Peg, was simply there, and being there, like Woody Allen's showing up, is the stuff of life and a badge of honor.

But I tell you, what remains in my memory is after I left St. Mary's. On occasions, usually funerals, unfortunately, I would come back. Mike, who always attended daily Mass, would always intercept me afterward. And the routine was always the same: I can picture it now. Silently, in the back of church, with that manly grin on his face, he would stand directly in front of me, extend his right hand to my right hand to hold, take his left hand and place it on my shoulder and look me straight in the eye and say sincerely, "How are you? It's good to see you." He meant every word.

I mention this because he in fact, like some others have done, said to me after one of those funerals, "Father, I liked that story. When I die I want you to come back and tell it to my family." I replied casually, "OK, Mike, it's a deal. And if I go before you, I hereby give you permission to read it at *my* funeral." And we both laughed. And afterward, whenever I came back for a funeral, he would point his finger at me and say, "Remember!" and I would give him a thumbs up.

And here I am, unexpectedly, with heavy heart, redeeming my promise. Ironically, as some of you here will recall, the story he wanted is one I gave here precisely a week ago in this same church in connection with a lenten series I was giving. The story is a variation on the gospel I read. You recall, Jesus, likely with his own next-day death in mind, knowing what abandonment and fear were like as he would experience them in the garden of Gethsemane, wanted to give some comfort to his soon-to-be bereaved disciples. So, as you heard, he said, "Do not let your hearts be troubled…in my Father's house there are many dwelling places….I go to prepare a place for you….I will come again and take you to myself so that where I am you may be also…."

So here, for Mike and his family, is that gospel dressed up in the story he wanted.

A long time ago there lived a little boy whose parents had died. He was taken in by an aunt who raised him as her own child. Years later, after he had grown up and left his aunt, he received a letter from her. She was in terminal illness and, from the tone of her letter, he knew she was afraid of death. This man, whom she had raised and touched, wrote her a letter in which he said:

It is now thirty-five years since I, a little boy of six, was left quite alone in the world. You sent me word that you would give me a home and be a mother to me. I've never forgotten the day when I made the long journey of ten miles to your house. I can still recall my disappointment when, instead of coming for me yourself, you sent your servant, Caesar, a dark man, to fetch me. I well remember my tears and my anxiety as, perched high on your horse and clinging tight to Caesar, I rode off to my new home.

Night fell before we finished the journey and as it grew dark, I became even more afraid. "Do you think she'll go to bed before I get there?" I asked Caesar anxiously.

"Oh, no," said Caesar, "she's sure to stay up for you. When we get out of these woods, you'll see her light shining in the window."

Presently, we did ride out into the clearing and there was your light. I remember that you were waiting at the door, that you put your arms tight around me, that you lifted me, a tired, frightened little boy, down from the horse. You had a fire burning on the hearth, a hot supper waiting on the stove. After supper you took me to my new room. You heard me say my prayers. Then you sat with me until I fell asleep.

You probably realize why I am trying to recall this to your memory now. Very soon, God is going to send for you, and take you to a new home. I'm trying to tell you that you needn't be afraid of the summons or of the strange journey or of the dark messenger of death. God can be trusted. God can be trusted to do as much for you as you did for me so many years ago.

At the end of the road you'll find love and a welcome waiting. And you'll be safe in God's care. I'm going to watch and pray for you until you're out of sight. And I shall wait for the day when I make the same journey myself and find you waiting at the end of the road to greet me.

Notice the metaphors and symbols: Caesar, the dark figure, is death; the light at the end of he journey is Jesus, the light of the world. The house is the "many rooms" in the Father's house that Jesus promised. The supper is the heavenly banquet. God is the loving aunt. It's a homecoming story. It is gospel.

Well, I hope you are pleased, Mike, not only that I kept my promise, but that you have found the story to be true and have arrived at your Father's house safely. And as for you, Peg—and also for you, Frances, Michael, Lorri, and John; and Josephine, Grace, Rocco, Alfred, and Sonny and the in-laws and grandchildren—I hope the comfort this thoughtful man wanted me to convey to you has found its mark in your hearts.

What more can I say? Be sad that he's gone. Be glad that he's home.

Ralph Imholte: Deep Down

John 20:19–21

I've included the gospel here to show that I shortened it for my purposes. This homily was very well received and, to my surprise, it struck a note with some in the congregation whose parents had fallen into dementia or Alzheimer's disease. The homily was, I found, an enormous comfort to survivors to know that God reached "deep down" into the mental sickness and dimness to bring peace to their loved ones. Recommended for people who did have mind-destroying diseases.

> On the evening of that first day of the week, when the doors were closed where the disciples were, for fear of the authorities, Jesus came and stood in their midst and said to them, "Peace be with you." When he said this, he showed them his hands and his side. The disciples rejoiced when they saw the Lord. Jesus said to them again, "Peace be with you. As the Father has sent me, so I send you." And when he had said this he breathed on them and said to them, "Receive the holy Spirit...."
> The Gospel of the Lord.

There is, I suppose, some significance that Ralph Imholte—husband, father, grandfather, deacon, friend—died just as the Easter season was beginning, Holy Saturday morning to be exact, because he was, as you know, very much an Easter person. He was springtime with his booming voice, his athletic prowess, his contagious hugs which he scattered like Johnny Appleseed. He was sometimes stubborn, quite sentimental, always sensitive. He was a passionate man, passionate with people, passionate with God. I knew that right off when I first met him.

You recall, as I mentioned at the funeral of Rosemary, his childhood sweetheart, his lifelong love, that I first encountered Ralph when, a transplant from Minnesota and a fugitive from St. Leo's at that time, he snuck over here to St. Mary's, and eventually, like Caesar, he came, he saw, he liked, and he conquered.

He asked outright if I would sponsor him as a deacon and I agreed on the condition that he find and dedicate himself to a particular ministry. In tribute to his wife, he said proudly that he was happily married and would like to share that. So the parish sent him to Iona College and then to Seton Hall to get his degree in counseling and in 1977 he was ordained a deacon.

To make a long, familiar story short, he became so good that we hired him to do all our marriage preparation and counseling, and what an asset over the years he was to the parish! Then, to keep him around all the time, I made him Parish Administrator. A good deal, I thought: deacon, counselor, parish administrator, and eventually friend, all in one package! How lucky could we get? He had settled in to St. Mary's and we were never the same.

Ralph, as you know, was a force, a glue. With his six-foot physique and bald head, looking for all the world like an understudy for Mr. Clean, later to be graced by a beard, he was hard not to notice. His buoyant presence was always signaled by a hearty laugh, a shouted exclamation, unbounded energy. He was part of a loyal faith-sharing group, went off annually to Weston Priory with his friends, gave Pre-Cana conferences and various courses. Many a happy marriage today owes itself to his ministrations. He was a trusted collaborator, a co-laborer, very much an essential part of the color and charism of St. Mary's.

It was, therefore, for all of us, a shock when this jock, this jogger, this competitive player who gave his sons a run for their money on the handball and tennis courts, had a stroke. Well, the long and short of it was that, despite our hopes, he never recovered. Rosemary put her ills on the back burner and ministered to him and, when she died, he died inside. We could all see that.

The seamless trip from hospital to rehab to nursing home was as inevitable as it was sad. To see this once big, vital man reduced to helplessness, this marathon man confined to a wheelchair, was hard to take. His loving and faithful family and his loyal friends could sense the slow decline. When I saw him last, it was clear that he had almost completely collapsed into his inner core, that he no longer could focus or recognize outside.

Yet speaking of that, there is, I suggest, some significance that Ralph did die on Holy Saturday. Let me digress as I tell you why. When I was a little boy the old pious folk used to call Holy Saturday "Deep-Down Day," an odd term. I used to wonder what it meant, so one day I asked my uncle. In his funny accent he said to me, "Little One"—he always called me "Little One—it means that Jesus, you know, went deep, deep down, went down there." He pointed to the ground. Seeing my blank face, he went on. "Jesus, you know, after he died, went to the deep hell."

Immediately I recognized that phase from the creed, "He descended into hell," and I remember Sister telling us in school that it meant that, after he died, Jesus went to the underworld to rescue all those waiting in a kind of antechamber to lead them triumphantly to a heretofore closed paradise. When I repeated that to my uncle, trying to enlighten him, he shook his head and, being a better theologian than Sister was, said patiently, "No, Little One, it means that there is no place Jesus cannot be." And much, much later I understood what he was saying.

I came to understand that Jesus, going deep down, descending into hell, means that when we are paralyzed by fear or sickness, locked behind the closed doors of our broken bodies and dimmed minds, God can still come, stand inside our fears and paralysis, and breathe out peace. "He descended into hell" means there is no hell where Jesus cannot, will not, be. As we heard in the gospel, they haven't built a door yet that his love cannot pass through.

So when Ralph died on "Deep-Down Saturday" I knew right away that this is what happened to him. In the last months and weeks of his life, our beloved friend had slowly faded behind closed doors—his diminishing body, his vacant eyes—and we were no longer able to enter. But Deep-Down Saturday tells me that there was one who *could* enter, who *did* enter, to stand in the middle of his fear, his darkness, to give him comfort and to breathe peace into the depths of his soul.

Jesus went through Ralph's closed doors to be with him, exhale the Spirit, and lead him home. I knew then that Saturday's deep-down love had brought Sunday's resurrection to my friend and I cried and smiled at the same time.

Whitey, Kathy, Mary Jo, Tom, Mark, and all Ralph's family and friends, hold that image in mind: the Easter Triduum—Good Friday, Deep-Down Saturday, and Risen Sunday—will always be linked to father, deacon, friend Ralph Imholte and each anniversary will give us sufficient reason through our tears to sing the Easter Alleluia.

Amen.

As I end and depart this pulpit, I must admit that there are two things that tease my mind: First, what must be his meeting with Rosemary? Second, was even Jesus prepared for his bear hug?

Easter peace, dear friend.

Mary Vanderbilt: Wife and Weaver

The deceased was a lovely, quiet woman of the parish. The imagery here is that of a weaver, one who quietly weaves together the fabric of a holy life. She had buried a son, Peter, a year or so before.

I first met Mary, or rather, perhaps, I was first more aware of her when, at church a long time ago, I was trying to build a sense of community. She always sat around the fourth or fifth pew to my right in those days. It was the feast of Epiphany, the feast of strangers from a strange place coming to Christ, and I said that Epiphany *still* takes place and we're all proofs of that. Then I proceeded to say that my father was of German descent, an orphan early on who wound up in Hightstown and he met my mother, an immigrant from Italy. And here I am in Colts Neck. And then I went around and invited other people to reveal their distant origins.

And people, some of you might recall, stood up and called out their country of ancestry: Ireland, Spain, Italy, France, Chile, Belgium, and so on. I said, "See, we're from all over, but united here in the same search and faith, just like the Wise Men. I guess we've covered all the countries." Then a timid woman raised her hand. I looked at her and asked, "Did we forget someone? She smiled, gave that little-girl shrug, and said, "American Indian." I shot back, "Foreigner!" It was, of course, Mary Vanderbilt slyly letting me know that I had overlooked the obvious. I made a mental note to keep an eye on that woman.

I did, and over time I found out that she was a rather remarkable woman and that her frail frame belied someone who had a long and hard journey from harsh poverty to tragic widowhood, to marriage to a man who would worship her all her life, and to motherhood that produced a large family she would nurture in good times and in bad. In fact, Mary reminded me of a TV interview I once saw.

The person being interviewed happened to be an heroic mother who had single-handedly raised a large family. In spite of all the frustrations, disappointments, and obstacles, she had persevered, and every one of her children had remarkable achievements not only in their schooling, but also in their vocation. It was an inspiring story worth celebrating, for it revealed the heights and depths of human greatness. During the interview, the reporter asked the mother her secret: 'I suppose you loved all your children equally, making sure that all got the same treatment?" The mother replied, "I loved them. I loved them all, each one of them, but not equally. I loved the one the most who was down until he was up. I loved the one the most who was weak until she was strong. I loved the one the most who was hurt until he was healed. I loved the one the most who was lost until she was found." That was Mary Vanderbilt.

That love wasn't confined to her husband and children either. In my book, she took a giant step up when I learned that she was wild about dogs and she would often bring Lady, who always remained ladylike, even when my dog barked at her to let her know she was on his property. And, I discovered, she had a deft way with antiques and would come over to the annual Chinese auction and appraise the hidden treasures among the junk.

But mostly I learned what great faith she and Doug had when together they ministered to their son Peter, embraced his illness, and eventually buried him, not, however, before Peter, true son of his mother and father, volunteered to refinish for me the wood altar in the spiritual center chapel. And then she would ferry the leftover food from Delicious Orchards to the place in Neptune that had been so supportive of Peter. Faith, hope, and love seemed to ride easy with her.

I want to confess something. I have this automatic mental habit of labeling people, a kind of seeing people in symbolic occupations and so, quite unconsciously, somewhere along the way—I don't remember when—I got this mental image of Mary Vanderbilt as a *weaver*. Yes, that was it. Perfect. Like an invisible thread, she quietly wove together a family and this community. She was always a background person helping out here and there, stuffing bulletins, cleaning up, making life easier. Yes, no doubt, she was a weaver of lives, of faith, of joy.

I was stunned when I heard she was in the hospital. That, to no one's surprise, her husband and her children rallied around her so attentively, took tender care of her to the end, and were generous in their love says a great deal about the way she raised them. And still, you know what? Even in the hospital, when she rallied slightly, she sent me this birthday card—What a woman!—I have here. The front, showing berries and butterflies, reads, "How blessed we are with little gifts from God." And then, inside, in her handwriting, these words, "Dear Father, We shall be forever grateful for all that you have brought to our lives. Our appreciation for you and our affection for you run so very, very deep. Our warmest love, Mary and Doug."

Here she is, with a few days left in her life, taking time to express love. How like her, how *very* like her, this weaver to the last. I shall always cherish this card and save it not only for its message, but because those words on the front say everything I could possibly say about Mary Vanderbilt, "How blessed we are with little gifts from God."

Amen to that.

Doug Vanderbilt: The Waiter

To no one's surprise Mary's husband died about two years later. They were in love and he could not endure the separation. The imagery here, as one might expect, is that of a waiter.

There are all kinds of waiters. I don't mean the folk who wait on your table at restaurants, but people who wait. Period. They fall into several distinctive categories and styles.

There are those who remain patient and calm no matter what the circumstance, but they are rare. Far more common are the impatient who pace and foot-tap and steal glances at their watches; who, when you finally arrive, let you know exactly how late you are; who maddeningly weave in and out of parkway traffic, trying to get one car ahead of the others; who jockey to get into the express lane at the supermarket with their far over-twelve limit; who, like the White Rabbit, are always in a hurry.

Then there are the waiters who bring something to read. Next there are the multi-taskers with their ubiquitous cell phones and Palm Pilots who, conditioned by society's incessant noise, can't abide the solitude and silence so necessary for emotional and spiritual growth. There are those who practice a Zen-like calm, whose motto is, "When they arrive, they arrive." Their opposite is the overanxious, who spend their time letting their imagination run wild, sure that something terrible and disastrous has happened, like the kidnapping of their awaited friend or their falling through an open manhole or being abducted by aliens. There are those who simply can't wait at all, like the child asking "Are we there yet?" or "When is Santa coming?"

Finally, there are those for whom waiting is sublime, like a woman awaiting the birth of a child who is taken in by the experience, or like a husband awaiting reunion with his wife.

That's how I think of this gentle man, Doug Vanderbilt. Waiter. Doug was never the same after Mary died. He became essentially a year-and-a half-long Advent person, yearning for the wife of many years and the God who would make them one again. Perhaps, therefore, it is fitting that he would go to his spouse and to the Lord during the season of expectation, the time of holy longing. His wait is over.

You know, I can still picture him at Mary's funeral in March of last year, how he perked up and looked at me when I read a note they had both sent me, a note made even more precious because Mary was at that time in the hospital and Doug was faithfully at her side, morning, noon, and night. Yet they took time to send a card which I still have and cherish. How I remember its words: "Dear Father, we shall be forever grateful for all that you have brought into our lives. Our appreciation for you and our affection for you run so very, very deep. Our warmest love. Mary and Doug." I brought to *their* lives? That still embarrasses me. What about all they brought to the lives of their children, to the lives of their friends, to the lives of this community, to my life and yours?

In Mary's homily, some may remember, I called her a weaver, a thread that wove together family, friends, and community. Now I call Doug a waiter, an Advent waiter who, according to Kip, when the doctor told him that he had a few weeks to live, protested that it was too long. He was leaving sooner. You cannot frustrate love.

I was privileged to anoint Doug last Sunday, to bring him the presence and comfort of the church, the fruits of Jesus' death and resurrection. He was quite conscious of my being there—our being there—and rewarded me with a smile of recognition. With the anointing done, I knew it was the last thing to be tucked away and he was ready and willing to depart. He had a reunion to attend.

Weaver and waiter, joined by the power of that Child we all yearn for at this holy season, the Child who one day would declare, "Come to me, all of you who labor and are burdened and I will give you rest." And whose resurrection would be a promise of our own.

Advent expectation has been met even before the season is over. May he rest in the faith that he practiced. May he rest in the hope that he kept. May he rest in the lady-love that he cherished. May this good man, this husband, father, grandfather, this friend, rest in peace. Amen.

Helen Owendoff:
On the Road to Emmaus

Luke 24:13–35

Helen was part of the "Morning Group," those people who came to daily Mass and who so generously took on many domestic and parochial tasks, such as stuffing the bulletin every Friday. We always had a pot of coffee going and people took turns bringing goodies. The imagery here is drawn from the powerful Emmaus story and I have used its divisions as points of commentary.

When St. Luke sat down to write this gospel story, it was not just a fancy and interesting telling of a post-resurrection tale. He was writing for his community that, like so many other communities—like our own today—had to face the question of death. And with death, the feeling of isolation, loss, shattering distress, and, often, as in the case of Helen, relief, for it was a hard departure. And in his finely wrought story Luke has proposed three elements as to how a community, a family, can find its own inner healing when faced with death, as the apostles did when faced with the death of its leader, Jesus Christ.

Notice the first element in Luke's story: the Scriptures. When these bewildered and distressed and grieving disciples were excitedly talking on the way to Emmaus, the stranger approached, and after their exchange of news, what did he do after he listened to their distress, anxiety, and hurt? *He opened to them the Scriptures.* And thus Luke is saying, in effect, in *your* grief, in *your* facing death—the death of your mother, your sister, your aunt, your grandmom—the first step to healing is to open up the Scriptures. And so we open them and as we cast our eye here and there, what is it we read? We read of Jesus saying: "I am the resurrection and the life; he who believes in me shall never die." Helen believed in Jesus. Or again, "The one who would save his life will lose it, but the one who loses his life for my sake shall find it." Helen, in her gifts to her family and to her church, often "lost" her life. And again in the Scriptures through Isaiah: "Though your sins be as red as scarlet I will make them as white as snow." Or yet, in Jeremiah, "Behold, tell the people I have loved you with an everlasting love." Helen was much loved, by God and by us.

And so Luke is right: The Scriptures give us comfort, and that is why through those words we can celebrate this woman's death in hope, because Jesus is now her resurrection and new life. And because of this we take our very human tears and our deep sorrow and freely mingle them with hope and, in a certain sense, even with joy. Which is why, from the very beginning, Christians have always displayed that double feeling about death: the profound sorrow at losing someone they have known and loved, right along with a very distinct undercurrent of joy. And the church, you observe, picks that up in its liturgy. For example, we have flowers that we normally associate with joyous times. And we are wearing the white vestments that we associate with weddings. And, what's more, in the early church, if they had had newspapers, the headline for Helen would even have been: "Helen Owendoff Celebrates Her Birthday Today." Because in the old days, they considered the day you died your birth-day, when you were really born again, when, without encumbrance and without obliqueness, without hospitals and medications, without pain and machines, without tubes and coma, directly face to face, as Paul says, you would look on the vision and the face of the Father. And all this because the Scriptures opened up to us the meaning of life and death in Jesus.

The second element that Luke gives for healing is the teaching that the distraught and grieving disciples finally recognized Jesus in the breaking of the bread. That is, in the Eucharist we get a glimpse—we always do—that we are not alone either in life or death, but that we recognize, however dimly, that One is at table with us, abides with us: "I am the bread of life. The one who eats this bread and drinks this blood abides in me and I will raise him up on the last day." Helen, who so often broke bread here around this very altar and therefore had intimations that she was never alone, now knows for sure. The Christ who came to her in the shadow of bread and wine is now there in the brightness of full humanity and friendship. She sees clearly now what she only surmised when she worshipped with us. And it is glorious.

The final element that Luke gives us in coming to terms with death is community. You notice at the end of his story, the first thing the disciples did when they got the good news of the Scriptures and recognized Jesus in the breaking of the bread, they turned around and went back to the community at Jerusalem. And here's the final element in the healing of the grieving heart, immersion in the community: the community of one's family and friends, the community of the church, the community we call parish. It is in this faith community that we freely exchange our hurts, our pains, our hopes, our love, and, in the context of such faith, healing eventually takes place.

But Helen knew all about that because she was certainly a force in this community. Oh, without any effort I can easily see her now all over the place: the counter of money, the reader of the Scriptures, the stuffer of bulletins, the Martha/Mary member, the chatty reporter of news far and wide, the bright and witty energy of the morning group. And I can see her too as the pray-er in the pews, the mother who twenty-three years ago buried a son in this very church, the wife who mourned a husband four years ago, the pilgrim whom God wondrously led from Brooklyn to Morris Plains to ultimately grace us at St. Mary's and then who journeyed from Lincroft to Monroe Township, the remarkably young looking and agile senior citizen who was an inspiration to us all. She was no doubt a vital strand in the fabric of community.

The Scriptures, Eucharist, Community: Luke's formula still works. And so, having tested it once more, we now we say goodbye to this woman of fourscore and six years. She mattered to her family and friends. She mattered to us. She made a difference, and that is high praise. She made us laugh, which is even higher. She cherished the Scriptures, ate at the table of the Lord, and enlarged community, which is the highest praise. She is now the journey completed. May she rest in peace.

Bill Kozabo: Another Ananias

LUKE 12:32–34

This homily also taps into the "behind the scene" theme, this time using the comparison to the scriptural Ananias. The first reading was a condensed form of his story from the Acts of the Apostles.

I have but a few, brief, very simple words as befits a man who would cringe at any long, flowery oration, so here they are. As many of you know, the Christian world is celebrating the afterglow of Easter. In this period our daily Scripture readings are taken from Luke's idealized early church history, the Acts of the Apostles.

In the first part of his work, he focuses on Peter and in the second part, just begun, he focuses on Paul. He starts with Paul's conversion. He relates how Paul, an enemy of his fellow Jews who claimed Jesus as Messiah, went around harassing and arresting them. But on the way to Damascus to claim more victims, he has a vision of Jesus, is struck blind, and told to wait for further instructions.

Meanwhile, in a little side street, a little unknown shoemaker, obviously a recent convert to the Way, as the Jesus Movement was called, has a vision. His name in Ananias. He's told to go to a street named Straight—easy to find in a city notorious for its wickedly crooked alleys—to find Paul and cure him. Ananias protests, citing Paul's murderous reputation toward his kind. He's overruled, gets himself moving, and with great trepidation finds Paul, cures his blindness (physical and spiritual), and baptizes him. Paul, as we know, eventually goes on to fame, if not fortune, on Oprah and the cover of *Time*.

409

And Ananias? The truth is, he goes on to nothing. His task done, he simply goes back to his shoe shop, lives, works, and dies. Period. This man, a non-entity, comes and goes and is never heard of again. There is, as far as I know, no *Saint* Ananias. No church named after him, no statue, no feast day. And yet—yet—we have to stop and ponder this deep truth about this little man of Scripture: He was there when God needed him and, in the end, that was all that mattered.

When you come to think of it, the Bible, life itself, is full of such "Ananias" people who are simply "there" when needed, with a capital "T."

You can see where I'm heading. I'm heading to Bill Kozabo, who, along with Helen, was a true Ananias, the best praise I can bestow. This quiet man of St. Joseph's trade was there when his country needed him: He was a sailor in the war. He was there when his community needed him: years as a fire and first aid volunteer. And finally and gratefully, to come to my personal experience, he was there when St Mary's needed him, when I needed him.

When I first met Bill and Helen some thirty-five years ago—is it that long?—I knew I had met my Ananias. From the beginning, they were emotionally and spiritually with me and were delighted with the new life beginning at St. Mary's. They readily embraced all the activities, the "coming alive" as Helen said more than once. There they were when we navigated Manhattan on the Circle Line. They were there in one of the dozen buses taking us to the old Madison Square Garden or Radio City. They were there at every event. Good and prayerful people, they were there every Sunday, They were there in the parish ministries and in every phase of St. Mary's journey to this very day.

What I'm trying to say, perhaps not too well, is that their "thereness," the simple, loyal, precious fact of it, was such a support and comfort and a grace, an outward sign of God's fidelity. As a result, over the years, like so many of you, we grew beyond parish priest and parishioner into friends. And then, I recall, in those days when Margaret was sick, I went many times to the Kozabo house to care for her and wound up being cared for. I never left the house without a treat.

And what do you say about people who for thirty-five years, uninterruptedly, have sent me a card, not only every Christmas, but on every single anniversary and every birthday?

We have had, thank God, our St. Pauls from this parish, names known and celebrated. But we have also had, and do have, thank God, our Ananiases, the "there" people, and this quiet man of integrity and faith, Bill Kozabo, was near the top of the list. People like him are simply glue, fabric weavers, mosaics in the grand design of love, life, and God's kingdom and that's all that matters.

I liked Bill, loved him and Helen and Margaret Buckelew. I was sorry to hear about his illness. When I did, I visited him in the Care One Home. He was alert, kidded about Helen's visit at the hairdressers when I asked about her. It was a nice visit, alas, my last one. Then apparently things grew worse and the last months were painful and excruciating for everyone and I'm sure that Helen and family and friends have to be relieved that at last Bill is relieved.

And now we come to pray for and bury this man thus relieved, noting that as St. Luke had his Acts of the Apostles and his Ananias, St. Mary's has its memories and its Bill Kozabos.

It is a sad time for all of us, but the happy note as I end my simple words for a simple man is this: The one thing I am absolutely sure of is that when God needed Bill, Bill was there for God. And now that Bill needs God, God is there for him. You can count on it.

Husband, uncle, carpenter, sailor, volunteer, parishioner, friend—good and faithful servant, may you rest in peace. Amen.

Hans Ziegler: The Blessed

In this homily I explore the theme of Advent for a gentle man waiting to die.

The gospel I just read is from the first Sunday of Advent and it ended, as you heard, with the words, "What I say to you, I say to all: 'Watch.'" Hans Ziegler was an Advent man, a watchful man. Not a fatalist who embraced cynicism but a realist who embraced acceptance.

He was eighty-nine years old. His health was failing. He was four years in a convalescent home, and he knew he would never leave. But as he wrote so typically in his Christmas note this year, "This is the fourth Christmas I am spending in a nursing home, and thanks to the continued care, and especially the loving help from my dear family and loyal friends, I have been fortunate to adjust to this limited lifestyle as an acceptable old-age solution. The fourth year passed without any major medical crisis and to expect at age eighty-nine further significant health improvements would seem to be unrealistic. (A lovely understatement.) It is time to count one's blessings!"

That's Hans Ziegler. That's a man at peace with himself. I always found him with that peace, for he used his time to pray and to count those blessings. Among his blessings he counted, above all, his family. He missed his beloved wife, Frederica, but he was mightily interested in the children and their children. Many times when I went to visit him, he would give me chapter and verse about each member: their travel, address changes, love lives. He delighted to see them unfold into mature adults. He was very proud of you.

He counted his friends a blessing too. The staff at the home, the visitors, Sister Agnes, and others. He also counted as a blessing and felt vindicated and proud when a book came out this year entitled *From Space to Earth*, in which the author mentioned him by name and his activities, some forty years ago, in the Signal Corps' Space Program. He was quite pleased with that.

Most of all, I know, he counted his faith a blessing. He spent his forced contemplative time in bed in prayer, in thought, in preparation, and in deepening that faith. Knowing that the time was coming near, but not when, he stayed alert as a faithful disciple. To me, he was a kind of living Advent: waiting and watching. Coincidentally, I saw him four days before he died. Sister Agnes had called to tell me he was taken to Jersey Shore Hospital. She thought I'd like to know, although she kidded that the last time she called me and I rushed over he returned from the hospital better than before! Still, I didn't want to take chances and I left immediately. When I got to the emergency ward he was not there. He was having x-rays taken. I ran into an old St. Mary's parishioner who was a nurse there and a parishioner from St. Denis where I helped out. We chatted as I waited and they brought Hans back. As they rolled him around into the cubicle where he could see me—I can still see his expression—he was delighted. Tired but still sharp—his mind was always clear—he spoke to me. He said it was hard, all these ups and downs, but what can you do?

He talked about his family as always, accepted with great joy and faith the blessing I gave and thanked me dearly for coming. He profoundly embarrassed me—I was glad no one was around to overhear him—when he said it was like a visit from Jesus Christ. Whatever his impression, I left an eighty-nine-year-old man who sensed he was dying at peace. And as I left, I must say, under my breath, I thanked him for his friendship and example and inspiration and wondered who was the real Christ.

I don't want to canonize the man. I've only known him for about twenty-some years. I don't know his early life and whether he was mean at times or had a temper or what weaknesses he had. I only know what I saw from the time I met him: a man with a keen mind who in years developed a deep faith and in his illness a profound belief that, in the end, love would be stronger than death. And so it has been.

The Lord of the house has come suddenly during Advent and found Hans not sleeping, but watching, and because he did heed the Lord's words of warning to watch, I am sure he has also heard the Lord's words of promise for those who do: "Well done, good and faithful servant. Enter into the joy of the Lord." Amen.

Bob Heller: Classmate and Priest

Bob, a classmate for part of my seminary days, went to a different seminary for his theology. We knew each other but were not close. That's why I was surprised when he had left instructions that I should preach not at this funeral Mass, but at the special memorial Mass that is customary the day or so before the main funeral. I exploit my lack of common friendship to explore the larger bonds that unite priests.

It is only right that I should be forthright with you. When Father Jawidzik called me the other night not only to tell me that Father Heller had died—he had been ill for about ten years, I understand—but that he had left it in his will that I should give the homily at this commemoration Mass, I was dumbfounded. Was this some kind of a mischievous, impish thing he would do on occasion? What did the man have in mind? Was he of sound mind when he put that in his will?

You see, the truth of the matter is that, beyond the accident of us being classmates and being ordained together forty years ago on June 4, 1955, as the last class to be ordained there before the old cathedral burned down—some, I confess, saw that as a judgment—we never had much contact. Hardly any. We went our separate ways. We did not go out socially, did not meet, and I think the last time I saw him was some twenty years ago when he was pastor at St. Ambrose in Browntown and I spoke at Father Ed Griswold's first Mass there. Father Griswold was the alternative preacher for this homily in case I couldn't make it, but he is away, I understand, and so I am here. But why, I am not sure. Bob and I were not close.

Which means, as I hinted, because of my social and physical distance from Father Heller, that I am here as one not only perplexed as to why he choose me, but as one also really unable to speak of personal things or give a eulogy. Fortunately, tomorrow at his funeral Mass, Father Bill Haughney, who knew him better, will do such homiletic honors.

So I stand here before you and my deceased classmate, slightly embarrassed and quite humbled, with nothing in common to talk about, which spares you many words, and maybe, when you come down to it, that might be his last and cunning gift to you.

Nothing in common…except, perhaps, when I think about it, two things that we *do* share: our human journey and our priesthood.

For our human journeys necessarily coincide: from childhood to youth to adulthood and mature years with all of their successes and failures, health and sickness, sins and repentances. To that degree I recognize that body before us and know its spirit: It is you and me. A lifetime is squeezed into that little box, but it is, of course, a lifetime larger than that container, for it's a lifetime that has changed lives, forged friendships, made its mark, and left its traces in the hearts of many. To that degree you and I share common humanity with Bob Heller and, to that degree, we are not strangers and I am perhaps closer to him than I think. I can resonate with that life, gone, but not gone entirely.

But, of course, as I suggested, we share something else beyond the common human journey. We share the priesthood of Jesus Christ. Our mutual life in the priesthood has taken us though five popes, one ecumenical council, and the heady and dissonant aftermath in both church and society that hasn't settled yet. We started out, Bob and I, celebrating the Holy Mass in Latin and wound up celebrating it in English. We turned our backs twice: once to the people, the other to the wall. We saw a full class in 1955 of 109 young men, our peers and classmates, dwindle to half, as many have gone through death or departure. From the Diocese of Trenton we were thirteen ordained in that cathedral forty years ago, six of whom, including now Robert, are deceased, two of whom who have left the active priesthood, leaving five of us original thirteen still active.

That's the physical parameters of the priesthood we shared. But with all the upheavals, big and small, there was one commonality: quiet fidelity and steadfast service. Think of his career: the countless Masses celebrated, the word preached, the sorrowful comforted, the ignorant instructed, the poor tended to, the babies baptized, the reconciliations effected, the marital unions consecrated, the sick anointed, the eyes closed, the comfort given, the dead buried. Bob's career, his priesthood, his ministrations were what counted, the proof that he *was* worth something, that his life was justified. All this is what we *do* have in common with each other—and with Christ. For the only living proof Jesus himself could come up with when challenged to give an account of *his* life and ministry was precisely and simply to recount:

> Go and tell John what you have seen and heard:
> the blind recover their sight
> the cripples walk
> lepers are cured
> the deaf hear
> the dead are raised to life
> and the poor have the good news preached to them
> And blessed are those who find no stumbling block in me.

That's a legacy to bequeath to the world, and one that is descriptive of this man, one that lives on, and one that tells us that Father Heller has not only reaped the rewards of his ministry, but also tells me that maybe he was right. Maybe he picked a name at random from his list of classmates, sensing that *any* of us would know what *all* of us would know, that the human journey is God-touched, that Christ's priesthood is powerful, and that a life given in service has every reason to expect resurrection.

That truth, that gospel, that hope are what we have in common. I guess that's why I'm here and you're here and that's why he is here. Here, but not quite, for this man of fallible faults and priestly service is now the recipient of those words, "Come, good and faithful servant, enter into the joy of the Lord." Words, by the way, uttered in chorus by Jesus Christ and five excited classmates.

Vi Tweedale: The Pilgrim

LUKE 2:22–40

This homily exploits the Simeon and Anna theme of Luke's infancy narrative.

There was also a prophetess, Anna...advanced in years...a widow...she never left the Temple but worshiped night and day with fasting and prayer. She gave thanks to God and spoke about the child....

There was also a prophetess, one who speaks forth the truth, Vi Tweedale, advanced in years—she would be ninety-four next month—a widow who lost her husband and a mother who lost her son, Robert, six years ago. She *always* left the temple especially if there was a bargain at the Acme, but she worshiped in her heart day and night with prayer and gave thanks to God and spoke with her life about that Child we call the Christ.

There's another similarity to a scriptural woman: Like Mary fleeing into Egypt, Vi too left her native land of England when a young girl and brought with her fond memories, her strong faith, and her sharp intelligence. In her ninety-three plus years she had, of course, like many of us, many journeys, happy and sad, winding up, fortunately for us, at St. Mary's becoming one more memorable and colorful figure for which St. Mary's is noted. She had hoped to get back to England someday to see her beloved brother, Sidney, but never made it. His lovely bouquet of flowers here today is his testimony to his sister.

For those of us who do remember, we can still see her slightly bent figure coming faithfully into church. Like many of her era, she would never think of *not* being here. She sat, if I recall, in the second pew and was not happy with anyone who took her seat. She was, to all appearances, obviously a

417

woman of age, but, as we know, not an old woman. There is a difference. Right up to the end she always made us laugh. She was a remarkably avid reader. For years this little old widow volunteered at Lunch Break to help the less fortunate. Right up to the last, she entertained friends—and attracted friends.

One of the stories I like is the story of when she was at Lutman Towers and went to the Acme and on the way there had a slight fainting spell. Mary Ellen Hintz and her daughter spotted her and they swung around again to see if Vi needed help. By the time they got her back into her apartment Vi had quite recovered and, as a proper English lady, served them tea and, as the saying goes, the rest is history. They became friends and Mary Ellen, like some of you, took her all over: to my neck of the woods; to the Manasquan inlet watching the boats come in and out, with Vi recalling stories of her childhood; recently to Holmdel Park Christmas display; and, forever and ever, shopping at the Acme, with Vi sitting in the child's seat in the shopping cart while Mary Ellen wheeled her around.

When finally she wound up for the past four years at the nursing home, God sent her a roommate, Ida Hall, a woman as mentally alert as Vi and they became not only fast friends, but enjoyable companions who made life in the home actually pleasant for themselves and for others. And then she died.

This is but the barest sketch of a woman who, we say, was born abroad, came to America, lived here, and expired in a nursing home. But what we're really celebrating here in this liturgy is a pilgrimage of a soul who has at last gone home. And it is, thankfully, an oft-repeated story, the story of quiet faithful people who, like Anna of our gospel, give thanks and speak of better things with their lives and charity.

What we're really celebrating here are the Vis and Annas of our world, flawed as they may be, who keep the light burning in a dark world, the little faithful Temple people who make differences, the Child-worshipers who anchor us all in terrible times of moral chaos and displacements. It's people like Vi—and you here today (and it is important that you know this)—who are the seeds of life. Vi didn't quite make the millennium, but who and what she was—and who and what you are—will make the millennium better. What more can you ask of a person?

So what I am saying is that we are not just remembering and burying an old friend. We are celebrating a prophetess, a life with imperfections and sorrows, but a steady, faithful life for all that. One who lived among us, helped us to define ourselves, and showed us the way. Like Old Simeon and old Anna, she has now received her reward: She too has at last looked into the face of Christ and the words of Scripture are now her words: "Now, Master, you may let your servant go in peace according to your word, for my eyes have seen your salvation." Amen.

John Friconi: Before His Time

MARK 15:33–37

I witnessed the marriage of John and Roberta and then, almost a dozen years later, John got a brain tumor and died leaving his wife and small child behind. The motif here is Mark's stark gospel counterbalanced with a little humor at the end.

I, who with a light heart presided here almost eleven years ago—it was September 3, 1993, to be exact—to witness the vows of John and Roberta, have returned today with a very heavy heart to preside at John's funeral. As a homilist then and now, I have a job to do. A homilist, as you know, must break open the word of God to the occasion and I must say that finding a word to break open was, in John's case, all too easy. It was easy to know instinctively what Scripture to pick. What else but, as you heard, a section of the passion narrative from the gospel of Mark.

Why Mark? Because Mark gives us a picture of Jesus being systematically stripped away of everything: clothes, friends, blood, dignity, consolation, life itself. Stripped little by little, minute after minute, hour after hour, till nothing was left.

But there's more. Intriguingly, there is an ancient legend connected with Mark's stark account. The legend says that the dying took so long—the torture, the carrying of the cross, the crucifixion, the horrible three-hour agony—and Jesus knew the pain it was causing so many, especially his mother. So at the end of the three hours, the legend says, he searched out her eyes among the crowd to ask permission to die. She, knowing that it had to be, nodded. Satisfied, he let out his cry, his last words, "It is finished!"

Then he was then taken down from the cross, from his bed of pain, and placed in the arms of that same mother. And so we have the *Pietà*, humanity embracing its dreaded enemy, death, and wondering if this is all there is. Finally, however, in that sad embrace, Mary too had to repeat her Son's words, "It is finished," and let him go. She had to let others take him and put him away, out of sight if not out of mind.

And the moment he was laid in the tomb and the stone rolled in place, the legend goes on to say, a strange thing happened. Both Jesus *in* the tomb and Mary *without*, and all the others who were there, in a kind of Greek chorus shouted together with relief, "It is finished! It is finished!"

> They had watched so long,
> cried so often,
> comforted so frequently,
> agonized so deeply,
> journeyed so far,
> prayed so hard,
> spoken so much,
> until they were exhausted.

Until death just *had* to be, because behind its release was blessed peace. For Jesus. For Mary. For friends. For all on that hill of Calvary, "it is finished." But, as they were to learn, not quite.

What a remarkably personal gospel for John, for Roberta, and his family! How it fits!

First, for John, just like Jesus—both about the same age when they died—everything was slowly stripped away. Seventeen months ago this young husband and father, housing manager, hockey enthusiast, music lover, competitive golfer—ask his brother—received the dreaded news of a brain tumor. For seventeen months he and Roberta, and little Sal in his own way, and his family and in-laws confronted the sickness, its ups and downs, its alternating times of hope and despair. Months of operations, doctor and hospital visits, medications, sickness, confinement, incapacity, loss. Loss of facile movements, at times loss of recognition, identity, and control. Like Jesus on Calvary.

All during this time his family watched, suffered, laughed, comforted, journeyed, prayed, and prepared. More than that. They tried to make life as normal as possible and continued to celebrate its daily rhythms. They even, for Sal's sake, threw him a birthday party last week, even though John was unaware of what was going on. They arranged for Father Ed to come and confirm him, something he dearly desired.

They did all they could and continued to do what they could amidst hope and prayer, all the while ultimately recognizing that, standing daily on John's hill of Calvary, death simply *had* to be.

And so there came a point, as it were, when the gospel legend of Jerusalem had to be replayed in Colts Neck, when John and Roberta and his family and friends and had to search out each other's eyes and nod permission to die. They gave it freely.

John said his "It is finished." He had let go. He died on his birth day and birthed his death day. His family and friends who were with him, surrounding him with prayers and love, had let go. And, finally, at this community liturgy, like Mary of the *Pietà*, we cradle John in our collective arms for the last time and then we too will let him go. We all chorus, "It is finished."

But not quite, any more than it was on Calvary because, in the Jesus story, remember, something else happened. For at the precise moment of his total emptiness, Mark's gospel suggests, Jesus was raised up to a new life. Like the seed which in its moment of death begins to sprout, so was it for Jesus. The grave was his seeding place. The love in Jesus' heart was too strong. Death could not hold him. And so there was a resurrection for Jesus and for all who believe in him. And then, as day follows night, rejoicing. Why rejoicing? Because death, dear friends, dear John, had been defeated and always would be. And that was something to laugh about.

A family went to Easter Mass and on the way home, the husband and wife were in the front seat and the six- and twelve-year-olds were in the back seat. The twelve-year-old brought up a question. "You know, we celebrated Jesus rising from the dead. I wonder when he rose from the dead and came out of the tomb, what was the first thing he said?"

The parents said, "Gee, we don't know. That's an interesting question: 'What was the first thing Jesus said rising from the tomb?' We don't know. It's a great question. Let's go back and ask the pastor because we have a smart pastor." (Pastors were smarter in those days.)

They got to the pastor and they asked him and he said, "I really don't know. I don't think anybody knows. But we're lucky. The bishop of the diocese is here today. The bishop is a very smart man and we'll go ask him." (Bishops were smarter in those days.)

And they went to the bishop and said, "When Jesus rose from the dead, does anybody know what his first words were? What was the first thing he said?"

The bishop said, "I don't know. I don't think anybody knows. It's not in the Bible. No one was there."

At this point, the six-year-old speaks up and he says, "Wait a minute. I know what he said." They looked at him. "I know exactly what Jesus said when he came out of the tomb." They said, "You do? What did he say?" "When Jesus came out of the tomb he said, 'Ta-dah!'"

That's a distinctively Christian story: for the moment we moved together from sadness to laughter, aridity to fullness, isolation to community. In a word, from a full tomb to an empty one. Our laughter is Jesus' promise that it will be longer than a moment.

The story also helps us to focus on the positive side of John's scatttered graces, the legacies he left us. There is his enduring love for Roberta and the fruit of their love, Salvatore. There are the loving services he evoked from Roberta's siblings: Luke, Elena, Jeanine; and his parents, Susan and Tom; and his two brothers and his in-laws, Linda and Bob. There is the support and service he drew from the unique community of St. Mary's. There are his doctors, nurses, and hospice caregivers who were made even more gracefully splendid by their compassion and care of John. John brought out the best in them all.

Finally, we might say, John gave us the gift of holy relief. His suffering is ended and on one level so is ours, our anxious, daily vigil. Sad as we are, we are glad to see him go into that place where there are no more tears, only brightness, fullness, and the endless embrace of God. Life has been given to John and, as Jesus promised, given abundantly. For there indeed is Jesus who no longer says, "It is finished," but who says, "I make all things new again."

Let me end with another smile by quoting a cemetery epitaph. On a tombstone are inscribed these words:

Remember, man, as you walk by
As you are now so once was I.
As I am now, so shall you be.
Remember this and follow me.

To which some wit replied by scribbling underneath:

To follow you I'll not consent
Until I know which way you went.

Faith tells us that we know which way Christ went. We know which way John went. We miss him terribly, grievously, deeply, but were privileged to help his journey and to have been blessed by his.

It is finished. It has just begun.

Pat Costigan:
Making Ready the Way

This homily offers a nod to the Advent season and the context of some words (transferable to other similar situations) of author Stephen King. Pat was a beloved secretary at a local Catholic high school who died in a car accident and I wanted my words to nudge the high school kids as well as the adults.

> *John the Baptist appeared preaching in the desert of Judea and saying, "Repent, for the kingdom of heaven is at hand....produce good fruit as evidence of your repentance, for the tree that that does not bear good fruit will be thrown into the fire."*

This is the gospel, as you might recognize, from this past Sunday. When I preached it I started out by saying, "Ho hum, we mentally tell John we've heard it all before." But wait a minute, I went on. I recall that at Vassar College graduation this year—to those young folk with the world at their fingertips, those privileged people who will shortly be running the globe—our country's most successful and popular writer, Stephen King, spoke. And you know what? Still recovering from a serious automobile accident, he sounded, in his own way, very much like John the Baptist in today's gospel, putting a modern spin on John's words. John the Baptist and Stephen King, it seems, have spanned the centuries and joined forces. Anyway, this is what Stephen King, sounding like John the Baptist, said to the graduates:

> What will you do? Well, I'll tell you one thing you're not going to do, and that's take it with you. I'm worth I don't exactly know

425

how many millions of dollars. I'm still in the third world compared to Bill Gates, but on the whole I'm doing okay and a couple of years ago I found out what "you can't take it with you" means. I found out while I was lying in the ditch at the side of a country road, covered with mud and blood and with the tibia of my right leg poking out the side of my jeans like the branch of a tree taken down in a thunderstorm. I had a MasterCard in my wallet, but when you're lying in the ditch with broken glass in your hair, no one accepts MasterCard....

We all know that life is ephemeral, but on that particular day and in the months that followed, I got a painful but extremely valuable look at life's simple backstage truths. We come in naked and broke. We may be dressed when we go out, but we're just as broke. Warren Buffett? Going to go out broke. Bill Gates? Going to go out broke. Tom Hanks? Going out broke. Steve King? Broke. Not a crying dime. And how long in-between?

How long have you got to be in the chips?...Just the blink of an eye. Yet for a short period, let's say forty years, but the merest blink in the larger course of things, you and your contemporaries will wield enormous power....Of all the power which will shortly come into your hands gradually at first, but then with a speed that will take your breath away, the greatest is undoubtedly the power of compassion, the ability to give. We have enormous resources in this country, resources you yourselves will soon command but they are only yours on loan. Only yours to give for a short while....

Not that long ago, we would have dismissed first-century John the Baptist and twenty-first-century Stephen King as full of rhetoric, if not something else. But since the World Trade disaster on September 11, the crash of American Airlines flight 794 on November 12, fears of terrorism and wars in Afghanistan and in Israel, we're not so ready to do that, are we? The current Advent theme of repentance, of making ready for a Savior through the works of compassion while we have time comes closer to home. In our brief time on earth, as King put it, it's up to us—it's our calling—to make ready the Lord's coming in grace, love, and service.

Why this long homiletic preamble? Because it was easy, so easy, for me to think of Pat Costigan on reading this gospel and preaching those words. She, taken in the blink of an eye, *was* ready, for, simply put, she was an Advent person, always preparing the way of the Lord for *somebody*: her children, her grandchildren, her neighbors, her many friends, the staff and students at St. John Vianney. Her family, for example, for which she lived, came first. I knew that. She was Christmas shopping for them just last week, buying for them things she could not afford, but, as she typically said, "What the heck; it's Christmas." She was knitting hats for the grandchildren. That kind of thing.

This was a woman who had her priorities straight: God, family, friends, and job, and it showed in her optimism and her wonderfully quick smile. I cannot help but think that it surely must have been a comfort for students at St. John's to encounter that smile when they walked into the office. She was a strongly faith-filled person and one of the *least* materialistic and *most* down-to-earth persons I knew, utterly without guile. Her life was as open a book as the lunch on her clothes.

When I heard of her tragic death, and almost witnessed it—I was waved around the accident by the police not knowing who it was—for some reason I instinctively thought of her Irish counterpart, someone very much like her: Father Mychal Judge, the New York City Fire Department chaplain, and I remembered the wondrous eulogy transmitted worldwide at his funeral service. This heroic priest, like Pat, also lost his life suddenly. You recall that he was killed while administering the last rites to a dying firefighter at the World Trade Center. In tribute to this fallen hero, the eulogist beautifully pointed out that at his final moments, Father Mychal Judge was 1) where the action was, 2) praying, 3) talking to God, 4) serving his fellow human. The eulogist then added wistfully, "Can anyone think of a better way to die?"

I thought to myself: That's Pat. Those words fit her perfectly. She was always where the action was: at home, neighborhood, school, church. She prayed with us and often talked to God. I would frequently see her at church. We would hug, she would smile and say everything's great. And she certainly served others: her family, friends, and the principals and students at St. John Vianney. A good woman, a smiling lady, even when at times there was little to smile about, who bore life's burdens and joys with deep faith, she was prepared. Death caught *us* off guard, not her.

As a sign of that, I want to share something with the family. As I was being detoured around the block at the accident scene, a woman, Dottie Voorhees, who comes to daily Mass, happened to be walking to church that fateful day. The accident happened right in front of her. She saw a gentleman go over to Pat, apparently asking her something. Pat nodded and then she, quite peacefully, laid her head back and closed her eyes. And that was all. The woman who witnessed this stood there all the while and prayed long and deeply for Pat, and finally, unable to continue to church, went back home. I mention this because I want the family to know that, at the precise hour of tragedy, there also was a pray-er present, one who did not let Pat Costigan make the transition alone but, like an angel in disguise, was there standing by to commend her to God. Chaos was present and police and ambulance personnel and first aid folk, but I wanted you to know that, at that exact moment, prayer was deeply present; spirit, love, compassion, and commendation were there. God had provided for his good and faithful servant. For all the distress in your hearts, cherish that scene.

Finally, I want to go back to Father Judge because he offers another comparison: His, as you may know, was the first recorded death from the disaster and there remains, you might recollect, that vivid image of his being carried from the rubble by distraught, determined rescue workers. His body is slumped in a chair, carried by two strong, dirt-covered men and followed by others. They brought him to a nearby church, processed up the aisle, and laid him before the altar, and covered him with a white alb. His earthly life spent, they presented him before the Lord.

I just want to remind you that, today, here, liturgically, we are doing the same thing. Pat spent her earthly life by preparing for her death, and we have brought her to church, processed up the aisle, laid her before this altar, and covered her with a white cloth. What we also are doing here— with tears and love, grief, and faith—is presenting Pat Costigan before the Lord: like Father Judge, a sudden but pleasing and very worthy gift, quite as heroic in her own way.

May this Advent woman rest in peace. May she who prepared the way for others find a place prepared for her. May her intercession bless us on earth. May her smile add to the brightness of heaven. Amen.

Tom Gassert:
The Music Maker

Again I wanted to take advantage of the Advent season, the time of this funeral, as well as offering a connecting story of interest. Tom was a musician and often played the piano and organ at church.

> *John the Baptist appeared preaching in the desert of Judea....It was of him that the prophet Isaiah had spoken..., "A voice of one crying in the desert, Prepare the way of the Lord...." John wore clothing of camel hair. His food was locusts and wild honey....*

The Christian world, as you know, is right now celebrating the season of Advent, a time of yearning, of longing, of desire, of hope. Its chief figure, as you just heard in the gospel, is John the Baptist, one summoned to "prepare the way of the Lord and make straight his paths." That was John's job description, his reason for living: a precursor, a forerunner, a preparer for something, for Someone greater than himself. No mean calling.

John the Baptist. He projects a definite first-century image: camel hair, a diet of wild locusts and honey, a solitary inhabitant of the demanding and unforgiving desert. An ascetic. Not one you would cozy up to. Be that as it may, there's no question that everything about the man *was* geared to one object: to prepare others for the fullness of grace, to open their hearts to possibilities. That was John's calling, his vocation, ultimately his glory. I mention this because I want to remind you that there are others like John the Baptist in every age, including our own, others with his same thrust, same mission. They just live at different times and in different places. They have different images and ways about them, but they're there, burdened with the ancient calling to prepare hearts and minds for something more, something greater, something better in life.

Maybe it's the context of the season, but that is why when I think of Tom Gassert, I think of John the Baptist. Does that surprise you? True enough, in many ways they couldn't be more different. John was first century. Tom was very much this century. John was stern and ascetic. Tom was gentle and kind. John was rough and ready. Tom was sensitive and cultured. John ate locusts. Tom ate home cooking. John wore camel hair. Tom wore blazers. John was a solitary figure in the desert. Tom was well known and respected in the city.

But in one respect, deeply and profoundly, wondrously, gloriously, they shared one thing in common. When you come right down to it, they were both preparers of hearts. Both made crooked paths straight and rough ways smooth. That was their life's work, their calling, and ultimately their glory. In this sense, both were prophets. That's why, were I to introduce Tom to those who did not know him, I would not, of course, as the first-century gospel writer, Matthew, tell the story of distant deserts and wild locusts, but I would introduce him in his time and place by telling another story that tells *his* story.

It goes like this. There is a statue in a certain town square in Eastern Europe that is not what you would ever expect to find there because it's not a statue in honor of a war hero, a politician, a famous athlete, or even a rock star. Rather, the statue is a tribute to a John the Baptist-like figure and here's its history.

One day during the war in Sarajevo, a bomb was dropped on a bakery where twenty-two people were waiting in line to buy bread. All twenty-two people were killed. A citizen of Sarajevo, a man named Vedran Smialiavic, decided that he wanted to do something to mark the death of these innocent victims. He said, "I am a simple man. What can I do?"

Before the war, Smialiavic played in the Sarajevo orchestra, but once the war started everyone was afraid to venture out just to hear music. With no music to perform, he walked the streets near his home and tried to find things to keep himself busy. But when he heard about the bakery bombing, Smialiavic dressed up in his tux and tails, took his cello and a chair, and marched to the site. He sat there amid the pile of debris for twenty-two days, one for each of the victims of the bombing, and played his favorite piece of music, Albinoni's "Adagio in G." He braved the artillery fire and ducked snipers' bullets and went on playing his cello, trying to show people a better way. Try to picture that in your imagination.

So, the statue in the town square is a statue of this musician, sitting on his chair playing his cello. People today often bring flowers to put around the base of the statue, always twenty-two flowers to honor those twenty-two people. He's a hero to them because he made beautiful music among the rubble.

This is *my* take on Tom Gassert, my gospel version of a modern John the Baptist. Before these latter years and recent illnesses sapped him of his energy and zest for living—his heart attack, pacemaker, leg trouble, and all the things that age bequeaths us—this was a man who literally and figuratively made beautiful music among the rubble and prepared hope in the lives of many, not the least of whom was his wife, Anita, and eight children who cherish their private memories and will pass them on like precious heirlooms. He didn't *have* to be a member and then chairman of the state Board of Higher Education, but he took it on to fight for the right, John-the-Baptist-like, to prepare minorities for their place in society. He didn't *have* to serve as a member and eventually president of the Sierra Club, work as counsel for the Archdiocese of Newark, serve on the Board of Trustees of Seton Hall University and countless other boards and committees, except that he felt he could make a difference, prepare the world for a better future, play a sweeter note among the discords of life.

And he played John the Baptist in secret as well. What few know, except those who benefited, was his consistent, ongoing help to individuals who needed it. More than one person has stepped forward since Tom's death to reveal personal and heartfelt gratitude for all that he did for them, for making very rough ways smooth. He has his own scripture in the hearts of many. And, of course, yes, there was *literally* his music. How many Masses did he play over many, many years to prepare us for profound worship? How many congregations did he inspire to prepare them for singing? How many brides and grooms did he send off to prepare them for a future? How many funerals like this did he play at, sitting at that very organ on that very same seat, to prepare the bereaved for eternal life? And, in the interest of full disclosure, how many times did he raise his eyebrows when he spotted an ashtray on the organ? (Tom was an unapologetic smoker and always had an ashtray on the organ and, as the rext said, likely as not, a cigarette up his sleeve. His eyebrows wouldn't have been raised but those in the congregation who spotted the ashtray would have.)

I come back to where I started. There are John the Baptists in every age. Thank heaven. Their noble if unsung task is still to prepare the way of the Lord. Tom Gassert was among us as one of them. This basically gentle and kind man had enough faith to accept his calling, enough hope to play among the rubble, enough love to believe that he could make a difference. I think the best and final thing we can say about him was that he was right and successful on all counts.

May this Advent man rest in peace. May he who prepared the way for others find a place prepared for him. May his intercession continue to smooth out rough ways and prepare hearts. May his music enhance the heavenly choirs. Amen.

Swede Chevalier: Casualty of 9/11

I repeat this homily from a previous collection because it still resonates with the tragedy of 9/11.

For decades we have seen in the movies and watched on television the horrors of war. We winced as whole villages were burned to the ground, the billowy smoke the only indication that men, women, and children once lived there. We looked aghast at the continuous black fumes from the Nazi gas chambers. We sat in horror to watch the footage of the bombings of Britain, Poland, France, Germany, the Netherlands. Cities, towns, hamlets, great castles, museums, cathedrals all up in smoke. We watched in fascination the death-dealing mushroom clouds over Japan. In *Life* magazine we checked out the photographs of the massive mounds of human skulls in the Cambodian killing fields. And eventually we all began to watch those horrors with a certain detachment, even those who lost loved ones in the wars, as Hollywood turned carnage into entertainment and killings into box office, mass exterminations into discussion panels, and unspeakable horrors into cash receipts. So we flipped the pages of *Life* magazine to see what Madonna was doing.

And, in a way, no wonder. All those things, those terrible, terrible unmentionable things, were "over there" in Europe and Africa and Asia and South America. We were never bombed. We were never invaded. Our skies never saw war smoke, war ash, explosions. Our cities were never wiped out. Our family members' body parts were never scattered among the debris. So we tightened our belts, used our ration stamps, bought our bonds,

433

mourned our dead soldiers who died "over there," but in our land we were free of the personal horrors of war and could never quite resonate with the wild language and metaphors and desperate prose of our allies who walked stone-eyed and ash-dusted amid the half houses and half bodies of their neighbors.

That is, till ten days ago. The unbelievable had happened. America had been violated. America had been terrorized. In the very blue skies of a beautiful day there was sudden black smoke; and where there were two massive towers housing thousands of people—nothing. The halls of Congress were evacuated, leaders were led to bunkers, the Pentagon was airplane-smashed and set afire, airlines shut down, and a continent of dismay and an ocean of tears flooded the land as people simply couldn't believe what they were seeing on TV.

The country was brought to a standstill. It was like a bad movie come true and we're still reeling from its impact. Terror had arrived at our doorstep and we will never be the same; our travel, our security, our innocence will never be the same. Who among us will ever forget those images of the jets crashing the towers, the fireballs of flame, the towers themselves collapsing before our very eyes, the ash-covered streets, the people jumping to their deaths from high windows, the herds of people walking zombie-like on the bridges away from suffocating smoke, the reports of brave people killed by falling concrete: 350 firefighters, 200 Port Authority employees, 40 police officers, 700 workers each from various financial companies, 266 people on the airplanes, nearly 200 at the Pentagon?

And these—it's so hard to say—are only preliminary figures as New York has ordered more body bags for what is to come. These "preliminary figures" are, of course, people: our parents, spouses, children, lovers, relatives, friends with names, faces, and histories, violently and terrifyingly cut short.

It was within this horrific scenario, this national tragedy that Elaine called to tell me that her son—her wonderful son, Swede—worked on the 100th floor of the Twin Towers. They are no more and at that time she was sick at heart fearing that *he* was also no more. The people at the Armory, where they stack bodies and what's left of them, had asked her for his dental records and his comb to check the hairs for his DNA so they could measure them against body parts. She and her family waited in anguished hope, as did thousands of those others pitifully holding up photographs of their loved ones pleading, Have you seen my husband? Have you seen my daughter? Have you seen my father? Have you seen my niece? Have you seen my friend?

Like the palmist of old they cry out, "My heart is in anguish within me, the terrors of death have fallen upon me. Fear and trembling come upon me and horror overwhelms me. And I say, 'O that I had wings like a dove! I would fly way and be at rest'" (Ps 55:4–6). But there is no rest. At least, not for a while.

For Swede *was* found, his intact but charred body identified, and if the family no longer has to wait for news to come, they now have to bear the news that has been. They have lost a son, a bright, intelligent young man whose business savvy, loyalty, and integrity I remember so well that marked him out as an unusual boy. They have lost this son. As they say, no child should die before its parents. But it happens. And we are here because it did, and we don't know what to do about it except in faith, in our ritual liturgy, try to grab firmly hold of St. Paul's words, he who knew a thing or two about terror: "We are afflicted in every way, but not crushed; perplexed but not driven to despair; persecuted, but not forsaken; struck down, but not destroyed; always carrying in the body the death of Jesus, so that the life of Jesus may also be made visible in our bodies" (2 Cor 4:5–10).

"Afflicted, but not crushed," said St. Paul. And these words came true in a most striking way because several nights ago Elaine, his mother, had a vivid dream. Three, she revealed, were in that dream: First, there was Swede, twenty-six-year-old Swede, looking quite happy. Then there was an archangel at this side. It is very significant who the archangel was. It wasn't Gabriel, the Announcer, or Michael, the Warrior. It was Raphael, the protector and guide of young men. Then, last but not least, was their dog, "Holly," the yellow lab who had died a few months before.

Thus, her dream. If all this sounds familiar, it should. It's right out of the Bible, the book of Tobit, our first reading, the story of a good but fussy, self-righteous father who sends his son to seek his fortune and a bride but is worried that he, young Tobit, about the same age as Swede, is inexperienced and wishes he had a guide to go with him. And, lo and behold, in answer to his prayers, a certain man, who passes himself off as Azariah but who is really the archangel Raphael in disguise, comes and offers his services, promising that he will be with, protect, guide, and bring Tobit's son to safety. Which, by the end of the story, he does. And so the Scripture, as you heard, tells the beginning of their journey: "The young man went out and the angel went with him and the dog came out with him and went along with him."

Thus the three of them: the family dog, an archangel whose specialty is young men, and a happy son. Quite a biblical story. Quite a peaceful sight. Quite a significant dream. Quite a current sign from God that all is well, that, in St. Paul's words, Swede, like so many others, was struck down by terrorist madness but not destroyed.

This is our belief, our celebration, if you will.

So, remember Swede. Remember him in life. Remember him as your son: handsome, confident, hardworking, honest. Remember him as your blood brother. Remember him as your fraternity brother. Remember him as your best friend. Remember him as your landscaper. Remember him as one who made a difference. Remember him as a good listener, a gentle person, a witty young man. Finally, remember him not in the hell of terrorist fire—that was only momentary—but as he is, in the heaven of peace and joy with his angelic guide and his faithful dog, Holly. That a dog should be in heaven is, of course, no surprise to dog owners. They are more surprised that *people* are there. But that's another story.

A lot of young people came to the wake. I see a lot of young people here today, each with your own personal memories and stories about Swede. Many of you, I suspect, have come a distance. How fine, how decent, how noble of you. Truly. You buoy my faith in the next generation. I thank you for that.

But as I end, I want to charge you with something. I want to challenge you to gradually move beyond your personal grief and momentary sorrow. I want you to take this life, what you knew and loved of Swede, and use it to motivate yourselves to become more than you think, more than you would have been without him. I pray that you will not have *your* lives shortened, but live them out to their fullest, allotted years, and when you are old I want you to look back on this sorrowful day as a beacon that made a difference to you.

In Steven Spielberg's movie *Saving Private Ryan*, a squadron of young soldiers, you remember, is sent on a mission to find one soldier behind enemy lines and bring him home. Most of the young men in the squadron, including the captain, die in the rescue attempt. As he lay dying, the captain's last words to Private Ryan are, "Earn this." Many years later, Private Ryan, now an old man, visits the grave of his captain. As he kneels at the grave, he says, "Not a day goes by I don't think about what happened....And I just want you to know...I've tried. Tried to live my life the best I could. I hope that's enough. I didn't invent anything. I didn't cure any diseases. I worked a farm. I raised a family. I lived a life. I only hope, in your eyes at least, I earned what you did for me."

Young men and women, the best tribute you can give your friend is to earn what Swede has meant to you.

Jim Bausch:
The Brother

JULY 22, 2006
ST. MICHAEL THE ARCHANGEL CHURCH,
SIESTA KEY, FLORIDA

This homily is included simply as a personal tribute to a beloved and gifted brother who died after a four-year struggle with pancreatic cancer.

As much as, like all of us, I had ample time to grasp and prepare for Jim's death, and as much as I thought that by this time I was emotionally depleted and cried out, I still find it painfully difficult to stand here today without fear of losing control. As Jim was near death, I told him of my weakness and misgivings and he suggested that I tape my words and have Father Brubaker lip-sync them. And we laughed together before we told each other, once more, how much we loved each other.

That wit and that declaration of love was Jim to the end. When people ask me what he was like I would always call up in my mind a favorite passage from Chaim Potok's celebrated novel, *The Chosen*. In a famous scene, the father is complaining in anguish to his friend Reuven about his precociously brilliant son Daniel, recalling how Daniel, at four years old, was able to read a tale in Yiddish about a poor Jew and his pitiable struggle to get to Israel before he died. And the boy, proud of himself, repeated the story back to his father from memory like he was reciting the phone book. And the father is smitten to the heart and cries out to God, "What have you done to me? A mind like this I need for a son? A heart I need for a son, a soul I need for a son. Compassion I want from my son, righteousness, mercy, strength to suffer and carry pain, that I want from my son, not a mind without a soul!"

I doubt if Jim's father—my father—ever prayed that, although he was a very prayerful man, or that he ever read *The Chosen*, although he read and spoke Yiddish fluently. But it is the most perfect reverse description of Jim Bausch that I know. He *was* a Daniel, very bright and intelligent, but, oh, he was a Daniel with heart, compassion, righteousness, mercy, and strength that carried suffering and pain, his own and others'. He was a mind with a very deep soul.

Yes, he *was* a Daniel. This blue-eyed child, this engaging, witty, intelligent man of open and generous heart, character and integrity; this gourmet cook and raconteur whom I used to describe to my friends as a "Renaissance Man," so wide was his knowledge: from The Beach Boys to Beethoven, from Thomas Aquinas to Tommy Lasorda, from John Rockefeller, whom he knew, to John LeCarré, about whom he knew everything. What he didn't know was only an Internet click away. That is why it was the most natural thing in the world for him to be involved in the USF Academy of Lifelong Learning in Sarasota. On the home front we in the family called him "Dr. Jim," for every ailment we had, he had read something about it, quoted the research, and suggested the right medicine. Even though he was practicing without a license, he was our consultant in residence.

Jim was instinctively compassionate. He was the idealist who was among the first to join the Peace Corps, became CEO of Save the Children, worked at the Ford Foundation and chaired other foundations. In short, Jim gave back abundantly to the community. He was genuinely generous and genetically moral. This Daniel with a laughing heart would show up and wash your floor, send you a helpful gadget, look up information that could aid you. He was uncannily sensitive to the needs of others. He remembered not only birthdays and anniversaries, but also the in-between things: when you were about to go to college, when exam time approached, when a marriage was troubled, when you needed money, when you were sick. About a half-dozen years ago I was rushed to the hospital for an emergency operation. When I awoke in the post-op room in Freehold, New Jersey, the first one I saw as I opened my eyes was my brother

Jim from Siesta Key, Florida. He was like that. It's no small wonder that he asked that donations in his name be made to the Child Health Foundation in Maryland.

Jim was a presence, a brightness. He had personality when that word meant wit and sensitivity anchored to character. When I called him two days before he died, he could no longer speak, only grunt to acknowledge my comments. I called my brother Charlie afterward and told him that I didn't know how Jim could continue. He must have a strong heart, I commented. Charlie agreed and then added, "and a big heart." Indeed.

He also had faith. He was a religious person. In one of our many conversations, he told me how all his life he prayed every day. He made his peace with the church, went to Mass, was grateful for the kindly ministrations of his pastor and my classmate, Father Brubaker, received the sacraments and gave himself over to God. In his last weeks his faith deepened profoundly and my last words to him were, "May God ease your passage." This Mass is his fervent wish. His ashes, to be scattered directly in front of this church, is his returned gift to God of a gifted life, a reminder to all who daily pass them by that a righteous person is there.

He was a long time dying. About four years ago, as you know, the possibility and then the actuality of cancer began to surface, and about two years ago it metastasized into one of the worst kind, fourth-level pancreatic cancer. Few live beyond four of five months. But Jim did and confounded everybody. With great support from his wife, Janet, and a group of truly extraordinary doctors who dispensed medicine, compassion, and hugs in equal amounts, he faced every challenge. And, for a long time, he succeeded. Jim in fact became the Poster Boy among the medical community for surviving so long, even appearing in the university newsletter. Again, you usually don't last beyond five or six months with that kind of cancer.

Last year his amazed doctor told him that he shouldn't be there in his office talking. Jim replied that three things kept him alive: good genes, lots of prayer, and determination. And determination he had, as he took on every new experimental procedure and medication. He was supposed to die in 2002, for sure in 2004. He made it to 2006. Characteristically this ever-sensitive man did not want to die on a holiday. Janet's mother died on Mother's Day and he didn't want to repeat that kind of an association. Stunningly, he did avoid the holidays for his departure. In 2005 he was delighted that he made Thanksgiving and then Christmas and Chanukah. He made New Year's and even, unexpectedly, his seventieth birthday on May 1. He wrote, "I didn't think I'd see last Christmas, Chanukah, or the New Year. Now, to everyone's surprise, I am about to fulfill the biblical lifespan of three score and ten years, a birthday I had no realistic hope of celebrating."

But if that long-time dying, especially these last few months, was a hardship, especially to Janet and his family, at the same time it was also a gift in more ways than one. It gave us all, family and friends, a chance to say many times how much we loved one another; to reminisce, to laugh and cry, to draw closer together. Not all families and friends get that chance.

I said Jim was an idealist, a world-fixer. There is a phrase that comes out of the mystic tradition in Judaism, the Kabbalah, called *tikkun olam*. It translates into something like "fixing up the world." It rests on the assumption that the world is imperfect, even that God intentionally left it imperfect, because he had created human beings to become God's agents in making creation proper. Moreover, the Master of the Universe, knowing human beings couldn't do it alone, insisted they must join up with others, look for friends, companions.

Jim was, as I said, a world-fixer and he had a talent for finding such world-fixing companions, for making fast and lifelong friends. His friendships from St. Peter's College, as you heard so ably, are legendary: John Fanning, Frank Mertz, Dick Keating, Dick Jeanneret, Harry Vitting—an awesome sextet by any standards—presided over by the late eccentric, Father Murphy, S.J. His friends from the places he worked, the Academy of Lifelong Learning, neighbors, his doctors, are many; and there are special friends such as Barry Gaberman, Joe Manhurter, Marilyn Harwell, Sid Landau, Bill Hooker, Lois Selden, Steve Schlossberg, and others too numerous to mention. That you are all here, from every background, tradition, and way of life is testimony to our common humanity and compassion that transcend all the boundaries human beings can invent. You are the folk who accompanied him while he was fixing up the world and now you accompany us and, on behalf of the family, I thank you deeply and sincerely.

Finally, even with all of his family and friends and remarkable endurance, time ran out as it had to. At the beginning of June he and his doctors decided to end all further procedures. He gave himself over to God and to the lovely ministrations of hospice. If, as I said, the gifted time we did have enabled us to say what we should have, it also gave Jim a time to plan. Jim was, if nothing, a planer, a researcher. He liked to have things all spelled out, a characteristic I share. He wrote e-mails and letters, took care of all legalities, and, much to my minor dismay, even planned every aspect of this funeral. Mildly exasperated at one point, I complained to him that while he was at it, why didn't he write this homily. Like Jack Benny, when confronted by a thug snarling, "Your money or your life!" there was a pause: "I'm thinking! I'm thinking!" he said. We laughed.

He put me very much in mind of the American writer E.B. White, best known as the author of the children's classic, *Charlotte's Web*. In a moving piece that was written late in his life, he mused about his wife's gardening:

> As the years went by and age overtook her, there was something comical yet touching in her bedraggled appearance on this awesome occasion…the small hunched-over figure, her studied absorption in the implausible notion that there would be yet another spring, oblivious to the ending of her own days, which she knew perfectly well was near at hand, sitting there with her detailed chart under those dark skies in the dying October, calmly plotting the resurrection.

That was Jim. That was my brother, calmly plotting his resurrection.

Yes, he was my brother, but beyond that, he was, first and foremost, profoundly and endearingly, Janet's husband—she was his sun, moon, and stars—and he was Jennifer and David's precious father, Rachel's grandfather, nieces' and nephews' uncle, godchildren's godfather, and dearest friends' dearest friend. His was a good life. His was a good death.

Jim agreed. He could write near the end:

> Janet and I have been looking back over these past years and it is clear that while others might live longer than I seem destined to, no one could have had it better than we. It has been a wonderful life together, blessed with Jennifer and David, being part of two terrific families, having marvelously supportive friends, and reflecting with joy and gratitude on some accomplishments and experiences we have had. I wouldn't trade my life for anyone else's, nor would Janet, which says a lot.

And among his last words were these: "Dying is a part of life. I'm ready, and I surely have nothing to complain about. I'm still the luckiest, most blessed person I know."

That is, outside of us who were privileged to know him.

CRIES OF THE HEART
Addenda to the Funeral Homilies

This is a follow-up section containing homilies that properly belong to the "Twice Told Talks" section but they logically fit here in this funeral context as a kind of emotional addenda. That's because these homilies attempt to deal with the ancient (and insoluble) theodicy problem: How can a good God permit such evil as we see every day in our world? This theoretical problem becomes quite real for certain people at the time of a death in the family. I know one woman who left the church after her twenty-two-year-old son was killed in an automobile accident. She demanded to know why she, a good churchgoer, didn't deserve better than that. God either didn't care or was impotent.

The questions are angry and heartbreaking. We've all heard (felt?) them: Where was God when my son/daughter/spouse/parent/friend died? Why didn't God cure him or her when we all prayed so hard? How can I ever trust God again? How can I return to church?

Recoiling from any insensitive comments that it was "God's will" or "Your faith was not strong enough," I have no better answers than others. I can only offer approaches that circle the problem for those grieving and questioning. These four homilies, scattered throughout the liturgical year, are brought together here in the hope of providing some context when painful questions arise.

Bill Johnson: Love Trusts

MATTHEW 11:25-30

Some time ago, twenty-three-year-old Patrick Purdy killed five small children in a schoolyard. And then he turned the gun on himself and took his own life. So I ask you to imagine, however difficult it is because it's so uncomfortable, I ask you to imagine that you are the parent of one of those slain children. You run down the litany of the feelings you absolutely have to have gotten: total shock and disbelief; grief and horror; and then, of course, finally rage.

But if that weren't bad enough, there is one more pain, which is probably the worst of all, and that is you can't even vent your rage on anyone because the young man was irresponsible; he was psychotic; but worse than that, he is dead.

So you think of that. There's no place to put your anger, no place to release your hate. There's nobody's chest that you can pound; there's not even an idiot face that you can yell at. There's no human being left that you can curse. There's no one around that you can even prosecute or that you can imprison. It's extremely unfair, to say the least. There's just raw frustration, with no place to go; except you can go inward and poison your system, and that can deteriorate your health. And, of course, there's always the third outlet: God.

I thought of this when I heard Friday of the death of Bill Johnson, who was jogging along in good health at Brookdale College where he was the athletic director. And not only did he just drop dead, but it was a year ago that his own young son died of a brain tumor. And so you listen to things like that, and read stories of five innocent children slain playing in their schoolyard, and then you ask, if not out loud, How do you square that with God?

446

And I think the question gets extremely poignant when you add, How do you square these things with God, especially when you have been good, and you have kept the commandments; and feel, rightly so, that after all, you deserve some consideration? You can't help but think that a God who does not come across for the faithful ones is either pretty fickle or pretty powerless. Now that's understandable.

In the light of St. Paul's epistle (1 Corinthians 13), these incidents force us to the deep question, the question that you and I don't like to look at because, again, it's not a terribly comfortable question; and it's very challenging, and goes right to the heart of the matter. Beneath all these tragedies and anger, and rage and perplexity, is the question that sooner or later we have to try to wrestle with: What is your relationship with God?

And the only way to respond to that is to say, "Well, what is my relationship with other people?" Fundamentally, we all have to say that my relationship with other people has to at least try to rest on some kind of a trust, even in perplexing and strained times; and maybe *especially* in perplexing and strained times. We accept, without question, that our relationships with other human beings are not a "tit for tat" contract type of thing: "I will be loyal and so will you. I will be honest and so will you. I will be faithful and so will you. I will do everything I should and so will you." It just doesn't happen that neatly, does it? It just doesn't happen that way.

And because it doesn't, and because we know that relationships are imperfect and are not based on guarantees but on trust, we make considerable room for forgiveness and reconciliation, for change and growth; for uncertainty; for hope; and, ultimately, as St. Paul says, for love, a love that somehow will overcome all the deficiencies. But when it comes to our relationship with God, we change the rules, don't we? You think about that. We come up with this extremely odd "contract" notion. "God, I kept all the commandments, so how could you let my daughter get sick? How could you let my marriage fail, and disintegrate and break up? How could you let my innocent child get machine-gunned at school? *How could you?*"

It always amazes me when Christians say things like that, although I can understand it when they're under stress. For after all, Christians every single year celebrate a two-thousand-year-old story of a man who was faithful to God, who kept all the commandments, and who wound up being spit upon, and stripped, and scourged, and crowned with thorns, and hung on a cross to die; and this was one about whom God said, "This is my beloved son."

But anyway, what gets exposed here is the one-dimensional shallowness of our relationship with God, which we would not tolerate with other people. When we analyze it, our relationship with God is one of contract, not of trust. With God, somehow, we want not trust, but guarantee; not acceptance, but explanation; not faith, but certainty; not adventure, but predictability; not ambiguity, but a flow chart; not mystery, but a signed contract. Is that the way you treat other people in your life? Why do we do it with God?

Or are we ready to trust that God, being God, will have the last word in all the madness and absurdities of life, as God did in the absurdity and madness of what happened to God's beloved son? And even there, what's our view of Jesus? I have a feeling that for most of us it's a distorted view: Jesus is the great detached one, who up his sleeve had the master plan laid out, and he says, "Well, I can put up with a little bit of fuss because in the end we're all going to live happily ever after." But the fact is that Jesus was not the great detached one. If anything, Jesus comes across in Scripture as the great pilgrim, the authentic life who did not escape the human condition; who did not know the master plan; who did not have the completed script; who took life day by day and let life's evil have its full play, while his Father, who would not remove human freedom with all its potential for good and evil, wept at what happened to him.

And in the end, the Father dried his tears and raised Jesus up, as Jesus trusted that he would, although he had his last-minute doubts: "My God, my God, why have you forsaken me?" That's faith. Faith is belief surrounded by doubt, with doubt getting stronger in troubled times. But that's relationship. Just like husbands and wives, and brothers and sisters, and friends and lovers; with all the unfairness of life, you have to trust—or you die.

Let me share with you the true story of a soldier named Joseph Schultz. Just over one hundred years ago Adolph Hitler was born. In his fifty-six years on the planet he did incredible harm and was responsible for millions of terrible deaths. Yet in all of the horror that he unleashed, there are pinpoints of light and nobility. And this German soldier, Joseph Schultz, who was the same age as Patrick Purdy, who machine-gunned children in the schoolyard, was one of these pinpoints.

He was sent to Yugoslavia shortly after the invasion. He was a loyal, young German soldier on patrol, and one day the sergeant called out eight names, his among them. They thought they were going on a routine patrol, and as they hitched up their rifles, they came over a hill, still not knowing what their mission was. There were eight Yugoslavians there, standing on the brow of the hill; five men and three women. It was only when they got about fifty feet away from them, when any marksman could shoot out an eye of a pheasant, that the soldiers realized what their mission was.

The eight soldiers were lined up. The sergeant barked out, "Ready!" and they lifted up their rifles. "Aim," and they got their sights. And suddenly in the silence that prevailed, there was a thud of a rifle butt against the ground. The sergeant, and the seven other soldiers, and those eight Yugoslavians stopped and looked. And Private Joseph Schultz walked toward the Yugoslavians. His sergeant called after him and ordered him to come back, but he pretended not to hear him.

Instead, he walked the fifty feet to the mound of the hill, and he joined hands with the eight Yugoslavians. There was a moment of silence, then the sergeant yelled, "Fire!" And Private Joseph Schultz died, mingling his blood with those innocent men and women. What was found on his body was an excerpt from today's reading from St. Paul. The excerpt was: "Love does not delight in evil, but rejoices in the truth. It always protects, always trusts, always hopes, and always perseveres."

Private Joseph Schultz was drawn into a war that was absurd. He was drawn into an event that was evil that he did not understand. He was drawn into a perplexity and an unfairness of life, and he wondered what God could possibly have in mind. And yet he trusted that his sacrifice would make a difference, and that God would be faithful.

He had no guarantee. He had no special insight into any master plan. He had no assuredness, he only had a relationship with God, whom he trusted, even when he did not understand God. And I think that is what Paul is saying.

There is hardly anyone hearing this who cannot say that life has been unfair. Many of you are in a broken relationship; some of your children have bitterly disappointed you; others among you are dying of cancer. And you say, "Life is unfair," and you're right. And you say, "I've been faithful.

I go to church every Sunday and I follow all the rules. How could God do this to me? I've lost a relationship. I've lost a son. I've lost a spouse. I've lost a parent. I've lost a job. I've lost health. Is this the way God treats God's beloved ones?"

And all that I ask you to do as you get angry with God, is, for heaven's sake, look at the crucifix. This is his beloved son. In the crucifix is the message that you trust the relationship, as Jesus had to. It is permissible to get angry, and it is permissible to doubt, as Jesus did on the cross. But in the end you have to ask, What is your relationship with God? If it's a relationship of a contract, you have a right to abandon God and say, "You didn't keep your part of the bargain, and I'm not keeping mine. Goodbye. I've had it!"

But if it's a relationship, like with somebody you love, then you have to trust God. With people you love, even though you don't understand what they're doing and why they're doing it, or why they're acting that way, you stick with them, even when they're mentally and emotionally and physically ill. You hang in there even when you see no end and no light at the end of the tunnel. God asks for nothing less than that. God is friend, is beloved, is in relationship with you, and as in any relationship, God asks for your trust. The resurrection of Jesus Christ, who had his doubts, is proof that God will have the last word. So St. Paul is right, and Private Schultz is right, and Jesus is right. If God is love, love does not delight in evil, but love rejoices in the truth. Love always protects; love always trusts; love always hopes. And love always perseveres.

Carly:
When the Miracles Stop

Seventeenth Sunday in Ordinary Time, B, John 6:1–15

"Jesus went across the sea of Galilee. A large crowd followed him because they saw the miracles he was performing...."

It's vacation time. It's summer time when the livin' is easy. Should I try to tease your minds and hearts in such a context? Should I offer something challenging that this gospel provokes? Well, why not? You can always complain to the pastor.

It's those opening words of the gospel I just cited that raise the issue. "A large crowd followed Jesus because they saw the miracles...." Well, I ask, who wouldn't follow? You'd be dense not to. My challenging question is, What happens when the miracles cease? When they dry up? Will we follow Jesus when there are no more miracles? Will I follow when my child is born genetically defective and all the prayers in the world aren't pulling in the miracle that would make her any different than a prospect for lifelong care? When my spouse is killed in an automobile accident and there is no miracle of resurrection, when I am diagnosed with a terminal illness and no miraculous cure appears? When bad things happen to good people and there are no miracles to right the equation? When, in a word, there are no miracles and no more God, at least none that I can detect, when faith is shaken if not evaporated altogether. Will we follow then? So again, my question: Will we follow Jesus when we no longer see miracles?

A woman who lost her child at birth, and almost her faith, writes:

> All my multilayered, carefully constructed faith was stripped
> away as I focused on one thing: the injustice that our little girl
> didn't have a chance to take even a single breath....[Even] prayer
> seemed so futile, even unnecessary, like throwing a glass of water
> on a burning house. I had prayed my entire pregnancy for the
> baby to be healthy—and she was. Carly was perfect but she wasn't
> alive, cooing in my arms. How could I not feel betrayed?...
>
> In the weeks following Carly's death, well-meaning friends
> and relatives called and sent hundreds of cards and letters of-
> fering helpless words of condolence. Most of their efforts said
> the same thing: "It was God's will. We cannot understand God's
> will." Those words kept me up at night for months, spinning
> through my frantic mind, tying me in philosophical knots.
> I know they were trying to help, but every time the issue of
> God's will sprang up, I was miserable. It got to the point where
> I couldn't even numbly smile or nod any more when the phrase
> inevitably popped up. I just clenched my teeth to keep from
> saying something I'd regret.

Finally, exhausted, this woman who lost her child and almost her faith, punctuates her long sorrow with these plaintive words: "Some may wonder why, after our experience, I still want to make the painful effort to believe. I can only respond that, despite my doubts, having seen the breathtaking perfection of my daughter's peaceful face, it is impossible to think God was not there." Somehow, beyond the miracle that never came, she sensed Someone.

Let's hold that in mind while I move to a short story I once read about a doubt-ridden Jesuit priest. Since age ten, he has been plagued by doubts. Finally, however, he develops a doubt that will not pass; he begins to doubt the love of God. In the face of his doubt, he prays for faith, but none comes. So, he prays for hope, but when that is not given either, he simply goes on with his duties: teaching, preaching, saying Mass. Then, one bright, clear day, after saying Mass, he is driving home to the rectory when he comes across a terrible automobile accident. A young man lies dying, trapped in an overturned car. The priest is able to force open the crumpled car door and manages to cradle the dying man in his arms.

Taking a vial of holy oil from his pocket, the priest anoints the dying man, pronouncing, "I absolve you from all your sins. In the name of the Father and of the Son and of the Holy Ghost. Amen." But, then, *nothing happens.* There is no shift in the world, no change in the dire situation, no word from heaven, not even any human rescuers come. Only the silent world and the dying young man's harsh, half-choked breathing. The priest begins to pray recited prayers, rote prayers, prayers about Mary, prayers to the Father in heaven. He feels foolish, but what else can he do, what else can he say? He wants that miracle.

He wonders, What would God do at such a moment, if there were a God? "Well, do it!" he says aloud, and hears the fury in his voice. "Say something!" But there was silence from heaven....What could anyone say to this crushed, dying thing, he wondered. What would God say if he cared as much as I?...The priest could see death beginning across the face of the young man, who suddenly turned in some dying reflex, his head tilted in the priest's arms, trusting, like a lover. And at once the priest, faithless, unrepentant, gives up altogether and bends over him and whispers, fierce and burning, "*I* love you," and continues until there is no breath, "*I* love you, *I* love you, *I* love you." A cry that meant that even if God didn't come through with a miracle, *he* loved the dying young man. What now?

This is hard, but I suggest in this story that the priest is fundamentally a converted man, even though he doesn't know it. He is a man who has quite painfully moved from a childish faith to a mature and hopeful one.

What happened is that the priest, when you come right down to it, was forced to give up his immature idea of a God who comes with miracle in hand when we whistle to make everything all right, in favor of a God who summons the faithful to be present when a need arises, to be God's incarnate divine mercy at this time and place. In other words, the priest, lacking a miracle, *himself* becomes the miracle. God was there and held that dying man through his arms.

So today's gospel in its own way poses the question: Will we follow Jesus when the miracles stop? When our daughter dies, when our son is killed?

Will we, like the woman who lost her child, see the absent miracles as an invitation to seek the miracle-worker himself? Will we consider the possibility that, when all is said and done, after the shock is over and the tears are dried, *we* ourselves might be the miracle?

I don't know. It's tough to stand in someone else's shoes. I just know that, of course, the folks in the gospel story were sensible and savvy to follow Jesus *because* of the miracles he was performing, but I also know that folks are even more sensible and spiritually savvy to realize that the magic tricks are just that: tricks to get you to the magician and to be discarded once you have found him. We are challenged to learn to love Jesus for who he is rather than for the free bread he can give us. I think that dried up miracles can help us focus on the real miracle, that *we* are called to be the compassion and presence of God. It is, as I said, a tough call, but a call nevertheless.

Anyway, it's something to think about on a summer day. As you heard, the gospel story had a happy ending. Lots of people saw miracles and were fed with a new one. But it's also time to think about those who saw none and are left excruciatingly hungry. Hungry for some answers, some sign, some way, ultimately, to live without miracles and still live with Jesus.

John the Baptist and Second Thoughts

John the Baptist is the dominant figure in today's liturgy. He's a remarkable man in many ways. We know that he received a call from God. And he answered it. As a result, Matthew's gospel which we just heard starts off:

> When John the Baptizer made his appearance as a preacher in the desert of Judea, this was his theme: "Reform your lives! The reign of God is at hand." Then turning to the Pharisees and the Sadducees, he shouts, "You brood of vipers! Who told you to flee from the wrath to come? Give some evidence that you mean to reform….Every tree that is not fruitful will be cut down and thrown into the fire."

This obviously is not a man unsure of himself. On the contrary, this is a man on fire with purpose. This is God's prophet aiming for the jugular. A strong, confident man. He was called. He reacted without hesitation and began his mission. A straight man on a straight line.

But somewhere along the way—we don't know when—doubt began to creep in. Was he right? Was he called by God or was all this self-delusion, all his fervent preaching for naught? *Was* cousin Jesus the one he was paving the way for? He wasn't so sure anymore.

Maybe after so many years, he was at a low point. Things weren't working out well. After all, at this time, he was no longer found along the Jordan but languishing in jail, detained in Herod's fortress of Machaerus, situated on the lonely desert heights overlooking the Dead Sea, awaiting who knows what! Or, as Matthew writes sparingly a few chapters later, "John was in prison." He had time to think. Maybe he had been all wrong, chosen the wrong path, bet on the wrong Messiah. Doubts made for troubled dreams. He decided to act.

Matthew gives us the account: "John in prison…sent a message through his disciples to ask him, 'Are you he who is to come or do we look for another?'" There it was. Plain, simple, and direct. "Just like John," Jesus thought to himself. Out loud, Jesus answered the delegation the best way he could: "Go and tell John what you have seen and heard: the blind receive their sight, the lame walk. The lepers are cleansed, the deaf hear, and the dead are raised, the poor have the gospel preached to them." And then he pointedly added with softness and compassion, "And blessed is anyone who takes no offense in me." He looked long at the departing disciples of John and then, when they were out of sight, commented, "I tell you, among those born of women no one is greater than John…."

John of Advent is many people throughout the ages. He is the initial *yeah-sayers with second thoughts*. I have been faithful to God. I have kept trust. I have prayed. I have been active in ministry. I read all the right books, faithfully go to Mass, give to the poor. And things have not turned out all right. I recently received letters from two John the Baptist-type people. One woman is filling me in on her family. The boys are doing fine. But the girls. One is living with a man and is planning to marry him outside the church. The other married a Jewish man, had the children baptized Catholic, and now is converting to Judaism and is going to raise the kids—her grandchildren—Jewish. Another's daughter just has a baby six months ago. The doctors recently removed a tumor the size of a grapefruit from her daughter, who is very sick now with chemotherapy. The baby was born with a hole in her heart and a thumb that is dangling and has to be removed.

"Are you the one who is to come or shall we wait for another?" Throughout the ages how many have wondered this in their grief or bitterness or disappointment? Have I been wrong to be so faithful? Worse, have I been a fool? People prayed for my son, we had a prayer chain going, we believe in healing, pleaded for a miracle. He died anyway. Some whispered that it was because I didn't have enough faith. If I had only believed more firmly!

To come to terms with this quandary, especially for those of a charismatic spirituality bent, I invite you to listen to the words of a fine and insightful Southern Baptist minister named Al Staggs:

> My wife died in April of this year following a twelve-year battle with cancer, a particularly malignant melanoma. [Comments from well meaning-but-misguided friends about the healing power of faith] have compelled me once again to rethink my theology of healing. I confess that I have extremely low tolerance for the so-called faith healers or for the peddlers of healing. I'm aghast that anyone would dare to claim to understand the mind of God about any particular person or any particular illness.
>
> What these folks do to people is to hold out hope for a complete reversal of a person's physical condition. When the miracle does not occur, the lack of miraculous action can be attributed to a person's lack of faith, which only compounds the person's problems. Not only are these people terminally ill, but they are also being taught that they are not good Christians. In my weaker moments I am reminded of the passage from Matthew 7:22–23, where Jesus says, "Many will say to me on that day, 'Lord, Lord, did we not prophesy in your name, and in your name drive out demons and perform miracles?' Then I will tell them plainly, 'I never knew you. Away from me, you evildoers!'"
>
> A few weeks prior to my wife's death, visiting friends recounted story after story of "miraculous" answers to their prayers. After hearing a steady diet of incidents in which people were healed of their infirmities or found better-paying jobs, my wife looked over at both of them and said simply, "It hasn't worked that way for us."
>
> Sometimes I just want to ask these people who become so excited about miraculous healing, "Has your vaunted prayer program yet kept anyone alive forever?" Eventually we all die, including those who were healed of their particular disease. No one has yet managed to avoid the grim reaper. So why save our success stories for just those precious few who have been allowed

a few months or years longer than they would otherwise have had? There needs to be a major emphasis on God's grace and sufficiency for every illness and every situation. The Christian community should talk just as loud and long about God's Essence in the most hopeless situations as we do about the "miraculous healings."

[Henri] Nouwen had this to say about death: "Death does not have to be our final failure, our final defeat in the struggle of life, our unavoidable fate. If our deepest human desire is indeed to give ourselves to others, then we can make our death into a final gift. It is so wonderful to see how fruitful death is when it is a free gift."

Nouwen's words and his own approach to his life and to his recent death are a counterbalance against those whose "healing" hit-and-run ministries suggest that death is a defeat and that only miraculous cure is a victory.

Stories of miraculous healing have their place. The miracle of a believer's faith, however, in the face of terminal illness, and the faith of a loving family, is just as important as any story of a miraculous cure of an illness. Very few people experience a total reversal of illness. Most people diagnosed with terminal illness struggle through it to the very end. So let us hear the stories of the miraculous presence of God in the lives of these saints who are faithful to the end.

There is our key: holding onto the faithful presence of God in our worst moments, clinging to belief in the ultimate victory of his love which "will make all things new again." Look, no one is free of second thoughts, especially in times of crisis. Not even John the Baptist. Not even Jesus: "Father, if it is possible remove this cup from me." "My God, my God, why have you forsaken me!" But there is the response and life lesson: "Nevertheless, not my will but thine be done....Into your hands I commend my spirit—my gift."

In other words, as Staggs said, be assured of, and hold on to, the miraculous presence of God in times of seeming abandonment, in times when we are tempted to look for another. It's like the distraught woman who cried to the priest, "Where was God when my son died?" And he answered softly, "The same place when *his* Son died."

If John was one who received the call, reacted with certainly and then lapsed into doubt, he is legion. But he gave his life for truth and God was in his fidelity, despite his doubt. Truly, no greater man was born of a woman.

And so too for us. Yes, pray for the miracle, the sudden cure. It happens. But also pray to discern that Divine Presence in the rhythmic pain, suffering, and death, and offer them as a gift, a gift that will be forever accepted by a love that never falters in a place where there are more tears.

The Divine Absence

Isaiah 42:1-4, 6-7

"A bruised reed he shall not break and a smoldering wick he shall not quench."

There is a scene in the play called *Ma Rainey's Black Bottom* written by the African American playwright, August Wilson. It's about some African American jazz musicians who are rehearsing in a Chicago recording studio. At some point they take a break from their rehearsal and begin to tell stories. One of them tells the story about a cousin of his, a minister whose sister in Atlanta was desperately ill and so he took a train to visit her. The train stopped in a little Georgia town to take on water and the minister got off the train to use the bathroom. He went into the station and was told, "Colored people can't use the bathroom in here; you have to use the outhouse."

So he went to the outhouse and while he was there the train left the station. There's the minister standing on a south Georgia platform—no train, no friends. Across the tracks there's a group of hostile young white men, and not wanting trouble, the minister simply starts walking up the railroad track. The group of men follow him. They surround him. They demand to know who he is and what he's doing. He tells them, "I am a minister." He shows them his Bible, he shows them his cross, he tells them his sister in Atlanta is sick and he's been left by the train. No matter. "Dance for us," they say. "Dance! Why don't you dance for us?" Someone pulls out a pistol and begins to fire at the ground and they make him dance.

The one telling the story says, "Can you imagine that, can you believe they did that to a man of God?" One of the other musicians says, "What I can't believe is that if he were a man of God, why did God let them do that

460

to him? If he was God's own man, why didn't God bring fire down from heaven and destroy those crackers? That's what I want to know."

Ah, there it is. That's what we'd like to know. Why didn't God step in and nuke those creeps? Why, in fact, does God seem so indifferent to any suffering in this world? Why does he allow rampant injustice? At times, truth to tell, God seems like such an impotent God, an insensitive God. All this misery, innocent children abused, tortured, dying, and God does nothing. Cancer, September 11th, war, death, the evil prosper, the wicked climb to the top. The rich get richer and the poor get poorer. And death intrudes into the family. The list is endless.

In the face of so much unfairness there are times we'd like to throttle God, write him off, shake him up, shout at him, if the thought weren't so blasphemous and we weren't so scared. Yet at times we are angry with God or at the very least mightily perplexed, profoundly disappointed, and painfully hurt. Some God. Some divine justice.

I must tell you here in church and quite up front, I have no answers to the misery and unfairness of life and God's terrible silence. I can only offer these three considerations in a long and difficult homily.

First, as far as wicked people go, we say that all we want from God is simple justice. Bring down the dictators, imprison the embezzlers, give payback time to the murderers and cheats, the rapists, and drug dealers. But—be careful what you pray for. Do we, you and I, really want God's absolute justice? Here and now? Think again, because that justice would also come our way as well. Are we ready for that: to be judged strictly, fairly, right down the line? Do we want our every sin judged, our every failing punished, our every connivance, lie, and impurity exposed and punishment meted out? Are second chances to be denied, repentance foreshortened, mercy withheld? Do we really want that when we cry out for justice? It seems rather that when we cry, "Why doesn't God do something?" we are extremely selective. We really mean why doesn't God do something about *them*? You know, those "others." You know, rain down his justice on those wicked other people. Could it be, though, that God is giving them, even though they cause untold evil and harm, the same chances as ourselves when we cause our own minor brand of evil and harm? Is this seeming indifference a case of extreme divine patience? I don't know.

Second, as far as horrible events go, maybe we just don't see things as God does. In fact, of course, we don't and we can't. God, after all, is mysterious and puzzling. For example, while we're crying out for a just God and the righting of the awful tragedies of life from my retarded child to my spouse's lingering cancer, today's Scripture comes along with some exotic description of God saying of him, "…he shall bring forth justice to the nations"—but, notice—"not crying out, not shouting, not making his voice heard in the street. [Rather] a bruised reed he shall not break and a smoldering wick he shall not quench."

What is this? We *want* God to cry out and shout and make his voice heard in the street. Can't God see all the pain? But he doesn't. Instead he shows a puzzling sensitivity, an unwillingness to break a bruised reed or snuff out a smoldering wick as long as here is the hope of life. Yes, in the end, as promised in the Scriptures, God will bring forth justice for the nations, but apparently it will be worked out in ways we do not understand, because the God of the Bible has an inexplicably soft spot that seems to let this suffering go on in the hopes that the wick of human decency and kindness will flame again.

Third, it would seem—and this is a bold thought indeed—that in all of the overwhelming evil in the world, all the endless suffering, somehow God himself mysteriously seems to suffer along with us. We get the distinct impression that he is not abstracted from our hurts, not apart, looking on like some impotent spectator above it all, not distant from human suffering, but right in the middle of it. It would seem that, ever since God created us, identified with us by making us into his own image and likeness, and then coming into our flesh in the incarnation and taking on our human condition, he mysteriously suffers with us like any passionate lover, like a mother who echoes every hurt of her child in her heart. He throbs with our pain.

You get a sense of that in Eli Weisel's harrowing book *Night*, the story of life and death in a Nazi concentration camp. In one scene, in a reprisal for some misdemeanor the Nazis decided to teach a lesson by hanging three people, including a young boy. Elie Wiesel describes the terrible scene:

The SS seemed more preoccupied, more disturbed than usual. To hang a young boy in front of thousands of spectators was no light matter.

The head of the camp read the verdict. All eyes were on the child. He was lividly pale, almost calm, biting his lips. The gallows threw its shadow over him....The three victims mounted together onto the chairs. The three necks were placed at the same moment within the nooses. "Long live liberty!" cried the two adults. But the child was silent.

"Where is God? Where is He?" someone behind me asked.... The two adults were no longer alive but the third rope was still moving. Behind me I heard the same man asking: "Where is God now?" And I heard a voice within me answer him: "Where is He? There He is. He is hanging here on this gallows."

Can that be? Is somehow God not apart from human suffering but a part of it, still groaning with the pains of giving birth to a people who will do his will? Is it really true what faith says: God in a stinking manger, God crying out in despair in Gethsemane, "Father let this pass me by," and asking on Calvary our oft-asked question, "My God, my God, why have you forsaken me?" Is this God who is also hurting, beseeching, suffering, and dying? Is this God on the gallows of our lives?

But if God is suffering with us, then the next question that comes to mind is this: Is not his rising an answer? Is the resurrection, his resurrection, a sign, a foreshadowing, that God's ultimate justice will triumph when he makes, as he promised, all things new again? If, like any lover, he suffered our agony, cried and died with us, is his resurrection the final response to life's long history of unfairness and senseless pain? Does his resurrection become a sign, a hope, a promise that justice will finally be done, even though meanwhile we have to live with the anger, the puzzlement over the world's seemingly endless pain and suffering?

There is a story about the ancient rabbi Baal Shem-Tov and it goes like this. One day, the rabbi and his students were standing on a hill when they noticed foreign troops invading their town. From their vantage point on the hill they were able to see all the horror and violence of the attack. The rabbi looked up to heaven and cried out, "Oh, if only I were God." A student asked, "But, Master, if you were God, what would you do differently?" The rabbi answered him, "If I were God, I would do nothing differently. But if I were God, I would understand."

We're not God. We do not understand. All that we're left with—and it is much indeed—is Jesus' final act of hope prayed to his Father on our behalf, "Father, into you hands I commend my spirit," and Jesus' final act of vindication from his Father, the resurrection. The one says that God is somehow in the world's senseless pain. The other says that God will redeem it. Perhaps not a very satisfying answer, but it will have to do for now.

TWICE TOLD TALKS

This section contains homilies from my past books with which a new generation of preachers might not be familiar. To keep the number of them reasonable I have concentrated only on the highlighted times of the year, that is, the busy times when the rhythms of the normal liturgical year are out of kilter. At those times, preachers attending to programs, rehearsals, and schedules cannot always give full attention to the preparation of a homily. That's why they will find here homilies for the liturgical feasts of Christmas, Epiphany, Easter, and Pentecost, as well as for those necessary non-liturgical feasts such as Thanksgiving, Mother's Day, Father's Day, Memorial Day, and the like. They should think of these homilies as a scribal file to be used in case of an emergency—and, of course, to be cleverly adjusted to your needs and style.

Christmas:
Love Among the Ruins

So solemn and captivating was this feast of Christmas that the ancients held that cattle in stables fall to their knees at midnight, birds sing all night long, and trees and plants, especially those along the Jordan River, bow in reverence toward Bethlehem. On Christmas eve, water in wells and fountains is said to be blessed by God with healing powers. Mysterious bells chime joyfully in the depths of mines, while cheerful lights can be seen in caves. It was once believed that at midnight the gates of paradise are opened and anyone dying at that hour would enter heaven at once. Children born on this night are especially blessed; they were believed to have the power to see spirits and even command them. Animals were thought to be able to talk like humans at midnight, and even in Latin, while witches, evil spirits, and ghosts had their powers suspended and could work no harm to humans, beasts, or homes. Legends like this one abounded:

On the first Christmas night the animals were given the power of speech so they could praise God and tell everyone about the birth of Jesus. The first animal to speak was the cock, who flapped his wings and chanted, "Christ is born." And the crow heard the cock, and wanted to know what time it took place. So he cawed, "When, when?" In the forest, the mighty lion heard the news of Christ's birth and roared with all his might, "Today Christ is born." The cow wanted to know where the Christ Child was born, so she lowed, "Where, where?"

The sheep heard the angels telling the shepherds the "good news of great joy" and bleated the answer, "He is born in Bethlehem." And the donkey wanted all to visit the stable at Bethlehem and see the Holy Child, so he brayed, "Let us go to Bethlehem." A little lark rose high in the air, as if to lead the way, and trilled, "To adore him." The dogs barked, "We should go to Bethlehem," and the horse whinnied, "Hee…He is born in Bethlehem."

All the animals offered their services to the Holy Infant and the Blessed Mother Mary.

The lowliest of all God's creatures, the worm, was the first in the stable to offer service to the Holy Child. It was so dark in the stable that Mary could not see to put the little garments on the Baby Jesus. A little worm, seeing how hard it was for her, crept along the floor to a slit in the door through which the moonlight was shining. He took a ray of light and carried it along until he reached the Blessed Mother. Then he climbed up her cloak and settled on her knee so that she could see by the light. The Little Savior was so pleased, he said to the little worm, "Dear little worm, your kindness to my mother shall be rewarded. I make you a present of the light. You shall never lose it." Then the little worm was placed on the edge of the manger bed where it took the place of a nightlight. And ever since, it has been known as the glowworm.

Shakespeare, in Act 1, Scene 1 of *Hamlet*, echoed some of those common beliefs:

> Some say that ever 'gainst that season comes
> Wherein our Saviour's birth is celebrated,
> The bird of dawning singeth all night long:
> And then, they say, no spirit dare stir abroad;
> The nights are wholesome; then no planets strike,
> No fairy takes, no witch has power to charm,
> So hallow'd and so gracious is the time.

But from this kind of ancient awe, we moderns have spun a different picture of Christmas. We have commercialized it and we have sanitized it. It is, for example, very difficult to override the Christmas card images of the nativity scene of the lovely city of Bethlehem, a scene that is always presented like a tableau of richly dressed Wise Men with their fabulous gifts, angelic choirs, the Babe in the manger, Mary and Joseph in clean clothes, the humble, sweet shepherds and, like Elsie the cow, well scrubbed and properly posed animals.

That scene gives us Radio City, but not the forceful message behind the realities of the first Christmas. To begin with, those shepherds: They were the dregs, people who couldn't find better jobs, conniving thieves, several steps below the proverbial used-car salesmen, a rather nasty lot. Then there are the Wise Men, magi of a sort certainly, but equally as certainly, not Jews, *not* people of the prophecies and *not* people of the promise; in a word, outsiders.

As far as Mary and Joseph go, they were not Barbie and Ken, but poor peasants of the countryside wearing travel-worn, dusty, dirty clothes. In the stable the animals were not sanitized and people had to walk around the droppings. Bethlehem was not Darien, Connecticut, but a scruffy village of no account. Then there's the manger, which is not a crib from Toys Я Us but a feeding station. If we insist in dressing all of this mess up in Gucci accessories and a set designed by Dreamworld Studios we miss the point.

What is that point? The point is that God came into human existence and among human existence with all of its limitations and flaws. Christmas is a potent and palatable sign of God's desire to embrace our brokenness. After all, Jesus is the Word made flesh who dwelt among *us*. *Among us*, not some paid actors in a play; *among us*, nasty, untrustworthy shepherds, people who didn't belong, like the Magi, you know, the different, the oddball, the out-of-step folk; poor peasant parents who smelled from the journey. And it is no accident that such a God who desired to be with us as we are, with all of our flaws, was born in a feeding station. A nice touch, a nice symbol that that's what he came for: to nourish our brokenness, feed our hungry souls. Christmas truly shows us Love Among the Ruins.

Well, I tell you this: It's hard to break early habits, even for God. This child grew up and hadn't changed one bit. He was criticized for hobnobbing with the marginal, the outcasts, and those outside the pale. Still at the feeding station, he broke bread and fed sinners and publicans and hypocrites too, for he knew that there are no hypocrites. Just like there are no hypocrites who come to church, no matter what critics say to justify their own staying away. There are only people with addictions. He had the temerity to say outright, "I have come to call sinners, not the just." He flirted with the Samaritan prostitute at the well, gave a second chance to Zacchaeus, a corrupt politician, actually touched an untouchable, a leper, and he died between two thieves, probably a couple of shepherds. From the cradle to the grave, "the Word has dwelt among us," been where we are. How's that for consistency!

The big question for Christmas is, Why don't we pay attention to all this? Why do we allow ourselves to fall for commercial sentimentality when all the while for Jesus, as Dostoevsky said, "Love is a harsh and dreadful thing." Harsh as deliberately being born among the scum of the earth, and dreadful as dying naked on a cross with holes in your body.

That same great Russian writer Dostoevsky got the Christmas message right in his story called "'The House of the Dead" in which he described the coming of Christmas day to a Siberian camp. It was a dingy little settlement among frozen wastelands. From the grim prison at one end of a single muddy street the convicts peered through barred windows at the small cathedral on a hill on the other side of town. The bells rang merrily as that Christmas dawn arrived and villagers trooped in happy procession to the early church service. It was Christ's mass, Christmas. "But not for us, who are cut off from all humanity," the ragged prisoners wept, huddled together for comfort from the cold. Finally, however, when the long cathedral service was ended, a priest came to the prison, set up a crude altar, and began the service of worship. "Now God has come to us!" the convicts shouted in surprised joy. "Oh, yes," replied the priest. "This is where he lives all year long. You see he goes to the cathedral only on special occasions. "

The truth is, God lives all year long among us, but often, in practice, we deny it. We think we're beyond his concern, his care, his love. Arraying Jesus in royal trappings and, under the pressure of the media, placing him high in a stage setting under the strobe lights, leads us to think that he is removed from our shepherd lives and so we do not experience his care and embrace. How can we do this to a God who ached so badly to be among us that his first audience was the dregs of society?

Let me mention Marilyn Monroe in this Christmas homily not just to get your attention, but because she figures here. She has, as you know, become a kind of icon, a symbol, of the sensuality and emptiness of our time. Playwright Arthur Miller, one of her husbands, in his autobiography, *Timebends*, mentions that during the filming of *The Misfits* he watched

Marilyn descend into the depths of depression and despair. He was fearing for her life, as he watched their growing estrangement, her paranoia, and her growing dependence on barbiturates. One evening after a doctor had been persuaded to give her yet another shot, she was sleeping. Miller stood watching her, reflecting. He wrote: "I found myself straining to imagine miracles. What if she were to wake and I were able to say, 'God loves you, darling,' and she were able to believe it. How I wish I still had my religion and she hers."

The sadness is that Arthur Miller and Marilyn Monroe were a couple of shepherds who didn't know God was partial to them.

I suggest that the only way we'll find the meaning of Christmas is to jettison the pretty Christmas card images of the birth of Christ and rediscover that he is here where he's always wanted to be: among the small and among the straw, hanging out there, so to speak, because he knows that's where we hang out. That's what the stable scene of Jesus' birth is all about. The Word became flesh among us and for us. He wanted to be close. Love Among the Ruins.

Author Ian Maclaren tells the true story of a young woman in his book, *Beside the Bonnie Briar Brush*. She's raised in a Christian home, but she wants, as they say, to find her freedom: freedom from all those rules, freedom from religion, freedom from the old Puritanism, freedom from God. And so she leaves and finds the kind of life she thinks is free. She gets for herself all that she's ever desired. But the getting's never enough. And what she possesses begins to possess her. Now she doesn't even know what it means to be free.

Well, one day, like a Prodigal Daughter, she decides to go home. When she gets near the cottage of her birth, she wants to turn around. What's she looking for anyway? She's left this place behind! And her footsteps falter. She begins to turn her body. But then the dogs in the yard catch scent of her. And they haven't forgotten her, even though it's been so long. Then the light comes on at the door, and she knows she's caught. When the door opens, all she can see is her father bathed in the light. And he calls out her name, even though he doesn't have a reason to expect her. He calls out her name, and suddenly her feet take her running to him. And he takes her in his arms, and he sobs out blessings on her head.

When she tells her neighbor later what happened, she described it this way. She says, "It's a pity, Margaret, that you don't know Gaelic! That's the best of all languages for loving. There are fifty words for 'darling,' and my father could be calling me every one of them that night I came home."

Jesus has fifty-plus words for us; that's what the stable scene is all about, what Christmas is all about. But to hear them, we've got to get close and find our rightful place among the shepherds, the wise men, and the animals and other outcasts he came to save. We've got to go to the Feeding Station.

So, it comes down to this: There is no way in TV land that you'll find anything but a tinseled tableau of that first Christmas. But here, tonight, gathered in a faith community where Jesus still comes humbly in his spoken word and in the size of a piece of bread, we know that he bends to shepherds, outcasts, and glowworms. In Christmas he has fulfilled his desire to be near us, to be with us.

Christmas is not a tableau in a store window; it is the celebration of the Word made flesh, our flesh. It is the celebration of Love Among the Ruins.

Christmas Storytime

LUKE 2:1–14

A kindly ninety-year-old grandmother found buying presents for family and friends a bit much one Christmas, so she wrote out checks for all of them to put in their Christmas cards. In each card she carefully wrote, "Buy your own present," and then sent them off. After the Christmas festivities were over, she found the checks under a pile of papers on her desk! Which means that everyone on her gift list had received a beautiful Christmas card from her with "Buy your own present" written inside, but without the checks! I'm sure that's a Christmas they will long remember!

On this Christmas 2001, I start off with a smile because, as you know, it's different kind of a Christmas this year, isn't it? Who would have thought this time last year, for example, that we would have seared into the national consciousness the date of September 11? That police and firefighters, Ground Zero, Taliban, Amtrak, terror, Afghanistan, hitherto unknown or unattended to, would become national buzzwords? Who would have thought that, for so many, this Christmas would carry gaping holes, deep emptiness, a visit to the gravesite, and an empty place around the festive table?

Well, the way we all deal with these tragedies, whether we realize it or not, the way humankind has *always*, from time immemorial, dealt with tragedies is to turn to storytelling. We instinctively turn to storytelling as a way of coping, as a way of reassuring ourselves and others that we are alive and that the world goes on. Which is why we tell stories of the deceased at funerals. We use stories to mesh emotion and intellect, heart and mind, in the face of a world turned upside down. I might add that children especially need stories. They spend hours, sometimes alone, watching graphic images of destruction. Unlike adults, children process grief by talking out

472

loud. Our tendency is to silence or distract them, which means the children end up processing their emotions alone. But we need to give them the opportunity to tell their stories and, above all, to listen to stories of hope and renewal. This is why we have to carve out space in all of the hectic comings and goings of these days to be with our children and story them.

And surely at this season, beyond the manufactured TV stories, we must tell the deeper good news stories of the nativity we celebrate: of a perplexed Mary and a bewildered Joseph, of wicked kings and crafty Magi, of mean innkeepers and sweet-singing angels—and, most of all, about this baby, this Jesus, this Son of God, who would make all things new again and whose love would always be the last word, no matter how bad things got. We must also tell those derivative stories that sound the same good news of redemption and hope and the power of love and draw their inspiration from the Christ Child.

There is, for example, the story of a black man from long ago walking along 42nd Street in New York, from the railroad to the hotel, carrying a heavy suitcase and a heavier valise. Suddenly, a hand took hold of the valise and a pleasant voice said, "Pretty heavy, brother! Suppose you let me take one. I'm going your way." The black man resisted but finally allowed the young white man to assist him in carrying his burden, and for several blocks they walked along, chatting together like cronies. "And *that*," said Booker T. Washington years afterward, "was the first time I ever saw Theodore Roosevelt." We don't have to spell out the meaning or the deeper significance of one man carrying another's burden. The story speaks for itself.

Then there's that marvelous story about a certain statue in a town square in Eastern Europe that is not what you would ever expect to find in a town square because it's not a statue in honor of a war hero, prime minister, or a famous athlete or even a rock star. Rather, the statue is a tribute to beauty in the midst of horror and here's its story.

One day during the war in Sarajevo, a bomb was dropped on a bakery where twenty-two people were waiting in line to buy bread. All twenty-two people were killed. A citizen of Sarajevo, a man named Vedran Smialiavic, decided that he wanted to do something to mark the death of these innocent victims. But, he said to himself, "I am a simple man. What can I do?"

Before the war, Smialiavic played in the Sarajevo orchestra, but once the war started everyone was afraid to venture out just to hear music. With no music to perform, he walked the streets near his home and tried to find things to keep busy. But when he heard about the bakery bombing, Smialiavic came up with an answer to his question. He dressed up in his tuxedo and took his cello and a chair and marched to the site.

He sat there amid the debris for twenty-two days, one for each of the victims of the bombing, and played his favorite piece of music, Albinoni's "Adagio in G." He braved the artillery fire and ducked the snipers' bullets and went on playing his cello.

So, the statue in the town square is a statue of Vedran Smialiavic. It shows him sitting on his chair playing his cello. People often bring flowers to put around the base of the statue, always twenty-two flowers to honor those twenty-two people. He's a hero because, little man that he was, he made a difference doing what he could do. His fame is that he made beautiful music among the rubble. He gave people hope.

Does this remind you of a tiny infant born in a stable, lying on a bed of straw, being heavenly music among the earth's rubble? Our story, like the Christmas story, challenges us and becomes a story to live by. It's the kind of story that asks you to imagine yourself all dressed up in a tux or evening gown, taking your cello and playing, say, at Ground Zero. Or anywhere for that matter, you as a Christian having the mission of making beautiful music wherever there is rubble.

"Merry Christmas," said the small boy as he handed over his Christmas present to his mother. Earlier that Christmas eve, he had shyly presented himself to a department store clerk. "I would like to buy my mom some pajamas," he said bravely. "Very nice," said the clerk, "but first I'll need to know more about your mother. Tell me, is she short or tall?" To which the boy replied, "She's perfect." Whereupon the clerk wrapped a nifty size medium for him. A few days later, mom returned the nifty-size medium and exchanged it for a size extra large.

We smile, but this story is also a variation of the Christmas story and its kernel of truth sticks out: *Could we not learn to see as that child?* Not a fat lady, not a loser, not a bum, not a nerd, not a sinner, but someone who, as God's image and likeness, is perfect? Is this what Jesus meant when he said, "Unless you become like a little child you cannot enter the kingdom of heaven"? Isn't this the way God sees *us*? Isn't this what the Christmas story is really all about with its helter-skelter mix of elegant Magi, bottom-of-the-pit shepherds, stinking animals, and heavenly angels? With that motley crew around the manger, is *anyone* excluded from the love of God materialized in this Child?

Looking over this vast congregation tonight, I can't think of any.

Merry Christmas!

Epiphany:
The Magi, Our Story

We three Kings of Orient are,
Bearing gifts we traverse afar.
Field and fountain, moor and mountain
Following yonder star.

O star of wonder, star of night,
Star with royal beauty bright,
Westward leading, still proceeding
Guide us to thy perfect light.

Picturesque, delightful, the stuff of fantasy movies…

I suspect that, next to the manger scene, nothing has caught the Christian imagination more than the Magi story. It's not just that they are so colorful that each succeeding generation had to add more and more hues; it's not just that they are so mysterious that we simply had to give them gorgeous names; it's not just that they are so wonderfully exotic that we had to count their number as the mystical three; it's not just that they come from a faraway land that we had to make them—what else—kings!

It's not just all of these things that have captivated us, but rather, deep down, whether we realize it or not, we instinctively know that the Magi story is *our* story and that's why we are mesmerized by it. The Magi, basically, are you and I and everyone born into this world. Their timeless tale follows the time-honored, indelible, irreplaceable human storyline of everybody.

Consider: First, for every human being, from the very moment of birth, there is a call to answer, a vision to follow, a goal to be reached, an ideal to be fulfilled. In a very real sense, we are all born with a vocation. It may be to become a mechanic, an engineer, a teacher, a dancer, whatever.

The goal may be one's lady love, the jewel in the eye of the idol, Emerald City for Dorothy Gale, the Holy Grail for Dr. Jones, the sorcerer's stone for Harry Potter, the King of the Jews for the Three Searchers. All are born with a goal to be reached. Or to put it another way, beneath all these symbols, there is, simply put, the human ache for God. We share that with the Magi.

Second, the Magi, in order to seek their goal, must embark on a journey and so take on the risks of doing so. So too, sooner or later, we modern Magi also have to leave *our* securities to venture out into the unknown. From birth to death, like it or not, life is one inexorable journey with very discernible and identifiable stages from infancy to adolescence to adulthood. And each stage has its set of risks.

Shall the child cling to the comfort and security of mother or take on the risks of the neighborhood and school? Can the adolescent leave his or her self-absorption and run the risk of trust of others? Can the adult pull back from the all-absorbing money-making career and take the time to foster fidelity and intimacy with another? These are risks all up and down the line.

Third, on a journey, *any* journey, there are always both obstacles and aids. For the Magi, there was a wicked King who lyingly sweet-talked them: "Please, go find this adorable child you are seeking and by all means come back and tell me. There is nothing more I want than to fall at those infant feet and adore him." And Herod, dreaming murder, wiped away a sentimental tear. And the Magi left thinking, "Such a decent, sincere man."

For us, the obstacles to our true goal are the lyingly sweet-talking commercials that try to convince us that we are what we purchase and what we purchase makes us what we are. It's the rationalistic hucksters in our universities or on our TVs who preach that we *have* no goal, that all is here and now. There *is* no journey. It's all an illusion. There's only a straight line to oblivion, so make the most of it.

There are the stimulating highs of drugs, the idolatry of celebrity, the lure of exciting, uncommitted sex, and the constant din provided by the ubiquitous noisemakers: their loud music and machines, their hectoring to buy, their heady success in teaching us to equate busyness with importance: "You must be terribly busy" has become a sort of compliment, a hint that we are indispensable. "Always on the go" and "There's never enough time" are badges we wearily but proudly wear. The noisemakers smile. In no way do they want us to flirt with silence and solitude wherein we might discover our true selves and sense the real goal of our journey. Such obstacles are, if you will, the spiritual steroids that puff up our self-importance, inflate our desire for power, and make us deaf to the cry of the poor.

But there are helps too, as we said. For the Magi, it was an angel who warned them not to return to oily Herod but to take another path. For us, there are our moral heroes and shapers—hopefully, beginning with our parents—who have taught us by word and example also to take another path, the path of Jesus, and who have taught us who we really are: God-imaged folk made to know, love, and serve God in this life and be happy with God forever in heaven. And in the best scenario, our parents are mightily aided by a faith community, the inspiration of the saints, common and faithful worship, prayer and the sacraments.

Finally, of course, there is the end of the journey. For the Magi it was to engage the sacred, to look into the face of Christ and, falling down, to offer him their gifts and worship him. For us, it is the same: to offer our gifts and talents and to minister to Jesus, which in fact we do whenever we forget ourselves and our culturally calibrated image to feed the hungry, give drink to the thirsty, and clothe the freezing because when we do these things for the very least of humanity, we are doing them for Jesus himself. So our heart's desire says.

So there we are.

> Beginning, middle, end.
> Birth, growth, death.
> Risk, obstacles, help,
> the face of God.

It's all there in today's gospel.

That's why the story of the Magi is so captivating, so resonants.

Deep in our subconscious, you see, we recognize ourselves: *We* are the

Magi still enroute, and that recognition forces us to examine where we are right now on our spiritual journey, what risks we have taken for the sake of the kingdom of God, or even perhaps how our quest for God has been replaced by false idols or sidetracked by modern King Herods.

We are made to pause in our life's journey, face up to our Herods, and ask: Is it possible that have we gained the whole world at the expense of our own souls? If so, we pray:

> O star of wonder, star of night
> Star with royal beauty bright,
> Westward leading, still proceeding…
> Guide us to thy perfect light.

Epiphany: Slouching toward Bethlehem

MATTHEW 2:1–12

The gorgeous story of the Wise Men is among the favorites of us Christian people. We love to hear it. We love to see the Wise Men's appearance at our crib with their royal clothes, elegant servants, and precious gifts. We love to point them out to our children and grandchildren. We love to weave romantic stories about them.

Gospel writer Matthew has indeed left us figures of high imagination. But through all the traditions, can we make any educated guesses as to who they really were? Yes, there's a hint. Matthew says in his gospel that when Jesus was born, Wise Men came from the East to Jerusalem asking, "Where is he who has been born the King of the Jews? We have seen his star in the East."

Now, although many translations are given—Magi, magicians, astrologers—it is very likely that these so-called wise men were priests of the Zoroastrian religion who worship the god of light. And they believed that every great person had a guiding light in heaven that appeared as a star—and the greater the person born, the brighter the star—and so no wonder, when they saw this extraordinary star, they trekked across the desert in search of the one who must be very great indeed.

Their number? That has varied with imagination. Sometimes the number was given as twelve and sometimes the number was given as six. The six got entrenched for a long time because in Milan, Italy, there supposedly three relics of the Magi were honored. But in 1164 there was an uprising and the relics were moved to Cologne, Germany. But as time went by, people didn't know that bit of history and so they figured there were three relics in Italy and three in Germany and that equals six Magi.

Finally, however, imagination worked backward and figured that since there were *three gifts* mentioned—gold, frankincense, and myrrh—the three gifts suggested three givers. Thus our Zoroastrian priests of uncertain number have come down to us as the Three Wise Men.

But the impulse of storytelling could never let Matthew's tale rest there, and in fact it took a clue from Matthew himself by reaching back to the Old Testament. There it found a psalm, the very responsorial psalm we used today, Psalm 72, whose refrain says, "The Kings of Arabia will come bearing gifts." This psalm was applied to the Magi and so the three priests of Zoroaster were turned into Three Kings of the East. "We Three Kings of Orient Are" is our musical testimony to this development.

How about their names? In Matthew's version there are no names. Some would speculate that this was done on purpose and was consistent with Matthew's story. Since King Herod was running all over, killing anybody connected with the Christ Child, Matthew didn't want to use the names of the Magi since they and their descendants would thereby be in peril of their lives.

But once more imagination could not abide that lack for long, and so, long after wicked Herod died, names were found. In fact, the names we have today were first found in those fabulous sixth-century mosaics in Ravenna, Italy: Balthazar, Melchior, and Gasper.

Even the gifts took on symbolism. Gold equals the virtue of these travelers. Frankincense, which is like incense going up to heaven, says they were a people of prayer, daily lifting their prayers to God. And myrrh, which is bitter and a kind of mineral, means they were willing to take on the bitterness and sacrifice necessary in their pursuit of the Holy One of Light.

Other stories and legends clustered around these very exotic people. One legend says that when they were over a hundred years old, they met again in A.D. 54 in Armenia to attend Midnight Mass, and then died shortly after. Another says they went to India where they were consecrated bishops by Thomas the Apostle and they died in their dioceses.

Another legend, which is appealing, says that they were of three different ages. Gasper was a very young man. Balthazar was in his middle age, and Melchior was an old man. When they arrived at Bethlehem, the three of them betook themselves into the cave of the Savior's birth, and they went in one at a time. When Melchior, the old man, went into the cave, there was no one there but a very old man his own age with whom he was quickly at home. And they spoke together of memory and of gratitude. The middle-aged Balthazar encountered a middle-aged teacher when he went into the cave and they talked passionately of leadership and responsibility. And when young Gasper entered, he met a young prophet, and they spoke words of reform and promise.

And then when they had all got outside after going in one by one, the three of them took their gifts and went in together. And when they went in together there was nobody there but a twelve-day-old infant. And later on they understood, and so should we: The Savior speaks to every stage of life. The old hear the call to integrity and wisdom. The middle-aged hear the call to generativity and responsibility. And the young hear the call to identity and intimacy.

So, truly the Three Wise Men have caught our imagination, and, when you think about it, noticeably more so than the other group in Matthew's Christmas story. And there is, I think, a powerful reason for that.

That other group is the shepherds. Have you noticed that the shepherds have never really caught our imaginations and that we have few stories about them? The reason is that, in the gospels, the shepherds are told everything. They are encountered by an extremely talkative angel. And this angel tells them every detail: where the Child is to be found, who's there, how to get there. When the shepherds arrive at the cave, the angel appears again to verify the place and when the shepherds return they're guided by a whole heavenly choir of angels singing to them along the way. So these shepherds have no doubts, no questions, no problems, no persecutors, no mystery. They didn't have to seek information. It was handed to them. They had it made.

That's not our experience. The easy-come, easy-go shepherds are not for us. Our experience is more like that of the struggling Magi, for we, like them, are searchers. We have difficulty with the large questions of life. We too are harassed by our modern Herods who seek to destroy our children with consumerism, pornography, materialism, greed, offering them hedonism for heart, sensation for substance, celebrity for character.

And we worry and wonder about family life, AIDS, crime in the streets, illness, cancer, war, recession, terrorism, death. Yes, we too would like heavenly messengers and heavenly assurances such as the shepherds got, but the fact is we experience neither.

No, no doubt about it, it's the Magi, the struggling band crossing a hot desert with only a vision and hope to guide them that resonate with us. They're our kind of people and we'll never tire of telling stories about them. So, we'll stick with them, for the bottom line is this: The Magi didn't have all the answers. Neither do we. They had a wicked King after them. In many ways, so do we. But on their life's travels what they did have was fellowship and the light of Christ to guide them. And so do we.

But the best part of the wondrous Magi story comes at the end. For at last they found what they were looking for. And so shall we.

The Holy Family: Fear of Glory

First Sunday after Christmas, C, Luke 2:41–51

The story of Jesus in the Temple besting the teachers belongs to a long list of ancient stories of kids getting the better of adults. Kids, naturally, love such stories. So Jack outsmarts the giant, a symbol of all adults who, in children's eyes, are giants. Little Red Riding Hood puts one over on the wolf. Little David gets the best of the big man, Goliath.

And here is Jesus, from a small town, with no formal schooling, who didn't get to read the Great Books of the Western World, confounding the university people. All those who do not do well on the SATs, who have no access to power and wealth, should love this story. Still, what's this incident doing here in the Scriptures? Do we need another story of a wise kid putting down adults? In the Bible yet. Doesn't it belong to fairy tales? No. It belongs to grace.

It tells the old God-story that the small, the weak, the vulnerable have God and have glory and should never settle for less. As the boy's mother sang of her own nothingness before he was born, "God has looked upon the lowliness of his handmaid, for he who is mighty has down great things for the likes of me....He has scattered the proud, brought down the powerful and lifted up the lowly...and all generations shall call me blessed."

And that's what I want to talk to you about: about all generations calling you blessed, about calling *yourself* blessed, provided you claim God and claim glory and stop denying it. To get what I'm driving at, let me begin, as I shall end, with reference to the splendid words of Marianne Williamson where she reminds us that our deep-down fear is not that we're inadequate but that, on the contrary, we are powerful. Powerful because we are children of God designated and destined to make manifest his glory. She therefore warns us:

> Your playing small doesn't serve the world.
> There's nothing enlightened about shrinking
> So that other people won't feel insecure around you....

On the contrary, letting our light shine gives permission for others to do the same.

Wise words. And she is right. And she is scriptural. Deep down, we *are* afraid *not* of our inadequacy, but of our glory; *not* of our darkness, but of our light, and so we "play it small." We play it small. What a shame, what a pity. And, someday, what a judgment. But we *do* play it small. To escape our glory, which will make others feel insecure, we embrace what an insecure world forces us to embrace to be accepted.

We wear the same uniform designer clothes, drink the same Starbucks coffee, collect the same accessories, envy *Baywatch* bodies, embrace our careers rather than our children, cut the same corners to get ahead, talk the same talk, value the same commercially induced values and, in the process, lose our identity and, sooner or later, no longer make manifest the glory of God within us. Indeed, we *suppress* our glory, can't even name it any more. The light no longer shines, for we, fearful of our own light, have become a part of the attractive darkness.

The glory, of course, cannot be completely suppressed—after all, we *are* children of God, no matter how we cover it up—and so at times we find ourselves flirting with New Age paraphernalia, watching *Touched by an Angel* and even going to church on Christmas.

But it's no good, is it? It's not enough. Not nearly enough. Something is wrong and Williamson puts her finger on it. We act and live the way we do because it is our light, not our darkness, that frightens us most.

How *dare* we be brilliant, gorgeous, talented, and fabulous, a child of God? How *dare* we be the kid who slays the giant, the little girl who bests the wolf, the backwoods boy who confounds the university teachers in the Temple? How dare we be civil in a vulgar world, chaste in a sex-saturated media, sober in a besotted place, honest in a bottom-line economy, simple in a city that offers us fifty kinds of mustard at the supermarket, sharingly compassionate in a planet of greed?

How *dare* we be bold enough to pull out the mechanical attachments which, plugged into us like so many intravenous tubes, keep us not only incessantly attached to Big Brother marketplace but *detached* from human relationships: the laptop, fax, cell phone, e-mail and beepers, all of which we take home with us like a patient forever strolling the hospital wards with a pole full of IV bags, not realizing that they make us work 160 hours more each year than we did twenty years ago, and spend 160 hours less with the people nearest to us. How *dare* we liberate ourselves from the machines that are supposed to be our servants but which have become our masters. How *dare* we honor vows in a divorce culture, embrace a "good enough" lifestyle in a consumerist society?

How *dare* we feed the hungry, give drink to the thirsty, clothe the naked, visit the sick, comfort the sorrowful, and publicly pray out our aching need for a God of infinite concern, forgiveness, and love.

How *dare* we embrace all these things that make manifest the glory of God within us when the world tells us, *programs* us to believe, that not only do we really have no time for all these godly fundamental ways—after all, our career is a god demanding total allegiance—but who do we think we are trying to play it big that way when everyone else is playing it small?

Do we want to make them feel insecure? We're no kid in the Temple letting his light shine through. We cannot admit that we are brilliant, gorgeous, talented, and fabulous. Were we to do so, would we live the way we are?

Back to the gospel. What do you see there now? A budding adolescent confounding the establishment or, what it is *really* about: an about-to-be young man from poor parents and a backward town who is simply *knowing* who he is: powerful beyond measure and *being* who he is: brilliant, gorgeous, talented, and fabulous? He put it right when he asked, "Did you not know I must be about my Father's business?" The Father's business is relationships, caring, peacemaking, forgiveness, healing, and love. More to the point, do we see ourselves there? Are we about our Father's business, or are our fears exposed, the fear that maybe we *are* children of God, the fear of the glory within us?

This gospel is like that grand old musical, *Man of La Mancha*, the story of the ridiculed Don Quixote who lives with the illusion of being a knight of old, battling windmills that he imagines are dragons. Near the end of the musical, Don Quixote is dying and at his side is Aldonza, a worthless slut he had idealized by calling her "Dulcinea," Sweet One, much to the howling laughter of the townsfolk. But Don Quixote had loved her in a way unlike anything she had ever experienced. When Quixote breaths his last, Aldonza begins to sing the haunting "Impossible Dream." As the last echo of the song dies away, someone shouts to her, "Aldonza!" But she pulls herself up proud and responds, "My name is Dulcinea."

This gospel is like that. It reminds us that although the culture calls us Aldonza and wants us to live as such, God calls us Dulcinea—My Beloved—and asks us to live *that* way. He wants to liberate us from what we fear and remind us who we are and how we must live.

Today's gospel wants us to think about all this. What or who made us forget who we are, urged us to settle for less? Who made us settle for Aldonza? Maybe that should be our New Year's resolution, our theme for a new year: to reclaim our dignity, to recognize our fears, to be about our Father's business by living as who we are: sons and daughters of God who were put here on earth to liberate others from rejection, separation, loneliness, and hurt.

So remember Marianne Williamson's poignant words about our fear of being powerful, powerful with the very light of God; that to play beneath ourselves is not worthy of ourselves or of God. Rather, to be liberated from our fear of our God-given dignity is to challenge others to be who they are: children of God destined to manifest his glory..

The Holy Family:
The Family Album

Picture this. It's Christmas. The family has gathered, exchanged pleasantries, shared a good meal, opened gifts, and then, sooner or later, as everyone knew would happen, Grandma starts the annual ritual. She goes to the dresser, opens the drawer and drags out the family album and sits on the couch. Soon, as required by long custom, everyone surrounds her as she begins to intone the familiar litany of her favorite reminisences. She turns with anticipation to the first page. There they are. Babies, all babies. "Look, there's Joan, there's Alfred and Bobby. And look, there *you* are, such an adorable baby!"

"How cute!" everyone chimes in. And, lingering over the sweet scenes, everyone oohs and aahs over the darling infants.

Then, smiling to herself, Grandma gleefully turns to the next pages. Are you ready for this? These pages couldn't be more of a contrast. But there they are in all of their graphic horror: There's one large blown-up photo and several smaller ones at different angles of a young man sprawled out in an alley, dead, the body all bloodied, hardly recognizable. It's easy to see that he was beat to a pulp. "Ah," says Grandma wistfully, "your brother Stephen. So young to die. Some gang got to him. Look at all that blood. Look at that nasty gash on his forehead." And for a long while the family scrutinizes and studies each terrible detail.

Then she turns to the next pages. It's several pictures of uncle John on a slab. They all strain to get a look, their mouths open. Uncle John had been boiled in oil. "So lifelike," comments Grandma, as they all gaze mesmerized at the pictures. After a while, she turns to the next page and she chortles to herself as they all gasp, as they never fail to do. It's lots of pictures of their little cousins killed in a bus accident two years ago. Grandma finally turns to the last page and there he is again: their sister's husband, Tom, who had had a sordid past, assassinated in the foyer of his own home. Mess everywhere. Blood everywhere. A mob hit. One last look and, satisfied, Grandma closes the album. Her annual ritual is over. Another holiday gathering. Another year looking at the family album.

Now you're wondering. What in the world am I getting at? Is this some kind of a ghoulish joke? This is something from the Addams family, isn't it? Or the Munsters. That's *their* idea of family fun, of "home for Christmas!" Well, you're right to be puzzled, but you know that somewhere I have a point. And the point is this: I wasn't, I confess, talking about the Munster or Addams families, and in fact that weird album really doesn't belong to them. The truth is, I'm afraid, I was setting you up. Fellow Christians, the album belongs to us. Yes, to us, the *Christian* family. And, don't you realize, we do this family album thing every year, every single year. It's an annual ritual.

Let me review it for you. There is, as you know, December 25 when we all gather and delight in the baby, that sweet Christ Child in the manger surrounded by loving parents and shepherds, angels, and exotic Wise Men. So far, so good. So far, so pleasing. So far, so sentimental. But then, without warning, the very next day, December 26, like Grandma dramatically turning the page of the family album, the church shoves into our faces the feast of the first Christian martyr, St. Stephen, who was brutally stoned to death, beaten to a pulp. Blood all over the place.

Then in rapid succession on December 27, the church celebrates the feast of St. John who was thrown into boiling oil for believing in Jesus, and on the day after that, December 28, the church celebrates, if you want to call it that, the slaughter of the Holy Innocents, those tiny harmless babies killed on orders of a deranged King Herod; and finally, on December 29, the church celebrates the martyrdom of Thomas à Becket, one-time womanizer and crook who became archbishop and saint and was assassinated by a mob of soldiers in the foyer of his own cathedral, Canterbury Cathedral, where even today you can see the mark on the floor where he fell.

Not much of an improvement over the Munster or Addams families, you might say, this surrounding of the Christ Child with all that blood, and not much different, this Christian family album, which starts off white and ends up red. But, listen up: Unlike the Munster or Addams families, which are seeking laughs, the church has a serious point when it forces us to look at our family album each year at Christmas week. The point the church has in mind is as simple as it is common: *Embracing the Babe of Bethlehem costs.*

Embrace a spouse and it will cost you. Embrace a friend and it will cost you. Embrace a child and it will cost you. Embrace a country and it will cost you. Embrace a cause and it will cost you. Embrace Jesus Christ and it will cost you. Don't overlinger at the manger on Christmas day, says the church, but move hastily on to the rest of the week to see what the manger implies. Look also at Stephen, John, the Holy Innocents, Thomas.

This week between the celebration of Christmas and the celebration of the feast of the Holy Family, then, is loyalty-test time. Are we part of the Holy Family? Have we earned membership? Have we moved beyond the sentimentality of Christmas? How much blood have we shed for Christ? Oh, I don't mean physically, although, Lord knows, in the Sudan, in China, in Africa and other parts of the world, people are still being tortured and killed simply for being Christian, but I mean spiritually. How much has being a Christian cost us? A little? A great deal? Nothing? Can people tell from our wounds that we are Christian? Our speech, our honesty, our decisions? The church's Christmas card is not framed in red for nothing.

In his book *Living Faith* former President Jimmy Carter provides a simple test that tells us whether we might be included in the family album. He tells about a group of Christian laymen involved in missionary work who approached a small village near an Amish settlement. Seeking a possible convert, they confronted an Amish farmer and asked him, "Brother, are you a Christian?" The farmer thought for a moment and then said, "Wait just a few minutes." He wrote down a list of names on a tablet and handed it to the missionary. "Here is a list of people who know me best. Please ask them if I am a Christian." Are we ready to make our list?

It's the feast of the Holy Family. Open up the family liturgical album. It's just not sweet Jesus, Mary, and Joseph there. It's the whole bloody clan: Stephen, John, the Holy Innocents, Thomas, and all those who, like ourselves, carry the same family name. They let it mean something to them. So should we.

Lent: The Scandal of the Cross

I have a favor to ask you this morning. I want you to use your imagination. And here's what I want you to imagine. Imagine that you have you have met new neighbors who just moved in next door. They seem like very nice people, and after you have gotten to know them for a while, they invite you to worship with them on Sunday. You have never heard of their religion, something entirely new and different. And yet, on the other hand, you feel somewhat honored that they want to share their faith. And so, perhaps as much out of curiosity as out of your newfound friendship, you go to their place of worship.

Well, imagine your surprise, your horrifying surprise, when, the very first thing that you see as you enter the front door and look up into the sanctuary, is not, for example, an altar. In fact, what you see shocks you, utterly shocks you. The whole sanctuary is bare. There is nothing in it except, placed dead center, an electric chair! My God, you feel like turning right around and running for your life. At the very least, you feel like excusing yourself, wondering what in the world you've gotten into. What kind of strange cult is this to have such a bizarre thing in their place of worship? What kind of people are these? And yet, on the other hand, for some reason, you hesitate. You hesitate between disgust and interest, between fear and curiosity. You find yourself torn because these people and everyone else don't seem weird.

In fact, as you look around, they seem to be rather nice; more than nice, they seem to be rather loving people, and it is obvious from the others who have gathered with them, that they show a great deal of love and concern for one another, and they're bringing, obviously, some kind of a spirit of worship to this day And so you're torn, but you finally decide to stay. And your host picks up something from the pew and hands you a small pamphlet. And in it they explain the group's belief. In the pamphlet you read that at the center of their faith and worship is a man who was strapped to and electrocuted in the electric chair through the machinations of a political and social system that saw this man as a threat to their lives of privilege and of power.

But subsequently these followers have somehow discovered that when they gather together, this man is present in spirit, pouring out his love and his grace into their lives. It begins to slowly dawn on you that to them the electric chair, a horrifying symbol of the state's power over life and death, a symbol of disgrace and condemnation and fear, has been inverted for these people and transformed into something entirely different from its common and accepted meaning. It's quite a shock, quite a reversal: to make an electric chair a point of veneration and inspiration. You're baffled. You're in a state of wonder and disbelief that something so monstrous could represent for your newfound friends the very power and the very wisdom of God for them.

It strikes you as bazaar, as nonsense and folly. You begin to reason to yourself about it and you try to figure it out in terms of society's accepted signs of power, the usual tokens of value and meaning that you see every day on television. Instead of the lifestyles of the rich and famous on TV, instead of yachts and villas and mountains and perks and private jets, instead of sleek automobiles and perfectly toned bodies, instead of these…the electric chair is the center of life's meaning? You find yourself baffled by the symbol. It's beyond all explanation.

And now I want to tell you that in that moment of perplexity and in the unnerving experience of the shock of walking into a church and seeing an electric chair center stage, you have instantly put yourself back into the experience of those incredulous people of the first century when they walked into a gathering of people called Christians, whose center of attention was the "electric chair" of the time: the cross. Visitors then would be shocked to see that the cross—the hated, disgraceful, shameful, and feared symbol of death—would be cherished, would be the means of revelation, redemption, and inspiration for these people on how they are to live.

We've gotten so used to the symbol of the cross—truly, familiarity breeds contempt—that we take it for granted. We decorate it, encrust it with diamonds and make a bauble out of it, another rock-concert artifact like a nose ring or earring. We have lost the ability to sense its shock value and what it cost Jesus to die on it, and the demands the cross makes for those who embrace it as their symbol. Look, there it is, above the altar, in the window in front of the purple cloth and we don't even notice it. It's on top of your church tower and over the side door, and we don't realize any more what a gross object it is.

Think of coming in here today and seeing instead an electric chair up there and on the tower and over the side door and then you'll get a sense of what the first Christians were dealing with; a sense of shock and scandal that the cross is a sign that suggests powerfully that the world's got it all backward. God is not coming to us through MTV and shiny cars; rather, God comes to us in the most outlandish and the most scandalizing way and behavior. He comes in sacrifice and self-giving and total love. Innocent and able to duck it, he nevertheless accepts his society's "electric chair," the cross, to show us how low he will sink for us, how high he will be raised for us, how far he will go for us, and where he expects us to follow. He offers us a sign of contradiction.

The world has its own symbols:

> Blessed are the rich in spirit.
> Blessed are the financially secure.
> Blessed are those who rejoice.
> Blessed are those who are proud.
> Blessed are the clever, the tricky.
> Blessed, especially are the celebrities.
> Blessed are Donald Trump, Hugh Hefner, Princess Di, and
> Monica Lewinsky.

The cross gives the opposite message:

> Blessed are the poor in spirit; they'll see God.
> Blessed are those who sorrow when they see the swollen bodies
> in Somalia and brother and sister killing each other in
> Bosnia.

Blessed are the homeless and the lowly.

Blessed are those who have a deep thirst for justice and are not
    content to live with the way things are.

Blessed are those who do not pick up guns and kill,
    but who show mercy.

Blessed are those who do not return hurt and an eye for an eye,
    but are peacemakers.

Blessed are the chaste, the faithful, the honest,
    those who keep their word.

And blessed are those who are willing to put themselves on the line and suffer persecution and ridicule and the name-calling in order to embrace this way of life, the worst name probably being, "You belong to that weird group that has in its church a cross."

That's what the cross means. And if we really don't want to accept it or want to get around it, we neutralize it and trivialize it and make it mere decoration and go about our business.

But during these latter days of Lent, I suggest that we might ponder anew what we take so lightly; that we renew our sense of scandal and outrage that the center of our religion is a shameful cross. Once more we have to come to terms with the reality that the cross is not a pendant, not a decoration. It's the sign of a radical way of living that demands decisions and when we sign that cross on our bodies we declare to the world our radical stance, that we are willing to die to self, are willing to be countercultural.

King Henry VIII in Robert Bolt's play *A Man for All Seasons* is trying to persuade his chancellor, Thomas More, to agree with his decision to divorce his wife and marry Anne Boleyn. He says: "You must consider, Thomas, that I stand in peril of my soul. It was no marriage; she was my brother's widow...."

More responds, "Your Grace, I'm not fit to meddle in these matters; to me it seems a matter for the Holy See...."

Henry interrupts: "Thomas, Thomas, does a man need a pope to tell him when he's sinned? It was a sin, Thomas; I admit it. I repent. And God has punished me; I have no son....Son after son she's borne me, Thomas, all dead at birth, or dead within the month; I never saw the hand of God so clear in anything.…I have a daughter, she's my good child—a well-set child—but I have no son. It is my bounden duty to put away the Queen, and all the popes back to St. Peter shall not come between me and my duty!"

Then he adds these powerful words, "How is it that you cannot see? Everyone else does."

More answers quietly, "Why, then, does Your Grace need my poor support?"

And here comes Henry's answer and, in effect, the challenge to Thomas More as to whether he will take up the cross or not. Henry says, "Because you are honest. What's more to the purpose, you're known to be honest.… Look, there are those like Norfolk who follow me because I wear the crown, and there are those like Master Cromwell who follow me because they are jackals with sharp teeth and I am their lion, and there is a mass that follows me because it follows anything that moves—and then there is you."

The cross looms up for More. He can reject the cross and live in fame and riches the rest of his life, or he can defy the king and face certain death. He embraces the cross. That's what the cross means: "And then there is you. You're one of those weird people whose leader died on a cross." Do people say that about us? Thomas More lived in the sixteenth century. Let me bring you closer to home. Most of you do not know the name of Nichelle Nichols. But you'll know her when I tell you that she played Uhura in that wonderful original *Star Trek* TV program and she was in six *Star Trek* movies.

What is significant about her was that she was one of the first black woman regularly featured on a weekly TV show. As such, she had some obstacles to overcome. A few studio executives, for example, were hostile toward her character, which was often diminished by script rewrites, and the studio even withheld tons of her fan mail. With that sort of thing going on after one year on the program, she was fed up. Nichols, who was also an extremely talented professional singer and dancer, told Gene Roddenberry she was going to quit and pursue her performing career.

Before she did, however, she happened to go to a fundraiser for the NAACP. There she happened to meet Dr. Martin Luther King, who urged her not to leave the show because she was a role model for many. Says Nichols, "When you have a man like Dr. Martin Luther King say you can't leave a show, it's daunting." She was in effect offered the cross. She continues, "It humbled my heart, and I couldn't leave. God had charged me with something more important than my own career."

The rest, as they say, is history. Not only did she become a fixture on *Star Trek*, she actually influenced NASA, challenging them to hire blacks and women for their astronaut corps. By embracing the cross in giving up her plans to sing and dance—a stupid, scandalous thing to do according to worldly wisdom—Nichols found the defining role of her career, Uhura, in one of the most popular TV shows ever, and influenced a nation.

Like the electric chair, the cross is scandalous. Jesus died on it and we are asked to embrace it. So look at it for what it is and don't sanitize it and realize how bizarre you and I are to center our lives around it. And yet it is precisely that terrible, shameful symbol that is offered us by our Master: "Unless you take up your cross daily and follow me, you are not worthy of me."

The cross is not a pendant. It is not a decoration. It is not pretty. It is a challenge—for More, for Nichols, for you, and for me. It's a risky thing to sign yourself: In the name of the Father, and of the Son, and of the Holy Spirit. Amen.

Lent: Lent Blesses

"All the families of the earth shall find a blessing in you."

That quotation is from the book of Genesis. The full quotation, spoken to Abraham is, "I will make of you a great nation and I will bless you. I will make your name great so that you will be a blessing…all the families of the earth shall find blessing in you." Blessing. Abraham, even though others might never have heard of him, was to be a blessing to others. In him others, whether they realized it or not, would find their lives blessed.

What a nice program for the followers of Jesus. What a good motto or life-theme. What a resolution for Lent. What a core conviction to carry within oneself and to try to live by: to be a blessing to others. This is my calling, my destiny. Me, little me, insignificant me: My vocation through baptism is to be a blessing to others, to bless others. And, in turn, I am to be gratefully conscious that others have blessed me, are blessing me every day of my life, even though I am not aware of it. I must remember to show gratitude.

Let me give you a concrete example of a hidden blessing. I don't know if you know the story of Charles Plumb. He was a U.S. Navy jet pilot in Vietnam. After seventy-five combat missions, his plane was destroyed by a surface-to-air missile. Plumb ejected and parachuted into enemy hands. He was captured and spent six years in a Communist Vietnamese prison. He survived the ordeal and now he spends his time lecturing on the lessons he has learned from that experience. He didn't know it, but he was about to learn and preach another lesson. It happened this way.

One day, when Plumb and his wife were sitting in a restaurant, a man at another table came up and said excitedly, "You're Plumb! You flew jet fighters in Vietnam from the aircraft carrier Kitty Hawk. You were shot down!"

"How in the world did you know that?" asked the amazed Plumb.

The man replied, "I packed your parachute."

Plumb gasped in surprise and gratitude. While he was speechless, the man pumped his hand and said, "Well, guess it worked!"

Plumb regained his composure and assured him, "It sure did. If your chute hadn't worked, I wouldn't be here today." And they parted.

End of coincidence, end of story? Not quite. You see, Plumb couldn't sleep that night. He kept thinking about that man. Plumb says, "I kept wondering what he might have looked like back then in a Navy uniform: a white hat, a bib in the back, and bell-bottom trousers. I wonder how many times I might have seen him and not even said 'Good morning. How are you?' or anything because, you see, I was a fighter pilot and he was just a sailor." Plumb then began to think of the many hours that ordinary sailor had spent on a long wooden table in the bowels of the ship, carefully weaving the shrouds and folding the silks of each chute, holding in his hands each time the fate of someone he didn't know.

So Plumb, having thought long and hard about this meeting, now asks his audience when he lectures, "Who's packing your parachute?" His point is that everyone has someone who has packed their parachutes, who has blessed them, who has provided what they need to make it through the day. Plumb points out that in fact he needed many kinds of parachutes when his plane was shot down over enemy territory. He needed his physical parachute, his mental parachute, his emotional parachute, and his spiritual parachute. He called on all these supports before reaching safety. And somebody had put them there, had richly blessed him. And he was grateful and determined to pass on that blessing.

A story with a point: Who blessed you this week? Think. Who made your lunch, did your laundry, fixed your car, cleaned your streets, picked up your garbage, took your pulse, opened your door, waited on your table, brought your mail? Who blessed you today, yesterday? Who packed your parachute?

Then, of course, the lenten question: Whose parachute did we pack? Or should have? Whom did we bless this week, or fail to bless? Sometimes, in the daily challenges that life gives us, we miss what is really important. We may fail to say hello, please, or thank you, congratulate someone on something wonderful that has happened to them, give a compliment, or just do something nice for no reason.

Remember, like Abraham, blessing is our calling. Of us it was also predicted, "All the families on earth shall find a blessing in you." Lent is the time to recall how we are blessed and how we bless others, and, if there is a failure to bless, to repent, to confess, to promise to do better. But most of all, Lent is simply a time to recall our awesome Abrahamic vocation. We are here on earth to be a blessing to others. It's a deep calling.

And at judgment time, as Jesus describes it, it will be wonderfully nice when he asks the standard question about blessing, "And whose parachute did you pack?" to be able to list a whole bunch of folks. Jesus, of course, will use other words even though they mean the same thing. He will say, "When I was hungry, you gave me to eat; when I was thirsty, you gave me to drink, when I was sick, you visited me...." Same thing, same thought.

The moral for Lent? Start packing parachutes. Start blessing those who packed yours.

Lent:
The Weeping Christ

LUKE 13:1–9

Once more we find ourselves, in the course of our Christian pilgrimage, almost midway through Lent, that time of our communal forty-day journey of special intensity. And sometimes—in fact, most times, I suggest—it helps us to have a rallying theme, a particular kind of focus, an inspiration, to get us through these days with encouragement and determination; that is to say, it helps us to have an overriding image that moves with us and compels us forward, an image that suggests both the journey and its goal. For some who saw Mel Gibson's *The Passion of the Christ,* a powerful image to carry with you through Lent might be the suffering Jesus. Hold on to that if you wish. But I would like to offer you another image. So allow me to explore with you two items that might lead you to the image I suggest. The first item is a poem and the other a story. First, the poem.

It was written in England and it carries a reference to the industrial city of Birmingham, which is something akin to our Pittsburgh or any large American city. It goes like this:

> When Jesus came to Golgotha,
> They hanged him on a tree.
> They drove great nails through hands and feet,
> And made a Calvary.
> They crowned him with a crown of thorns,
> Red were his wounds and deep:
> For those were crude and cruel days,
> And human flesh was cheap.

When Jesus came to Birmingham
They simply passed him by.
They never hurt a hair of him,
They only let him die.
For men had grown more tender,
And they would not give him pain;
They only just passed down the street
And left him in the rain.
Still, Jesus cried, "Forgive them,
For they know not what they do."
And still it rained a winter rain
That drenched him through and through.
The crowds went home and left the streets,
Without a soul to see.
And Jesus crouched against the wall
And cried for Calvary.

Of course, the point of the poem is that the indifference of the people was worse than their active hostility when they nailed him to the cross. And so Jesus wept as we would—and do—when people are indifferent to us, treat us as a sideline, see right past us, ignore us as if we didn't exist or count. Indifference is a particular kind of pain and Jesus feels it every day and weeps every day. Keep that Weeping Jesus in mind as I move to the story.

It comes from a writer named Walter Wangerin who tells of his little son, Matthew, a whirlwind of lad, willful and determined. When Matthew decided to do something he just dashed headlong in and did what he wanted to do without too much thinking of the consequences.

So one day, Walter relates, he went into his son's room and found him sitting on the bed with a whole stack of comic books around him. He said to Matthew, "Where did you get the comic books?"

Matthew said, "I took them out of the library."

"You took them out of the library?"

"Yes."

"You mean you *stole* them from the library."

"Yes."

So the father called the librarian and said that he was going to march his son, Matthew, right down with the comic books and apologize and restore what he had stolen. He did precisely that and the librarian gave little Matthew a stern lecture about stealing.

Well, the following summer they vacationed at a small community in Vermont where there was a general store. When they returned home after the summer, at the beginning of the fall, the father went into Matthew's room and he found a pile of comic books in his dresser drawer. And Matthew said, "I stole them from the store this summer." So the father took the comic books and he went into the den and he started a fire in the fireplace and he threw the comic books into the flames, and with each comic book that he threw into the flames, he reminded little Matthew of the seventh commandment, "Thou shall not steal."

A year later, Matthew again stole some comic books, and this time his father told him that he was going to have to spank him. He sent him into the study and put him over his knee, and spanked him five times with his bare hand. Why five times? Because he felt that if he did any less he would be too soft, and if he was really angry he might do too many, so he limited himself to five. He spanked Matthew and he sat him down, and he could see his son's head hanging; and it was obvious that Matthew did not want to shed a tear in front of his father.

And the father understood that. And so not wanting to see little Matthew cry, he said, "Matthew, I'm going to leave you alone for a while, but I'll be back in a few minutes." And after he stepped out of the room and closed the door behind him, the father himself began to cry and began to cry really hard. And he went into the bathroom and washed his face and went back into the study and talked to his little son, Matthew.

Years later when Matthew was an older teenager and he and his mother were driving back from a shopping trip, as often happens, they were reminiscing. And the reminiscence happened to come around to those early days when Matthew was a rascal stealing comic books. And Matthew said to his mother, "You know, after that incident with Dad, I really never stole anything again."

And his mother made the comment, "I suppose that the reason was because your father spanked you."

"Oh, no," replied Matthew, "it was because when he stepped out of the room I could hear him crying."

That poem and this story, I suggest, might provide us with a deep image, a personal focus as we continue to move though Lent. The image I propose is simply Jesus Weeping.

In the gospels, you recall, Jesus overlooked the city of Jerusalem and wept. "Oh, Jerusalem, Jerusalem," he cried, "how often I would have gathered you as a mother hen gathers her chicks, but you would not." He wept too over his friend Lazarus, over his death, over what death did to his sisters and neighbors and that entire village. On the night before he died he said, "I no longer call your servants but friends" and when one of those friends betrayed him, it's not hard to sense not only the pained voice but the tears in his eyes as he said, "Judas, do you betray the Son of Man with a kiss?" The friendship kiss at that.

This weeping of Jesus stayed with the Christian community. Peter cried his tears basically because he could not stand Jesus'. The image got translated into popular piety recognized anywhere from the Dürer woodcuts where the thorn-crowned and sobbing Christ is sitting holding his head in his hands, to the First Friday devotions which told of the visions of St. Margaret Mary Alacoque who saw Jesus with his wounded heart complaining, "Behold the heart which has loved people so much and has received so little love in return." And he wept.

So I suggest that this image of the Weeping Christ might be ours for the rest of this lenten journey.

It will help remind us that what we do for Lent, what we surrender, is not for its own sake or for our own self-improvement. What we do: the good deeds done, the prayers said, the sacrifices given—all have as their goal a deep and personal relationship with Jesus Christ. To know him with a burning desire, to love him with a burning passion. And that's why an image of Jesus is important. It places him at the center, and at the center as friend and lover. And the phenomenon of weeping tells us that Jesus is someone with feelings, someone who cares enough to be pained by what his friends do; who is highly susceptible, because of his love for us, to our betrayals that quite reduce him to tears.

For he weeps over our version of stealing comic books; he doesn't like what it is making us become and the hurt we are giving others. Like Walter, he cries not from hatred of his son, but from love. So the Weeping Christ becomes our mantra, if you will, our mental image to take along on the remaining days of Lent. If we contemplate the Weeping Christ long enough we will turn from our sins. It won't be because we fear the spanking. It will be because we can hear Jesus crying.

Lent: The Prodigal Son's Brother

The youngster was assigned in his high school to read a Shakespeare play. To his immense surprise he discovered that he actually *liked* it except, he complained, " it was full of trite sayings." Indeed it is, like "every dog has its day," and so on. Of course the lad missed the point: Shakespeare is the originator, not the one who made them trite.

We have the same problem with today's parable. It has become trite because we have heard it so much and its phrases have fallen into common lore such as "the prodigal son" or "the fatted calf." Still, there are always riches here to be explored and so today I want to take you to a different vantage point. I want to talk about the three sinners in the story, but especially about the sinner who got a bum rap. That's the elder son. He justifiably complained, "Look, all these years I served you and not once did I disobey your orders; yet you never gave me even a young goat to feast on with my friends," and the Father admitted, "Yes, son, you *are* here with me always; everything I have is yours." But that wasn't enough.

Let's hear it for the elder son. He's steady and obedient and faithful and has served well. He's there when you need him. He works hard behind the scenes. You don't have to follow after him or remind him. He's dependable. He's a rock. He's loyal. He's the kind of son parents dream of. And all this means that his wonderfully forgiving father is not without sin and has something to answer for. And that something is that he *has* obviously taken the elder son for granted. When was the last time he praised him, told him how much he meant to him, that things around here would be in a pretty sorry mess without him, that he is grateful. More, that he's proud of him. Even more, that he loves him and thanks God every day for him. Never.

So we can resonate with that elder son and our sympathies are with him. And he is legion. He is the housewife or mother who keeps the family together emotionally and physically and is utterly taken for granted, like an unpaid servant. He is the father who works hard to raise his family, putting in long hours, sacrificing his own wants and pleasures so his kids can go to a good school. And he is taken for granted. He is the loyal worker who is there every day, takes no phony sick leaves, gives more than his or her time and energy, over and above what is required, and is taken for granted. He is the teacher who stays long after the bell, the crossing guard in the freezing weather, the little league coach rushing home from work, the mailman who comes through the snow, the nurse on the midnight shift, the garbage man who simply comes and does his job, the friend you can count on, borrow from, and walk in on—all taken for granted.

And, then, let someone else do one little thing out of the ordinary or let someone who is self-centered, manipulative, or uncaring do a good deed almost by accident or do something decent for the first time in his life or fall into some good luck and the whole world throws a party for him. And the elder sons and daughters of this world look on and shake their heads. It's not fair.

So, you see, there is sin all around in this parable. The sin of the younger son who insulted and fled and hurt his father deeply, the sin of the father who graciously forgave this son but forgot to hug his other son and tell him what a right arm he was. And the decent elder son: What was his sin? His sin is one that plagues good people. It's the sin of the constricted heart, the ungenerous spirit.

Mary was upset with herself. Her sister was moving home. She should, after all, be happy, as happy as her mother was. But she wasn't. It just didn't make any sense. Since her father had died three years ago, Mary had taken care of her mother all by herself. She did everything for her mother. She talked to her on the telephone twice a day. She had her over for dinner two or three times a week. She bought her groceries, made her appointments and saw to it that she got to them, cleaned her apartment, and even handled her finances. Now that her sister was coming home, she wouldn't have to do everything by herself. She should be happy that she was going to have help. But she wasn't. What was wrong with her?

What was wrong with her is understandable. Now she has to share. She is no longer the limelight. Mary can no longer have her mom so exclusively, and besides, she, *not her sister,* has been there all the time like the elder son, day in and day out caring for mom and being a real support. And now this younger sister is returning home and displacing her and people will forget all she did. And, worst of all, her mother will probably throw a homecoming party for her.

You see, like Mary in our story, so often our identity is threatened. Our place in the sun. Our hope for appreciation evaporates as our steady, faithful deeds are forgotten. Our dedication is taken for granted as another moves in. It's a deep and irradicable sense that we all have, that if someone else goes up on the seesaw of life, we go down, and down there no one thanks us. And we feel a twinge of resentment, of hurt even, as we try to smile.

But, as we travel the spiritual path, we must resist this contraction of heart because sooner or later, if we don't, we will become like the elder brother who so let it get to him that, as noble as he was, he would not even come into the ancestral home, a grave insult in that culture. He could not even bring himself to call his sibling "brother"; he used the oblique phrase, *"your* son." Worst of all, he could not really be pleased that something truly wonderful had happened: the momentous gift of grace his brother received and the generous outpouring of his father, that a sinner was redeemed.

Well, the truth is, none of us elder brothers and sisters ever really outgrows that constricting "if-another-goes-up-I-must-go-down" syndrome, but we can go a long way toward peace and a truly generous spirit if during Lent we remember that God is in charge, that God sees what we do, that God is pleased with us, that God never takes us for granted. Rather, God invites us to laugh and rejoice wherever beauty, truth, and goodness reveal themselves—even in arrogant prodigal sons—because that is what makes us like most like the One who sends rain on the just and the unjust alike.

Lent: Mark Becomes a Christian

RCIA

During these forty days of Lent, as you know, the RCIA candidates—that is, those in the Rite of Christian Initiation of Adults—are going through several steps in a process that will culminate with their baptisms on Holy Saturday night. This process of initiation is a very ancient one, based on the catechumenate of the early centuries of Christianity. The catechumenate was a long training period that included instruction, prayer, fasting, and conversion, as well as learning how to live as a Christian. It was a spiritual internship.

Here is how it worked back then. Someone from the Christian community would sponsor a candidate and give the name of this candidate to the bishop. The sponsor testified to the candidate's honesty and worthiness. Bishops had to be careful in those days, lest they unwittingly took in a Roman spy who would eventually turn in all the Christians of the area. Over the years that followed, the sponsor worked, prayed, and fasted along with the candidate until the candidate made a final decision to become a Christian. This process could last for many years. To catch something of the spirit of this preparation, right through to the completion of the Christian initiation rites, let us follow an imaginary candidate through the steps. We'll call him Mark.

Mark is twenty-six years old now. For a long time, he has been distressed at the empty paganism in which he was brought up. Like many a young man of our own times, Mark has been searching for meaning in his life. Well, three years ago he heard about the new Christian religion. Carefully, he has ascertained a person to whom he could speak. With much caution, he found a sponsor to instruct, guide, and pray with him.

And so, for the last three years, Mark has met with the Christian community. First, he has undertaken a serious routine of prayer, scrutinies, and exorcisms. At the same time, he has been investigating the Christian community itself. Does he want to be like these people? Are they living what they profess? (It is worth remembering that the RCIA candidates today are doing the same with us, that is, putting us under investigation to see if it's worthwhile to become Catholic.)

Now Mark has arrived at the beginning of Lent. He has to decide whether he will become a Christian, whether or not to hand in his name and request baptism. After much prayer, he decides to do just that. Mark is now ready for forty days of intensive learning. He will be allowed to come to the first part of Mass to hear the Scripture readings, after which he will be dismissed for prayer, meditation, and fasting almost daily during Lent. He and the other candidates are led before the bishop, who questions them as to the sincerity of their motives and the worthiness of their characters. This questioning is called the "scrutinies."

The bishop also asks the candidate's neighbors, "Does this man live a good life? Does he respect his parents? Is he a drunkard or untrustworthy?" Once the bishop finds that the candidate is free from all the faults about which he has questioned the witnesses, he writes down the candidate's name. As he watches the bishop write his name, Mark's heart jumps. Why? Because he knows full well that in these times of persecution, should this book be found, it would be his death warrant. To have one's name written down in the baptismal register is a most serious commitment. It means risking one's life. (Being a Christian back then was no small matter.)

The exorcisms follow the scrutinies. To the ancients, the spirit of evil was no abstraction. Evil existed then as it does now, in the form of hatred and war and famine and injustice and corruption. But exorcism then did not imply devil possession. Rather, it implied that the candidates were in the bondage of sin. Exorcism was meant to help the candidates break away from sinfulness, to dramatize their determination to "put on Christ."

At last, Holy Week, the time for the culmination of all this preparation, the great week, arrives. The candidates will actually be baptized on Saturday night, the Easter Vigil. The joyful tension is mounting.

On Holy Thursday, as he has been instructed, Mark takes a bath, not an ordinary bath, but one done consciously as a sign of ritual purification. Then, on Good Friday and Holy Saturday, Mark fasts and prays. At about ten o'clock on Holy Saturday night, Mark goes to a preappointed place. There, along with about seventy-five other young boys and men (the women are meeting elsewhere), he is brought into a large room. The sponsors are there, along with the bishop. The room is darkened and the ceremony begins.

As a body, the seventy-five men rise and face west. (Mark's teacher has told him that the west is the symbol of darkness and therefore, the abode of Satan, the place of evil.) Then one of the deacons shouts, "Stretch out your hands!" As the men stretch out their hands in the dark they try to feel the evil spirits and ward them off. They then expel their breath in an effort to blow the spirits away. On cue, all the candidates speak firmly out loud with one voice: "I detach myself from you, Satan, from your pomp, your worship, and your angels." There is a collective sigh of relief at that bold declaration. Mark feels it, and knows there will be no more pagan games, pagan idols, or pagan devil worship in his life.

The group suddenly makes an about-face. They turn noisily to the east and say, with even more firmness and volume, "And I attach myself to you, O Christ!" Their faces are brighter now, for they all know that the east is a sign of life and therefore a sign of Christ. It was in the east that the Garden of Eden had been planted, the place of original innocence to which they all aspire. As it rises in the east, the sun brings newness, life, and brightness, the very things that are the fruits of baptism. They all know the Scripture, "As the lightening appears from the east, so shall the Son of man appear." Turning away from the west (Satan) and toward the east (Christ) is a dramatic way of spelling out conversion, a word which means "a turning around."

Having thus turned from west to east, from darkness to light, and professed their faith, the men now stand with hands at their sides. Mark watches the bishop approach him and the others. He anoints Mark on the head with oil. This is the seal, the *sphragis*. This is the mark of Christ, his brand. After all, shepherds put their mark on their animals and owners on their slaves. Why should it not be so for Christ?

The group now moves further into a pre-chamber to the baptistry. Here they strip off all their clothing to symbolize the words of Paul: You have stripped off the old self with its practices." This is also a sign of returning to the primitive innocence of Adam and Eve, who went naked and felt no shame before sin entered into the world. Taking off one's clothes is a decisive gesture that means putting off vanity, frivolous ornaments, luxury, bad habits, in a word, anything that is incompatible with new life as a Christian. After the baptism, the candidates will be clothed with linen robes, a sign of new life.

Deacons now approach Mark and begin to anoint him once more with oil, this time from the top of his head to his toes. Oil is a preservative, and this anointing is a sign of preservation from sin. Rubbing the body with oil is common among the Greek athletes, especially wrestlers. Because these new Christians will have to wrestle with the power of evil, they too are rubbed all over and made, in Paul's words, "athletes for Christ."

After this anointing, Mark and the other candidates are led to the baptistry itself. While he awaits his turn, Mark notices how the shape of the pool is like a tomb or even a womb, a sign of rebirth in water and the Spirit. He recalls Jesus' words: "Unless a man is born again of water and the Spirit he cannot be saved." There is a brief blessing of the pool by the bishop. Now the baptism is at hand.

Just before midnight, so it will be finished by the first moments of Easter Sunday, the baptism begins. Mark steps into the water, which comes up to his chest. The bishop kneels by the side of the pool and puts his hand on Mark's head. He applies a little pressure. Taking his cue, Mark ducks under the water and comes up. The bishop asks, "Do you believe in the Father?" Mark answers yes, and is ducked into the pool. "Do you believe in the Son?" "Do you believe in the Holy Spirit?" Mark answers yes to these questions, too. And so the bishop says, "Mark is baptized in the name of the Father, and of the Son, and of the Holy Spirit."

Mark comes out of the pool. It is now Easter. He is dried off and then anointed with *myron,* a special perfumed oil, on his five senses. This anointing is given with the prayer that Mark receive the Holy Spirit. The very name "Christ" is Greek for "anointed one," and so in this last anointing Mark is reminded that he has received the Spirit of Jesus. Now Mark is clothed in a white linen robe that denotes the risen Christ, purity of life, and the forgiveness of sin. This robe will be worn for a full week until Low Sunday.

Mark is handed a lighted candle and given a kiss of peace. On this Easter Sunday morn, like the risen Lord, Mark is now radiant with his new life of faith. With the others, Mark is led to the awaiting assembly—the same people who had so impressed him with their style of living—to be greeted by them and partake, for the first time, of the Eucharist with them. And this is the completion of Mark's initiation into the Christian religion.

So that's the way it was back in the second century. And this is still the way it is today for hundreds of thousands of converts throughout the world who are preparing to be received into the church through the RCIA process. We cradle Catholics take all this for granted, but by following the story of Mark through the process of initiation into the church, I hope you get a renewed sense of what means to be a Christian. Contemplate what it costs, what it promises, most of all, the importance of your role as witnesses to Jesus Christ.

Easter: Easter Hilarity

A few years ago, I began an Easter homily like this:

The cruise ship docked at a Mexican port during a very high tide. Everyone on board was forced to use the ship's narrow gangplank to the dock far below. The staff stood motionless when a passenger in her eighties appeared at the top of the plank. There wasn't room enough for anyone to assist her, so she edged along slowly and finally made it to the dock safely, to everyone's relief.

As she stepped down, she turned, looked back at the top of the plank and shouted, "It's okay, Mother, you can come down now!"

Then there was Rube Goldberg who tells about the time he traveled to Europe on an ocean liner. He was assigned to a table with another single passenger. His companion was a Frenchman who spoke no English. Goldberg spoke no French.

Each night the Frenchman would be the last to arrive for dinner and he would come to the table, click his heels, bow and say, *"Bon appetit."* Goldberg says, "I would get up and reply, 'Goldberg' and shake his hand and sit down."

This routine went on for three or four nights. Then one day Goldberg happened to mention this to an acquaintance. "You know, it's the strangest thing. I'm sitting with a Frenchman in the dining room and at each meal he tells me his name's 'Bon Appetit' and I have to tell him who I am."

"No, no," said the other man, "that's not his name. That's a French phrase for good appetite."

"Oh," said Goldberg, "I feel so stupid. Well, I'm going to have to correct that."

That night, Goldberg came to the table late and the Frenchman was already seated. Goldberg bowed, clicked his heels, and said, *"Bon appetit."*

514

The Frenchmen stood up and said, "Goldberg."

Then there was a shepherd who was herding his flock in a remote pasture when suddenly a brand-new BMW advanced out of the dust cloud toward him. The driver, a young man in a Broni suit, Gucci shoes, Ray Ban sunglasses, and YSL tie leaned out the window and asked the shepherd, "If I tell you exactly how many sheep you have in your flock, will you give me one?"

The shepherd looked at the man, obviously a yuppie, then looked at his peacefully grazing flock and calmly answered, "Sure."

The yuppie parked his car, whipped out his notebook and connected it to a cell phone, then he surfed to a NASA page on the Internet where he called up a GPS satellite navigation system, scanned the area, and then opened up a database and an Excel spreadsheet with complex formulas. He sent an email on his Blackberry and, after a few minutes, received a response. Finally, he prints out a 150-page report on his hi-tech, miniaturized printer, then turns to the shepherd and says, "You have exactly 1586 sheep."

"That is correct; take one of the sheep," said the shepherd. He watches the young man select one of the animals and bundle it into his car. Then the shepherd says, "If I can tell you exactly what your business is, will you give me back my animal?"

"OK, why not?" answered the young man.

"Clearly, you are a consultant," said the shepherd.

"That's correct," says the yuppie, "but how did you guess that?"

"No guessing required," answers the shepherd. "You turned up here although nobody called you. You want to get paid for an answer I already knew, to a question I never asked, and you don't know diddly about my business. Now give me back my dog."

Finally, there's the Irish comedian who says his mother in-law is so backward that she thinks that Manual Labor is the name of the Spanish Ambassador.

What was I doing telling jokes on Easter Sunday? I was borrowing from the ancient Russian Orthodox tradition when the day after Easter was devoted to sitting around the table and telling jokes. Even in church they told them. And why? Well, this was the way, they felt, that they were imitating that cosmic joke that God pulled on Satan in the resurrection.

You see, witnessing Calvary which he had engineered, Satan thought he had won and was smug in his victory, smiling to himself for having had the last word: death. So he thought. Then God raised up Jesus from the dead, and life and salvation became the last words. And the whole world laughed at the devil's come-uppance and discomfort.

And this attitude passed into the medieval concept of *hilaritas*, which did not mean mindless giggling, but rather that, even at the moment of disaster, one may wink because he or she knows there is a God who makes all things new again. *Hilaritas* is an Easter response to life triumphing over death, and that's the origin of the Easter Sunday jokes.

This means that Christians, as believers in the resurrection, are by definition deeply committed to that hope grounded in a suffering Messiah who rose again; a hope that is evidenced in four of the most famous post-Easter stories in the New Testament: the stories of the Gardener, the Cook, the Stranger, and the Housebreaker. All four appear at moments of disaster, of profound sadness and disillusionment. And all four bear unexpected witness to God's presence and love. All are high comedy.

You remember the first story. The Gardener says one word to the weeping woman in his garden. He calls her by name, "Mary!" Out of her grief she recognizes the Lord. Gone to mourn the dead, she finds life. Thinking at first she is talking to the gardener, she winds up clinging to the Lord. What a joke on her!

The second story is where the depressed apostles have gone fishing for the lack of something better to do. They are dropping in their nets without much enthusiasm, for their Master has just been put to a terrible death. But they begin to sniff the air. They smell something. On the shores of the lake where they are fishing, someone is cooking fish! They draw near to the shore and they begin to make out the cook. John, younger with the sharper eyes, exclaims to Peter, "It is the Lord!" Think of that. In an off-shore cook-out, God called to them when they least expected it, when they were in the midst of despondency. When they had lost all taste for life, he served them a meal. Now *that's* hilarious.

In the third story there are two young disciples, quite dejected, on the way to Emmaus. A stranger joins them. He speaks to them, attracts them, eats with them, breaks bread with them—and they recognize the stranger!

They had broken hearts. The stranger who breaks bread and not hearts, smiles and disappears. What could be more fun than that?

Then in the fourth and final Easter story, the apostles were, as the Scriptures tell it, hiding behind closed doors for fear of the establishment. Suddenly Jesus appears out of nowhere. I know the gospels say his words to them were "Peace be with you," but my guess is that his first words were "Gotcha!"—and he laughed heartily. Here they were, cringing in fear behind locked doors, because everything was in shambles when the risen Housebreaker surprises them with a visit. It must have taken their breath away. They must have laughed and cried at the same time.

Easter is all of these stories and all of those surprises and all of those jokes. Easter tells us of one who silently comes into the human situation hiding himself as the Gardener, the Cook, the Stranger, and the housebreaker who lifts us up and brings hope out of despair, new beginnings out of old disappointments, life out of death, and laughter out of tears.

And that's the basic Easter joke. When all seems lost, it may just be found. At the moment when sickness and death proclaim their victory, they meet their defeat. All because of the power of the resurrection.

No wonder today we share cosmic jokes, the hilarious joy of an Easter faith.

Easter: Easter Validation

Some people like to collect the more interesting tombstone epitaphs. Like the one in New Mexico that plays with names. It says:
> Here lies Johnny Yeast.
> Pardon me for not rising.

Another, obviously in memory of an accident:
> Here lies the body of Jonathan Blake.
> Stepped on the gas
> Instead of the brake.

Another from Boot Hill, Arizona:
> Here lies Lester Moore.
> Four slugs from a .44,
> No Les no more.

Finally, another word play from Massachusetts:
> Under the sod and under the trees
> Lies the body of Jonathan Pease.
> He is not here, there's only the pod
> Pease shelled out and went to God.

These, of course, are light gallows humor that disguise our innate fear of death. What do they have in common with the following true story?

A man was standing in line at the bank, he overheard a commotion at the counter. A woman was quite distressed, exclaiming, "Where will I put my money?! Where will I put my money? I have all my money and my mortgage here! What will happen to my mortgage?!" She was all upset. Well, it turned out that she had misunderstood a small sign on the counter. The sign read, We Will Be Closed For Good Friday. I guess Easter was not uppermost in her thoughts, because she thought that the bank was going to close "for good"—that coming Friday.

What do both episodes have to do with Easter? Two things. One is the fact that at least in faith we *can* laugh at death because Easter says it's lost its ultimate power. The other is that people, like the misunderstanding woman at the bank, continue to misunderstand Easter as well. But at least here, in this faith community, we can try to get some focus. So let me say three things about Easter and why Christians can laugh.

First, Easter is a testimony to the force of love. I know that sounds trite, but it is profoundly true. And that's not a novel idea to us.

In a cemetery in Hanover, Germany, is a grave on which were placed huge slabs of granite and marble cemented together and fastened with heavy steel clasps. Why? Because it belonged to a woman who vehemently did not believe in the resurrection of the dead. So she directed in her will that her grave be made so secure that if there *were* a resurrection, it could not reach her. On the marker were inscribed these words: "This burial place must never be opened." Ah, but in time, you see, what happened was that an infinitesimal seed, covered over by the stones, began to grow. Slowly it pushed its way through the soil and out from beneath them. As it grew and its trunk enlarged, the great slabs were gradually shifted so that the steel clasps were wrenched from their sockets and, there it was, the grave was exposed. A tiny seed had pushed aside those enormous stones.

Easter says that if nature can move huge stones, God can move the huge stone at Jesus' grave. And ours as well. Such is the force of God's love.

Second, Easter is not only a validation of the life and horrible death of Jesus but a statement that goodness and beauty will endure. Jesus did his best. He washed the feet of the apostles and kissed Judas. He healed the ear of Malchus and answered Pilate's questions. He looked silently at Herod and admonished the women on his way to the cross. He thanked Simon of Cyrene. He forgave the soldiers and prayed for his murderers. He encouraged the robber on the cross next to him. But, finally, ugly and bruised, he bent his head and gave up his heart. Bleeding and disfigured, he fell and did not come up again. But God rescued him. Today we celebrate God's validation of his life and all that he stood for. Today Easter celebrates not the ugliness of his suffering and death and what people did to him, but the enduring and compelling beauty of his life and love that surmounted it all.

The luminous paintings of the great artist Renoir are, as you know, aglow with life and light and color. He seemed to put light inside the people he painted. Remarkably, as you may know, for the last twenty years or so of his life, his most productive years, Renoir was terribly crippled with arthritis. His hands were twisted and gnarled. His wrists, his arms, his spine even were ravaged by the disease. He couldn't even stand as he worked. He had to sit and be shifted about in his chair by assistants as he painted. At times the pain was so great as he worked that beads of perspiration would stand out on his face. On one occasion, one of his students, the great artist Matisse, said to him, "Why do you go on and torture yourself like this?" Renoir looked at the canvas on which he was working and replied, "The pain passes, but the beauty remains."

Easter is the celebration of the life-giving beauty of Jesus that remains beyond the pain. For Jesus and for us.

Third, Easter is hope. What I am about to say won't impress the young folks here today, but it will their parents and especially their grandparents and, in time, themselves. A celebrity of his time, playboy, wit, editor of the famous British publication *Punch*, Malcolm Muggeridge "got religion." Because he was so famous, the elite, who felt betrayed by him, couldn't ignore him. They gave him his fifteen minutes of fame and then dropped him. He had committed the unpardonable sin. Not only did he get religion, he became a Catholic. Not only did he become a Catholic, but he did so because he was inspired by the presence and work of Mother Teresa. Anyway, elderly when he converted, he wrote many lovely things. This is one of them:

> As I approach my end, I find Jesus' outrageous claim ever more captivating and meaningful. Quite often, waking up in the night as the old do, I feel myself to be half out of my body, hovering between life and death, with eternity rising in the distance. I see my ancient carcass, prone between the sheets, stained and worn like a scrap of paper dropped in the gutter and, hovering over it, myself, like a butterfly released from its chrysalis stage and ready

to fly away. Are caterpillars told of their impending resurrection? How in dying they will be transformed from poor earth crawlers into creatures of the air with exquisitely painted wings? If told, do they believe it? I imagine the wise old caterpillars shaking their heads: No, it can't be; it's a fantasy. Yet in the limbo between living and dying, as the night clocks tick remorselessly on, and the black sky implacably shows not one single scratch of gray, I hear those words: "I am the resurrection" and I feel myself to be carried along on a great tide of joy and peace.

Easter is such promise. For him and for us.

Easter, then, is a testimony to the power of love.

Easter is a restoration of beauty, Jesus' and ours.

Easter is promise of resurrection.

Let me end with a final epitaph, this one from England, a rather somber one you may have heard before:

Remember man, as you walk by
As you are now, so once was I.
As I am now, so shall you be,
Remember this and follow me.

To which some wag replied by scribbling on the tombstone:

To follow you I'll not consent
Until I know which way you went.

Easter says we know which way Jesus went, and where we shall follow because of him. *That's* what it's all about and why we laugh and shout the joyous "Alleluia!"

Happy Easter.

Easter: The Themes of Passiontide

The themes of Lent and Passiontide always resurrect an old scenario embedded deep in the minds of Catholics, at least in the older ones. It goes like this. As a consequence of original sin, the gates of heaven were closed so that, from the time of Adam and Eve until the moment of Jesus' death, nobody could enter paradise. Only a divine act of reparation could give human beings access to heaven, and that act of reparation was Jesus' death, which paid the debt of sin and so opened the gates of heaven. Sound familiar?

In this view of things, all the just people who had died from the time of Adam and Eve until Jesus' death were asleep somewhere, in a Hades of sorts or a kind of antechamber. Immediately following his death, Jesus descends to that underworld and awakens these souls and then triumphantly leads them into paradise. That descent is what we understand as "the descent into hell," a phrase that we recite whenever we say the Apostles' Creed, not the Nicene Creed we recite at Mass: "He descended into hell and on the third day he rose again."

But I want you to consider that that "descending into hell" is an image, something that captures a deeper reality. It's not a videotape of an actual happening, so how is it to be interpreted? *How* did Jesus descend into hell? What does it mean? I suggest that he "descended into hell" means two things.

For the first, let me offer three images: The first is a story, a tragic one. Some years ago the daughter of my friend committed suicide. She was in her early twenties and away from home when she first attempted to kill herself. The family rushed to her, flew her home, surrounded her with loving solicitude, took her to doctors of every kind, and generally tried every possible way to love and coax her out of her deadly depression. Despite their efforts, she killed herself. Strong as human love can be, sometimes it stands helpless, exhausted, before a door it can't open.

My second image is taken from John's gospel. After Jesus rises from the dead, he appears to the disciples who, as John describes, are huddled together in a room, in fear, with the doors locked. Jesus comes right through the locked doors, stands inside the middle of their fear, and breathes out peace. A week later, he does it again.

A third image: When I was a young boy, my mother gave me a holy card, an adaptation of a famous painting by Holman Hunt, "The Christ Who Knocks." In it, we see a man huddled behind a locked door, paralyzed by fear and darkness. Outside the door Jesus stands with a lantern, knocking, ready to relieve the man of his burden, but there's a hitch: The door only has a knob on the inside. Jesus cannot enter unless the man unlocks the door from his side. There's the implication that God cannot help unless we first let God in. Fair enough? Not exactly and here's why.

The cross of Christ reveals that when we are so paralyzed by fear and overcome by darkness that we can no longer help ourselves, God can still come through our locked doors, stand inside our fear and paralysis, and breathe out peace. The love that is revealed in Jesus' suffering and death is so other-centered that it can forgive and embrace its executioners, pass through locked doors, melt frozen hearts, and penetrate the walls of fear. In a word, it can descend into our private hells and breathe peace.

There it is, there is the key: He "descended into hell" means that there is no hell where Jesus cannot, will not be. They haven't invented the hell yet where his love cannot penetrate. They haven't built the door yet that his love cannot pass through. *That's* what the phrase means. The young woman who committed suicide had reached a point where she was frozen inside a private hell, behind doors that her family's love and professional doctors could no longer open. I have no doubt that when she awoke on the other side she found Christ standing inside her fear and darkness, breathing out peace. You see, he "descended into hell" means that Jesus' love—God's presence—is in the worst places of our lives.

The second meaning of that phrase, he "descended into hell," is that, as disciples of Jesus, we must do the same. Let me illustrate by sharing a story about that wonderful man, Pope John XXIII, now Blessed Pope John.

Shortly after he was elected pope, he visited the Regina Coeli Prison outside Rome, setting off an international orgy of press reporting. There he is on film, a confident, cheerful old man, his soft brown eyes alight, completely at ease with himself and his audience, gesturing expressively with his big farmer's hands, and speaking with spontaneity, obviously making up his comments as he goes along. Since they couldn't come to see him, he tells the prisoners, he came to see them.

He said that he came from poor people. Then he added, "There are only three ways of losing money in Italy: farming, gambling, and women. My father chose the least interesting way." He told them that one of his brothers had been caught poaching; an uncle had done time. "These are the things that happen to poor people," he said, and then added, "but we are all children of God. And I, John, I am your brother."

The audience—from priests to politicians, from convicts to jailers—wept openly, and in the film you can see copious tears coursing down hardened faces. Then suddenly a murderer dared approach the pope to ask, "Can there be forgiveness for me?" In answer, the pope just took the murderer in his arms and hugged him, heedless of all danger to his person, let alone to his dignity. Truly a pope such as the world had never seen, but a pope who "descended into hell," who went into a prison to release those awaiting salvation.

Pope John even went into the hell of atheism because, unlike his predecessors, he received Khrushchev's daughter, Rada, and her husband, Alexis. When they came into the room the pope heard Rada Khrushchevska whisper to her husband in Russian to look closely at the pope's hands, which she described as "the beautiful hands of a Russian peasant." She could not know that her host understood her native language, and the pope was deeply moved.

The pope then asked Rada to tell him the names of her children, not because he didn't already know them (he did), but "because," he said, "when a mother speaks the names of her children, something exceptional happens." He then asked her to caress her children for him, especially the one named

Ivan (Russian for John). As his gift, John gave her, the atheist, a rosary, saying he knew she wouldn't wish to use it but he wanted her to have it nonetheless, "because," he said, "it reminds me of peace in the home and of my mother who used to say it by the fireside when I was a child."

Then he asked the couple to accept his blessing, not the blessing of a pope, which he knew they as official atheists could not accept, just the blessing of an old man. They left smiling and in tears; and to this day Rada has kept the rosary and calls it "one of my most precious possessions." That's the kind of man Pope John was. Like Jesus, he "descended into hell."

So there is no part of our lives into which Jesus cannot and will not come. That is so because he loves us. There is no reason why we cannot visit the private hells of others and offer kindness, compassion, and a blessing. And be a sign of that love.

"He descended into hell." A mysterious phrase embedded in our creed. Yet, when we understand it, what a reassurance to take with us as we journey. What an inspiration as we journey with others.

Pentecost:
The Janitor's Hands

Two stories from my childhood help shed light on this feast of Pentecost.

When I was a child, my parish church of the Sacred Heart in New Brunswick was an attractive semi-Gothic building with pillars forming arches inside the body of the church and the nave. In the highest part of the arch in the sanctuary there was this very large triangle with rays of lights emanating from it and inside this triangle was this single enormous eye. Since I went to the school behind the church and my home was the apartment above our bakery shop a block away, I would, as Sister urged us, stop in for a quick visit on my way home. Although I liked the church and its smells and sights, I was, like any little boy of six or seven, always intimidated by that large eye high above the altar always looking at me.

One day when I shot in for a quick visit, an old woman was there saying her rosary. She noticed me gaping apprehensively at that eye and she motioned me to come over to her. "You're one of the Bausch boys, aren't you?" she asked. I nodded. She sat me down beside her and holding my hand and looking up at that eye she said, "Son, some people will tell you that that eye means that God is always watching to see you when you are doing wrong so he can punish you." Then she paused and looked at me. "I don't want you to think of it that way. Every time you see that eye, I would rather have you remember that God loves you so much that he can't take his eyes off you."

What a difference that made! God was in love with me, just like my mother and father were. I was the apple of his eye. And ever after when I went in for my visit I would wave at the eye and say, "Here I am. It's me, Billy."

My other childhood memory is when our pastor visited us in class one day bringing in behind him, much to our surprise, Mr. Curry, the janitor. "I want you children," Monsignor said, "to look at this man's hands." The janitor, obviously embarrassed, but an obedient member of the flock, held out his palms for us to see. They were the type of hands, I thought, that marked you for immediate dismissal from the dinner table in my house. They were calloused and dirty. Monsignor held the Mr. Curry's right hand up for us to see. "These hands," he said, "do the Lord's work." We looked at each other. Some of us were thinking of those very same hands grasping a mop to clean up a third-grader's spilled lunch and wondered about the extent of the Lord's interest in the task.

"This man's hands," Monsignor continued, "have cleaned our church, kept your school running, and have washed the statues of Jesus, Mary, and Joseph that grace our lawn. This man's hands—this man's life—are dedicated to the Lord in each and everything he does. Take a good look at your hands and see that they do the same."

These two stories point up a forgotten truth about the feast of Pentecost and underscore an enervating misunderstanding we have about it. For when we say, as we were taught, that Pentecost is the feast of the birthday of the church, what we really mean, what we really have in mind, the image that immediately pops up, is that Pentecost is the birthday of the hierarchy, those institutional caretakers—bishops, priests, and religious—who form less than one percent out of the total Catholic population. Pentecost, we feel, is their feast, the celebration of the hierarchal structure of what we call the church: popes, cardinals, archbishops, bishops, monsignors, pastors, associates, brothers, and nuns.

As a result, we tend to think that the more we imitate them, the ordained holy ones, the closer we are to the things they do, the closer we are to the altar, so to speak, the more we are engaged in churchy, institutional things, the holier we are. On the other hand, the less we are engaged in churchy things—we really don't have time to teach CCD or be a lector or eucharistic minister or clean the church—the less we are near God. And it hasn't helped our attitude, I admit, that of 177 saints in the official liturgical calendar, 172 are celibate clergy and religious and the other five are widows or widowers.

The result of this mindset is that, starting from the pinnacle of full-time church work, everything seems to devolve in descending order of unworthiness, if not moral pollution, as far as holiness and mission go. I mean, if you made time and were devout, you would squeeze in some spirituality on Sunday or the annual mission, but never in the real world. As a kid, I remember that the most we non-churchy folk could hope for was that, when our time came, we could sneak into purgatory with a scorched rump. Even the retreats for the laity gave this message by focusing mainly on prayer and the sacraments and seldom, if ever, on the gifts of the people for public witness and service where they were. The equation came down to this: churchy activity equals heightened spirituality; worldly activity equals danger.

When you think of it, even our charitable "good works" unintentionally give the wrong message. For example, the parish social ministry calls people out of their daily lives and neighborhoods into working at soup kitchens, homeless shelters, AIDS residences, nursing homes, Catholic Charities agencies, peace groups, and so forth. Which, by all means, is a wonderful and noble response. But the unintended effect is often that ordinary people conclude that ministry and service and gospel living is something that falls into such extracurricular activities apart from their lives, is something they must seek outside of their day-to-day routines if they want to live the gospel.

The result is that we have never developed a spirituality of everydayness, an understanding of God planted-where-you-are; a sense of calling and mission, of co-creation; a sense of God loving us so much at every moment that he can't take his eyes off us; a sense, in short, of being church.

I mentioned this once before but it's worth repeating here on Pentecost. Years ago when I used to give the Cana Conferences to married couples, I would always remind parents that, according to Jesus, they have, above all the others, the best chance of salvation. Why? Because in the famous Matthew 25 passage, Jesus gives us the only measurements for salvation—and all of them are right there in the boring routine of everyday living.

They are what we call today, you recall, the corporal and spiritual works of mercy. The beautiful part, I reminded the parents, is that they're built right into normal family life. You couldn't escape them if you wanted to.

Parents, in raising children, can't avoid heaven. Feeding the hungry, giving drink to the thirsty—they're all right there, not the sanctuary, not in the foreign missions, not in the hierarchy, but right there in the home and neighborhood. So:

The 2 AM bottle = giving drink to the thirsty.

Diapering = clothing the naked.

Cough medicine to the bedroom = visiting the sick.

Preparing meals = feeding the hungry.

"Dad, can you help me with my homework?" = instructing the ignorant.

"Mom, what'll I wear?" = counseling the doubtful.

The cat died = burying the dead.

Hearing the kids' prayers = praying for the living and the dead (endlessly).

Are you still in the bathroom? = visiting the imprisoned.

This is being church. This is what church is. This is where church is. The Spirit fell on us at baptism to both uncover and witness to God in our daily lives, in our world. The great writer Dorothy Sayers was on target when she once remarked that it is unfortunate that a carpenter hears on Sunday, "Don't get drunk on Saturday night and be sure to give enough in the collection" instead of hearing, "Be the best carpenter you can be."

But we resist the notion that we are church when we do these things. It's just not so, well, exotic or exciting. Church holiness has to be elsewhere than my home, neighborhood, school, or job. But that's not so. God has loving eyes on us at every moment. He's given us blessed hands to be church where we are, in our calling, not somewhere else.

But it is hard to convince people of that. For example, during a weekend retreat some years ago, l listened as a lawyer spelled out his understanding of and satisfaction with the ministries in which he was involved. They all had to do with efforts like the retreats in which he was engaged, the Cursillo Movement, the RCIA in his parish, and so on. At one point in the retreat I asked this obviously good-willed man about the everyday, workaday world of his professional life. That is, did he encounter values and practices contrary to the gospel there? And, if so, what did he as a Catholic do about them? The man's answer was revealing. "I don't think I even want to look at that question." Then I knew. Somewhere along the line, like so many others, he had interiorized the erroneous interpretation of being church and the path of holiness as confined to church activities, not something that should be the witness and fabric of his own everyday routine life.

Actually, all this is quite surprising because our original roots show us an almost exclusive "lay" vocation. Some people were indeed called to follow Jesus, but most of those New Testament people, remember, were grounded and remained grounded in their world. Think, for example, of Zacchaeus, Simon's mother-in law, the centurion, Jairus and his daughter, the Jericho blind man, the widow (of the mite fame), the woman with the hemorrhage, the woman at the well, even Martha, Mary, and Lazarus.

The point is God established his church as a people, as all of us, you and I—not as a clerical few—who are called to live decently and morally and bear witness in the place where we are, in the trenches of everyday living: loving, hurting, struggling, and dying. Recall, after all, St. Paul's words in today's second reading that "there are different kinds of spiritual gifts but the same Spirit....To each individual the manifestation of the Spirit is given for some benefit....For in one Spirit we were all baptized into one body... we were all given to drink of one [Pentecostal] Spirit."

So it comes down to this. Today is *our* feast, not a feast of the hierarchy. Pentecost is the public manifestation and declaration that God loves all of us so much that he can't take his eyes off us, and, as a result, he's poured out his Spirit on all of us and has given us, so to speak, janitor hands to share that love. Pentecost is God's official delegation of us as his church in the everydayness of life.

"[At Pentecost] they were all filled with the Holy Spirit and began to speak in different tongues as the Spirit enabled them to proclaim." Thus today's Scripture. Pentecost is the inaugural feast that has filled us all with the Holy Spirit so that we the church who speak in different tongues, that is, in our various walks of life and in our different accents, speak the same hopeful messages of love and redemption.

So, my advice? Go home today and look in the mirror and exclaim, "Happy Birthday, Church!"

Pentecost: The Subterranean Spirit

Today is the feast of Pentecost, sometimes called the Birthday of the Church. It's been around for twenty centuries, displaying large tableau of sin and sanctity as you might expect of a church made up of human beings and not angels.

As the secular media never lets us forget, at this point in history, two thousand years after the coming of the Holy Spirit, the world once again is unsafe and the church is once more battered by scandal and shame and has lost power, influence, and members. It is tempting to parade its faults and predict its demise.

But I want to suggest to you this morning that, however we describe this Third Person—Paraclete, Comforter, Breath, Advocate, and so on—the one description that is most accurate and meaningful is "The Subterranean Spirit." Which is to say, like an ever-moving silent stream under civilization's debris and chaos, the Spirit flows on in the great and in the lowly, and the work of Jesus goes on in spite of all.

Under the Spirit, the church has seen the commencement of all the existing governments on this planet. It was there before the Saxons set foot in Britain, before the Franks crossed the Rhine, and before Grecian eloquence flourished in Antioch. No scandal has destroyed it; no betrayal by intimates has completely stilled its voice.

The church, the People of God, moves on steadily in spite of the worst horrors man could inflict on man. The early Christians, a minority, persecuted fringe group, amid the greed and pride of the Roman Empire, were so caring and so giving, so kind to the sick and needy that they forced

531

even their enemies to exclaim, "See those Christians; how they love one another."

There were the folk who established the monasteries, the Holiday Inns of the Dark Ages, that served as places of learning, refuge, hospice, and hospitality for many in a dangerous age when vandals and brigands freely roamed and pillaged the land. There were the Irish monks bringing civilization back to a Europe collapsed by war and conflict.

There were Aquinas and Ignatius who helped the church recover its intellectual and spiritual footings when it stumbled badly. And Michelangelo and Dante left us beauty in the midst of moral ugliness. And Francis and Dominic, living in terrible, corrupt times, breathed into us a new spirit. There was Hildegard of Bingen, forerunner of the Broadway musical; and the Passion Plays, the forerunner of the modern theater. There was Thomas More, husband and father, laying down his life for principle while others rationalized.

There was Vincent de Paul and the Daughters of Charity taking in the homeless and poor, to be followed in another age by a Mother Cabrini and a Mother Teresa. Abraham Lincoln had high praise for the Catholic nuns who ministered heroically during the Civil War. There was homely Peter Claver caring for the slaves when others thought they were animals, divorced Rose Hawthorne caring for cancer victims society had abandoned, and widowed Elizabeth Ann Seton opening schools for disenfranchised children.

My point is that, in unspeakable horrors, there are always instances of touching heroism when the Spirit surges. Who does not remember, for example, that moments after the Twin Towers fell, medical and emergency professionals were on the scene? Hordes of volunteers raced to help rescue the injured buried beneath the rubble. Thousands of doctors, nurses, medical students, police, firefighters, clergy, blood donors, and structural engineers rushed to provide whatever their expertise offered. Church and social service agencies across the country mobilized their networks to provide donations of food, clothing, and equipment. Doctors, nurses, and firefighters risked life and limb, crawling into airless clefts to treat someone found still alive. People stood in line for six hours to give blood at the Red Cross. A sporting goods store cleaned out its inventory of kneepads and sent them to the rescuers who were scouring the wreckage. Local restaurants supplied food faster than it could be eaten.

This, I maintain, is the Spirit of God at work within the rank and file. A nobility is secreted in the human spirit that invariably springs to life in the face of catastrophe. This feast of Pentecost celebrates the perpetual movement of that ever-present Subterranean Spirit.

And that Spirit is non-elitist; anyone is fair game. The communist wino catches God's breath when he shares his raggedy coat with a shivering buddy. Erin Brockovich, brazen, profane, minimally educated, twice divorced, mother of three, takes on a billion-dollar corporation, bringing it to its knees for lying to the people about poisoning their water supply.

My friends, among war and betrayal within and without the church, betrayals that would have toppled any other institution long ago, I tell you that Pentecost lives in the quiet heroism of many men and women, boys and girls of this age as it has in all the ages past.

And, as far as the church goes, perhaps the best modern toast to the Subterranean Spirit I can think of comes from Jesuit octogenarian, Father Walter Burghardt. He writes:

> In the course of a half century, I have seen more Christian corruption than you have read of. I have tasted it. I have been reasonably corrupt myself. And yet, I love this Church, this living, pulsing, sinning people of God with a crucifying passion. Why? For all the Christian hate, I experience here a community of love. For all the institutional idiocy, I find here a tradition of reason. For all the individual repressions, I breathe here an air of freedom.
>
> For all the fear of sex, I discover here the redemption of my body. In an age so inhuman, I touch here tears of compassion. In a world so grim and humorless, I share here rich joy and earthy laughter. In the midst of death, I hear here an incomparable stress on life. For all the apparent absence of God, I sense here the real presence of Christ.

After two thousand or so years of inhumanity, only the enduring Pentecostal Spirit could still invite us here and, amid our bewilderment and fear, bring us to celebrate a happy birthday.

So, let the red you are wearing cause you to take heart, give hope, and never cease to pray, "Come, Holy Spirit!"

Corpus Christi

This past Monday was Memorial Day and this Sunday is the feast of Corpus Christi. One day celebrates the deeds of the dead and the other celebrates unity of all the baptized in one Body of Christ. I would like to join the two concepts together.

Let me start off with some unpleasant facts: Soldiers left home, lived in barracks, ate military food, suffered hardships in the jungles and deserts, were wounded, and some died far from home. And because they did all these things, we are free. What they did affected us all. In some kind of spiritual joining, in some kind of deep connection, the soldier dying on the fields of Gettysburg or in the deserts of Saudi Arabia or Iraq has touched our lives. There's no doubt about it: There is a synergy, a deep action and reaction that binds the human race.

This common experience contradicts the popular philosophy that we are independent, that we live in a world where each person is a separate atom and a solitary individual, that we are free-floating organisms, a bundle of selfish genes, that we are unrelated and unconnected to others. And in such a scenario, of course, pain becomes utterly without meaning and utterly ridiculous.

But we don't believe that for a moment. In fact, in the religious terms of our feast, we are the Body of Christ. We are members of the same body, interconnected by baptism, joined by grace, united by a common Spirit. What we do or fail to do affects others: our love, our rejection, our prayer, our suffering, our pain.

When we sense that we are connected, united, the very Body of Christ, suffering and pain become powerful agents of grace. Nobody wants it, but when it comes, it is spiritual barter and spiritual power. That's why, in the old days, we had something else to do with pain and suffering and, if you promise not to laugh, I'll tell you what it is: We could offer it up for the souls in purgatory, and anyone else, for that matter. Modern folk find this a quaint thought. It provokes ridicule and smiles. Offering up sufferings for others does quite boggle the modern, individualistic mind.

Christian truth is different. Simply put, it is this: We *are* the Body of Christ and we *are* all connected. The Christian witness says that we are in physical, psychical, spiritual relationship with one another. We can plead for one another, we can pray for one another. We can offer up acts of courage, endurance, and sufferings for others. Why, we can even die, and somehow in the great cycle of life and love, it can benefit others.

It is not just that Sidney Carton took the place of his friend at the guillotine in Dickens's *A Tale of Two Cities*. It's not just that St. Maximilian Kolbe took the place of a prisoner in a concentration camp and died in his stead. It's not just that innumerable United States soldiers in World War I and II, and in the Korean and Viet Nam wars, and in all the other wars, died for us that "we might be free." What's important for us to remember today is that human beings can do things that affect others because we are spiritually joined. Because we are spiritually united, we can direct our energies, and our prayers, and our sufferings and deaths.

Is it absurd that, if you have asthma, let us say, to offer some of your discomfort for those who are suffocating in New York tenements on a hot summer's day? Is it silly for you, lying on your hospital bed, to offer your pain for those who are languishing in nursing homes? Is it ridiculous for you, when you are hungry, to offer up some of your hunger for those who daily go to sleep without anything to eat? Is it outrageous for you to offer up your migraine headache, your pain, your cancer, your sickness, for hardened sinners? And for those you love? And for those you hate?

A society that sells drugs, facelifts, and pills for every occasion, says, "Yes, it is absurd. Suffering has no meaning. It has no redemptive value." But we say it does. By the grace of God, suffering can be redemptive, and that in an unknown way, we can gain graces for countless others, for we are the Body of Christ.

Let me put what I'm saying in the form of a story. After the usual Sunday evening hymns, the church's pastor slowly stood up, walked over to the pulpit and, before he gave his sermon, briefly introduced a guest minister who was in the service that evening. The pastor told the congregation that the guest minister was one of his dearest childhood friends and that he wanted him to have a few moments to greet the church and share whatever he felt would be appropriate for the service.

With that, an elderly man stepped up to the pulpit and began to speak. "Once upon a time, a father, his son, and a friend of his son were sailing off the Pacific coast," he began, "when a fast-approaching storm blocked any attempt to get back to the shore. The waves were so high that even though the father was an experienced sailor, he could not keep the boat upright and the three were swept into the ocean as the boat capsized."

The old man hesitated for a moment, making eye contact with two teenagers who were, for the first time since the service began, looking somewhat interested in his story. The aged minister continued, "Grabbing a rescue line, the father had to make the most excruciating decision of his life: *to which boy he would throw the other end of the lifeline?*

"He only had seconds to make the decision. The father knew that his son was a believer in Jesus, a good Christian, and he also knew that his son's friend was not and was living a sinful life. The agony of his decision could not be matched by the torrent of waves. Finally, as the father yelled out, 'I love you, son!' he threw out the lifeline to his son's friend. By the time the father had pulled the friend back to the capsized boat, his son had disappeared beneath the raging swells into the black of night. His body was never recovered."

By this time, the two teenagers were sitting up straight in the pew, anxiously waiting for the next words to come out of the old minister's mouth. "The father," he continued, "knew his son would step into eternity with Jesus but he could not bear the thought of his son's friend stepping into an eternity without Jesus. Therefore, he sacrificed his son to save the son's friend."

He then paused and said with fervor, "How great is the love of God that he should do the same for us. Our heavenly Father sacrificed his only begotten son that we could be saved. I urge you to accept his offer to rescue you and take a hold of the lifeline he is throwing out to you in this service."

With that, the old man turned and sat back down in his chair as silence filled the room. Well, within minutes after the service ended, the two teenagers were at the old man's side. "That was a nice story," politely stated one of the boys, "but I don't think it was very realistic for a father to give up his only son's life in hopes that the other boy would become a Christian."

"Well, you've got a point there," the old man replied, glancing down at his worn Bible. As a soft smile broadened his narrow face, he once again looked up at the boys and said, "It sure isn't very realistic, is it? But I'm standing here today to tell you that that story gives me a glimpse of what it must have been like for God to give up his son for me. You see, I was that father and your pastor over there...he is my son's friend."

St. John Lateran: Mother Church

NOVEMBER 9

Today's feast, November 9, which this year has displaced the usual Sunday, may seem strange to us with its strange name: Dedication of St. John Lateran. Who was he? What could St. Mary's in Colts Neck, U.S.A., have to do with an almost 2000-year-old church in Rome? The answer is: a great deal.

First, some background. You will recall that for the first three hundred years Christianity was illegal. It was an off-again, on-again persecuted religion with penalties of torture and death. In fact, the Roman Empire unleashed some ten persecutions against it, catching not only Peter and Paul but all those whose names we will mention in the first canon. The Christians, during this time, had to go underground. They had no temples, no churches, no public places of gathering and worship. They met secretly in homes, barns, cemeteries. But in the year 313 the Roman Emperor, Constantine, became a Christian, even though a heretical one. He granted religious tolerance to Christianity and eventually his successor granted it freedom.

Once Christianity was politically free to worship openly and publicly, it needed to build its own churches, especially when it became the national religion. Now there was a palace in Rome, formerly owned by the Laterani family that was now used by Constantine and his mother, St. Helena. He turned a wing of that palace over to the church, making it the first public church in Rome that was Christian. More precisely, he gave it to the bishop of Rome, Pope Melchiades, along with an adjacent basilica. There the pope presided and resided as did all the popes after him—except for a forty-year hiatus when the popes were in Avignon, France—until 1871 when Pope

Pius IX, during the Italian Revolution, fled to the Vatican Hill where the popes have lived ever since. Most of the popes have been crowned at St. John Lateran. To this day, restored many times over, it remains the pope's official church in his capacity as Bishop of Rome and to this day the Holy Thursday ceremonies are held there. It is called St. John Lateran Basilica in honor of St. John the Baptist and the original Laterani family name. It has inscribed over its door the words, "The mother church of Rome and of all the churches in the world."

We celebrate this feast of St. John Lateran, then, because it is the first Christian church, the mother church. But that is only the surface reason. We celebrate this feast because it reminds us of our origins. Rome was evangelized by Peter and Paul and by countless missionaries before and after them. In turn, Rome, being the world center at the time, the heart of the Roman Empire, sent missionaries out to the west. Most of us are European in origin, although that is fading, and so the faith comes to us by way of Rome. Not directly from Jerusalem where the faith started, nor from Antioch in Syria which sent missionaries to the east, to the Balkans, and to Turkey, but from Rome, and we celebrate that fact. We have been evangelized from Rome, the mother church.

"To be in union with Rome," as the saying goes, does not necessarily mean to take commands from Rome or have the same system of government as Rome, or use the same liturgy, style, dress, and customs, although we surely are influenced in these matters and perhaps too narrowly so. But it does mean to be in union with our origins, with that faith proclaimed by Rome's imports from the Mideast, Peter and Paul. Rome is where Peter eventually lived and died and passed on the faith. The Lateran Palace, or St. John Lateran, is the place where Peter's successors have lived and died and passed on the faith. It's our Christian equivalent of the Governor's Palace in Williamsburg or Independence Hall in Philadelphia. It's a historical sign and symbol of our deep-rootedness, our connection with the past, our touchstone of faith with the long line of popes who have presided there.

St. John Lateran Basilica, therefore, reminds us of our catholicity, our relationship with the center and from the center to the rest of Christianity. It reminds us here in our little parish in Colts Neck, New Jersey, that, through our connection with that mother church, we belong to a vast brotherhood and sisterhood both to the past and to the present. And in these days of almost pathological individualism, of atomistic existence, this is no small thing indeed. We're part of a wide community. We are Catholic with both a small and big C. St. John Lateran tells us that.

There's another reason why the Catholic world celebrates a church building in another part of the world. We are reminded that the building of temples and churches is a natural, poetic instinct we humans have. We need symbols and rituals in order to live, and would sooner do without food and water. The poor of France know the Eiffel Tower could be melted down and the money given to them, but they would resist, knowing they do not live by bread alone. The Dome of the Rock for the Arabs, the Wailing Wall for the Jews, Westminster Abbey for the Anglicans, Sancta Sophia for the Turks are all more than buildings. They enshrine national history and aspirations and house celebrations and rituals. They give identity and cohesion. Which is why tyrants' and invaders' first act is to destroy a people's shrines and literature. Without them, the people are nothing. At times, people have lost their moorings and declared that all buildings are human vanity.

The Puritans wrought terrible havoc by destroying many masterpieces, smashing stained-glass windows, and burning priceless works of art. They forgot that churches and cathedrals were not the products of human vanity, although at times they were, but truly the expression of human faith. Men, women, boys and girls, people from all walks of life, the whole town, for example, helped build Chartres Cathedral, stone by stone, love by love. This feast reminds us that our church, however grand or humble, is a sign of transcendence, a gathering for us to worship and say out loud what we are pressured to deny openly: Jesus Christ is Lord!

A final reason we celebrate this feast of our mother church, St. John Lateran, is that it reminds us that we ourselves are unfinished temples. We indeed have a great history of grandeur. Over the centuries the church has been responsible for more good and decency and help than will ever be realized. The constant media focus on our failings should not blind us to the enormous good we have done throughout the ages, and still do. Realize that Catholic Relief Services is the largest private relief service in the world. Think of all the Mother Teresas there are, the countless Catholic hospitals, schools, and clinics, leprosaria. Perhaps the biggest assistance to

AIDS patients is the Catholic church, although you would never know it. We have taught people to read and write and sing. We have healed, consoled, buried, and converted. We're in every part of the globe ministering to others, day and night, endlessly. We have done Christ's work.

But of course, we are, as I said, unfinished. Just as St. John Lateran had to be restored many times throughout the centuries because of the ravages of time and vandals, so has the whole church. We have sinned and we have constant reforms and renewals to call us back to our origins. This is the reason we celebrate this feast. It recalls struggles, countless martyrs, sacrifice, Peter and Paul, missionaries, and it challenges us to see how far we have strayed from the message they left us at so great a price. To that extent, this feast beckons us to reform.

St. John Lateran. It's a shame many people, many Catholics, do not know it and are perplexed as to why it's a weekend feast day and why we take the time to celebrate it. But now you know and in the knowing you should have pride and resolve: pride in our ancient heritage that keeps us grounded to the truth, and resolve that our spiritual ancestors will not, as one of our Presidents said, have died in vain.

End Times

The sun will be darkened and the moon will not give its light and the stars will be falling from the heavens, the powers of heaven will be shaken and they will see the Son of Man with great power and glory.

A darkened sun, a blank moon, crashing stars, planetary collapse, Jesus' fateful return on the clouds: You know when you hear this that you're in the exotic realm of apocalyptic literature.

This genre of cosmic dooms-daying and the imminent return of Christ to rapture the good and nuke the bad is a variation of the age-old battle between good and evil, light and darkness; between Arthur and Mordred, Holmes and Moriarty, Luke Skywalker and Darth Vader, Simba and Uncle Scar, Christ and Antichrist, with the underdog being ultimately triumphant.

It's Eliza Doolittle's "Just you wait, 'enry 'iggins, just you wait!" Someday things will be reversed and *we'll* be rewarded and you'll be punished. Mary sang this very theme in her Magnificat: "He has scattered the proud in the thoughts of their hearts. He has brought down the powerful from their thrones, and lifted up the lowly" (Lk 1:51–52), and her Son inveighed: "But woe to you who are rich, for you have received your consolation. Woe to you who are full now, for you will be hungry. Woe to you who are laughing now, for you will mourn and weep" (Lk 6:25–25).

And in apocalyptic literature the underdogs even know *when* these reversals will happen, which the top dogs don't because they, the underdogs, alone possess the key to the books, especially the book of Daniel and the book of Revelation, which unlock to them the signs and the timetable of the end time.

542

It's an old story, isn't it? Predictions of the end of the world are a staple of the ages from the writings of the early Church fathers, the twelfth-century so-called Prophecies of St. Malachi, sixteenth-century Nostradamus, Archbishop James Usher who predicted the end of the world to occur in 1996, the Jehovah Witnesses who predicted it with great regularity till they threw in the towel in 1994, to David Koresh and his end-of-the-world sect in the Waco tragedy of 1993, the 1997 Heaven's Gate disaster whose members committed mass suicide to speed up the second coming, to Jerry Falwell, to the Fatima secrets and the mumbo-jumbo nonsense of Hal Lindsey's *The Late Great Planet Earth*, which has sold over 35 million copies, and the current multi-million bestsellers, equally nonsensical, the Left Behind stories of Tim LeHaye. Obviously, end-of-the-world scenarios have a hold on the public imagination.

These end-of-the-world themes are as old as ancient Jewish and Greek literature and are found deeply embedded in our New Testament from Jesus to St. Paul, even enshrined in our liturgy. Every Sunday we all unthinkingly recite our creed which says, "He *will* come again in glory to judge the living and the dead" and our acclamation after the consecration cries out, "Christ has died, Christ is risen, Christ *will* come again." Besides, since there are always signs of disaster, from the Holocaust, global warming, tornados and tidal waves to 9/11, there will always be people reading into them signs of the last times and reversals of fortune and, with their tortured arithmetic and imaginative fantasies, will always capture an audience, especially among society's have-nots who look forward, after the dust has settled, to being on top and seeing Bill Gates on the bottom.

For the "haves," however, whose signs of the end are a dip in the Dow Jones or a dent in their Mercedes, it's a different story. They look upon these sign-carrying prophets of doom and their long list of consistently failed predictions with benign indifference or patronizing smirks, as cartoon characters sidelined to the nut fringe. Alas, they sigh, as they go about their business, these fanatics will always be with us.

But they should be. Listen up here: They should be, because, behind all the exaggerations and fanaticism, there lies a truth that we desperately need to be reminded of and cling to. The truth the crazies fervently proclaim is that God is God, not us.

We need to hear that because we, with our portfolios and insurance plans, our Platinum cards and bonuses, our frequent flyer miles and second houses generate a certain hubris, a certain pride, that we are insulated from life's tragedies and entertain the fantasy that we are in charge. And yet, all of the Fannie Maes, stock options, and self-made satisfactions plummet into insignificance when: we leave the doctor's office stunned with the news that we have breast or prostate cancer; we learn that our spouse is divorcing us or our son is on drugs or our marriage has grown cold; death has snatched away a husband or wife or child in the prime of life, like the 170 youth whose ski train suddenly turned into an oven; we have been downsized; our toys have become boring and empty.

And all these tragic interruptions to our complacency pale into nothing when, like lightning out of the blue, grace strikes and Saul, breathing the fire of persecution, finds himself as Paul breathing the Spirit of the risen Lord; and the libertine, out-of-wedlock father Augustine blubbers his first confession to St. Ambrose; and the rich merchant's son Francis shocks his parents as he embraces Lady Poverty; and the slave dealer and womanizer John Newton gives us our unofficial national religious anthem and sings of Amazing Grace; and ex-communist and unwed mother Dorothy Day astounds her bohemian friends by converting to Catholicism and shoving the poor in our faces; and Charles Colson, the second most powerful man in America, ministers to prisoners; and the late Cardinal O'Connor takes off his ermine and changes the bedpans of AIDS patients.

And, remember, these people too once had other plans and thought they were in charge. The apocalyptic strain rightly says to all this, "What did you expect? Foolish ones, you were never in charge to begin with. *God* is in charge of times and seasons and lives."

Go ahead and live your lives. Just don't hug the illusion that you're in charge. Live piously, justly, and in the fear of the Lord, as Scripture says. Do your best, but be humble enough to give glory to God. Be open to the Spirit. Even learn to embrace your cross, knowing that God can tease glory out of all that radiation and chemo and broken ribs and broken hearts. God is sovereign.

Thus evangelical fundamentalists and their weird apocalyptic messages have the virtue of putting human life and human experience and human history into the context of faith. There *is* a plan. We *are* going somewhere. Justice *will* triumph. Life *has* ultimate meaning. Even though we're a speck in the endless cosmos, we're a special, privileged, and beloved speck awaiting redemption and the fullness of love.

Timetables belong to God. We indeed may take the howling of Scripture and the cosmic chaos it portrays in today's gospel and place them smugly on the shelf with our Star Wars trilogy but, if we do, we will miss the point.

The point is that "submit" and "obey" and "trust" and "open to the Spirit" are not favorite words in a culture raised on the "Self" as the measure of all things whatsoever and a Self daily proclaimed to be the center of the universe. Apocalyptic language and thought simply remind us that this is the greatest illusion of all.

Christic the King

The gospel is a rich tapestry of a scene. It's fraught with drama and color as the two protagonists square off. Pilate is nervous. Seven times he's in and out the praetorium, the governor's residence, between the people and the prisoner. In his heart he knows Jesus is innocent—after all, his wife had a dream about that—and in his head he knows he must play the game of politics and from the two he mixes up a compromise: he washes his hands and then sends Jesus off to his death. Pontius Pilate comes down in history as the great compromiser, the symbol of all those who compromise their principles and so continue to sentence the Christ to his death to this day.

On the other hand, there are those who would not—do not—compromise, those who demonstrate in their lives and deaths that, given a choice, Christ is King and they will follow him. When Jesus really matters to such people, where Christ is King, the compromises fall away before the truth. Let me share some of their stories.

In April 1940, Nazi Germany invaded Denmark. There was little resistance because the Danes felt it would be hopeless. A puppet Danish government got on as best it could. As in all the occupied territories, Danish people nowadays recount tales from those days of the necessary compromises they made to survive.

But then, in 1943, German policy toughened. It was decided to impose on Denmark the same "final solution" policy of exterminating Jews as elsewhere. And suddenly there was a remarkable transformation. German officers leaked the plan to the Danish resistance. Escape routes were quickly organized. Jewish people tell how complete strangers approached them in the streets with the keys to their houses so they could hide. Train guards and boat captains joined the plan.

Within a few weeks all but a few of the 7000 Jews had been whisked over the Oresund to safety in Sweden. Some even tell how their escape boats were boarded and searched by German patrol vessels, yet the Germans let them through. For many Danes it eventually meant the concentration camp and death. But faced with the very human need of the Jews, it seemed that a whole nation and many Germans too turned their backs on political compromise and performed a true and great act of love.

Another war-time hero, a German soldier, Joseph Schultz. He was sent to Yugoslavia shortly after the invasion. He was a loyal, young German soldier on patrol, and one day the sergeant called out eight names, his among them. They thought they were going on a routine patrol, and as they hitched up their rifles, they came over a hill, still not knowing what their mission was. There were eight Yugoslavians there, standing on the brow of the hill; five men and three women. It was only when they got about fifty feet away from them, when any marksman could shoot out an eye of a pheasant, that the soldiers realized what their mission was.

The eight soldiers were lined up. The sergeant barked, "Ready!" and they lifted their rifles. "Aim," and they got their sights. And suddenly in the silence that prevailed, there was a thud of a rifle butt against the ground. The sergeant, and the seven other soldiers, and those eight Yugoslavians stopped and looked. And Private Joseph Shultz walked toward the Yugoslavians. His sergeant called after him and ordered him to come back, but he pretended not to hear him.

Instead he walked the fifty feet to the mound of the hill, and he joined hands with the eight Yugoslavians. There was a moment of silence, then the sergeant yelled, "Fire!" And Private Joseph Schultz died, mingling his blood with those innocent men and women. Later, you know what was found on his body sewn into his coat? An excerpt from St. Paul: "Love does not delight in evil, but rejoices in the truth. It always protects, always trusts, always hopes, and always perseveres."

Another instance. During the prime days of the struggle for racial integration in the South, black civil rights workers—"freedom riders" they were called—would travel on buses from city to city, challenging segregationist laws. Sometimes they were greeted with violence; often they were arrested. In one town, the police halted a bus and the passengers were booked and jailed.

The jailers did everything possible to make the prisoners miserable and to break their spirits. They tried to deprive them of sleep with noise and light during the nights. They intentionally oversalted their food to make it distasteful. They gradually took away their mattresses, one by one, hoping to create conflict over the remaining ones.

Eventually the strategies seemed to be taking hold. Morale in the jail cells was beginning to sag. One of the jailed leaders, looking around one day at his dispirited fellow prisoners, began softly to sing a spiritual. Slowly, others joined in until the whole group was singing at the top of their voices and the puzzled jailers felt the entire cellblock vibrating with the sounds of a joyful gospel song. When they went to see what was happening, the prisoners triumphantly pushed the remaining mattresses through the cell bars, saying, "You can take our mattresses, but you can't take our souls."

It was the hymn singers who were in jail, but it was the jailers who were guilty. It was the prisoners who were suffering, but the jailers who were defeated. It was the prisoners who were in a position of weakness, but it was the broken and bigoted world of the jailers and of all the Pontius Pilates of history that was perishing.

We have to ask ourselves, what makes people take such stands in life when others do not? What makes them spurn the role of Pilate when others embrace it? I don't think there's much of a mystery here. The answer is as simple as it is true, as this little bit of wisdom tells us:

When you thought I wasn't looking, I saw you hang my first painting on the refrigerator, and I wanted to paint another one.

When you thought I wasn't looking, I saw you feed a stray cat, and I thought it was good to be kind to animals.

When you thought I wasn't looking, I saw you make my favorite cake just for me, and I knew that little things are special things.

When you thought I wasn't looking, I heard you say a prayer, and I believed there is a God I could always talk to.

When you thought I wasn't looking, I felt you kiss me good night, and I felt loved.

When you thought I wasn't looking, I saw tears come from your eyes, and I learned that sometimes things hurt, but it's all right to cry.

When you thought I wasn't looking, I saw that you cared and I wanted to
be everything that I could be.

When you thought I wasn't looking, *I looked*…and wanted to say thanks
for all the things I saw when you thought I wasn't looking.

In her book *Out of Africa,* Isak Dinesen tells the story of a young man
from the Kikuyu tribe who worked for her on her farm for three months.
Suddenly he announced that he was leaving her to go to work for a Muslim
man nearby. Surprised, Dinesen asked him if he was unhappy working for
her. He told her that all was well, but that he had decided to work for a
Christian for three months to study the ways of Christians and then work
for a Muslim for three months to study the ways of a Muslim. After experiencing both, he was going to decide whether to be a Christian or a
Muslim.

What about that? What would he choose if he lived among us and saw,
when we thought he wasn't looking, what we did and how we acted and
how we treated others at home, at school, the neighborhood and the workplace? I wonder. I wonder if he would see Pontius Pilate or, say, Private
Schultz?

So, as always, the gospel comes back to haunt us, doesn't it? Light and
darkness, right and wrong, principle or compromise, Pilate or Jesus—it
was all there then. It's all here now. Every day.

"The reason I was born" said Jesus in this morning's gospel, in reply to
Pilate, "the reason why I came into the world, is to testify to the truth." That
is what we're here for, isn't it?

New Year's Day

A parable for a New Year that is only four days away.

On the first day God created the cow. God said, "You must go to the field with the farmer all day long and suffer under the sun, have calves, and give milk to support the farmer and I will give you a life span of sixty years." The cow said, "That's a kind of a tough life you want me to live for sixty years. Let me have twenty years and I'll give back the other forty." And God agreed.

On the second day God created the dog. God said, "Sit all day by the door of your house and bark at anyone who comes in or walks past. I will give you a life span of twenty years." The dog said, "That's too long to be barking. Give me ten years and I'll give back the other ten." So God agreed (sigh).

On the third day God created the monkey. God said, "Entertain people, do monkey tricks, make them laugh. I'll give you a twenty-year life span." The monkey said, "How boring, monkey tricks for twenty years? I don't think so. The dog gave you back ten, so that's what I'll do too. Okay?" And God agreed again.

On the fourth day God created man. God said, "Eat, sleep, play, and enjoy life. Do nothing, just enjoy. I'll give you twenty years." The man said, "What? Only twenty years? No way, man. Tell you what, I'll take my twenty, and the forty the cow gave back, and the ten the dog gave back and the ten the monkey gave back. That makes eighty, okay?" "Okay," said God. "You've got a deal."

So that's why for the first twenty years we eat, sleep, play, and enjoy life, and do nothing; for the next forty years we slave in the sun to support our family; for the next ten years we do monkey tricks to entertain our grandchildren; and for the last ten years we sit in front of the house and bark at everybody!

Where does time go? The new year is a few days away. Another year that inevitably transitions us from one timeframe to another. I don't know if

550

the parable holds true—although it has a certain identifiable ring to it—or where we currently are in the cow-monkey-dog stages, but I do know that time is a gift and that a New Year is always a New Beginning and, since grace abounds, that spiritual opportunity will always be around the next calendar corner. Or to put it in terms of our comments, this new year we will be invited to another stage of our life, to a more profound involvement with the Spirit, to a deeper degree of conversion, to a challenge of being holier at the end of next year than we are at the end of this year.

To assist you in this goal, I want to suggest to you, in the tradition of the New Year, three resolutions for Christians. I call them "Pull Back," "Pick Up," and "Put Down."

First: Pull Back. Dr. Gerald Jampolsky wrote a book a few years ago entitled *Love Is Letting Go of Fear*. In that book he asks this question: "Have you ever given yourself the opportunity of going through just one day concentrating on totally accepting everyone and making no judgments?" He goes on to say, "Everything we think or say reacts on us like a boomerang. When we send out judgment in the form of criticism, fury or other attack-thoughts, they come back to us. When we send out only love, it comes back to us." So I suggest this. Try this once a month—I don't think we can really handle this more than that—for one day, say, the third Tuesday of each month: *suspend all judgments*. Spend one day of acceptance. Pull back from judging and just look and accept. See the difference it makes in your life. Pull Back.

The second resolution is this: Pick Up. Pick up on what others have started. Some of you have known losses. You've lost spouses, you've lost children, you've lost relationships, you've lost health, you've lost equilibrium. You name it: There are losses scattered all over the landscape. But you have your choice about these losses. Your choice is either to turn in on yourself and forever cry "Woe is me," or you can pick up on those who turn tragedy into growth.

Let me share a story my uncle told me about Puccini, the great Italian composer, the author of such masterpieces as *Madame Butterfly* and *La Bohème*. Puccini had contracted cancer early in life and spent his last days writing his masterwork, *Turandot*, his most accomplished piece. When told to take it easy, he would reply, "I am going to do as much as I can on my great masterwork, and it is up to you, my friends, to finish it." He did die and so his friends had a decision to make. They could either mourn forever or they could make beautiful music building on his melody. They chose the latter.

So in 1926 at the famed La Scala opera house in Milan (my uncle was there) the masterwork was first played under the great conductor, Arturo Toscanini. When it came to that part in the opera where the Master had stopped because of his early death, Toscanini stopped everything. He turned around to the audience and with tears streaming down his cheeks, said, "Here is where the Master ends." Then, after a long pause, he lifted up his head, smiled broadly and said, "and this is where his friends begin."

Pick up on what others have done. Pick up and make life better for others. You have a new year in which to rewrite the tune. Some have left you the precious melodies of memories that will never leave you. Don't turn in on yourself and feel sorry for yourself. No, pick up and honor those memories by sharing the music of love and service. Pick Up.

The third resolution is this: Put Down. Put down last year's garbage. A woman relates: I was telling my new workplace friend, Alice, about how awful my former boss had been, when she laughed and said, "So forget him. Why not just enjoy it here?" Then she went on to tell me a little story about herself. "I'm reminded of the time I moved a few years ago," she began. "I was making enough money to have a professional mover pack for me and when he asked what I wanted him to pack, I just waved my arm and said, 'Everything!' So when I got to my new place, I saw that he had taken me literally. Along with my furniture he had packed up all my trash bins as well, and there I was in my beautiful new place with all my old garbage, including old newspapers, empty ketchup bottles, and grapefruit peels!"

It's a little story, all right, but it packs a big meaning. You have a beautiful New Year ahead of you. Leave the emotional garbage behind.

So, there you are. Three succinct New Year's resolutions: Pull Back. Pick Up. Put Down. Pull back from judgment. Pick up the positive. Put down the emotional garbage.

My friends, all told, we have been given, on the average, some 25,000 days to live. Some portion of that has already run out. But a New Year, remember, wipes out all of the yesterdays and offers us, shinning new, 365 tomorrows in which to be finer, more focused, more faithful Christians.

There is a new year ahead: time to pull back, pick up, and put down.

Mother's Day — 1

"I give you a new commandment: Love one another. Such as my love has been for you, so must your love be for one another."

Thus the summary of the Christian message is that we are to love *as* Jesus loves us. That word "as" pops up several times in Jesus' teaching: "Love one another *as* I have loved you....Forgive us our trespasses *as* we forgive those who trespass against us....Be compassionate *as* your Heavenly Father is compassionate...." There is a standard, then, by which our moral lives are to be measured. We are to love *as* Jesus did, and if we want to see the full force of that word, we look to Calvary.

It is worthwhile to remember, however, that love is not instinctive, not inborn. It is a learned response. Just like in those animal documentaries you see on TV, catching and eating prey is not automatic. The cubs have to learn that. And it is not without merit today to ask, from whom do they learn it? Who protects them, moves them from den to den, defends them to the point of death, teaches them survival skills? Their mothers. Human mothers, it should be noted on Mother's Day, do the same. They teach survival skills. But more than that. They teach love. And they teach it the only effective way one teaches anything: by doing loving things. They, like Jesus, become the measurement, which is why, I suspect. we give them such honor.

If Jesus said, "Such as my love has been for you, so must your love be for one another," so every mother silently says the same. "Watch me and you'll learn how to love. Let me move you from inbred selfishness to loving, sharing, and giving and concern for others. Watch me and I'll show you how to do it." To this extent, every mother furthers the gospel. For, as Ann Taylor's ditty catches it:

Who ran to help me when I fell,
And would some pretty story tell,
Or kiss the place to make it well?
My mother!

She could just as well have said "Jesus."
Or how about Kipling's poem:

If I were hanged on the highest hill,
Mother o' mine, O mother o' mine!
I know whose love would follow me still,
Mother o' mine, O mother o' mine!
If I were drowned in the deepest sea,
Mother o' mine, O mother o' mine!
I know whose tears would come down to me,
Mother o' mine, O mother o' mine!
If I were damned by body and soul,
I know whose prayers would make me whole,
Mother o' mine, O mother o' mine!

"As I have loved you, so you are to love one another."
Out of the French Revolution came the story of a mother who had wandered through the woods for three days with her two children, trying to survive on roots and leaves. On the third day, she heard some soldiers approaching and quickly hid herself and the children behind some bushes. The sergeant in charge prodded the bushes to see what was stirring behind them. When he saw the starving woman and children he immediately gave them a loaf of brown bread. The mother took it eagerly, broke in into two pieces, and gave one piece to each of the children. "She has kept none for herself," the sergeant said. "Because she is not hungry?" a soldier asked. "Because she is a mother," the sergeant replied.
"Be compassionate as your heavenly Father is compassionate."
Love is taught by loving actions and our first experience of love in this life comes from our mothers. We instinctively recognize that. Have you ever noticed what's the first thing that someone says when they get in front of a video camera? Why, of course, it's "Hi, Mom!" Guess who the most important person in their lives is. But, I must hasten to add, love is taught

by *lots* of moms and dads, even childless, single people like myself. For Mother's Day and Father's Day really celebrate all those people who have mothered and fathered us and taught us how to love. I think of my fourth-grade teacher, Mr. McElliott, who never married but who was a dear father to us boys seeking guidance and understanding. I think of Miss Consolvo, who mothered many a teenager, and now that she is retired, still gets invitations, letters, and visits from her now adult students who have never forgotten her kindness. Such people have many children in the Lord.

Still, it's our mothers who preeminently teach us how to love, which is why this adult child said, "I finally found a Mother's Day card that expressed my feelings for my mother in real terms." The card said, "Now that we have a mature, adult relationship, there's something I'd like to tell you. You're still the first person I think of when I fall down and go boom!"

But perhaps nobody catches both the mood and the happy interplay of today's gospel and of Mother's Day like the late Erma Bombeck. She writes:

> On Mother's Day all over the country, grateful moms are pushed back into their pillows, the flower on their bird-of-paradise plant (which blooms every other year for fifteen minutes) is snipped and put in a shot glass, and a strange assortment of food comes out of a kitchen destined to take the sight from a good eye. A mixer whirls, out of control, then stops abruptly as a voice cries, "I'm telling." A dog barks and another voice says, "Get his paws out of there. Mom has to eat that!" Minutes pass and finally, "Dad! Where's the chili sauce?" Then, "Don't you dare bleed on Mom's breakfast!" The rest is a blur of banging doors, running water, rapid footsteps and a high pitched, "YOU started the fire! YOU put it out! " The breakfast is fairly standard: a water tumbler of juice, five pieces of black bacon that snap in half when you breathe on them, a mound of eggs that would feed a Marine division, and four pieces of cold toast. The kids line up by the bed to watch you eat and from time to time ask why you're not drinking your Kool-Aid or touching the cantaloupe with black olives on top spelling M-O-M.

Now comes the punch line of today's gospel as Bombeck continues:

> Later in the day, after you have decided it's easier to move to a new house than clean the kitchen, you return to your bed where, if you're wise, you'll reflect on this day. For the first time, your children have given instead of received. They have offered to you the sincerest form of flattery: trying to emulate what you do for them. And they have presented you with the greatest gift people can give: themselves.

That's the meaning and message of today's gospel: "Such as my love has been for you, so must your love be for one another."

It's a perfect gospel for Mother's Day. Why? Because mothers do it best.

Mother's Day — 2

Beyond the sentimentality and especially the commercialism of Mother's Day there lies a deeper religious reality, an example of which we find in today's gospel: "I give you a new commandment. As I have loved you, so you also should love one another." The operative word is, of course, "as," and if you want to know the content of "as," you look at Jesus washing his disciples' feet or the crucifixion. That explains "as." Jesus, in short, was wise enough to know that he couldn't just say something abstract about love. He had to make it concrete. Love has to have a content, a pattern, a demonstration for it to mean anything, to catch on. So he used his own life and death as an example of love.

This, of course, is a common truism: We learn how to love from being loved, from seeing love in action. It's as simple and profound as that. And that's why I said that behind the Mother's Day hype lies a deeper religious reality: We honor mother because, in almost all cases—there are rare exceptions—her love is the first to touch us and is the first concrete lesson we have in it. So, to this extent, Mother's Day is a celebration of all those, parents or not, who nourish or cherish others and teach them the meaning of love. It's just that mothers are the most evident, most visible, most endearing teachers and that's why we honor them, remember them and their concrete love examples.

One daughter wrote this about her mother:

> A few years ago when my mother was visiting, she asked me to go shopping with her because she needed a new dress. I don't normally like to go shopping with other people, and I'm not a patient person, but we set off for the mall together nonetheless. We visited nearly every store that carried ladies' dresses, and my

mother tried on dress after dress, rejecting them all. As the day wore on, I grew weary and my mother grew frustrated. Finally, at our last stop, my mother tried on a lovely blue three-piece dress. The blouse had a bow at the neckline, and as I stood in the dressing room with her, I watched as she tried, with much difficulty, to tie the bow. Her hands were so badly crippled from arthritis that she couldn't do it.

Suddenly, as I watched her fumbling with her arthritic hands, it hit me. Suddenly my impatience gave way to an overwhelming wave of compassion for this woman, my mother. I went over to tie the bow for her. The dress was beautiful, and she bought it. Our shopping trip was over, but the event was etched indelibly in my memory. For the rest of the day, my mind kept returning to that moment in the dressing room and to the vision of my mother's hands trying to tie that bow. They are old and stiff now, but I couldn't get it out of my mind that these were the loving hands that had fed me, bathed me, dressed me, tied my shoelaces and bows, caressed and comforted me, and, most of all, prayed for me.

Later in the evening, I went to my mother's room, took her hands in mine, kissed them and, much to her surprise, told her that to me they were the most beautiful hands in the world.

She continues with this comment. "I'm so grateful that God let me see with new eyes what a precious, priceless gift a loving, self-sacrificing mother is. I can only pray that some day my hands, and my heart, will have earned such a beauty of their own." This daughter was learning to love others *as* her mother loved her.

Alicia Sferrino was just twenty years old when she was diagnosed with severe kidney failure. Although dialysis would help for a while, doctors made it clear to Alicia's family that she would die without a kidney transplant. Like any loving parents, Deanne and Vincent Sferrino would have gladly given a vital organ to save their precious daughter. But they couldn't. You see, Alicia was adopted, and they had no idea who her real parents were.

So began an arduous search to connect with Alicia's birth mother. All they had was her name, Ruth Chiasson, and the state in which she gave birth. After making extensive telephone calls to this town, they learned that Ruth had married and now her last name was Foisy. But they couldn't find a Foisy anywhere. Finally, Deanne and Vincent tracked down the priest who had married Ruth and her husband. He agreed to send her a letter from the Sferrinos.

When Ruth Foisy first opened the Sferrino's letter, she was stunned. At seventeen, she had become pregnant and given birth to a baby girl. Her parents pressured her to give the baby away. Ruth had never gotten over the heartbreak and guilt of that act, and for twenty years she had burned a candle on the date of Alicia's birth. Now the child she had given life to needed her to give that gift a second time. Ruth, the mother, knew what she must do for her child of long ago. It wasn't easy to gather her present children around and tell them that they had a half-sister they never knew. It wasn't easy to relive the story of giving away her baby for adoption. But when she was finished, Ruth's children rallied around her. They would support her all the way.

Ruth went through with the donation, and today both women are doing well. Alicia Sferrino is healthy, her new kidney functioning fine. She is married now, and the mother of a baby daughter herself. In a time of physical and emotional crisis, these two women gave each other a special gift. Ruth gave Alicia life a second time; Alicia gave Ruth the forgiveness she sought for so long.

Love is like that and that's how we learn it. It's today's gospel in another guise.

Finally, on a lighter note, in these days, when in some quarters, motherhood is devalued, let me end with one woman's account.

> A friend of mine went to the County Clerk's office to renew her driver's license. "Do you have a job, or are you just a...?" the recorder asked her.
>
> My friend, fuming, snapped: "Of course I have a job. I'm a mother."
>
> The recorder replied, "We don't list 'mother' as an occupation. 'Housewife' covers it."

The woman goes on:

Well, I found myself in the same situation one day when I was at our own town hall. The clerk was obviously a career woman, poised, efficient, and possessed of a high-sounding title, like Official Interrogator or Town Registrar.

She asked, "And what is your occupation?"

I don't know where they came from, but all of a sudden the words popped out of my mouth: "I'm a Research Associate in the field of Child Development and Human Relations."

The clerk paused, pen frozen in midair. I repeated the title slowly: "I'm a Research Associate in the field of Child Development and Human Relations." The clerk wrote my pompous title in bold, black ink on the official questionnaire.

The clerk said, "Might I ask just what you do in your field?"

I replied, "I have a continuing program of research in the laboratory and in the field. I'm working for my Masters (the whole family) and already have four credits (all daughters). Of course, the job is one of the most demanding in the humanities, and I often work fourteen hours a day. But the job is more challenging than most run-of-the-mill careers and the rewards are in satisfaction rather than just money."

There was an increasing note of respect in the clerk's voice. She completed the form, stood up, and personally ushered me to the door. As I drove into our driveway, buoyed by my glamorous new career, I was greeted by three of my lab assistants—ages thirteen, seven, and three. And upstairs, I could hear our next experimental model (six months old) in the child development program, testing out a new vocal pattern.

I felt triumphant. I had scored a beat on bureaucracy. And I had gone down on the official records as someone more distinguished and indispensable to society than anyone else. I was a mother.

Father's Day

Comedian Johnny Carson said his son gave him a paper that read, "To the man who has inspired me with his fatherly wisdom."

Carson said, "Son, I didn't know you felt that way about me."

His son said, "I don't. Can you fax this to Bill Cosby?"

Well, today *is* Father's Day and we usually spend it praising Dad and, on your behalf, preachers like myself extol him. The emphasis is always on us-to-him. Today, if you will bear with me, I want to do something different. I want to do the opposite.

Much to Dad's chagrin, I want to deliver a message from him to us, a message he often finds it difficult to give himself, which is why I will speak for him. To make this easier on you and me and Dad, I want to tell this message through the medium of a son's story, a true one. So just relax and let the story, which is every father's story, come to you.

My father lived a hard-working, middle-class life. He had served his country during World War II and held tight to the moral values he gained through the struggles of that era. In all the years of my youth, I knew of only two days of work that Dad missed.

His honorable work ethic and quiet, solid manner also gave rise to one of his flaws: my father's inability to express his feelings or to speak aloud about the love he felt for his family. Yet there was one exception to this rule that I will never forget.

One Sunday, my sister, one of my brothers, and my wife and I had gathered at my parents' house for dinner. During the normal chatter, I noticed that my father slurred his words now and then when he spoke. No one mentioned this during dinner, but I felt compelled to discuss it with my mother afterward, as we sipped coffee alone together in the kitchen.

"He says his dentures don't fit any more," Mom explained. "I've been bugging him for weeks to make an appointment with the dentist, but he keeps putting it off."

"The problem isn't his teeth, Mom. I don't know what's wrong, but he needs to see his doctor, not his dentist. I know he hates to go to the doctor, and I'll help you drag him in if we have to. I'm really worried."

Drawing on the lessons learned from her many years of marriage to a stubborn man, my mother devised a plan to deliver him to the doctor's office without a struggle. She made an appointment with the dentist, and then called the doctor to explain the situation. The doctor, well aware of the difficulty in getting my father to keep an appointment, went along with the plan.

Waiving the normal rules for a specific appointment time, he agreed to see my father immediately after his dental appointment. The dentist, also clued into the conspiracy, pretended to adjust my father's dentures and then sent him on his way.

Mom took the "scenic route" home, and before he suspected a thing, Dad found himself in the parking lot of the medical complex. After the standard protest, he quietly followed my mother into the doctor's office. She phoned me two days later.

"I'd like you to come over this evening. We need to talk," she said. I rushed over after work. My mother motioned me into the kitchen. She spoke softly so my father could not hear.

"They found a brain tumor," she said. "It's too large at this point to operate. They're going to try to shrink it with radiation and chemotherapy; maybe they can do something then." She stopped to wipe tears from her eyes.

My father soon began to undergo a barrage of treatments. One of the side effects was the loss of almost all of his thick black hair. One of the lighter moments we experienced during this ordeal was when my wife Michele gave birth to our first child, and we all laughed to discover what had happened to Dad's hair: Chelsey arrived in the world wearing it.

My father's condition worsened, and the doctors finally informed us that his condition was terminal. During one of his prolonged stays in the hospital, we brought Chelsey with us when we visited him. By this time his speech had deteriorated to the point where interpreting the words he tried to form was virtually impossible. Lying in bed, my father's head propped up on pillows, he tried to communicate with me through grunts and hand gestures. I finally figured out that he wanted me to set Chelsey on his stomach so he could make faces at her.

With my father's hands wrapped around her tiny waist, Chelsey sat on her grandpa and they jabbered nonsense-talk back and forth. Chelsey's vocabulary was restricted by her youth, my father's by the horrible disease that was stealing a larger part of his brain with each passing day.

Dad remained in control of his laughter, however, if not his speech. And how he laughed that day. He mumbled and cooed to Chelsey; she returned the volley with a stream of gurgles and slobbery consonants. Then they'd both erupt into deep belly laughs. The bond that grew between grandfather and granddaughter never required a formal language. Dad discovered an ally who fell in love with him completely and unconditionally. Chelsey possessed the child's knack of knowing a grandfather's loving touch when she felt it.

After Dad escaped the hospital for the familiar and comfortable surroundings of his own home, the Grandpa/Chelsey comedy routine became a regular part of our visits. Both participants found it hilarious. They laughed every time they played the game, each trying to out-silly the other.

Finally, on a visit to my parents' home during what we all knew were my father's last days, my mother took Chelsey from my arms and announced, "Your father would like to see you alone for a minute." I entered the bedroom where my father lay on a rented hospital bed. He appeared even weaker than the day before. "How are you feeling, Dad?" I asked. "Mom said you wanted to see me. Can I do anything for you?" He tried to speak, but I couldn't make out a word. "I'm sorry, but I can't understand you," I said. "You want your pad and pen?"

Ignoring my suggestion for his pad and pen, he slowly and with great effort pulled himself higher in the bed. Moved by the intensity of his struggle as he again tried and failed to speak, I reached out to hold his hand. Our eyes met and locked, both of us suddenly forced to face the painful reality that all the years we'd spent together, as I'd grown from a child to a man with a child of my own, had come down to this one last father-and-son moment.

Tears glistened in my father's eyes. He shook his head and smiled at me as if to say, "Ain't this just the damnedest thing?" Then Dad took a deep breath and won one final battle with the disease that would soon win the war. He softly spoke three little words with crystal clarity: "I love you."

The son goes on and gives us the point of the story.

> We don't learn courage from heroes on the evening news. We learn true courage from watching ordinary people rise above hopeless situations, overcoming obstacles they never knew they could. I saw the courage my mother possessed when she chose to fight the battle that would allow her husband to remain at home where he belonged. I gained courage from our friends, neighbors, and relatives as they drew closer, circling wagons of love around until the last days of my father's life. Most of all, I learned about courage from my father, who simply refused to leave this world until he overcame his greatest obstacle: sharing his heart with his son.

Dads don't always openly share their love. On Father's Day I just wanted to remind you that it's there. Oh, yes, children, it is there.

Memorial Day

The famous ship, the Queen Mary, now sits at a dock in Long Beach, California, and is enjoying life as an exclusive restaurant attraction, after sailing for over a half century on the high seas. The Queen Mary has a fabled history. Let me recall it. The ship was built in Scotland and launched in 1934. After Her Majesty Queen Mary presented her personal standard, it embarked on its maiden voyage on May 27, 1936, departing Southampton. It took only a record five days to reach New York. The Queen Mary has four propellers weighing 35 tons each, a 140-ton rudder and weighs 81,234 tons. In its glory days it carried nearly two thousand passengers serviced by a crew of over a thousand.

It was *the* premier luxury liner of the time. Something was to change all that, however. World War II broke out, and so the Queen Mary underwent a transformation. The ship became known as the "Grey Ghost" when it was camouflage-painted and its portholes blacked out. Because its four 40,000 horsepower turbine steam engines could outrun German U-boats, it became a military transport. Servicing the war effort, it traveled more than 600,000 miles and carried over 800,000 troops. One historic journey to New York on May 1943 included passenger Winston Churchill and 5000 German prisoners of war. Quite a history.

Is there something here for us to contemplate? Yes. When given the choice between becoming a museum for gawking curiosity seekers and being a ship on the high seas outrunning the enemy, bringing glory to the British crown, the Queen Mary opted for glory. And now once again, when the Queen Mary's use as both luxury liner and transport carrier are clearly no longer possible, she is creatively surviving as a floating restaurant attracting thousands of tourists every year and exposing them to her past, present, and future glory. She's no museum; she's earning her way in yet another life or adaptation.

Why do I tell you that story? Because, for our purposes today, the story of the Queen Mary functions on three deep spiritual levels. First, on this Memorial Day weekend, it reminds us of all those men and women whose lives, like the Queen Mary, were changed when war broke out. Their placid everyday routines were dramatically impacted and turned upside down. Thousands of men and women were called to be, as it were, camouflage-painted into a hundred different jobs, campaigns, and service here and abroad.

With unified purpose, they sailed the seas in high adventure and constant danger. They all knew that, like the mighty ship, they had their choice of selfishness or service, and they choose service and many of them paid with their lives. And now, just as the Queen Mary sits in the dock as a reminder of its former glory as a civilian and a soldier, so we build our monuments, celebrate our holidays, and call up our memories to remind us of the dreadful glory earned on the battlefields of the world and those who paid the price for it.

But as I said, the story of the Queen Mary functions on a second level as well, a different, more personal one. It's a paradigm of what happens to us. We too, like that ship, start out great, so to speak, and then, as life goes on, we find that the unexpected comes along and we must keep on making adaptations. We simply didn't bargain, for example, for our personal wars any more than the Queen Mary bargained for a global war: sickness, depression, a divorce, a child on drugs, financial setback, loss, widowhood, the relentless ravages of time and aging—but there they are.

Suddenly, we have a decision to make: to forever keep on looking back like a perennial Baby Jane, keep propping up our old persona like an aging movie star loading the makeup on a face that won't lie any more; or, like the Queen Mary, to adapt to new circumstances, new challenges, to new stages in our lives, and to adapt creatively, that is, in a way that both serves others and makes us grow. For example, Audrey Hepburn, after her marketable looks wore out, became an advocate for poor children. The Queen Mary story forces us to ask in life's changing circumstances, how can I grow *now*? How can I serve *now*? How can I love *now*? What is God calling me to *now*? Not then, but now.

Finally, realize it or not, the Queen Mary story functions as a challenge. We are making our future now. While we must rightfully strive for immediate success in our chosen field, we must always at the same time be building for the future. Which is to say, as I work and live now, what kind of person am I turning into? If I am successful and am gaining fame and fortune, which I must let go of sooner or later, what values that endure have I embraced and nourished along the way?

Here's a true story that catches what I'm trying to say. While at the park one day, a woman sat down next to a man on a bench near a playground. "That's my son over there," she said, pointing to a little boy in a red sweater who was gliding down the slide.

"He's a fine looking boy," the man said. "That's *my* son on the swing in the blue sweater." Then, looking at his watch, he called to his son. "What do you say we go, Todd."

Todd pleaded, "Just five more minutes, Dad. Please? Just five more minutes." The man nodded and Todd continued to swing to his heart's content.

Minutes passed and the father stood and called again to his son. 'Time to go now."

Again Todd pleaded, "Five more minutes, Dad. Just five more minutes." The man smiled and said, "O.K."

"My, you certainly are a patient father," the woman responded.

The man smiled and then said, "My older son Tommy was killed by a drunk driver last year while he was riding his bike near here. I never spent much time with Tommy and now I'd give anything for just five more minutes with him. I've vowed not to make the same mistake with Todd. *He* thinks he has five more minutes to swing. The truth is, I get five more minutes to watch him play."

Catch my meaning? Like the Queen Mary which didn't realize it at the time, we are making our future now and "now" can never be recaptured. Fame and fortune, career and corporation are good goals, but not the most important, and when we are forced—*and we will be*—to let go and adapt to a new way of living and being, will we have built the resources and cherished the precious moments and precious people to find grace in the new moment and opportunity to love and grow in a new way?

Over and above our jobs, over and above our "image," which is so important today, in a world without substance, over and above our fashion statements, this larger truth, which I read somewhere, endures:

> Every person who ever came into this world was sent into this world by God to do some special task. Every person is, as it has been put, a dream of God. That task need not be a task which is great as the world uses the word great. It may be to care for a child, to make someone else happy, to teach someone's mind, to cure someone's body, to bring sunshine into the lives of others across a counter or in an office, to make a home. To make a difference.

The Queen Mary never dreamed it would be anything but a playground for the rich and famous. But when war broke out and courage was called for and service was demanded, it came through. We remember that, which is why we have Memorial Day. The Queen Mary didn't stay stuck in one category. A terrible war intruded but it learned to respond to the moment. And so must we respond to new chapters in our lives. The Queen Mary with its hyper-design and forward-looking engineering didn't realize at the time that it was also being built for future service in a way it didn't expect. As are we.

Let me sum it all up by fittingly recalling a war movie, Steven Spielberg's movie *Saving Private Ryan*, where a squadron of young soldiers, you recall, is sent on a mission to find one soldier behind enemy lines and bring him home. Most of the young men in the squadron, including the captain, die in the rescue attempt. As he lies dying, the captain's last words to Private Ryan are, "Earn this." Many years later, Private Ryan, now an old man, visits the grave of his captain. As he kneels at the grave, he says, "Not a day goes by I don't think about what happened....And I just want you to know...I've tried. Tried to live my life the best I could. I hope that's enough. I didn't invent anything. I didn't cure any diseases. I worked a farm. I raised a family. I lived a life. I only hope, in your eyes at least, I earned what you did for me."

A good sentiment for us today on Memorial Day. A hoped-for sentiment for someone tomorrow who will remember us.

Fourth of July

I have two set-up stories, both true, to tell you first. On January 13, 1982, Air Force Flight 90 crashed on a takeoff and fell into the icy waters of the Potomac River. Some of you recall that incident. Martin Skutnik was there and he saw the plane go down. He stood with the other spectators on the river bank watching a woman who had survived the crash and was struggling to swim in the cold water. Skutnik plunged into the river and rescued her.

He had never taken a life-saving course, but he saved the woman's life. He didn't use the proper form or technique when he swam to the woman's side, at least as professional swim instructors would teach it. He may not have followed the Red Cross Manual in the method he used to grab the woman and bring her back to the safety of the shore. But he saved her.

My second story. An Italian fisherman named John Napoli was returning with his catch of fish one foggy morning. He piloted his boat beneath the Golden Gate Bridge into San Francisco harbor. What he saw next horrified him. There were people everywhere in the water. A hospital ship, The Netherlands, had collided with an oil tanker. People were shouting, "Help me! Save me! I'm drowning! "

John Napoli carefully guided his fishing vessel to a cluster of drowning men. Quickly he began to pull them aboard one by one. Soon the small fishing boat was overcrowded. And then John Napoli made one of the hardest decisions of his life. He knew that the lives of those men were far more important than his small fortune of fish. Within minutes he dumped his entire cargo of 2000 pounds of fish, worth thousands of dollars, into the waters of San Francisco Bay and pulled more than seventy people aboard his boat.

It's the Fourth of July week. These two stories set you up for my final story, fittingly enough, from the annals of war. And then we shall draw our conclusions.

It was an unforgettable photo. You know it well. The raising of the flag on Iwo Jima. In fact, if you had to pick ten photographs to tell the story of our country, this one featuring U.S. soldiers lifting up an American flag would be one of them, even if it was a posed re-enactment of the real thing.

Iwo Jima is a dot in the Pacific where the United States needed a landing strip for bombers striking Japan during World War II . Some 70,000 marines were sent to take it from a dug-in enemy. "The thing I'll remember forever," recounts retired Major General Fred Hayes, "was the courage and the guts of the kids…and these were young kids." They were kids but also heroes. There are six flag raisers in the photo. The front four are Ira Hayes, Franklin Sousley, John Bradley, and Harlon Block. The back two are Michael Strank and Rene Gagnon.

Strank was subsequently hit by a mortar shortly afterward and died and is buried in Arlington Cemetery. Block, who had enlisted in the Marine Corps with twelve of his teammates, was also killed by a mortar blast just hours after the flag-raising. Franklin Sousley also died at age nineteen on Iwo Jima. Bradley, Hayes, and Gagnon survived and became national heroes within weeks.

What is most amazing is how ordinary each of these flawed heroes were. Mike Strank played the French horn and once slugged a baseball out of Points Stadium in Johnstown, Pennsylvania. Harlon Block was an outgoing daredevil with many friends at Weslaco High School in Texas. Franklin Sousley was a red-haired, freckled-face "Opie Taylor"-type kid, raised on a tobacco farm in Kentucky. All that's left of him are a few pictures and two letters he wrote home to his widowed mother. In one he wrote, "Mother, you said you were sick. I want you to stay out of that field and look real pretty when I come home. You can grow a crop of tobacco every summer, but I sure as hell can't grow another mother like you."

Ira Hayes was a Pima Indian from Arizona who was told by his chief to be an "honorable warrior," but he had deep emotional problems with being dubbed as a hero and going on money-raising tours to promote the war effort. He felt he was no hero but rather that his buddies who died on

Iwo Jima were the real heroes. He went back to the reservation but the war and the searing memory of his fallen buddies had taken its toll on him. He turned to alcohol and he died at age thirty-two after a night of drinking.

Rene Gagnon was just a kid from Manchester, New Hampshire, who ended up being the youngest of the survivors. He was the one who carried the flag up Mt. Suribachi. And John Bradley was a Navy Corpsman from Wisconsin who "just jumped in to lend a hand," as he put it. He was wounded in both legs and won the Navy Cross for heroism. He returned to his home in the Midwest, became a farmer and businessman, was married for forty-seven years and had eight children.

So we have three stories of ordinary people. At the time, Michael Skutnik was only twenty-eight. He was a general office worker. He had a wife and two children and lived in a rented house. An ordinary man. For the Italian fisherman there was something more important to him than profits. He deliberately lost his profits in order to save people. An ordinary man. Then there's that handful of kids on Iwo Jima and a famous image of a flag-raising among the dead bodies of their comrades. Ordinary kids.

And here we contemplate and we pray deep within ourselves, for, my people, remember this: *that's* where freedom arises: spiritual freedom, personal freedom, national freedom. Not from programs. Not from training. Not from manuals. But, as Jesus taught us, from the selfless heart, something we should pray for at this Mass.

When *we* move beyond our own personal concerns to save others, when we put people before profits, when we reach out—even if we have to pay for it with our lives—to raise the flag of decency and truth, there is release, newness, spirit, freedom. True freedom.

What these stories are saying is that this Fourth of July you can have all the patriotic speeches you want. You can wave the stars and stripes till the cows come home. You can march in parades till you drop, but freedom is always won on the one-to-one level of the daily small heroisms of ordinary people. Like Martin Shutnik, John Napoli, Ira, Franklin, John, Harlon, Michael, and Rene—and us.

Don't forget us.

Halloween

Tomorrow is Halloween. All throughout the land there will be pint-sized goblins, ghosts, and ghouls patrolling our neighborhoods, asking for tricks or treats. But behind this rather commercial, rather secular fun day, is there a religious challenge, a religious posture in disguise? To answer that, I'd like to share with you a lesson on the origins of Halloween, and accordingly, what we can do from a faith perspective to place it in our lives.

As far as we can tell, Halloween comes to us from the old Celtic celebrations held at the end of summer. The reason they had a celebration to mark the end of summer was because it was then when the spirits were beginning more actively to stir. You see, according to popular lore, the spirits come out at night and as summer wanes and the days get shorter and the winter nights get longer, it gives the goblins and ghouls more dark time to work their mischief.

To appease such spirits who now had a longer haunting time, the pagans offered them treats so that they would not be the objects of their tricks. Of course, among the Celts, as always, there were those cunning citizens who were not above a little deceit. That is, they took to disguising themselves as evil spirits so that, for one thing, they hoped to fool the real spirits into leaving them, fellow ghosts, alone, but also so that they, so disguised, could go around stealing the treats the people left for the real spirits. That's where we get the "trick or treat " tradition.

Anyway, it was this kind of pagan thing that the Christians met when the came to the Emerald Isle and, as was their wise custom, they did not do away with Halloween altogether, but rather they baptized it; that is, they sifted out what was true and shucked off the superstitions. After all, the Christians figured, there *is* a spirit world—the angels, the saints in heaven—so maybe it was a good opportunity to draw these pagans into remembering all the spirits, but as kindly, as friends, as members of the Mystical Body, the communion of saints, as all of God's people, both living and dead, now united with us in his love. So the pagan custom of *appeasing* the spirits became the Christian holy time of *remembering* them; that is to say, to re-member, to rejoin them in a vast holy community. So we get All Hallows Eve, the word "hallow" meaning "holy," as in "hallowed be thy name." It was now a holy time of connection rather than an unholy time of fear.

And once that was in place—remembering the holy ones now deceased—then around the fourth century it was easy to introduce the feast of those spirits who weren't going around shouting "boo!" but who were going around interceding for us. And so we got the Feast of All Saints which they placed also at the end of summer, right next to this general remembering of the spirit world. And then a few centuries later it was easy to introduce what we call the feast of All Souls on the next day, the spirits on the way to God but who needed help.

The whole mix ultimately reminded everybody—a reminder especially needed in these days of rampant individualism—of what incredible connections we have, that everyone on earth, in purgatory, and heaven are all part of one family of God. We are indeed what Jesus said: vine and branches. So, Halloween, All Saints, All Souls say we're all connected. We are never alone. We interact. We form one vast communion of saints and these festive days remind us of that great Catholic truth.

What else can we say about Halloween? For one thing, even though we never think about it, dressing up for Halloween—yourself, your children and grandchildren—ritually connects us to that spirit world. In other words, in dressing up we are symbolically joined to the community of the invisible world. And that's a good thing. Second, when we don those scary masks, try to remember, from a Christian point of view, that they are a symbol of human disfigurement brought on by sin, betrayal, sickness, and death. But faith reminds us that someday those masks, by the grace of God and our faith, will be removed and we shall be made beautiful as ugliness dissolves, sin is cleansed, and even the last enemy, death, falls before the everlasting mercy of Christ.

Finally, as an aside, I'd like to call to your attention that at Halloween a lot of very worldly folk are really playing a cultural game, although they would be the first to deny it. That is to say, in a world in which the interior life is despised, faith ridiculed by the elite, and every vestige of organized religion is being legally eradicated, people still cannot find peace in the totally one-dimensional secular world. So, while denying the spiritual, the sophisticated secular people unconsciously sneak it in the back door by pretending to be playing Halloween games. This way they can flirt with the possibilities of another world and scratch a gnawing spiritual itch without losing face.

Halloween, of course, like Christmas, has been co-opted by the marketplace and lost much of its spiritual power, so much so that none of us even comes near to thinking in faith terms when we costume up. So, to help restore its place, I'd like to end by making four simple suggestions that might redirect yourselves and your family these next three days.

First, before you go out trick or treating, gather the whole family and offer a prayer for the deceased members and friends of your family, people of your past who meant something to you and who are very much present.

Second, bring out the family album for the triduum of Halloween, All Saints, and All Souls; or if you have a picture of grandma or grandpa or other deceased family members, take it off the wall or out of the album and put it on the coffee table with a little lit candle in front of it. The point is that you want to make some kind of statement to your children or grandchildren that we all come from a long line of people who loved us and that this is sacred as well as fun time, that we are a part of their journey and they ours.

Third, on All Saints Day, perhaps at the dinner table, have family members research their saints' names and tell everyone something about him or her.

Fourth and finally, you might bring some of the things you get by going around tricking or treating to a nursing home, send to the hurricane victims, or save as Christmas presents for the needy.

Halloween, All Saints, All Souls: a time of fun but don't forget the other "F," a time of faith.

All Saints

A, B, C, REVELATION 7:2–4, 9–14

Today's feast of All Saints is one of my favorite feasts because it conjures up that great panoramic and majestic scene that was presented to us in the first reading. It conjures up those vast multitudes of 144,000 multiplied endlessly. It conjures up the fact that, with all this incredible, astronomical number of people whom we call holy, that this feast is, when you come right down to it, a paean to God's mercy, to God's all-inclusiveness; and when we sing *When the Saints Come Marching In,* indeed it provokes an inspiring and truly awesome feeling.

The feast of All Saints evokes many observations. Wise ones, like this from Sidney Harris: "The saint loves people and uses things. The sinner loves things and uses people." Or the always quotable Oscar Wilde: "The only difference between a saint and a sinner is that every saint has a past and every sinner has a future." So this feast is a fascinating and colorful tableau to contemplate.

But this morning I would like to forgo the grandeur and the pageantry that the feast of trillions of saints evokes in our minds and I would like to offer a different focus and imagery of the saints, the saints of the past, the saints who are present among us. And the imagery I would like you to think about when you reflect on this feast of All Saints is that of a *chorus.*

Get into the mood. Close your eyes for a moment, if you wish, and picture yourself standing in a chorus of an endless 144,000 people, singing a song of faith, singing aloud, if you will, the Creed. And I ask you to be aware of two things that will be operating as each of us belts out our song, and you must listen to this seriously and carefully to catch its meaning.

The first is this: No one believes it all. No one believes it all. Each of us in the chorus is gifted with only a partial understanding of the mystery of God among us; and so, in our large chorus, one sings with great intensity and assurance, another sings with little attention and conviction. Or perhaps today we're caught by the words and melody because we happen emotionally and spiritually to be in a good place. But, at another time, in another mental or emotional place, we feel doubtful and alienated and we can hardly get the words out of our mouths. That's O.K. No one believes it all, but together we sing more than we can sing alone. Together we sing more than we can sing alone.

And so the saints, you see, the saints are a chorus, a communion, that sings what we cannot and believes those parts we cannot accept. They chant the song of faith with us when we can join them and they hum the song of faith when we cannot. Together, we, the saints of yesterday and today, sing more than we can sing alone, for no one believes it all, but all believe.

The second thing that operates is this: If no one believes it all, so also no one believes all the time. Our journey of faith is seldom smooth and uninterrupted. At times it fluctuates between belief and unbelief. A few years ago a friend of mine lost her son in an automobile accident. She says that she can no longer believe in God, in a God who would let her son lose his life, especially since she and her family are faithful Catholics and good churchgoers. How could God do this to her? There are three responses to this woman.

The first is to say, "Well, if you can no longer believe, you are no longer a Catholic. You no longer belong." That's a harsh view. That's to deny the seriousness of her loss. A second response is to say to her, "You haven't really lost your faith. You're just temporarily depressed. Everything will be fine." Everything will *not* be fine. This is to deny her pain. But the third response is to honor her losses, the loss of her son, the loss, or at least, the shock to her faith. The fact of the matter is that tragedy has indeed broken her trust in a loving, provident God.

Meanwhile? Meanwhile, the community believes for her. The saintly chorus picks up her faltering verses. The collective faith of the saints sustains her though her period of unbelief; and as she slowly encounters these saints of yesterday and today, she will begin to see *their* scars and sense *their* resilience and they will help her believe once more, in the face of tragic absurdity, in a new and different way. They will help her sing with a different modulation. They will sing the louder the phrases that she can only sing softly, if at all.

So, you see, no one here, you or I, believes it all. And no one here believes all the time. No one accepts every verse and no one can sing every note all the time. But the chorus does. The chorus, or the community of saints, sings when you and I are unwilling or unable to do so.

Peter sang for Doubting Thomas until he could believe again. Thomas sang for Denying Peter until he could embrace again. Monica sang for her son Augustine when he was in his period of sinfulness and unbelief until he could repent again. Clare sang for Francis when he was sad until he was glad again. We are a whole community. We are a chorus of saints. That's what we're celebrating today. We support each other and we become more than the sum total of our individual selves as the Communion of Saints.

You exhibit the gifts I don't have and I exhibit those you don't have. You cry the tears I cannot cry and I laugh the laughter you cannot laugh. You believe when I struggle with doubts. I believe when you struggle with doubts. You smile when I am in tragedy. I grieve when you are in joy. Our individual pieces are partial. Our faith, our hope, and our love are quite incomplete. But this feast of the saints, of *all* the saints—past, present, and future, those in heaven, earth, and purgatory—tells us something. This feast gives us support. It reminds us of our faith family, that we belong to a vast community of time and space. It becomes a revelation and a comfort. It tells us a mighty truth: Together we sing more than we sing alone.

A Week of Super Saints

As some of you may know, this past week has offered an unusual array of some of our most popular and fascinating saints who have just paraded across the church's liturgical calendar.

On September 29, we had the angelic trio, the archangels St. Michael who in the book of Daniel defends Israel against its enemies and in the book of Revelation leads God's army to victory over Satan; St. Gabriel, also appearing in the book of Daniel and then later to a frightened little girl in Nazareth to announce some startling news; and finally, St. Raphael who was little Tobit's disguised traveling companion through a series of adventures that included the healing of his father's blindness and, at the very end of the story, as in an exciting novel, he reveals his true identity.

On September 30, there was the feast of St. Jerome. Irascible, cantankerous, ill-tempered, he was noted for his sharp tongue and sharper pen. He skewered more than one well-known personage. He fought with everyone from Pope Damasus to his friend St. Augustine. Yet he was captivated by the word of God and, after years of study and five years in the desert, he finally wound up in a cave outside Bethlehem where he died. Meanwhile, his claim to fame is that he translated the Bible into Latin from the Greek and gave us the famous Vulgate version that held sway in the church for many centuries.

Then, the next day, October 1 there was lovely St. Thérèse, the Little Flower, as unknown in her lifetime as Jerome was famous in his, and as gentle as he was harsh. She was young, in poor health, cloistered in an obscure Carmelite convent in Lisieux, France, doing nothing but routine chores, but infusing that routine with the love of God. "I prefer the monotony of obscure sacrifice to all ecstasies. To pick up a pin for love can convert a soul," she was to write later in her famous autobiography. Before her untimely death she wrote, "I want to spend my heaven doing good on earth," and that "good" is symbolized by that shower of roses she is pictured with.

She is followed the next day, October 2, by the feast of the Guardian Angels, first given their feast in the early seventeenth century, though honored way back in the sixth century by St. Benedict and in the twelfth by St. Bernard. They are our invisible guides on our daily paths.

The feast of the exalted angels was followed by a rather unexalted John Bernadone, a foppish young man with rich merchant father who regaled his companions in the local taverns, who so liked French finery that his friends nicknamed him "Frenchy" and eventually Francis. But this Francis from Assisi, a Don Diego become Zorro, after a bout with illness and imprisonment, which revealed to him the emptiness of his life, became a wandering beggar, at first an embarrassment to his old friends and held as a religious nut by his neighbors. But he won them all over, for he had discovered Jesus and it showed. Although he died early—half blind and seriously ill, he died at age forty-four—he became the troubadour of God and the modern world's favorite saint and left us not only the Christmas crèche and a love for animals but a respect and love for the environment.

October 6 will see the feast of a saint less known to us, the early thirteenth-century St. Bruno, a hermit. He has the distinction of founding the Carthusians, which he established so well that it's the one order in the church that has never had need of a reform. Quite a feat.

October 7 is the feast of Our Lady of the Rosary, established in 1573 to thank God for the victory of the Christians over the Turks at Lepanto. Mary's rosary rose from an old practice of saying 150 Our Fathers in imitation of the 150 psalms and then the parallel of saying 150 Hail Marys with a mystery of Jesus' life attached to each Hail Mary. In the thirteenth century, although the story of Mary giving her rosary to St. Dominic is unhistorical, there is no doubt that Dominic's followers propagated this form of prayer two hundred years later and, finally, in another hundred years, in the sixteenth century, we got the rosary we know today.

Finally, there is the minor feast of St. Denis. It's the feast of third-century St. Denis, held to be the first bishop of France, who was beheaded in the persecution under the Roman Emperor Valerius in 258. One of the more exotic legends about St. Denis says that after he was martyred on Montmartre in Paris, he carried his head to a village northeast of the city where in the sixth century St. Genevieve built a basilica. Which is why, Halloween-like, you see pictures of him carrying his head.

So there we have a remarkable ten days graced by some remarkable people: Michael, Gabriel, and Raphael, the mighty archangels; Jerome, the scold; Thérèse, the consumptive; Francis, the playboy; Bruno, the hermit; Denis, the martyr, a motley crew from different centuries, countries, and walks of life, no different from anyone else in their time—except for one thing, which is why I am telling you about them. The one thing these flawed people had in common was that, at one point in their careers, they let go of their titles and toys, their securities and images, their lies and deceits, and surrendered to Jesus Christ. Instead of the "I" dominating their lives, they switched to "Thou" and they were never the same. Nor was the world.

The "Thou," the beloved Christ, became their holy obsession and that made all the difference. One thinks, for example, of the wealthy playboy, Francis, literally shucking off his fine rich clothes right there in the public square to walk into a new life with Lady Poverty and Brother Sun and Master Jesus.

Well, at this point, I have a fable that fits these saints, and every saint, and I'd like to end with it. Remember, the fable is not an entertainment or a distraction. It must be heard as a challenge. It was their story and maybe someday, we must pray it will be ours as well. Listen.

Once long ago in a distant land, a prince was riding through a deep forest far from his home with his company of soldiers, looking for new lands to conquer. Quite suddenly he came upon a clearing in the trees. There before him stretched a meadow leading to a glorious hill. The meadow and hill were covered with blossoming trees, bushes, and wildflowers that seemed made of pure gold. It so sparkled in the sunlight that the prince was nearly blinded.

Fascinated, the prince signaled to his regiment, and together they rode closer and closer, and up the hill toward the castle. The birds sang sweetly, the perfume of flowers was lovely. As they drew near the castle, he saw that a window opened for a moment in the wall and a face appeared, a face that shone more brilliantly than the sun and yet more gently than any flower. Then it was gone. Instantly he fell in love.

He knocked on the castle door. "Who is there?" came a voice softer than the bluest sky.

"It is I, Prince Rindleheart. I am known throughout the land for my bravery. My armies are the strongest, my wealth is enormous. My castle is but two days ride from here. May I please come and be with you?"

"There is only room for one of us here," was the reply.

He left downcast and in his desperation he sought the wisdom of a wise woman. "Perhaps your armies intimidate her," she suggested.

"Of course," he thought. He returned to the castle alone and knocked upon the door.

"Who is there?" came the sweet voice.

"It is I, the mighty prince, alone," he replied.

"There is only room for one of us here," said the sweet voice.

He went away again, dejected and confused. He roamed the wilderness for some years until he met a famous wizard. "Perhaps she cannot know you with all of your armor and weaponry," he suggested.

"Of course!" said the prince.

So he returned and laid down his armor, his shield, and his sword. He walked humbly to the castle door and knocked.

"Who is there?" asked the voice.

"It is I. No soldier, just a man."

"There is only room for one of us here," came the reply.

For seven more years the prince wandered alone in the wilderness, forsaking his kingdom, thinking only of his beloved. He sought wisdom only from the stars in the sky and the wildness inside him. Finally, one day the prince returned to the castle on the hill. He had no armies, no armor, no horse, no nothing. He slowly walked up the hill, past the bushes heavily laden with fruit, and knocked upon the door.

"Who is there?" came the sweet voice.

The prince took a breath—and said, "It is *thou*."

And the door was opened to him.

Mary

The woman named Mary whom we honor today and about whom we know so little has intrigued us for twenty centuries. We don't know when she was born or when she died, but we can place her in history; we know where she lived and who were some of her friends and family. But why does she persist through the ages? What is her appeal? The answer is to be found in her human journey with God, which is in reality our journey.

When we first meet her, Mary is the object of an ugly rumor: She is pregnant without a husband. Her fiancé, Joseph, is minded officially to deny her and anything about the pregnancy and put her at a distance. That she was innocent, invaded by the Spirit, was not believed. So right away, people down the ages who have suffered from false rumors, who have had their reputations soiled, who have been misunderstood and maligned, unwed mothers, have identified with her.

Then, too, there was her very human anxiety and fear. What's this all about anyway, this Mother of God business? "How can this be?" she asked the angel incredulously. "What does God want? What about Joseph? How can this happen? How can I do this?" Confused and scared and full of questions, Mary is all those throughout the ages who have cried out, "How can I tackle this challenge? How can I survive? What does God want of me? What's it all about, Alfie?"

When her son was born, shepherds and angels rejoiced but power-brokers seethed and conspired to kill her baby. They wanted his life, his spirit. And right away, parents today and down the ages, faced with so many soul assassins, have identified with Mary. They know well enough that there are people out there waiting to kill their children. The people who are waiting to sell their children drugs, the media that glamorizes uncommitted sex, the hawkers, with cash registers for hearts, who teach them that we *do* live by bread alone, the soul snatchers of false values—all are after their children to kill their spirits. Parents know what Mary knew and fear what she feared.

Mary has to flee with her husband and child and become a refugee in a foreign land and immediately joins the countless displaced persons, the homeless huddling in the world's doorways and sleeping on the nation's grates and the twenty-seven million refugees walking the earth today—these lowly people who need to be lifted up. They are cousins under the skin and they can identify with Mary.

When Jesus is an adolescent, Mary loses her child, can't find him in a crowded city. She becomes every parent, every teacher, every mentor in history who can't communicate with a teenager, who loses them to gangs or drugs; whose kids have joined the small army of runaways roaming the streets, exploited by the sex trade, abused and beaten. Many can identify with Mary here.

At some point—we don't know when—this wife and mother became a widow. She buried her husband, and everyone who has lost a spouse, cried Mary's tears, felt the gnawing void in their belly, and returned to an empty bed can identify with her.

When her son is old enough he leaves home to begin his mission and he leaves a widowed mother behind and suddenly every mother and father who see their children grow up and leave them behind, especially those in nursing homes, know what she is feeling in her heart.

When she walks the streets, now that she is alone, she has to give way to the rough Roman soldiers and leering men passing by. She has to move quickly and live in the shadows. As a minority woman in an occupied territory, as a widow with no man around, she is always subject to sexual and physical exploitation and discrimination. Everyone with no rights, every minority figure who has to swallow their pride, everyone ever called nigger or wop or fag can identify with Mary.

When she hears rumors that her son is preaching nearby, she goes with some relatives to see him but can't get near him because of the crowds. She has to be content with sending word that she's out there on the fringe. The message tells Jesus that his mother and relatives want to see him and he, gesturing to the crowd, asks, "Who are my mother and brothers and sisters? Everyone who does the will of God is my mother and brother and sister." It sounded like a putdown, a message to tell his mother to go home, but she read it for what it said, what she always knew: her glory was not primarily that she was his biological mother, but that she was closer to him than anyone else because she loved God and, even when she didn't understand it, did his will. And every little person on the sideline, off-center, on the fringe who doesn't understand what's going on but simply clings fast to God's will can identify with Mary.

And then that son is caught, betrayed by one she had had over for dinner many a time, brought to a mock trial, beaten and humiliated, and hung on a public cross. She arrives in time to see him hanging there, every inch of her mind and body straining to go to him, but she is forced by the soldiers to keep her distance. And suddenly, every parent who has seen their child on a cross, every parent who has seen their child carted off to prison, every parent who wants more than anything else to help their grown children dealing with alcoholism, living in sin, raising their children on nothing, not even having them baptized, going through a divorce—every parent who witnesses such "crucifixions" but who must keep their distance, who are *told* to keep their distance, can identify with Mary and have to pray and suffer in silence.

And finally she cradles the broken dead body of her only son in her arms and sobs uncontrollably and there she is once more: every parent who has lost a child, any friend who has lost a friend, any classmate who has lost a classmate through overdose or gunshot can identify with Mary of the Pietà.

This is the woman—this pilgrim who savored the ups and downs of life—this is the ageless woman who has been given to us as a legacy. "Son, behold thy mother." And here we are today beholding her. But it's good to remember that we're beholding her now that it's all over. In this feast the church has frankly romanticized her. It clothes her with the sun, puts the moon beneath her feet, halos her head with stars, dresses her in medieval robes, paints in winged cherubs to do her bidding, places her against a background of Italian villas, and has her whisked up into heaven to the sound of Handel's *Messiah*.

But we should understand that that's all metaphor, figures of speech, storytelling. What it means to say, all this heavenly glamour, is that Mary who is Everywoman, Everyman, is blessed now because, unblessed in many ways in life, she remained faithful. In all of the unfairness of life, she clung to God. In virginity, in motherhood, in widowhood, at home, a wanderer in a foreign land, with living child, with dead child, she clung to God. So she becomes a woman for all ages and that is the secret of her enduring popularity and her appeal. The church elevates her not because she started out as great and traveled a privileged path, but because she was a handmaid of the Lord and traveled the lowly path. But then, he who is mighty has done great things for her. God has lifted her up when down, fed her when hungry, and because she responded to his loving invitation wherever life would lead her, saw to it that all generations would call her blessed.

That's what we're doing right now: calling this woman of our flesh and blood, our experience, blessed. Which is not honoring someone far away and high above us. No, we're calling blessed someone near and right with us at every human step. And the message of this feast, the celebration of God's taking her into heaven, is a sign of hope for us. It is meant to be a preview of coming attractions for all who cling to God in perplexity and adversity. Mary, the church says in this feast, is what we shall be. She is promise fulfilled, humanity completed, faithfulness rewarded. Simply put, she is us at the end of the journey we are traveling. That is why Mary is so compelling. She is indeed a Woman for All Times and All Seasons.

Joseph

"This is how the birth of Jesus Christ came about." Thus begins St. Matthew's account. And his account, unlike another evangelist, St. Luke, sees the event from the eyes of Joseph, not Mary.

Joseph. His name is mentioned four times in a few verses in today's gospel and yet we know so little about him. But what we do know forms our solemn reflection for this Sunday before Christmas. And whatever else we can say about Joseph, three things initially stand out about this man: he was perplexed, he was marginal, he was a loser.

He was perplexed. His fiancée was pregnant by another man, as far as he could tell. He was torn between his trust in her and what seemed like the obvious facts. He was afraid to take her as wife, as the angel noted. Between his knowledge of Mary's condition and that dream of his, he spent tortured days and sleepless nights. There was so much he didn't understand.

He was marginal. He comes and goes so quickly in the gospel stories. Gone and forgotten. There is not even one recorded word of his. Everyone else has something to say: the angel, Mary, the shepherds, Herod, the Magi. But not Joseph. Silence. The spotlight, literally and figuratively, shines on Jesus and Mary. He's not even the child's real father. He's a stepdad. The manger scene often puts him in the shadows. Like the Lone Ranger, everyone asks, who was that masked man? We really don't know.

Finally, he was, to put it mildly, a loser. He had to fall in love with a mystic, someone claimed by a higher power. He had to struggle with doubts and desperately search for answers. He lost his wife to God, as it were. Then he, the so-called great family man, lost his only son and had to go looking for him down the alleys of Jerusalem. Finally, he lost his life, somewhere between that search for Jesus and Jesus' start of his public ministry. He was gone. Deceased. He left his wife a widow and his son fatherless. Not a great track record. Joseph the loser.

And yet, in this particular Advent of the year 2001, laced with memories of terrorism and death, it is this Joseph who, of all the characters who appear in the Nativity story, speaks to many, resonates with many, identifies with many.

Let us look. We said that Joseph was perplexed, and we also are perplexed. There is so much we don't understand in today's world: the ramifications of human cloning, why other peoples hate us, why September 11 happened, why families break up, why children kill children, why parents divorce, why a child is on drugs. Why, in short, so much evil? But notice, Joseph, the also perplexed, just didn't stand there paralyzed. His perplexity did not stop him from doing what he could. He led his pregnant wife on a long caravan journey to Bethlehem, found a place for her to have a baby, fled with his family to Egypt like the Trapp family fleeing the Nazis, supported them by his handiwork, taught his son a trade. The point is, in spite of so much he didn't understand, he did what he could to make this world a better place. He did his duty. Simply, faithfully, loyally, dependably. To that extent, Joseph speaks to all who at the beginning of this new century are perplexed by it all, and he says, "Do what you can do to be caring, compassionate, and helpful. Stay loyal and faithful to your beliefs and convictions. Do your duty. *You* make this world a better place."

We said he was marginal but, remember, this man also had dreams, just like another marginal person of this century who proclaimed, "I have a dream." As such, he speaks to today's hopeless, today's marginal. Not just those shunted aside because of the color of their skin or their nationality but the slow, the unpopular, the unattractive, the disappointed, the poor, the hurting, those considered on the fringes of nerdville, beyond the social pale—anyone who desperately dreams that things could be better. Joseph speaks to them all. He reminds them to hold on to and cherish their dreams. Have faith, he would say. Look: Mary of Nazareth became queen of heaven, Jesus, the infant in danger of death, became Savior. And Joseph himself, dreamer that he was, eventually emerged from the shadows so that the whole world now knows him as *Saint* Joseph. So have faith in God. Remember Joseph. Cherish your dreams.

Finally, we said he was a loser, a man who knew loss. He speaks deeply to all others who are losers, who also have suffered loss. He knows, for example, that this Christmas will be hard on the thousands upon thousands who have lost their jobs in the ripple effect from September 11, who will experience a leaner holiday, smaller meals, fewer presents, perhaps feelings of failure, of desperation. He knows this Christmas will also be a blue one for those who have lost family members and friends in the World Trade Center disaster, especially those with no closure, or any family member or friends for any reason. With sorrow he sees that there will be empty places at the festive table, empty spaces under the tree, empty beds, empty hearts, perhaps a photograph with a vigil candle on the coffee table. It is so unbearably sad. Joseph, who almost lost a wife and did at one time lose a son, knows the feeling. But, again, he also knew that God would have the last word; that God in time could make loss the very condition of compassion, service, and growth; that, although scars would remain and grief would now and then openly assert itself, loss would be the seeding place of quiet greatness.

So this Advent of the year of the Lord, 2001, Matthew has fortunately presented us with a role model, a man for our seasons. He asks, in effect, "Are you, like Joseph, perplexed? Marginalized? Hurting over losses?" Let Joseph's steadfastness and example be yours, for he is the kind who, many times, would have the occasion to utter this ancient Gallic prayer that may fit some of you today. Listen as I close with it.

> As the rain hides the stars,
> as the autumn mist hides the hills,
> as the clouds veil the blue of the sky—
> so the dark happenings of my life hide
> the shining of Thy face from me.
> Yet if I may hold Thy hand in the darkness,
> it is enough.
> Even though I may stumble in my going,
> Thou dost not fall. Thou dost not fall.

Peter and Paul

Firmum est cor meum. "My heart is firm" [faithful]. These are the words on the seal of the North American College, the American seminary in Rome. A fitting motto for us to remember on the church's celebration of Founders Day.

The fact is, Peter and Paul—one called by the Sea of Galilee and the other on the road to Damascus; one the blue-collar fisherman and the other a learned scholar—are founding apostles and we celebrate them as any country or corporation or organization celebrates the people whose genius gave the original vision and supplied the witness and hard work to make a lasting contribution. We link them together because the two of them single-handedly cemented the foundation of the church and literally bet their lives on its future.

Some facts. We know for sure that these two did not establish the church in Rome; it was already there when they arrived, founded by one of the other apostles or disciples of Jesus. But we also know for sure that Peter and Paul went there to take their message to the center of civilization and they died there as the church's two preeminent apostles—thus enhancing Rome's preeminence—one crucified upside down and the other beheaded. They gave their lives, these two, for the One who gave his life for them.

St. Paul was buried beneath the church we know today as St. Paul's Outside the Walls and St. Peter is buried, of course, under St. Peter's. We know this because for centuries architects have always wondered why they built the first church on such an uncongenial spot of land which required tons of fill dirt to make the ground even when there was already level ground not too far away. Except, of course, that that particular spot, from the very beginning, must have been special.

Investigations in the past century have uncovered the cemetery of Emperor Diocletian. In a Christian section they found a box of bones—according to the graffiti on the walls, they turned out to be Peter's—buried directly with mathematical accuracy, layers and layers down, beneath the high altar of St. Peter's. So now we know why they built the church in such an awkward place. It was ground hallowed by the presence of Peter's grave. We know all these things. What we don't know is when all this happened, when Peter and Paul gave their lives for Jesus. Certainly it was not on the same day.

As usual the early Christians were inventive. They solved that mystery by taking advantage of what was already there, namely, a secular feast day. They chose June 29 for Peter and Paul's deaths because June 28 was already being celebrated as the day Rome was founded by Romulus. The message was that if Romulus founded an old empire, Peter and Paul laid the foundation for a new one: the Christian Church which, like the Roman Empire, quickly spread all over the world. So that's what we're celebrating today: the founder of physical Rome and the founders of spiritual Rome.

We know other things too about Peter and Paul. They were flawed men who had their names changed, highly significant in those days. One was weak, "Depart from me for I am a sinful man, O Lord," and the other a hothead, "I persecuted the church of Christ." But Simon was summoned to go beyond his historical weaknesses and become Peter, a rock on which the church would rest. Saul was summoned to go beyond his fervor as a persecutor squelching the new Jesus movement and become Paul, Apostle to the Gentiles, a promoter of the new movement.

Unlikely candidates for Founding Fathers, but maybe G.K. Chesterton had it right when he wrote: "All the empires and the kingdoms have failed because of this inherent and continual weakness, that they were founded by strong men and upon strong men. But this one thing, the historical Christian Church, was founded on a weak man and for that reason it is indestructible. For no chain is stronger than its weakest link." So we remember them. We remember them for the same reason anyone has Founders Days: We look back and we ask, "Can we recapture their original genius and insights? Can we recapture once more the vision that urged them on and made them tick?" We seemed to have strayed.

One example will do. The full title of Prince Charles, the future king of Great Britain, is his Royal Highness Prince Charles Philip Arthur George, Prince of Wales and Earl of Chester, Duke of Cornwall and Duke of Rothesay, Earl of Carrick, Baron of Renfrew and Lord of the Isles, Prince and Great Steward of Scotland. When Jesus was crucified *his* title, scratched on a simple wooden piece attached to the cross, was "Jesus of Nazareth, the King of the Jews." And when Peter and Paul were martyred in Rome, their titles were simply "apostles." The grander titles would come later: Holiness, Supreme Pontiff, Eminence, Most Reverend, Your Grace, My Lord, or in French, Mon Signore, in English, Monsignor, and the rest.

You catch the difference in this comparison. Before the titles, Peter was walking along the street when, you recall, a lame man begged alms and Peter famously replied, "Silver and gold I have none, but what I do have I can give: In the name of Jesus Christ, rise up and walk." And the man did. After the titles, under his successor Julius II, centuries later, a poor monk traveled to Rome and interviewed this pope who showed him the vast riches and priceless treasures of the church. The amazed monk was shown room after room filled with treasures of art, sculpture, jewels, gold, and silver. The proud pope said to the monk, "You see, my friend, the successor of Peter does not have to say, 'Silver and gold I have none.'" "Yes, Holy Father," replied the monk, "but by the same token, he can no longer say, 'In the name of Jesus Christ, rise up and walk.'"

That's the kind of a story that makes us ask, "Have we lost something on the way? What *was* it that made Peter and Paul tick?" Jesus. "How can we regain their vision?" Jesus.

For Peter, it was, "Lord, to whom shall we go? We have come to believe that you have the words of eternal life." For Paul, is was, "It is no longer I that live, but Christ lives in me," and "I am determined to know nothing else but Jesus Christ and him crucified." The feast day of our spiritual Founding Fathers reminds us that if we as the church have fallen on hard times, could it be because Jesus is no longer the center of our lives as he was for them? It's a thought not just for the day, but for *this* day, *this* time, *this* place, *this* heart of yours and mine.

Flo and Tess

Love of God and neighbor equals the whole law, says Jesus. Let us see, then, how it works out in real life, And to this end, I want to talk about two influential women from the 1800s. In my more irreverent moments, I call them Flo and Tess. Separated by sixty-three years one was a Protestant, the other a Catholic. One was in the public eye, the other was hidden. One lived till ninety, the other only until twenty-four. These very different women of the same century didn't know each other, of course, but what an impact they made on the world.

First, the Protestant lady. Her name is Florence Nightingale. I don't know about you, but when I hear that name, I think of a slender young woman holding an oil lamp, with a peaches-and-cream complexion under an old-fashioned bonnet, and, of course, the face of an angel. That's the popular image of Florence Nightingale, but it probably gilds the lily. Florence must have been made of much sterner stuff, with a feisty, resilient spirit, because the conditions she had to contend with would surely have broken a lesser person.

She was born in Florence (hence her Christian name) in 1810, but spent most of her childhood in England. Then, at the age of seventeen, she felt God's call to nursing. That's about the age that many of today's nurses begin their training, but Florence waited until she was thirty before she received her first nursing training in Germany.

A few years later she returned to London as superintendent of a hospital but that was only for a short while. The Crimean War broke out, you see, and was inflicting terrible casualties, and so, at the age of thirty-four, Florence volunteered to organize all the nursing services for the British Army.

I wonder whether she knew what she was letting herself into. She landed in Turkey with a team of thirty-eight young nurses and took over the military hospital at Scutari. And so began a daily struggle for life within the hell of human suffering. Rooms and corridors were filled with the horribly injured soldiers, there was no sanitation and precious little medical treatment. If that weren't enough, Florence and her nurses had to contend with open hostility from some of the doctors, who probably believed that women weren't fit for such work. But Florence and her nurses proved them wrong. They scrubbed, they cleaned, they nursed, and they comforted. You could say they went where no man had gone before. And the quality of their caring actually began to lower the death rate in the military hospital. Finally, even Florence's most prejudiced opponents couldn't fault her efforts, so she soon became a legend in her own time. The "Lady with the Lamp," they called her, a symbol of light in a dark, despairing world .

Florence lived to the age of ninety, having written the definitive textbook on nursing training and founded the world's first school of nursing at St. Thomas Hospital of London. And that, of course, was only the beginning, for since that time nursing has grown into both a profession and a vocation, for men as well as women. A remarkable woman who made a difference.

Sixty-three years later another woman felt a call from God. She couldn't be more different. Her name is Thérèse and we know her as Thérèse of Lisieux or St. Thérèse of the Child Jesus or St. Thérèse, the Little Flower. Her life, unlike Florence's was quiet. It was hidden. It was uneventful. Unlike Florence's, it was brief. She died just over a hundred years ago, in 1897 at age twenty-four.

She didn't go on any great missions like Florence. She didn't perform any great works like Florence. In fact, when she died in her small convent, the superior in charge of writing the obituary was very troubled because there was nothing to say about her. They asked one of the nuns there about her and she said, "Thérèse was a sweet little sister who never did anything."

And yet, she became easily one of the most popular figures of the entire twentieth century, rivaling that of Florence Nightingale. Within twenty-five years, she was named a saint by the church. She had a terrific impact on a whole variety of people's lives. There was, for example, James Keller, a priest born and raised in Oakland, California, who became the founder and director of the Christopher Movement. He attributes his whole direction and vision to St. Thérèse. Dorothy Day, up for canonization, attributes her conversion to Saint Thérèse and wrote a biography of her. Another person who had Saint Thérèse as a favorite, Jack Kerouac. He was the Poet Laureate of the Beat Generation. And, for him, St. Thérèse was very important.

Florence Nightingale had vision and dedication and a core of compassionate followers. What is Therese's legacy? What's her discovery? What lesson does she have for us? Well, the first lesson, I think, comes from the very fact of her age. She was very young. She was only fifteen when she entered the Carmelite convent. She lived there only nine years. She died, as I said, at the age of twenty-four.

She taught us that you don't have to be old to be holy, that young people are equally called to the greatest of holiness.

Her second lesson came when, about three years before she died, her superior ordered her to write an autobiography. Her brief life and that small journal called *A Story of the Soul* really revolutionized modern thinking about holiness, for she taught us what was revolutionary at the time, that every single Christian is called to holiness. We are all called to holiness, not just people in religious orders, not just missionaries, and not just martyrs. We are all called to great holiness.

For Thérèse, the key to holiness was the ordinary. She called it the "little way." She wrote, "In my 'little way' are only very ordinary things. And little souls can do everything I do....Doing one's ordinary work, our ordinary life is quite enough provided we do it with great love and great joy." And that's exactly what she did. For her, it was washing laundry and sweeping corridors and trying to stay awake at meditation time.

Most of the statues, paintings, and pictures of Thérèse show her with a bouquet of roses or roses at her feet or a rose in her hand. It's a sign of her caring and loving for her community and people all over the world, for she had said, "I will send roses from heaven. I intend to spend my entire life in heaven continuing to do good work on earth." And so she has.

Two commandments: love of God and love of neighbor. Two paths, one public and the other private, that led to that goal. Two saints, one canonized, the other not. Two women, Florence and Thérèse, Flo and Tess, who showed us in their own way how it's done.

Rose

This past month we've had some stellar saints to celebrate in the Catholic world: St. Alphonsus, founder of the Redemptorists; St. Dominic, founder of the Dominicans; St. Lawrence, St. Maximilian Kolbe, St. Bernard, St. Pius X, St. Bartholomew, St. Monica, St. Augustine—all heavy hitters. But today I want to speak to you about an uncanonized saint, an ordinary spiritual star who was married, though not happily or, unfortunately, lastingly. She happened to carry a celebrity name before celebrities were invented. Her name is Rose Hawthorne, the daughter of the very famous American author, Nathaniel Hawthorne. Remember, he wrote *The House of the Seven Gables* and *The Scarlet Letter*.

Her story, briefly, goes like this. At age twenty, Rose met a young American writer in Europe and married him. They had one son together who died of diphtheria at the age of four. And her husband, throughout their marriage, was a confirmed alcoholic. After twenty years of very difficult married life, both of them, in 1891, were converted to the Catholic Church, and became very prominent and active Catholics. And while it may have been good for their faith life, it didn't do anything special for their marriage. And three years later, their separation was permanent and it was final.

Rose was now in her early forties. After a life devoted to her husband and to society events and entertaining in high society in New England and New York, she began to look for meaning and service to give value to her days and nights. And she found it in a very surprising and even frightening place. She found meaning and service among victims of cancer in the poorest slums of New York City. Today cancer still frightens us, but in 1890 it was considered and viewed not just as incurable, but also as contagious. And the moment a patient in a hospital was diagnosed with cancer, the patient was released and moved out. They were barred from entry to any other hospital in the city. If you had a lot of wealth, your family could take care of you. Otherwise, you were exiled to an island in the middle of the East River, or you lived with other cancer patients in the slums.

Rose took a three-month course in nursing, and then rented a three-room tenement apartment in the very tough Lower East Side of New York. She began visiting cancer patients, tenement by tenement. She wrote about some of the things she did on a typical day. For example, in October 1896, she said that she fed and clothed a starving mother and daughter; she changed the dressings of a cancer patient two times; she visited an elderly woman dying of cancer; she prevented the eviction of a tenant because he had cancer; and she brought food to a child dying of meningitis. Before long, she was inviting the patients into her three little rooms, into her apartment. Day after day, she spent washing the cancerous sores and changing the bedclothes of her impoverished guests.

But even more important, she was determined to offer friendship and respect and a sense of worth and a sense of value to those whom others considered outcasts. She drew a motto from the writing of St. Vincent de Paul, "I am for God and the poor." She expanded her work and rented a larger building, opened it, and named it, "St. Rose's Free Home for Incurable Cancer." She later funded more buildings by begging from her acquaintances and friends in society and by advertising in the New York papers. One of her most generous and constant benefactors was Mark Twain.

She set two rules for those who wanted to work with her. If you worked with her, you had to live with the poor and accept no salary. And the second rule was that you would accept no payment ever from a patient or from their family or from the state.

In 1900, she and her helpers joined a community of women religious Dominicans. But after six years with them she left and she founded her own community that she named "The Servants for the Relief of Incurable Cancer." She died in 1926 at the age of seventy-five, and today her community continues her work. They are usually referred to as the "Hawthorne Dominicans." They continue to be faithful to Rose Hawthorne, serving the poor and refusing to accept any payment from families or from the government.

Her engagement ring and her wedding ring are exactly where she left them, on the hand of a statue of Jesus in one of the principal buildings that they staff in New York.

Well, what lessons do we learn from Rose Hawthorne? I'd say the first one has to be about marriage. Just because a marriage doesn't work out, or because our family is dysfunctional, it doesn't mean that our life doesn't work out and that we have to be dysfunctional. It means that we can begin again and find a new life.

Second, we learn that there is so much quiet love going on all the time. What strikes me is how anonymous Rose is! I mean, this weekend, I guess I've spoken to close to 1000 people and I bet there aren't more than two that ever heard of her before.

What it tells me, in our history as a community, as a church, is that there *is* a tremendous amount of good being done in very quiet ways by anonymous people. There is an enormous amount of good work and good people, an untold amount, of which we can be very proud.

The third lesson is about the poor. The American bishops said that the test of a healthy country, the test of a healthy society, is not how high its standard of living is or how well off the well-off are. The test of a healthy country is how it treats its poorest and weakest citizens. Rose Hawthorne says the same thing.

A test for Christians, for those who try to follow the gospel is this: How do you stand with the poor? And where are your concerns with the poor?

Bottom line: We are encouraged and challenged to know that our God has walked and has worked in the courage, the compassion, and the care of these people. But, even more to know, that our God, beyond scandal, terrorism, hurt, and disappointment, continues to work with and to walk among us when we show care and compassion for one another. Let us give thanks to the Lord who is so good. Amen.

Homily for a Young Suicide

LUKE 7:17

As I look out over this congregation brought here by the common bond of the tragic death of someone we knew, I know that words are inadequate to temper our grief. Therefore, I shall try to make my words brief and address them to three groups of people. My first words concern John; my second thoughts concern John's friends and peers and classmates who are here in great numbers, to the great credit of your friendship and sympathy for his family; and my third thoughts concern all of us, but especially John's family.

As for John, I presume that no one here is unaware that he took his own life. I think we ought to say that out loud so that we can hear it publicly and not just whisper this open secret among ourselves, and so that we can try to deal with it. But I want to share with you that often this deed, in the confused mind of a troubled person, is done out of love. A misguided and wrong-headed love, but love nevertheless.

The thinking of a person who is deeply troubled frequently goes like this: "I am a burden. I'm hurting people. I'm in the way. I'm making a mess of things. I'm unhappy and making others unhappy. I worry those nearest to me. It would be kinder for everyone if I took the burden off their shoulders, if I weren't here, if I ceased to be." That's the understandable but backward logic that often is at work in a person so troubled that he or she doesn't see or think dearly.

And that's at least good to know. As painful as suicide is for us, at bottom there is the truth that it is often done out of love and concern for others. It's not good thinking, but bad thinking that nevertheless has its roots in

598

charity, not malice. And we ought to remember that about John. His tender love, as he understood it, did him in.

As for you young people here in such great numbers, John's friends and companions, for you, John's death raises a question. It is this: What are you going to do about your friend's death? I mean, after the pain and the shock, after the anger—maybe at John himself, probably at God—after the hurt and tears, what are you going to do about your friend's death? It's easy to cry in his memory. What are you going to do with your life in his memory when your tears have dried?

I want to share with you a story an uncle of mine, dead himself many years now, told me because he had been there. It might suggest an answer. He told me the story of Puccini, the great Italian writer of such classic operas as *Madame Butterfly* and *La Bohème*. It seems when Puccini was fairly young he contracted cancer, and so he decided to spend his last days writing his final opera, *Turandot*, which is one of his most polished pieces. When his friends and disciples would say to him, "You are ailing; take it easy and rest," he would always respond, "I'm going to do as much as I can on my great masterwork and it's up to you, my friends, to finish it if I don't."

Well, Puccini died before the opera was completed. Now his friends had a decision to make. They could forever mourn their friend and return to life as usual, or they could build on his melody and complete what he started. They chose the latter. And so, in 1926, my uncle was there at the famous La Scala Opera House in Milan, Italy, when Puccini's opera was played for the first time, conducted by the famed conductor Arturo Toscanini. And when it came to the part in the opera where the master had stopped because he died, Toscanini stopped everything, turned around with eyes welling up with tears, and said to the large audience, "This is where the master ends." And he wept. But then, after a few moments, he lifted up his head, smiled broadly, and said, "And this is where his friends began." And he finished the opera.

You see the point of the question I asked you: What are you going to do about John's death? What are you going to do about his unfinished masterpiece? Will it be, in a month or so, life as usual? Or can you build on his humor, his ability, his fun, his unrealized dreams? I would suggest that if there is any fitting response to the shock of your friend's death it is life, your life, a life that's lived better, a life lived more selflessly, a life that makes a difference, a life that is honest and decent, a life that makes beautiful music for John and for the Lord. Across the chasm of death you can make John live. The music doesn't have to stop here today and doesn't have to be buried with John. You have your choice.

Finally, to all of you, to all of us, but especially to John's family, in this sad moment I leave you with an image of hope, of perspective. Picture yourselves standing on a dock beside one of those great old-time sailing vessels. It's standing there, sails folded, waiting for the wind. Suddenly a breeze comes up. When the captain senses the breeze as a forerunner of the necessary wind, he quickly orders the sails to be hoisted and sure enough the wind comes, catches the sails full force, and carries the ship away from the dock where you are standing. Inevitably you or someone on that dock is bound to say, "Well, there she goes!" And from our point of view it does indeed go.

Soon the mighty ship, laden with its crew and goods, is on the horizon where water and sky meet and it looks like a speck before it disappears. It's still mighty and grand, still filled with life and goods, but it's left us. We're standing on the dock quite alone.

But on the other side of the ocean people are standing in anticipation, and as that speck on the horizon becomes larger and larger they begin to cry something different. They are crying with joy, not abandonment, "Here she comes!" And at the landing there is welcome, joy, embracing, and celebration.

We miss John. He is quickly receding from our sight, and this funeral and his burial at the cemetery are our farewells, our versions of "There he goes." But goes where? From our sight, from our embrace, from our care and love and friendship. How we miss that, how we will miss him! But he is not diminished, nor made poorer. We must remember on faith that "Here he comes!" is the cry on the eternal shore where Jesus, who understands the human heart even when it goes wrong, is waiting. And there is John, now forever larger than life, filled with life, intoxicated with life and laughter and in the arms of the One who makes all things new again, the One who says, "Welcome, John. Welcome home."

Credits and Comments

Introducing Matthew

I always hesitate to give one of these "teaching" homilies, but when I do, the people, as in this instance, are pleased and full of compliments. Such response signals how hungry people are for instruction and maybe we preachers should give more of it, since very few come to parish courses.

How Starbucks Saved My Life

Except that it would be distracting I had all I could do not to add that, if I were pope, I would require every candidate for bishop or pastor to take a workshop on Starbucks's philosophy and managing techniques to be followed by a one year's apprenticeship at a local Starbucks. In a few years the church would change dramatically, for the good. The book is published by Gotham Books, 2007.

The Ten Commandments of Forgiveness

This is the only homily not my own. I have, with his characteristic gracious permission, modified it from a homily given by Father Brian Joyce of Christ the King Church in Pleasant Hill, California. Brian is one of the nation's outstanding pastors.

Wildflowers

In the body of this homily I mention "corruption is everywhere from Congress to churches, from boardrooms to baseball." It was a timely reference. Just the week before this homily (December 2007) the sensational "Mitchell Report" appeared (named after Senator Mitchell). It was a searing revelation of the extensive use of steroids among baseball players, and it actually listed the names of some forty-five of them. Steroid use among other athletes was also in the news.

CEOs: Achievement and Challenge
Chaim Potok's *The Chosen* was published by Simon and Shuster in 1967.

What Should We Do?
This is one of several instances when I shortened the gospel because the second half beginning with "Now the people were filled with expectation..." was, in this case, irrelevant and therefore a distraction from the main point I was trying to make.

Overture
The Fourth Sunday of Advent this year (2007) was the day before Christmas Eve; hence, the thrust of this homily.

Have an Upside-Down Christmas!
I was very apprehensive about this homily. After all, it's Christmas. People—many strangers—are there crowding the church, looking for a sentimental tale; you know, the crippled kid who leaves his crutches at the crèche kind of thing. The people want to be comforted and go home and open presents. I decided (nervously) on some minor shock therapy to get at that "real meaning" of Christmas. I exchanged the beloved Lucan Christmas gospel for the visitation gospel right to the very end of Mary's song. Before I began, I told the congregation two things. First: "The gospel you are about to hear is 2000 years old. Since they didn't have cell phones back then, to preserve the mood, please take a few seconds to turn off your cell phones." (As I said, the crowds were there and many young people for whom the cell phone is like another appendage.) Second, I said, "Put down your missalettes because I am going to read a different gospel and I ask you to listen to it carefully because it is quite subversive."

As you noticed, I started with a joke and a warning and then immediately launched into my message.

I delivered the rather strong homily and, to my genuine surprise, the congregation received it well and applauded!

The Bells of Christmas
Like most preachers, I have never used Matthew's genealogy gospel, not quite knowing what to do with it and fearful of mystifying, if not boring, the mixed congregation (regulars and irregulars). But this year I decided to tackle it. As you have noted in the introduction to the gospel, I did not want to start it cold and leave the people perplexed. So I prepared the people for what was coming

and I read a shortened version stopping at verse 17, omitting the actual birth story. I also added Bathsheba's name ("David became the father of Solomon whose mother, Bathsheba, had been the wife..."). I read the genealogy taking audible breaths between paragraphs.

Seldom do I do this—there are only two other instances in this book—but I reused the Anne Lamott story from Christ the King Sunday because it fit here so well. The homily proved challenging and impressive.

Same Time Next Year

This was an opportunity to take the "after-it's-all-over" congregation into some background and, I hope, some spiritual insight of what we celebrated. The suggestions at the conclusion I owe to Bruce David Forbes's book, *Christmas: A Candid History* (University of California Press, 2007).

Take Congress

A homily that reflects the headlines. There will be, alas, always examples to use. My reference to the Atlantic City of my state can be easily transferred to other locations.

Lenten Anger

The five suggestions for Lent I got from my friend and notable preacher, Father Pat Connor, S.V.D.

Transformation

A good homily with a good story. Unfortunately, I can't trace for certain the origin of the story of the cabbie. I understand there are two authors who claim ownership. When it's settled, I will be happy to give proper credit.

God So Loved the World

The Lewis Grizzard story is adapted from Thomas G. Long's book, *Whispering the Lyrics: Sermons for Lent and Easter, Cycle A* (Lima, OH: CSS Publishing, 1995).

The Stations Pilgrims

I have used some of this material before. The people very much resonated with the message of each station. They readily found identification with one or more of them.

Lazarus: Death and Life

First of all, I read a condensed version of the long Lazarus gospel, enough to make my point in the homily. Second, in one of the very infrequent instances that I do this, you will notice that I culled the individual stories from other homilies in this collection and wove them into a new configuration for the purposes of this homily. Finally, to be consistent with the theme of death I used in the Mass the first preface of the Masses for Christian Burial. The story of the boy and his aunt is from Arthur Gordon in his book, *A Touch of Wonder* (Jove, 1986).

Easter

The fabulous story is from Walter Wangerin's book *The Ragman* (San Francisco: HarperCollins, 2002).

Easter: God's Choice

Once more the examples used can always be left undated. Some readers may recognize the homily as an expression of the work of Dominic Crossan and Marcus Borg. The homily was met with applause from a mixed crowd of regulars and visitors.

Threes and Tragedies

Again, I read a shortened version of the gospel assigned. I left out the "Peter, do you love me" episode. This homily was made especially powerful by its wrenching social context: In the previous week thirty-three people were gunned down at Virginia Tech.

The Ninety-Seven Percent Solution

This brought not only a round of applause, but a lot of buzz for weeks. Which is only another example of the depth of religious illiteracy and the lack of knowledge of church history.

Promised Presence

Since this Sunday was so near Ascension I used the Ascension gospel for my remarks instead of the Sunday gospel.

The Holy Spirit and Papa God

The introductory paragraphs are modified from J. Ronald Knott's wise collection of homilies titled, *An Encouraging Word* (New York: Crossroad, 1995, p. 185).

The story "Papa God" I heard in several versions. I had written down the one I knew, until I came across Hugh Lipton's retelling in his wonderful book, *Tales of Wisdom Wonder* (New York: Barefoot Books, 1998). His retelling influenced my retelling. A book worth owning.

Moorings

The thoughts about the movie *Into Great Silence* I owe to John Garvey writing in *Commonweal* magazine, May 8, 2007, p. 7.

The data on college alcohol and drug abuse comes from an article in *America* magazine, May 28, 2007, by Joseph A. Califano, Jr., "Wasting the Best and the Brightest," p. 16.

The Dan Yashinsky's story can be found in *Storytelling Magazine*, May/June 2007, "Suddenly They Heard Footsteps," p. 35.

The visit to the monk story is modified from Rabbi Zalman Schachter-Shalomi on the website, spiritualityhealth.com, April 2007.

The Call

I have reprised some stories here from a previous homily into a new configuration.

Beyond the Pew

The T.S. Eliot lines are from *Choruses from "The Rock,"* published in 1934.

A Day in the Life of Jesus

The Ram Dass quote is from his book, *Still Here: Embracing Aging, Changing, and Dying*, edited by Mark Matousek and Marielle Roeder (New York: Riverhead Books, 2000, p. 67).

The John Updike poem can be found in *Collected Poems 1953–1993* (New York: Knopf, 1993).

The Fred story is from Peter M. Senge and others in *Presence: Human Purpose and the Field of the Future* (Cambridge, MA, 2004).

Valentines

The start-off introduction is from James Wallace, C.Ss.R., in *Lift Up Your Hearts* (Mahwah, NJ: Paulist Press, 2006) and "Life After Football, Hello Real World" is from a column by Richard Justice in the *Houston Chronicle*, January 21, 2004.

WHAT SIMON SAW

I owe the information about St. Callixtus and Hippolytus to Thomas J. Craughwell's delightful book, *Saints Behaving Badly* (New York: Doubleday, 2006).

LEGENDS

In 2007 the Sunday liturgy was bumped by the feast of St. John the Baptist. Because I didn't have any thoughts on John I moved to an independent theme. I owe the Dismas chronicle to Thomas J Craughwell's *Saints Behaving Badly*.

NEVERTHELESS

This strong homily—again, the homilist can update the references—finds its roots in three must-read books: Bill McKibben's *Deep Economy: The Wealth of Communities and the Durable Future* (New York: Times Books, 2007); Robert Putnam's *Bowling Alone* (New York: Simon and Schuster, 2001); and Dick Morris's *Outrage* (San Francisco: HarperCollins, 2007).

DUST

Moss Hart's recollection is from *Act One: An Autobiography* (Random House, 2002).

THE VIEW FROM THE DITCH

The remarkable insight in this homily comes from Barbara Reid's book, *Parables for Preachers* (Collegeville, MN: Liturgical Press, 2000, p. 117).

SABBATH REST

The Little Prince by Antoine de Saint-Exupery was published by Gallimard in 1943. The translator was Katherine Woods.

YIN AND YANG

The "home" visits to Martha and Mary I have expanded from Alice Camille, *God's Word Is Alive!* (Mystic, CT: Twenty-Third Publications, 1998). I remember reading somewhere in his works Scripture scholar Raymond Brown's commentary on Martha's profession of faith.

TREASURES

Once more I shortened the gospel, ending with "When he finds of pearl of great price, he goes and sells all he has and buys it." The rest of the text didn't add anything to what I wanted to say.

Snakes and Fish

Because Bill McKibben's book *Deep Economy* was so much on my mind, I forsook the obvious theme of today's Scripture that clearly called for a homily on prayer and used his data to weave a homily around the (rather forced) gospel words of the snake and scorpion. Despite my initial disclaimer, the homily was well received.

Higher Calling

The opening reference to the *New Yorker* cover I took from James Wallace's homily "The Clock's Ticking," in *Lift Up Your Hearts* (Mahwah, NJ: Paulist Press, 2006).

Elijah

The full text of Crowell's poem appears in her book, *Poems of Inspiration and Courage* (New York: Continuum, 1999).

Reference Point

I skipped the first two paragraphs of this Sunday's gospel and started with, "At that time Jesus said, 'Who, then, is the faithful and prudent steward...?'" It added better focus to my remarks. In the headline from the local paper, "Jenks, cops unite to curb teen drinking," "Jenks" refers to Jenkinson's, a beach and entertainment (rides, arcades, Tiki Bar, etc.) enterprise at the shore where I live.

I Beg to Differ

In July 2007, two career criminals, serial burglars with drug habits, broke into a two-story home in Cheshire, Connecticut. They raped and strangled Jennifer Pettit and her two daughters, poured gasoline over them, tied them to their beds, and lit the gasoline. The husband, Dr. William Pettit, bloodied with his legs bound stumbled out of the house shouting for a neighbor. It was an especially horrific crime, shocking the nation. The two criminals were caught. Their long list of criminal offenses has raised questions on their routine paroles. In August of that year, a heavily traveled, main bridge in Minneapolis dramatically collapsed sending cars into the river. So far, about seven people have been declared dead and scores were injured. It was the most serious bridge collapse that the country has seen. In its aftermath, the inspection of many bridges in the country has found that many are seriously in need of upgrading and repair, spotlighting, as I say in the homily, the distorted priorities of some politicians and members of Congress. This homily was well received.

SAVED OR SPENT?

I owe the Matt Talbot story to Janice McGrane's fine book, *Saints to Lean On: Spiritual Companions for Illness and Disability* (Cincinnati: St. Anthony Messenger Press, 2006).

HYPOCRISY

I ended the gospel right after the Isaiah quotation. The story of the boy and his policeman father comes from John Shea. This wasn't an especially good homily.

MOVING UP LOWER

This homily was given during the presidential campaign when Hillary Clinton, Rudy Giuliani, and others were running. Once again, I am indebted to Tom Craughwell's book for the life of Peter Claver.

"OH"

The first three stories in this homily are modified from the wonderful stories of famed preacher, Fred Craddock. The Ellsberg excerpt is from his book, *All Saints* (New York: Crossroad, 1997).

DIVINE OBSESSION

I owe the biblical information here once more to Barbara Reid. For the gospel, I cut it short and omitted the sentence "Then the celebration began" and the following incident of the older brother. I wanted to concentrate only on the three God figures in order to make my point.

A TRICKSTER TALE

I omitted the last paragraph of the gospel, basically because it contains some early editors' fumbling attempt to justify this puzzling gospel and really doesn't advance any understanding. I ended with "And the master commended that dishonest steward for acting prudently."

JESUS AND WARREN BUFFETT

I'm indebted to some of this material to John Kavanaugh, S.J., in *America* (August 27–September 3, 2007, p. 10). The reference to the migrant workers is especially relevant to my state of New Jersey where every day they gather at outposts waiting to be hired.

SERVANT LEADERSHIP

This is one of those homilies that reflect times of deep corruption in government, the UN, sports, and corporations. Many of the real names in this homily are from my own corrupt state of New Jersey. The reader wanting to appropriate this homily for his or her own use will always have new replacement names.

THE JUSTICE WOMAN

I owe this interpretation to Barbara Reid, *Parables for Preachers.*

BRITNEY AND THE PUBLICAN

I left off the last phrase of the gospel, Luke's interpretative gloss that "whoever exalts himself…." It was a distraction from what I was trying to develop.

IT MIGHT HAVE BEEN

I changed the word "grumble" in the gospel to "murmur." It had a better sound here and in the homily and recalls the crowd murmuring against Moses.

To continue the theme of the homily I stongly suggest that the presider, especially if he is the homilist, use the first reconciliation preface. Omit the two internal paragraphs for greater effect.

GOLDEN JUBILEE: PRIESTHOOD

The Little Prince by Antoine de Saint-Exupery was published by Gallimard in 1943. The translator was Katherine Woods.

WHERE'S BOB?

I have taken and modified the example of the woman from John Shea, *The Relentless Widow: The Spiritual Wisdom of the Gospel for Christian Preachers and Teachers, Year C* (Collegeville, MN: Liturgical Press, 2006).

Sr. Jose Hobday's words are from her book, *Stories of Awe and Abundance* (New York: Continuum, 1999).

FATHER'S DAY: THE MEN

While preaching this homily I was conscious of the men and young males who were in fact in the congregation and so at the end of Mass I made it a point to praise them and thank them for their witness. They beamed and the congregation applauded in approval.

9/11 Anniversary and Father Mychal Judge
The three homilies, "Hurricanes and Such," "Katrina," and "Father Judge," all centering around the same event, resonated deeply with many, showing that the wounds and memories are still there.

Second Time Around: Marriage
This homily for the wedding of a widow and widower garnered many words of praise for its sensitivity. The story was a great ice-breaker.

Jim Bausch: The Brother
Chaim Potok's *The Chosen* was published by Simon and Schuster in 1967.

John the Baptist and Second Thoughts
Al Staggs is quoted by Martin Marty in *Context* (November 15, 1998).

Christmas: Love Among the Ruins
The story by Ian McLaren is from his book *Beside the Bonnie Briar Bush* (Barse and Hopkins, 1894).

The Holy Family: Fear of Glory
Williamson's lines are from her book, *A Return to Love: Reflections on the Principles of a Course in Miracles* (San Francisco: HarperCollins, 1992).

Lent: The Weeping Christ
The poem is by Geoffrey Studdert Kennedy, who died in 1929.

Easter: The Themes of Passiontide
The insights for the first part of this homily come from the spiritual writer Ronald Rohlheiser. I have lost the source but I wanted to give him credit.

Mother's Day — 1
Kipling's verse, "Mother o' mine," appears in his novel, *The Light That Failed* (Bel Air, CA: Bibliobazaar, 2007).

Father's Day
The moving story is from *A Cup of Comfort* by Ed Nickum.